PATRICK HENRY

CHAMPION OF LIBERTY

JON KUKLA

Simon & Schuster

NEW YORK · LONDON · TORONTO
SYDNEY · NEW DELHI

Simon & Schuster
1230 Avenue of the Americas
New York, NY 10020

First Simon & Schuster hardcover edition July 2017

SIMON & SCHUSTER and colophon are
registered trademarks of Simon & Schuster, Inc.

For information about special discounts for bulk purchases,
please contact Simon & Schuster Special Sales at
1-866-506-1949 or business@simonandschuster.com.

The Simon & Schuster Speakers Bureau can bring authors to your
live event. For more information or to book an event, contact the
Simon & Schuster Speakers Bureau at 1-866-248-3049
or visit our website at www.simonspeakers.com.

Interior design by Paul Dippolito

Manufactured in the United States of America

1   3   5   7   9   10   8   6   4   2

Library of Congress Cataloging-in-Publication Data

Names: Kukla, Jon, 1948– author.
Title: Patrick Henry : champion of liberty / Jon Kukla.
Description: New York : Simon and Schuster, [2017] |
Includes bibliographical references and index.
Identifiers: LCCN 2016027735| ISBN 9781439190814 | ISBN 143919081X
Subjects: LCSH: Henry, Patrick, 1736–1799. | Governors—Virginia—
Biography. | Legislators—Virginia—Biography. | Virginia—
History—Revolution, 1775–1783.
Classification: LCC E302.6.H5 K86 2017 | DDC 973.3092 [B] —
dc23 LC record available at https://lccn.loc.gov/2016027735

ISBN 978-1-4391-9081-4
ISBN 978-1-4391-9083-8 (ebook)

Frontispiece art: Dodge, Mary Mapes *St. Nicholas an Illustrated
Magazine for Young Folks* (New York, New York: The Century Co., 1886)/
Clip Art Etc. Florida Center for Instructional Technology, College
of Education, University of South Florida.

For Sandy

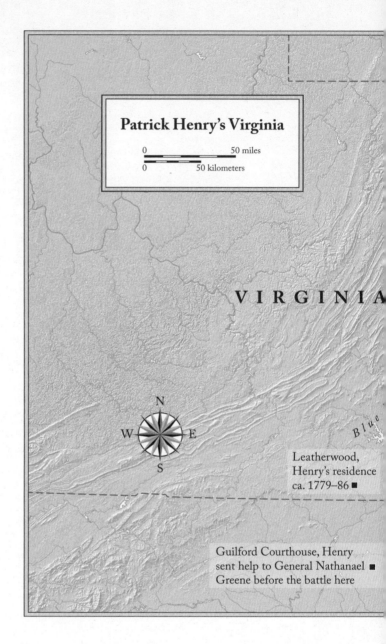

Patrick Henry's Virginia

0   50 miles

0   50 kilometers

VIRGINIA

N
W   E
S

Leatherwood,
Henry's residence
ca. 1779–86 ▪

Guilford Courthouse, Henry
sent help to General Nathanael ▪
Greene before the battle here

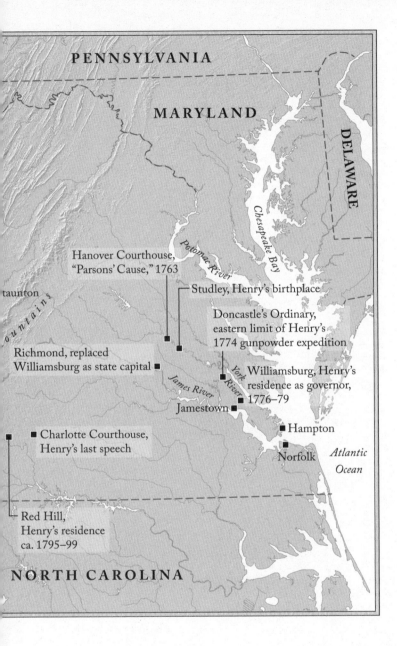

PENNSYLVANIA

MARYLAND

DELAWARE

Chesapeake Bay

Potomac River

Hanover Courthouse,
"Parsons' Cause," 1763

taunton

Studley, Henry's birthplace

Doncastle's Ordinary,
eastern limit of Henry's
1774 gunpowder expedition

Richmond, replaced
Williamsburg as state capital

James River

York River

Williamsburg, Henry's
residence as governor,
1776–79

Jamestown

Charlotte Courthouse,
Henry's last speech

Hampton

Norfolk

*Atlantic
Ocean*

Red Hill,
Henry's residence
ca. 1795–99

NORTH CAROLINA

Contents

Preface

IN *1882 HENRY ADAMS*, one of America's great historians and certainly the finest writer among them, offered a distinct opinion about how to write a biography of Patrick Henry—an opinion directly informed by his own experience. Although a Philadelphia publisher had just issued the twenty-third edition of William Wirt's *Sketches of the Life and Character of Patrick Henry* since its original appearance in 1817, Henry Adams demanded something better. "Henry's life is still unwritten," Adams declared in a letter to editor John T. Morse, Jr., "as indeed is the case with all the Virginians except G.W."—and one other.

Adams could "also except" John Randolph of Roanoke, "whose life can now be read" in the biography that he had just published in the American Statesman series, which Morse edited for Houghton, Mifflin and Company—though neither man was happy with the book's presentation of Patrick Henry's eccentric Charlotte County neighbor. Randolph himself caused one of the book's problems. "The acidity is much too decided," Adams lamented, even if its tone had really been determined "by the subject and the excess of acid is his." The other problem Adams attributed to his biography of John Randolph was his own identity as the Boston-born great-grandson of President John Adams and grandson of President John Quincy Adams. "A man who really understood his material could do a great deal with Patrick Henry," Adams suggested, "but he ought to be a Virginian and a hard student"—"it needs a Virginian to write of Virginia, if he would write the truth."

To be sure, several good books about Patrick Henry have appeared in the century and a third since the great historian declared that Henry's life was still unwritten, but there is some truth in the qualifications Adams highlighted. A Wisconsin-born author may be forgiven for supposing that Henry Adams had something more in mind than geographic place of birth when he advocated "a Virginian and a hard student"—even if the

Badger State had still been a part of the Old Dominion during Henry's first three terms as governor of the commonwealth. By testing everything against the best available primary sources, this book attempts to avoid the accumulated errors that mar many previous biographies. Many newly discovered sources provide fresh insights about Henry and his times. Finally, a greater appreciation of the social and political contexts of Henry's activities enriches this narrative of his life and career. If a historian who has devoted four decades to the study of Virginia counts as a "hard student," then perhaps these pages can provide a fresh approximation of the truth about Patrick Henry. Toward that end, as Henry Adams counseled, an author can only "do his best."

Jon Kukla
Richmond, Virginia

CHAPTER ONE

A Serious Loss

AFTER SWALLOWING A DOSE of liquid mercury on Thursday morning, June 6, 1799, Patrick Henry sat calmly near a window at the northeast corner of his modest house in Charlotte County, Virginia. As he pondered the blood congealing under his fingernails, Henry whispered words of comfort to his wife and children and waited for the mercury to cure him or kill him.

Henry was sixty-three. He had been seriously ill since early April, when he described his symptoms to physician George Cabell, of Lynchburg, as something "like the Gravel." Kidney stones large and small—*the stone* and *the gravel*—were common afflictions in the eighteenth century, painful or annoying but rarely fatal. Pharmacy ads in the *Virginia Gazette* touted cures and treatments such as tincture of goldenrod, Blackrie's Lixivium, and Swinsen's Electuary for the Stone and Gravel.

By the first of June, Dr. Cabell's diagnosis was more grim. Henry was now suffering from a life-threatening intestinal obstruction called intussusception. Part of his intestine had telescoped into itself, blocking the digestive tract. Infection and death were imminent unless the blockage could be relieved. The remedy was risky. With luck the weight of a large dose of liquid mercury, which is 20 percent heavier than lead, might unravel the intestinal knot, pass through his bowels, and save Henry's life. If the blockage persisted, however, Henry's body would absorb the mercury, the muscles of his chest would fail, and he would die by suffocation.

Family members who gathered at Red Hill that morning left a poignant record of the final conversation between the dying patriot and his physician.

"I suppose, doctor, this is your last resort," Henry said as he accepted the vial of mercury.

"I am sorry to say, governor, that it is," Dr. Cabell replied. "Acute inflammation of the intestines has already taken place; and unless it is removed mortification will ensue, if it has not already commenced, which I fear."

"What will be the effect of this medicine?" Henry asked.

"It will give you immediate relief, or . . ." Cabell was unable to finish his sentence.

"You mean," Henry said, "that it will give relief or will prove fatal immediately?"

"You can only live a very short time without it," Cabell explained, "and it may possibly relieve you."

"Excuse me, doctor, for a few minutes," Henry replied, drawing his silk cap down over his eyes. Holding the vial of mercury in his hand, Henry prayed briefly for his family, his country, and himself. He swallowed the medicine and spoke quietly for a while with his family and physician. Finally he breathed "very softly for some moments" and died.

ooooo

For half a dozen years Patrick Henry had regarded Red Hill, the last of the twelve places he had lived since his birth in Hanover County in 1736, as "one of the garden spots of the world." Five hundred feet above sea level, the plantation's 2,900 acres straddled the line between Campbell and Charlotte counties. The southern vista from his house looked down on the ferry across the Staunton River and the wooded hills of Halifax County. Just beyond the southern horizon lay the Virginia–North Carolina border, drawn in a 1728 feat of exploration celebrated in William Byrd II's *History of the Dividing Line.*

To the north, through the window nearest the corner where he spent the last hours of his life, Henry could see a century-old osage-orange tree, which has since grown into the gnarled giant designated as an American champion for the species. Visible to his right were young figs ripening along the walkway that linked Henry's house and its adjacent kitchen, a small clapboard shed dominated by its massive brick fireplace and oven, with the two-room frame structure that served as his law office. There, on his desk, Patrick Henry had left two messages for posterity—testaments both to his private religious faith and his hopes for America's future.

Patrick Henry's will, written entirely in his own hand, provided his widow and his seventeen children with legacies sufficient to support them in comfort and independence. After disposing of his property—including nearly eighty slaves—Henry's will also conveyed a private assurance to his wife and children: "This is all the inheritance I can give to my dear family," its final clause explained. "The religion of Christ can give them one which will make them rich indeed."

On the desk next to his will Henry had left a sealed envelope addressed to his executors. It contained a single sheet of paper. One side bore the text of his 1765 resolutions against the Stamp Act, which men and women of his day acknowledged as a starting point of the American Revolution. The other side offered a message to his fellow citizens that Henry knew could only be read after his death.

Henry's message to posterity began with a short commentary about the past. His Stamp Act Resolutions had spread an alarm "throughout America with astonishing Quickness," Henry recalled. They had successfully united the thirteen colonies behind "the great point of resistance to British taxation" that "brought on the War which finally separated the two Countrys and gave Independence to ours."

Then Henry turned his thoughts toward the future—on a subject he had been thinking about since 1765 or 1766. "Whether [independence] will prove a Blessing or a Curse," he wrote, "will depend on the Use our people make of the Blessings which a gracious God hath bestowed on us." If American citizens act with wisdom, he believed, "they will be great and happy." If not, he warned, "they will be miserable. Righteousness alone can exalt them as a Nation." The message closed with a final admonition:

> Reader! whoever thou art, remember this,
> and in thy Sphere, practice Virtue thyself,
> and encourage it in others.
> P. HENRY

At his death as through his life, Patrick Henry affirmed the interaction of personal faith and civic responsibility—Christian virtue and classical-republican *virtù*—that sustained many eighteenth-century Americans.

Patrick Henry was only sixty-three when he died, but he had outlived virtually all the leaders who had challenged Parliament and the crown in the early 1760s. John Dickinson, Benjamin Franklin, John Hancock, and James Otis, Jr., were dead—as were such Virginia comrades as Richard

Bland, Landon Carter, George Mason, Richard Henry Lee, and Peyton Randolph. Only three other prominent men from the very earliest controversy over the Stamp Act were still alive when Patrick Henry died: George Washington, George Wythe, and George III. Hundreds of younger American participants in the American Revolution, such as Alexander Hamilton, John Jay, Gouverneur Morris, and even John Adams, were relative latecomers to the struggle against England—as were such living Virginians as Thomas Jefferson, James Madison, John Marshall, Edmund Pendleton, and Edmund Randolph.

The Patrick Henry that most people remember today was the eloquent slaveholder who defied George III and Great Britain with his call for liberty or death in 1775. The spellbinding orator who insisted—a few weeks before the patriots at Lexington and Concord, Massachusetts, fired the shots heard round the world—that "the war is actually begun!" The man who called Virginians to arm themselves in defiance of Parliament and king by predicting that the next gale that swept from the north would "bring to their ears the clash of resounding arms!"

Students of the Constitution and its ratification by the states also remember Patrick Henry, a dozen years later, as the critic whose thundering arguments nearly kept Virginia from ratifying the plan—and whose political clout kept James Madison out of the new Senate and forced him to promise the voters a Bill of Rights and push it through Congress. The great debates of 1787–1788 remind us again of Henry's long career on the center stage of American history. Of all the major participants in the drafting and ratification of the Constitution, only Patrick Henry, Samuel Adams, and Benjamin Franklin had been prominent in the opposition to the Stamp Act a quarter of a century earlier.

Throughout his life, Patrick Henry adhered to a cluster of five tactical ideas that drove him and his neighbors first to resist and then to declare themselves independent of Great Britain. He believed that the burgesses and councilors who comprised Virginia's legislative assembly spoke for the people of Virginia just as members of the House of Lords and House of Commons served as the constitutional legislature for the people of England, Scotland, and Wales—and that Parliament had no legitimate authority in Virginia's internal government. Second, he acknowledged allegiance to the British monarch based on the compact, enshrined in the coronation oath, by which kings promised to protect their subjects in exchange for their allegiance—and by which, as John Locke had written, a monarch who broke that promise forfeited his subjects' allegiance and degenerated from a king into a tyrant. Third, Henry believed that the protection of American liberty demanded unanimity between the people of Virginia and their compatriots in the other colonies or states. Fourth, Henry recognized the necessity of invoking sanctions against enemies of the community in defense of liberty and the common good. And finally, Henry genuinely respected the will of the people when expressed fairly through democratic institutions.

None of these ideas was unique to Henry, and many other ideas figured prominently in his life and career (including concepts of liberty, equality, rule of law, freedom of conscience, religious toleration, representation, federalism, separation of powers, and the list of republican virtues he enshrined in the Virginia Declaration of Rights: justice, moderation, temperance, frugality, virtue, and a "frequent recurrence to fundamental principles"). In support of these and other civic principles, nevertheless, the five tactical elements sustained Patrick Henry's course during Virginia's transition from the oldest and largest of Great Britain's American colonies when he was born in 1736 to the largest and arguably still most influential of the American states when he died in 1799.

When Patrick Henry left the copy of his 1765 resolutions in his law office at Red Hill he was reasonably confident that his contemporaries remembered their back story and recognized their significance. Henry saw no need to explain how his words (or the five concepts behind them) had eventually "brought on the War which finally separated the two Countrys," for countless Americans equated Virginia's resistance to the Stamp Act with the beginning of the American Revolution. Typical was the Harvard-educated author Jeremy Belknap, a founder of the Massachusetts Historical Society, who believed that his two-volume chronicle, *History of New Hampshire*, required this grateful nod toward Patrick Henry and the Old Dominion: "The first proposal [for a union of the colonies] came from Virginia," Belknap declared, "where American liberty was first publicly asserted when it was flagrantly violated by the stamp-act"—a contribution to the destiny of the Granite State for which Belknap believed "the name of Patrick Henry will ever be illustrious."

ooooo

Dorothea Dandridge Henry buried her husband at the edge of a garden east of the house and law office at Red Hill. "Virginia has sustained a very serious loss," wrote John Marshall, the future chief justice, when he conveyed news of Henry's death to George Washington. "Not only Virginia," Washington replied, "but our country at large has sustained a very serious loss. I sincerely lament his death as a friend, and the loss of his eminent talents as a patriot." Thomas Jefferson and his friends kept silent, but one Richmond newspaper, the pro-Federalist *Virginia Gazette*, mourned the great orator. Its editor put heavy black borders around the obituary. "As long as our rivers flow, or mountains stand," proclaimed the *Gazette*, "Virginia . . . will say to rising generations, imitate my HENRY." Decades later Patrick and Dorothea's youngest son, John, marked his father's grave with a marble tablet, visible today at Red Hill, with the simple inscription "His fame his best epitaph."

Patrick Henry's fame endured throughout the nineteenth century, despite some political enmity from Jefferson and his supporters, so long as Americans continued to appreciate the powers of great oratory. But fame is fleeting—at best a transient epitaph—and written texts outlast spoken words. Patrick Henry could leave a copy of his Stamp Act Resolutions in his law office, and he could write a message to posterity about virtue, but some of the powerful speeches with which he made history were lost forever. Jeremy Belknap and other Americans remembered that Henry's resolutions had rallied the colonies to resist Great Britain in 1765 and 1775, but few Americans knew how Henry's earlier participation in the Parsons' Cause of 1763 set the stage for Virginia's decisive reaction to the Stamp Act. And fewer still could see beyond his oratorical prowess to his frequent acts of statesmanship.

Even today, more than two centuries after Patrick Henry's death, it remains true that the American Revolution in Virginia (as Richard R. Beeman wrote in 1974) "has, surprisingly, produced numerous specialized works, but very few synthetic, interpretive books." And throughout those centuries, Henry's proper place in American history has been obscured by the popular myths concocted by his first biographer, William Wirt, in 1817. Readers who are familiar with modern scholarship about the American Revolution, or specialized studies of Virginia, or the biographies of

Henry's famous contemporaries, will likely be surprised (as I often was while laboring to get this story right) by the accuracy of Thomas Jefferson's grudging admission, ten years before his own death, that "Mr. Henry's transcendent eminence as an Orator and Statesman, and especially his unquestioned primacy in bringing on the revolution, give him a mass of fame sufficient to satisfy any ambition."

CHAPTER TWO

Totopotomoy Creek

THE ROMANTIC POET Lord Byron knew little about the geography of Patrick Henry's birthplace when he compared the reactionary European statesmen of the 1820s who were reviving the monarchies of the Old World after the Napoleonic Wars with four heroes who personified the virtues of the New World: Benjamin Franklin, George Washington, Simón Bolívar, and Patrick Henry—"the forest-born Demosthenes whose thunder shook the Philip of the seas." A century earlier, high on a ridge in eastern Hanover County, Virginia, John Syme had built a commodious house at Studley plantation about 1720. Named perhaps after Studley Park, a fashionable resort in Yorkshire, England, Syme's plantation overlooked Totopotomoy Creek a few miles upstream from the Pamunkey River. It was there, a few years after she remarried, that Syme's widow gave birth to Patrick Henry, her third child, on Saturday, May 29, 1736.

Hanover County lies a few dozen miles west of the lands in the York River Valley that the infant's earliest immigrant ancestors had settled in the previous century. The county straddles the fall line that separates Virginia's coastal plain, known as the Tidewater, from the hills of the Piedmont that extend west to the Blue Ridge Mountains, the first line of peaks in the Appalachian chain. Eighteenth-century Hanover was a booming agricultural county, created in 1721 from the western districts of New Kent County, which in 1654 had been carved from York County, one of the colony's original shires of 1634. Hanover's aspiring planters, yeoman farmers, and enslaved laborers tilled fields of tobacco for export to London and other British ports, grew corn for export to the British islands of the Caribbean, and raised fruits, vegetables, and domestic animals for local consumption. They looked east for markets, manufactured goods, culture, and governance, despite the avid interest they shared with their neighbors in colonies stretching from Georgia to Massachusetts in the fresh lands of the west, especially the rolling foothills that in 1742 became Louisa County. The tobacco wharves and warehouses on the Pamunkey River at Newcastle, about six miles east of Studley, and at Page's Warehouse, about four miles to the northwest, connected the plantation's fields and produce with the markets of London, Glasgow, and the ports of Europe. Page's Warehouse, later known as Hanovertown, marked the westernmost point of navigation on the Pamunkey. That river, which still defines most of Hanover County's northern boundary, is a major tributary of the stately York River, one of the four great waterways (including the James, Rappahannock, and Potomac Rivers) that divide Tidewater Virginia into distinct peninsulas as they flow easterly toward the Chesapeake Bay and the Atlantic beyond. A public road along the south banks of the Pamunkey and York connected Hanover County with the provincial capital at Williamsburg, and on several occasions powerful colonial legislators nearly succeeded in moving the seat of government to Newcastle.

The man who built Studley came to Virginia about 1715 from Aberdeenshire. John Syme was one of the thousands of aspiring Scots who swarmed into the middle Atlantic colonies after the 1707 union of Scotland and England. Trained as a surveyor, Syme (pronounced Simm) prospered in the colony, amassing extensive landholdings, a considerable number of slaves, and a stylish and impressive house. When Hanover County was carved from New Kent in 1720, Governor Alexander Spotswood appointed Colonel Syme as a founding justice and militia officer in the new jurisdiction. Between 1722 and 1730, while he served as the county's official surveyor, Syme's neighbors repeatedly elected him to the House of Burgesses, the lower chamber of Virginia's colonial legislature.

Young Patrick Henry lived his first fifteen years in one of Hanover County's finest homes. Studley's three thousand square feet of living space made it seven times larger than the average house in the county—a gentry household similar in size and complexity to all but the grandest of Virginia's Tidewater mansions.

Lord Byron exercised a poet's license when he imagined Patrick Henry's birth in the wild forests of the New World. The real boy— along with his half-brother John Syme, Jr., and nine siblings—grew up in a prominent gentry family living in a spacious household with a well-stocked library and a very English kitchen garden that supplied a bounty of fashionable vegetables for the dining room. William Byrd II, a gentleman of letters who cherished good conversation, was a frequent guest at Studley, a few hours' carriage ride from his elegant home on the banks of the James River. Byrd's first recorded visit was in October 1732, about a year after Colonel Syme's death. Byrd described Sarah Winston Syme as "a portly, handsome dame ... who seemed not to pine too much for the death of her husband." Byrd wrote that they "tossed off a bottle of honest port" before he retired for his evening devotions and described his "obliging landlady" as "a person of lively and cheerful conversation, with much less reserve than her countrywomen." The next morning Byrd declined the widow's invitation to join her at church with the playful suggestion that "she would certainly spoil [his] devotion," but he readily accepted her invitation "to make her house my home" whenever Byrd had occasion to visit his landholdings in Hanover.

∞∞∞∞

Aside from his physical appearance, no person endowed with Patrick Henry's famous genius for oratory could be described as *average*. Henry was of medium build and average height, with deep-set but piercing steel-blue eyes, a dark complexion, and strong features. His face was described not as handsome but as "agreeable and full of intelligence and interest." Neither uncouth nor genteel in his appearance, the young Patrick Henry seemed indifferent to fashions and clothing beyond a marked preference for "clean linen and stockings." In his thirties Henry donned a brown wig and experimented with more colorful and fashionable clothing, including the bright red cape he sported when elected the first governor of the commonwealth (a synonym for *republic* chosen for the Virginia constitution of 1776 and associated with the English government created after the execution of Charles I). Henry's later penchant for plain black apparel often lent him the appearance of a country parson or common planter.

From the moment of his birth Henry was in many ways representative of the freeborn population of eighteenth-century Virginia by virtue of his ancestry, family, education, religion, and politics. His mother's English ancestors had lived in Virginia for generations. Her great-grandfather William Winston had come to the colony in the 1660s from the English west country near Bristol. The immigrant quickly acquired 1,800 acres near the mouth of the York River, downstream from the lands that later comprised New Kent and Hanover counties. Cornelius Dabney, a maternal great-grandfather, came to the colony a few years later from the eastern coast of England near Cambridge or Norfolk. Dabney acquired tracts of land along Totopotomoy Creek (then near the western frontier of European settlement) and lived with the Pamunkey tribe long enough to learn their language and serve as interpreter for their queen, Cockacoeske, when she negotiated a peace treaty with colonial authorities at Jamestown in 1678. By 1720, when Hanover County was created from the western parts of New Kent County, the Winston and Dabney families had accumulated land, political power, and social prestige along the upper tributaries of the York.

Sarah Winston Syme Henry was born about 1709 or 1710 to Isaac Winston and his first wife (whose identity has been lost) and was raised by his second wife, Mary Dabney. Sarah's five siblings—Isaac Jr., William, Mary Ann, Lucy, and Anthony—remained prominent in the colony, especially in Hanover and Buckingham Counties. At seventeen, Sarah married the widower John Syme, and on Christmas Day 1727 she gave birth to their only child, John Syme, Jr. Sarah's cousins and uncles were prominent among the county's justices, sheriffs, and vestrymen throughout the mid-eighteenth century, and Winston family connections bolstered the civic careers of both her husbands and her children, especially among religious dissenters. Sarah and at least one of her brothers shared her father's inclination toward evangelical doctrine and worship: her father, Isaac Winston, was brought before the governor in 1747 on charges of promoting the itinerant Presbyterian preacher John Roan; her brother Isaac Jr. declined election to the Anglican vestry of Henrico Parish in 1751; and Sarah herself preferred the preaching of the New Light evangelist Samuel Davies at his Pole Green meetinghouse over her brother-in-law's sermons at St. Paul's Anglican Church.

Patrick Henry's father, Sarah's second husband, was born about 1704 in windswept Foveran Parish on the North Sea, a dozen miles north of Aberdeen and a hundred north of Edinburgh. John Henry was the younger of two sons and three daughters born to Jane Robertson and Patrick Alexander Henry. The girls stayed in Scotland. Two died before adulthood, but the surviving girl, Isabel, married a local miller, corresponded occasionally with her Virginia relations, and died near Aberdeen in 1777. Education was the ticket by which John Henry and his elder brother, Patrick, escaped a bleak future in Aberdeen, with its feudal agricultural practices, impoverished soils, and hardscrabble landscape near the mouth of the Ythan River—not to mention the lingering political turmoil in the shire after the Jacobite uprising of 1715.

After a few years of instruction in a parish school, both boys won scholarships to the universities in Aberdeen, where virtually the entire curriculum was conducted in Latin as late as the 1730s. Patrick Henry studied at Marischal College from 1713 to 1718, took the degree of Master of Arts, and was subsequently ordained in the Episcopal Church of Scotland. His younger brother studied four years at King's College from 1720 to 1724, but declined to pay the additional fees required for a formal diploma and official Bachelor's degree. Unless they contemplated careers in the universities or the church, frugal Scots such as John Henry valued what they had learned at university without paying extra for sheepskin certificates.

Arriving in Virginia about 1727, John Henry was in his mid-twenties when he found work as a surveyor's assistant and lodging at Studley, helping John and Sarah Syme run the plantation. Within a year of his arrival John Henry began acquiring land in his own name, and by the close of his second decade in the colony he had acquired 23,338 acres in Hanover, Goochland, and Albemarle counties. He also participated in more speculative claims for sixty thousand acres of land in western Goochland and northern Albemarle counties and, with fifty other investors in 1772, an unsuccessful attempt to claim 59,000 acres in Kentucky. In 1739 John Henry used his skills as a surveyor to lay out the streets and fifty-two lots of Newcastle on the Pamunkey River. William Parks, founding publisher of the colony's first *Virginia Gazette*, and other Williamsburg residents were among the Virginians who purchased lots and built houses in Newcastle. A fire in 1747 that gutted the capitol prompted a serious attempt to move the seat of government to Newcastle—an effort that reflected the port town's mercantile prosperity in its heyday (before agricultural erosion clogged the upper Pamunkey River with silt).

Governor Sir William Gooch named John Henry as a justice of the peace, militia officer, and member of Hanover County court in April 1737. Two months later Major Henry took the oath of a vestryman of St. Paul's Parish, which then embraced most of Hanover County, at the same meeting that his elder brother, who had followed him to the colony five years earlier, was named as minister of the parish. As was common Virginia practice, the clergyman used the name *Patrick Henry* and generally signed his name *Pat Henry* throughout his forty-year career, while his nephew used *Patrick Henry, Jr.* until his uncle's death in 1777. Meanwhile, John Henry's rise in stature continued with his designation as a member of the quorum, or senior justice, of the Hanover court in 1741 and his appointment as county sheriff for 1744–1745. By the 1760s, his longevity made Colonel Henry the senior and presiding justice of the county court.

Young Patrick Henry's social standing benefited substantially from his mother's extended gentry family, but his father's talents and education carried weight as well. Wealthy Tidewater gentlemen and upcountry planters, a Princeton-educated tutor observed, valued educational attainments and civic honors above "blind stupid fortune." College-educated men traveling in Virginia, he explained to a northern classmate, could expect to keep company in society as though they possessed estates worth £10,000—and "be despised and slighted if you rated yourself a farthing cheaper." Colonel Henry made the most of his skills as a surveyor (as did Peter Jefferson, the future president's father, George Washington, and other similarly talented Virginians), but he could also exploit his university education, and especially his proficiency in Latin, by opening a school for young men of the neighborhood.

The Presbyterian evangelist Samuel Davies, whose eloquence and faith attracted Sarah Syme Henry to his services at Pole Green meetinghouse, a few miles south of Studley, described her steadfast Anglican husband as "more intimately conversant with his Horace than with his Bible." Perhaps Davies was aware of Colonel Henry's engagement in a private philosophical debate about doctrines of eternal rewards and punishment with his clergyman brother and two prominent vestrymen and legislators— Richard Bland, a senior member of the House of Burgesses (the popularly elected lower house of the colonial legislature), and John Blair, Jr., a ranking member of the powerful colonial Council (which served the governor as his executive Council, functioned as the upper house of the legislature, or General Assembly, and also comprised the General Court, highest appellate court in the colony). The private circulation of letters and essays within circles of gentlemen interested in subjects ranging from theology and politics to poetry, gardening, or botany was a characteristic of gentry culture in eighteenth-century England and Virginia. This Virginia debate was part of a transatlantic dispute within the Church of England over the

nature of Christian salvation and eternal punishments that harked back to
the third-century churchman Origen of Alexandria and had been revived
by John Locke, Isaac Newton, and other voices of the Enlightenment.
The theological debate had its secular parallel in the growing recognition,
which culminated in William Blackstone's legal treatises of 1769, that severity of punishment was not an effective deterrent to crime. According to
literary historian Kevin J. Hayes: "Patrick Henry was raised among men
who . . . recognized the value of their education and its importance for understanding both the here and the hereafter."

Patrick Henry's neighbor and lifelong friend Samuel Meredith, four
years his senior, recalled that Henry learned reading, writing, and arithme-
tic at "a common English school" in Hanover by the age of ten and thereafter studied with his father as "his only tutor." Meredith, who grew up
near Studley and eventually married Henry's sister Jane, contended that
his boyhood friend "never went to any other school, public or private" but
acquired from his father by age fifteen a "knowledge of the Latin language and a smattering of the Greek," a mastery of mathematics, "of which
he was very fond," and a solid grounding in ancient and modern history.
Aside from the Anglican catechetical instruction that his uncle the Reverend Patrick Henry, Sr., offered to the children of St. Paul's parish every
spring, Meredith insisted that Henry's uncle "had nothing to do with his
education." George Dabney, eight years younger than Meredith and four
younger than Henry, remembered the colonel as "a man of a liberal education" who, to support his large family, "kept a grammar school at his
own house in which his son Patrick took the rudiments of his education."
Henry's knowledge extended well beyond government and politics, a visiting Italian statesman observed in 1787, to embrace "literature and the sciences, the study of which he still pursues in hours free of [public] affairs."

Despite occasional self-deprecating comments to such bookish men as
John Adams (to whom Henry claimed to have read Virgil and Livy at fifteen but "not looked into a Latin Book since"), Henry's mastery of Latin
extended to verse as well as history. The pages of Henry's now lost copy
of Virgil—last seen in the nineteenth century—were extensively marked
with his closely written marginalia.

Young Patrick Henry and his brothers and friends hunted, fished, and
explored the countryside. Henry spent pleasant afternoons fishing along
the Pamunkey, and he later told a curious acquaintance that he had sought

to "learn the language of the birds." He enjoyed innocent fun and the occasional prank but never, his companions recalled, displayed "the least spice of ill-nature or malevolence." His cousins Charles and George Dabney, however, did remember a favorite stretch of the South Anna River, a tributary of the Pamunkey, where their canoe seemed prone to capsize and throw them all into the river. Only later did the Dabney boys realize that while they always tumbled into the water fully clothed, Henry "under some pretext or other, was generally divested of his."

ooooo

Growing up on a farm in Piedmont, Virginia, in the 1730s and 1740s also meant growing up with slavery, an everyday reality so familiar and ordinary that Henry's youthful friends and acquaintances said nothing about it in their recollections and memoirs. Henry, to the best of our knowledge, recorded no comments about slavery until he was about thirty, but his anxieties about Virginia becoming "the gloomy retreat of slaves" were rooted in his earliest personal experiences. Enslaved persons, many of them newly imported and therefore especially alien to their British owners, comprised between 30 and 40 percent of his county's population during Henry's youth. Slaves probably outnumbered the free residents of Studley plantation. Their labor surely cushioned Henry's life (as it did for his gentry siblings and neighbors), and the grim realities of chattel slavery cannot have escaped the notice of a boy remembered for "his invariable habit of close and attentive observation."

By his tenth birthday, for example, Henry had surely witnessed enslaved children of his own age sleeping in rude cabins, beginning their long days of hard work tending fields of tobacco and corn, and eating a monotonous fare of corn, root vegetables, and small quantities of pork and fish. The stark differences in clothing could not have escaped his notice. Although toddlers of virtually all ranks in society wore similar unisex smocks in the seventeenth and eighteenth centuries, free white boys soon began wearing britches, shirts, and shoes like their fathers. Their enslaved counterparts, however, boys and girls alike, typically wore no underwear until adulthood (a practice variously attributed to slaveholders' parsimony or a deliberate strategy of degradation and humiliation).

Incidents in the neighborhood left no question about the implicit violence that sustained Virginia's slave regime—or the cultural, linguistic, and religious differences that separated Henry and his siblings from the strange dark-skinned men and women who disembarked from slave ships and were sold on the docks at Newcastle, just a few miles from Studley. When Henry was ten, his county was alerted to the escape of a "very artful and cunning" sixteen-year-old slave named Stephen, who "has been much whipt, which his Back will shew, and has several Scars in his Face." When Henry was three, a thirty-year-old Angolan named Roger escaped with his Virginia-born wife, Moll, from John Shelton, Henry's future father-in-law. Six years later other neighbors advertised for the capture and return of a young slave named Will, who "speaks but little English and . . . can't tell his Masters Name," and for two newly imported Gambians "who understand no English." By the time he was twenty, Patrick Henry could understand the anxiety some Virginians expressed about being overrun with "ignorant Heathens . . . transplanted from the barbarous Wilds of Africa."

In time Henry would lament that Virginia had not done more to encourage the immigration of "Europeans, instead of Africans." He came to believe that "the evils" plaguing Virginia included "the disadvantage from the great number of slaves," but that "to re-export them [was] now impracticable, and sorry I am for it." Quietly observant about the behavior of people he encountered, Patrick Henry seldom volunteered his own impressions, whether in conversation or in writing. From what we know that he did say about slavery, however, Henry clearly joined his contemporaries in the belief that slavery was detrimental to everyone it touched. Slavery and racial prejudice nourished "vanity and sloth," a visiting Frenchman observed. Even before they learned to walk, another French visitor wrote, white children in Virginia learned "to tyrranize over the blacks." The presence of slavery discouraged arts and manufacturing, impelled prospective white workers to despise honest physical labor, and, as Henry's political soul mate George Mason put it, exerted a "most pernicious effect on manners" throughout the community. "Every master of slaves is born a petty tyrant."

Regardless of what Patrick Henry may have thought about it as an adolescent, slavery was widely accepted throughout the British empire in the mid-eighteenth century. His attitudes toward slavery and race were inevitably shaped by the two clergymen who figured most prominently in the young man's religious upbringing—uncle Patrick Henry, Sr., and the

Presbyterian evangelist Samuel Davies, both of whom bought and owned slaves. We do not know how many slaves Patrick Henry's parents held, but his uncle listed two dozen as bequests to his daughter. And throughout the century, even the Society for the Propagation of the Gospel in Foreign Parts (responsible for promoting Anglican ministries in North America) owned and operated a Barbados sugar plantation with hundreds of enslaved laborers, some of them branded across the chest with the letters "S-O-C-I-E-T-Y."

In order to encourage the baptism and religious training for enslaved persons, Anglican bishops proclaimed (and Davies agreed) that slaveholders should have "no fear of losing the Service and Profit of their Slaves by letting them become Christians." Slavery, and even the slave trade, spokesmen for the church argued, was an accepted and natural condition. Slavery had existed throughout the ages and had been accepted by the apostles, especially Saint Paul. "The better Christian a Negro became," another prominent Anglican announced in London when Patrick Henry was two years old, "the more honest, the more contented, the more submissive, the more industrious he will prove." The duty of a Christian was not to set slaves free but to treat them decently, the bishop of Oxford declared when Henry was six.

The Reverend Samuel Davies owned fewer slaves than Henry's uncle, but he upheld the institution of slavery with equal vigor. Christ had died "for poor *Slaves* as well as for their Masters," Davies preached, "for the contemptible *Negroes* as well as Whites." Providence, nevertheless, had implemented "civil Distinctions among Mankind, that some should rule and some be subject, that some should be Masters and some Servants." Echoing Saint Paul, Davies asserted that "Christianity made no Alterations in matters of Property, in civil Distinctions, or Employments." A true Christian could be happy even in slavery, for "Liberty, the sweetest and most valuable of all Blessings, is not essential to his Happiness" because Christ's sacrifice "made him free from the Tyranny of Sin and Satan." Inviting his listeners to "ask my own negroes whether I treat them kindly or no," Davies urged slaveholders to teach their slaves to read the Bible and provide them with books—as he did with the support of English donors. Christianity, Davies bluntly advised Virginians, "will make them better Servants than the Terror of the Lash and all the servile and mercenary Measures you can use against them." The hours that some masters spent "tying them up and whipping them," Davies urged, were better spent leading slaves in worship and teaching them to read. "Certainly," the evangelist noted, "he that can lay out Forty or Fifty pounds to purchase a Slave, is able to spare a few Shillings to furnish him with a few Books for his instruction." From his own experience as a slaveholder and a pastor, Davies announced that "making Allowance for their low and barbarous Education, their imperfect Acquaintance with our language, their having no Opportunity for intellectual Improvements, and the like, they are generally as capable of instruction as the white People."

ooooo

Patrick Henry's boyhood friends apparently said nothing about their enslaved contemporaries, but they did remember that Henry was "remarkably fond of hunting, fishing, and playing on the violin." After decades of unrestricted hunting by the English colonists, deer were more scarce in eighteenth-century Hanover County than they are today, but young men found year-round opportunities to hunt small game and vermin—including wolves, foxes, raccoons, and possums—with shotguns or fowling pieces. Tidewater Virginians "never hunt with hounds," a colonial clergyman reported in the 1680s, but every household kept three or four mongrel dogs to destroy vermin. By Henry's day some Piedmont Virginians were raising hounds for foxhunting "as you do in England," but the rituals of scarlet jackets, velvet hats, and cocktails on silver trays were introduced to the upper Piedmont counties known today as Virginia's horse country early in the twentieth century by wealthy northerners.

Henry had a good ear for music and in that regard his enthusiasm was, again, representative of his contemporaries. "All Virginians are fond of music," a German officer commented during the Revolution. After breaking his collarbone at the age of twelve, Henry during his convalescence taught himself to play the flute, though only for his private enjoyment. "He was also an excellent performer on the violin," his friends recalled, an instrument better suited to social occasions in Virginia, where dancing was extremely popular. Gentry parents and guardians (including George Washington and Thomas Jefferson) insisted that their sons and nephews be taught dancing, music, and fencing, and their daughters and nieces dancing, music, and drawing. Virginians preferred the minuet, reels, and French quadrilles over the simpler country dances that were popular in northern colonies—and they were prepared to pay for their fashionable tastes. Dozens of dancing masters and music teachers flourished in eighteenth-century Virginia, conducting classes in Williamsburg and various county seats and traveling circuits from plantation to plantation throughout the colony. Shortly before Henry's birth a newly arrived royal governor reported that there was "not an ill Dancer in my Government."

ooooo

Possessed of talents and intelligence that his friends eventually recognized as "far-soaring above those of ordinary men," young Patrick Henry nevertheless seemed to his neighbors and acquaintances a typical Virginia teenager with "nothing very remarkable [about his] person, mind, or manners." He was "fond of society," and friends described his disposition as benevolent, humane, mild, quiet, and thoughtful. Henry cared about the happiness of others, Sam Meredith recalled, particularly his seven younger sisters—Jane (Meredith's future wife), Anne, Sarah, Lucy, Mary, Elizabeth, and Susannah. Henry took great pleasure in reading, contrary to the opinions voiced by political rivals misled by his modesty about flaunting one's talents or learning. Like Thomas Jefferson (later one of his major detractors) Henry spent hours "lying with his back upon a bed" reading Laurence Sterne's popular and risqué comic novel, *The Life and Opinions of Tristram Shandy*, Miguel Cervantes's *Don Quixote*, or Daniel Defoe's *Adventures of Robinson Crusoe*.

Patrick Henry combined the capacious memory of a thespian with the contemplative temperament of a preacher. He was an intensive rather than an extensive reader. He read, reread, and contemplated books of proven value and importance (an approach that many people bring to the scriptures or favorite works of poetry and literature), and he often gave away the books themselves after he had mastered their content. Like a preacher focusing on a few lines of scripture as the theme of a sermon, his son-in-law Spencer Roane concluded, Henry "read good books as it were for a text." It was in this spirit that Henry commended Montesquieu's *Spirit of the Laws*, that sprawling compendium of classical history and politics, as "a good book for one traveling in a stage-coach" because one could "read as much of it in half an hour as would serve you to reflect upon a whole day." Henry's reading habits reflect his mind and character—and his genius was routinely misunderstood by those whose eloquence required quill and paper, who amassed huge personal libraries, and who habitually filled their commonplace books with pages of quotations and notes.

Of all the comments made about young Patrick Henry's personality and character, the most penetrating insight came from his boyhood friend and brother-in-law Samuel Meredith. "There was nothing in early life for which he was remarkable, except his invariable habit of close and attentive observation," Meredith explained. "From his earliest days he was an attentive observer of everything of consequence that passed before him. Nothing escaped his attention." Henry possessed a capacity that his countrymen had prized from the moment that an Anglican priest wrote from Jamestown, their earliest capital, that Virginians "for want of bookes read men the more." The secret of Henry's persuasive oratory (and his effective leadership) was rooted less in his talents as a speaker than his skills as an empathetic listener and observer.

Whether in a tavern, a drawing room, or the halls of government, Henry relied upon his bantering conversation that "often appeared to be irrelevant to the subject" to gauge the sentiments of others without revealing his own opinions. He became a formidable trial lawyer because he had studied men as well as books, knew that the law was what a jury believed it was, and knew that scoring legal points against opposing counsel meant little compared to winning the jury, the verdict, and the damages. In court, Henry looked deep into the eyes of the jurors, farmers and planters who felt that he was one of them, and they rewarded his empathy with subtle reactions from which he discerned what to say, what not to say, and how best to win his client's case. In public or legislative debate (as we will see), Henry's contemporaries repeatedly struggled to describe the "bold, grand and overwhelming eloquence" of his oratory. Henry's "consummate knoledge of the human heart," Jefferson wrote in 1805, directed his eloquence and made him "the greatest orator that ever lived."

ooooo

Indirectly, Patrick Henry also owed his persuasive skills to his mother's religious outlook. During his teenage years, Sarah Henry (and others in her family) preferred the Presbyterian preaching of the Princeton-educated evangelist Samuel Davies over the stately Anglican cadences of her brother-in-law. On many Sundays during his teens, Patrick Henry watched his father mount up for the seven-mile ride to worship at St. Paul's Church, near the courthouse about seven miles north of Studley plantation, as he took the reins of his mother's carriage for the five-mile trip southwest across Totopotomoy Creek to Pole Green meetinghouse.

The eighteenth-century religious revival known as the Great Awakening came to Hanover County in the 1740s and swiftly penetrated young Patrick Henry's family. Triggered by the emotional preaching of George Whitefield, a protégé of John and Samuel Wesley, the founders of Methodism, the movement was fueled by its adherents' dissatisfaction with what they perceived as the flat and formal sermons of established clergymen throughout America. In December 1739 Whitefield had preached to a crowded audience at Bruton Parish Church in Williamsburg on the theme *What think ye of Christ?*—one of his most popular sermons. "His extraordinary Manner of Preaching," William Parks reported in the *Virginia Gazette*, "gains him the Admiration and Applause of *most* of his Hearers"—except those stung by his harsh words about some of his Anglican colleagues. At first the chasm that split evangelical "New Light" challengers from established "Old Light" clergy (whether Virginia Anglicans or New England Congregationalists) had more to do with rhetoric than theology. A clergyman's preaching style seemed to reveal more about his faith than the doctrines he espoused.

Patrick Henry was nine years old when his uncle registered Virginia's earliest complaints about "the New Preachers that have lately seduced some unwary people in this Parish." He was ten when his uncle let George Whitefield preach from his pulpit at St. Paul's Church—and when the colony's General Court indicted his grandfather Isaac Winston (who had been repeatedly fined by county authorities for skipping Anglican services and attending dissenting meetings) for allowing a Presbyterian itinerant, John Roan, to preach in his house without the required license from the governor and Council. No family in central Virginia felt the impact of the Great Awakening more intensely than did Henry's kin.

According to Pastor Henry's report in February 1745, the "Enthusiastick Preachers" who came to Hanover County from the New Light Synod of New Brunswick condemned the Anglican liturgy and Book of Prayer as an "abundance of lies" and maligned the established clergy as impostors with "no authority to meddle with Holy things." They claimed that as "true believers" they could distinguish hypocrites from sincere Christians—and they were certain that both Pastor Henry and the bishop of London were damned and unconverted men.

The avuncular pastor was an easy target. Parishioners who absented themselves from his Sunday services (including Sarah Henry and her father, Isaac Winston) regarded him as a lackluster preacher (and his only surviving sermon tends to confirm that impression). Evangelicals regarded him as one of the "hirelings and false prophets" that George Whitefield and his followers believed were driving people out of the Church of England "into the wilderness" of dissent. Within the Anglican establishment, the bishop of London believed that Pastor Henry had come to the colonies "more out of necessity than choice," and in Virginia the bishop's administrative representative, or commissary, thought he was one of those churchmen who exhibited less "regard for the Church's Interests [than] their own."

For his part, however, Pastor Henry criticized the evangelical visitors for preaching "the terrors of the law" and insisting that sinners "be brought to despair by way of preparation for Gospel grace." They frightened their listeners with "a violent agitation," he reported, stamping their feet and pounding their fists until their impressionable listeners "fall down and froth like people in convulsion fits." Repeatedly working their audiences into a violent frenzy, they welcomed the "penitent Souls who came to Christ" and condemned the rest as hard-hearted sinners "beyond the reach of mercy."

Unlike the itinerants of the 1740s, however, Samuel Davies discouraged the "religious Phrenzy" that accompanied religious revivals in many American communities. Upon his arrival in Virginia, Davies promptly sought and obtained licenses to preach at four locations in the county. He moved gracefully in the gentry society of Tidewater Virginia, owned slaves, published poems as well as sermons, and was firm but not combative about theology. He won the respect and friendship of governors and legislators, and after his first wife died in childbirth, Davies married the Anglican daughter of the mayor of Williamsburg. Only twice, Davies confided to his brother-in-law, the newspaperman John Holt, did he ever preach to Virginians about the Calvinist doctrine of predestination, "that tremendously unpopular Subject."

Davies called people to repentance and salvation, of course, but he also encouraged Virginians to work hard, lead moral lives, treat their slaves and neighbors decently, and sing to the Lord both the ancient psalms of David and the new hymns of Isaac Watts. He urged young men to join the army and the militia and everyone to support Britain's war against Catholic France. He also founded the Hanover Presbytery as the institutional hub of Presbyterianism in the American south. In all these ways, Samuel Davies distanced his ministry from the unsettling conduct of earlier itinerants such as John Roan while demonstrating that his followers were patriotic citizens who deserved religious toleration. Toleration was the sole object of their political activity. Beyond their support for Protestantism and quest for religious toleration, Virginia evangelicals in the 1750s and 1760s had as yet no other political agenda.

Samuel Davies had no idea how the example of his preaching helped change the course of American history. During their carriage rides home from the Presbyterian services that Davies conducted at Pole Green and Ground Squirrel meetinghouses, Sarah Henry cultivated her son's analytic and rhetorical skills by having him recapitulate both the biblical text and the substance of every sermon. Samuel Davies transformed Patrick Henry's life not by a religious conversion (for Henry remained a lifelong communicant in the Anglican, later Episcopal, Church) but by the example of his preaching style. Davies taught Henry an insight when he described the task of an effective preacher: "There is not so much Need," Davies told his listeners, "to convince your Reason of [God's] Truth," as to . . . make your Hearts sensible of it." Jefferson sounded a similar note many years later. "The secret of this singular power," he told a young lawyer in 1822, "was not produced by the force of intellect" but by Henry's unique capacity for "completely seizing the sympathies of the hearers" and exercising "some magnetic power over them." When Patrick Henry employed the impassioned oratorical style of Samuel Davies in defense of English liberties and Virginia traditions, the result was revolutionary.

In the end, however, those Sunday outings with his mother gave Patrick Henry something far more substantial than lessons in effective public speaking. As practiced by George Whitefield, Jonathan Edwards, and Samuel Davies (and arguably by all their American successors), a revivalist preacher surveyed the dire state of fallen humanity and called upon individual believers to repent and change their ways in order to save themselves *and* the world that God created. "He will execute Justice upon

Sinners as Individuals in the eternal World, but *now* is the Time for him
to deal with them as a *Society*," Davies declared. God punishes "impenitent
Nations . . . with his righteous Judgments, for their national Sins, in this
World," he concluded, "for it is only in this World that they subsist in a
national Capacity."

The secret of Patrick Henry's extraordinary power was that he hitched
the dynamic engine of personal reform—Christian virtue and civic republican *virtù*—to the defense of political and social ills that had been,
as Henry saw it, thrust upon the freeholders of Virginia's healthy commonwealth by the corrupt external instruments of a royal tyrant and an
autocratic Parliament. By harnessing the transformative drive for private
redemption to the reform and perfection of an existing but threatened
civic republican status quo, this unlikely marriage gave Henry the perplex-
ing amalgam of radical ideals supporting conservative ends that set the
American Revolution apart from all the subsequent radical revolutions
aimed at transforming both individuals and the world.

CHAPTER THREE

Decade of Misfortunes

COMPARED TO STUDLEY, Mount Brilliant was a modest residence on a 630-acre plantation in the Piedmont section of Hanover County. Designed by Henry's father in "an English style," Mount Brilliant was a story-and-a-half structure built on brick foundations with sturdy hand-hewn oak framing secured by wooden pins rather than nails. From its dormer windows one could survey the plantation's fertile lands sloping gently north toward the South Anna River and east toward Stone Horse Creek, which divided St. Paul's from St. Martin's Parish. The exact date of their relocation is unknown but Patrick Henry's family had certainly moved to Mount Brilliant by the autumn of 1751, when the St. Paul's Parish vestry elected a replacement for Colonel Henry, "who hath left the parish." If the adolescent Patrick Henry ever really lived in a forest, it was here. A Frenchman riding near Mount Brilliant complained about having to cut his way through "a forest of full-grown trees" fully three decades later. About three miles from the new home was Ground Squirrel Meeting-house, a twenty-by-twenty-foot log structure to which Sarah Henry could once more bring Patrick and his siblings to hear Samuel Davies. The Fork Church of St. Martin's Parish, where Colonel John Henry and his children attended Anglican services, stood where the confluence of the North Anna and South Anna forms the Pamunkey River about a dozen miles northeast of Mount Brilliant.

Patrick Henry's new haunts were more sparsely settled than his old neighborhood because several of the county's wealthiest families held huge tracts of land along the South Anna River. Scotchtown (now remembered as Patrick Henry's home from 1771 to 1776) was the earliest manor house in the upper county. Built about 1719, Scotchtown, after subsequent enlargement, was a "large commodious dwelling house" with eight rooms and a large central hall above a ground-level cellar, or English basement. Directly across the South Anna from Mount Brilliant, Thomas Nelson of Yorktown kept a country house on nearly twelve thousand acres. One of the county's largest landowners, Nelson was a member of the colonial Council and secretary of the colony.

The move to Mount Brilliant also introduced Patrick Henry to the families of *both* his future wives. Little is known of their courtship, but eighteen-year-old Henry married sixteen-year-old Sarah Shelton at her home near the Forks of Hanover in 1754. Her parents, John and Eleanor Parks Shelton, owned properties throughout the county—including the tavern across the street from the courthouse they inherited from William Parks, Sarah's grandfather and founding editor of the first *Virginia Gazette*. Although other generations of the Shelton family lived on Totopotomy Creek near Studley plantation, accounts that place the couple's wedding at Rural Plains have been shown to be twentieth-century inventions.

A few miles upriver from Mount Brilliant stood the home of Nathaniel West Dandridge, who would become one of Patrick Henry's earliest legal clients, and in 1777 would witness the marriage of his daughter Dorothea (born in 1755) as Henry's second wife. At the Dandridge house during Christmas celebrations in 1760 Patrick Henry first met young Thomas Jefferson, a second-year student at the College of William and Mary. "On my way to the college," Jefferson informed William Wirt long after Henry's death, "I passed the Christmas holidays at Col. Dandridge's in Hanover, to whom Mr. Henry was a near neighbor. During the festivity of the season, I met him in society every day, and we became well acquainted, altho' I was much his junior, being then but in my seventeenth year, and he a married man." As often happened, Jefferson betrayed flashes of hostility in his recollections about Henry, in this instance by faulting Henry for passing up opportunities for "conversations on scientific subjects" during the Christmas revelry. Henry excelled as a conversationalist, Jefferson grumbled, "and it attached every one to him"—as though anyone else could expect holiday partygoers to favor the scientific musings of a bright college sophomore over the social agility that he disparaged as Henry's "passion [for] music, dancing, and pleasantry."

ooooo

The 1750s were a challenging decade for Virginia, the British empire, and young Patrick Henry, too. Recurrent droughts throughout the decade decimated Virginia's tobacco, corn, and other crops, afflicting virtually every family in the overwhelmingly agricultural province. Then came the French and Indian War, triggered by a bloody clash between Virginia militia, Mingo warriors, and French troops near the Monongahela River in May of 1754. Nine years of imperial warfare raged from the Ohio Country and Great Lakes to the Caribbean, Europe, and far beyond the Bay of Bengal to the Philippine archipelago. Eventually the war terminated French control of Canada, set expansive boundaries for the British empire, and left the imperial government a huge debt. But the catastrophic July 1755 defeat of the British army and Virginia militia led by General Edward Braddock about 180 miles northwest of Hanover County was only the first in a series of reverses and failures that threatened Virginia with direct attack by the French throughout the decade. Finally, amid anxieties born of war, economic dislocation, and religious ferment, an attempt by the colonial legislature, General Assembly, to mitigate the effects of the drought sparked a political tempest that would became an early precursor of the American Revolution—and that launched Patrick Henry's political career.

Aside from a happy and advantageous marriage to the daughter of a prominent gentry family, and the prompt arrival of their daughter Martha in 1755 and their son John in 1757, Patrick Henry spent the 1750s struggling to find his place in the world.

"About the age of fifteen," according to his friend Samuel Meredith, Henry "became clerk for some merchant in Hanover"—the essential first step by which aspiring storekeepers in Virginia and Maryland (sometimes legally indentured as apprentices) learned the mercantile business. The young Scotsmen who comprised Henry's competitors generally began their careers with a five-year apprenticeship to an experienced factor, or resident merchant, who typically represented a transatlantic enterprise such as William Cuninghame and Company of Glasgow. Henry, by contrast, "continued in that employment for [only] one year," Meredith recalled, before "his father purchased a parcel of goods for him and his brother William, and they commenced business on their own account" with a store near the New Kent county line a few miles south of Newcastle.

We have no details about William and Patrick Henry's storekeeping beyond their friend Meredith's recollections—and that void has proved itself an irresistible temptation for the invention or repetition of spurious anecdotes by writers from William Wirt's day to the present. Regardless of the brevity of their mercantile training, however, their store was doomed by realities other than the inexperience (or imagined indolence) of its teenage managers. The transatlantic tobacco economy of the eighteenth-century Chesapeake ran on long-term credit. The London merchants who worked principally with Tidewater planters had established the basic system by supplying Virginians with English goods of all kinds on credit throughout the year and then settling accounts after they sold the previous year's consignment of sweet-scented tobacco for the English market. Well intentioned as Colonel John Henry may have been, his sons lacked their competitors' networks of local stores, their transatlantic shipping connections, or their deep corporate pockets secured by sophisticated London and Glasgow bankers.

When Henry married sixteen-year-old Sarah Parks Shelton in the autumn of 1754, "a woman of some fortune and much respectability," her family gave the couple "a tract of land and fourteen or fifteen Negroes" and his parents gave them another piece of land and four or five slaves. The couple made their first home at Pine Slash, a three-hundred-acre farm about midway between Studley and the Shelton property at Rural Plains. Sharing the daily experience of Virginia's other yeoman farmers, Henry labored in the fields with his slaves to grow tobacco and corn on the farm's indifferent soil—transplanting the delicate tobacco seedlings, hoeing weeds, picking off worms and suckers (buds that would otherwise form small unwanted leaves), and topping the mature plants (removing the flowers to encourage continued leaf growth).

The 1750s were difficult years for farmers in Virginia, however, especially novices like Henry. The decade brought a "variety of bad seasons," the Tidewater planter Landon Carter lamented in his diary, and the droughts of 1755 and 1758 were especially devastating. Samuel Davies spoke of seeing "parched and fading" tobacco plants and "fields that in former Seasons . . . were rich in stately, blooming Corn, now withering." Lieutenant Governor Robert Dinwiddie responded to the poor harvests and "great Scarcity of all Grain" in 1755 by prohibiting shipments to the Caribbean islands of the "Flour, Bread, Grain, or Pulse" (peas, beans, and legumes) that comprised nearly a third of the colony's export trade. "Alas! What shall I do ... to support my Family?" desperate planters wondered. One option for Henry and many of his neighbors was to "Sell some of my Slaves, or any thing in my Possession, to secure a sure Supply."

While Virginians complained about the stagnation of trade, the scarcity of money, burdensome taxes, and the high prices of goods, Samuel Davies observed that the colony's poor families were caught "in the very Jaws of Famine." But the widening war between Great Britain and France for control of North America posed equally severe threats to Virginia. General Braddock's disastrous campaign against Fort Duquesne (modern Pittsburgh) had left the entire colony vulnerable to attack. "Languishing with Drought and alarmed with the Terrors of War," as Davies exclaimed, Virginians faced the prospect "that Indian Savages and French Papists ... should rule Protestants and Britons with a rod of iron." Denied any support from imperial troops, the colony was repeatedly pressed to raise men and money for its own defense—"almost double the sum of the other colonies put together," Dinwiddie reported.

Struggling to feed and clothe his family, Patrick Henry could not answer the call to arms, but many of his neighbors rallied to defend themselves and the frontier—with strong encouragement from Samuel Davies and support among religious dissenters eager to demonstrate their patriotism against Catholic France and her Native allies. Hanover took the lead in August 1755 when Captain Samuel Overton's Independent Company of Hanover Volunteers marched westward after a rousing sermon. Davies called upon the volunteers to defend their religion "against Ignorance, Superstition, Idolatry, Tyranny over Conscience, Massacre, Fire and Sword, and all the Mischiefs ... with which Popery is pregnant"—to protect "the inestimable Blessings of Liberty, *British Liberty*, from the Chains of French Slavery"—and to keep their property and families "from falling Prey to greedy Vultures, Indians, Priests, Friars, and hungry Gallic slaves."

Three years later, however, while Davies and Henry's boyhood friend and future brother-in-law Captain Samuel Meredith were recruiting their neighbors to guard the frontier, another bout of frigid weather was drying up the plants at Pine Slash and farms throughout the colony. As late as mid-May killing frosts devastated delicate tobacco seedlings before Henry and his contemporaries could get them transplanted to their fields. Then

came "Millions of Flyes" feeding upon what was left, followed by "a terrible gust"—a term the colonists applied to major storms or hurricanes.
Wheat and oats turned yellow. Moles ravaged the corn. By early summer
many farmers had given up on tobacco and replanted their fields in corn—
Henry likely among them—but summer brought withering drought.
"Mighty hot and very drye," Landon Carter complained in July. "Grass
all burnt and every other vegetable," he grumbled in August. "Tis well we
have no tobacco to aggravate this misfortune by seeing it all dye." For all
the hard work that Henry and his slaves devoted to the fields at Pine Slash
during the droughts, only in 1757 did he manage to deliver a single hogshead of tobacco, worth slightly more than £10, to the inspectors at Page's
Warehouse.

That same year, three years into Henry's career as a farmer, fire consumed the dwelling at Pine Slash, destroying the family's household goods
and most of their furniture. At first Henry and Sarah moved their family
into a vacant overseer's house a hundred yards from the ruins—a story-
and-a-half cabin with two rooms (expanded to three rooms about 1800)
that survives to this day on a cul-de-sac a few miles south of his birthplace.
Soon thereafter the family moved to Shelton's ordinary, the sprawling inn
adjacent to the county courthouse, which Sarah's parents had purchased
from the estate of her maternal grandfather, William Parks.

Hard pressed for money, Henry and Sarah sold some of their slaves,
bought a stock of goods, and early in 1758 he opened a second country
store about a mile south of Hanover Courthouse. During its two years
of operation, from July 1758 through September 1760, Patrick Henry's
second store had mixed success—income of more than £150 against expenses of less than £50 for the first year, followed by a net loss of £57 for
the second year. The names of family and friends leap from the pages of
the earliest surviving account book: Colonel Henry and brother William;
father-in-law, John Shelton; uncles Patrick Henry, Sr., and Isaac Winston;
the reader at the lower church of St. Paul's Parish, Charles Crenshaw; the
clerk of the county court, William Pollard; and one of Henry's slaves, Jean,
buying items on his own account. After augmenting his family income
and household supplies during two otherwise bleak years, Henry sold the
store's remaining stock to a rival merchant partnership in 1760 for £25 and
change. Henry's experience as a storekeeper gave him insights into the
day-to-day realities of Virginia and the pressures felt by local planters,

farmers, merchants, and their families. And he seems to have closed the book on his mercantile career in good humor. When Henry opened a new account book for his law practice he inscribed a line from the epitaph of the poet and playwright John Gay, author of *The Beggar's Opera*, who had died in 1732, inside the front cover: "Life's a jest & all things show it."

ooooo

As a licensed ordinary (the antique English word that Virginians still used for their inns or hotels), John Shelton's establishment at Hanover Court-house was required to provide "good, wholesome, and clean lodging and diet for travelers" as well as "pasturage, fodder, provender, and stableage for their horses." Ordinaries were "indispensable" for travelers in "a country so thinly inhabited that the houses are often at a distance of two or three miles from each other," a French visitor remarked, and Shelton's ordinary was "a rather good inn" with "a very large hall and a covered portico." The main building was the 82-by-21-foot "wooden tavern" with a ground-level brick cellar, or English basement, with a 24-by-24-foot addition at the back and the porch extending along the front of the building. Nearby were a stable large enough for two dozen horses, a 54-by-32-foot wooden barn with lean-to sheds on either side, a 32-by-20-foot freestanding kitchen, and a 25-by-17-foot "private house"—all on 330 acres of land. Because Patrick and Sarah Henry assisted with day-to-day operations at the complex that came to be known as Hanover Tavern, however, and because the ordinary served beer and liquor as well as meals, Henry's brief connection with the ordinary across the road from the courthouse has long been mired in silly controversy.

"Patrick Henry was originally a bar-keeper," Thomas Jefferson told Massachusetts congressman Daniel Webster in 1824, as he had contended in a letter to biographer William Wirt twenty years earlier. Another of Wirt's informants, Hanover resident William Overton Winston, went further, attesting that he had frequently seen Henry acting as a bartender for his father-in-law "clad in a coarse shirt or jump jacket" (a short coat of jute or linen) and "very frequently barefooted." Henry "was very active and attentive to his guests," this Winston cousin claimed, "and very frequently amused them with his violin on which he performed very well."

On the other hand, three reliable observers (Edmund Winston and the Dabney brothers) said nothing at all about Shelton's ordinary. Samuel Meredith declared that "the whole story of his keeping the bar of a tavern is utterly false" and "that there is no man to whom such an occupation would have been more abhorrent." Judge Spencer Roane echoed that assessment when he told William Wirt that he had "never heard that [Henry] was ever a barkeeper, nor do I believe it," for no person "would have been more abhorrent at mixing toddy and seeing it drunk in a tavern than Patrick Henry." In the end, although Henry's first biographer embraced some dubious reports about his subject, Wirt rejected Jefferson's insinuation that Henry "was a bar-keeper by profession." Wirt recognized that John Shelton's ordinary was an eighteenth-century tavern not a nineteenth-century saloon and that it was "very natural in Mr. Henry's situation" for an obliging and gregarious son-in-law to step in if his father-in-law were absent, welcome the guests, and see that travelers (and their horses) were properly bedded, fed, and refreshed.

ooooo

In the closing months of the 1750s, while working the farm at Pine Slash, closing down the store, and helping out at Shelton's ordinary, Patrick Henry also found time (how much time remains a matter of dispute) to school himself for the practice of law. "Necessity compelled him to practice Law," one of Henry's friends recalled, "for the support of a Wife and children." Except for the wealthy few who studied law in London or Edinburgh, aspiring attorneys in colonial America generally "read the law" by apprenticing themselves to an established lawyer. Writing in the *Virginia Gazette*, an advocate for educational reform summarized the training that was typical in Henry's Virginia: "When a young gentleman has resolved to study the law," a Country Justice wrote, "he applies to some attorney for his advice, assists him in copying a few declarations, reads the first book of Coke upon Lyttleton, and the Virginia laws, and then applies for a license, and begins to practice a profession . . . which he is perhaps utterly unacquainted with." Henry's training differed from this formula only insofar as he "did not read law under the direction of any person," according to his friend Meredith, and did not even mention his aspirations to his family and friends until he had studied enough to consider applying for the bar examination.

Henry's silence surely contributed to his contemporaries' uncertainty about how extensive his legal studies had been. Edmund Winston guessed that Henry studied for six weeks, "reading such books as he could borrow." Samuel Meredith and George Dabney guessed six to eight months, "during which time he secluded himself from the world, availing himself of the use of a few law books owned by his father." Nathaniel Pope, who spoke to many of Henry's boyhood friends, believed he had studied for nine months. Much later, Henry reportedly told Judge John Tyler, father of the future president, that he had studied for a month and Jefferson that he had studied for six weeks—to which Spencer Roane replied that "if he got a license after six week's reading, that was the very reason he would not mention it, as it would look like boasting."

True to the formula described by A Country Justice, Henry focused his studies chiefly on Edward Coke's classic *First Part of the Institutes of the Laws of England, or A Commentarie upon Littleton* and the Virginia laws adopted by the General Assembly. By a curious coincidence, William Parks—owner both of the first *Virginia Gazette* and Hanover Tavern—had begun printing a new edition of the Virginia code when he died, and had directed his son-in-law, John Shelton, to oversee its completion. Literary historian Kevin Hayes plausibly speculates that some imprints from the Williamsburg press may well have stayed in the family and found their way to Shelton's ordinary—including John Mercer of Marlborough's *Exact Abridgement of All the Public Acts of Assembly*, which Parks published in 1737, and *The Acts of Assembly, Now in Force in the Colony of Virginia*, which Shelton saw through to completion in 1752. Regardless of how long Henry read the law (or where he found the books), Henry sought the advice of a rising Fredericksburg attorney, John Lewis, when he thought he might be ready for the examination early in 1760. Lewis was about seven years older than Henry and had apparently won his admiration (as well as the epithet the "Honest Attorney") for his strict refusal to defend clients he thought were wrong. Lewis encouraged Henry to apply for a license.

In spring of 1760, bearing 20 shillings for the examiners' fees and a certificate from his county court attesting to his "probity, honesty, and good demeanor," Patrick Henry went to Williamsburg in pursuit of his law license. The four gatekeepers who would decide his future were designated by the governor and his Council from the eight or ten elite attorneys who practiced only before them when they met as the General Court. Chosen because they were "learned in the law"—not simply because they were powerful Tidewater grandees—the examiners were sworn to "well and truly examine into the capacity, ability, and fitness" of candidates and decide whether an applicant was "fit and qualified or not."

If ever Henry felt awed by his surroundings or the men he was about to encounter, it might have been at this moment early in April 1760 when he ventured into a Williamsburg neighborhood designed to overawe visitors with symbols of imperial authority and Tidewater privilege. Virginia's imposing Governor's Palace, then the residence of the urbane royal governor Francis Fauquier since 1758 and home to his predecessors since 1722, stood at the north end of Palace Street, its approach framed by the town's only tree-lined boulevard. At the south end of the street stood Bruton Parish Church, built in 1715 midway between the college and the capitol along the town's main street. Commanding the west side of Palace Street between the palace and the church stood the grand homes of two examiners, and the other two lived nearby on England Street, a block to the east.

Henry's first interview was with the king's attorney general, thirty-nine-year-old Peyton Randolph, at his house a block from the palace on North England Street. After studying at the College of William and Mary and the Middle Temple in London, Randolph had followed his father, Sir John Randolph, to a career at the bar. Appointed attorney general of Virginia by George II in 1744, Randolph held that office for twenty-two years until his election as Speaker of the House of Burgesses in 1766. The second examiner was the respected jurist George Wythe, now thirty-four, who lived on Palace Street next to Bruton Parish Church. Although Wythe now enjoyed an extensive and lucrative law practice before the General Court and represented the College of William and Mary in the House of Burgesses, he had close connections with Henry's friend John Lewis. After reading law as an apprentice to a local attorney and passing the examination he was now administering, Wythe had begun practicing law in Fredericksburg in partnership with Zachary Lewis and his son, the Honest Attorney, before moving back to the capital area after the death of his first wife, John Lewis's sister Ann.

Henry's third examiner was Robert Carter Nicholas, now thirty-two, whose "large and commodious" home, enclosed garden, and outbuildings filled eight city lots between Wythe's house and the Governor's Palace. A grandson of the phenomenally wealthy planter Robert "King" Carter, a late member of the Governor's Council who had left his descendants some thirty thousand acres of land, Nicholas had studied at William and Mary and was now representing York County in the House of Burgesses. A devout Anglican with a reputation for scrupulous honesty, Nicholas would become treasurer of the colony in 1766, and when his new responsibilities overwhelmed his practice before the General Court he would assign his caseload to Henry. For the moment, it was Nicholas who accepted the candidates' fees and saw that each examiner got his share. Henry's fourth interview was at Tazewell Hall, the elegant home of John Randolph, now thirty-two, on England Street three blocks south of his brother's house. Educated at the College of William and Mary and the Middle Temple in London, Randolph was clerk of the House of Burgesses and would succeed his brother as attorney general.

Three of these four examiners were destined to become Henry's colleagues in the Revolution—Peyton Randolph as moderator of Virginia's revolutionary conventions and first president of the Continental Congress, Nicholas as treasurer of the colony, and George Wythe as clerk of the House of Burgesses, a signer of the Declaration of Independence, and in 1779 America's first professor of law at the College of William and Mary. John Randolph, however, chose exile, sailing for England as a loyalist in 1775.

Henry readily admitted, as Thomas Jefferson recalled, that he passed the examinations for his law license only "after much entreaty and many promises of future study." Beyond that generalization, however, the details of Jefferson's recollections wavered over the years. He may have been correct that Peyton Randolph "signed his license with . . . reluctance," and that Robert Carter Nicholas signed only after Henry's "repeated importunity and promises of further reading." On the other hand, Jefferson's contention that George Wythe "absolutely refused" is utterly contradicted by Wythe's signature on the license Henry presented to the Goochland County court later that month. Finally, however, Henry's own account of his interview with Attorney General John Randolph confirms George Dabney's statement (as well as Jefferson's general impression) that "one of the Gentlemen who licensed him [said] that he was so Ignorant of Law at the time, that he should not have passed him if he had not discovered his great genius."

Patrick Henry himself recounted the story of his interview with Attorney General Randolph to his friend John Tyler. Put off by Henry's appearance and his plain country clothes, Randolph was not inclined to examine Henry at all. When Henry told him that he already had two signatures, however, Randolph reluctantly agreed to ask him some questions. A few minutes of conversation persuaded the Tidewater gentleman that he may have drawn premature and "erroneous" conclusions based on Henry's appearance. With increasing surprise occasioned by "the peculiar texture and strength of Mr. Henry's style, and the boldness and originality of his combinations," Randolph "continued the examination for several hours," interrogating Henry less on the details of statute law than "on the laws of nature and of nations, on the policy of the feudal system, and on general history," which Randolph found to be Henry's "stronghold."

Focusing for a moment on the common law, Randolph professed to disagree with one of Henry's answers and challenged him to defend his opinion. This produced a debate in which the experienced attorney subjected Henry to all the techniques that Randolph used in court, drawing Henry out with questions, attempting to confuse him with subtleties, confronting him with assertions, and all the while watching the defensive operations of Henry's mind.

"You defend your opinions well, sir," Randolph finally declared, "but now to the law and to the testimony." Guiding Henry into his library and opening several volumes, Randolph said, "Behold the force of natural reason; you have never seen these books, nor this principle of the law—yet you are right and I am wrong. . . . Mr. Henry, if your industry be only half equal to your genius I augur that you will do well, and become an ornament and an honor to your profession." Thirty years later, long after he had fulfilled the attorney general's prediction, Henry reflected upon his experience in a letter to a beleaguered acquaintance. Maturity grew not from "uninterrupted tranquility," Henry wrote, but from hardships that "compel an exertion of mental power. . . . Adversity toughens manhood— and the characteristic of the good or the great man is not that he has been exempted from the evils of life, but that he has surmounted them."

At the time, however, the newly licensed attorney was too busy for sustained reflection. Henry formally presented his law license to the Goochland county court on Tuesday, April 15, 1760, and promptly represented his first client in a lawsuit. Henry almost certainly presented his license to the next meeting of the Hanover county court on Thursday, May 1, and probably when the Louisa county court met on Tuesday, May 27—and within two years his clients hailed from a dozen counties. Nor did Henry forget his promise about continuing his studies. Three days after he registered with the Goochland court, Henry's kinsman Peter Fontaine presented him with a celebratory gift of William Bohun's *Declarations and Pleadings* (London, 1733)—a working manual that showed how to write the necessary legal documents for debt actions, cases of slander, and other common-law proceedings. Henry grandly inscribed the volume with his signatures in English and in French: "Patrick Henry's Book April 18 1760, Patrice Henry le Juene son Livre avrille 18th. 1760." Within a few years, however, having mastered the techniques of declarations and pleadings in the course of his burgeoning law practice, Henry gave his copy of Bohun's treatise to another attorney, and it passed through several hands before it was acquired by the Library of Virginia.

A year later Henry inscribed his name and date—"P. Henry Jr. May 1761"—in a copy of the standard English manual for equity law, Giles Jacob's *Compleat Chancery-Practiser* (London, 1730), a complement to his books about the common law. As his practice grew, Henry accumulated nineteen volumes of law reports summarizing the arguments in trials from the days of Queen Elizabeth to the reign of George III (many of them now bearing Henry's extensive marginal comments or his bookplate), and dozens of volumes of statutes and treaties, specialized reference works, and dictionaries.

As a newly minted attorney, Henry faced stiff competition at the bar in his home county, where John Lewis, Peter Lyons, and John Semple had well-established practices. This situation prompted a few of Henry's friends to imagine that his legal career started slowly. In fact, however, by traveling to engage clients in Goochland, Louisa, and counties as distant as Augusta, Cumberland, and Orange, Patrick Henry quickly built a lucrative practice. According to his ledgers, Henry's caseload climbed from 176 cases in 1760 to 493 in 1763. During his first three years at the bar, Henry charged £1,255 in fees for 1,185 suits, as well as legal advice and the preparation of papers out of court such as wills or deeds. Henry, like other Virginia attorneys, received prompt payments from about half his clients. His cash receipts for these years totaled £634, not counting payments in kind from clients who gave him ten gallons of peach brandy, a "barren cow," a pair of breeches, a silver watch, a hogshead of tobacco, or a miscellaneous parcel of "sundries," pepper, and rhubarb.

By the close of 1763, Patrick and Sarah Henry and their children—

Martha, John, and the newborn William—were thriving. Henry found himself able to lend money to clients and help both his father and his father-in-law as they encountered financial reverses. And then, in November 1763, the Honest Attorney, John Lewis, gave Patrick Henry an opportunity to demonstrate talents that no one knew he had.

CHAPTER FOUR

The Parsons' Cause

HANOVER COUNTY'S PICTURESQUE eighteenth-century court-house now hugs the eastern shoulder of a busy modern highway that tracks the old colonial road between Richmond and Fredericksburg, from the falls of the James River to the falls of the Rappahannock. The court-house dates from about 1735, fifteen years after the county was named in honor of George I, Great Britain's German-speaking monarch and elector of Hannover. Beneath its steep hip roof with tall chimneys at either end, Hanover's original courthouse had a central courtroom flanked by two small jury chambers. Across the front of the building, a series of brick arches created a sheltered porch, or loggia, that reflected the distinctive Flemish-bond masonry of the capitol and other public buildings at Williamsburg.

On the west side of the modern highway stands a rambling wood-frame structure, greatly expanded after the American Revolution, now known as Hanover Tavern. John Shelton's ordinary offered lodging, food, and beverage to visitors who flocked into the tiny village when the county court met on the first Thursday of the month—and on December 1, 1763, it was still home to twenty-seven-year-old Patrick Henry and his family. With three years of experience in court, Henry was about to argue his first major case, a complex lawsuit brought by the Reverend James Maury, rector of Fredericksville Parish, against his Anglican vestry, or parish council. On that chilly morning Henry and his boyhood friend Sam Meredith may have taken shelter on the porch of the tavern or beneath the loggia of the courthouse as they awaited the arrival of the Reverend Patrick Henry, the rector of Hanover's largest Anglican parish.

At last, as Meredith later recalled, the Reverend Patrick Henry arrived in an impressive horse-drawn carriage, the potent symbol of an eighteenth-century gentleman. As his uncle's carriage rolled to a stop, the young attorney rushed forward and asked him not to enter the courthouse.

"Why?" the clergyman asked.

"Because I am engaged in opposition to the clergy," Henry replied, "and your appearance there might strike me with such awe as to prevent me from doing justice to my cause."

Meredith's recollection of the conversation might have been overly polite. Another account hinted at the religious and political tensions within the Henry family and forecast the "disagreeable things" the young attorney was about to assert: "I will enforce this day the rights of the people," Patrick Henry is reported to have warned his uncle, "and expose the avarice and ambition of the priests. I know them, [and] they shall have justice done this day *upon them.*"

Although posterity may never be certain about the exact words exchanged outside Hanover Courthouse on that December morning, the Reverend Patrick Henry did turn his carriage around and go home. And young Patrick Henry vindicated his clients—and the constitutional claims of the rights of the people and legislature of Virginia—with damning aspersions against the provincial clergy and the king of England.

At the heart of the Parsons' Cause was a dispute over the legitimacy of legislation adopted by the Assembly of Virginia and signed by the governor. The controversy triggered an extended public debate in Virginia and prompted five Virginia clergymen to sue their vestries for the salaries they would have received if the General Assembly had not intervened. The statutes at issue were known as the Two-Penny Acts of 1755 and 1758. Each was a temporary measure intended to aid Virginia taxpayers by adjusting fees and salaries that were normally paid to public officials (both secular and clerical) in quantities of tobacco because crop failures had more than tripled the commodity's market value in those years. Rather than lobbying against the 1758 legislation during the General Assembly session, a group of disgruntled clergy led by the Reverend John Camm, rector of York-Hampton parish near Williamsburg, chose to protest Virginia's second Two-Penny Act to the Board of Trade in London.

Camm traveled to England and there easily enlisted the support of Thomas Sherlock, bishop of London, a high-church Tory in the House of Lords. Sherlock favored both the creation of an American bishop and the extension of ecclesiastical courts into the colonies (prospects that delighted John Camm as much as they horrified many American colonists) and had enlisted his friend Queen Caroline to enforce the strict payment of tithes to Anglican clergy in England. Based on Camm's reports, Sherlock obligingly declared to the Board of Trade that he regarded Virginia's law as tantamount to "Treason"—language that elevated a provincial dispute over salaries into constitutional arguments about imperial authority in the colony.

Bolstered by the bishop's opinion, crown officials overruled Virginia's Two-Penny Act—though they ducked the question of whether the law was void from the beginning (*ab initio*) or invalid only after their ruling. After the Board of Trade's opinion reached Virginia, the five Anglican clergymen brought their suit for back pay. Each of the cases differed slightly, and four of the five plaintiffs were completely unsuccessful.

The fourth of the five plaintiffs was the Reverend James Maury, the only clergyman who won a formal ruling against the Two-Penny Act. The justices of Hanover County ruled that the Reverend James Maury's vestry and taxpaying parishioners owed him £288 in back pay—a decision that was effectively nullified by the jury a month later after Patrick Henry took charge of the vestry's defense. One result of Henry's success was that only the intrepid John Camm continued to press his lawsuit on appeals until 1766, when the Privy Council in London finally ruled against him.

After his uncle's departure, Henry encountered the usual crowd of planters and merchants, lawyers and litigants, debtors and creditors, aspiring political candidates and prospective voters who turned out for the familiar rituals of Court Days, the Old Dominion's civic equivalent of a New England town meeting. But on this December morning the usual crowd was augmented by a dozen or more Anglican parsons eager to see how much money they might hope to recover if they sued their own vestries. A month earlier, when the Hanover court had ruled in favor of Parson Maury at its November session, the vestry's original attorney, Henry's friend John Lewis, had then withdrawn from the case. Now the jury's decision about Maury's damages could set a precedent for the claims paid to ministers throughout Virginia. By law, the base salary for Virginia's Anglican clergy was set at 16,000 pounds of tobacco. In accord with the contested statute, however, they all had been paid £144 in money, computed at the legislated rate of 2 pence a pound rather than the actual, higher market value of tobacco in 1758.

Maury's suit was on the docket for the December session for the very limited purpose of having a jury determine how much back pay the vestry owed him. Maury was once again represented by Hanover's most experienced lawyer, Peter Lyons. The vestrymen entrusted their interests to a local twenty-seven-year-old attorney with just three years of litigation under his belt.

After the sheriff empaneled a jury and Colonel John Henry, the senior justice, called the court to order, the straightforward process began. Peter Lyons presented two of the area's leading tobacco merchants, Samuel Gist and James McDowall, who testified that the market price of tobacco in 1758 had been 6 pence a pound. Henry then presented a receipt bearing Maury's signature indicating that the vestry had paid him £144 in money, computed at the rate of 2 pence a pound in accord with the contested statute. Had things then gone as the clergy expected, the jury should have declared that the vestry owed Maury the difference—the substantial sum of £288, roughly twice his annual salary.

James Maury was reasonably successful in his ministry, but he and his ever-growing family were never entirely comfortable on his salary. Educated at the College of William and Mary, Maury had taken holy orders in England and begun his ministry downstream from Hanover in King and Queen County. In about 1752, "to advance his fortune," he had moved west to Fredericksville Parish, where he bolstered his salary and educated his own children—all twelve of them—by establishing a well-regarded school near the Louisa-Albemarle county line. Students there included Thomas Jefferson, James Monroe, and James Madison, first Episcopal bishop of Virginia and a cousin of the future president.

Jefferson remembered James Maury as an excellent teacher, and by all accounts he was a decent and conscientious servant of his Lord and church. Perhaps for that reason his attorney, Peter Lyons, himself an exemplary gentleman and friend of the church, chose to say a few words in court about his client's benevolence. It proved a fateful decision, for it gave Patrick Henry an opportunity to answer Lyons on behalf of his vestry clients and their parishioners—and to reassert the Virginia's claims for the legitimacy of the Two-Penny Acts.

Oral arguments presented in a county courtroom, then or now, are seldom noticed by contemporaries much less preserved for posterity. Henry's remarks in the Parsons' Cause in December 1763 proved a rare exception on both counts. Well into the nineteenth century, Hanover residents praised public speakers by allowing that an orator might be "almost equal to Patrick, when he plead[ed] against the Parsons." And the gist of Henry's arguments have been preserved for posterity because James Maury reported the details of the hearing to his fellow clergymen.

After Peter Lyons sat down, Maury reported, Patrick Henry "harangued the jury for near an hour . . . upon points as much out of his own depth . . . as they were foreign from the purpose." Maury and the clergy in the audience were appalled. Relying on the published arguments of Landon Carter and Richard Bland in defense of the Two-Penny Acts, Henry invoked the English constitutional principles advocated by John Locke when Parliament deposed James II as a tyrant in the Glorious Revolution of 1688–1689.

The Two-Penny Act of 1758 "had every characteristic of a good law," Patrick Henry asserted. "It was a law of general utility." Virginia's law was "consistent" with what Henry called "the original compact between King and people, stipulating protection on the one hand and obedience on the other"—again echoing Locke as he challenged the misuse of royal authority. "By disallowing Acts of this salutary nature," Henry declared, the king had forsaken his responsibilities and thereby "degenerated into a Tyrant." A king who fails to protect his people, Henry concluded, "forfeits all right to his subjects' obedience."

At this point in Henry's speech, Maury and "the more sober part of the audience were struck with horror." Attorney Peter Lyons vehemently declared "that the gentleman had spoken treason." Others in the crowded courtroom echoed the charge in "a confused murmur of Treason, Treason!" Maury reported. "Yet Mr. Henry went on in the same treasonable and licentious strain, without interruption from the Bench."

Henry's rhetoric was radical. His accusations were serious. But not necessarily treason. Henry's words alarmed Maury and his friends, but the king's promise to protect his subjects in exchange for their allegiance was a sacred contract enshrined in the coronation oaths sworn by European monarchs. Theorists such as Samuel Pufendorf and John Locke agreed that any monarch who commits a serious breach of trust against the well-being of his subjects, in Locke's words, "becomes no King; and loses all Power and Regal Authority over his People." The second idea, which made Henry's arguments treasonous in the eyes of James Maury, was his insistence that while Virginians owed loyalty to their legitimate monarch, the General Assembly of Virginia was coequal with the British Parliament. This part of Henry's argument was not novel, at least to most of his audience. Henry could count on the widespread acceptance of this crucial principle as it had emerged in the extensive pamphlet and newspaper debate over the legitimacy of the Two-Penny Acts.

It took another dozen years for the patriots of the Second Continental Congress to reach full consensus in May of 1775 about America's "dependence on the Crown" but independence from Parliament. And many Americans declined until the spring of 1776 to hold George III responsible for the actions of his government. The fact that Henry borrowed some of his arguments from recent pamphlets that Landon Carter and Richard Bland had written in response to the clergy's attacks on the Two-Penny Acts merely confirms the oft-forgotten truth that too much originality is a liability with judges, juries, and voters. Henry knew that familiar and dog-eared principles usually got better results in the real world than the innovative theories that so often delight academicians.

In reply to Peter Lyons's remarks about his client's benevolence, Henry chided Maury and his colleagues for betraying their official responsibilities to the community. Directly challenging the opinion expressed by John Camm, self-styled agent for the clergy in the public debate over the Two-Penny Acts, Henry characterized Virginia's established clergy as pastors not priests—public officials called to a vocation of service to their parishioners not an exalted status before God. "The only Use of an Established Church and Clergy in Society," Henry proclaimed, was to enforce "Obedience to civil Sanctions" and encourage what he called "Duties of imperfect Obligation." According to mainstream eighteenth-century Anglican doctrine, the church did two things for society in exchange for governmental support. First, as Bishop William Warburton wrote in 1736, the church reinforced law and order by teaching that God was "the Rewarder of good Men and the Punisher of ill." Second, religion encouraged sociable behavior and the "several Sorts of Duties that Civil Laws could not inforce. Such as the Duties of *imperfect Obligation*." Although many listeners may have been puzzled by Henry's use of the philosophical distinction between perfect and imperfect obligations, the court's presiding justice knew what his son meant. The distinction between perfect obligations (duties enforceable by civil, criminal, or international law) and imperfect obligations had been introduced into western thought by Samuel Pufendorf, whose writings had dominated the Scottish university curriculum when Patrick Henry's father and uncle studied at the University of Aberdeen. Imperfect obligations, Pufendorf had written, were those "left to a man's sense of decency and conscience" and not "extorted by a threat of the law." By refusing to accept the legitimacy of Virginia's Two-Penny Acts, the Anglican clergy revealed their greedy disregard for the public good. "Instead of useful members of the state," Henry declared, the litigious clergymen "ought to be considered as enemies of the community."

"We have heard a great deal about the Benevolence and holy Zeal of our reverend Clergy," Henry declared, "but how is this manifested?

> Do they manifest their Zeal . . . by practising the mild and benevolent precepts of the Gospel of Jesus? do they feed the Hungry and Clothe the naked? Oh no, gentlemen! . . . These rapacious Harpies would, were their power equal to their will, snatch from the Hearth of their poorest parishioner, his last Hoe-Cake! from the Widow and her Orphan Children, their last Milch Cow! the last Bed, nay, the last blanket from the lying-in Woman!

Henry implored the jury to stand firm in defense of the local vestry and the colonial legislature against dictatorial intervention by the crown lest they "rivet the chains of bondage on their own necks." The jury's verdict, Henry demanded, should make "such an example of [Pastor Maury] as might, hereafter, be a warning to himself and his brethren." The verdict should affirm the validity of laws adopted for the good of the colony by Virginia's own General Assembly and duly signed by their benevolent and patriotic royal governor.

But how could the jury send this message? For regardless of Henry's eloquence, the court had already ruled that the vestry of Fredericksville Parish, and all the parishioners whose taxes supported that parish, owed back pay to the Reverend James Maury. Maury's report of the hearing reveals Henry's solution. "*If they must find* . . . for the Plaintiff," Henry advised the jury, they "need not find more than one farthing."

Accordingly, Maury wrote in disgust, the jury "went out, and, according to instruction (though whether according to evidence or not, I leave you to judge), in less than five minutes brought in a verdict for the Plaintiff, one penny damages."

After hearing the verdict, Maury claimed that the sheriff stacked the jury against him by excluding gentlemen and recruiting jurymen "among the vulgar herd," including three or four "Dissenters of that denomination called *New Lights.*" When he disputed the sheriff's choices, Maury told his friends, "Patrick Henry (one of the Defendant's lawyers) insisted they were honest men, and therefore unexceptionable, they were immediately called to the book and sworn." On this detail, modern scholarship sides with Henry. A thorough examination of courtroom procedures and personnel in Goochland County demonstrates that demographic composition of Maury's jury was typical of area juries in the eighteenth century.

James Maury and the Anglican clergy had sought royal intervention to win their case against the people of Virginia and their elected representatives. The bishop of London and Board of Trade had ventured the king's authority in support of their position. Now they all were appalled to discover that Patrick Henry's radical language reflected ideas that were widely shared among the people of Virginia. "The ready road to popularity here," Maury lamented, "is to trample under foot the interests of religion, the rights of the church, and the prerogative of the Crown."

The people of Hanover and Louisa counties felt differently. The crowd burst into celebration after the jury returned its verdict, carrying Patrick Henry from the courthouse on their shoulders. Then, at their first opportunity—a by-election in 1765—the grateful voters of adjacent Louisa County sent him to his first term in the House of Burgesses. Henry had articulated what would become the colonies' fundamental constitutional justification for the American Revolution. Within eighteen months, the murmurs of "Treason!" voiced in Hanover County, Virginia, on the wintry morning of December 1, 1763, would soon resound through the capitol in Williamsburg when Patrick Henry transferred the lessons of the Parsons' Cause to the British Parliament and the Stamp Act.

CHAPTER FIVE

Visit to Williamsburg

IN THE WEEKS after the December 1763 decision in the Parsons' Cause, Henry's neighbors had begun to recognize his potential as a candidate to succeed Nathaniel Dandridge in the Assembly. For the moment at least, Henry disagreed, for he had much to learn about politics. As events played out through the summer, however, Henry was able to school himself on provincial and imperial affairs from the *Virginia Gazette*s and in conversation as he conducted his business at monthly meetings of the county courts. Then, come autumn, Henry took advantage of a three-week sojourn in Williamsburg by transforming the trip into an inconspicuous political reconnaissance mission.

Henry was not entirely a stranger to the members of the Assembly. His half-brother John Syme, Jr., was representing Hanover County in the House of Burgesses, and Henry had grown close to the brothers sitting for Louisa County, Thomas and William Johnson. November 1764 was, nevertheless, the occasion of Henry's first opportunity to see the General Assembly in action. At the capitol he could attend deliberations in the House of Burgesses, witness the subtle protocols of parliamentary debate, and comprehend the practical uses of procedural measures such as petitions, resolutions, and committee reports.

Hanover County's midcentury elections for burgesses were often contentious, sometimes triggering disputes that had to be decided by the Assembly's Committee of Privileges and Elections. February 1764 was such an occasion, which prompted Henry's friend Nathaniel West Dandridge to challenge his defeat by James Littlepage, a prominent Hanover planter and former clerk of neighboring Louisa County. By *promising* to alter "the damned Inspecting Law" that regulated the quality of marketable tobacco, Littlepage ran afoul of colonial Virginia's election laws. Although modern voters admire candidates who make and keep their promises, eighteenth-century regulations meant to guarantee the independence of Virginia legislators prohibited candidates from offering voters not only "money, meat, drink, entertainment or provisions" but also "any promise, agreement, obligation or engagement" about legislation or policy. When the Assembly convened eight months after the disputed election, Dandridge's challenge to Littlepage's apparent violation of this rule brought Patrick Henry to Williamsburg.

On several mornings in November, one burgess noticed "an ill-dressed Young Man sauntering in the Lobby" of the capitol at Williamsburg. The young man "seemed to be a Stranger to every Body," the burgess told Edmund Winston. Soon thereafter, however, when the Committee on Privileges and Elections met about Hanover's disputed election on Friday, November 23, Winston's acquaintance was "surprised to find this same Person was Counsel for one of the Parties, and still more so, when he delivered an Argument superior to any Thing [the member] had ever heard." Judge John Tyler, then a seventeen-year-old reading law in Williamsburg, recalled that Patrick Henry appeared before the burgesses wearing "very coarse apparel," but that his eloquence "on the great subject of the rights of suffrage . . . from a man so very plain and ordinary in appearance struck the committee with amazement." Although the committee report that Chairman Richard Bland presented to the burgesses on Monday, November 26, respected the cogency of Henry's arguments, Dandridge lost his appeal. Henry's predilection toward a strict enforcement of public morality (which he voiced again in the capitol on many occasions) apparently envisaged a higher standard for compliance with campaign laws than the House of Burgesses cared to enforce.

Henry was already acquainted with Attorney General Peyton Randolph and Elizabeth City county burgess George Wythe, who had examined him for his law license. His presence as Dandridge's counsel also brought him into contact with the provincial leaders who served with Richard Bland on the Committee of Privileges and Elections. Several other committeemen would figure prominently in his subsequent career as well. Edmund Pendleton was a self-made Caroline County attorney who had chosen to advance himself by a close political alignment with the Tidewater elite and especially his client, Speaker John Robinson, Jr. Pendleton outlived Henry by three years and became his virtual nemesis in many political encounters. Colonel Landon Carter of Richmond County, an extremely wealthy planter famous for his essays in the Parsons' Cause, would share Henry's opposition toward Parliament but abhor his populist tactics. Richard Henry Lee, of Westmoreland County, and his elder brother Thomas Ludwell Lee, of Stafford County, would become frequent political allies and occasional rivals. John Page of Rosewell in Gloucester County would eventually serve as Henry's lieutenant governor. In the more immediate future, George Johnston of Fairfax County would soon endorse and support Henry's resolutions against the Stamp Act.

Henry's visit to Williamsburg was the first time he met the chair of the Committee on Privileges and Elections. But more importantly it was the occasion when Henry bought the copy of Richard Bland's month-old pamphlet, *The Colonel Dismounted: or The Rector Vindicated . . . containing A Dissertation upon the Constitution of the Colony* that remained in his personal library for the rest of his life. Henry had already drawn upon Bland's and Carter's earlier essays for his courtroom arguments in the Parsons' Cause—he now acquired Bland's new and ultimately revolutionary explication of the Virginia constitution from the shop on Duke of Gloucester Street where Joseph Royle published the *Virginia Gazette*.

Purportedly written "purely for amusement" as his final rejoinder in the pamphlet skirmishes over the Two-Penny Acts, *The Colonel Dismounted* was a third-person report of an imaginary dialogue between Bland and the Reverend John Camm, the outspoken parson who had stirred up the controversy. After twenty pages laden with twists of eighteenth-century humor that exhaust today's readers, Bland ended his invented conversation with five straightforward pages on the constitution of the colony. Bland's exposition advanced the ideas about the autonomy of Virginia's legislature and the responsibilities of kingship that he and Landon Carter had sketched earlier and that Patrick Henry had espoused in the Parsons' Cause.

The Colonel Dismounted explained how Virginians saw their constitutional position within the British empire months before anyone in Virginia would learn that Parliament contemplated taxing the American colonies. His dissertation on the constitution was a straightforward attempt to determine which spheres of government action were appropriate to colonial and imperial executives and legislatures—but, as historian Bernard Bailyn recognized, the constitutional principles that Bland articulated in *The Colonel Dismounted* also "lay at the heart of the Anglo-American struggle" that began in Williamsburg that autumn. With Richard Bland's 1764 pamphlet in hand, and his defense of Virginia's constitution in mind, Patrick Henry was well armed for the political disputes of the coming months. When melded with the Lockean assessment of kings and tyrants that Henry had asserted at Hanover Courthouse, these arguments for Virginia's legislative autonomy were principles that Patrick Henry would sustain throughout the decade of imperial controversy that ended with American independence.

Richard Bland began his examination "into THE POWER OF THE GENERAL ASSEMBLY TO ENACT LAWS" with the basic constitutional principle of the colony's founding. It was a mistake to suppose that "the present inhabitants of Virginia [were] a people conquered by British arms" and therefore subject to the governance by right of conquest. Virginians were, rather, "the descendants of Englishmen who by their own consent and at the expense of their own blood and treasure undertook to settle this new region" and "they were as much freemen and had as good a right to the liberties of Englishmen after *their* [*own*] conquest as they had before" coming to America. Rooted in the colony's charters of 1606, 1609, and 1612 and reinforced by a century and a half of colonial experience, this denial of government by conquest reflected an essential element of English constitutional thought. "Under an English government all men are born free," Bland wrote, and "only subject to laws made with their own consent." Thus it followed that freeborn Virginians, who enjoyed all the liberties and privileges of English subjects, "must necessarily have a legal constitution" with "a legislature composed in part of the representatives of the people" empowered to "enact laws for the INTERNAL government of the colony." Richard Bland was forthright about the implications of these fundamental principles: "Without such a representative [component], I am bold enough to say, no law can be made." On the other hand, based on the incontrovertible principles that he deduced from the nature of the English constitution, Bland asserted "that the legislature of the colony have a right to enact ANY law they shall think necessary for their INTERNAL government."

For the "EXTERNAL Government" of the empire, Bland recognized, Virginians were "subject to the Authority of the British Parliament." But if Parliament tried to impose laws upon the colonists for their "INTERNAL

Government" that would deprive Virginians "of our Birthright as English-men, of being governed by, Laws made with our own Consent." Parlia-ment, "as the stronger Power, can force any Laws it shall think fit upon us," Bland conceded, but the important question was "not what it can do, but what constitutional Right it has to do so." Bland expressed confidence that Virginians had "nothing of this Sort to fear from those Guardians of the Rights and Liberties of Mankind." Nevertheless, he warned explicitly that Parliament had no constitutional right to impose legislation or levy taxes within the colony of Virginia: "Any tax respecting our INTERNAL polity which may hereafter be imposed on us by act of Parliament is arbitrary," Bland announced, "and may be opposed"—a principle that Patrick Henry embraced.

ooooo

The consequences of Patrick Henry's three weeks in Williamsburg were profoundly important. Henry witnessed both levels—one public and the other confidential—of Virginia's very first opposition to the announce-ment by George Grenville, leader of the king's government in Parliament, that he intended to impose stamp duties on the colonies. The burgesses began formulating their public response while Henry was in Williams-burg and finished the job after he had gone home. But for those who cared to examine it (as the ill-dressed young man sauntering in the lobby surely did), the entire file of correspondence between the Assembly leadership and their agent in London lay open for review on the clerk's table in the chamber of the House of Burgesses from mid-November to the end of the legislative session on December 21.

The new crisis had begun in England on Friday evening, March 9, 1764, when several hundred members of Parliament from England, Scot-land, and Wales crowded into St. Stephen's Chapel of Westminster Palace, meeting place of the House of Commons, to hear George Grenville, first lord of the Treasury, describe his plans for coping with the nation's bal-looning postwar debt. The title of prime minister was not yet in use, but as the third leader of His Majesty's government in the three years since George III had ascended the throne, Grenville had charge of an empire that now stretched from Canada and the Caribbean to the Indian Ocean by virtue of Great Britain's recent defeat of France and her various allies. But the victory had not come cheap.

In a speech that lasted two hours and thirty-five minutes, Grenville attributed half the national debt of £146 million to the recent war—and since America "gave birth" to that war, he declared, Parliament needed to raise revenues in the colonies to pay down the debt and offset future expenses for imperial defense. Not surprisingly, Grenville's audience welcomed his unexpected announcement that when Parliament reconvened in 1765—a full year later—he would introduce a program of stamp duties for America. Although Grenville was brazenly ignoring some long-acknowledged constitutional requirements about obtaining revenue by consent, his audience comprised men whose families owned most of the land in Great Britain, paid most of the land tax that supported the government, and welcomed the prospect of sharing that burden with the American colonists.

Englishmen had been familiar with domestic stamp duties for nearly a century, and for two years George III and his ministers had been deliberating in private about how to impose taxes on the colonies. Although Grenville announced his plan for stamp duties long before his aides even began drafting the legislation, his slapdash approach didn't bother Englishmen at the time because everyone in Parliament knew how stamp duties worked. In retrospect this was the first of many arrogant blunders that would undermine the Stamp Act of 1765 and instigate rebellion. Of the options they considered for raising a revenue in America, British leaders agreed that a stamp tax was "the least exceptionable" because "it requires few officers and even collects itself"—an assessment that was another overconfident blunder because the colonists had no prior experience, aside from duties on imported goods, with any forms of direct parliamentary taxation.

In response to Grenville's proposal, the House of Commons adopted a formal resolution that said only that "towards defraying the necessary expenses of defending, protecting, and securing the *British* Colonies and Plantations in *America* . . . it may be proper to charge certain Stamp Duties in the said colonies and plantations." This vague statement fostered confusion about the ministry's intentions, and this confusion was compounded by the fact that parliamentary debates and proceedings were not yet routinely published, so there was no accepted record of what Grenville had said.

In a subsequent meeting with the official agents that many colonial legislatures hired to represent their interests in London, Grenville seemed to invite suggestions from "the several provinces" about the "modes best suited to their circumstances [to] raise a sum adequate to the expense of their defense." Although Virginia's agent described this invitation to his clients, in fact it was another of the mixups that cloaked Grenville's real intentions throughout the Stamp Act fiasco. According to an experienced parliamentarian's notes, Grenville expressed only his vague "wish to follow to a certain degree the inclination of the people in North America, if they will agree to the end"—which turned out to mean that the only information he really wanted was to make sure that no unfamiliar American documents escaped his duties. When the colonial agents asked Grenville for copies of the bill so their clients "might have the whole, both substance and form under their deliberation," Grenville begged off because "the Bill was not yet thoroughly digested." In fact, work on the final bill did not begin until five months later; a full year passed before the colonial agents saw the legislation, and the American public first saw the Stamp Act of 1765 as a fait accompli in colonial newspapers several weeks after its enactment.

During 1764 only two aspects of the ministry's program *were* clear. Grenville had asked the members of the House of Commons whether anyone doubted "the power and sovereignty of Parliament over every part of the British dominions for the purpose of raising or collecting any tax" rather than "suffer objections of that nature at a future day." The only MP who spoke against a stamp duty was a prominent London merchant who preferred other ways of raising a revenue in America. No one disputed the constitutional principle. Virginia's agent emphasized the depth of Parliament's support in his urgent dispatch after Grenville's speech: "The House appeared so unanimous in opinion that America should ease the revenue of this annual expense," Edward Montague cautioned his Virginia clients, "that I am persuaded they will not listen to any remonstrance against it." The second obvious aspect of Grenville's program was an open secret—a concept so familiar that no one mentioned it in open debate. The great significance of Stamp Act was the precedent it created, according to barrister Thomas Whately, the most able of Grenville's lieutenants, the man responsible for drafting the legislation, and the anonymous pamphleteer who invented the idea of virtual representation in its defense. The Stamp Act was "a great measure," Whately boasted to a friend in private, "on account of the important point it establishes, the right of Parliament to lay an internal tax on the colonies."

ooooo

Virginia's response to this threat of parliamentary taxation began in June 1764 after the ship bearing Edward Montague's urgent dispatch docked at Yorktown. During their contest over the Two-Penny Acts the House of Burgesses had hired Montague in 1759 as its own agent in London, winning the acquiescence of Governor Fauquier and the Council (who already had their own agent) to Montague's appointment by welcoming several members of the Council to a new Committee of Correspondence responsible for monitoring events between Assembly sessions and directing the agent's lobbying efforts in London. As a result, Montague's warning about stamp duties came directly to the attention of the colony's most powerful leaders when they gathered for a hastily called meeting on Friday, June 15, 1764.

In the months since they last met, their agent Edward Montague had sent them six reports from London, culminating with the March 10, 1764, warning about Grenville's stamp duty that had just arrived in Williamsburg. "Much alarmed" by Grenville's intended duties, "particularly on Madeira Wine and the proposal for a Stamp Duty," the committee wanted Montague to oppose them "with all his Influence" and especially to "insist on the Injustice of laying any Duties on us and particularly taxing the internal Trade of the Colony without their Consent." The prospect of a stamp duty was "truly alarming" because it contradicted "the most vital Principle of the British Constitution," that the king's subjects were "subservient" only to laws or taxes enacted with their consent. To help their agent press their objections with his "whole weight and influence so far as Decency will allow," the committee gave George Wythe and Robert Carter Nicholas six weeks to draft detailed instructions to Montague that addressed both principles and tactics.

Wythe and Nicholas presented a draft that reflected all of Richard Bland's thoughts about the constitutionality of internal and external taxation and legislation when the Committee of Correspondence met again on Saturday, July 28, 1764. Both the draft text and the committee's subtle revisions show how skillfully Virginia legislators began their protest against Grenville's plan. At this early moment in the dispute, they had to decide about how hard to press their constitutional objections. Lest they seem too strident, the committee added a few words (shown here in italics) softening the instruction that Montague exert his "whole weight and influence *so far as Decency will allow* in opposing this and every other Measure of the Sort." As experienced parliamentarians the committee wanted Virginia's protest to be firm but diplomatic, manly but polite. Only civility had any chance of success. As spokesmen for an institution that had modeled itself upon the House of Commons since the 1640s, however, these Virginians also wanted to present themselves as Virginia gentlemen addressing their English political equals. With the burgesses slated to meet that autumn, the committee hoped their London agent could persuade the ministry to "postpone any Determination on this Subject till we can furnish you with their Sentiments." In the meantime they also asked Montague to comb the British archives for copies of Virginia's charters and grants going back to 1606, which may be "useful to us not only upon the present Dispute but upon any other Occasion."

As Henry examined the draft letter he could see the committee's intense fear (emphasized by another alteration shown here in italics) that if Parliament could establish a precedent for taxing America, "not only we and our Children, but our latest Posterity may *and will* probably be involved in its fatal Consequences." Virginians felt they had taxed themselves with "greatest Chearfulness" to support the recent war. What worried them was not the money a stamp duty might raise but the creation of a precedent for "taxing the Colonies at pleasure." Parliament's intention of imposing "internal" taxes was not "a little step" against the constitution but "a long and hasty Stride . . . of the first Importance."

Eighteenth-century British politicians were obsessed with precedent, especially men like Patrick Henry with training and experience as lawyers or legislators. The knack for anticipating dangerous or advantageous precedents was an elemental feature of jurisprudence and governance in a civic culture that venerated the common law. Precedent was "the first ground and chief cornerstone" both of the common law and of Britain's celebrated unwritten constitution according to the preeminent legal authority Sir William Blackstone. If Parliament could create a precedent for easing the tax burden of its English, Welsh, and Scots constituents at the expense of the king's American subjects, where would it end? "What makes the approaching Storm appear still more gloomy and dismal," the

Virginians lamented, was that a successful precedent for taxing Americans would have dire and lasting consequences.

Time and again in the years leading up to the American Revolution, participants based their decisions not only on their assessment of an immediate situation but also upon their experience with analogous situations in the past and, especially, their anticipation of how future adversaries or friends would take advantage of whatever precedent might be inferred from today's decision. Jousting over the creation or avoidance of precedents was central to eighteenth-century constitutional discourse. A precedent for taxing America was far more valuable to the ministry and dangerous to the colonists than the revenue itself.

Rather than admit a precedent for taxation by Parliament, Virginia's Committee of Correspondence was confident that when the General Assembly convened in October it "would rather agree to lay on themselves any reasonable Apportionment of the Sum intended to be raised in the Colonies." Conversely, the principal draftsman of Grenville's Stamp Act had assessed his handiwork in a private letter as "a great measure on account of the important point it establishes, the right of Parliament to lay an internal tax on the colonies." To explain why American colonists were almost paranoid about threats to liberty, historians often point to the influence of civic republican ideas and radical Whig traditions from the seventeenth century. The transatlantic obsession with precedent, however, fueled the deep mistrust to which minds schooled in the common law and parliamentary practice easily fell victim—especially when the actions of men like George Grenville inspired reasonable suspicions in the minds of men like Patrick Henry (and vice versa).

Henry and his contemporaries—both British and American—were prone to the impassioned informal logic that philosophers and ethicists describe as slippery-slope reasoning—the prospect that a small first step will inevitably trigger a chain of events leading to a drastic and usually catastrophic result. Henry and his Virginia colleagues feared that the slightest acquiescence about taxation would inevitably result in tyranny and slavery—while their counterparts in Great Britain acted as though any limit whatsoever upon parliamentary sovereignty would destroy both Britain's delicately balanced constitution and the empire. This rift between Great Britain and the colonies became as turbulent as the storms of the North Atlantic, and Edward Montague's grim forecast that Parliament *will not listen* to Virginia's objections would be confirmed time and again in the years ahead.

Thanks to the Parsons' Cause, Virginia leaders reacted to Grenville more decisively than their sister colonies with well-developed arguments rooted in their own colony's history—to the point of echoing Richard Bland's and Patrick Henry's scorn for rapacious clergymen as enemies of the community. At the close of their letter to Montague, the committeemen reiterated their worries. "Every mention of the Parliament's Intention to lay an Inland Duty upon us," the committee advised Montague, "gives us fresh Apprehension of the fatal Consequences that may arise to Posterity from such a precedent." If money "must be raised in the Colonies," they asked, "why not in a constitutional Way?" Great Britain might be powerful enough to extort money by military force, as Richard Bland would argue in his next essay, but surely no man "dared be such an *Enemy to his Country* as to say that [Parliament] have a Right to . . . the Destruction of the Constitution." "These things we write to you with great Freedom," the committee advised its agent at the end of its letter, "but your Discretion will teach you to make prudent use of them."

References to *enemies of the country* on both sides of the Atlantic reflected the deep-seated clash between Virginians and Parliament over the nature of the imperial authority in the decades since the Glorious Revolution. As events played out between 1765 and 1776, Virginians would discover many occasions when radical Whig perceptions of parliamentary corruption and imperial decadence fit their perceptions of British political conduct. On the other hand, the blunt truth was that the Virginians were correct in 1764 about Grenville's unprecedented determination to impose direct taxes within the American colonies. He and Whately *did* seek a strong precedent for taxing America, and Grenville himself told George III privately in 1765 that anyone who opposed his Stamp Act was a "criminal" and "betrayer of his country."

ooooo

After the burgesses rejected his client's electoral challenge in November 1764, Patrick Henry had no compelling reason to linger in Williamsburg. He could mount his horse and ride west to Hanover County thoroughly familiar with Virginia's prospective reaction to the proposed stamp duties and aware that the burgesses were delaying final action on a threefold public response until all their other business was complete. Landon Carter had adapted the arguments he and Richard Bland had developed over the years into an address to the king and a memorial to the House of Lords. Richard Henry Lee, a rising leader from the Northern Neck, had pushed for and helped draft a memorial to the House of Commons, despite the misgivings of Speaker John Robinson and Attorney General Peyton Randolph, who saw no point in addressing any protest to the very institution whose authority Virginians were denying. The quill of George Wythe certainly touched all three documents, too, but weeks of deliberation erased any hallmarks of individual authorship in the final texts that all the members of the House of Burgesses and the Governor's Council could accept.

Written as though the burgesses were kneeling before their king, Carter's polite address asked first for permission to approach the throne and then for his gracious protection of Virginia's "ancient and inestimable Right of being governed by such Laws respecting their internal Polity and Taxation as are derived from their own Consent, with the Approbation of their Sovereign or his Substitute." The address closed with humble expressions of hope that in a reign already distinguished by his majesty's "gracious Attention to the Liberties of the People," the "invaluable Birthright . . . will not be suffered to receive an Injury."

Virginia's legislators had more trouble formulating their memorials to the Lords and Commons "in a respectful Manner, but with decent Firmness." What was the proper way to inform the House of Lords that while Virginians regarded "their connection with Great Britain, the Seat of Liberty, as their greatest Happiness," nevertheless Parliament had no right to tax or legislate for them? How graciously could the burgesses insist upon their sole authority for internal legislation while reminding the House of Commons that "British Patriots will never consent to the Exercise of anticonstitutional Power"? While New York and Massachusetts legislators asked Parliament to respect American control of its own taxation as "a matter of favour . . . and not a claim of right," the Virginians insisted upon "their just and undoubted rights as Britons" and their duty to resist "subversive" measures threatening "that Freedom which all Men, especially those who derive their Constitution from Britain, have a right to enjoy."

Eager to get home for the holidays, Virginia's burgesses and councilors settled upon the final wording of their protests on December 18 and directed the Committee of Correspondence to have Edward Montague arrange "their being respectively presented" to the king, lords, and commons. Three days later Governor Fauquier adjourned the Assembly until May after signing all the legislation completed in the busy weeks since October. Then, on Christmas Eve, Fauquier penned a cautionary note to the Board of Trade about the Assembly's protests, although he had "not yet seen them." The governor was skeptical about assurances offered by a few legislators who had worked to "mollify" the protests that there was "nothing now in them which will give the least Offence." Fauquier rather expected that the king, Lords, and Commons would regard the tone of Virginia's protests as "very warm and indecent."

ooooo

Before leaving Williamsburg, Patrick Henry had taken another revealing step toward his entry into politics. On Saturday, November 24, 1764—the day after the Assembly hearing about the Dandridge-Littlepage election—Henry visited the *Virginia Gazette* print shop and paid £3 2s for the eight-hundred-page folio volume of Baron Samuel von Pufendorf's *Law of Nature and Nations*, one of the great seventeenth-century treatises on natural law, morality, jurisprudence, and government. An influential predecessor of John Locke (and Virginia's most popular continental author on legal subjects), Pufendorf insisted that nature created all men equal and that civil society began when free individuals in a state of nature gave their consent to a social contract. Henry later celebrated the likes of Pufendorf, Hugo Grotius, and Emmerich de Vattel as "illustrious writers" and benevolent spirits who "held up the torch of science to a benighted world." As Henry read Pufendorf over the winter of 1764–1765 for insights about Virginia's situation, however, several parts of the massive compendium had special significance.

As a practicing lawyer, Patrick Henry had much to contemplate in Pufendorf's sophisticated discussion of the legal ethics in a chapter entitled "Speech and the Obligations which attends it." In criminal cases (which later comprised a significant and lucrative part of Henry's practice) Pufendorf endorsed an accused person's right to counsel and an attorney's responsibility for defending clients charged with criminal behavior regardless of their likely guilt or innocence. For civil suits, however, Pufendorf stood closer to Henry's friend John Lewis, the Honest Attorney, by condemning any tactics that impeded "the injured party from obtaining his Right as soon as possibly he may."

As a rising advocate for Virginia's constitutional principles, Henry found many passages in Pufendorf's *Law of Nature* that refuted ancient ideas about the divine right of kings and endorsed the standards of royal conduct that Henry had articulated in the Parsons' Cause. Pufendorf's language was more ponderous than Locke's or Henry's, but his opinion about "*Dereliction* or *Desertion* on the Part of the Sovereign" was clear. If a monarch failed to protect his community, the baron wrote, "the [authority] of the said Sovereign doth expire."

In the context of the issues raised by the impending stamp duties, however, the most significant passage that Patrick Henry encountered in *The Law of Nature* was Pufendorf's succinct discussion of the relationship between colonies and their parent states—the very same passage that the combative Boston lawyer James Otis quoted that summer in a pamphlet entitled *The Rights of the British Colonies Asserted and Proved*. Pufendorf identified three situations. First, a colony might remain "a Part of the *Commonwealth* it was sent out from." Second, a colony might "pay dutiful Respect to the *Mother Commonwealth*" within "a sort of *unequal Confederacy*." Third, a colony might transform itself "into a *separate Commonwealth* and assume the same *Rights* with the *State* it is descended from."

Patrick Henry and his contemporaries were not advocating American independence in 1764 (indeed James Otis contended that America's duty was "to submit and patiently bear" Parliament's exertion of authority), but clearly they recognized that independence was a logical possibility—and a possibility that struck fear in the hearts of many eighteenth-century British observers. A dozen years earlier, James Abercromby, who served as agent for Virginia's governor and Council in London and also supported Grenville's stamp duties as a member of the House of Commons, "laid it out as a fundamental Maxim" that maintaining the "Subserviency" of Britain's colonies was the chief objective of colonial governance. Americans were not yet "disposed to throw off their Dependency and to Assume to themselves sole . . . Sovereignty," Abercromby wrote in 1752. Nevertheless, "they are Subjects under peculiar Circumstances, formed into Separate Societys, that in time may feel their new Strength."

Henry's encounter with Pufendorf's ideas about colonies and independence came on the heels of widespread speculation as to whether Britian's retention of Canada as a prize of war would weaken colonial ties to the mother country. Most observers thought not. If independence came at all, surely it would be far in the future—"in the space of thirty or fifty years" (according to a visiting Swedish scientist) or "at too great a distance to be dreaded" (according to a North Carolina pamphleteer). Far in the future, with just one lethal caveat. Independence "can never reasonably be supposed to happen," an anonymous pamphleteer wrote in 1755, unless Americans "were driven to that extremity by usage which would make *Britons* themselves impatient of subjection." Although Baron Pufendorf invited Patrick Henry and other readers to recognize the abstract *possibility* of colonial independence, no Americans were advocating separation from Great Britain in 1764. The colonies would remain "dutiful and obedient," Benjamin Franklin contended, so long as imperial "government is mild and just" and "important civil and religious rights are secure." Only "the most grievous tyranny and oppression" could shake America's confidence in their king and mother country.

CHAPTER SIX

Scandal and Protest

IN OCTOBER OF 1764 John Shelton sold the tavern at Hanover Courthouse where Patrick Henry and his family lived while he initiated his law practice and prepared himself for politics. Henry used the necessity of moving his family into a new residence to make his move toward elected office. While he was in Williamsburg in November, Henry had his mulatto overseer, James Matthews, buy enough lumber—650 boards at £1 6s per hundred—to build a new house on 1,700 acres that Henry had acquired from his father to settle an outstanding loan. A local carpenter, John Gilbert, began work in March of 1765 at Roundabout Creek some forty miles northwest of Mount Brilliant. The family's new house stood near Major Thomas Johnson's plantation, Roundabout Castle, about half a dozen miles south of Louisa county courthouse. When completed the following autumn it was a modest residence—twenty by eighteen feet according to a neighbor—with two large rooms at the front of the house, each with a fireplace; children's bedrooms in the half-story upstairs; and Patrick and Sarah's bedroom beneath a sloping shedlike roof at the back. By 1769 Henry had expanded his holdings at Roundabout to two thousand acres, although his ten slave laborers—Ben, Dick, Isaac, Ben, Dinah, Beck, Jenny, James, Will, and Pedro—had as yet only cleared and cultivated about thirty acres of tobacco by 1771, when Henry bought Scotchtown plantation and moved his family back across the county line to northwestern Hanover.

Henry's triumph in the Parsons' Cause had won him immense popularity among Louisa County voters, especially among the Reverend James Maury's parishioners and the county's religious dissenters. That victory had also won him the friendship and gratitude of the influential Johnson family. Henry's new neighbor was the same Thomas Johnson who, as collector of the parish levies, had been the specific target of Maury's lawsuit. He and his younger brother William had also represented Louisa County at the autumn session of the House of Burgesses and were slated to return when the Assembly reconvened in the spring of 1765. More significantly, Patrick Henry and the Johnson brothers were political soul mates, sharing as they did a populist skepticism about some of the Tidewater grandees and their profligate spending that would surface anew during Henry's first days in the Assembly.

By a vote of 37 to 32, the burgesses in 1759 had censured Thomas Johnson for disparaging their honor with allegedly "false, scandalous, and malicious" statements made at his home on the evening after an election in November 1758. In addition to his claims that another burgess and frontier leader had "cheated the Country out of eleven Hundred Pounds" and yet retained his prominence in the Assembly (charges that were regarded as substantially true), Johnson had described the Assembly as a place of "Plots, Schemes, and Contrivances" where "one holds the Lamb while the other skins." Too many burgesses exploited the public trust for personal gain, Johnson told his neighbors, "and it would surprize any Man to see how the Country's Money is squandered away." Among Johnson's specific targets was the most rapacious royal careerist, John Randolph, clerk of the House of Burgesses and later attorney general. When the burgesses were deliberating about Randolph's salary, the clerk had strolled through the chamber and "nodded to his Creatures or Partizans on each Side," Johnson complained, encouraging their generosity in respect to his salary. Although Johnson, too, "was solicited by Mr. Randolph, the Clerk, and many of the Members, to be for the largest Sum which was proposed for the Clerk's Salary," he had refused and thereby incurred the wrath of the powerful Tidewater burgesses allied with Speaker John Robinson and the Randolphs.

Owning property was the minimal threshold for participating in the political life of colonial Virginia, and the laws allowed freeholders to vote and seek office in any county where they owned property. Although Patrick Henry did not move his family into their new home until November or December of 1765, he was eligible for election to the vacancy occasioned by the convenient resignation of Louisa County's junior burgess, William Johnson. Early in May the grateful Louisa residents who had carried Henry on their shoulders after his triumph in the Parsons' Cause got their

chance to send him to Williamsburg. Despite his popularity and the backing of the powerful Johnson family, Henry took no chances at the polls. At
least forty-one Hanover residents with sufficient landholdings in Louisa
traveled west to vote for Henry. On May 20, three weeks into the Assembly session, Patrick Henry took the oaths required of a new burgess—
swearing his allegiance to king and country, his acceptance of the Anglican
faith, and his denial of Roman Catholicism—and was named to the standing committee on courts of justice.

ooooo

No one had expected much to happen when the House of Burgesses reconvened on Wednesday, May 1, 1765. Attendance was slim. Fewer than
sixty of the 113 elected members made the trip back to Williamsburg after
their pre-Christmas adjournment. Their business was expected to be routine. One burgess had died since the last session and three had resigned,
including William Johnson, to accept appointments as sheriffs or coro-
ners. After the house asked the governor to issue writs for the customary
by-elections to fill these vacancies, it turned its attention to legislation it
had nearly completed before its Christmas recess—including provisions
for improving the colony's credit. The three weeks before Patrick Henry
arrived were uneventful. It seemed too early to expect a report from the
Virginia agent Edward Montague about the protests against the Stamp
Act sent to London in December. And despite some general anxieties
about the economy, few people outside the mercantile community were
alarmed by rumors about the careless administration of Virginia's paper
currency by the powerful Speaker, John Robinson, who had also served as
treasurer of the colony since 1738.

Late in the 1750s the General Assembly had financed Virginia's wartime expenses by issuing paper currency meant to circulate for limited pe-
riods of time (specified by expiration dates printed on each note) and then
be destroyed as the money came back to the Treasury either in tax payments or in exchange for new bills bearing a later expiration date. English
merchants and crown officials were always skeptical about paper money
issued by the colonies, but Virginia's currency had held its value better
than most—until the autumn of 1764. Responding to new imperial restrictions on colonial money, the governor had instructed Virginians who
held expired notes to exchange them for currency bearing later dates—but

unfortunately the treasurer ran out of money. "When People brought in their Notes, there was no Money of any Sort to redeem it," a member of the Governor's Council wrote in horror. The fiasco had "the Appearance of a Bankruptcy" and "caused a great deal of noise amongst the Trading people."

Three days before Henry entered the Assembly, Joseph Royle's *Virginia Gazette* published an anonymous article proposing an audacious quarter-of-a-million-pound scheme to create a Loan Office and restore the treasury. Speaker Robinson and his cronies proposed to have the colony borrow £240,000, use £100,000 to buy up the existing currency, invest £140,000 in circulating "Bank Notes," and pay off the entire plan over thirty years through a combination of poll taxes and increased export duties on tobacco. When Attorney General Peyton Randolph suddenly introduced the plan to the House of Burgesses on Friday, May 24, scarcely anyone knew the full extent of the illicit personal loans that Robinson had made by recirculating expired currency that he was supposed to burn. On the other hand, three of the ten legislators who represented their chambers in conference about the plan were deeply indebted to Robinson: Carter Braxton and Archibald Cary each owed more than £3,400 and councilor William Byrd III owed a whopping £10,166 (slightly more than one tenth of all Robinson's illicit loans).

Had the Loan Office plan succeeded, Thomas Jefferson later explained, "the debts due to Robinson on these loans would have been transferred to the public, and his deficit thus compleately covered." Instead, forewarned by the previous week's newspaper article, Patrick Henry was ready to attack the plan on his third day as a burgess "in that style of bold grand and overwhelming eloquence for which he became so justly celebrated afterwards."

A frequent spectator at Assembly sessions while he was studying law in Williamsburg, Jefferson witnessed the debate over the Loan Office from the lobby of the burgesses' chamber and mistakenly credited Henry with its defeat. In fact the resolutions authorizing the Loan Office passed the House of Burgesses and were rejected by the Governor's Council, though Jefferson was doubtless correct that Henry found stronger support from "members of the upper counties" than from "the aristocracy of the country."

Jefferson described Patrick Henry's bold affront to the Speaker and his allies as "indelibly impressed on [his] memory." Proponents of the loan scheme urged that many planters had debts that would ruin them if forced to immediate payment but "with a little indulgence of time might be paid with ease." Henry responded by denouncing both "the spirit of favoritism on which the proposition was founded and the abuses to which it would lead." Jefferson wrote that he could "never forget [the] particular exclamation" with which Henry "electrified his hearers"—"What, Sir!" Henry demanded, "is it proposed then to reclaim the spendthrift from his dissipation and extravagance, by filling his pockets with money?" Although Henry's eloquence did not crush the Loan Office "in its birth," as Jefferson later claimed, key members of the Governor's Council shared Henry's concerns about fairness, integrity, and virtue. Few Virginians had a better grasp of the colony's fiscal situation than Richard Corbin, a member of the Governor's Council and receiver-general of His Majesty's quit-rents, the annual fee due from landholders that comprised a major portion of the provincial operating budget. The Council regarded the Loan Office "as a Tax upon the frugal to promote Luxury and Extravagance." Corbin privately suspected that the scheme had been devised "only to help the [treasurer] out of the mire in which he has plunged himself." On this subject, the outspoken young burgess and the shrewd imperial bureaucrat were of one mind: Only "Industry and frugality," Corbin wrote and Henry believed, "can relieve us and make us a Happy People."

ooooo

Soon after the vote on the Loan Office, when the business of the Assembly session seemed over, Edmund Pendleton recalled that he and "many of the Members retired" to their homes and left behind a bare quorum of thirty-nine burgesses, according to Governor Fauquier's headcount. And just days after their exodus a ship docked near Williamsburg about Tuesday, May 28, carrying an urgent letter from Edward Montague along with the final text of the Stamp Act, which itemized no fewer than fifty-five direct taxes scheduled to take effect throughout the colonies on November 1.

The House of Commons had silenced Montague when he attempted to present Virginia's "manly but decent" protest from the Committee of Correspondence. And both houses of Parliament had spurned the memorials that the General Assembly sent in December. Only Virginia's petition to George III remained unanswered. Its authors, whom Thomas

Jefferson regarded as "the cyphers of the Aristocracy" as he remembered these events many years later, still insisted that a favorable response to Virginia's eloquent petition "was daily expected." Others were skeptical, and in fact the king steadfastly refused to acknowledge any American petition that challenged British authority over the colonies.

Sensing the hesitation among Virginia's established leadership, Patrick Henry reacted immediately. Taking a blank page from an old law book, as he told the story in the note he left with his will, Henry drafted seven resolutions against the Stamp Act. Colonel Robert Munford, of Mecklenburg County, and George Johnston, of Fairfax County, may also have conferred with Henry and helped draft the resolves, but the principles Henry espoused were the same that he had borrowed from Richard Bland and Landon Carter for his speech at Hanover Courthouse in 1763, that the Committee of Correspondence had conveyed to Virginia's agent in 1764, and that the burgesses had expressed in their December address to the king and memorials to Parliament. Patrick Henry did put an aggressive spin on these earlier arguments, and he did not tailor his language to English sensitivities. Each resolution was succinct and forceful.

While the Committee of Correspondence had *privately* advised the London agent that they regarded anyone who thought Parliament had a right to tax Virginia as an enemy of the colony, Henry's seventh and final resolution thrust that revolutionary idea into the public discourse. Already at odds with Speaker Robinson and his friends over the Loan Office, the brash new member from Louisa County also backed his resolutions with shocking oratory that fearlessly implicated George III as a tyrant in regard to the Stamp Act. On Wednesday, May 29, Patrick Henry and his allies moved that the House of Burgesses resolve itself into a committee of the whole "in Consequence of the Resolution of the House of Commons of Great Britain . . . charging certain Stamp Duties in the Colonies and Plantations in America." Thomas Johnson seconded Henry's motion.

As a procedural measure, the committee of the whole facilitated discussion of complex issues by relaxing some of the rules of ordinary debate. Members were allowed to speak more than once on the matter in question, for example, and the terms of proposals and resolutions were easier to amend or refine. In England the Speaker left the chair when the House of Commons went into committee of the whole (and sometimes retired from the chamber) while the house chose a chairman who presided from the

clerk's table. In Virginia the chairman—in this instance Attorney General
Peyton Randolph—seems to have presided from the Speaker's chair while
Speaker John Robinson often participated in committee debate—a privilege otherwise denied to the presiding officer. Finally, like any other committee, once the committee of the whole had finished its deliberations, its
chairman reported its conclusions to the house for deliberation and debate
in regular session. These procedural rules meant that the burgesses debated Patrick Henry's resolutions against the Stamp Act in committee on
May 29 and again in regular session on May 30.

After Peyton Randolph took the chair, Henry introduced his resolutions one by one and urged their adoption. Johnson supported him with
"solid reasoning," according to young Thomas Jefferson, who had taken
a break from his law books to witness the debate from the door to the
lobby along with his friend John Tyler. The opposition came principally
from Richard Bland, Robert Carter Nicholas, George Wythe, the powerful Speaker John Robinson, and committee chair Peyton Randolph—men
whom Jefferson described as the "old members whose influence in the
house had till then been unbroken." The old guard's strongest argument
was that Henry's resolutions were redundant and inflammatory, merely re-
peating sentiments they had expressed "in a more conciliatory form" in the
December address and memorials "to which the answers were not yet received." Governor Fauquier would report a similar rift between his loyal
friends and the "young, hot and Giddy members" he believed Henry had
beguiled, but the deeper reason for the intense clash over Henry's resolutions was the passage of the Stamp Act itself. For Speaker Robinson and
his conservative friends, it had been one thing to dispute pending legislation and was now quite another to defy an act of Parliament. In 1764 the
burgesses had vigorously protested against pending legislation. Opposition to the Stamp Act now threatened to cross the line between legal protest and extralegal defiance. One was the respectable conduct of statesmen
and citizens, the other was the notorious behavior of criminals and rebels.

Patrick Henry's first resolution, which closely echoed the memorials
adopted in December, passed without much controversy. Virginians had
long agreed that their earliest ancestors "brought with them, and transmitted to their Posterity" all the rights and privileges enjoyed by the people
of Great Britain. The second resolution was similar. Royal charters from
James I guaranteed Virginia settlers the liberties and privileges "of Den-

izens and natural Subjects, as if they had been abiding and born within the Realm of England." This, too, was constitutional gospel straight from Carter and Bland, the Committee of Correspondence's letters to Montague, and the Assembly's December protests.

The burgesses also endorsed Henry's third resolution. "Taxation of the People by themselves, or by Persons chosen by themselves to represent them," was a "distinguishing Characteristick of British Freedom, without which the ancient Constitution cannot exist." Parliament disagreed, but Virginians believed that only their own provincial legislature knew "what Taxes the People are able to bear." Only Virginia's General Assembly knew "the easiest Mode of raising them." Only the burgesses of Virginia, whose lives and property were directly "affected by every Tax laid on the People," could offer their constituents "Security against a burdensome Taxation."

Henry's fourth resolution again crossed swords with Parliament by asserting principles widely accepted in His Majesty's most ancient and loyal colony. The authority for Virginia's laws of "internal Polity and Taxation" rested upon "their own Consent, with the Approbation of their Sovereign, or his Substitute." A heritage of self-governance stretching back without interruption for a century and a half and enshrined in the county courts and General Assembly had "never been forfeited or yielded up." Henry's fifth resolution—which passed by one vote on May 30 and was then rescinded and expunged from the official journal the next day—bluntly declared that Virginians were not bound to obey "any Law or Ordinance ... designed to impose any Taxation whatsoever upon them" except for legislation adopted by their own General Assembly.

Having summed up Virginia's constitutional arguments in five increasingly vigorous resolutions, Patrick Henry sensed that he had pushed the burgesses as far as they were willing to go toward outright resistance to Parliament. "The Gentlemen had two more resolutions in their pocket," Governor Fauquier reported to the Board of Trade, but "knowing them to be more virulent and inflammatory, they did not produce them."

Patrick Henry's sixth resolution would have declared that any attempt to shift the authority for taxation and legislation away from the General Assembly toward "any other Person" (such as George III) "or Persons whatsoever" (such as Parliament) was unjust, illegal, unconstitutional, and likely to "destroy British as well as American freedom." Henry's final resolution, advocating social pressure and coercion as weapons in defense

of colonial liberty, was the most radical of them all. Echoing the private
sentiments expressed by the Committee of Correspondence (as well as
his own strictures against the established clergy in the Parsons' Cause),
Henry proposed that any person who contended "by speaking or writing" that the king or Parliament had "any Right or Power to impose or
lay any Taxation on the People . . . shall be deemed an Enemy to this his
Majesty's colony."

ooooo

Thomas Jefferson and John Tyler came back at ten the next morning,
Thursday, May 30, when a bare quorum of the burgesses reconvened to
consider the resolutions discussed in committee the day before. Two thirds
of the elected members were absent, but word of the impending debate
had spread around town and attracted a crowd. One new face in the lobby
that morning was a Scottish wine merchant in his early thirties who had
been touring the American colonies since December. Charles Murray,
who later served as British consul to Madeira, was traveling on business
for the Madeira-based firm of Scott, Pringle, Cheap & Company and had
spent the previous week in Portsmouth recuperating from a carriage ac-
cident. After stopping for breakfast at Yorktown, Murray had arrived in
Williamsburg late that morning. Hurrying past the bodies of three slaves
hanged for felony theft at the gallows near the public jail, Murray "went
immediately" to the capitol to witness a debate that would shake the foundations of the British empire.

The burgesses endorsed Henry's first resolutions by votes of 22 to 17,
Speaker John Robinson opened the historic debate by calling upon
Peyton Randolph for a report from the committee of the whole. Randolph rose from his seat, read the previous evening's resolutions aloud,
and delivered the text to the clerk's table. Substantive parliamentary debate, whether in Williamsburg or in Westminster, customarily began after
the second reading. Accordingly, while Clerk John Randolph read each
resolution in turn for the second and third times, Murray, Jefferson, and
Tyler found themselves "entertained with very strong Debates" and Patrick Henry's "torrents of sublime eloquence."

The burgesses endorsed Henry's first resolutions by votes of 22 to 17,
but as John Randolph continued the readings, Henry's majorities grew
narrower. Debate on the fifth resolution "was most bloody," Jefferson recalled. Its declaration that Virginians owed allegiance only to laws enacted

by their own General Assembly passed only by a vote of 20 to 19. "By God, I would have given 100 guineas for a single vote," Jefferson heard Peyton Randolph exclaim as he left the chamber after the debate. One more negative vote would have "divided the house" and allowed Speaker Robinson to break the tie and reject Henry's fifth resolution outright.

The torrents of eloquence that Henry discharged against the Stamp Act were even more radical than his resolutions. The language of his resolutions challenged Parliament and the Grenville ministry without attacking the king—an opposition strategy perfected over the centuries by Englishmen seeking to oppose the king's ministers and *their* policies without risking the gruesome penalties for treason by directly opposing the king. Patrick Henry, by contrast, lambasted the king himself as ultimately responsible for the conduct of his government, based upon the fundamental contract between a legitimate monarch and his loyal subjects that Henry had described at Hanover Courthouse in the Parsons' Cause. Henry bolstered his arguments against the Stamp Act with stunning references to civic-republican heroes. Lucius Junius Brutus was regarded as the founder of the Roman Republic for overthrowing the tyrant Lucius Tarquinius Superbus in 509 BC. Marcus Junius Brutus was prominent among Julius Caesar's assassins in 44 BC. And Oliver Cromwell was the parliamentary leader and general associated with the trial and execution of Charles I in 1649. Invoking these historic figures as a warning for the future, Henry denounced the Stamp Act every bit as dramatically as he would clinch his reputation with his speech about Liberty or Death a decade later.

"Tarquin and Caesar had each his Brutus!" Henry thundered.

"Charles the first, his Cromwell!

"And George the Third ..."

"Treason!" shouted Speaker Robinson, and cries of "Treason! Treason!" echoed through the chamber.

Henry paused. It was "one of those trying moments which is decisive of character," according to John Tyler, who was listening in the lobby with Jefferson. Both men agreed that Henry did not waver. Fixing his eye on the Speaker he finished his sentence with firm emphasis: "... and George the Third may profit by their example. If this be treason, make the most of it."

ooooo

The Caesar-Brutus speech against the Stamp Act was a "splendid display of Mr. Henry's talents," Jefferson recalled, "such as I have never heard from any other man. He appeared to me to speak as Homer wrote." Edmund Pendleton, who had left the session days earlier, wrote that he "heard a Gentleman commend Mr. Henry's dexterity in playing on the line of treason, without passing it." Asked by Henry's first biographer to confirm Paul Carrington's and John Tyler's accounts of the speech, Jefferson remembered "the cry of treason, the pause of Mr. Henry at the name of George the Third, and the presence of mind with which he closed his sentence, and baffled the charge vociferated."

Charles Murray, however, left a slightly different account of the Caesar-Brutus speech and especially of Patrick Henry's response to Speaker Robinson's intervention. "Shortly after I came in," Murray wrote, "one of the members stood up and said he had read that in former times tarquin and Julius had their Brutus, Charles had his Cromwell, and he Did not Doubt but some good american would stand up, in favour of his country." At that moment, according to Murray, Speaker Robinson scolded the burgesses because "the last [member] had spoke traison, and [he] was sorry to see that not one of the members of the house was loyal Enough to stop him, before he had gone so far"!

"Upon which," Murray's diary continued, "the Same member stood up again (his name is henery) and said that if he had affronted the speaker, or the house, he *was ready* to ask pardon." Henry then reaffirmed his loyalty to George III, Murray reported, attributing his strong language to the "heat of passion" and "the interest of his Countrys Dying liberty which he had at heart." Henry also ventured that "he might have said more than he intended, but, again, *if* he said anything wrong, he begged the speaker and the houses pardon." Finally, Murray wrote, several other burgesses spoke up in Henry's defense and "that affair was dropped."

Historians writing in 1953 pounced on this passage in the "French Traveller's" diary as evidence of cowardice or insincerity on Henry's part—an oft-repeated accusation that is naive on two counts. First, the accusation ignores centuries of parliamentary etiquette. Like their English brethren, Virginia burgesses routinely embellished their oratory with oh-so-gracious offers of apology for their zingers. Second, Patrick Henry was on his way to becoming one of the most effective trial lawyers in modern history. Like an attorney apologizing for an outburst that supplies jurors with information they are not supposed to hear, Henry said he "*was ready* to ask pardon ... *if* he said anything wrong." When necessary, wrote the Williamsburg jurist St. George Tucker, Patrick Henry could bow to the authority of a court "with a grace that would have done honour to the most polished courtier in Westminster Hall." His proffered apology in the Caesar-Brutus speech was neither cowardly nor duplicitous. It was the gambit of a quick-witted and skillful lawyer. "A tactical retreat that took nothing away from the audacity of the speech," historian Rhys Isaac concluded. A familiar trick, says an experienced lawyer, for any viewer "who has ever watched a courtroom drama on television."

ooooo

Having secured the passage of his first five resolutions against the Stamp Act, Henry rose early on Friday morning and headed home. Jefferson had risen early, too, more intrigued by events at the capitol than the black-letter pages of Coke's Institutes or his recently purchased copies of the *Complete Dictionary of Arts and Sciences* and William Cheselden's *Anatomy of the Human Body*. At about ten o'clock on May 31, Jefferson watched his distant cousin, Peter Randolph, enter the burgesses' chamber and thumb through the journals at the clerk's table. Now a member of the Governor's Council, Randolph came in search of a precedent for expunging a decision that he remembered from his tenure as clerk of the house in the 1740s. The curious law student stood at one end of the table as Randolph searched the journals for the telltale erasure, but Jefferson did not recall whether Randolph ever found it.

When the bell rang and Speaker Robinson called the house to order, however, the house apparently accepted whatever precedent Peter Randolph had found. "Some of the timid members, who had voted for the strongest resolution," now moved to rescind Henry's fifth resolution and erase it from the record. Henry's fifth resolution utterly disappeared from the official journal of the House of Burgesses, and the successful motion and vote to rescind it were never recorded.

Despite this effort to rewrite history in the pages of the house journal, however, the Speaker and his allies could not control what witnesses saw and said. Although Charles Murray was puzzled by the dispute over precedents for "entering resolves on the records," he was present again that Friday morning for what he described as "very hot debates *stil* about the

Stamp Dutys." And the text of Murray's diary leaves no doubt that people in Williamsburg were openly and accurately discussing the gist of Henry's *seventh* resolution. "One of the resolves" that some burgesses still favored, the young merchant wrote,

> was that any person that would offer to sustain that the parle-
> ment of Engl[an]d had a right to impose or lay any tax or Dutys
> whats[oeve]r on the american Colonys, without the Consent of
> the inhabitants thereof, Should be looked upon as a traitor, and
> Deemed an Enemy to his Country.

Once the house journal had been sanitized, Governor Fauquier summoned the burgesses to the council chamber on Saturday, June 1, and dissolved the Assembly. The following Tuesday evening he opened the palace for the customary celebration of the king's birthday, an event that usually drew crowds of burgesses and townspeople. Charles Murray attended "in Expectation of seeing a great Deal of Company" on his last night in the capital, "but was disappointed for there was not above a Dozen of people."

ooooo

As the young wine merchant left Williamsburg for the last time on Wednesday morning, Governor Francis Fauquier began drafting a report for the Board of Trade about the recent Assembly session. With it he enclosed a copy of Virginia's four official resolutions against the Stamp Act. "Very indecent Language was used by a Mr. Henry," Fauquier wrote, "who carried all the young Members with him." Speaker Robinson, Attorney General Randolph, and George Wythe offered a spirited opposition to "this rash heat," the governor explained, but they "were overpowered." If more burgesses had stayed for the end of the session, Fauquier suggested, "there is cause at least to doubt, whether [Patrick Henry's resolutions] would have been the Sense of the Colony"—a statement that stretched the truth if only to shield Fauquier's friends in the Assembly from imperial censure because he knew his administration could not function without their support.

Governor Fauquier also managed to keep the four official resolutions out of the *Virginia Gazette*. Its aging publisher, Joseph Royle, was not about to risk an annual stipend of £375 as printer for the colony by offending the governor and senior leaders of the Assembly. Fauquier's attempted suppression of the official texts backfired, however, as secrecy often does. Had Royle published the four resolutions from the journal of the House of Burgesses, newspaper editors in other colonies would have reprinted them. Instead, when denied access to these official texts, newspapers throughout the colonies disseminated unofficial versions of *all seven* resolutions, thereby portraying Patrick Henry's views, and especially his denunciation of the enemies of the people, as the authentic voice of His Majesty's most ancient and loyal colony. Royle's deference toward the governor also cost him his business monopoly when several Virginians encouraged Maryland printer William Rind to establish a second, independent *Virginia Gazette* in 1766 with the motto "Open to All Parties, but Influenced by None."

The radical version of Patrick Henry's resolutions against the Stamp Act first appeared in print in Newport, Rhode Island, in June 1765. Newspapers in Annapolis, Boston, Philadelphia, and New York published them in July—and other printings may yet be discovered in the unexplored files of provincial newspapers from Georgia to New Hampshire or in the Caribbean, Scotland, and Ireland. By mid-August the full original version of Henry's resolutions reached London, where their impact was heightened because they gave British readers their first glimpse of America's reaction to the Stamp Act.

"Mr. Henry has lately blazed out in the Assembly," the *London Gazetteer* declared on August 13, "where he compared George III to a Tarquin, a Caesar, a Charles the First, threatening him with a Brutus, or an Oliver Cromwell." That same day, Thomas Whately sent a version of the Virginia resolutions to George Grenville, who immediately reacted to Henry's seventh resolution as an example of Virginia's "dangerous and desperate doctrines." Thrown out of office in July after he had exasperated George III, Grenville wondered how the new ministry under Lord Rockingham would respond. "Have you seen the Resolutions of the assembly of Virginia declaring the Parliament of Great Britain [as] Enemies of their Country and that the sole right of imposing Taxes is in themselves?" Grenville asked a cousin and political ally. The ousted minister wondered "what answer our new ministry will give" to the Virginia resolutions and Patrick Henry's "new fangled and desperate Doctrines."

ooooo

The old guard's bitter opposition to Patrick Henry, historian Thad Tate has suggested, reveals the political consequences of the debates of May 1765. Beyond matters of tone and tactics, none of Henry's resolutions departed from the principles held dear by most Virginians. And although Henry and his strongest supporters were freshman burgesses, the traditional disdain of veteran legislators for upstart newcomers does not account for their anger. Despite Governor Fauquier's depiction of Henry's group as young, hot, and giddy, Virginia's burgesses routinely favored talent over seniority. Promising newcomers were often given opportunities to grow into their responsibilities. Indeed Henry himself, having arrived three weeks into his first session, was nevertheless immediately offered an important committee assignment often denied to senior members of more modest talents.

Clerk John Randolph's son Edmund pointed toward a more significant shift in his posthumously published *History of Virginia*. As the colony expanded and new counties were created, Randolph detected the gradual emergence of a new generation of legislators whose political outlooks diverged most notably from the men around Speaker Robinson and Attorney General Randolph in their views about public spending: "While one would pay a public servant upon a strict calculation of the labor to be performed," Edmund Randolph observed, "the other would augment the stipend for the sake of dignity." At issue was less a clash of crass economic interest than of two differing styles of politics, one emphasizing the representation of one's constituents and the other one's responsibilities as a magistrate.

In addition to their focus on the dignity of office, Henry's adversaries were experienced with the politics of a transatlantic imperial world in which they had enjoyed significant influence with royal officials in the colony as well as consignment merchants and policymakers in London—a realm of experience exemplified by the knighthood conferred in 1732 upon Peyton and John Randolph's father (Edmund's grandfather) for his support of the Robert Walpole administration's legislative program in Parliament. Patrick Henry and his allies, on the other hand, had little direct experience with imperial politics and saw the empire as a more remote and intrusive element in provincial affairs. They and their constituents traded with Scottish factors at local stores in situations that fostered distrust rather than confidence, and their perceptions of imperial issues tended to be more abrupt and plainspoken than nuanced or subtle. At bottom, the fundamental differences in May 1765 focused not on constitutional principle or resentment toward newcomers but on the strategic implications of the three resolutions that were kept off the official record. By refusing to accept the Stamp Act and branding its supporters as traitors, Henry and his allies showed themselves willing to abandon the older leaders' familiar lines of imperial communication and incite open defiance of British law. Henry suddenly provided effective leadership for an emerging style of American politics that seemed, to rivals such as John Robinson or Edmund Pendleton, akin to demagoguery. For many years these new men had meandered without a leader, Edmund Randolph concluded, until "at this critical moment, Patrick Henry appeared as a member from the county of Louisa."

As newspapers throughout the colonies reprinted versions of Patrick Henry's resolutions during the summer of 1765, their principles galvanized American resistance to the Stamp Act. Between September and December 1765, eight colonial legislatures followed Virginia's example with denunciations of the stamp duties. Well into the summer of 1765, Patrick Henry's defiant language inspired and emboldened patriots in the other colonies as it echoed through the newspapers, taverns, and coffeehouses of North America. Maryland statesman Daniel Dulany folded Henry's arguments into his well-known pamphlet, *Considerations on the Propriety of Imposing Taxes in the British Colonies*, published anonymously in Annapolis on October 24 and promptly denounced in Boston by the mercurial firebrand James Otis, Jr., "as a Species of high Treason."

Far more vivid than the testimony of dusty newspapers and pamphlets, however, were the lively observations that Charles Murray recorded in his diary as he continued his tour up the Atlantic coast. After celebrating the king's birthday with Governor Fauquier in Williamsburg, the young Madeira merchant witnessed the spreading ripples of Henry's resolutions as he feasted his way northward through the Old Dominion, Maryland, Pennsylvania, and New York before sailing for home in October 1765. Murray "was realy surprised to hear the people talk so freely" about their opposition to Parliament, but quickly learned that "this is Common in all the Country."

Early in June Murray spent several days in Hanover County, trapped by heavy spring rains, where "nothing [was] talked of but the stamp Duties." He heard "a great deal said about the Noble Patriot Mr. henery, who lives in this County," and he spoke with planters who declared they would defend Henry "to the last Drop of their blood." Defiant Hanoverians "muttered betwixt their teeth, let the worst Come to the worst we'll Call the french to our sucour."

Feasting near Annapolis on Tuesday, June 18, Murray raised his glass as Maryland leaders offered toasts to "the King's health, the virginia assembly, and then Damnation to the Stamp act." En route to Baltimore, Murray dined the next Monday at the Patapsco ferry with a large group of gentry planters and their families whose conversation was "Continually on the Stamp Dutys." As the evening grew late and liquid, Murray caroused with tipsy Maryland planters cursing the Stamp Act, "Damning their souls if they would pay," and boasting to their ladies that "they would fight to the last Drop of their blood before they would Consent to any such slavery." At a dinner in Annapolis, James Tilghman, father of the chief justice of Pennsylvania, told Murray that the newly favored afterdinner toast in Boston was to "the virginia assembly!"

ooooo

Patrick Henry's vigorous constitutional objections to the Stamp Act found a friendly audience among Massachusetts patriots whose own attempted protest had been gutted by Lieutenant Governor Thomas Hutchinson. The distinguished attorney Oxenbridge Thacher was overjoyed when he discovered Virginia's resolutions in a Boston paper. "They are men! They are noble spirits!" Thacher exclaimed. "It kills me to think of the lethargy and stupidity that prevails here." Bay State patriots welcomed the prospect of a political partnership with Virginia. John Adams never wavered from his belief that Virginia's resolutions and "the eminent patriot Patrick Henry, Esq. who composed them" expressed "the universal opinion of the continent."

In a backhanded way, even New England's friends of the British ministry testified to the impact of Patrick Henry's resolutions. Many people walking along King Street in Boston that July witnessed James Otis, Jr., in a fit of rage railing against the Virginians for treason. Thomas Hutchinson later claimed that Virginia's declaration, "that all who maintained the right of parliament should be deemed enemies to the colony," was responsible for "those acts of violence which soon after were committed in Boston."

Another Harvard-educated attorney also blamed the Virginia resolutions for a transforming public opinion throughout the colonies. "We were happy in our subordination," Daniel Leonard wrote, "but in an evil hour, under the influence of some malignant planet . . . some resolves of the house of burgesses in Virginia, denying the right of parliament to tax the colonies, made their appearance.

"We read them with wonder" for "they savoured of independence," Leonard recalled, but the people of Massachusetts "and almost all Americans, followed [Virginia's] example, in resolving that the parliament had no such right." Suddenly it "became unpopular to suggest the contrary," Leonard complained. In the wake of Patrick Henry's resolutions mere sympathy for Parliament could put a Yankee's life in danger—as it eventually did for Leonard when his neighbors attacked his house in Taunton, Massachusetts, and forced him first into wartime sanctuary in British-occupied Boston and eventually into postwar exile in Bermuda.

American resistance was accelerating faster than news under sail could across the Atlantic. "I thought that this people would submit to the Stamp Act," Massachusetts governor Francis Bernard informed British authorities, but "the Virginia Resolves proved an Alarm bell to the disaffected." "Murmurs on account of the Stamp Duty are not confined to Virginia," a London newspaper informed its readers in mid-August. "All the Colonies consider it as a most intolerable burthen." Reporting from New York City, where he commanded the British army in North America, General Thomas Gage wrote that "the Resolves of the Assembly of Virginia . . . gave the signal for a general out-cry over the Continent, and . . . they have been applauded as the Protectors and Assertors of American Liberty." While British officials shook their heads in dismay at the rapid dissemination of Patrick Henry's newfangled and desperate doctrines, angry colonists began translating his bold rhetoric into direct action against the newest enemies of American freedom—thirteen freshly appointed stamp distributors whose names were conveniently supplied by Treasury authorities in London.

CHAPTER SEVEN

The Stamp Act

A FEW HOURS AFTER the passage of his resolutions against the Stamp Act on Thursday, May 30, 1765, Patrick Henry had walked with a fellow first-time burgess from Charlotte County, in the southern Piedmont, as they left Williamsburg together, just as Edmund Pendleton and others had departed a few days earlier after the debate on the Loan Office. Clad in leather britches for the ride home, as his companion recalled, the reins of his horse in hand and saddlebags over his arm, Henry was twenty-nine, having spent his birthday in committee debate over the Stamp Act. He had accomplished remarkable things during his first ten days as a burgess. But when Governor Fauquier dissolved the Assembly that Saturday, Henry and his compatriots reverted to their private status as ordinary subjects pending the outcome of a new election.

Governor Fauquier's attempt to suppress Henry's resolutions against the Stamp Act backfired, but the governor effectively prevented Virginians from participating in the wider rebellion inspired by those resolutions. Calling for new elections in July, Fauquier sought a more compliant House of Burgesses led by "the more enlightened and sensible Men of the Colony." Instead, the freeholders of Virginia endorsed Henry's tactics by throwing out more than one third of the incumbent burgesses in favor of more assertive candidates. Still hoping that "the Madness of the people shall abate," Fauquier repeatedly postponed the Assembly over a period of sixteen months until the crisis had run its course. By the time the burgesses finally met again in November 1766, George Grenville had been forced out of office, Parliament had repealed the Stamp Act, and the death of Speaker John Robinson had exposed the full extent of his financial transgressions.

Forced to the sidelines for better than a year, Patrick Henry could do little more than watch attentively as other men in other colonies acted upon the principles expressed in his resolutions. At least half the men he had served with in the House of Burgesses also held local office as magistrates in their county courts. Aside from his joining the vestry of St. Martin's Parish in Louisa in 1766, however, Henry never held local office and never served as a county justice of the peace. After leaving Hanover he never lived long enough in any single locality to warrant a formal appointment to its county court—and although Henry derived enormous influence from his identification with the interests of gentry and yeoman throughout the colony, his political stature soon transcended localities. For the most part (except during his confrontation with Governor John Murray, Earl of Dunmore, in the revolutionary crisis of 1775 and his brief stint as commander of the militia in 1776) Henry exercised legislative or executive leadership at a provincial level—developing a distinctive style of leadership that deepened his reliance upon persuasion and his empathetic sensitivity to public opinion.

ooooo

Royal authorities in London seldom gave colonial governors the full support they deserved, but the Board of Trade hit a new low in the summer of 1765. At the end of every parliamentary session the colonial office customarily sent the governors copies of all new laws that affected America. That June, however, the transmission was delayed while the king was recruiting Grenville's successor, thirty-one-year-old Charles Watson-Wentworth, Marquess of Rockingham. In July, after the new ministry summarily dismissed all of Grenville's men at the Treasury and the Board of Trade, the newcomers gave no thought to sending copies of the Stamp Act to the American governors. Eager for advice from imperial authorities "to guide me through this wilderness," Virginia's governor expressed the frustration common to all his colleagues. High British officials were too caught up in ministerial politics to help the American governors implement the Stamp Act. "I have never in the course of my Life been in a Situation which required so much Circumspection," Fauquier complained from Williamsburg. Although Edward Montague had sent a copy of the Stamp Act to the Committee of Correspondence, the governor "had not the common Notice of there being such an Act, as it has never been sent to me."

From Fauquier's perspective, keeping the Assembly at bay obstructed

Virginia's support for her sister colonies during the crisis—and specifically prevented the Old Dominion from sending representatives to an intercolonial Stamp Act Congress in New York that October. On the other hand, Fauquier's strategy undermined the colony's older leaders, long accustomed to directing Virginia affairs through their control of the Assembly. Hamstrung by the interruptions of provincial and local government during colonial resistance to the Stamp Act, older provincial leaders would have no occasions to confer and act together. "Mr. Henry," Jefferson later recalled, "took the lead out of the hands of those who had heretofore guided the proceedings of the House." Meanwhile the political forces unleashed that May—especially the advocacy of coercive pressure upon enemies of the community—fostered experiments with egalitarian forms of political protest and alternative means of social control in Virginia and beyond.

ooooo

As though chanting a reassuring mantra, British officials had repeatedly asserted that a stamp duty "in a great degree executes itself" because documents "not stamped are null and void." The logic was plausible—and there was just enough truth in that opinion to invite disaster. Under the new system, if one of Patrick Henry's clients wanted to buy a house, the validity of the deed required a tax stamp. His client might grumble about the tax but surely Henry and his client would insist upon its payment to ensure that his title to the property held up in court. Similarly, newspapers and decks of cards were discretionary purchases, so Henry's neighbors were expected to accept the stamp duty on those commodities just as modern American consumers unthinkingly accept the tax stamp on a bottle of liquor or a pack of cigarettes. Individual attempts to resist a stamp duty were self-defeating. Aside from forgery, which was unlikely and infrequent, the only thing that could defeat a stamp duty was the persistent and virtually unanimous defiance of an entire population—a prospect that never crossed the mind of George Grenville although it was the inherent strategy behind Henry's resolutions.

The duties fell most onerously upon lawyers and printers, two groups that savvy politicians usually try not to alienate. "It was fortunate for the liberties of America that Newspapers were the subject of a heavy stamp duty," wrote historian David Ramsay of South Carolina, for printers (and many lawyers) generally cared about two things—"the side of liberty" and "the profits of their profession." By threatening both, the Stamp Act "provoked their united zealous opposition."

Patrick Henry and his neighbors were shocked by the details of the Stamp Act itself—eight dense pages of small print listing fifty-five specific taxes that would take effect on November 1, 1765. Henry's practice as an attorney was subject to forty particular duties ranging from 2 pence to £10 on every kind of legal document from wills and deeds, bills of sale, and even college diplomas. The taxes on newspapers, almanacs, calendars, broadsides, and pamphlets ranged from half a penny to 2 shillings for each sheet of paper, and double that for imprints in a foreign language. "Poor America!" lamented his fellow attorney and burgess Edmund Pendleton. "Every kind of business transacted on paper is taxed."

But Grenville's scheme did not stop there. The stamp duty on a deck of playing cards was one shilling, on a pair of dice 10 shillings. And the Stamp Act levied a 2-shilling tax on "every advertisement . . . in any gazette, news paper, or other paper, or any pamphlet"—a fee equal to what most printers charged for the advertisements themselves. Compounding this affront to American liberty, violations were subject to the jurisdiction of the British admiralty courts, which operated without juries.

Inspired by the principles of Henry's resolutions, acts of resistance to the Stamp Act in several colonies relied on four things that British officials had failed to anticipate. First, although stamp duties could be self-enforcing in some situations, they were susceptible to failure if met with a complete and effective wholesale repudiation. Second, because the absence of a tax stamp rendered so many routine business and legal transactions invalid, this punitive aspect of Grenville's plan actually helped the colonists enforce an economic boycott against the Stamp Act. Third, the interruption of American trade had a devastating effort on merchants, manufacturers, and laborers in the British Isles, and it threatened starvation and unrest in the slave-based economies of the British sugar islands, which were dependent upon food and supplies from Virginia, Pennsylvania, and New York. Finally, the twenty-six officers named to implement the Stamp Act were far too few to enforce the act in the North American and Caribbean colonies.

By appointing prominent native-born Americans rather than office-seeking Englishmen to the lucrative posts of stamp officers, Grenville had hoped to curry favor for his duties among "the most respectable people in their several provinces." In practice, however, the list of stamp distributors provided American communities a convenient roll call of their enemies.

Emboldened by Virginia's resolutions and angered by the duties themselves, colonial newspapermen rallied their communities against Parliament during the summer of 1765. "The People of Virginia have spoke very sensibly, and the frozen Politicians of a more northern Government say they have spoke Treason," declared a July essay in Benjamin Edes's *Boston Gazette and Country Journal*. "Pray Gentlemen, is it Treason for the Deputies of the People to assert their Liberties?" Then, a month later, urban crowds in a northern port city demonstrated the implicitly revolutionary threat in Henry's call for action against the enemies of the people.

America's first Stamp Act riot began in Boston on August 14 when the sun rose upon an effigy of Andrew Oliver—designated stamp officer for the colony, secretary of the province, and brother-in-law of Lieutenant Governor Thomas Hutchinson—hanging from a great tree near Boston Common. Nearby was a figure of the devil inside a large black boot (a visual pun mocking George III's unpopular favorite, the Earl of Bute) with a brightly painted "Green-ville sole." By the next morning crowds of laborers, artisans, and more than a few gentlemen disguised in working-class garb had torn down a brick dockside building that Oliver intended as the provincial stamp office; destroyed his stable and coach, and then finally "surrounded Mr. Oliver's House, Broke his Windows and Entred the House and destroyed a great part of the Furniture." Oliver had not yet received his formal commission as stamp officer, but he promised to refuse the appointment.

Nearly two weeks later, a less disciplined mob primed with alcohol attacked three other houses on the evening of August 26–27. Instigated by a few merchants accused of smuggling, the second mob burned vice-admiralty records when they destroyed William Story's house, customs records when they destroyed Benjamin Hallowell's house, and virtually everything from the garden to the cupola when they gutted the lieutenant governor's Georgian mansion. Eighteenth-century men and women knew how to distinguish between unruly mobs and crowds of citizens defending their communities. Hutchinson himself recognized that "the encouragers of the *first mob* never intended matters should go this length" and that "people in general express the utmost detestation" of the second riot as an "unparalleled outrage" that historians rank as the most violent of the entire period.

Inspired by the Virginia resolutions (which the Rhode Island Assembly had formally endorsed) and the example of Andrew Oliver's resignation in Boston, three prominent Newport merchants planned America's third Stamp Act riot against "Enemies to the liberties of North America." On Tuesday, August 27, a crowd of protesters hanged and burned effigies of the stamp officer and two vocal supporters of Parliament from a gallows near the statehouse. The next evening "a chosen band of Ruffians" with painted faces descended upon the loyalist's house with "axes and other tools of desolation," plundered every room, destroyed all the furniture, carried off all the clothing and table linen, and finally broke into his cellars and "carried away all his wines and other liquors." By midnight, with one house now "a miserable shell" and the second exhibiting "the same scene of ruin," the crowds converged on the residence of the stamp officer, "but were diverted from destroying it by an assurance solemnly given that he would renounce the stamp office tomorrow for ever." As promised, two weeks after Oliver's resignation in Boston, the designated stamp officer for Rhode Island announced that he would "retire immediately to Boston and be incognito," while his loyalist acquaintances boarded merchant ships headed for Bristol and London.

Within a few days this pattern of intimidation and resignation surfaced in Maryland, where Charles Murray had repeatedly witnessed Marylanders raising their glasses to the Virginia Assembly and "Damnation to the Stamp act." From the first hint of its passage, printer Jonathan Green had regarded the Stamp Act as a direct attack on his *Maryland Gazette*, and Governor Horatio Sharpe had reported in July that his colony's lawyers "are most violent in their Out Cries against it." In mid-August, Annapolis merchant Zachariah Hood had returned from London bearing his appointment as stamp officer, which the governor anticipated "will probably be worth many hundreds a year" but "extremely unpopular." Within days of his arrival, effigies of Hood were whipped, burned, and hanged in a dozen Maryland localities by protesters calling themselves Sons of Liberty, and on September 2 three or four hundred people destroyed his store in Annapolis. Escaping with only the clothes on his back, Hood fled to New York City, where the local Sons of Liberty threatened him with further violence and forced his formal resignation.

Contrary to the ministry's assumption that stamp duties implemented themselves, Governor Sharpe reported that the Stamp Act would never be enforced "without a considerable Military Force in each Colony." Protesters everywhere focused on forcing the resignation of officers responsible for implementing the tax. "The Inhabitants of all the Colonies," Governor Sharpe concluded, seemed to be acting "in Concert." More than sixty riots throughout America in the months between the destruction of Andrew Oliver's house in August 1765 and Philadelphia's rowdy celebration of the repeal of the Stamp Act in May 1766 sent a consistent message. "A perfect Frenzy seems to have seized the Mind of the People," wrote "Civis" from Connecticut. Except for a brief moment in Georgia, Britain's stamp distributors made no headway in the thirteen colonies.

ooooo

While Patrick Henry patiently monitored the news from other colonies, chance circumstances delayed Virginia's confrontation with its own stamp distributor until the very end of October. Colonel George Mercer had served with distinction throughout the French and Indian War and represented Frederick County in the House of Burgesses with his friend George Washington in 1761. After the war he had sought his fortune in London, bearing enthusiastic references from the governor and Council. While Mercer was visiting Irish relatives in his increasingly anxious search for employment, the Treasury Department named him as stamp officer for Virginia on May 27, 1765, six weeks before the king sacked Grenville. Delayed by the changing personnel in the ministry, months passed before Colonel Mercer got his formal commission in August—and then contrary winds and other complications delayed his departure until September 12, just six weeks before the Stamp Act took force. By the time Mercer sailed on the merchant vessel *Leeds* (with several tons of stamps and stamped paper for Virginia, Maryland, and North Carolina secure in its hold), London newspapers were publishing the first reports of Virginia's protest and Patrick Henry's Caesar-Brutus speech. By October, as the *Leeds* hauled westward toward the Chesapeake, the papers were reporting news of effigies, riots, and the coerced resignations of American stamp officers. Colonel James Mercer was sailing into a tumult.

On September 2 Mercer had been burned in effigy at Dumfries, a port town on the Potomac ten miles north of his father's plantation at

Marlborough and fifteen miles south of Mount Vernon. The protesters of Prince William County mounted Mercer's effigy on horseback with its face toward the tail, a sign of disgrace, and tied a copy of the Stamp Act to a halter around its neck. "Accompanied by hundreds of all ranks," the ringleaders paraded Mercer's effigy through the streets of Dumfries and subjected it to what Anglo-American protesters called "Mosaic Law"— caning and whipping and then "pillorying, cropping, hanging and burning, etc., etc." Three weeks later Richard Henry Lee had organized Virginia's second Stamp Act "riot" at the county seat of Westmoreland County during the Court Days of September, the only time one could hope for a crowd in the rural village of Montross. Adopting many of the conventional symbols of protest used by English crowds and satirical printmakers alike, these demonstrations in Dumfries and Westmoreland County were ceremonial media events (unlike the destructive riots in Boston and Newport) meant to proclaim the colony's united opposition to their still absent stamp officer.

The procession in Montross began on Tuesday with African American slaves from Richard Henry Lee's plantation dragging effigies of George Grenville and George Mercer in a cart to the gallows near the courthouse. Placards identified Grenville as "the infamous Projector of AMERICAN SLAVERY" and Mercer as the stamp officer for Virginia. Signs affixed to Mercer's effigy read "MONEY is my GOD" and "SLAVERY I LOVE." At the courthouse, the effigies were hanged to the "Acclamations and Applause of a large Concourse of People, of all Ranks and Denominations"— including the slaves Lee had brought from Chantilly to swell the ranks of protest against Grenville's plan to enslave America! The drama continued on Wednesday when an "Audience of all Ranks and Degrees of People" assembled at the courthouse to hear "the dying Speech of George Mercer," written and performed by Richard Henry Lee, before his effigy was burned "for Traitorously aiding and assisting in the Destruction of his Country's Liberty." Lee's script portrayed Mercer standing "on the verge of Eternity," confessing that an "inordinate Love of Gold" had tempted him away from "Honour, Virtue, and Patriotism" before accepting "the Propriety of my Punishment." Lee's invented speech was brief and its civic lessons suited the moment. The sentiments that Lee imagined as Mercer's final thoughts are layered with irony, however, for we now know, as the crowd at Montross did not, that only a year earlier Richard Henry Lee had

himself sought the post of stamp officer before, as he later claimed, realizing the pernicious nature of Grenville's stamp taxes.

Intelligent and well educated, tall and austere, Lee became Patrick
Henry's equal as a zealous patriot and his closest rival as an orator—
contemporaries compared him to Cicero and Henry to Demosthenes. But
unlike Henry, Lee was notoriously persistent in his quest for gainful political employment. Born at Stratford Hall in 1733 as the scion of an illustrious Virginia family, Richard Henry was the sixth of his parents' eight
children and therefore a victim of the Anglo-American law of primogen-
iture, an element of inheritance law designed to sustain aristocratic family
dynasties through the generations by transmitting entire landed estates to
the eldest son rather than allowing their division into parcels too small to
sustain a great house and family. Lee and his siblings had obviously benefited from the wealth and status of their father, but only the eldest brother
would inherit Stratford Hall and its acreage and slaves.

While Henry earned his fortune by practicing law, Lee enjoyed only
a modest income from his plantation and became, in effect, an ambitious
professional politician. Named a justice of the peace at twenty-six in 1757,
he had been elected to the House of Burgesses the next year. Lee had repeatedly sought an appointment to the Governor's Council before anyone
else thought him ready for the honor, and in 1764 he had welcomed Richard Corbin's nomination for the office of stamp officer. Even Lee's subsequent turn against the Stamp Act had a self-serving dimension as well,
for he believed that visible leadership against British authority would advance his aspiration to succeed the aging John Robinson as Speaker of the
House of Burgesses.

On the other hand, Richard Henry Lee's domestic obligations but-
tressed a genuine commitment to frugality as a civic-republican virtue
that he shared with Patrick Henry. "Having a large family to support,"
Lee openly admired the "wise, attentive, sober, diligent and frugal" residents of New England, and in time he grew so affectionate toward "the
eastern part of this Union" that political rivals at home claimed he "favored
New England to the injury of Virginia." The Stamp Act demonstration
Lee staged at Montross certainly echoed its northern antecedents—and at
Congress the friendship that he and his brother Arthur felt toward Samuel and John Adams cemented Virginia's political alliance with New England leaders throughout the struggle for independence.

More significant than the planters and slaves frolicking with effigies of Grenville and Mercer outside the Westmoreland courthouse, however, was the substantive protest that Richard Henry Lee and his fellow justices adopted inside the building on September 24. In a letter to Governor Fauquier and the Council, the justices of Westmoreland announced that compliance with the Stamp Act would "impose on us a Necessity, in Consequence of the Judicial Oath we take, of Acting ... in the Destruction of our Country's most essential Rights and Liberties." Honor and virtue compelled them, they reasoned, to close the county court effective November 1 rather than conduct any business that would generate documents that required the new tax stamps.

In October the justices of Stafford and Culpeper counties ventured further than their colleagues in Westmoreland. Rather than abide by the Stamp Act, they offered Governor Fauquier their resignations en masse. John Mercer of Marlborough, father of the soon-to-arrive stamp master and one of the colony's leading jurists, drafted the Stafford letter, which reminded Fauquier that their county seal bore a motto from Magna Carta—*We will deny or delay no one justice or right*—that was "utterly inconsistent with the Stamp Act." Culpeper County's justices declared that the stamp duties shook "the very foundation of our Liberties." If Parliament could levy taxes without their consent, Americans became "merely the Property of those whom we formerly lookt upon as our fellow Subjects."

Virginians were demonstrating that Patrick Henry's admonition against enemies of the people had real teeth even without destructive riots. Good government in Virginia depended upon the participation of "properly educated and qualified gentlemen," Governor Fauquier reminded the Board of Trade. If they quit in protest, he doubted that anyone could recruit replacements, even from the "meaner Sort of people," for the plantation gentry generally set the tone for polite society. "If the first Gentlemen of the Counties refused to act" as justices of the peace, Fauquier explained, "it would have become a fashion for the others to follow their Examples." Rather than accept resignations from any county courts, Fauquier and his Council tabled these letters "till affairs were better settled, and peace should take the place of Disorder and Confusion." Attorney Edmund Pendleton confirmed Fauquier's assessment. If the governor attempted to replace justices who threatened to resign, Pendleton wrote, "none that are fit for [office] will and others dare not succeed them."

County magistrates on the Eastern Shore, between Chesapeake Bay
and the Atlantic Ocean, took a more radical approach that reflected
Henry's sixth resolution, which had declared that "the inhabitants of this
Colony, are not bound to yield obedience to any Law or Ordinance whatever, designed to impose any Taxation whatsoever upon them, other than
the Laws or Ordinances of the General Assembly." Rather than close
their court or submit their resignations, the seven justices of Northampton County attacked the authority of Parliament. On the question of
"whether they . . . should incur any penalties by not using stamped paper,"
in compliance with the Stamp Act, the court unanimously declared "their
opinion that the said act did not bind, affect, or concern the inhabitants
of this colony, inasmuch as they conceive the same to be unconstitutional,
and that the . . . officers may proceed to the execution of their respective
offices without incurring any penalties."

ooooo

Much of Virginia's colonial archive burned when Richmond fell to the
Union armies in April 1865, but fortunately an October 1765 fragment from
the records of the General Court survives to reveal Governor Fauquier's
worries about the implications of the Stamp Act. Williamsburg was bus-
tling that autumn. Every morning dawned with anticipation. "Colonel
Mercer is not yet arrived but daily expected," and a persistent rumor held
that the Sons of Liberty were poised to descend upon the capital from all
parts of the colony to seize and destroy the tax stamps. Patrick Henry's
exact whereabouts cannot be documented, but there is every reason to suppose that he and other colony leaders were in town. The fragment shows
that in the absence of any instructions from British authorities, Fauquier
turned to his Council for guidance on three questions in advance of the
stamp distributor's arrival and the upcoming session of the General Court.

Whether the Stamp Act took effect on November 1 "or not till the
Day after"?
    Whether, if stamps were not available, the General Court could
"sit and continue to do Business"? And,
    Whether the judges could meet, adjourn, and have their clerk
make an unstamped record of their adjournment "without being
subject to the penalty in the Act"?

The councilors suggested that Fauquier pose his queries to the small group of elite attorneys licensed to practice before the General Court. No record of their advice survives, but clearly someone decided that the Stamp Act took effect on the 1st, and that without stamps the General Court (like the county courts) could do nothing beyond instructing its clerk to record its adjournment—for that is exactly what happened at the capitol on Friday, November 1, two days after the *Leeds* docked near Yorktown after seven weeks at sea.

Two surprises awaited Colonel George Mercer as he approached Williamsburg on Wednesday, October 30. First, he quickly learned that British officials had botched the implementation of the new tax. Governor Fauquier had received no information about the Stamp Act whatsoever—nor had Governor William Bull of South Carolina or Governor James Wright of Georgia. Virtually everything most colonial governors knew about the Stamp Act came from the newspapers. Second, although he had witnessed jealousies during the French and Indian War that had prompted Mercer to dismiss the likelihood of intercolonial cooperation as an "Absurdity," he soon discovered that the colonies were remarkably united in their resistance to the Stamp Act. Since August, stamp officers had been harried into resignation from the Carolinas to Massachusetts, often with the destruction of their property and threats of violence. Now it was his turn.

Arriving from Yorktown late that afternoon, George Mercer encountered a crowd of some two thousand people near the Exchange, the open meeting space near the east end of Duke of Gloucester Street where merchants and planters gathered at Marot's and Burdett's ordinaries and Richard Charlton's coffeehouse whenever the Assembly or General Court was in session. "This Concourse of people I should call a Mob," Governor Fauquier reported to the Board of Trade, except that "it was chiefly if not altogether composed of Gentlemen of property." Anticipating the confrontation, Governor Fauquier was sitting on the open porch of the coffeehouse, where he was an occasional customer, as Mercer approached. Ostensibly wanting to "be an Eye witness of what did really pass," Fauquier also positioned himself and a cluster of senior leaders to intervene if Mercer needed help.

People were all gathered at the Exchange as usual, Fauquier wrote, when someone cried "One and all"—a signal that sent the crowd in search of Colonel Mercer, who was known to be staying at his father's favorite inn on Waller Street behind the capitol, probably Christina Camp-bell's. As the throng of planters and merchants passed the capitol, they met Colonel Mercer walking toward the coffeehouse—one of many small coincidences that suggest the likelihood of prior arrangements between a few of Virginia's senior statesmen, if not Fauquier himself, and responsi-ble gentlemen (probably including Henry) among the protesters. At first the confrontation echoed the early moments of the northern Stamp Act riots. The crowd stopped Mercer and demanded "whether he would resign or act in his Office as Distributor of the Stamps." With the poise of a gen-tleman and courage of an officer, Colonel Mercer promised that he would return to the Exchange after consulting his friends and "give them an an-swer at ten o'clock Friday morning."

Dissatisfied with Mercer's promise, the crowd followed him to the cof-feehouse where Fauquier beckoned him to join him on the porch along with several councilors who had voiced Virginia's earliest opposition to the Stamp Act as members of the Committee of Correspondence and John Robinson, Speaker of the House of Burgesses, "who had posted himself between the Crowd" and the governor. Faces in the crowd went sullen. A tense silence was occasionally broken by a voice complaining that "Friday was too late," by then "the act would take place," or demanding "an answer to morrow."

"The leading men of the crowd" repeatedly urged Mercer to resign, but each time the colonel replied that "he had already given an answer and would have no other extorted from him." As the tension escalated toward possible violence, the gentlemen on the porch heard someone cry, "Let us rush in." Fauquier and his companions "advanced to the Edge of the Steps" as the crowd surged toward the porch—then someone shouted *Be careful of the governor!* "and those who before were pushing up the Steps immedi-ately fell back."

Now it was getting dark, and the confrontation could easily spin out of control. Mercer had upheld his honor, and now the crowd needed some small concession toward reconciliation as a reward for its civility. Rather than waiting until Friday, as he had promised, Fauquier's companions pre-vailed upon Mercer, "against his own Inclination . . . to promise them an Answer at the Capitol the next Evening at Five." As Mercer's token con-cession closed this act of political theater, it was time to leave the stage. Stepping to the edge of the porch, Fauquier announced his belief that no man would do him any harm and that the colonel would accompany him home. The walled gardens around the Governor's Palace lay several blocks to the west, but the two men walked "side by side through the thickest of the people," Fauquier recounted, without incident "tho' there was some little murmurs."

On Thursday afternoon at five o'clock George Mercer walked to the Exchange, as promised, to announce his decision to a crowd much larger than the night before, "messengers having been sent into the neighbour-hood for that purpose." Mercer explained that he had never encouraged the passage of the Stamp Act, had been in Ireland during the parliamen-tary session, and he had not sought the appointment as stamp distributor. Shortly before sailing to Virginia he had seen "some resolves which were said to be made by the House of Burgesses." Uncertain about their au-thenticity, however, he figured that once he arrived in the colony he would learn "the real sentiments of my countrymen from themselves." Mercer commanded sufficient respect from his neighbors to speak candidly about his dilemma. How could he satisfy both his "friends and countrymen here, and the authority which appointed me," he wondered. "I have not yet been able to discover that happy medium," he admitted, so until he got "further orders from England" he pledged not to "proceed in the execution of the act"—"and not then without the assent of the General Assembly of this colony."

On Friday, the day the Stamp Act took effect, the scene of protest shifted to the chamber of the General Court. Fauquier and his councilors took their customary seats in their judicial capacity as the colony's highest court with Attorney General Peyton Randolph at his table before them. The courtroom was full of spectators when the bailiff voiced the rit-ual proclamation—"Oyes, Oyes, Oyes! All manner of persons that have anything to do at this court draw near and give your attendance"—a sig-nal that usually sent attorneys rushing toward the bar of the court to place their cases on the docket. On this fateful day, however, nothing happened.

Fauquier waited. He ordered the bailiff to repeat the proclamation. Nothing happened. He waited a bit longer, then sent the bailiff to re-peat his proclamation at the outer door of the capitol. "Oyes, Oyes, Oyes," echoed toward the Exchange, where hundreds of Virginians had sur-rounded George Mercer on the two previous evenings. Once again, noth-ing happened.

Now Fauquier had to do something as governor lest he seem to relinquish control of the General Court and erode his exercise of the king's authority. Fauquier called for Colonel Mercer and asked whether he could supply the General Court with the stamps necessary to comply with the new law? Mercer replied that he could not. He then repeated his promise not to act as stamp distributor without further advice from British authorities and permission from the General Assembly of Virginia. Fauquier turned to Benjamin Waller, clerk of the court and a member of the Committee of Correspondence, and asked whether he could carry out his duties without the new stamps? No, Waller answered, not without subjecting himself to penalties that he found unacceptable. Finally Fauquier polled the members of the General Court itself, asking each judge in turn whether, "as there was no Business before us," they might legally adjourn until April? One judge wondered whether Fauquier had received "any particular Instructions or Directions how to act on this Occasion." Fauquier replied that he had not.

As the court unanimously rose to adjourn, however, George Mercer stepped toward the governor and suddenly offered to resign his commission. "I did not expect this," Fauquier hastily replied, then scrambled for a response "proper to give in public." The best he could do was to suggest that his authority to accept resignations extended only to his own appointments "but not those of his Majesty or his Ministers at home." All the while Fauquier was actually thinking (as he informed the Board of Trade) that by accepting Mercer's resignation he become responsible for finding his replacement, "and I was well convinced, I could not find one." George Grenville's Stamp Act was dead in Virginia—the enemy of the people was vanquished.

On the following Sunday, Fauquier sized things up for the Board of Trade. Events had moved at a startling pace during the long weekend since Mercer's arrival on Thursday. The resignations of county justices, intimidation of the stamp officer, and forced adjournment of the General Court meant that Virginia's united opposition to the tax stamps would effectively close all the colony's courts and ports. Beyond that, Fauquier saw only "Disorder, Confusion, and Misery . . . unless this poor unhappy deluded People in the Colonies in general should change their Plan." And there was scant chance of that. "The Flame had spread so universally throughout the Colonies" that Virginia merchants stood adamant against the Stamp Act even in the face of financial ruin with a stoppage of trade.

General Thomas Gage extended Fauquier's observation to a continental perspective. Reporting from New York City, where he commanded the British troops in North America, Gage wrote that the Americans had a plan. First, they would compel stamp distributors to resign "by Menace or Force." Then they would destroy the stamps as they arrived, giving them an excuse for conducting business as usual. Finally, before replacement stamps could be sent to America, the colonists hoped that "the Clamor and outcry of the People" as well as "Addresses and Remonstrances from the Assemblys might procure a Repeal of the Act." Deftly shielding himself from the 20-20 hindsight of London's armchair generals, Gage also reminded the ministry that enforcing the Stamp Act by military force was not an option. His army was "scattered and divided, over this vast Continent" and could not rally to the support of any colonial governor "in Case of sudden Emergencys."

ooooo

The task of cleaning up Grenville's mess fell to the Marquess of Rockingham, only five years older than his king and with little experience in government and none in the House of Commons. At twenty he had inherited his father's title and seat in the House of Lords, along with huge estates in Yorkshire and Ireland, a passion for horse racing, and a bent for politics. George III regarded Rockingham as the least objectionable of the men who could organize a government after Grenville's dismissal, but from the American perspective Rockingham looked like a friend of the colonies, with solid credentials as a Whig and strong support among British merchants.

The fresh memories of Britain's logistical difficulties in the French and Indian War discouraged talk of military intervention across the wintery Atlantic, but a Parliament obsessed with precedent and wary of slippery slopes was not about to reverse itself in the face of American constitutional defiance and reports of mob violence. Rockingham's strategy took shape early in 1766. Bristol and London merchants would mount a petition campaign for repeal of the Stamp Act because of its devastating impact on the British economy. The ministry would play down American constitutional claims and violence. Repeal would be linked, Rockingham wrote in January, with "a declaratory act in general terms." Finally, just as the passage of the Stamp Act had prompted Thomas Whately's invention of virtual representation, its repeal now required the face-saving discovery of a distinction between internal and external taxation that Benjamin Franklin, "the celebrated electric philosopher," was happy to supply.

Virginians savored every detail of the king's acceptance of the repeal on the front page of Alexander Purdie and John Dixon's *Virginia Gazette.* Cheered by jubilant crowds, George III had processed in full regalia to the Lords' chamber at Westminster on Tuesday, March 18, and taken his seat "on the throne with the usual solemnity." After the Speaker and members of the House of Commons entered, "his Majesty was pleased to give the Royal assent" both to the repeal of the Stamp Act—four days short of its first anniversary—and to the accompanying Declaratory Act "for securing the dependencies of the British Colonies in America, on the Crown and Parliament of Great Britain."

Throughout the crisis, from the arrival of Patrick Henry's resolutions early in August to the receipt of the memorials and petitions of the Stamp Act Congress in December, Parliament had stubbornly refused to hear and consider, much less answer, America's constitutional objections to the Stamp Act. The final clause of the Declaratory Act ended that silence on a note of imperious disdain. "And be it further declared," the Declaratory Act stipulated,

> That all resolutions, votes, orders, and proceedings in any of the said colonies or plantations, whereby the power and authority of the parliament of Great Britain is denied or drawn into question . . . are hereby declared to be utterly null and void to all intents and purposes whatsoever.

As if that addressed Virginia's position that only the colonial legislatures, as representatives of the people, held legitimate authority for American taxation and legislation.

Edmund Burke, whose constituents in Bristol had close ties to the Old Dominion, had Virginia pegged when he recognized the role of elite leaders at the beginning of the Stamp Act rebellion. "The principal people" taught "the lower sort," Burke wrote, to comprehend how the Stamp

Act threatened "much greater evils than they, probably, were liable to feel." As the decade progressed, however, the officeholders who had dominated the provincial and local institutions of Virginia's participatory oligarchy increasingly found themselves pushed by their constituents toward more vigorous resistance to Parliament in favor of American liberty. By focusing on the rights of the people at large, Patrick Henry bypassed the old guard and charted a path to prominence that no longer depended upon the favor of the king and his agents. As Henry explained these principles later in life, he believed that regardless of a statesman's individual sentiments, if the wishes of the people were clear their representative needed to respect their wishes. Henry informed his legislative colleagues in 1788 that he had always sought "to bow, with the utmost deference, to the majesty of the people."

CHAPTER EIGHT

Europeans or Africans?

PARLIAMENT LINKED ITS REPEAL of the Stamp Act in 1766 with a Declaratory Act that affirmed its claims of authority to tax America, but Americans were ready to hope that the new Rockingham ministry might follow the example of Robert Walpole and the advice of William Pitt by choosing not to exert the constitutional authorities that Parliament claimed in theory. Although Patrick Henry and his neighbors kept a vigilant eye on the new ministry, for the moment it was as easy for Virginians as it was for English merchants and artisans to celebrate the reopening of trade and to dream that the clash between the colonies and Parliament was over.

Daily life in the Old Dominion, nevertheless, seemed different and unsettling. Controversies in the columns of the *Virginia Gazette* had exposed the aristocratic vanity of the Tidewater elite in the scandal of John Robinson's mismanagement of the Treasury. Ordinary planters worried about inequities and exploitation. Indentured servants and slaves often felt the lash of injustice or abuse. Population growth, increasing religious diversity, friction between rich and poor, and the rapid expansion of slavery all posed disquieting implications for the colony's future. Virginians also worried that their haven for virtuous Englishmen was being tarnished by a "degeneracy in morals which is so conspicuous all around us."

The Reverend Richard Hartswell, of Prince George County, pointed toward an emerging ideal of public honor based more on virtue and talent than wealth, family, and "outward grandeur." Hartswell acknowledged that wealthy men were capable of meritorious public service, but when they neglected the public good or brought injury upon their country "they cannot justly be called *great men.*" Scandal eroded the old Virginia model of distinction based on fortune, birth, and social station, Edmund Randolph explained in his *History of Virginia*, in favor of a new standard based on patriotism, talent, and virtue—and it was in this context that Randolph identified Patrick Henry as the man who first "broke the influence" of the Tidewater aristocracy.

Prior to the French and Indian War, colonial Virginians had been fond of imagining their province as an English country estate on the western bank of the North Atlantic, its residents living in pastoral simplicity and domestic independence far from the corrupting temptations of London. William Byrd II had translated this bucolic dream into a popular metaphor when he portrayed the planters of Tidewater Virginia as Old Testament patriarchs resting beneath their vines and their fig trees, surrounded by their flocks and herds, kindred and slaves, "in a kind of independence [from] everyone but Providence," with their "bond-men and bond-women" engaged in every sort of trade. Despite its increasing divergence from the slave society in which they lived, Byrd's fanciful vines and fig trees remained a favorite image for George Washington, Patrick Henry, Thomas Jefferson, and countless other Virginians.

During and after the Stamp Act rebellion, nostalgia for the comfortable imperial world the colonies had enjoyed before 1763 became a recurrent theme in Virginia's protests about imperial authority, but America's new wine proved too effervescent for the empire's old bottles. The searing experience of the Stamp Act Crisis and growing anxieties about slavery required fresh assessments of Virginia's society, economy, and political life; as well as its relationship with the western frontier, with its sister colonies, and its place within (or perhaps separated from) Britain's transatlantic empire. "Wherefore is it," Henry asked in an essay contemplating Virginia's plight, "that a country . . . blest with a soil producing not only the necessarys but the luxurys of life; full of rivers, havens and inlets that invite the visits of commerce"—a country "that might be covered with magnificent citys . . . instead of lonely scattered huts"—"should want the common conveniencys, the necessarys of life?"

Henry's perspective on Virginia's situation was international. And his thoughts about slavery, religious liberty, property values, and American manufacturing embodied the progressive agenda of his generation. Virginia needed to embrace the "social intercourse among nations" that cements the civilized world together "like one great family." The Old Dominion needed to encourage the "sciences and arts that embellish and sweeten human life." Diversified agriculture, immigration, and domestic manufacturing offered a better future than slaves and tobacco—and he found "the example of the Northern Colonys striking."

"Away with the schemes of paper money and the loan office," Henry wrote, dismissing measures favored by the late Speaker John Robinson's generation. Virginia enjoyed the happiest situation on the continent, with farms capable of producing grain, livestock, wool, hemp, flax, corn, rice, fruits, and wine. Its rivers and creeks invited "the visits of commerce for the products of industry." If only Virginians would seize the opportunity, their lonely farmsteads could be transformed into "magnificent cities." By highlighting America's dependence upon British merchants and manufacturers, the Stamp Act Crisis had demonstrated the importance of domestic industry and, as Henry put it, "the necessity of home manufacturers." Imported goods were ruining a colony blessed with "the means of becoming the most prosperous on the continent." Henry believed that the old guard's attempts to encourage industry with "premiums"—cash incentives, bounties, bonuses, or tax exemptions—were doomed. Virginia's problem was not a lack of raw materials but the absence of skilled laborers.

"Our country will be peopled," Henry began. "The question is, shall it be with Europeans or Africans?" Just as England had once imported skilled Flemish and French artisans, Virginia now needed skilled immigrants from the British Isles and the Continent. Suppose a planter wanted to reduce his dependence on tobacco by investing in textile production. Where would he find "spinners of wool and flax, a tanner, a shoemaker, a weaver, a fuller, etc." Was anyone "so degenerate," Henry asked, "as to wish to see his country [remain] the gloomy retreat of slaves" when Virginia should be welcoming skilled immigrants as contributing members of a free society?

The most visible contradiction to colonial Virginians' bucolic self-image was the presence of "vast shoals of Negroes who are employed as Slaves." During Virginia's first century white colonists and indentured servants from England had performed most of the hard labor of clearing fields and cultivating tobacco and other crops. By the 1720s, however, slaves comprised 30 percent of the population and had become Virginia's "chief Instruments of Labour." Wealthy families made huge investments in slaves, who performed all the field labor and many of the skilled tasks required for tobacco production at about one third the cost of free labor.

"To live in Virginia without slaves," a Huguenot refugee and planter observed, was simply "impossible."

Two weeks after Patrick Henry's birth, his mother's admirer William Byrd II set aside his earlier reveries about vines and fig trees and confessed the deep anxieties Virginians felt about slavery—recurrent anxieties heard from every generation of property-owning whites about how slavery affected *them*. Among the "many bad consequences of multiplying these Ethiopians among us," Byrd told John Perceval, Earl of Egmont, a trustee engaged in the founding of the new proprietary colony of Georgia, slavery "ruin[s] the industry of our white people, who . . . detest work for fear it should make them look like slaves." Faced with a growing proportion of slaves in the overall population, too many slave owners were adopting the methods of Caribbean slave drivers, Byrd lamented. If Virginians embraced "the necessity of being severe" and "the inhumanity . . . that is practiced in the islands," the result would be "terrible to a good natured man." Nevertheless, Byrd shrugged, "Numbers make them insolent, and then foul means must do."

Byrd closed his letter by expressing both the eternal dread of rebellion that haunted slave owners everywhere and the facile self-delusion embraced by generations of Virginians that somehow someone else might find some effortless way to reverse their long-standing commitment to slavery. Because he was writing forty years before the Stamp Act Crisis, Byrd could thoughtlessly invite the Earl of Egmont to share his dilemma by venturing the hope that Parliament might "put an end to this unchristian traffick of makeing merchandize of our fellow creatures"—but his ultimate concern was that "these private mischiefs are nothing if compared to the publick danger."

"Their numbers increase every day as well by birth as importation," Byrd wrote. "And in case there should arise a man of desperate courage amongst us, exasperated by a desperate fortune, he might with more advantage than Cataline, kindle a servile war . . . before any opposition could be formed against him, and tinge our rivers as wide as they are with blood." Virginians "import so many Negroes hither," William Byrd II wrote in 1736, "that I fear this colony will some time or other be confirmed by the name of New Guinea." Three decades later virtually the same question perplexed Patrick Henry and his generation. Could Virginia escape becoming "the gloomy retreat of slaves"?

Like other southerners then or later, Henry had no realistic plan for reducing Virginia's existing slave population. Apart from later advocating intermarriage between free white Virginians and Native Americans, he was no more able to imagine a transition to a multiracial society than most of his contemporaries, though unlike the sage of Monticello, Henry never placed any confidence in colonization schemes. "The disadvantage from the great number of [our] slaves may perhaps wear off, when the present stock and their descendents are scattered through the immense deserts in the West," Henry wrote. "To re-export them is now impracticable, and sorry I am for it."

Henry asked why farmland in Pennsylvania sold for "five times the value of ours?" Why was land in the newly settled areas of the Shenandoah Valley "almost as dear as at Williamsburg," despite its distance from the coasts and urban markets? Henry's answer was a severe indictment of Virginia society. The immigrant from Germany, Ireland, or Scotland who settled in Pennsylvania or ventured down the Great Wagon Road into the Valley of Virginia, he wrote, "finds there his religion, his priest, his language, his manners, and everything but [the] poverty and oppression he left at home." As the son and nephew of Anglicans who had fled Scotland's religious strife and established Presbyterian Kirk, Henry knew firsthand that religious toleration had profoundly important social and economic implications. Neither Patrick Henry's religious faith nor his commitment to toleration can ever be denied, but he also respected the practical consequences of religious liberty "as the best means of peopling our country." It was obvious that "free exercise of religion hath stocked the Northern part of the continent with inhabitants." The oppressed European Calvinist, Lutheran, or Quaker, Henry concluded, "sails not to Virginia."

ooooo

Patrick Henry's personal interest in western lands coincided with the imperial crisis triggered by the Stamp Act. From their earliest settlements, Virginians had vaguely regarded the Pacific Ocean as their western boundary. "Virginia," acting governor Thomas Lee, Richard Henry Lee's father, had informed the Board of Trade in 1750, "is Bounded by the Great Atlantic Ocean to the East, by North Carolina to the South, by Maryland and Pennsylvania to the North, and by the South Sea [or Pacific Ocean] to the West including California." The Mississippi River supplanted the

Pacific as the colony's western boundary according to the treaty that ended the French and Indian War. Before and during that war, land speculation by the Virginia gentry, seeking to enhance their estates and provide for their descendants, increasingly focused on southwestern Virginia (near the North Carolina–Tennessee line) and the Ohio River Valley—despite an ineffectual and short-lived British attempt to close the area to further settlement in 1763.

Patrick Henry's father had speculated closer to home, in the foothills of the Blue Ridge west of the new house at Roundabout, but Henry owed his introduction to land speculation in southwestern Virginia to the financial difficulties of his father-in-law, John Shelton. Flush with income from his prospering law practice—he collected more than £5,300 in legal fees between 1764 and 1771—Henry had lent significant amounts of money to his father, father-in-law, half-brother, and a web of cousins and clients. Early in 1766 Shelton engaged Henry to help him sell 3,400 acres in Holston River Valley (a dozen miles northwest of modern Kingsport, Tennessee) at risk of confiscation by British merchants to whom Shelton owed more than £350. To help Shelton avoid bankruptcy, Henry bought four tracts on Moccasin Creek and the Holston River and had his friend Thomas Jefferson witness the paperwork.

Eight years before Daniel Boone blazed the Wilderness Trail into Kentucky, Patrick Henry made his first expedition to the frontier accompanied by his older brother, William, and Colonel William Fleming, a veteran of frontier campaigns in the French and Indian War. Henry and his brother rode from Louisa across the Blue Ridge to Staunton, where Fleming practiced medicine near the courthouse of Augusta County. The party then rode southwesterly through the Valley of Virginia, following the Great Wagon Road that connected central Pennsylvania with the Carolina backcountry. After passing Fleming's Bellmont estate north of Big Lick (now the city of Roanoke) they finally reached Moccasin Gap and the Holston River Valley—all without setting a foot outside the boundaries of the sprawling frontier county named for George III's mother, Augusta of Saxe-Gotha. On this first venture into dangerous territory still prone to bloody clashes between colonists and Native Americans, Henry could locate only one of the Shelton tracts, but within a few years he had secured his claim to all 3,400 acres.

After returning from his southwestern adventure, Henry also acquired his father-in-law's share in a more ambitious speculative project in Kentucky. In partnership with the celebrated explorer Dr. Thomas Walker, who had discovered and named the Cumberland Gap, Henry engaged William Fleming "to reconnoitre the lands lying on the Mississippi near its junction with the Ohio." Henry and Walker delegated to Fleming the choice of a suitable location for settlement, but first they wanted appealing details about "the face of the Country" to recruit settlers for their "first company of adventurers." "Pardon me if I recommend to you a diary," Henry wrote, for "even the trees, herbs, grass, stones, hills, etc. . . . ought to be described." Henry and Walker intended to publish "a succinct account of [Fleming's] Journal . . . in order to invite our countrymen to become settlers." Henry recognized that "the Jaunt" would give Fleming "much trouble, hazard, and fatigue," but he was confident it would win him (and their project) "the favourable notice of every gentleman engaged in the scheme." Henry also used his growing influence in the House of Burgesses to promote "an act for the encouragement of settlement in the upper parts of Augusta County" in April of 1767.

In addition to Henry's speculative interest in western lands, he developed strong connections to the frontier inhabitants, many of whom were friends or family. His favorite sister, Annie, settled in the southwestern highlands (near modern Roanoke) after she married William Christian in 1768.

Henry's seven sisters had a thing for men in uniform or frontier hunting shirts. Another sister, Elizabeth, met her first husband, William Campbell, when he was a captain in her brother's revolutionary regiment. Later renowned as a hero of the battle of King's Mountain, South Carolina, Campbell owned large tracts of land at Aspenvale on the Great Wagon Road twenty miles north of modern Abingdon. Two years after Campbell's death in 1781, Elizabeth married another military man, General William Russell, who lived near Aspenvale and would share the conversion to Methodism that led to Elizabeth Henry Campbell Russell's prominence as a religious leader in the new republic. Henry's sister Jane stayed in Hanover County after marrying his boyhood friend and militia leader Colonel Samuel Meredith. His sister Susannah married Captain (and later General) Thomas Madison, of Augusta and Botetourt County, and died in Bowling Green, Kentucky. Henry's sister Mary wed Luke Bowyer, one of the first attorneys admitted to practice in Botetourt

County, and his youngest sister, Lucy, married Valentine Wood, clerk of Goochland County and colonel of the county militia. Except for Sarah, who married an English merchant from Bristol and lived at Newcastle in Hanover County, Patrick Henry's sisters all moved west and comprised a network of family and friends that extended Henry's political connections in the Piedmont and the western frontier.

ooooo

Although the Council rejected Henry's bill to encourage western settlement in the closing hours of the April 1767 Assembly session, the fact that the thirty-one-year-old legislator had successfully guided it through the House of Burgesses was an indication of his growing political influence. Eighteen months after the governor had dissolved the Assembly for passing Henry's resolutions against the Stamp Act, Fauquier worried that the people of Virginia seemed in a "sour" mood "spirited up by the news papers." Virginians were arguing with one another over just about everything as "a Matter of heat and Party Faction," Fauquier told the Board of Trade. He had hoped that a fresh election of burgesses and Parliament's repeal of the Stamp Act might temper the "Spirit of Discontent" embodied by Henry and his companions. Instead the electorate had thrown out more than a third of the burgesses and sent new faces to Williamsburg in their places. "The Blood of the People is soured," Fauquier lamented, and "Party feuds will run high."

Patrick Henry and his new friend Richard Henry Lee were unable to deliver the Speaker's chair to their nominee, Richard Bland, but on Lee's motion and Henry's second the burgesses did detach the Treasury from the speakership. "In a warm debate on continuing the union of the chair and Treasury," George Dabney recalled, "Henry by his eloquence prevented it." Speaker Peyton Randolph got an annual salary of £500 to replace the income associated with the Treasury, while the devout and incorruptible Robert Carter Nicholas took charge of the late John Robinson's office and accounts. Randolph also gave Robinson's critics a leading role in the investigation of the Robinson scandal, naming Richard Bland as chair of the eleven-man panel, accompanied by the staunchly independent Landon Carter and the vocal critics Richard Henry Lee and Patrick Henry. Committeemen Archibald Cary (who owed the Robinson estate £3,975) and George Wythe were two obvious friends of the present and former Speakers, and Edmund Pendleton was his protégé and executor. The settlement of Robinson's estate would take years, but Peyton Randolph's evenhanded management of the investigation minimized partisan bickering over the scandal.

With less than two weeks' experience in the previous Assembly and no experience whatsoever as a county justice, Henry had bypassed the usual political apprenticeship by which established Virginia leaders guided the careers of aspiring officeholders. Henry's political clout, as evidenced by prestigious committee assignments, far exceeded expectations for a junior burgess. He served with Bland, George Washington, Richard Henry Lee, Pendleton, Wythe, and Peyton Randolph on the committees that controlled legislation. And surely Henry took delight in his appointment to a special committee charged with erecting a statue of George III "to perpetuate the Glorious Repeal of the late unconstitutional act"—a project abandoned after the assembly recognized William Pitt's role in the repeal by naming Pittsylvania County and Chatham, the county seat, in honor of the Great Commoner.

ooooo

Patrick Henry was not alone in his anxiety over seeing Virginia become "the gloomy retreat of slaves." By the 1760s, slaves comprised nearly half the population of most of Tidewater and Piedmont counties, and (in stark contrast to South Carolina and the Caribbean islands) Virginia's slaves were increasingly likely to have been born in the colony rather than imported from Africa. An essay about slavery and the slave trade by Richard Henry Lee's brother Arthur, published in William Rind's *Virginia Gazette*, echoed Henry's themes in support of greater restrictions on slave importation: justice, public safety, religion, and a preference for European artisans. We would be "more strenuous in our Opposition to ministerial Tyranny," a planter contended in the *Virginia Gazette*, "had we not been conscious that we ourselves were absolute Tyrants, and held Numbers of poor Souls in the most abject and endless State of Slavery."

Exotic as the images of African stevedores toting hogsheads of tobacco may have seemed to Englishmen admiring the maps of Virginia published by Joshua Fry and Peter Jefferson in 1751 or John Henry in 1770, those wharf-side scenes were all too familiar in the Old Dominion. The physical and cultural presence of enslaved Africans fueled the anxieties of free men and women whose world seemed increasingly enslaved and black. White Virginians who cherished their British identities, British liberties, and imported British clothing, furniture, tableware, and fineries readily accepted the racist attitudes that permeated British and American society.

Apparently "slavery was a little less brutal in the Chesapeake than in the Lowcountry," and it certainly was true that most slaves fared better in Virginia than on the sugar plantations of the Caribbean. Nevertheless, Virginia slaves clearly were "treated by too many of their Owners as so many Beasts of Burthen"—and as the imperial crisis called attention to ideas about liberty and justice, many white Virginians grew uneasy about their dependence upon a labor system that contradicted humanitarian values.

Slavery seemed to undermine Virginia's capacity to resist tyranny. John Mercer of Marlborough, father of the colony's hapless stamp agent, feared that Virginians were already too "Infatuated and Abandoned" to act decisively against slavery and its effects. Henry certainly agreed with Arthur Lee that slavery was always "dangerous to the safety" of any community in which it existed, "destructive to the growth of arts and Sciences," and responsible for a "very fatal train of Vices both in the Slave and in his Master." Virginians felt powerless to rid the colony of slavery, but they could strike at the Atlantic slave trade. The General Assembly voted in 1766 to double Virginia's import duty upon slaves to 10 percent and three years later to double it again to 20 percent. Henry and his legislative contemporaries embraced these impediments to the slave trade as an admirable step toward "the Policy of encouraging the Importation of free People and discouraging that of Slaves."

Both Henry's disdain for slavery and his sympathy for religious dissenters won him lasting respect among Virginia's Quakers, who had recently begun sending representatives to Williamsburg to lobby against slavery. An entry in Rachel Wilson's diary, for example, described her visit to Williamsburg in March of 1769 "to see one of the Assemblymen, who was a man of great moderation, and had appeared in Friends' favour; his name was Patrick Henry. He received us with great civility, and made some sensible remarks." Wilson began a dialogue with Henry about slavery and manumission that her Quaker brethren sustained for two decades.

CHAPTER NINE

Organizing Resistance

BY VIRTUE OF the Declaratory Act of 1766, Virginia and Parliament had reached a constitutional deadlock. Neither party felt it could waver without admitting a fatal precedent that would bring catastrophe. Only by backing away from abstractions could the contestants sustain a tenuous stalemate that kept the peace. What Virginians feared, however, was that "some Bungler in politics" would "Experiment" with enforcing Parliament's claims "by military Power"—and the result would trigger "a general Revolt in America." Unfortunately, in the summer of 1767, just a year after Henry's political soul mate George Mason made that forecast, Charles Townshend, a newly appointed chancellor of the exchequer, leapt eagerly into the role of imperial bungler.

Prudence and constitutional principles be damned, Charles Townshend meant to enforce the claims of the Declaratory Act with taxation and legislation. The quarrel between Great Britain and her colonies "must soon come to an issue," he believed, and by *soon* he meant *now*. British authority, he told the House of Commons, "can at no time be better exerted than now." Without raising a farthing for imperial defense (the ostensible reason that Grenville had advocated the Stamp Tax) Townshend put forward a slapdash three-part program that historians recognize as "the most futile and inept laws of the age." One part imposed a cluster of miscellaneous taxes on paper, paint, glass, lead, and tea exported to the colonies. A second provision created a board of customs commissioners armed with writs of assistance. The third element suspended the elected assembly of New York as punishment for its earlier refusal to provide quarters for British troops.

The Townshend Acts confirmed Patrick Henry's worst fears about British motives and intentions, though their author did not live to see their damage. Early in September, just days after his forty-second birthday, Charles Townshend died of "a putrid fever," probably typhus. George III promptly named Frederick Lord North as the next chancellor of the exchequer. Had the fatal disease struck Townshend earlier, North Americans today might be singing "God Save the Queen," drinking tea, and driving on the wrong side of the road. Instead, Americans reacted to the Townshend Duties by reasserting the basic constitutional arguments advanced in Henry's resolutions against the Stamp Act. John Dickinson's famous *Letters from a Farmer in Pennsylvania* denied Parliament's authority for taxing the colonies but conceded its claims for regulating trade and industry—positions that Virginians had embraced years earlier—while Arthur Lee expressed views closer to Henry's in a series of essays published over the pen name Monitor.

Dickinson predicted that another round of legislative resolutions, instructions to colonial agents, and petitions to the king and Parliament "will have the same success now that they had in the time of the STAMP ACT." Arthur Lee, by contrast, had recently lived in London, had witnessed George III's and Parliament's refusals even to read protests from the colonies, and knew that the British repeal of the Stamp Act had been driven by "their own interests" rather than "friendship to our liberties and rights." Lee and Henry were on the same page in every respect. His "Monitor" essays began with praise for Dickinson's "excellent" constitutional principles (just as Henry's early resolutions had endorsed the Assembly's earlier protests against the Stamp Act) but then pressed for more aggressive, democratic, and inherently revolutionary action. Where Dickinson advocated legislative protests, Lee pressed for energetic resistance from "the people of every county" (just as Henry had called for action against enemies of the people). Where Dickinson mentioned John Locke only in a footnote quoting someone's speech about taxation and representation, Lee boldly quoted the same justification for armed revolution that Henry had invoked at Hanover Courthouse in 1763—*"an appeal to Heaven, that is, to the sword."* The question Americans now faced was whether they would "bequeath bondage or liberty to our children."

But the most significant aspect of Lee's Monitor essays was a call for community mobilization consonant with Patrick Henry's style of political leadership. As Henry had done for the Stamp Act, Lee advocated unanimous and determined opposition to the Townshend

Acts' "subversion of our constitutional freedom and happiness." Echoing Henry's Caesar-Brutus speech, Lee exhorted Virginians to demand from their representatives a petition of rights akin to the Petition of Right devised "on a similar occasion in the time of Charles the First." Then, recognizing that economics rather than eloquence had pushed Parliament to repeal the Stamp Act, Lee urged his neighbors to organize themselves in civic associations to encourage domestic manufacturing and boycott British imported goods. In short, the Monitor essays articulated Virginia's transition from protest to radical resistance between 1768 and 1770. The emergence of strong local organizations mobilized for resistance foreshadowed the nonimportation movement of the 1770s and strengthened Henry's hand by pushing Virginia's traditional leaders toward radical measures and eventual revolution. In a shrewd observation about Henry's leadership and its compatibility with Virginia's increasingly democratic political culture, Edmund Randolph compared him to the great orator and prime minister William Pitt. Henry's nature would have denied him "the capacity of becoming Pitt," Randolph wrote, "while Pitt himself would have been but a defective instrument in a revolution the essence of which was deep and pervading popular sentiment."

ooooo

Early in 1768 hundreds of freeholders gathered in four Piedmont counties—Amelia, Chesterfield, Dinwiddie, and Henrico—to sign petitions urging the House of Burgesses to "implore his Majesty" (whose sovereignty they regarded as their sole connection with the mother country) to deflect Parliament's attack on the legislature of New York. The Townshend Acts, and especially their assault upon the existence of a colonial legislature, were "so destructive of the Liberty of a free People" that the inhabitants of these Virginia counties directly felt "the Danger of losing their antient Rights and Privileges as Freemen." A similar petition from Westmoreland County, ancestral home of Arthur Lee's extended family, addressed the burgesses as "the only true and constitutional Representatives of the People of Virginia" and therefore the only legislature capable of imposing taxes upon Virginians "consistently with Law and Liberty." It protested the Townshend Acts as measures that menaced "*American* Freedom and Happiness."

These county petitions marked the beginning of an important democratic mobilization. In partnership with men such as Henry and the Lee brothers—and in advance of the more hesitant members of the General Assembly—ordinary Virginia freeholders, united as "the people of every county," began insisting that their own legislative assembly, "the Constitutional Guardians of the Liberty of Virginia," take the lead in organizing resistance to British tyranny. The 1768 session of the Assembly was sparsely attended (probably owing to its last-minute summons after the death of Governor Fauquier) but those present took heed of popular sentiment. In effect the county petitions of 1768 rallied Virginia freeholders to the first step in what began as an organized program of resistance but would end in revolution: The petitions led to the creation of nonimportation committees of 1769–1771 and then the powerful local committees of the Virginia Association of August 1774, which in turn would culminate both in the Continental Association that Virginia recommended to the First Continental Congress in September 1774 and in the county and provincial Committees of Safety that guided the Old Dominion to independence.

"Don't you think the Virginians have behaved like Men?" a North Carolinian exclaimed in a letter that found its way into newspapers as far north as Salem, Massachusetts. "Titles, Burgundy, and a gilt Coach"—references to Virginia's newly appointed governor, Norborne Berkeley, Baron de Botetourt—"will not be sufficient Inducements to bribe Men out of their Liberties." By autumn, assemblies in Delaware, North Carolina, and Maryland had endorsed and adopted, unanimously and verbatim, Virginia's resolutions against the Townshend Acts. The popular toast in good company throughout New England was to "The brave VIRGINIANS."

By December of 1768 all the colonies from Georgia to New Hampshire had endorsed Virginia's call for unified defense of the rights and liberties of British North America—and with this coordinated response to the Townshend Acts, the Old Dominion and the Bay State resumed their leading partnership in resistance to British measures. According to the observant gadfly Horace Walpole, whose father had arranged a knighthood for Peyton and John Randolph's father, the Old Dominion had both "the best heads and the principal *boutesfeux*," or incendiaries, in North America.

ooooo

Virginia's strident and unified response to the Townshend Acts startled crown officials. The Earl of Hillsborough, then secretary of state for the American colonies, found the Old Dominion's unified resistance and its demonstrated capacity for intercolonial leadership especially troubling. "The *Council* as well as the Assembly of Virginia have joined in the most indecent remonstrances" against the Townshend Acts, "and they have called on the other colonies to make it a common cause." While worrying that Virginia might now be "in a much worse state than even the colony of Massachusetts Bay," Hillsborough dreamed of drawing the Old Dominion's aristocratic planters away from their New England brethren. While the administration debated what to do with the Townshend Duties, Hillsborough toyed with lifting all of the duties for Virginia and a few other colonies that already provided permanent salaries for their crown-appointed officials. This time, however, the king had apparently read Virginia's petition. "The conduct of the Virginians was so offensive," George III advised his cabinet, that "altering the Revenue Act in their favour ... would not be proper." George III was especially affronted by the Council's endorsement of those "indecent remonstrances." When Hillsborough suggested sending "four or five ships of war and a body of mariners" to Williamsburg, both George III and his minister recognized that the commander of British forces in North America, General Thomas Gage, was incapable of sending "a great force to any part of America"—and that if military force against Virginia proved unsuccessful ("if that force should meet with a check") it was "but too likely that the whole continent would join in actual opposition to government." As their conversation continued, however, George III did agree with Hillsborough's plan to send a full-fledged resident governor to Virginia for the first time in six decades.

Although Hillsborough promptly embarrassed the king with his abrupt removal of Virginia's longtime absentee governor, General Jeffrey Amherst (who had been given the sinecure office by George II as a reward for his service in the French and Indian War), his appointment of Norborne Berkeley, Baron de Botetourt, as governor of Virginia was one appealing element of an ambitious new plan for the colonies. As the ministry sought to isolate the northern port cities from their southern allies, Boston felt the iron fist and Williamsburg the silk glove. Early in October two regiments from Halifax disembarked at Boston Harbor, followed in November by two more from Ireland—a mobilization of more than one thousand British troops intended to intimidate New York and Philadelphia, as well. Things were far different at Yorktown on Wednesday, October 26, 1768, when Governor Botetourt disembarked from the warship *Rippon* not with companies of armed redcoats but with his servants, his baggage, and an impressive carriage "gilded in every part" and emblazoned with the Virginia coat of arms.

Governor Botetourt enjoyed two remarkably cordial years in Virginia before his sudden death at fifty-two from erysipelas, a bacterial infection known as St. Anthony's Fire that also claimed the lives of Queen Anne, John Dryden, and George III's daughter Princess Amelia. Talented as Botetourt may have been, however, the disease ended his tenure in Virginia before the intractable clash between Virginia and Parliament could dim his popularity. As it was, Botetourt arrived with secret instructions directly from George III (whose initials are visible on the original document) directing him to challenge the constitutional principles that Patrick Henry had been preaching since the Parsons' Cause. His charge was to dissolve the old Assembly, call new elections, and somehow charm the House of Burgesses into reversing its course, endorsing the Declaratory Act of 1766, and recognizing the king's authority "to enact Laws by and with the Advice and Consent of Our Parliament, to bind all and every part of Our Empire in all Cases whatsoever." To accomplish this miracle George III encouraged Botetourt to talk "separately and personnally" with influential Virginians, as the king sometimes did with his own ministers, and persuade them "to disclaim the erroneous and dangerous Principles which they appear to have adopted." If the new governor did initiate private talks with Virginia leaders, he left no record for posterity. We can only imagine the conversation Botetourt may have had with Patrick Henry.

ooooo

Dogwoods, redbuds, and spring flowers brightened the trails in the spring of 1769 when Patrick Henry rode to Williamsburg to welcome Lord Botetourt to the capitol on Monday, May 8. He and his family still lived at Roundabout—where Sarah gave birth to their fourth and fifth children, Anne and Elizabeth—but Henry had been elected to the House of Burgesses from his native Hanover County, where he owned property and had many enthusiastic supporters, while his friend Thomas Johnson returned to the Assembly from Louisa.

The new governor had a flair for ceremony: clad in a bright red coat bespangled with gold trim for the short ride from the Governor's Palace in a gilded carriage, he opened the new Assembly by announcing the royal birth of Princess Augusta Sophia and encouraging Henry and the other 107 burgesses (including a lanky, sandy-haired first-time representative from Albemarle County) to focus "without Passion or Prejudices [upon] the *real interests* of those you have the Honour to represent."

Eight days later Henry's friend John Blair, Jr. (who was also his partner in the ownership of a huge tract of land near the Cumberland Gap), presented four resolutions written by a committee that represented the full range of temperaments among the burgesses, from assertive voices such as Patrick Henry, Richard Henry Lee, and Thomson Mason (George Mason's younger brother and author of a recently published essay denying parliamentary authority in America) to the conciliatory treasurer Robert Carter Nicholas and the Speaker's close friend and brother-in-law Benjamin Harrison. The first resolution reiterated the fundamental principle that Virginians had learned from Richard Bland, Landon Carter, and Patrick Henry: the sole right of imposing taxes in Virginia "is now, and ever hath been, legally and constitutionally vested in the House of Burgesses." The three remaining resolutions addressed recent developments. The burgesses reaffirmed their right to petition the king for "Royal Interposition in Favour of the violated Rights of America." They invoked the rights of Englishmen to declare that any Virginian accused of treason must be tried in the colony by a local jury. Finally, the burgesses asked George III to quiet the minds of his loyal subjects by assuring them that no Americans accused of crimes would be transported across the Atlantic for trial. Despite Botetourt's aristocratic title and personal charm, the Assembly's unanimous adoption of these four resolutions underscored the magnitude of the governor's impending political defeat. When the burgesses were summoned before him the next day, the governor's message was brief: "Mr. Speaker and Gentlemen of the House of Burgesses," Botetourt said, "I have heard of your Resolves, and augur ill of their Effect: You have made it my Duty to dissolve you; and you are dissolved accordingly."

Botetourt's apparent equanimity was a careful deception. Within a few days he dispatched a "Secret and Confidential" report to Lord Hillsborough. "My duty to the King obliges me to inform Your Lordship," Botetourt warned the ministry, "that Opinions of Independency of the

Legislature of the Colonies are grown to such a Height in this Country, that it becomes Great Britain, if ever she intends it, immediately to assert her Supremacy in a manner which may be felt." The time had come either to enforce or surrender Parliament's claim of authority in America. "Great Britain needed to assert her supremacy firmly," Botetourt wrote, "and to loose no more time in Declarations which irritate but do not decide."

ooooo

Because Botetourt's dissolution of the Assembly stripped the former burgesses of all official authority, what happened next on Wednesday, May 17, 1769, was inherently rebellious, perhaps revolutionary. After they followed Speaker Peyton Randolph down the stairs from the Council chamber, Patrick Henry and virtually all his colleagues left the capitol, walked a hundred yards together past the Exchange and Charlton's coffeehouse on Duke of Gloucester Street, and gathered in the Apollo Room of Anthony Hay's Raleigh Tavern, the largest privately owned meeting place in town. There the former burgesses organized themselves as an extralegal convention— as members of Parliament had frequently done in their various struggles against Stuart tyranny—to enforce their protests with economic pressure. They elected their former Speaker as a presiding "Moderator," put a select committee to work drafting regulations for a boycott of British imports, and agreed to reconvene the next morning. Patrick Henry, Richard Henry Lee, and the rest of the committee worked late into the evening, polishing and perfecting a document whose first draft had been written in George Mason's study at Gunston Hall. George Washington, whose diary entries were always terse (and in this instance prudently cryptic), noted only that he dined with Treasurer Nicholas that evening and then met with "a Committee at Hay's till ten o'clock."

On Thursday morning the committee presented its work—eight regulations creating an Association to enforce a boycott against the importation and consumption of British manufactured goods—which the gossipy merchant James Parker of Norfolk attributed to the pens of Washington, Lee, and Henry. The agreement accused Britain of "reducing us from a free and happy People to a wretched and miserable State of Slavery." Unless Americans curtailed their consumption of British goods, as they had against the Stamp Act, there was "little reason to expect a Redress of those Grievances." Accordingly, effective September 1, 1769, the Virginia Associators (as they described themselves) agreed not to purchase anything taxed by Parliament "for the Purpose of raising a Revenue," wines "of any kind," and a long list of specifically prohibited commodities from spirits, ale, candles, and pickles to clocks, jewelry, fabrics, shoes, and saddles. In addition, expanding upon the intended goal of their recently augmented import duties, the Associators agreed "that they will not import any Slaves . . . until the said Acts of Parliament are repealed."

Henry's situation was far different than it had been just four years earlier when Governor Fauquier dissolved the Assembly in 1765 and tried to suppress his resolves against the Stamp Act. Fauquier had enjoyed considerable support from John Robinson, Peyton Randolph, and Richard Bland. Now Robinson was dead and his memory disgraced. Bland had challenged Randolph for the Speaker's chair with support from Patrick Henry and Richard Henry Lee. And Henry's bold vision of Virginia's legislative autonomy within the British empire had gained unanimous concurrence in the General Assembly as well as a wide circulation among the people at large—whose defiance of British policy increasingly threatened reluctant candidates with electoral defeat. Back in 1765, when Virginians disputed among themselves about how best to persuade the king and Parliament to respect their rights as Englishmen, the cries of treason aroused by Henry's Caesar-Brutus speech might have seemed extravagant. Four short years later, however, the burgesses who were contending that Parliament had no authority to tax or legislate for America were also taking precautions to defend their leaders against formal prosecution for treason. The biggest difference between 1765 and 1769, however, was that after Fauquier dissolved the Assembly the former burgesses had left the capitol and gone home.

ooooo

Just as the meeting at Raleigh Tavern marked a turning point in Virginia's path toward independence, far across the Atlantic a meeting that same month of George III's cabinet marked "the point of no return," according to British historian P. D. G. Thomas, in the series of ministerial decisions that led to the American Revolution. By a contentious vote of 5 to 4 on Monday, May 1, Hillsborough and Lord North won support for the policies that ultimately led to war. They would repeal all the Townshend Duties except the tax on tea, which the king regarded as an essential token of British authority and Lord North cherished as the only duty that was actually raising significant revenue. The ministry also agreed not to impose any new taxes on the colonies (a shift in policy that might have done some good a few years earlier) and to express goodwill toward America in a "soothing" letter to the colonial governors.

With Parliament threatening to indict Americans for treason and drag them to London for trial, Henry and other forward-thinking Virginians rarely committed their thoughts about armed resistance, war, or independence to paper. Even in a hand-delivered private letter to his trusted friend George Mason, for example, George Washington took care to cloak the incriminating word *arms* when he confided in April 1769 that if economic sanctions proved ineffective, "no man should scruple or hesitate a moment to use a—ms in defence of so valuable blessing" as American liberty, "yet A—ms I would beg leave to add, should be the last . . . resort." The prospects of war and independence had become the subject of whispered conversations for a wide range of Virginians—not just Henrys, Washingtons, Masons, and Lees—in the decades since the Earl of Halifax took charge of the Board of Trade in 1748. Although Halifax and a few British politicians worried that Americans were seeking political separation from Great Britain, the colonists were careful to share their thoughts only with those whom they trusted.

Of only seventeen public remarks about political independence in colonial newspapers between 1769 and 1771, twelve were English accusations about American intentions and five were American denials. However, one-third of all statements about political independence specifically mentioned Virginia. A Bostonian touring the Chesapeake in 1769 reported that a private disposition toward "a total independency [from] their mother country" was rampant in Virginia and Maryland. A year later, two future members of the Continental Congress described Virginia's resolutions against the Stamp Act as assertions of "*an absolute Independence of the Mother Country*" because they proclaimed Virginia's exclusive authority over both taxation "*and internal police.*" Everyone knew that "internal police" meant the whole system of laws regulating public and private matters in civil society, so that Virginians "in effect maintain an absolute Independence of the Mother Country." Posterity may never be certain about colonial attitudes toward war and independence at the beginning of the 1770s, but even Patrick Henry (so far as we know) withheld his *public* advocacy of independence until the first week of January 1776.

ooooo

The Virginia Association of 1769 made a critically important transition from eloquent protest to economic resistance. Virginia's organization differed from the nonimportation agreements among merchants in Boston, New York, and Philadelphia—mercantile associations that soon collapsed as a result of local factionalism and regional rivalries in the northern ports. Henry and his colleagues cast a broader net that aimed at gathering all their constituents—not just the merchants—behind the promise neither to import *or consume* a long list of specific goods until Parliament repealed the Townshend Duties. Their list of prohibited commodities (including imported liquor, wine, and ale; clocks, looking glasses, and jewelry; cheese, pickles, and candies; lace, linens, and ribbons; shoes, boots, saddles; and much more) made the Virginia agreement of 1769 twice as long as its northern antecedents. Until those duties were repealed, signers promised to cancel all orders from British merchants and return any shipments of proscribed goods. Virginians also promised not to import or purchase slaves, a provision not found in the northern or Maryland agreements that reflected the Assembly's repeated attempts to impose prohibitive duties on the slave trade. The sixth clause banned imported wines, an obvious luxury, and the seventh halted the butchering of spring lambs to encourage greater reliance upon local wool and homespun clothing or "Virginia cloth."

Once the plan had been affirmed with a unanimous vote, Henry and the former burgesses lined up to sign the Association document (an innovative ritual that we now take for granted) as representatives of the community in the spirit of John Locke's theories about social and political contracts. Moderator Peyton Randolph had the honor of signing first, and in the printed version of the Association his name is followed immediately by Treasurer Nicholas and Richard Bland. Richard Henry Lee was fifth, Washington was seventh, and Henry was eleventh. Attorney General John Randolph's name was conspicuously absent. Equally as significant as the eighty-eight printed signatures, however, was the space left at the bottom of the printed handbill that invited additional signatures from freeholders throughout the colony. Henry and his colleagues in the Apollo Room recognized the importance of enlisting their constituents in the boycott. "The Association is Sent to every County in Virginia," Norfolk's James Parker told a business associate, "there is hardly a tayler or Cobler in town but what have Signed it."

Whether present with Henry at Raleigh Tavern or subscribing a circulating copy at a courthouse or church service, every signer promised "upon his Word and Honor" to uphold the boycott until the Townshend Duties were repealed and the Association disbanded. Every signature strengthened the Association as symbol of the social compact among the people of Virginia. Political deference did not happen by chance in eighteenth-century Virginia—when present it was rooted in a measure of respect between the yeoman farmers and their gentry neighbors that ordinary planters were quick to demand (as in the Robinson scandal) when would-be aristocrats overstepped their authority.

More than one thousand residents of Dinwiddie County, on the Appomattox River west of Petersburg, signed the Association by early July 1769. Only two rare copies of the circulating broadside are known to survive. The Association handbill at the Library of Virginia bears nineteen autograph signatures from residents of four counties in the Potomac watershed. Another at the Library of Congress bears 101 autograph signatures from a somewhat wider area including Fairfax, Hanover, King George, Loudoun, Stafford, and Westmoreland counties.

Other bits of evidence provide glimpses of heightened resistance to British authority and the public campaign for the nonimportation Association. When the burgess who represented the port of Norfolk returned from Williamsburg after helping create the Association, the borough's "principal inhabitants" honored him with an elegant dinner celebrating "their entire approbation of his conduct in the late Assembly." Significant support for the Association also came from Virginia women, who routinely managed many details of domestic consumption and production on farms and plantations. William Rind's *Gazette* celebrated five prominent "widow Ladies" whose endorsement of the boycott set an "example of public spirit" bolstered by their family connections. By endorsing it these patriotic widows elevated the Association above the realm of ordinary politics. Encouraged by their example, gentry women and their seamstresses throughout the colony also organized stylish demonstrations of community support for frugality and the boycott. "I expect to be dressed in Virginia cloth [i.e., homespun] very soon," Martha Jacquelin wrote from Yorktown in August. Four months later, when the burgesses honored Botetourt with a ball at the capitol, his councilors and their wives "made a genteel appearance" along with the ladies and gentlemen of Williamsburg "chiefly dressed in Virginia cloth." That spring, at another formal ball in honor of the governor, "upwards of a hundred Ladies appeared in home-spun dresses" fashioned "for the entertainment of Lord Botetourt."

Patrick Henry was by no means alone in his purchases of a flax sickle, loom, and enough seed to harvest five hundred pounds of linen fiber a year in 1768 and 1769. Henry's penchant for down-to-earth clothing became the patriotic fashion as well. In a well-coordinated domestic campaign for liberty and frugality, gentry women "apparelled in Virginia growth" urged "the middle rank" to forgo "the extravagance and folly" of imported finer-ies in favor of "agreeable dress created by the labour of their own families." A letter from "Buckskin" in Rind's *Gazette* suggested that "deer skins make as good and commendable waistcoats as they do breeches." And Landon Carter admired the crowds who gathered at Virginia courthouses "warmly clad in the produce of their wives and daughters" for their contributions to "the preservation of our future liberties."

By the winter of 1769 Virginians had created an informal network of local committees reporting to a central committee in Williamsburg that would be formally confirmed in a revised agreement in 1770. It bears re-peating, a quarter of a millennium later, that all these activities—gathering signatures in localities throughout the colony, affirmations of support in the newspapers, endorsements by prominent widows, and all the rest—point toward the Association of 1769–1771 as the experience by which Virginia men and women began mobilizing their families, counties, and colony for collective resistance to British authority and enemies of the community.

The nonimportation movement also confirmed several lessons that de-fined Henry's future resistance to British policies. Petitions and constitu-tional arguments had little influence with British policymakers. Acts of oppression against other colonies were direct threats to liberty in Virginia. Intercolonial unity was essential, as was cooperation between the capital and the counties and harmony among Virginia freeholders. Gentry plant-ers and ordinary farmers could join in the work on elected local committees founded in civic principles. Old-fashioned homespun virtues, industry and frugality as well as Virginia cloth and buckskin clothing, contributed to the common good by shielding Virginians from the luxury and corruption so rampant in British society and politics.

Events also convinced candid Virginians that George III and "both Houses of Parliament [were] united in a design to enslave us." Although not yet apparent to everyone, the prospect for genuine reconciliation between Great Britain and the American colonies had passed. Virginians found themselves radicalized in ways they had not anticipated earlier. The Association and its extralegal provincial and local committees began to supplant the regular machinery of government. Emboldened by their partial success and frustrated by the backsliding of their northern brethren in 1770 and 1771, Patrick Henry and the Associators of the Old Dominion were emerging as a cadre of incipient revolutionaries.

CHAPTER TEN

Good and Evil

WHILE PATRICK HENRY and some of his colleagues worried about Virginia's dependence upon slavery, the colony's small community of Quakers was setting its sights on abolition. At their yearly meeting in 1768, the Old Dominion's Society of Friends decided that members should no longer purchase slaves, and the following spring they began lobbying for a law permitting manumission, or voluntary emancipation, of individual slaves. Since the 1720s, Virginia law had only permitted the governor and Council to set a slave free as a reward for "meritorious services" to the colony. In advance of the short-lived Assembly session that May, Rachel Wilson and Petersburg Quaker Edward Stabler, clerk of Virginia's yearly meeting, met with Patrick Henry, who received them "with great civility, and made some sensible remarks" when they were lobbying the burgesses to adopt legislation encouraging manumission. Robert Pleasants, a prominent Virginia Quaker who eventually founded an Abolition Society in Richmond, advanced the Quakers' effort the following year by sending the veteran legislator Richard Bland copies of Maryland's manumission law and an antislavery pamphlet by the Quaker John Woolman. Pleasants entertained the wildly optimistic hope that Bland might persuade the burgesses not only to lift the legal restrictions on manumission but to embrace the "Noble sentiments of liberty" and free all Virginia slaves from bondage.

With the support of burgesses like Henry and young Thomas Jefferson, Bland *did* propose easing the restrictions on private manumissions, but the reaction from many legislators was ferocious. Four decades later, amid the growing national debate about slavery in advance of the Missouri Compromise of 1820, Thomas Jefferson remembered the vicious personal assaults on Bland and his proposed legislation. Angry burgesses denounced Bland "with the grossest indecorum" as an "enemy of his country" for suggesting that slaves be afforded "certain moderate extensions of the protection of the laws." It was a vivid and nasty episode, too often repeated in southern history, that taught Henry's generation a fateful lesson about the political hazards associated with slavery and race in Virginia.

Although Robert Pleasants and the Quakers continued their campaign against slavery, the example of Bland's vilification certainly informed Henry's subsequent dialogue with them. Few contradictions in American history are more stark than the existence of slavery in a nation ostensibly committed to liberty—and Patrick Henry was acutely aware of this dissonance. From the vantage point of the twenty-first century, some are inclined to dismiss all slaveholders as hypocrites. Virginians of Henry's generation believed that leadership often meant doing the good one can, when one cannot do all one might wish—a lesson they could trace back to Aristotle. Conduct often fell short of aspirations, then as now, but Henry's candor about slavery in these early years of his dialogue with Robert Pleasants is instructive. We frequently forget that by declaring that slavery was morally wrong, the founders themselves set the standard against which subsequent generations gauge their moral failures.

Labor systems based on personal bondage enforced by violence (slavery, serfdom, feudalism, and indentured servitude) had been prevalent throughout the world for centuries prior to the American Revolution, but in the 1760s and early 1770s there was "a remarkable shift in moral consciousness," according to Yale historian David Brion Davis. "What was unprecedented," Davis concluded, "was the emergence of a widespread conviction that New World slavery symbolized all the forces that threatened the true destiny of man."

Patrick Henry expressed his most revealing thoughts about slavery in a January 1773 letter to Robert Pleasants acknowledging the gift of a copy of "Anthony Benezet's book against the slave trade"—*Some Historical Account of Guinea . . . With an Inquiry into the Rise and Progress of the Slave-Trade, Its Nature and Lamentable Effects*, published in Philadelphia in 1771. "It is not a little surprising," Henry said of the early church fathers, "that the professors of Christianity, whose chief excellence consists in softening the human heart . . . should encourage a practice so totally repugnant to the first impressions of right and wrong." Even more surprising "is that this practice has been introduced in the most enlightened ages." Modern men and women proud of their "improvements in the arts and sciences and refined morality," Henry observed, have "brought into general use, and guarded by many laws, a species of violence and tyranny which our more rude and barbarous but more honest ancestors detested."

"Is it not amazing," Henry continued, "that at a time when the rights of humanity are stated and understood with precision, in a country above all others fond of liberty, that in such an age and in such a country, we find men professing a religion the most humane, mild, gentle and generous, [while] adopting a principle as repugnant to humanity as it is inconsistent with the bible and destructive to morality? Every thinking, honest man rejects [slavery] in speculation"—that is in abstract theory—but "how few in practice from conscientious motives!"

Then came Henry's candid assessment of his own involvement with the evil of slavery—entirely free of the rationalization often invoked by Tidewater gentlemen who had inherited their slaves along with their plantations. "Would anyone believe," Henry wrote, that "I am the master of slaves of my own purchase. I am drawn along by the general inconvenience of living here without them. I will not, I cannot justify it. However culpable my conduct, I will so far pay my d[uty] to virtue, as to [acknowledge] the excellence and rectitude of [virtue's] precepts and lament my want of conformity to them."

Despite the initial promise of Henry's reply, however, it soon became evident that although Henry regarded slavery as wicked, neither he nor his contemporaries could decide how to end it. He expressed hope that "a time will come when an opportunity will be offered to abolish this lamentable evil." Like many other southerners, Henry professed to welcome the end of slavery, "if it happens in our day," but aside from his genuine efforts to end the importation of slaves, he saw no realistic path toward its abolition—no way of "reduc[ing] this wished-for reformation to practice." Any serious consideration of slavery "gives a gloomy perspective to future times," Henry admitted. Ending the slave trade was a step in the right direction, but unless the institution somehow disappeared on its own, Henry could only urge that his generation "transmit to our descendants, together with our slaves, a pity for their unhappy lot and an abhorrence of slavery." "The furthest advance we can make toward justice," Henry concluded, was to "treat the unhappy victims with lenity." Slavery was an evil, and the decent treatment of its victims was a debt that slaveholders owed "to the purity of our religion, to show that [Christian morality] is at variance with that law which warrants slavery."

ooooo

The conviction shared by Patrick Henry and his contemporaries that by attacking the slave trade they were effectively attacking the institution of slavery itself gains some plausibility from recent scholarship comparing slavery in the Chesapeake with slavery in the Caribbean. Because Virginians had only begun importing large numbers of slaves in the early decades of the century, the troubling and growing presence of Virginia's "vast shoals of Negroes," as the Reverend Hugh Jones lamented in 1724, seemed obviously to be the immediate result of the slave trade. In a broader geographic perspective, it has become apparent that the sugar plantations of the Caribbean required periodic importations of slaves to replace laborers who died in that brutal system, just as Virginia planters of the previous century had continued to import indentured servants to replace laborers who died or completed their terms of service. Despite their similar origins, however, plantation slavery in the sugar islands and the Chesapeake became "radically different." The "increasingly dysfunctional" slave labor system of the sugar islands, where slave deaths far exceeded births, collapsed after Great Britain closed its African slave trade in 1807 and ended with compensated emancipation in 1834. By contrast, despite the fact that the Old Dominion terminated its participation in the Atlantic slave trade in the 1770s, slave births in Virginia so greatly outnumbered deaths that the state's black population doubled during the quarter century after the American Revolution. The eventual result, especially after the Louisiana Purchase and the War of 1812, was the phenomenal growth of the antebellum *internal* slave trade, which drove half a million enslaved Americans from Virginia and the Chesapeake to the cotton fields of the Mississippi River Valley—a development that may obscure from our view the impressions that had once encouraged the naive hope embraced by Patrick Henry's generation that ending the Atlantic slave trade might eventually put an end to slavery.

Despite the now obvious limits of his aversion to slavery, Henry did genuinely oppose the slave trade and would in time embrace legislation encouraging private manumissions. He also supported both the prohibition of slave imports by Virginia's nonimportation associations and the

1772 declaration by the House of Burgesses that "the interest of the Country would manifestly require the total expulsion" of slaves, whose presence "greatly retards the Settlement of the Colonies with more useful Inhabitants." Always more eager to protect their society than their slaves, Virginia legislators focused on curtailing the importation of Africans—and despite decades of objections from British merchants engaged in the slave trade, crown authorities had never interfered with Virginia's import duties on slaves prior to 1769. In that year, however, the Board of Trade began siding with the protests from Liverpool and Bristol without offering any objection "in point of law." British officials began vetoing Virginia's import duties on slaves because they impeded "the importation of a considerable article of British Commerce." From 1769 to independence, George III and his ministers yielded to the clamor of British slave traders and vetoed every one of the very limited steps against slavery taken by the General Assembly of Virginia. Not until 1778 was the independent Commonwealth of Virginia able to end the international slave trade by prohibiting the importation of slaves "by sea or land" from Africa or neighboring states.

ooooo

In the summer of 1768, soon after the Quakers began lobbying Patrick Henry and others about slavery, half a dozen self-taught Baptist preachers began testing the limits of religious toleration in Anglican Virginia. Wandering the colony preaching their vision of the Gospels, these intrepid souls seemed especially eager to validate their faith by suffering as "prisoners for Christ." Unlike Samuel Davies, the Presbyterian evangelist who had earned the respect of the Tidewater gentry by complying with the law, the Separate Baptists, as they were known, refused to preach in registered meetinghouses as required by law. They regarded their preaching as subject only to God's direction and the restrictions of the English Toleration Act of 1689 as an affront to Jesus as lord of the church. Unlike the Quakers, whose quiet ways won them legal exemptions from oath taking and military service, the Separate Baptist preachers welcomed beatings, humiliation, whippings, and imprisonment at the hands of public officials, Anglican priests, and common bullies.

The Separate Baptist preachers "are great disturbers of the peace," a Spotsylvania attorney complained to the county court in June 1768. "They cannot meet a man upon the road, but they must ram a text of scripture down his throat." An Anglican rector in Caroline County, where the itinerant Baptists faced an orchestrated campaign of religious persecution, compared them to "the gnats that buzz around us in a summer's evening"—"little insignificant animals" with a noisy capacity "to tease, to sting, and to torment." Foremost among the preachers' few defenders was Patrick Henry—and chief among their persecutors were Edmund Pendleton and Archibald Cary.

As senior justice of the Caroline County court and a vestryman of Drysdale Parish, Pendleton and his pastor, the Reverend Andrew Moreton, encouraged a climate of religious persecution in the central Piedmont. Pendleton's court began levying fines against people who skipped Anglican worship or attended illegal Baptist services in 1768. Within the next three years Pendleton and his fellow justices indicted more than three dozen worshippers—far more than suffered in other counties—and preachers fared much worse. They sent John Young to jail in June after he admitted to preaching the Gospel without being licensed as a dissenting preacher. Laden with penalties and security bonds that totaled a whopping £100, Young was still incarcerated in July, preaching through the bars of the jailhouse window, when Pendleton imprisoned another Baptist preacher and three laymen with bonds of £20 each. Early in August Pendleton sent a sixth preacher, Lewis Craig, to jail in lieu of another £20 bond.

By consigning six devout Baptists to jail in the summer heat "for preaching the laws of God while violating the laws of the Anglicans," as Pendleton's admiring biographer put it, Caroline County took a leading role in Virginia's prosecutions of religious dissenters. Of about 150 acts of religious persecution perpetrated against Virginia Baptists in the decade before the Declaration of Independence, 21 percent occurred in Caroline County, where Pendleton, a friend later recalled, "drank deeply of the enthusiasm of orthodoxy" and fully "concurred in these persecutions." The most notorious episode happened in the spring of 1771, when the Reverend Andrew Moreton, Pendleton's pastor, rode his horse into a Sunday service led by the itinerant John Waller. Accompanied by his parish clerk and the county sheriff, Moreton flicked his whip across the pages of Waller's psalm book at the lectern while the congregation was singing. When Waller began to pray Moreton forced the butt end of his whip into Waller's mouth. Then the parish clerk pulled Waller off the stage and dragged him to the sheriff, who "whipped him in so violent a manner that poor Waller was presently in a gore of blood." Twenty lashes from the sheriff's horsewhip gave Waller scars that he carried to his grave, but after his assailants left he returned to the stage and finished the service, "singing praises to Jehovah" and rejoicing, like Saint Paul, "that he was worthy to suffer for his dear Lord and Master."

South of the James River, the Baptists confronted another formidable churchman in the person of Archibald Cary of Ampthill, senior justice, vestryman, county lieutenant, influential burgess, and later president of the Virginia Senate. Cary signed most of the warrants for the Baptists fined and jailed in Chesterfield County between 1770 and 1774. When people gathered at the windows to hear seven incarcerated ministers preach through the bars, Cary had a high brick wall built around the jail. The public example of magistrates such as Cary and Pendleton unleashed private acts of violence and intimidation against Baptist worshippers throughout the colony. More than thirty Baptist preachers were imprisoned in Middlesex, Orange, Spotsylvania, and other counties before 1778. Beatings and whippings were common. Crowds carrying clubs and whips drove Samuel Harris out of Culpeper County, and in Orange County he was "pulled down as he was preaching and dragged about by the hair of his head." Someone threw a hornet's nest into one prayer meeting and a poisonous snake into another. Men on horseback rode into streams and disrupted baptisms, mocking the practice of baptism by immersion. Mobs dunked preachers, "holding them underwater until they were nearly drowned, asking them *if they believed.*"

And believe they did, with a courage that confirmed Tertullian's adage about the blood of martyrs as the seed of the Church: "The more ye mow us down, the more we grow." In the tumultuous years between 1768 and 1774, the Separate Baptists in the Old Dominion grew from a few itinerant ministers to fifty-four congregations with as many as four thousand members. Among their friends in Hanover County were the Presbyterian Isaac Winston, who was hauled into court for welcoming itinerant preachers to his property, and Patrick Henry, Winston's grandson and Virginia's foremost advocate for the Baptists' freedom of worship. Time and again, Henry either defended itinerant preachers in court or quietly arranged for their release by paying the fines they could not afford or that they refused as a matter of conscience.

Well into the twentieth century Baptist historians have celebrated Patrick Henry's defense of one itinerant preacher, either John Weatherford at Chesterfield Courthouse or John Waller in Fredericksburg. Arriving after a long ride, one story goes, Henry entered the courtroom just as the clerk was reading aloud the formal charge for disturbing the peace. "May it please the court, what did I hear read?" Henry interrupted. "Did I hear an expression, as if a crime," the account continues, "that these men, whom your worships are about to try for a misdemeanor, are charged with . . . preaching the gospel of the Son of God!" Whether or not Patrick Henry spoke those words, Virginia Baptists recognized and appreciated his efforts on behalf of religious freedom. From those days of persecution "until the day of their complete emancipation from the shackles of tyranny," the denomination's pioneering historian wrote in 1810, "the Baptists found in Patrick Henry an unwavering friend. May his name descend to posterity with unsullied honour!"

The persecution of Virginia Baptists got occasional notice in the newspapers. Purdie and Dixon published in their *Gazette* the earliest statement of support for "men of all religious persuasions" in June 1770. Signed by "A Citizen of the World," the essay invoked Pennsylvania's record as evidence for the importance of immigration and religious toleration—arguments expressed earlier by Patrick Henry, who could well have been the author. Virginia needed to encourage immigration by assuring that no one suffered "on account of their religious tenets, which in all men differ as much as their faces." Sounding a note that would reverberate in Henry's speeches at the First Continental Congress, A Citizen of the World invited his countrymen to overcome their religious, ethnic, and political differences and "glory in name of Americans."

On the other hand, a lengthy "Address to the Anabaptists imprisoned in Caroline County" that coincided with Edmund Pendleton's August 1771 imprisonment of the itinerant preacher Lewis Craig urged Baptist preachers throughout the colony to comply with the licensing laws as other dissenters had done. Its author (probably Pendleton) identified himself as "one among the few Lawyers in the Country" who thought the itinerants were entitled to the full benefit of the English Toleration Act of 1689 if they complied with its requirements. "The private Opinions of Men are not the Objects of Law or Government," he acknowledged, but when "*every One* undertakes to preach *every Where*" and by preaching doctrines "subversive of all Religion and Morality," they could expect to be prosecuted "as the Law directs" for disturbing the peace.

But what exactly did the law direct? A Virginian writing as "Timoleon," the name of a hero who overthrew tyrants in Corinth, Syracuse, and Sicily in the fourth century BC, posed that question two weeks after Pendleton sent Craig to jail. If the Act of Toleration did not apply to Virginia Baptists, then neither did the penal laws being cited to jail them. Alluding to the many places where dissenting denominations lived in harmony with their Anglican neighbors, Timoleon believed it was wrong to suppose that society required "a Sameness of Religion" or to categorize any dissenter as "an Enemy to the State." Liberty of conscience was the sacred property of every man, "which none can take from him without being guilty of Sacrilege and Tyranny."

Patrick Henry was outnumbered in the House of Burgesses when the new standing committee on religion grappled in February 1772 with religious toleration and "the State of the established Religion in this Colony." Confronted with a dozen Baptist petitions seeking the same treatment "in religious matters as Quakers, Presbyterians, and other Protestant Dissenters enjoy," the burgesses decided that their overall request was "reasonable." But of course the devil lurked in the details. Chaired by the conservative churchman Robert Carter Nicholas and stacked with like-minded burgesses such as Archibald Cary and Richard Bland, the committee on religion presented a formidable "Bill for Extending the Benefit of Several Acts of Toleration to His Majesty's Protestant Subjects in the Colony" while Henry was out of town with an excused absence.

The art of labeling repressive measures with attractive titles is nothing new. The proposed bill would have reinforced all the legal impediments to genuine religious toleration, especially the restrictions upon interracial evening meetings. The Assembly's handling of the bill reflected its controversial nature. Unable to defeat it outright when Nicholas presented the bill for a final reading on March 17, Henry and his allies were able to have it published to test public opinion and "laid on the table" until July 1—months after the Assembly session ended. Without public support, the repressive proposal remained dead on the table after William Rind gave it half the front page of his *Virginia Gazette* on March 26, 1772.

In the years ahead, Virginians would grapple with the proper relationship of church and state, the appropriate measure of state support for churches or education to promote public virtue, the degree to which religious uniformity contributed to social order, the merits of religious toleration and freedom of conscience. In a curious way, however, the first immediate result of these religious quarrels was to gird the freeholders of Virginia for imperial battles that were about to resume. Religious persecution by the likes of Edmund Pendleton and Archibald Cary boosted the cause of toleration in Virginia, but their repressive actions also demonstrated how extralegal methods of persuasion might be used to enforce an economic boycott or intimidate intransigent friends of king and Parliament.

CHAPTER ELEVEN

Hurrying Toward a Crisis

THE EXEMPLARY CAREERS of Governors Fauquier and Botetourt, who had died in Williamsburg after devoting their final years to the Old Dominion, set a daunting standard for any successor, but John Murray, Earl of Dunmore, did himself no favors after receiving notice from London in 1771 of his reassignment to the Old Dominion. The ambitious Scot had just begun to exploit the lucrative governorship of New York. In nine months he had already amassed a 51,000-acre tract on Lake Champlain and £14,000 in fees for land patents and he wanted more. A report that preceded him to Virginia told of his drunken rant in a Manhattan street on the night that William Tryon, formerly governor of North Carolina, had taken the oath of office as his successor: "Damn Virginia—Did I ever seek it?" Dunmore roared. "I asked for New York—New York I took, and they have robbed me of it without my Consent."

When George III had learned of Botetourt's death, he wanted the Williamsburg vacancy filled immediately. Dunmore's proximity, his stature as an earl, his energy and military experience, and his relative youth at thirty-nine were considerations that supported his appointment. On the other hand, Dunmore's character flaws included greed, impulsiveness, manners more suited to a garrison than a drawing room, and a chronic inability to keep his fly buttoned while separated from the beautiful Lady Charlotte Dunmore and their seven children, who had not yet followed him to America. During the seven months that Dunmore delayed his departure from New York, the gossip heard by Norfolk merchants engaged in the coastal trade held that the short, muscular earl who dismounted his horse at the Governor's Palace on September 25, 1771, was "a gamester, a whoremaster and a Drunkard."

The gossip was only two-thirds accurate. Dunmore seldom wagered on cards, horses, or dice. Patrick Henry and Richard Bland had formed "a very unfavorable opinion" of Dunmore in 1770 at an aborted conference about western lands in New York City. Richard Henry Lee pronounced history's verdict about Virginia's last royal governor in a letter to the sympathetic English historian Catherine Macaulay in 1773. Had George III and Lord North "searched through the world for a person the best fitted to ruin their cause and procure union and success for these Colonies," Lee concluded, "they could not have found a more complete Agent than Lord Dunmore."

ooooo

The first of Patrick Henry's clashes with Governor Dunmore began in February 1773. Acting upon the testimony of an informant (and against his councilors' advice about summoning the General Assembly to provide legal sanction for his actions) the governor had dispatched several soldiers as a "strong guard" to assist Pittsylvania County authorities in the arrest of a gang of counterfeiters, including the engraver, papermaker, and printer as well as their "plates, tools, and implements of every kind." Dunmore had then compounded the affront by having the offenders transported immediately to Williamsburg for trial before the General Court—"knowing how ineffectual it would have been," as he later explained to Lord Dartmouth, "to examine them in the County where they were taken, *which is the usual mode.*"

After Dunmore summoned the Assembly to repair the economic dislocation caused by the counterfeiters, Patrick Henry and the burgesses expressed alarm about the governor's departures from that "usual mode." Dunmore claimed that he had followed the advice of Speaker Peyton Randolph, Attorney General John Randolph, and Treasurer Robert Carter Nicholas "in every part of my conduct in this affair," but his reliance upon those capitol insiders only revived anxieties about the fair administration of justice from earlier scandals among Henry's colleagues in the House of Burgesses.

The house assigned the drafting of its warning for the new governor to an unusually powerful committee of eight—including Patrick Henry, Richard Henry Lee, Richard Bland, Archibald Cary, and Edmund Pendleton, as well as Treasurer Nicholas (whose advice was being corrected), Bartholomew Dandridge (a Henry ally and brother-in-law of George

Washington), and Benjamin Harrison of Berkeley (soon to be distinguished from four namesake ancestors as "The Signer" of the Declaration of Independence). The committee's reprimand was succinct, polite, and firm. Although grateful for the arrest of the counterfeiters, the burgesses reminded Dunmore that government was responsible for "the safety of the innocent" as well as "punishing the Guilty." The "usual mode" of Virginia procedure (which favored local elites over Williamsburg insiders) stipulated that accused criminals be examined first in the county where their crime was committed or arrest made. Inconsistencies in the application of criminal law were destructive. Disdain for what we now call due process threatened American liberties. And governors needed to respect the authority of the county courts. Finally, to emphasize the intensity of their concern the burgesses took the unusual step of delivering their admonition "to his Excellency *by the whole House*"—a gesture that also shielded any individual messenger from Dunmore's already notorious temper.

Anxiety about Dunmore's intervention in Pittsylvania County and the fair administration of British justice was heightened by news from Rhode Island. Early in 1772 the skipper of a customs schooner, HMS *Gaspee*, had begun targeting smugglers sailing out of Providence and Newport. When the *Gaspee* ran aground about four miles below Providence while chasing a suspicious packet boat, however, forty or fifty Rhode Islanders immediately jumped into longboats and rowed south toward the stricken schooner. The watermen wounded the hated lieutenant, evacuated his crew to safety, and then burned the *Gaspee* to the waterline. As its flames sparkled across Narragansett Bay in June of 1772, the Rhode Islanders could scarcely have imagined that their revenge would catapult the aristocratic planters of Virginia into the vanguard of America's final round of resistance to Great Britain.

Lord North's attorney general assessed the *Gaspee* crisis as a political disaster "five times the magnitude of the Stamp Act." After contemplating the revocation of Rhode Island's charter, the ministry sent a commission of inquiry to bring the offenders to justice—*imperial* justice that ignored and overrode American judicial institutions. The commission was to send suspected perpetrators to England for trial on charges of treason in accord with laws that dated to Henry VIII—the same statutes invoked by Botetourt when Virginians created the Association of 1769. Back then the Rhode Island legislature had endorsed Virginia's defense of "the inestimable privilege of being tried by a Jury of their Vicinage." Now the *Providence Gazette* lambasted the new royal commission with language again borrowed from Virginia: sending anyone "beyond the Sea to be tried is highly derogatory to the Rights of British Subjects." For Patrick Henry, Dunmore's energetic prosecution of the Pittsylvania County counterfeiting ring had raised the same fundamental questions about the administration of justice and the rights of the accused as the *Gaspee* commission's intention of sending accused Americans overseas for trial.

ooooo

Soon after the burgesses adopted their admonition about Governor Dunmore's handling of the counterfeiters, Henry and a few others met in a private room at Raleigh Tavern to discuss the British reaction to the *Gaspee* incident. Present in addition to Henry were Richard Henry Lee and his brother Francis Lightfoot Lee, from the Northern Neck, Thomas Jefferson and his dear friend and brother-in-law Dabney Carr, representing Albemarle and Louisa counties respectively, and perhaps one or two other progressive souls. All were fearful that the "old and leading members" (especially the three officeholders who had advised Dunmore about the Pittsylvania arrests) lacked the "forwardness and zeal that the times required"—and that colonists everywhere lacked timely and reliable information about the *Gaspee* commission and other potential challenges to American liberty.

The political situation in the House of Burgesses was delicate during the second week of March 1773. The British reaction to the *Gaspee* incident posed three dilemmas for men like Peyton Randolph and Richard Bland. How could the burgesses protest that a commission of inquiry was unconstitutional without appearing to sanction a mob's destruction of the king's schooner? How could they denounce the burning of a navy vessel without undercutting Virginia's stalwart resistance to tyranny? And how could they advocate for the adjudication of the *Gaspee* case in the "usual mode" when it was obvious that Rhode Island authorities were unlikely to identify anyone responsible for the destruction of royal property?

Henry and the younger men at the Raleigh evaded their elders' dilemmas with an understated approach that condemned the mob by implication, ignored the destruction, and admitted nothing—all while reaffirming the basic tenets of Virginia's past decade of resistance. Perceiving the

Gaspee crisis as yet another step in the North administration's march toward tyranny, Henry and his collaborators embraced the Old Dominion's time-tested strategy of encouraging "an understanding with all the other colonies to consider the British claims as a common cause to all, and to produce an unity of action." As Richard Henry Lee explained to John Dickinson, the caucus at the Raleigh "contrived" their language to avoid having their "honest attempt to defend ourselves from their tyrannous designs" treated as though they sought to unleash a "vortex of treason." Intercolonial "union" and the colonies' "perfect understanding of each other" were among the principles "on which the political salvation of America so eminently depends."

Henry and his colleagues at the Raleigh drafted a call for *intercolonial* committees of correspondence and inquiry, modeled on the committee that had managed Virginia's agent in London since 1759. He and the Lee brothers, who had taken the lead in the Pittsylvania confrontation, suggested that Jefferson introduce the proposal, but Jefferson disliked public speaking and persuaded them to afford his brother-in-law this opportunity to demonstrate "his great worth and talents."

On March 12, 1773, twenty-eight-year-old Dabney Carr proposed the creation of a Standing Committee of Correspondence and Inquiry responsible for maintaining "correspondence and communication with our sister colonies" and monitoring the actions of Parliament and the North ministry as they "relate to or affect the British colonies in America." More immediately, the committee would also examine the legality of the royal commission "lately held in Rhode Island with powers to transport persons accused of offences committed in America to places beyond the seas." Patrick Henry, wearing a fashionable peach-blossom-colored coat and a dark wig (according to a law student who witnessed the debate), and Richard Henry Lee supported the plan with short but eloquent speeches. The House of Burgesses endorsed the plan unanimously—indeed with "too much unanimity," the student recalled, for the orators to exert "all the[ir] strength."

Carr's resolution not only created the Committee of Correspondence but usurped the Speaker's customary prerogative of naming its members. The list began with eight of the Assembly's most influential burgesses (seven of whom had written the warning to Dunmore): Speaker Randolph, Treasurer Nicholas, Richard Bland, Richard Henry Lee, Benjamin Harrison, Edmund Pendleton, Patrick Henry, and Archibald Cary. The ninth member was Dudley Digges of Yorktown, a twenty-year veteran of the house and descendant of three generations of councilors to the governor. Jefferson was tenth, and the final member was the worthy and talented Dabney Carr, making his first and only significant mark upon the pages of history before his sudden death two months later of a "bilious fever." On March 19 Virginia's new committee dispatched copies of the house resolution to the other mainland colonies with a cover letter bearing the increasingly familiar signature of Peyton Randolph. "If the other colonies shall think fit," the Virginians hoped their legislatures would also create standing committees "to communicate from time to time with the corresponding committee of Virginia." Not surprisingly, Rhode Island's House of Deputies was the first to reply.

The committees of correspondence created in response to Virginia's invitation laid a foundation for American union and served as the first permanent machinery for coordinated resistance to British measures. The committees could respond to events more quickly than provincial assemblies or extralegal conventions, and they could not be disrupted by royal governors. Virginia's call for intercolonial committees of correspondence also bolstered a widespread expectation that "a Congress will grow out of this measure." Ezra Stiles, a founder of Brown University and future president of Yale, predicted that the "Measures proposed by the Virginia Assembly . . . will finally terminate in a General Congress."

ooooo

Governor Dunmore remained as indifferent to the worsening imperial crisis as he was uninterested in its constitutional wrangles. "The Americans would soon be quiet," he had decided, "if they were only left to themselves." Patrick Henry did not share the governor's blissful delusion.

Returning from Williamsburg after the Assembly session, Henry closeted himself in conversation with four prominent neighbors at the home of Colonel Samuel Overton, an experienced militia leader who had led the company of volunteers in the French and Indian War for whom the Reverend Samuel Davies preached his famous recruiting sermon. The colonel's nephew John Overton, who recounted the conversation for Henry's first biographer, was a militia leader destined for service as a captain in the Revolutionary War. Also present were John Hawkins, a prominent

Hanover slave trader who would soon devote his mercantile experience to the war effort as a highly respected commissary officer, and Richard Morris, the younger Overton's brother-in-law and a rising politician who served on the county committee of safety and later in the General Assembly and was building Green Spring plantation in the beautiful rolling hills of Louisa County.

In light of the ministry's reaction to the *Gaspee* incident, Colonel Overton asked Henry "whether he supposed that Great Britain would drive her colonies to extremities?" And if so, "what he thought would be the issue of the war?" Overton and his companions were stunned by Henry's response. After looking around to make sure he would not be overheard, Henry whispered confidentially, "She will drive us to extremities! No accommodation will ever take place! Hostilities will soon commence—and a desperate and bloody *Touch* it will be."

"But do you think," Overton asked, it "possible for us . . . to oppose successfully the fleets and armies of Great Britain?"

"I will be candid with you," Henry replied. "I doubt whether we shall be able *alone* to cope with so powerful a Nation!" Then Henry rose from his chair and spoke "with great animation" in a voice that his listeners could never forget. "Where is France? Where is Spain? Where is Holland? The natural enemies of Great Britain? . . . Do you suppose they will stand by idle and Indifferent Spectators to the contest? . . . Believe me, no!" Once Louis XVI became convinced that Americans were serious about independence and "that all prospect of reconciliation is gone," Henry continued, "he will send his Fleets and Armies to fight our Battles for us [and] he will form with us a Treaty offensive and defensive. . . . Spain and Holland will join the confederation! Our Independence will be established, and we shall take our stand among the Nations of the Earth."

The company was startled, Colonel Overton recalled. For ten years Virginians had insisted on their loyalty to George III while defending their claims to the rights of Englishmen. Now Lord North's ministry was threatening to drag Americans across the Atlantic and hang them for treason. Nevertheless, hearing the word *independence* spoken aloud in Samuel Overton's parlor in Hanover County came as a shock. Henry's startling forecast about British intentions and America's prospects would soon prove true.

ooooo

Fortuitously, Patrick Henry was in Williamsburg for the General Assembly session in May of 1774 when news of Parliament's adoption of the Boston Port Act reached him. By shutting down the city's port, the British aimed to punish the inhabitants of Boston for their tea party with the first of five measures that came to be known as the Intolerable Acts or Coercive Acts. Without waiting for America's new committee network to lurch into action, Henry and his colleagues decided that Parliament's aggression against the city of Boston demanded an immediate response from Virginia. On Monday evening, May 23, he and others who had engineered the response to the *Gaspee* commission, including Richard Henry Lee, Francis Lightfoot Lee, and Thomas Jefferson, slipped into the capitol and "rummaged" through the Council library in search of suitable English precedents for a day of fasting and prayer.

Thomas Jefferson wrote his familiar account of their evening's work in an autobiography begun forty-seven years after the fact. Ever the bibliophile, Jefferson emphasized how they turned through eight volumes of John Rushworth's *Historical Collections* and found texts from the days of Charles I with which they "cooked up a resolution, somewhat modernizing their phrases." In a letter written just three days after the event, however, George Mason, who had just come to town on business, gave a neighbor and close friend a more accurate summary of the evening in the Council library than Jefferson's. Williamsburg was entirely "engrossed by the Boston affair," Mason reported, but profound secrecy surrounded the measures being contemplated for the preservation of American liberty. "Matters of that sort here are conducted and prepared with a great deal of privacy and by very few members," Mason told his friend, "of whom Patrick Henry is the principal."

Although Mason was not a burgess, Henry and the others welcomed his assistance when they began work that Monday evening. Mason found himself delighted by the "opportunity of conversing with Mr. Henry and knowing his sentiments." Hearing him in debate at the capitol a few days later, Mason wrote that Henry was "by far the most powerful speaker I ever heard."

> Every word he says not only engages but commands the attention; and your passions are no longer your own when he addresses them. But his eloquence is the smallest part of his merit. He is in my opin-

ion the first man upon this continent, as well in abilities as public
virtues.

Here was the beginning of a civic partnership that lasted until Mason's
death in 1792.

Early Tuesday morning Henry, Mason, the Lees, and Jefferson waited
upon Robert Carter Nicholas, "whose grave and religious character was
more in unison with the tone of our resolution," and asked him to move
for the adoption of their protest against "the hostile Invasion of the City of
Boston." Later that day the House of Burgesses unanimously designated
June 1—the date set for the closing of Boston's port—as a "Day of Fasting,
Humiliation, and Prayer" for divine intervention to avert both the destruction of American liberties and the evils of civil war. The burgesses prayed
for unity of heart and mind "firmly to oppose . . . every Injury to American Rights." More pointedly, Virginians also asked God to inspire the king
and Parliament "with Wisdom, Moderation, and Justice" and safeguard
"the loyal People of America . . . from a continued Pursuit of Measures
pregnant with their Ruin."

Attorney General John Randolph, who owed his seat as a burgess for
the College of William and Mary to Dunmore's influence with the faculty,
neither spoke against nor voted against the cooked-up resolution, though
he later denounced it in an anonymous pamphlet. In Landon Carter's bitter phrase, however, "the College Member traitorously informed" Dunmore that the burgesses were trying to complete their routine business
before they risked a dissolution by adopting additional resolutions against
British measures. On Thursday, with a copy of their call for fasting and
prayer in his hand, Dunmore summoned the burgesses to his office and
dissolved the legislature. "It certainly deserves notice," Carter observed in
his diary, that Dunmore castigated the burgesses for praying for "his Majesty and his Parliament . . . in an established Church, whose Liturgy pro-
poses [prayers] for that very purpose and in words almost tantamount."

Once again the former burgesses marched up Duke of Gloucester
Street to the Apollo Room at Raleigh Tavern, designated Peyton Randolph as their moderator, and set forth the principles for a revived nonimportation association. Their statement, signed on Friday by eighty-nine
former burgesses and twenty-one others, declared that "an attack made on
one of our sister colonies . . . threatens ruin to the rights of all." It outlined

several major objectives. They agreed to stop drinking tea. They agreed
to an immediate boycott of all East India Company commodities except
spices and saltpeter. They called for annual meetings of a "general congress" to promote "the united interests of America." But for the moment
the former burgesses decided *against* closing off "all commercial intercourse with Britain."

Barely three weeks separated the news of the Boston Port Act from its
enforcement by General Thomas Gage and a flotilla of British warships—
insufficient time for Americans to reach any consensus about how best to
protect themselves. "We were divided in our Opinions," Peyton Randolph
and two dozen Associators announced from Williamsburg on Tuesday,
May 31, the day before they knelt together at Bruton Parish Church to pray
for the beleaguered city of Boston. Despite disagreements about details,
however, Moderator Randolph and the few Associators still in town that
day made two momentous decisions. First, they invited "all the Members
of the late House of Burgesses to a general Meeting in this City on the
first Day of August next." Second, they urged their fellow Associators to
use the intervening weeks as an "Opportunity of collecting the Sense of
their respective Counties." Cloaked in these seemingly innocent phrases
was Virginia's historic call for the first of five revolutionary conventions
that would guide the colony from resistance to independence. "Things
seem to be hurrying to an alarming Crisis" that now required "the speedy,
united Councils of all those who have a Regard for the common cause."

Except for Virginia's few future loyalists, such as John Randolph,
Americans were sorting out three possible responses to what Landon Carter called "Parliament's war against the town of Boston." Samuel Adams,
the popular leader that crown officials regarded as the principal incendiary
in Massachusetts, hoped for a complete and immediate boycott of British
goods, a virtual impossibility in the time available. Throughout the colonies people also debated whether to stop importing British goods or to
stop exports as well. But that debate was more complicated in Virginia,
where Dunmore had effectively shut down Virginia's courts by dissolving the Assembly before it had renewed a law regulating and allowing the
payment of attorneys' fees. Patrick Henry, George Mason, Richard Henry
Lee, and Treasurer Nicholas favored an immediate end both to imports
and exports as well as keeping the courts closed as a means of enforcement. Speaker Randolph, Edmund Pendleton, Thomas Nelson, Carter

Braxton, and Paul Carrington took a more conservative position, advocating an immediate boycott of imports but a year's extension for exports so Virginians could sell their tobacco, pay their debts, and perhaps even reopen the county courts.

ooooo

The pace of events in the summer of 1774 *did* seem to be hurrying toward something, especially compared with the 1760s. Virginia's impending convention bolstered the ongoing substitution of popular sovereignty for royal authority, especially with Governor Dunmore absent from the capital for five eventful months. On July 10 the governor set out from Williamsburg to chastise the Shawnee in the Ohio River Valley and strengthen Virginia's claims to the contested territory around modern Pittsburgh, an expedition known as Dunmore's War. He did not return to Williamsburg until Sunday afternoon, December 4, thirty or forty hours after Lady Dunmore, who had rejoined her husband in February 1774, gave birth to the daughter they named Virginia.

While Dunmore prepared for his western adventure, Virginians rallied at their courthouses throughout June and July in support of American liberty and the "piteous and melancholy" inhabitants of Boston. Henry and other gentry leaders attended as much to ascertain as to influence the sentiments of their constituents, who in many places endorsed more radical measures than the former burgesses would have adopted on their own. Many counties gave explicit instructions to their representatives, as did the freeholders of Hanover County when they gave Patrick Henry and John Syme the "Plan of Conduct we wish you to observe."

Henry's constituents saw the Boston Port Act and other offensive measures as indications "of the future Policy of Britain towards all her Colonies"—a detestable system that, unless overthrown, "will probably be fixed upon us forever." Hanoverians wanted Henry and his half-brother to secure "the hearty Union of all our Countrymen and Sister Colonies," and to attain that goal they declared their "Readiness to sacrifice any lesser Interest arising from a Soil, Climate, Situation, or Productions peculiar to us." Specifically, they believed the African slave trade was "dangerous to Virtue and the Welfare of this Country," and "therefore most earnestly wish to see it totally discouraged."

All sixty-one Virginia counties favored vigorous and united resistance to the Boston Port Act. More than forty-eight localities sent detailed resolutions to Williamsburg, of which thirty-nine survive. Three localities—Accomack, Dinwiddie, and the town of Fredericksburg—expressed succinct support for "any measures" that the Virginia Convention decided upon in August. Everyone favored reinstating a boycott against British imports. Fourteen county committees also wanted a prompt or immediate end to Virginia's export trade. Four recommended imposing an export ban in October 1775 (Fairfax), November 1775 (Albemarle), or whatever date allowed "Time for the Discharge of British Debts" (Norfolk and Henrico).

Although many colonists and virtually all Englishmen regarded the complete denial of parliamentary authority in America as a radical viewpoint in the summer of 1774, this fundamental constitutional principle had become so thoroughly entrenched in Virginia that twenty-three-year-old James Madison, the future president, described it to a college friend as "political Orthodoxy."

The county resolutions that summer were similarly terse. "Let it suffice to say, once for all," the freeholders of Hanover reminded Patrick Henry and John Syme, "we will never be taxed but by our own Representatives." Since the colonies had "Parliaments of their own under the authority of the same King," Spotsylvania County noted, "the British Parliament can have no Power" in America. York County spelled out the parallel relationships of the king's British subjects through Parliament and his colonial subjects through "his American Assemblies by Laws adapted to their local Situation." Although only four of these working instructions for delegates to the August convention in Williamsburg were reprinted outside Virginia, with few exceptions these county resolutions temporarily interrupted the usual run of political essays in the *Virginia Gazettes* for June and July 1774.

On Friday, August 5, the convention selected seven delegates for the First Continental Congress in Philadelphia. Peyton Randolph got 107 votes (everyone's but his own) as the man who "should preside in Congress." Patrick Henry and George Washington tied with 104, and Richard Henry Lee had 102. Henry and Lee were expected to "display the different kinds of eloquence for which they were renowned," and Washington to "command the army, if an army should be raised." The meticulous Edmund Pendleton, with 100 votes, was sent as "the penman for business." Benjamin Harrison, with 94 votes, would speak "plain truths," and Richard

Bland, with 90, would lend the Congress his mastery of "the treasures of ancient colonial learning." Thomas Jefferson and Thomas Nelson, Jr., of Yorktown, runners-up with 18 and 16 votes, would be elected to the next Congress. Each Virginia county contributed £15 toward their expenses, so every delegate got about £100 for travel and lodging.

Virginia may have thrown George III and his ministers into a quandary, but patriots throughout America were delighted by the resolutions adopted at Williamsburg in August. "All America look up to Virginia," the Philadelphia Committee of Correspondence declared: "You are ancient, you are respected, you are animated in the Cause." John Adams, en route to Philadelphia as a Massachusetts delegate, had reached New York City August 23 when he "went to the Coffee House, and saw the Virginia Paper. The Spirit of the People is prodigious," Adams noted in his diary. "Their Resolutions are really grand."

CHAPTER TWELVE

Congress in Philadelphia

CURIOSITY ABOUT THE Virginia delegates ran strong among the congressmen gathering in the City of Brotherly Love for the opening of the First Continental Congress early in September of 1774. Thomas Lynch, Sr., of South Carolina found many opportunities to tell and retell his story about witnessing George Washington's eloquence in Williamsburg when he offered to raise an army with his own funds and march for the relief of Boston. The congressmen and their constituents had been reading and endorsing the Virginians' bold words for ten years, but few had ever met them. Governor Fauquier had prevented the General Assembly from electing representatives to the Stamp Act Congress eight years earlier. Few northern congressmen had ever visited the Old Dominion, and colonial Virginia gentry generally knew the city of London better than Boston, New York, or Philadelphia. Half the Virginia delegation had been schooled in the British Isles, though four of Virginia's congressional delegates had at least traveled briefly in the north. Peyton Randolph had visited Philadelphia and New York in 1769 when he served on a commission to resolve a boundary dispute, and George Washington had ventured as far north as Boston in 1756. Patrick Henry and Richard Bland had scarcely met anyone during a brief trip to Manhattan for an aborted meeting in 1770, but one of Richard Henry Lee's sisters had married into Philadelphia's prominent Shippen family (with whom Lee resided during the First Congress) and his brother Arthur had spent some time in Philadelphia with John Dickinson in the 1760s.

With Congress scheduled to convene the following Monday, John Adams enjoyed a "very sociable and happy" dinner with the South Carolina and Rhode Island delegates and their wives on Friday, September 2, at the home of Thomas Mifflin—but Adams wrote more enthusiastically about his chance encounter at the City Tavern after dinner with four Virginia delegates—Peyton Randolph, Benjamin Harrison, Richard Henry Lee, and Richard Bland. "These Gentlemen from Virginia appear to be the most spirited and consistent of any," Adams thought. "Randolph is a large, well looking Man. Lee is a tall, spare Man. Bland is a learned, bookish Man. Harrison said he would have come on foot rather than not come. Bland said he would have gone, upon this Occasion, if it had been to Jericho." Patrick Henry and Virginia's remaining delegates, Edmund Pendleton and George Washington, reached Philadelphia on Sunday afternoon after riding together from Mount Vernon.

Gathering temporarily at a tavern on Monday morning, the delegates elected Peyton Randolph as president of the First Continental Congress in recognition both of his merits and Virginia's strategic importance. The delegates snubbed Joseph Galloway, conservative Speaker of the Pennsylvania legislature, by rejecting his invitation to meet at the State House (now known as Independence Hall) in favor of the guild hall owned by the city's carpenters. Their choice of Charles Thomson as secretary of the Congress also sent a pointed message. Thomson was "the Sam. Adams of Phyladelphia," John Adams noted in his diary. While "highly agreeable to the Mechanics and Citizens in general," as Connecticut delegate Silas Deane informed his wife, Thomson was "mortifying to the last Degree to Mr. Galloway and his Party."

Character sketches that congressmen Silas Deane sent his wife demonstrate his admiration for the Virginia delegation. "They are sociable, sensible, and spirited Men, and . . . their Conversation gives Me the highest Idea of their principles and Character." Peyton Randolph presided with dignity and a "noble appearance." Benjamin Harrison was "an uncommonly large Man . . . rough in his address and speech." Washington was tall and spoke modestly in a "cool but determined Stile and Accent," with a stern face but "an easy Soldier-like Air and gesture." Colonel Bland was a sensible writer, a "tolerable Speaker in public," and deeply acquainted with the antiquities of Virginia and America in general. Pendleton was an eminent lawyer "of easy and chearful countenance, polite in address and elegant if not eloquent." Patrick Henry, raved Deane, was "the compleatest Speaker I ever heard . . . but in a Letter I can give You no Idea of the Music of his Voice, or the highwrought, yet Natural elegance of his Stile."

Richard Henry Lee was "said to be his Rival in Eloquence," and together they were regarded as "the Demosthenes and Cicero of America."

When Congress and its committees were not in session, America's largest city offered Henry and his colleagues more than coffeehouses and taverns. The forty-year-old Library Company of Philadelphia, founded by Benjamin Franklin a few blocks from Carpenter's Hall, had offered Congress "the use of such Books as they may have occasion for during their sitting"—as it would again when delegates gathered in 1787 to write a new constitution for the independent republic. Urban bookstores were another attraction for Henry. His purchases included Thomas Leland's edition of *The Orations of Demosthenes on Occasions of Public Deliberation* (London, 1763), one of many books about oratory that Henry used to improve his public speaking. The book now bears Henry's printed bookplate, signature, and his handwritten notation *Philadelphia 1774*. Beyond identifying his ownership, Patrick Henry generally refrained from marking up his books (unlike John Adams, who often argued with authors in his marginal notations) but Henry's copy of Demosthenes at the Library of Congress contains a dog-eared corner of a page at a passage that must have left an impression on Virginia's great orator: "When we take up arms against the Barbarian," Demosthenes proclaimed about 354 BC, "we take them up for our country, for our lives, for our customs, for our liberty, and all such sacred rights."

Patrick Henry's oratorical skills *were* impressive, of course, but the delegates placed greater weight on his ideas. Back in 1763 and 1765, Henry had contended that Parliament had no authority over America and that George III was in danger of violating the contract between a king and subjects. American sentiment had taken a decade to catch up. Now, as the colonies met in Congress and groped toward more unity in their resistance to Great Britain, Henry stood once again in the vanguard. Gone was the peach-blossom coat from the previous spring. Henry came to Congress clad in a dark suit of "minister's gray and an unpowdered wig." Secretary Charles Thomson later admitted that he winced in anticipation of a rural politician embarrassing himself before so distinguished an audience when someone who looked like a country parson rose to address the Congress. "But as he proceeded," Thomson recalled, the seemingly rustic speaker "evinced such [an] unusual force of argument, and such novel and impassioned eloquence, as soon electrified the whole house. Then the excited inquiry passed from man to man ... who is it? who is it? The answer from the few who knew him was, it is *Patrick Henry!*"

Wasting not a word on nostalgic hopes for reconciliation with Great Britain or idle dreams of turning the clock back to 1763, Henry pointed to the virtual collapse of parliamentary *and* royal authority in America. The British invasion and occupation of Boston revealed a stark truth. "Fleets and Armies," Henry declared in the opening moments of the first substantive debate of the First Continental Congress, "shew that Government is dissolved." Without speaking aloud of independence, Henry gazed unflinchingly toward a future that terrified Joseph Galloway. Petitions, memorials, and the economic boycott might buy needed time to prepare for armed resistance in defense of American liberty, but John Locke's appeal to heaven was at hand. "We are in a State of Nature," Henry declared on Tuesday, September 6, 1774, according to several delegates' notes of the congressional debates:

> Government is dissolved ... The Distinctions between Virginians, Pennsylvanians, New Yorkers and New Englanders, are no more. I am not a Virginian, but an American.

Henry was speaking in support of allocating votes in Congress by population, which would have benefited the larger colonies of Virginia, Pennsylvania, and Massachusetts. For an audience steeped in English constitutional history, however, the radical implications of his premise were obvious and, for many, unsettling. For public consumption, however, Congress would find consensus by expanding the basis for its claims of American rights to include "the laws of nature, the principles of the English Constitution, and charters and compacts."

ooooo

Bold as were Henry's assertions on the floor of Congress, he spoke as candidly in private conversation with trusted companions as he had at Samuel Overton's house in Hanover. When other congressmen conferred discreetly at the London Coffeehouse or City Tavern their voices were too soft to hear across the room and their spoken sentiments were lost to posterity. Philadelphia physician Benjamin Rush, who inoculated Henry against smallpox while he was in town, enjoyed many conversations with Henry. Rush described him as "amiable in his manners and a zealous advocate of the claims of his country," but he attached particular value to Henry's "private opinions upon men and things, [which] shewed a deep and correct knowledge of human nature."

Thanks to John Adams, however, we have a more detailed record of a remarkable private conversation with Henry. On his way from Quincy to Congress, Adams had ventured a bit west of the shortest route to visit Northampton and confer with Joseph Hawley, a power broker in the Massachusetts legislature and one of Adams's revered political allies. Long regarded as one of the "River Gods" of the Connecticut River Valley, Hawley was earning a reputation as a leading radical in the conflict with Britain. Although age and failing health precluded his own attendance at the First Congress, Hawley had presented Adams with a page of notes entitled "Broken Hints to be communicated to the Committee of Congress."

Patrick Henry listened "with great attention" when John Adams found an opportunity to share Hawley's thoughts with the Virginia orator. Britain's evil policies were intolerable, Hawley wrote. If British tyranny went unchallenged, Americans yet unborn would never know a free government. On the other hand, the colonies stood to lose everything if they were attacked and conquered before they could organize for victory. Reconciliation was impossible unless the king and Parliament restored American rights, which was unlikely. An immediate plunge into armed conflict was futile, too, so the prudent course was for Congress to negotiate with Britain while quietly making military plans for the battles that loomed ahead. America was not yet ready for war, but armed resistance was on the horizon. Victory would depend upon a sturdy intercolonial union, which the British sought to shatter, so it was essential that the colonies regard the grievances of their neighbors "as a grievance to the whole." But ultimately, Joseph Hawley contended, "We must *fight*."

"By God, I am of that man's mind!" Henry exclaimed when Adams read the words "we must fight." Adams then handed Hawley's notes to Henry, who reviewed them carefully and solemnly declared "that he agreed entirely in opinion with the writer." Henry's and Hawley's ideas were more radical than Adams's own opinions at the time, but the memory of that conversation, and of Henry's assertions that the dissolution of British authority had placed the colonies in a state of nature, remained vivid in John Adams's mind forty years later. "In the Congress of 1774," Adams informed Thomas Jefferson in 1813, "there was not one member, except Patrick Henry, who appeared to me sensible of . . . the Pinnacle on which he stood, and had candour and courage enough to acknowledge it."

ooooo

Patrick Henry's visit to Philadelphia also brought him into contact with the Quaker leaders of America's earliest abolitionist movement, thanks to letters of introduction from the Richmond antislavery lobbyist Robert Pleasants. The substance of Henry's conversations and correspondence with Virginia Quakers was widely known not only among Friends in Philadelphia but among Quakers at the Burlington meetinghouse, near Trenton, New Jersey, as well. Encouraged by congressional adoption of the Continental Association and its suspension of slave importation, one of the Burlington Quakers, Samuel Allinson, wrote Henry on October 17 in hope of persuading him to advance their antislavery agenda in Congress. "Although a stranger to [his] person," Allinson assured Henry that he was "not quite so to [his] Character." Allinson felt that Congress needed to consider "whether a Negro is not intitled to the same essential Justice with ourselves" at a moment when "the inhabitants of North America are groaning under unconstitutional impositions destructive of *their Liberty*." Though vague about specifics (as was characteristic of their lobbying efforts), Allinson hoped that Henry could persuade Congress "to give a Vital blow to the shameful custom of Slavery in America . . . by at least declaring their sentiments against the future infraction of the rights of others."

Echoing Henry's earlier observations about the incongruity of slavery in "this enlightened age," Allinson suggested that it would be a "lasting disgrace if so respectable a body of Men as the Congress . . . should spend so much time to secure their own *Liberties* and leave no vestiges of their regard to those of their *fellow men*." How could God look with favor upon "our endeavors to obtain our own rights when we act inconsistent with ourselves?" Allinson asked. Could Americans claim "that a *Limited* Slavery is injurious and disagreeable to ourselves," but "that *Absolute* Slavery is not unjust to a race of *fellow men* because they are black"? Allinson thought not—and in their hearts Patrick Henry and many of his colleagues agreed. With the delegates focused on sustaining a united opposition to British policies, the prospect of any congressional declaration against slavery was politically unlikely. Although Samuel Allinson's letter reflected the Quakers' respect for Henry—and perhaps his prominence in the public eye as well—by the time the letter reached him, the First Continental Congress was busily wrapping things up for its adjournment on October 26.

ooooo

Early in October, when Galloway's allies James Duane and John Jay moved for a conciliatory message to George III, Richard Henry Lee responded with an amendment instructing the colonies to raise, arm, and discipline their militias because it was unnecessary and improper for Great Britain to bear the expense of maintaining a standing army in America. Seconded by Henry, Lee's proposal triggered a frank discussion of military resistance. Edward Rutledge, of South Carolina, warned that Lee's amendment was virtually "a Declaration of Warr." Benjamin Harrison worried that the colonies were unable to defend themselves and that Lee's amendment would "tend only to irritate, whereas Our Business is to reconcile." Lee replied quickly that he saw it as their responsibility to encourage Americans to defend themselves—and then the presiding officer recognized the eloquent gentleman from Hanover County.

"Preparation for Warr is Necessary to obtain peace," Patrick Henry declared, for America was not in a state of peace. "All the Bulwarks of Our Safety [and] of Our Constitution are thrown down." The collapse of British government in America threatened to leave the colonists "in a State of Nature." Americans had to decide what to do if nonimportation and nonexportation—the economic sanctions that Henry, Lee, Mason, and Washington had years earlier identified as measures of last resort—fell short as they had before. "In that Case," Henry warned, "Arms are Necessary," and the time for defensive preparation was at hand. "Arms are a Resource to which We shall be forced," Henry predicted, a resource afforded to the colonists by God and Nature. "Why in the Name of both," Henry asked, should Americans hesitate now when it was "in our power" to prepare themselves for armed defense.

Congress eventually softened Lee's and Henry's call to arms, but not before Cicero and Demosthenes had their way on two significant points. Congress rejected Jay and Duane's call for repaying the East India Company for the property destroyed in the Boston Tea Party. It also rebuffed Duane's motion to acknowledge the legitimacy of the Navigation Acts, laws regulating seaborne trade within the British empire that had been widely accepted as legitimate since 1651. Not surprisingly, Patrick Henry had "a horrid Opinion of Galloway, Jay, and the Rutledges," John Adams confided to his diary after spending an evening in conversation with the Virginian. "Their System he says would ruin the Cause of America," and he found it difficult to contend with "such Fellows and not be at Liberty to describe them in their true Colours."

ooooo

Patrick Henry may have chafed at the rhetorical compromises forced upon him by the delicate balance of progressive and conservative opinions inside Carpenter's Hall, but it seems that he found another way, using the pseudonym "Scipio," to explain George III's direct responsibility for the imperial crisis to the American public. Circumstances and substance point to Henry as the author of a bold letter "To the KING" submitted to William Bradford in the third week of September and published on the front page of Bradford's *Pennsylvania Journal*, a fiercely partisan newspaper, on October 6, 1774. A leader in Philadelphia's Sons of Liberty along with Charles Thomson, Bradford was also proprietor of the London Coffeehouse, a frequent retreat for members of Congress meeting four blocks away at Carpenters' Hall.

In addition to its style and content—especially the bold challenge to the king that Henry had first voiced at Hanover Courthouse in 1763 and more recently in Congress—the author seems to have left two prominent clues to his identity and reputation. One was the display quotation from Shakespeare's *Julius Caesar*—"HEAR ME! *for* I WILL *speak*." The other was his chosen pen name, Scipio, a pseudonym honoring the Roman patriot and general praised by Cicero as an exemplary orator and leader. Three weeks after its appearance in Philadelphia, the Scipio essay was reprinted near Boston in the *Essex Journal and Merimack Packet* on October 26 and, notably, just a day later in John Pinkney's *Virginia Gazette* in distant Williamsburg.

Scipio's letter "To the KING" opened with a harsh Lockean judgment. When by negligence or "willful mal-administration" a king destroyed the respect that he "*ought* to command," his transgressions rendered him "a culprit before the awful tribunal of the Public." Even the sovereign of the British empire derived his ultimate authority from the people, who were "as much at liberty to arraign his conduct as . . . to approve it." Despite their hopes at the time of his coronation in 1760, millions of loyal subjects were now ready to "impeach" George III for his *unfaithful* execution" of duties he was bound by "nature, justice, and religion . . . to discharge with *fidelity.*"

In language that echoed Patrick Henry's speech in the Parsons' Cause, Scipio reminded George III that he had sworn a solemn oath to reign as "the Guardian of your people and secure them in their just rights, privileges, and religion"—specifically the Protestant faith of "the blessed reformation"—"but alas! How art thou fallen! How hast thou apostasized!" No longer praiseworthy as "the happy Guardian of your People, you are becoming their Tyrant and Oppressor!" Scipio thundered. "You are become the hated object of millions!—You have violated the most solemn engagements with God and your Subjects, your Coronation Oath!"

Scipio castigated George III for "the wickedly unconstitutional Laws which have been authorized under your *Royal sanction*" culminating in the recent "diabolical Act respecting the government of Canada," a reference to the Quebec Act of 1774, one of the Intolerable Acts, which endorsed Roman Catholicism in the French-speaking province. He deplored the king's "connivance" in the "bloody massacre" at Boston "of [his] own Subjects for bravely and honestly asserting their privileges as Englishmen and Freemen!" George III was guilty of corrupting Parliament with "a venal administration" and paying "a list of Pensioners, *of your own creation*, supported at the expence and poverty of one half of your Subjects to ruin the other half!" The king was also guilty, "particularly in America," of appointing "obnoxious" men to government offices.

"These, sir, and numberless other hideous calamities have generally been attributed to your Ministers," Scipio bluntly declared,

> but I am bold to say they become chargeable to YOU, as responsible for the conduct of men whom YOU,—YOURSELF, nominate to office.

Scipio even invoked madness (perhaps a disorder "called a *Catalepsis*, in which the patient is *void* of *sense*") to account for George III's failures. "The greater part of the world, particularly your own Subjects . . . have always attributed every miscarriage in the state to the weakness of your understanding," Scipio asserted, "unless what has been charged to the

weakness of your head, may, with more truth, be imputed to the wickedness of your heart."

If George III hoped to "perplex our councils and disturb our unanimity," Scipio warned, he was "much mistaken." From Massachusetts to
Georgia, the colonies were united with "a FIRMNESS which all the machinations of a corrupt Administration will *never* be able to shake.... Tyrant
authority will be impotent against the virtuous and persevering zeal of men
struggling for their religious rights and liberties—men incapable of feeling
dejection of mind from *threats*—stimulated from motives of liberty, justice, and conscience, and who owe no fear but to their God." The histories
of England, Scotland, and Ireland, as well as France, Spain, Germany, and
other countries all demonstrate "the fatal corruption and evils which have
been produced ... by an over-bearing Administration or Monarchy!"

Quoting John Trenchard and Thomas Gordon's *Cato's Letters*, popular essays about political liberty revered by eighteenth-century American
readers, Scipio pointedly reminded George III that "the breath of a tyrant
blasts and poisons every thing, changes blessings and plenty into curses
and misery, great cities into gloomy solitudes, and their rich citizens into
beggars and vagabonds."

> Your sun of glory is fast setting; your kingdoms at home
> depopulating ... [and] your American Subjects, whose prosperity
> and opulence would have been the pride and glory of *a wise and good
> Sovereign*, [are] determined rather to yield their lives, than make a
> sacrifice of their Liberty at the shrine of Despotism.—Good God,
> Sir, awake from your lethargy, and recede from the measures you
> have taken!... Your brave and free-born American Subjects ...
> profess for your sacred person a decent and loyal obedience as SUB-
> JECTS, but they *dare* tell you, they will never become your SLAVES.
> The sword, great Sire, is a dreadful umpire!

Finally, attributing the fatal conflict between Britain and the colonies to the king's "too easy concurrence" to his ministers' wicked schemes
and implicitly endorsing the petition that Henry was then drafting for
the Congress, Scipio called upon George III to "hear with your *own ears*,
and behold with your *own eyes* the humble and dutiful representations of
your petitioning Subjects." People throughout the colonies were willing to

stretch forth the hand of amity one last time if only the king decided to maintain his prerogative "*equitably*"—just as his subjects were steadfast in their resolve "to prevent the smallest violation of their civil and religious Liberties, and . . . avert the mischiefs of furious, unpitying, and destructive Tyranny."

ooooo

The final gesture from the First Congress was yet another petition to George III offering to end the dispute with Great Britain if he rolled imperial regulations back to the status quo in 1763. If Parliament stopped trying to raise revenue in America, rescinded the expansion of the admiralty courts, honored American rights of trial by jury, lifted the punitive measures against Boston, and reversed the extension of Canadian authority into the Ohio River Valley and the sanction of Roman Catholicism in Quebec, then Congress could lift the economic boycott and restore Anglo-American commerce. Early in October, while Congress continued its debate about military preparedness and while William Bradford was printing the Scipio essay, the select committee chaired by Richard Henry Lee gave Patrick Henry the task of preparing this address.

Ten days later Henry presented a polished and respectful draft that reflected the committee's original instructions. Sharply divided by the situation, however, the delegates now felt a need for something different, so Lee himself prepared a shorter second version that did not satisfy them either. Next up was John Dickinson, who composed the final text with some advice from Lee and Henry before they headed home with Bland and Harrison on Sunday, October 23. Three days later, as the delegates prepared to adjourn, Congress finally approved Dickinson's text. Charles Thomson promptly presented two copies of the address for signatures. Peyton Randolph signed for himself, Richard Henry Lee signed for himself and Henry, and George Washington signed for himself, Bland, Harrison, and Pendleton.

For all the effort expended upon the address to George III, however, nothing came of it on either side of the Atlantic. Protocol dictated that a formal address to the king be laid before the throne before its text was released to the public, so William Bradford could not print the address in the official journal that autumn, nor did it appear in the newspapers until mid-January 1775. In the meantime, Secretary Thomson sent the signed

originals to London, where Benjamin Franklin arranged for the Earl of
Dartmouth to present one to George III. The king gave it to Lord North,
who in January dumped it on the clerks' tables at Westminster—the final
item in "a great Heap" of nearly 150 "letters of Intelligence from Governors
and officers in America, Newspapers, Pamphlets, Handbills, etc." Rather
than hearing American grievances with his own ears or beholding them
with his own eyes, as Scipio had hoped, George III, his ministers, and his
Parliament once again rejected them out of hand.

ooooo

In a continuing effort to foster unanimity among the colonies, Patrick
Henry and other members of the First Continental Congress had been
careful not to flaunt the revolutionary consequences of their achievement.
Perhaps their most significant achievement was the simple fact that delegates from all the colonies north of Georgia had met together as an extralegal alternative to the king and Parliament, hoping for peace while
arming for war. Unlike the Stamp Act Congress of 1765, whose members met briefly and then dispersed, delegates to the First Continental Congress anticipated that British intransigence would force them to
meet again—for which they set a date in May 1775. "One general Congress has brought the Colonies to be acquainted with each other," Silas
Deane wrote Patrick Henry a few months after they adjourned. The next
meeting, Deane hoped, "may effect a lasting Confederation . . . and perfect American Constitution . . . whether connected with Great Britain,
or Not."

The second achievement of Congress was the creation of the Continental Association, closely based on the nonimportation and nonexportation program adopted by Virginia in August. To uphold American
economic sanctions against the British, the Association imposed oaths
of compliance, enforced by local committees, upon the residents of every
community in the American colonies—the same mechanisms that Virginia had pioneered in 1769 to undergird its remarkably unified resistance
to British measures. Just as the partnership between local committees and
the House of Burgesses cemented political unity in Virginia, the oaths and
committees of the Continental Association encouraged a broad shift in
public allegiance toward Congress and away from the king (Parliament

having long since been excluded) as the emerging locus of American sovereignty.

The effectiveness of the new continental boycott was astonishing. In 1774 the Chesapeake colonies imported European goods worth £690,000. Under the Continental Association, Virginia and Maryland imports for 1775 fell by more than 99 percent to £2,000. The Old Dominion's virtually universal compliance with nonimportation resulted from pervasive community support for the American cause and vigorous local enforcement. Illicit property was seized and auctioned, with any profit going either to the suffering poor of Boston or the purchase of weapons and powder for defense.

Third, the Congress of 1774 brought America's provincial leaders together in far-reaching conversations about the political and military future of the colonies. When Congress adjourned on October 26, 1774, the delegates from Virginia and Massachusetts had cemented a partnership between America's oldest and most influential colonies that would push all thirteen colonies toward independence and revolution. The British strategy of isolating New England had, instead, united the colonies at the First Continental Congress in a broad plan of political resistance, economic boycott, and military preparedness. Few congressmen were as bold as Patrick Henry (or Joseph Hawley), but even the cautious John Dickinson of Pennsylvania wrote a friend after Congress adjourned that "War is unavoidable unless there be a quick Change of British Measures."

The king's reaction to congressional support for the Bostonians came as no surprise to his ministers. George III declared that the colonies were "in a State of Rebellion." Lord Dartmouth, secretary of state for American affairs and North's step-brother, was equally blunt. Upon reading the full text of the Continental Association, Dartmouth proclaimed that "every one who had signed it was guilty of Treason"—an accusation that by 1774 had been ringing in Patrick Henry's ears for eleven years.

CHAPTER THIRTEEN

Blows Must Decide

WHEN SCIPIO ACCUSED George III of madness in the columns of William Bradford's *Pennsylvania Journal*, fears about insanity weighed heavily on Patrick Henry's spirit. After the birth in 1771 of their sixth child, Edward or "Neddy," Henry's beloved wife, Sarah, had begun to exhibit symptoms of mental instability. Although the new house at Roundabout was barely complete, Sarah's condition contributed to their decision to move back to Hanover County and the neighborhood near his parents at Mount Brilliant, his half-brother, John Syme, at Rocky Mills, and the Dandridges. In September 1771 Henry's mother informed his sister Annie that he had recently "bought the Scotchtown to live at."

The largest and grandest home that Patrick Henry ever owned, Scotchtown had come on the market in the estate settlements of its previous owners, Colonel John Chiswell and Speaker John Robinson. It was described in the *Virginia Gazette* as a "large commodious dwelling-house built of wood with ... a very large [central] passage" and "eight rooms upon the first floor, with most delightful cellars under them"—the spacious English basement—"together with a dairy and servants hall with fire-places." In addition to the great house, the 960-acre property included a water-driven grist mill, a full array of barns and outbuildings, and three subordinate "plantations cleared sufficient to work 20 or 30 hands, under good fences, with Negro quarters, tobacco houses, etc." Henry got it for a bargain price of about £600 that he paid to the Robinson estate in quarterly installments between November 1771 and November 1772. The family's first year at Scotchtown was happy. Henry's law practice was thriving, he was a respected country squire, and their children enjoyed the house, gardens, fields, and forests. "His children were on the most familiar footing with him, and he treated them as companions and friends," Samuel

Meredith recalled. "Mr. Henry seemed to think the most important thing is in the first place to give [children] good constitutions . . . before they were permitted to wear shoes and . . . confined to books."

Sarah Henry's illness brought heartbreak to Scotchtown. "My brother Pat is not returned from Philadelphia," his sister Annie advised their mother in October 1774, "yet his wife is extremely ill." Sarah's deterioration apparently began with puerperal psychosis, an extreme form of postpartum depression that afflicts one or two out of every thousand new mothers. In addition to general cognitive impairment and bizarre behavior, common symptoms associated with Sarah's illness were delusions of persecution, hallucinations, and violence—even suicide or infanticide. Patrick Henry's "beloved companion had lost her reason," their family physician Dr. Thomas Hinde told his son years later, "and [she] could only be restrained from self-destruction by a strait-dress."

Today's victims of postpartum depression or psychosis can be treated with medication, but Henry's choices for Sarah's care and treatment were grim. Virginia had proudly opened North America's first public asylum "for the support and maintenance of ideots, lunatics, and other persons of unsound minds" in 1773. Progressive for its day, the new Public Hospital at the edge of Williamsburg was specifically designed to protect the community from persons disposed toward dangerously violent behavior. The building had twenty-four brick cells, each with a stout door, barred window, mattress, chamber pot, and an iron ring in the wall to which patients were fettered by the wrist or ankle.

Not surprisingly, Henry chose to provide Sarah with more humane and loving care at Scotchtown. She was given a well-lit apartment on the ground floor, or English basement—a spacious room with a window, a large fireplace, and a pleasant view of the backyard. When not away on business, Henry could go downstairs several times a day to comfort his distressed wife, feed her, and converse with her when she was lucid. After three years of suffering that weighed heavily on everyone in the family, Sarah Shelton Henry died early in 1775 and was probably buried at Scotchtown. "The loss of his first wife," Henry told the Italian patriot Philip Mazzei, "led him to move away from all objects reminding him of her." Henry would return to Scotchtown for rest and recuperation during his first year as governor of the new commonwealth, but in August 1777 he put the plantation up for sale. With Hanover's property values enhanced

by the wartime risk of British raids in the Tidewater counties, Henry sold
Scotchtown in 1778 for £5,000 (eight times his purchase price) and thereby
"advanced his Fortune very considerably" and "rendered him[self] entirely
independent."

ooooo

Back in Hanover County after the First Continental Congress, Henry
demonstrated that his reputation as the Demosthenes of America was well
deserved in ways that his classically trained contemporaries appreciated
better than their twenty-first-century descendants. When asked about
the most essential element of oratory, according to the Roman historian
Plutarch, Demosthenes answered Action." The second? "Action." And
the third, "again he answered 'Action!'" A young Presbyterian clergyman
who heard Henry speak at Charlotte Courthouse made a similar observation. "Shall we call him the Cicero of Virginia?" asked the Reverend
Conrad Speece. "I think he resembled Demosthenes more strongly," for
"when Cicero finished a speech his hearers exclaimed, what a fine orator
Cicero is!" But when Demosthenes finished a speech "the universal cry
was, to arms, citizens, let us march!" Inevitably, Patrick Henry's leadership
in Congress also inspired several stanzas of verse in Clementina Rind's
Virginia Gazette:

> AMERICANS unite! Your dearest ties
> Demand you to be diligently wise. . . .
> Our delegates in general congress meet,
> And closely of momentous matters treat. . . .
> Say to what better end was HENRY born?
> . . . But that our most inveterate foes
> May learn Virginia wants not Ciceroes. . . .
> And to the spacious world it shall be shown,
> Although our belligerent powers are new,
> That we have Scipios and Caesars too.

Immediately after his return from Congress, Patrick Henry spread
the word among the county militiamen that he "wished to communicate
something to them of great importance" at Smith's tavern near Hanover

Courthouse. "A considerable number of the younger part of the militia attended," Charles Dabney recalled, "and [Henry] addressed them in a very animated speech, pointing out the necessity of our having recourse to arms in defence of our rights"—as recommended by the Continental Congress—"and recommending in strong terms that we should immediately form ourselves into a volunteer company."

For more than a century, Virginia's traditional militia companies had answered to the governor and the gentry leaders who populated the vestries and the county courts. Hanover's new independent company, like the others established in accord with the Continental Association, directed its allegiance instead toward the people, their county committee, and the Congress—not the governor. Disaffection from royal authority was so prevalent in some counties, Dunmore advised the ministry in December, that members of the independent companies were swearing oaths "to execute all orders which shall be given them from the committees of their county." In addition to their "avowed purpose of protecting their committees," Dunmore warned, they also stood ready "to be employed against [his] government."

Despite their approval of his successful frontier expedition against the Shawnee, Dunmore lamented that Virginians "universally supported" the Continental Congress and regarded its new institutions as "superior to all other authority." They spoke of their committees, conventions, and associations "with marks of reverence which they never bestowed on their legal government or the laws proceeding from it." As the year 1775 began, Dunmore recognized that he had no recourse against "the committees, independent companies, etc." without a contingent of British troops.

In a peculiar way, Dunmore's reveries about armed reinforcements lifted his spirits as he penned the final pages of a long letter to Lord Dartmouth on Christmas Eve 1774. Puffed up by the wilderness adventure of Dunmore's War, he imagined that making Virginia's "undutiful people" feel "the distress and misery of which they have themselves laid the foundation" would be as easy as chastising the Shawnee. Altogether ignoring the facts that his frontier comrades-in-arms overwhelmingly sided with Patrick Henry, or that Virginia merchants already had a two-year supply of English goods in their warehouses, the governor dreamed of turning the Association's program of nonimportation and nonexportation against its proponents. "Scarcity will ruin thousands of families," Dunmore forecast, as "the lower class of people . . . discover that they have been duped by the richer sort."

Finally, when the situation had generated enough social discord, Dunmore was convinced that Virginia's supposedly numerous "partisans of government" would rally to him and persuade their neighbors of the "necessity of depending on [their] mother country and of embracing its authority." Here Dunmore was succumbing to "the old and fatal delusion" that an aide to General Charles Cornwallis described as rampant among British military leaders—the fantasy "that our successes will enable our numerous Friends to exert themselves in the cause of Great Britain."

Late on Christmas Eve, grown fierce with despair, Dunmore set himself on his final destructive course. Virginia's "ports should be blocked up," he advised Dartmouth, "and their communication cut off by water even with their neighbouring colonies." For this he needed only a ship of the line and a few small tenders. Ashore, he and other royal officers should be withdrawn and the functions of government suspended ("which in fact are now entirely obstructed"). Then, when the resulting confusion reminded "the people . . . from what source their former happiness flowed," Virginians would "prostrate themselves before the power which they had so lately . . . treated with contempt."

ooooo

While Lord Dunmore dreamed of martial redemption at his desk in Williamsburg, George III and his chief ministers in London were also contemplating war with the colonies. On January 13, 1775, the cabinet agreed to reinforce General Thomas Gage's army in Massachusetts with regiments from Ireland. That same day, yielding to the king, the cabinet rejected the suggestion of negotiation toward reconciliation with the colonies and authorized the capture of prominent colonial leaders for trial in England, including Peyton Randolph of Virginia. According to Philip Mazzei, when Patrick Henry discovered that his name was missing from the roster of proscribed Americans "he flew into a rage, stamping his feet and shouting: 'What have I done not to be on that list?'"

Within two weeks they had the details in place. On the 27th, Dartmouth dispatched secret orders directing General Gage to send troops into the countryside from Boston and crush the rebellion. "Your object has hitherto been to act upon the Defensive," Dartmouth wrote, but now "the King's Dignity and the Honour and Safety of the Empire require that . . . Force should be repelled by Force." Should the Americans perceive the newly assertive policy as "a Signal for Hostilities," Dartmouth concluded, it was better to risk war now than when the colonies were "in a riper state of Rebellion." The king's long-awaited moment was at hand. "Blows must decide," George III had told Lord North in November, "whether they are to be subject to this country or independent."

Lord Dartmouth dispatched his secret orders to Gage aboard HMS *Falcon* late in January, with a duplicate set aboard HMS *Nautilus*—but adverse winds prevented either vessel from leaving the Thames and reaching the open sea until late March. Beating hard for New England, the sloops crossed the Atlantic in less than four weeks, with Captain John Collins bringing the *Nautilus* into Boston Harbor two days before the *Falcon*. On the 14th of April, General Gage opened the secret letter from Lord Dartmouth that would send redcoats marching toward Lexington and Concord.

ooooo

Dartmouth's secret was no surprise to Patrick Henry and other vigilant colonials in Massachusetts or Virginia. He and Richard Henry Lee had attempted to get Congress to encourage the colonies to organize their defenses against a British attack. By Christmas nearly every gazette in the colonies carried fragments of news heralding the advent of war. A single page of Purdie and Dixon's *Virginia Gazette* on December 8, for example, carried half a dozen news items that revealed British intentions—from the royal proclamation restricting the export to America of gunpowder, arms, ammunition, and saltpeter (an essential component of gunpowder) to the news of two regiments of light infantry heading for New York and 150 marines embarking for Boston. Excerpts reprinted from British papers reported that two vessels laden with gunpowder ordered by the colonists had been detained in the Thames and that quartermasters of the Royal Navy were contracting for one thousand oxen and three thousand hogs. Week after week the publication of clues about the ministry's "warlike preparations"—as Patrick Henry would soon proclaim—made it increasingly difficult for anyone to indulge in hopeful illusions of peace by shutting their eyes against the painful truth.

Richard Henry Lee's resolution for calling up the militia had been too bold for Congress in October 1774, but Virginians did it anyway in the months that followed. Local committees in the Old Dominion endorsed the Continental Association, embraced congressional authority as a foundation of constitutional legitimacy, and recruited and armed their independent volunteer companies. During these same months, as they responded to Peyton Randolph's invitation to elect delegates for another convention in March, Virginians throughout the colony also sent a clear message of strong opposition to Great Britain. Of all the county resolutions the delegates carried to Richmond for the Second Virginia Convention, the instructions from the inhabitants of Botetourt County (which then sprawled across the mountains from the Blue Ridge to the banks of the Ohio River at modern Parkersburg, West Virginia) best expressed the public opinion in Virginia. Lamenting that "a set of miscreants unworthy to administer the laws of Britain's empire" had eroded American confidence in George III by their cruel and tyrannical invasion of colonial rights, the freeholders of Botetourt County proclaimed a continental vision. "When the honest man of Boston . . . has his property wrested from him, the hunter on the Allegany must take alarm." Grateful for those "SONS of WORTH and FREEDOM who appeared for us at Philadelphia" in the Continental Congress, the frontiersmen of Botetourt County pledged to uphold the Association and "religiously observe their resolutions and obey their instructions." But if peaceful measures and economic pressure failed, *"we will stand prepared for every Contingency."*

CHAPTER FOURTEEN

Liberty or Death

THE VILLAGE OF RICHMOND had been founded in 1737 by William Byrd II at the rapids that comprise the falls of the James River. He named it for the London suburb where the view of the Thames reminded him of the vista at his father's old trading post. It was here on Monday, March 20, 1775, that Patrick Henry and ninety-four other delegates from Virginia's sixty-five counties and three of its four corporations (Jamestown, Norfolk, and Williamsburg) congregated at the parish church of Henrico County on Indian Town Hill (now Church Hill) overlooking Shockoe Creek. Across the creek bottom and immediately west of the church rose another steep hill that would become the site of a new capitol after Richmond became Virginia's permanent seat of government in 1780.

For Patrick Henry and his compatriots in 1775 the attractions of the meeting place now known as Saint John's Church were its size and location: large enough to accommodate their convention and fifty miles upriver from Williamsburg, beyond the range of a surprise raid by Dunmore if he tried to suppress the convention and enforce Lord Dartmouth's request that royal governors strive to prevent the election of delegates to another Continental Congress. By Wednesday, when Colonel Adam Stephen, author of the Fort Gower Resolutions, by which the officers and men fighting in Dunmore's War had endorsed the Continental Association, arrived from distant Berkeley County (now in West Virginia) the convention totaled 119 members. Attorney General John Randolph, who represented the College of William and Mary, stayed home.

Far from disrupting the Second Virginia Convention, Dunmore ignored Dartmouth's orders and avoided any confrontation with the delegates, whose popularity reflected a surge in patriotic feeling since the creation of the Virginia and Continental Associations. The seven-day convention was a hotbed of radicalism compared to that of many other colonies, but its actions merely confirmed the commitments already made by freeholders and county committees throughout Virginia between November 1774 and March 1775—the elections and local initiatives for defense that comprise the forgotten background of the Second Virginia Convention and the revolutionary public decision, clinched by Patrick Henry's famous Liberty or Death speech, to put the Old Dominion "into a posture of Defence."

ooooo

After Pastor Miles Selden, chairman of the Henrico County Committee, said Amen to the morning prayers from his pulpit on Thursday, March 23, Clerk John Tazewell read aloud a petition from the assembly of Jamaica to the king that Dixon and Hunter had published in their newspaper two weeks earlier. It was tame stuff, but intercolonial cooperation was important. Reminding George III that they had never countenanced riots or violent resistance, the islanders urged him to intervene as a "mediator" between his British and American subjects. Despite their "deep and silent sorrow" about Parliament's arbitrary measures, however, the Jamaicans candidly admitted that their "peculiar situation"—they spoke for "a very small number of white inhabitants" residing on a tropical island with more than 200,000 slaves—precluded any overt resistance to Great Britain.

While the ever-cautious Robert Carter Nicholas voiced a mild tribute to Jamaica's patriotism and his own ardent wish for a speedy return to those halcyon days before the Stamp Act "when we lived a free and happy people," the crowd that filled the church and spilled into the churchyard had more important things in mind. Back in October, Congress had declined Richard Henry Lee's call for defensive preparation, but with American liberties under attack Virginians had been organizing volunteer companies and arming themselves anyway. Would Virginia's provincial convention do better than Congress? Would it endorse the calls from the county committees for military readiness? Treasurer Nicholas had scarcely taken his seat when President Randolph acknowledged the gentleman from Hanover County. Consigning Jamaica's petition to virtual oblivion, Patrick Henry embraced Virginia's grassroots mobilization with a bold resolution demanding "that this Colony be immediately put into a posture of Defence." Richard Henry Lee seconded the motion, just as Henry had seconded Lee's proposal in Congress.

The first of four significant elements in Henry's resolution declared that "that a well regulated Militia composed of Gentlemen *and Yeomen* is the natural Strength and only Security of a free Government." By adding the yeomen of Virginia to a text whose lineage otherwise reached back to Lee's motion in Congress and its antecedents in year-old resolutions from Fairfax and Augusta counties, Henry reinforced the indispensable partnership between gentry leaders and ordinary freeholders that Virginia needed for the battles ahead.

Second, Henry's praise for a well-regulated militia as the natural strength of a free people packed another wallop. Phrases that we now associate with the Second Amendment to the Constitution had larger implications for Henry and his contemporaries. Keenly aware of the crown's recent suppression of local militias in England and Scotland, Henry was anticipating British attempts to hamstring the colonial militias by confiscating American weapons and powder. Third, Henry was recommending a reliance upon colonial militia units rather than British regulars for the general defense of North America to cancel that "Pretext of taxing us for their Support." And finally, pointing to Dunmore's failure to let the General Assembly protect the colony "in this time of Danger and Distress," Henry was asserting that the convention was forced to accept responsibility for putting Virginia "into a posture of Defence" by recruiting, arming, and organizing "such a Number of Men as may be sufficient for that purpose."

The old guard reacted immediately. Richard Bland, Treasurer Nicholas, Benjamin Harrison, and Edmund Pendleton charged that Henry's resolution was "premature," just as they thought his Stamp Act Resolutions had been nine years earlier. George III had not yet answered the recent petition from Congress. Henry was going too far. He and his allies, including Richard Henry Lee, Washington, and Jefferson, wanted more than an endorsement of county militia drills and the de facto creation of a defensive army. They were pushing the convention to abandon hope for any peaceful reconciliation and admit publicly that Virginia and the colonies were virtually at war with Great Britain.

When at last Henry took the floor, eyewitnesses describe him as starting "calmly," as was his usual practice. Praising the patriotism of the worthy gentlemen who had just spoken, Henry warned that his opinions were "very opposite to theirs." They had succumbed to the natural temptation to shut their eyes against painful realities. Henry wanted Virginians to face the whole truth, acknowledge the worst, and provide for it. Henry's speech, as one distinguished historian observed, "transformed resistance into revolution."

How, Henry wondered, could anyone still hope for reconciliation in light of the past conduct of the British ministry? "I have but one lamp by which my feet are guided, and that is the lamp of experience," Henry said. "I know of no way of judging the future but by the past"—especially the past decade. Were his timid friends seduced by the "insidious smile" with which George III and his ministers greeted the recent petition from Congress? What of the "warlike preparations" that covered American waters and darkened the land? Could force win back the colonists' affection? Were fleets and armies the instruments of love and reconciliation, Henry asked. "Let us not deceive ourselves. These are the implements of war and subjugation . . . the last arguments to which *kings* resort." Did Great Britain have enemies in this quarter of the world that required such a concentration of navies and armies? "No, sir, she has none. They are . . . sent over to bind and rivet upon us those chains which the British ministry have been so long forging."

How best could Americans resist British oppression? Henry ridiculed the advocates of petitions and memorials. "Shall we try argument? Sir, we have been trying that for the last ten years." Americans had addressed their disagreements with Britain in every possible light. Shall we try "humble supplication," he sneered. "What terms shall we find which have not been already exhausted?" Americans had done everything they could to avert the approaching storm. "We have petitioned. We have remonstrated. We have supplicated. We have prostrated ourselves before the throne" and repeatedly begged for George III's "interposition to arrest the tyrannical hands of the ministry and Parliament." All these efforts had failed.

"Our petitions have been slighted. Our remonstrances have produced additional violence and insult. Our supplications have been disregarded. And we have been spurned with contempt from the foot of the throne!" Hard experience proved there was no longer any prospect of peaceful reconciliation. "There is no longer any room for hope," Henry insisted—finally at liberty to announce in public the sentiments he had endorsed privately with John Adams in Philadelphia. "If we wish to be free, we must fight! I repeat it, sir, we must fight!" British aggression was forcing America to "an appeal to arms and to the God of hosts"—John Locke's solemn euphemisms for revolution—and the fault lay with the king, as Patrick Henry had been insisting since 1763.

"They tell us that we are weak and unable to cope with so formidable an adversary," Henry acknowledged. "But when shall we be stronger?" Will it be next week? or next year? or when the colonies were totally disarmed with a British guard stationed in every American home? Could the colonies gain strength by inaction? Could they resist tyranny by clinging idly to delusions of hope while their enemies bound them hand and foot? "We are not weak if we make a proper use of those means which the God of nature hath placed in our power," Henry thundered. "Three millions of people armed in the holy cause of liberty . . . are invincible by any force which our enemy can send against us."

Nor would America fight its battles alone. The God who decides the fates of nations—as Henry had assured Samuel Overton two years earlier—would assuredly raise up allies for the great struggle. Ready or not, however, it was now too late to evade the contest. "There is no retreat but in submission and slavery! Our chains are forged! Their clanking may be heard on the plains of Boston! The war is inevitable—and let it come! I repeat it, sir, let it come." When Henry paused, murmurs of "Peace! Peace!" emanated from the pews where some of his timid colleagues sat, punctuating the dramatic moment and prodding one of history's greatest orators toward the culmination of his most famous speech.

"Gentlemen may cry, Peace, Peace," Henry answered, echoing the Old Testament prophet Jeremiah, "but there is no peace. The war is actually begun! The next gale that sweeps from the north will bring to our ears the clash of resounding arms! Our brethren are already in the field!" he exclaimed, affirming once again Virginia's policy of steadfast unanimity with the other colonies. "Why stand we here idle?"

Slumping so vividly into the posture of a hopeless slave that onlookers perceived manacles "almost visible" on his wrists, Henry asked, "Is life so dear or peace so sweet as to be purchased at the price of chains and slavery?" He paused again, lifted his eyes and hands toward heaven and prayed,

Forbid it, Almighty God!—I know not what course others may take, but as for me . . . give me liberty, or give me death!

Then as his voice echoed through the church and his audience watched in stunned silence, Henry raised an ivory letter opener as if it were a dagger and plunged it toward his chest in imitation of the Roman patriot Cato.

The church fell silent. "Men looked beside themselves," one listener recalled. Another listener, standing outside a window after failing to find a seat inside, felt overwhelmed by Henry's oratory. "Let me be buried at this spot," exclaimed Edward Carrington, the younger brother of a Charlotte County delegate. Some thirty-five years later his family honored that request. Now, after two and a half centuries, his grave bears witness to the speech that burned itself into the memories of countless listeners—Give me liberty or give me death!—and carried Virginia further toward armed resistance and revolution.

ooooo

In any colony other than Virginia, Richard Henry Lee might have claimed the provincial crown for eloquence. Taking the floor after Henry, Lee fanned the blaze Henry had lit. Thomas Jefferson spoke, too, offering closely reasoned arguments for the civic role of the militia in a republic. George Washington had no need to address the convention. The determined expression on his face when Henry ridiculed dreams of peace left no doubt of his wholehearted agreement. Finally, just before the vote on Henry's resolution, the delegates heard from Yorktown's wealthy merchant Thomas Nelson, Jr. Born into Virginia's Tidewater elite and educated at Christ College, Oxford, "Young Tom Nelson" was the thirty-four-year-old son of the late councilor and acting governor William Nelson. Dunmore had vetoed his application for his late father's seat on the Council, and as chair of the county committee during the Stamp Act Crisis, Nelson was thought to have personally thrown a carton of tea into the river at Yorktown. Despite many layers of family connection to the leaders of the old guard, however, Nelson's quiet support for Patrick Henry had begun in the Stamp Act debates of 1765, his fourth year in the Assembly, though he had not said much at previous meetings. Now calling upon God as his witness, the future governor and signer of the Declaration of Independence proclaimed his support for Henry's resolution. If British troops landed in York

County, where he was county lieutenant, Thomas Nelson, Jr., declared that "he would wait for no orders" but "summon his militia and repel the invaders at the water edge."

Nelson's dramatic break with his moderate friends proved significant, for regardless of the widespread public enthusiasm for military readiness, the convention vote on Henry's resolution was close. James Parker, Norfolk's crusty but well-informed royalist, heard that the tally was 65 to 60—a statistical impossibility for a convention of 119 members but a clear indication of the narrow margin. Parker's other insights about the convention, however, suggest additional reasons that nearly half the members may have remained wary of Henry's resolution.

"What flattened their ardour," Parker reported, was the apprehension that Henry might present his militia resolution, as he had his Stamp Act resolves a decade earlier, as the first item of a more ambitiously radical plan for replacing Virginia's royal government with a revolutionary regime. The "Plan to be Presented by P. Henrie," as Parker described it, was "no less than the taking of Government into their hands, appointing Magistrates, and levying money." When Treasurer Nicholas caught wind of the rumored plan—along with Benjamin Harrison of Berkeley, Richard Bland, and Colonel Lemuel Riddick, a Suffolk lawyer and planter with nearly forty years experience in the Assembly who may have been Parker's source—they "formed an opposition which over Set the Scheme." Except for Parker's report there is no evidence that Henry had any such plan in mind, but Nicholas was unsuccessful in an attempt to replace Henry's militia resolution with his own alternative plan for raising several regiments of troops commanded by gentry officers.

Parker's informant also focused on two revealing elements of Henry's "infamously insolent" speech that are missing from William Wirt's familiar reconstructed text. Henry castigated George III as "a Tyrant, a fool, a puppet, and a Tool to the ministry"—charges like those he had used in the Parsons' Cause and that the Scipio author used to accuse the king of failing in his responsibilities as a monarch. Henry also condemned the rampant corruption of British society and politics with echoes of his assertions in Congress about the collapse of imperial governance and America's return to a state of nature. The once proud subjects of George III had "lost their natural courage" and were no longer able "to look the brave Americans in the face." Devoid of civic virtue, the British isles were home to "no Englishman, no Scots, no Britons" but only "a Set of wretches sunk in Luxury." America, the last bulwark of English liberties, stood in need of new institutions of government—but for now Henry and his allies in the convention had only enough votes to call out the militia.

ooooo

The convention debate between Henry and the moderates, as in the Stamp Act dispute, reflected differences of temperament and tactics but no lack of courage on either side. Henry was certain that war was imminent. His critics saw no advantage in broadcasting Virginia's preparations for resistance while there was any chance, however slim, of avoiding the conflict. They still believed in the efficacy of economic pressure for the redress of American grievances, as Edmund Pendleton explained to a frontier leader a few days later. Parliament would neither repeal the disputed measures nor "attempt to execute them by Force," Pendleton believed, but would engage to see which side "could longest endure the Commercial Struggle." Still seeking only "a redress of grievances and not a revolution of Government," Pendleton and his friends "endeavored to moderate the violent and fiery who were plunging us into rash measures." Pendleton's stance exasperated Jefferson's friend and fellow oenophile Philip Mazzei, then living in Albemarle County. "His doctrines could have undermined us," the volatile Florentine complained. Had Virginians heeded Pendleton's counsel "the English would have conquered us without any opposition," Mazzei said. "Clear-minded men called him *Moderation* instead of *Pendleton.*"

Although neither side won a complete victory in the convention debate at St. John's Church, General Gage promptly and Governor Dunmore soon thereafter confirmed the necessity of Patrick Henry's call to arms. War came to Massachusetts *and* Virginia about three weeks after the Liberty or Death speech when British redcoats moved simultaneously to disarm the colonists in the two major theaters of resistance. On April 18 a company of regulars marched twenty miles inland from Boston to seize a patriot arsenal at Concord. The next day they encountered the musket fire at Lexington celebrated by Ralph Waldo Emerson as the shot heard 'round the world. Less than forty-eight hours later, before dawn on April 21, Lord Dunmore dispatched a company of royal marines—the only troops available to him—to raid the Powder Magazine on the market square in the center of Williamsburg.

CHAPTER FIFTEEN

Gunpowder

IN THE DARK morning hours of Friday, April 21, 1775, Lieutenant Henry Colins, commander of the schooner HMS *Magdalen*, came ashore with a detachment of twenty armed marines at Burwell's Ferry (now known as Kingsmill) on the James River four miles southeast of Williamsburg. Following the Quarterpath Road into town about 4 a.m., Colins and his squad retrieved a horse-drawn wagon from the Governor's Palace and advanced quietly to the Powder Magazine, built in 1715 on the market square at the center of town about three blocks away. The heavy gate in the high brick wall around the octagonal magazine surrendered easily to its key, which Dunmore had supplied Colins after borrowing it from the magazine keeper. Inside were forty-three half barrels of powder, 342 new muskets, an array of small guns, and some old muskets.

Before someone woke up and sounded an alarm, the marines were able to remove fifteen half barrels of gunpowder. Then, scrambling onto the wagon, the raiding party escaped back to their anchorage at Burwell's Ferry. By 6 a.m. the stolen powder was secure aboard the *Magdalen*. The raiders had escaped successfully, save for the loss of a bayonet scabbard while the marines were carrying their weapons back to the boat. Colins's orders were to deliver the powder to the man-of-war HMS *Fowey*, then stationed at Norfolk. By early afternoon, anticipating retaliation by angry townspeople, Colins and his men had their vessel "in readiness," its guns loaded with round- and grape-shot. Conversely, a late-afternoon rumor to the effect that Colins and his marines were returning for the rest of the powder and weapons sent armed townspeople rallying to the magazine, "but soon dispersed except a few who acted as patrol that Night."

While Colins and his marines slipped away from the magazine amid beating drums, shouting residents, and rising tempers, the hastily dressed members of Williamsburg's independent company of volunteers had gathered nearby. Then, when an indiscriminate crowd began marching toward the palace to demand that Dunmore restore the powder, cooler heads quickly intervened, their successful intervention made possible only by the fact that news of Wednesday's bloodshed at Lexington and Concord had not yet reached Virginia. Peyton Randolph and Robert Carter Nicholas were eager to avoid an altercation that might mar the Old Dominion's reputation or impede an accommodation with Great Britain at the upcoming Second Continental Congress.

Hastily convening the Common Hall, the town's governing body, Mayor John Dixon, the printer, and his colleagues wrote a formal request for the return of the powder and carried it to the palace. With the independent company behind them "at a little distance," as Dunmore grimly observed, Speaker Randolph handed the paper to the governor. Its terms were milder than Dunmore had expected, though he complained to Secretary Dartmouth that the incident, "if not a treasonable proceeding," remained "one of the highest insults that could be offered to the authority of his majesty's Government."

After scanning the document, Dunmore offered Randolph and Dixon the first of several dubious justifications for his confiscation of the powder. Rumors of a slave insurrection in a neighboring county prompted his fears for the security of the magazine, so he had ordered the powder removed "to a place of perfect security." He had expressly ordered Lieutenant Colins to remove it "in the night time to prevent an alarm," but Dunmore now promised upon his word of honor (as if that meant much anymore) that he could return the powder in half an hour if needed. Expressing surprise that "the People" had taken up arms, Dunmore added "that he should not think it prudent to put powder into their hands in such a situation."

Though not persuaded by Dunmore's fabrications, the Speaker, the treasurer, Mayor Dixon, and the alderman repeated them to the crowd as they urged their neighbors to return to their homes in some measure of calm. In the days after the incident, despite Dunmore's subsequent exaggerations about the danger he faced, the governor and his chief aide, Edward Foy, as well as Lieutenant Colins and Captain George Montagu, who transported the powder to Norfolk on Sunday, all strolled the town unmolested. Even Lady Dunmore, Attorney General John Randolph later attested, "had no reason but the Timidity of her Sex" to worry about insults in the streets of Williamsburg.

Dunmore reported his actual motive for raiding the magazine in a letter to Secretary Dartmouth. Royal government in Virginia had been "entirely overturned" by the dangerous actions of "the People" and specifically by the convention's adoption of Patrick Henry's militia plan. "Their having come to a Resolution of raising a Body of armed Men in all the Counties," Dunmore wrote, "made me think it prudent to remove some gunpowder which was in a Magazine in this Place, where . . . I had Reason to believe the People intended to [seize it]."

Unfortunately for the remaining shreds of Dunmore's credibility, however, physician William Pasteur was called to attend a patient at the palace on the Sunday after Colins's raid. In a chance encounter with the governor, Dunmore expressed his exasperation that the people had taken up arms. When the doctor observed that they had acted in haste and confusion, and that many townspeople believed they may have overreacted, Dunmore exploded. "His Lordship then swore by the living God that if a Grain of Powder was burnt at Captain Foy or Captain Collins [*sic*], or if any Injury or insult was offered to himself, or either of them, that he would declare Freedom to the Slaves, and reduce the City of Williamsburg to Ashes."

As if that were not enough, Dunmore mentioned "setting up the Royal Standard" (the customary signal by which a king or his agent rallied the support of loyal subjects in the event of riot or rebellion) and then shocked Pasteur with his claim that he would have "a Majority of white People and all the Slaves on the side of Government." By God, Dunmore swore, referring to his expedition against the Shawnee, "he had once fought for the Virginians, and . . . would let them see that he could fight against them." Finally, Dunmore threatened to "depopulate the whole Country"—and ordered Pasteur immediately to convey his threats to the Speaker and other gentlemen "for there was not an Hour to spare."

By these impulsive actions and outbursts, the Earl of Dunmore turned the Governor's Palace into an armed fortress surrounded by a poisonous whirl of fear, anger, whispers, and threats. He alienated a vast majority of the king's white subjects in Virginia while exposing the reality that his own authority was increasingly dependent upon a small contingent of navy vessels and redcoats. Many townspeople feared that Dunmore would carry out his threat of arming the slaves. Others pointed to the flight of Lady Dunmore and her children from the palace to temporary refuge aboard the HMS *Fowey*, anchored off Yorktown, as a sign that her husband intended to summon warships to bombard the capital. Captain Montagu, commander of the *Fowey*, warned Secretary Thomas Nelson that he *would* fire upon Yorktown if anyone threatened the governor or the troops sent to protect him—and his threat quickly found its way into all three newspapers. For these rumors and the turmoil they caused, Governor Dunmore had only himself to blame. On Saturday, however, when John Pinkney published damaging excerpts in his *Virginia Gazette* from a letter Dunmore had written to Lord Dartmouth months earlier, responsibility for yet another blow to the governor's reputation lay entirely with Lord North's ministry, which had opened Dunmore's letter to public scrutiny by laying it before the House of Commons in February.

ooooo

On Monday morning, April 24, news of the gunpowder raid reached Fredericksburg, where the independent company of Spotsylvania County was drilling near the falls of the Rappahannock River under the command of Captain Hugh Mercer. Reacting promptly to this "very disagreeable intelligence," the militiamen voted unanimously to alert their comrades in neighboring counties and "hold themselves in readiness" to march toward Williamsburg the following Saturday. In the interim, Captain Mercer dispatched Mann Page, Jr., Lewis Willis, and young Benjamin Grymes, whose family stables provided three swift horses, to reconnoiter the situation at the capital.

Riding hard for twenty-four hours, the Spotsylvanians arrived in Williamsburg on Thursday, April 27, along with an unidentified rider on a similar errand from Hanover County. Page, a burgess since 1772 whose ancestors had served in the Assembly for twelve decades, and Willis, a member of the Westmoreland County committee who had signed the Association against the Stamp Act, promptly arranged a meeting with Peyton Randolph and reported that "upwards of 2000 men" were ready to march. The actual number at Fredericksburg was closer to six hundred, one of whom proudly wrote home that he had never before seen "so many brave hearty men" and that "every man Rich and poor" had turned out "with their hunting Shirts, Belts, and Tomahawks."

Thanking the messengers for their offers of assistance, Speaker Randolph explained that things were entirely under control. The capital was quiet and Dunmore continued to give private assurances that the powder would be made available if needed. Randolph was "firmly persuaded that perfect tranquility will be speedily restored" but, as always, apprehensive that violence could lead to consequences "which God only knows the effects of." Page and his companions hastened back to Fredericksburg, riding more than two hundred miles in a little more than forty-eight hours, and delivered the Speaker's letter late Friday afternoon.

That same day an express rider from the north reached Fredericksburg with the earliest fragmentary report of the bloodshed at Lexington and Concord on April 19. In another example of the democratizing interaction of Virginia's gentry leaders and patriotic yeomen, a council comprised of one sixth of the independent company's "well armed and disciplined men" convened on Saturday, April 29, and voted to postpone their march on Williamsburg. Instead, Spotsylvania's 102 militia officers, committee members, and other "friends of constitutional liberty and America" denounced Dunmore's actions as "full proof," confirmed by the news from Massachusetts, that royal governors everywhere, regardless of their private virtues, were agents of "the violent and hostile proceedings of an arbitrary Ministry."

For the moment, Spotsylvania's patriots resolved to return to their homes, vigilant and ready to reassemble at a moment's notice and "defend the laws, liberty, and rights of this, or any sister colony, from unjust and wicked invasion." Their fiery statement closed with two elements of revolutionary zeal. One was obvious: the phrase GOD SAVE THE LIBERTIES OF AMERICA in place of the customary *God save the King*. The second was perhaps more significant: a democratic assertion that their resolution, although already supported by one of every six patriots present, had also "been read at the head of each company" and "cordially and unanimously approved." Militia companies in Berkeley, Caroline, Frederick, and Dunmore counties stood down in similar readiness, guided either by the Speaker's advice, Spotsylvania's example, or both.

That same Saturday, Peyton Randolph left Williamsburg to meet Edmund Pendleton and Benjamin Harrison at Edmundsbury for their trip north to Philadelphia and the Second Continental Congress, scheduled to convene on May 10. Stopping briefly at Bowling Green in Caroline

County, they urged the volunteer company to follow the example of their Spotsylvania neighbors, then headed on their way escorted by armed militiamen and cheering crowds. George Washington, Richard Henry Lee, and Richard Bland made a similar departure from Mount Vernon on May 4. All six delegates agreed with the Speaker's counsel about a temperate response to Dunmore's raid on the magazine, although Colonel Washington had also packed his handsome militia uniforms and wore them conspicuously when Congress met. Virginia's seventh delegate, who delayed his departure from Scotchtown for Congress, felt differently about Dunmore's raid.

ooooo

Although Speaker Randolph had averted several potential violent confrontations in Williamsburg after Dunmore's confiscation of the colony's gunpowder, the governor's assurances wore thin as they spread with news of the raid far beyond the range of HMS *Fowey*'s twenty cannon. Committeemen in Gloucester County, across the river from Yorktown, denounced Dunmore's response to Mayor Dixon and the town councilmen as "unsatisfactory, disrespectful, and evasive." Further west, the committeemen of New Kent and Henrico counties cited his lordship's remarks as "an insult to every freeman in this country" and "proof that he was influenced by the worst motives," while the volunteer militia company in Albemarle County decided against Speaker Randolph's soothing advice. Popular opinion throughout the colony increasingly held that by his actions and his deceit Dunmore had "forfeited all title to the confidence of the good people of Virginia."

Upon receipt of Hugh Mercer's letter from Spotsylvania, Jefferson's neighbors put the matter to a vote of the volunteers assembled for the march to Williamsburg. All but two men "voted *for* a march," and the majority then had the pair who balked "drummed out of the company." Similar anger reigned in Hanover County, where Dunmore's attempt to disarm the colony confirmed all of Patrick Henry's warnings about the intentions of George III, his ministers, his minions, and his governor. Encouraged by his neighbors, Henry's reaction to the gunpowder crisis was the polar opposite of Peyton Randolph's.

In response to the raid, Henry's kinsman and lifelong friend Captain

Samuel Meredith summoned the county militia to meet at Newcastle on the Pamunkey River. By Tuesday, May 2, the ever-growing conclave numbered about 160 men, all eager to do *something* in defense of liberty. But what? Some volunteers talked of protecting the inhabitants of Williamsburg against Dunmore, others demanded restitution of the stolen powder, and an angry few advocated taking the governor hostage until he restored the powder or paid back its fair value.

Knowing that Henry had just departed for Congress in Philadelphia, Captain Meredith and Peter Lyons, who had represented James Maury in the Parsons' Cause, persuaded Colonel John Syme, Jr., Henry's half-brother, to dispatch a messenger imploring him to come back and join their meeting at Newcastle. The courier caught up with the orator, riding in the company of his cousin George Dabney and Colonel Richard Morris, both members of the Hanover County committee, before they crossed Littlepage's Bridge over the Pamunkey on the road to Bowling Green and all points north. By the time Henry arrived back at Newcastle, according to Meredith's recollection, the emerging consensus of the patriots favored marching on the capital and demanding payment for the powder from the crown's receiver-general, Richard Corbin. "As soon as these objects were made known," Meredith recalled, Henry "expressed the most hearty approbation of them."

Recounting their conversation on May 2, 1775, as he rode with Henry and Colonel Morris to meet with the Hanover volunteers, George Dabney remembered that Henry asserted privately that Virginia's gunpowder incident was "a fortunate circumstance" for America—a reaction similar to Samuel Adams's joyful response to the news from Lexington and Concord. It had been difficult to rally Americans to the dangerous implications of British duties on tea, Henry reminded Dabney and Morris, "but tell them of the Robbery of the Magazine and that the next step will be to disarm them, and they will be then ready to fly to Arms to defend themselves."

Recounting his conversation for Henry's first biographer, George Dabney recalled his cousin's apparent gift for anticipating the distant consequences of political events as well as Henry's resolute certainty, at this moment of crisis, that Britain and the colonies were heading toward a permanent separation. A military confrontation with Lord Dunmore "was generally condemned by most of our leading men as imprudent and impolitic," Dabney recalled, "but Henry's views extended further than recovering the [powder and arms]."

ooooo

How much further? In some respects the status of British authority was more frail in Virginia than in Massachusetts. General Gage had unsuccessfully dispatched a company of troops into the countryside but had a secure base in Boston with several thousand troops, a flotilla of warships, and good communications with his superiors at Whitehall. Dunmore's palace was full of weaponry but his military resources were limited to the *Fowey* at Yorktown, the *Magdalen* and *Liberty* in the James, and a maximum of two hundred navy and marine personnel—about forty of them encamped at the palace but most of them aboard ship. More significantly, while a small contingent of British troops had ventured out of Boston and clashed with American *defenders*, the growing contingent of angry volunteers and expert marksmen marching toward Williamsburg seemed poised for *attack*. Gage easily survived the embarrassment of his army's retreat from Lexington and Concord, but Dunmore's situation in the early days of May 1775 was far more tenuous. Virginians everywhere had taken up arms, Dunmore told Dartmouth, and he expected at "every Moment to be attacked."

Dunmore's greatest threat came from Patrick Henry, whom the governor portrayed as a man of desperate circumstances "actively encouraging disobedience and exciting a spirit of Revolt among the People for many years past." Henry's force was marching on the capital "with all the Appearances of actual War," Dunmore wrote. The most influential of Virginia's more cautious leaders were in Philadelphia, for after trying to defuse the crisis over the powder magazine raid they had departed for Congress. If the Hanover volunteers marched on Williamsburg (and especially if Dunmore did anything rash that angered their compatriots in other counties) the royal governor of Virginia faced the real prospect of a humiliating defeat and surrender. Dunmore knew that Patrick Henry had him by the short hairs. The critical question was what Henry intended to do.

ooooo

From their rally at Newcastle on Tuesday, May 2, Henry and some two hundred volunteers of the independent company of Hanover County followed the road along the south banks of the Pamunkey and York Rivers and stopped for the night at New Kent county courthouse. On Wednesday they continued their march and established camp at Doncastle's Ordinary, an easy sixteen-mile striking distance from the capital. While his main force marched toward a confrontation with Dunmore, Henry had also sent Ensign Parke Goodall and sixteen men eastward to Laneville, the imposing brick home of Receiver-General Richard Corbin in King and Queen County. Goodall's mission was either to collect £330 from crown revenues, the estimated value of the powder, or take Corbin prisoner and bring him to Doncastle's Ordinary with "strict orders . . . to do no injury to his person." The ensign's squad surrounded Corbin's mansion Tuesday night, but early Wednesday morning Mrs. Corbin told them her husband was in Williamsburg, where he kept the crown Treasury at his office in the capitol. Goodall declined her invitation to search the house and then reported back to Henry that afternoon.

While Henry awaited news from Laneville, a succession of messengers from Williamsburg, including Treasurer Nicholas's merchant son-in-law John Hatley Norton, urged him to hold his ground in New Kent. "Our thick-headed Treasurer," Dunmore's friend James Parker chuckled, "is in a terrible panic." Soon thereafter, Richard Corbin's son-in-law, Carter Braxton, rode in from Caroline County, where he had witnessed Edmund Pendleton, Benjamin Harrison, and Peyton Randolph pause on their way to Congress and dissuade the independent company from marching on the capital. Braxton urged Henry to halt his march "upon the strength of this precedent," but Henry insisted either that the powder be returned or the colony compensated for its loss. Braxton agreed to seek his father-in-law's agreement in Williamsburg, and Henry promised to wait in New Kent pending his return.

Braxton soon learned that Receiver-General Corbin had little cash on hand, but with the assistance of Secretary Thomas Nelson, Sr., president of the Council, he persuaded Corbin to offer Henry a bill of exchange. Henry, in turn, gave Corbin a formal receipt "for the gunpowder lately taken out of the public magazine." Dated Thursday, May 4, the receipt promised that Henry would deliver the bill of exchange to the Virginia delegates in Congress pending the next meeting of the General Assembly or a Virginia Convention.

"The affair of the powder is now settled," Henry wrote Treasurer Nicholas when he offered to bring the Hanover volunteers to the capitol if Nicholas thought it prudent to transfer the public Treasury to some location "more safe than the city of Williamsburg." Nicholas replied curtly that he "had no apprehension of the necessity or propriety of the proferred service." Nevertheless, more than a hundred townspeople patrolled the capital streets and guarded the Treasury that night—and the committees of Cumberland and Spotsylvania counties also recommended moving the Treasury to a more secure location. In general, though, Dunmore described the end of the episode accurately when he informed Lord Dartmouth that Henry and his volunteers "returned triumphantly to their respective habitations" crowing that "Justice [had been] done to the Country for the Insult he had committed."

ooooo

Wednesday, May 3, had been a busy day for the governor, too. After a contentious meeting with the members of his Council, Dunmore issued a proclamation justifying his removal of the powder and calling upon Virginians to "restore peace and harmony to this distracted country." Once again, however, his lordship undermined his posturing with angry rants. Reacting to councilor John Page's suggestion that he simply return the powder, Dunmore "flew into an outrageous passion, smiting his fist on the table." Later he blew up at Mayor John Dixon, swearing that if he were mayor he would march the town volunteers to New Kent to confront Henry, declare that he was "satisfied about the affair of the powder," and insist that Henry's volunteers "must not and shall not enter our town, which is now in peace and quietness." Dixon and the common hall chose instead just to ask Henry not to invade Williamsburg.

Before he learned of the Braxton-Nelson-Corbin-Henry negotiations, Governor Dunmore had convinced himself, based in part on faulty intelligence from excitable loyalists such as James Parker, that Henry planned to attack the palace at dawn on the 4th of May. Dunmore's animosity had become intensely personal. Henry "did actually bully him," the young councilor John Page observed, though he also thought the two antagonists were "mutually afraid of each other." His lordship's informants were more accurate about Henry's call for the people of York County to prevent communication between the palace and the *Fowey* and especially to thwart any "retreat to the Man of War." Despite that warning, however, one captain, one lieutenant, and forty-one sailors and marines were able to sneak as far as Porto Bello, the governor's private plantation on Queen's Creek midway between Yorktown and the capitol, where their presence was discovered about midnight.

Now it was Captain Montagu's turn for worry. Short of firearms and well aware of the weaponry stocked at the palace, Montagu had equipped the squad only with cutlasses, swords, and bayonets. Williamsburg's independent company under Captain James Innes was ready to confront the detachment from the *Fowey*, but Dunmore's aide, Captain Edward Foy, went house to house and defused the situation by promising that Montagu's sailors and marines would not trespass into the town itself. They would enter the palace through its gardens at the edge of town, Foy promised, and return promptly to the *Fowey* as soon as the governor's personal safety was assured. The next day, readers of Pinkney's *Gazette* were amused to learn that Montagu's sailors and marines "were so fatigued when they reached the confines of the Palace that several of them tumbled into a ditch" in the rugged terrain behind the governor's gardens.

Despite Lord Dunmore's fears for his personal safety and Edmund Pendleton's anxieties about fiery demagogues, once Patrick Henry had Corbin's receipt for the gunpowder in hand he promptly brought the crisis to a peaceful conclusion. Henry, it turns out, saw himself not as a self-important rebel but rather as a responsible popular leader constrained both by the will of his people and the expectations of his gentry colleagues. "The affair of the powder is now settled, so as to produce satisfaction to me, and I earnestly wish to the Colony in general . . . in a manner least liable to the imputation of violent extremity," Henry advised Robert Carter Nicholas—who promptly declined the volunteers' repeated offer of further protection for the Treasury.

The dispersal of Henry's Hanover volunteers and the arrival of Montagu's squadron at the palace presented Dunmore with a safe opportunity to reinflate his courage. Now that the immediate crisis had passed, Dunmore vented his anger in a proclamation against "a certain *Patrick Henry*, of the County of *Hanover*, and a Number of his deluded Followers." Issued in Williamsburg on Saturday, May 6, Dunmore's proclamation called on Virginians to "vindicate the constitutional Authority of Government," but the trend of events was moving against him.

ooooo

Patrick Henry had long ago accepted the inevitability of independence, but he knew it could happen safely only with the overwhelming consent of a unified American community. In that regard, the clashes of April 1775 played into his hands, as he remarked to Dabney and Morris while they rode back to the muster at Newcastle. The events set in motion by Gage's and Dunmore's attempts to disarm the colonies would soon persuade more Americans "to fly to arms to defend themselves." Henry knew that his detractors had been frightened by the march to Doncastle's Ordinary. Now he worried that while he was serving in Congress they might accuse him at Virginia's next convention of provoking a war with Britain. Henry sought help from his longtime friend Francis Lightfoot Lee, Richard Henry Lee's younger brother. Writing from Hanover on May 8, Henry told Frank Lee that some "who opposed the measure we took" were now contending "that the powder belonged to the King." Although that "pretence" was obviously false, Henry worried that in his absence "perhaps an attempt may be made to . . . misrepresent my conduct."

Henry knew that most Virginians approved his actions and that many felt that "the hostilities to the Northward would have justified much greater reprisals," such as an assault on Dunmore, which he "chose to decline." Pointing to the Hanover volunteers' "moderation and justice," Henry asked Lee to defend him in the convention "if you think it right," or at least try to postpone any action "until I am heard." Although Henry's immediate fear proved unfounded, for no one but Dunmore openly attacked him or the Hanover volunteers, Henry's letter to Frank Lee shows again his dutiful respect both for the concerns of his gentry colleagues and the collective civic authority exercised by Virginia's revolutionary conventions.

Using the pen name "Brutus," Frank Lee wrote an eloquent defense of Henry's actions. By the time Alexander Purdie could publish it, however, fifteen county committees had flooded the newspapers with spontaneous expressions of gratitude and "hearty approbation," as the frontier residents of Fincastle County put it, for the "spirited and meritorious conduct of Patrick Henry, esq., and the rest of the gentlemen volunteers." When Patrick Henry finally set out for Congress on May 11, a volunteer guard from Hanover, King William, and Caroline counties escorted him to the Potomac River and saluted him with repeated huzzas until his ferry landed safely on the Maryland side.

ooooo

Riding to the Potomac with Henry's volunteer guard was his friend Parke Goodall, to whom he had entrusted the mission to Richard Corbin's plantation during the gunpowder crisis. Henry spoke quietly to Goodall about his hopes for the Second Continental Congress. He had no doubt that a general confederation of the American colonies would be formed. He was equally certain that the northern colonies would not shirk from the impending war even if their southern brethren were so "pusillanimous" as to desert them. But if American military exertions fell short, Henry remained confident that the colonies would gain their independence with the assistance of foreign powers, as he had predicted months earlier in his Liberty or Death speech. Arriving in Philadelphia on May 18, Henry turned his attention to the business of Congress, though most of the working committees had already been appointed.

Back in Williamsburg, Lord Dunmore vented his frustrations with one last outrage at the Powder Magazine. The 4th of June was Pentecost, or Whitsuntide, a favorite Sunday for baptisms throughout the English-speaking world. In British villages everywhere, including Williamsburg, Fredericksburg, Alexandria, and Norfolk, the weekend was traditionally devoted to festivities such as games, dancing, races, food, and drink. About midnight on this Whitsunday Eve, however, the weary residents of Williamsburg were startled by the loud blast of a shotgun.

Once again vigilant townspeople and volunteers rushed toward the market square, expecting to interrupt another British raid on the Powder Magazine. Instead they discovered three young Virginians, one with two fingers blown off his right hand, one shot through the shoulder, and a third with minor injuries. A few local boys had broken into the magazine, unaware that Dunmore had secretly booby-trapped its doors with spring guns connected to trip-wires. Fortunately no lives were lost, though Alexander Purdie's newspaper tagged the unnamed perpetrators "with the opprobrious title of MURDERERS." Dunmore's conduct had reached a new low, and by the governor's own admission in a letter to Dartmouth, "the Cry among the People was for Vengeance." On Monday an angry crowd stormed the unguarded magazine and carried off its remaining inventory of musketry. "Old Dick Bland talked very fluently about hanging" Dunmore, the Norfolk loyalist James Parker reported. Even the staid and moderate Edmund Pendleton remarked, when details about the spring guns reached Congress, that Dunmore "deserved Assassination."

Once again feeling threatened, Dunmore asked his friends in the navy to send him another squadron of armed men. Hearing no prompt reply, however, at about two o'clock Thursday morning, June 8, Lord and Lady Dunmore, their children, and the long-suffering Captain Edward Foy slipped out of the palace and for the last time made their way along Queens Creek to the quiet anchorage of HMS *Magdalen.* Diverting the *Magdalen* from an intended mission to Delaware Bay (for which Captain Montagu was nearly court-martialed), the governor sent his wife and children home to England on Thursday, June 29. Two weeks later, when HMS *Mercury* arrived to relieve the *Fowey,* Captain Foy and his wife jumped aboard for home rather than share further in his lordship's disgrace. "I am no longer interested in the fate of Lord Dunmore," Foy announced bitterly. The other prominent defector who sailed for England that August was Attorney General John Randolph, whose daughter Susan was alleged to have been Dunmore's mistress and whose son Edmund was angling for an appointment as aide-de-camp to General Washington.

CHAPTER SIXTEEN

Commander in Chief

NEWS OF THE GUNPOWDER RAID in Williamsburg reached the northern press just as Patrick Henry belatedly arrived at the Second Continental Congress on May 18, 1775. Accounts of the march against Dunmore by "a number of armed people, all men of property, led by Patrick Henry, Esq." and of Lady Dunmore's initial flight to the *Fowey* shared space in the northern papers with the joyous reports of the capture of Fort Ticonderoga, America's first resounding victory in the Revolutionary War, that was now under way. A mountaintop bastion overlooking the road between Lake George and Lake Champlain, Ticonderoga was a strategic point in the Hudson River–Lake Champlain waterway targeted by British strategists hoping to isolate New England from New York and the colonies to the south.

While royal government was collapsing in Virginia, Patrick Henry, Samuel Adams, Richard Henry Lee, and other patriots at the Second Continental Congress had long ago decided, like John Adams's friend Joseph Hawley, that Americans must fight. George Washington wore his militia uniform to Congress every day. "We have nothing going on now but preparations for war," an observant Philadelphia housewife informed her nephew. Nevertheless, while both Edmund Pendleton and Benjamin Harrison remained wary about the radicalism they associated with Boston, moderates such as John Dickinson and John Jay were still hoping for reconciliation. Pendleton went so far as to speak against the choice of George Washington as commander of an American army—although he also helped the new general write his acceptance speech and update his will. Henry and most other congressmen welcomed the June 15 decision to put Washington in command of an army of ten thousand men at Boston and another five thousand at New York. His appointment "firmly Cements the

Southern to the Northern" colonies, a Connecticut delegate wrote, and eased sectional jealousies by removing any fears that a victorious northern general might "give law to the Southern and Western Gentry."

Only in deepest confidence, in letters to his wife, family, and trusted friends, did the newly appointed general express his apprehensions about ruining his reputation by falling short "of so important a trust." Henry stood within that intimate circle, according to the Philadelphia physician Benjamin Rush. "About this time I saw Patrick Henry at his lodgings," Rush recalled, "who told me that General Washington had . . . informed him that he was unequal to the station in which his country had placed him, and then added with tears in his eyes 'Remember, Mr. Henry, what I now tell you: From the day I enter upon the command of the American armies, I date my fall, and the ruin of my reputation.'"

Congress now grappled with how best to explain what American troops were fighting for. For two weeks John Dickinson and Thomas Jefferson (who took Peyton Randolph's seat on June 21 a month after the president went home to preside over the House of Burgesses) bickered over the wording of a "Declaration of the Causes and Necessity of Taking Up Arms." The result of their contention was a stronger statement than either man could have written alone. Adopted on July 6, 1775, the statement harked back to the glory days of William Pitt's administration under George II and culminated with an eloquent declaration of America's determination to fight for the preservation of endangered liberties. "Our cause is just. Our union is perfect. . . . Foreign Assistance is undoubtedly attainable." As to independence, although their private assessments varied, Henry and everyone in Congress could still agree with the *public* warning, from the pen of Dickinson, that "necessity has *not yet* driven us to that desperate Measure."

ooooo

Back in Virginia, the deliberations of the Third Convention at the parish church in Richmond had begun in mid-July and dragged on for five contentious weeks. "We are undoing one day, what we did the day before," a delegate complained to his father in August 1775. Except for Peyton Randolph, whose health was failing, and George Mason, who stepped into Washington's seat when his illustrious neighbor took command of the Continental Army, Virginia's most talented leaders were still at

Congress—and their absence made a difference. Not until mid-August did the return of Henry, Pendleton, Lee, Harrison, and Jefferson reinvigorate the convention, though it surely helped, as Mason informed Washington, that by then the "Bablers" had talked themselves hoarse.

Despite its limitations, the Third Convention had continued the shift away from royal governance toward a more substantial alternative by adopting *ordinances* (rather than *resolves* and *recommendations*) meant to give "obligatory Force to their Proceedings." One provided for regular annual elections of delegates and county committees. Another created an eleven-man provincial Committee of Safety that served as Virginia's executive body between conventions until the adoption of a new constitution in June 1776. The delegates also authorized the recruitment of two regiments totaling more than one thousand men as well as additional minutemen and militia—and then fell into rancorous disputes over the selection of the commanding officers. Patrick Henry's election as "commander in chief" of the Virginia army was controversial—and still is.

Henry and the other congressmen were traveling home from Philadelphia when the convention cast secret ballots on Saturday, August 5, to choose commanders for three (later reduced to two) new regiments. On the initial ballot the most experienced candidate, Hugh Mercer of Fredericksburg, got a plurality of forty-one votes to Patrick Henry's forty—with Thomas Nelson, Jr., and William Woodford sharing the remaining ten votes. The Scottish-born Mercer had begun his military career in the Jacobite uprising of 1745, fought in the French and Indian War, and more recently commanded the Spotsylvania Volunteer Company during the Powder Magazine crisis—but when Nelson's supporters shifted their votes in the runoff, "the Majority appeared in favour of Patrick Henry." After Mercer withdrew his name from consideration for command of the Second Regiment and Nelson declined the post in favor of a seat in Congress, however, the second election runoff pitted Patrick Henry's brother-in-law William Christian, a veteran of Dunmore's War from Fincastle County, against William Woodford, a protégé of Edmund Pendleton who had served under Washington in the French and Indian War and now commanded the independent volunteer company of Caroline County. Finally, after a majority of the delegates chose Woodford as commander of Virginia's Second Regiment, the convention decided against creating a third.

Although virtually every colony had some men with command experience from the French and Indian War, their numbers were few and many were too old for active duty. Patrick Henry's admirers at the Third Convention in Richmond believed him as capable as anyone else of leading Virginia's new army—especially after his highly visible conduct in the march against Dunmore. During the Revolution, as in subsequent American wars, several former civilians proved themselves exemplary officers. General Nathanael Greene had been raised a pacifist Quaker and was a journeyman blacksmith at his father's Rhode Island foundry until the war changed the course of his life. General Henry Knox had been an apprentice bookbinder and was running a book shop in Boston when he joined the local militia.

Without commenting on his qualifications, George Washington told an aide that in his private opinion the Virginia delegates "made a Capitol mistake when they took Henry out of the Senate to place him in the Field." But Henry was not the only civilian caught up in the *rage militaire* that swept the colonies in 1775 after ten years of civilian protest. "Oh that I was a Soldier!" John Adams confided to his wife, Abigail, that spring. "The military Spirit which runs through the Continent is truly amazing." Adams fretted that among his fellow congressmen "Dickinson is a Colonel. Mr. Reed a Lt. Colonel. Mr. Mifflin a Major." On the other hand, civic republican ideals and the experience of history testified to the risks of mixing civilian and military authority—as reflected in the Third Convention's new rule against military commanders holding provincial civil office or representing Virginia in Congress. Julius Caesar and Oliver Cromwell leapt to the eighteenth-century mind, as did the redcoats of the Boston Massacre and such military governors as General Thomas Gage and John Murray, Earl of Dunmore.

During the early weeks of the Third Convention, however, less edifying political maneuvering inflamed the dispute about Patrick Henry's overall command of the new Virginia regiments and, more generally, led George Mason to express his "Vexation and Disgust" with the "Partys and Faction that prevailed at Richmond" before the congressmen returned from Philadelphia. With elder statesmen such as Richard Bland and Peyton Randolph slipping toward retirement or the grave, the followers of Patrick Henry and Edmund Pendleton succumbed in their absence to squabbling over long-standing differences in policy, personality, and ambition.

From their common roots as struggling gentry in adjacent Piedmont counties, Henry and Pendleton had made their fortunes in law and politics. Pendleton, older by fifteen years, rose to prominence by attaching himself to the late Speaker John Robinson, Jr., whose mismanagement of the colonial Treasury was an early target of Henry's populist rhetoric. Both men were steadfastly religious, but their convictions about the toleration of evangelicals and power of Anglican discipline were as different as their personal temperaments and their attitudes toward the imperial crisis. Pendleton could not understand Henry's style of leadership, and his acute fear of demagoguery aggravated his misgivings about Henry's appointment as colonel of the First Regiment—as did his long friendship with his neighbor William Woodford. The tension between Henry and Pendleton complicated the Old Dominion's military response to Lord Dunmore in 1775 and 1776, especially after Pendleton declined reelection to Congress and became chairman of the newly created Committee of Safety, where he kept the colonel of the First Regiment on a very short leash. Colonel Henry might be commander in chief but the convention and its Committee of Safety retained "absolute direction of the troops."

CHAPTER SEVENTEEN

Norfolk Destroyed

ALEXANDER PURDIE DRAPED his newspaper in mourning on Friday, November 10, 1775, with heavy black rules between the columns that lamented the death of Peyton Randolph, longtime Speaker of Virginia's House of Burgesses and first president of Congress. Eulogized as a firm patriot, wise legislator, and benevolent public servant, Randolph was fifty-four when he fell victim to "a stroke of the palsey" in Philadelphia. His death removed the one man whose influence had cushioned the policy differences represented by Edmund Pendleton and Patrick Henry, and the somber columns of Purdie's *Gazette* carried four other dire reports as well. A brief notice claimed that Captain Mathew Squire's "ministerial squadron" lost twenty-one men "besides the seven prisoners" in a skirmish at Hampton—the first fatalities (although the numbers were inflated) in the clash with Dunmore. An item summarized George III's proclamation declaring America in a state of open and avowed rebellion. A letter on page three complained that George III and Parliament were forcing Virginians to choose between "slavery or independence." And finally, in a prominent place on the front page, the Committee of Safety cited recent "hostilities against his majesty's peaceable subjects" by Lord Dunmore and officers of the navy as reasons for imposing a quarantine on Norfolk and Portsmouth, severing all trade and communication between the port cities and the rest of the colony as a preliminary step toward military action.

Bypassing Colonel Henry, Edmund Pendleton and the committee dispatched William Woodford and his Second Regiment toward Norfolk while Henry and the First Regiment, minus some troops temporarily reassigned to Woodford, guarded the capital. Henry *might* have led the mission as capably as Woodford, but by a 7-to-4 vote after two days of agonizing discussion the committee decided to take no chances with Virginia's limited troops and finite resources. It was a decision that inevitably aroused hard feelings among proud men who cared deeply about honor— and within four months would lead to Colonel Henry's resignation. According to Paul Carrington, a member of the Committee of Safety from Charlotte County, no one doubted Patrick Henry's courage or commitment. Doubts did arise, however, from the perception that his approach to military command was too democratic. Career officers commonly held that "distance" was necessary between officers and enlisted men, and that "familiarity" was incompatible with proper military subordination and discipline. Political rivals already wary of Henry's alleged demagoguery worried that a popular commander who "regarded his soldiers as so many gentlemen" and "exacted from them little more than the courtesy that was proper among equals" would not be "conscious of the importance of strict discipline in the army."

Despite a detractor's claim that Henry's "studies had been directed to civil and not to military pursuits" and that he was "totally unacquainted with the art of war and had no knowledge of military discipline," the colonel's library tells us otherwise. Henry owned both *The New Art of War*, a translated compilation of four works by influential French military authors published in 1726, and Humphrey Bland's tried and true *Treatise of Military Discipline*, a favorite of eighteenth-century British officers that went through nine editions between 1727 and 1762. A veteran of the Duke of Marlborough's campaigns, Bland explained how to organize companies of infantry into battalions and train them for active service—how to march at various rates, move from one formation to another, form a line of battle, and fire effectively against a variety of adversaries—and how to arrange for shelter, provisions, posting guards, and keeping records. Bland's *Treatise* remained the standard British army manual throughout most of the century.

As commander in chief Henry also relied on Edward Harvey's *The Manual Exercise as Ordered by His Majesty in 1764*, the successor to Bland's *Treatise*, which set forth the most up-to-date methods of infantry drill and tactics. On the advice of George Washington, the Second Virginia Convention had specifically endorsed the 1764 manual for use by the militia units in accord with Henry's resolution for defense and his Liberty or Death speech. At the regimental camp in Williamsburg, Colonel Henry used *The Manual Exercise* for training his troops, but he also recognized its limits. Henry's general orders for October 10, 1775, for example, stipulated that his officers and troops spend one full hour learning "the Usual Exercise" according to the *Manual* but three hours learning "the Decipline of Woods fighting" from his experienced senior officers, many of whom had proven themselves in Dunmore's War and other frontier conflicts. Colonel Henry urged his lieutenants to "pay particular Attension" and devote "all possible Deligence" to woods fighting "as the most Likely method to make the Troops formidable to their Enemies."

ooooo

The Virginians of Colonel William Woodford's advance party approached the Great Bridge, about ten miles southwest of Norfolk and Portsmouth, on November 25. There stood the wooden bridge across a branch of the Elizabeth River that had had greatness thrust upon it as the only overland access to the port cities from Virginia and North Carolina. Long narrow causeways at either end of the bridge traversed the impassably marshy terrain. By December 2, when Woodford and the rest of the Second Regiment arrived, Dunmore had removed the plank decking from the bridge and erected at its north end a small stockade manned by a contingent of loyalist volunteers as well as runaway slaves and indentured servants hopeful of winning their freedom.

While Woodford's regiment marched toward Great Bridge, Dunmore had scored a lopsided victory a few miles closer to Norfolk in a skirmish at Kemp's Landing against ill-trained patriot militiamen who fired too soon and then fled into the woods. Flushed with triumph, Dunmore had chosen that moment to raise the king's standard, the signal calling upon loyal subjects to help suppress a rebellion. Although lacking a pennant bearing the king's arms and forced to substitute some regimental colors, Dunmore accompanied the ritual declaration of rebellion with a controversial proclamation, printed on the press his marines had stolen from Norfolk printer John Holt, promising freedom to "all indented Servants, Negroes, or others (appertaining to the Rebels)" willing to join his majesty's troops.

Dunmore's edict was a tactical act of war akin to Abraham Lincoln's Emancipation Proclamation nine decades later. The governor had prepared his text in advance and waited for an opportune moment. The skirmish at Kemp's Landing was his Antietam. Like Lincoln, Dunmore limited his offer of freedom to servants and slaves owned by his adversaries not by his loyalist allies, but unlike Lincoln he expressed no moral objections to slavery. In the absence of the widespread antislavery sentiments of Lincoln's day, Dunmore's conditional offer of freedom for indentured servants and slaves did his own cause far more harm than good. Indeed modern scholarship reveals that only a few hundred slaves responded to Dunmore's proclamation, and most of them died from disease.

At Patrick Henry's headquarters near the capitol in Williamsburg, where the Committee of Safety stood in recess, Alexander Purdie printed a broadside version of Dunmore's proclamation with a note from Colonel Henry for immediate distribution throughout the colony. Describing his lordship's proclamation as "fatal to the publick Safety," Henry alerted magistrates to the urgency of "unremitting Attention to the Government of the SLAVES" as well as "Constant and well directed Patrols." From a political perspective, Archibald Cary of Chesterfield County pointed to "the most extensive good consequence" of Dunmore's proclamation. "Nothing could have been more unwise than a declaration of that nature," Cary wrote. "Men of all ranks," including planters formerly sympathetic to the governor, saw Dunmore's proclamation as "a dagger to their Throats."

Dunmore's good fortune at Kemp's Landing blurred any lessons he might have learned from earlier skirmishes. Woodford's troops at the Great Bridge were miserable—beset with cold weather, wet ground, and inadequate shelter, food, and blankets—but within a few days they had erected earthworks seven feet high along the road and "a strong Breastworke" east of the causeway.

About 3 a.m. on Saturday, December 9—ignoring the skeptical counsel of the professional soldiers who later blamed his "absurd, ridiculous and unnecessary attack" on his dependence upon bad advice from "Scotch Pedlars"—Dunmore sent about 120 men of the British 14th Regiment of Foot to attack Woodford's entrenched troops. Marching six abreast to the cadence of two drummers, the regulars led by Captain Charles Fordice crossed the bridge and advanced down the causeway, followed by a ragged band of three hundred slaves and pro-British volunteers, or Tories.

Scrambling to their earthworks, Woodford and about forty riflemen held fire at the causeway until the redcoats came within fifty yards, while Lieutenant Colonel Edward Stevens and a hundred of his Culpeper minutemen dashed to the breastwork. "Bullets whistled on every side" when Woodford's men unleashed their devastating fire toward the bridge, while

Stevens's marksmen picked off redcoats, Tories, and slaves trapped on the causeway. Struck in the knee, Captain Fordice bravely advanced within five yards of the earthworks before collapsing in a hail of bullets. As his decimated unit broke into a disorderly retreat, the Culpeper minutemen rained fire upon the causeway, forcing back Captain Samuel Leslie and his reserve troops.

The fighting at the Great Bridge, the first land battle of the Revolutionary War in the southern colonies, ended within thirty minutes. Apprehensive about a rumor that five hundred Highlanders might be rushing to Leslie's rescue and mindful of his instructions "to risk the success of your arms as little as possible," Woodford sent a flag of truce and offered a cease-fire for the removal of dead and wounded. His decency left a deep impression on the British regulars, who had heard Dunmore's allegations that prisoners faced scalping and torture, especially because the Virginians did not need a cease-fire. One of Woodford's troops had a wounded finger, while Dunmore tallied the British losses at seventeen dead and forty-nine wounded—although the British officers counted 102 casualties and fifteen lost as prisoners.

At dusk the defeated remnants of Leslie's 14th Regiment began their slow withdrawal first to Norfolk and then to the refuge of warships anchored in the Elizabeth River while their seasoned officers vowed that they would never again be "sacrificed" to the governor's "whims." Dunmore reacted to the disaster at the Great Bridge with characteristic fury and finger-pointing. Raving "like the Mad Man he is," Dunmore condemned Leslie's tactics as imprudent and with appalling cruelty blamed Leslie's decision to withdraw upon "depression" over the death of his nephew, a lieutenant who died in his arms.

In a report to the nominal commander in chief, Patrick Henry, Woodford described the victory at the Great Bridge as "a second *Bunker's Hill* affair in miniature, with this difference, that we kept our post and had only one man wounded." The colony was far from secure, of course, and Virginians remained apprehensive about the future, but Woodford's success at the Great Bridge inspired the Old Dominion's first openly published call for independence in John Pinkney's *Gazette*. "Some people have expressed great uneasiness at the thoughts of being separated from Great Britain," but in light of their bloody efforts to oppress America, their role in the African slave trade, and their cruelties in the East and West Indies,

Pinkney's bold correspondent wanted "no connections with such a people as this."

By mid-December Dunmore and the British troops had evacuated Norfolk and taken refuge aboard a flotilla anchored offshore. Advancing carefully to avoid ambush or the rumored arrival of British reinforcements, Woodford's Second Regiment took possession of the city on December 14. That evening the Virginians welcomed Colonel Robert Howe and 250 troops from North Carolina, whose arrival swelled the occupying force to about 1,200 men. The next morning Colonel Woodford graciously yielded command of the American forces to Colonel Howe, whose continental commission outranked Woodford's provincial credentials. Eager to safeguard the mission against any confusion about command authority, Pendleton and the Third Virginia Convention had alerted Woodford to the "Rule of Congress" and urged him "not to suffer the good of the common cause to be interrupted by Punctilios of no real consequence." As a continental officer, the new commander was exempt from Colonel Henry's authority and could work directly with the Committee of Safety.

Working smoothly together, Woodford and Howe shared their troops' disdain for the city of Norfolk and especially the local Tories who had taken refuge with Dunmore and the army aboard the fleet of warships and merchantmen anchored just offshore. Ever since Dunmore fled from Williamsburg, the Tories who called themselves "Friends of Government" had become increasingly dominant in the port city. Letters intercepted from Norfolk correspondents revealed merchants eagerly stocking up for the retail boon they hoped would accompany a British invasion. Other enterprising loyalists wrote their English correspondents seeking appointments to government posts now held by patriots or touting the likely investment opportunities in confiscated Virginia estates once the rebels were crushed. Although the intercepted letters also disclosed a pervasive fear of attack and destruction, by autumn 1775 Thomas Jefferson spoke for the vast majority of Virginians when he echoed Cato the Elder's war cry against Carthage in a letter to his boyhood friend John Page, vice chairman of the Committee of Safety: "Delenda est Norfolk." Norfolk must be destroyed.

Within days after Dunmore evacuated the city, his floating refugee camps began running short of food and water. Messages from the fleet asked about replenishing the "Provisions and Water," "clean Cloths," and "fresh Provisions" for which the British had previously depended upon city merchants. Howe and Woodford replied firmly that their orders prohibited "any communication" with the "Troops and Ships of War." The commanders were equally blunt in the question they posed to the Virginia convention after they took control of Norfolk and Portsmouth. They recognized the port cities' importance in the economic life of Virginia and North Carolina and their strategic significance if the British held them as a garrison—but was the convention prepared to commit provisions, cannon, and the large "Boddy of Troops" necessary to establish an American fortress? Or should Norfolk be "Totally distroyed"?

While Howe and Woodford awaited instructions, Dunmore and his refugees, military and civilian, suffered from cramped and miserable conditions afloat. Constantly exposed to verbal taunts from shore, they were also vulnerable to snipers if they ventured to the deck to smoke, urinate, or breathe fresh air. By Christmas Day exasperated royalists aboard the *William* were forecasting that as punishment for the denial of provisions "the ships of war will destroy the town in a few days." About noon on New Year's Day 1776, patriot soldiers began a parade along Water Street, in full view of Dunmore's ships, confident that distance prevented British musketry from ruining their fun. Jeering at the navy, the soldiers stuck their hats on their bayonets, waved them in the air, and dared the British to shoot them off. The holiday spectacle destroyed any patience Dunmore had left. British muskets lacked the range or accuracy of American rifles, but rifles were no match for British cannon.

About three o'clock that Monday afternoon British cannon opened fire on Norfolk's waterfront buildings, aiming to dislodge Virginia's pesky sharpshooters. Small parties of redcoats in small boats sent to raid the docks were easily turned back, but cannon boomed steadily until midnight and intermittently through the dark hours of the next morning. A conflagration started by Dunmore's cannonade devastated the city during the first three days of 1776, destroying 914 buildings valued in excess of £125,000. On Tuesday and Wednesday, Woodford and Howe watched approvingly as torch-bearing Virginians made sure the obliteration was complete. Loyalist James Parker's house, with its stone steps, marble chimneys, and the city's finest garden, was one of the first they helped into ashes. Although both officers honestly reported their troops' active role in the destruction, the convention kept the full story quiet. In the court of American public opinion, as one disillusioned British officer complained,

Dunmore's bombardment of Norfolk transferred "the Inhumanity of the Action from American to British shoulders."

"Nine-tenths of the town are destroyed," Alexander Purdie's *Virginia Gazette* reported on Friday, January 5, "but the fire is now out." Acting upon secret orders from Pendleton and the Virginia convention, the American forces tore down or burned another 416 structures "to prevent our enemies from taking shelter in them" before evacuating the city a month later. Of the few habitable structures in Norfolk that survived the first months of 1776, only the borough church (now St. Paul's Episcopal Church) stands today—with a British cannonball lodged in its brickwork.

ooooo

Williamsburg printer Alexander Purdie highlighted Lord Dunmore's cruelty on behalf of George III in the first reports of the destruction of Norfolk published in a two-page supplement to his *Virginia Gazette* issued January 5, 1776. These initial reports began with excerpts from Colonel Woodford's description on Monday of the opening bombardment, followed by parts of a letter written on Tuesday by Colonel Howe. The third report, written on Thursday afternoon by an observer at Hampton, across the water from Norfolk, had a cover letter added by Patrick Henry on Friday. Purdie added a few anecdotes from Williamsburg, and then filled the remaining columns of his supplement with an essay by "An American" about the implications of the conflagration.

Significantly, An American's essay read like a speech: "I hope our countrymen will not be at all dispirited at the destruction of Norfolk," it began, "but rather rejoice that half the mischief our enemies can do us is done already!" The destruction revealed George III's malevolent intentions toward America: "Dunmore's plots against us . . . must have been authorised by a higher power." The burning of Norfolk clinched the argument for independence: "Most freely would I *cut the Gordian knot* which has hitherto formerly bound us to Britain," An American concluded, "and call on France and Spain for assistance against an *enemy* who seems bent on our destruction." Betraying the sacred contract between a monarch and his subjects, George III had made himself the enemy.

Like the Scipio letter in 1774, circumstances strongly suggest Patrick Henry's authorship of the essays by An American that Purdie published in 1776. The first essay especially has the cadences of oratory. As news of the bombardment of Norfolk filtered into Henry's regimental camp at Williamsburg during the first three days of 1776, Colonel Patrick Henry surely felt compelled to buck up the morale of his troops. Had Washington faced similar events he would likely have issued a written statement for his subordinates to share with his more numerous and dispersed forces, but for Colonel Henry what could have been more natural than an impromptu speech to reassure everyone in camp that Lord Dunmore's terrible malice actually bolstered their cause—that Virginians should not be "dispirited . . . but rather rejoice!"

Published within hours of the events it assessed, the essay could only have been composed by someone fully acquainted with the latest reports and present in Williamsburg at the moment they arrived. Considering both substance and circumstance, everything we know about the essay suggests that Alexander Purdie heard Patrick Henry address the First Virginia Regiment at their camp near Williamsburg with just enough time to summarize Henry's remarks and set them in type for immediate publication. The pseudonym recalled Henry's famous speech in Congress in 1774—"I am not a Virginian, but an American"—and the content matches Henry's known opinions in 1775 and 1776: Dunmore's violence was an example "of British cruelty, and American fortitude." America should make alliances with France and Spain. Virginians needed to share "the sufferings of our American brethren." The burning of Norfolk proved once and for all that George III was their enemy. The time for independence was at hand.

Weeks before excerpts from Thomas Paine's *Common Sense* would reach the Old Dominion, Virginians could agree with An American that the burning of Norfolk was proof of George III's responsibility for "Dunmore's plots" and that it was time to sever ties with Great Britain. The Boston patriot Samuel Adams thought the burning of Norfolk would "prevail more than a long Train of Reasoning to accomplish a Confederation." Many of his neighbors drew similar conclusions about the similar bombardment and destruction of Falmouth, Massachusetts (now Portland, Maine), by Admiral Samuel Graves and the British navy in October. "The destruction of Norfolk and threatened devastation of other places will . . . unite the whole Country in one indissoluble Band against a Nation which seems to be lost to every sense of Virtue," George Washington observed to an aide. "Such flaming Arguments as were exhibited at

Falmouth and Norfolk, added to the sound Doctrine and unanswerable reasoning contained in the pamphlet Common Sense," he believed, would compel Americans to accept "the Propriety of a Seperation."

ooooo

Virginia's Fourth Convention had met initially in Richmond on Friday, December 1, 1775, and then moved back to the greater comforts of Williamsburg until it adjourned on January 20. With Patrick Henry and the First Regiment camped near the College of William and Mary, convention leaders believed that Lord Dunmore was too preoccupied in Norfolk to attack the capital. With Edmund Pendleton in the chair after the death of Peyton Randolph, the Fourth Convention was better organized than its immediate predecessor but once again short of talent and experience. Five of Virginia's most skillful leaders—Benjamin Harrison, Thomas Jefferson, Richard Henry Lee, Thomas Nelson, Jr., and George Wythe—were away at Congress. George Mason was ill. Henry and Washington were ineligible by virtue of their military commands, and Treasurer Robert Carter Nicholas was overburdened with administrative work.

Day-to-day work in the convention fell heavily on the shoulders of the powerful moderate Edmund Pendleton and Archibald Cary, the autocrat of Chesterfield County, who shaped a cautious response to the escalating conflict and the increasingly radical turn of public sentiment. Despite an open-ended encouragement from Congress, for example, the Fourth Convention deferred the creation of any new system of government by reaffirming the Committee of Safety as an acting executive between conventions and authorizing greater sanctions against loyalists by the county committees. Hard feelings from the Henry-Woodford command decision had not dissipated, but military necessity in the war against Dunmore was top priority. The convention added seven new regiments to the provincial line, and Pendleton maintained an effective communication with Woodford and Howe, while Colonel Henry parlayed his rank and influence into a significant martial achievement: the creation of the Virginia navy. The idea had been discussed in the convention, but it was Henry who took action.

During a routine inspection of the defenses erected at Hampton after the British raid in October, two suspicious merchant ships had appeared on the horizon. Henry immediately sent James Barron, a local sea captain, and twenty militiamen in a small vessel to intercept the ships. Capturing nine prizes in ten days, Barron and his brother Richard soon put an end to British harassment of Virginia shipping in Hampton Roads. A few days before Christmas the convention endorsed Henry's initiative, gratefully placed three armed vessels under Barron's command, and directed the Committee of Safety to make the navy a separate branch of service. It also named three admiralty judges to rule on prize claims and help enforce the trade ban with Britain, and it endorsed a flotilla on the Potomac organized by Fairfax County. By the end of the Revolution, the legacy of Patrick Henry's navy comprised two major shipyards and a dozen smaller ones as well as scores of warships—brigs and brigantines, schooners and pilot boats, and cruisers and row galleys—all manned by more than seven hundred officers, sailors, and marines. Augmenting this official state navy, about a hundred Virginia privateers conducted patrols, blockade running, and raids under letters of marque.

February 1776 witnessed a flurry of activity in Tidewater Virginia—including the launch of the galley named the *Norfolk Revenge*. On the 6th, Colonel Robert Howe abandoned Norfolk and (after taking an inventory as a basis for future compensations to *patriot* owners) destroyed its remaining structures. Most of the army moved to Suffolk, where it could monitor land routes between Virginia, North Carolina, and the Norfolk-Portsmouth area. Dunmore offered to negotiate a peace agreement in a letter conveyed through Richard Corbin, the king's former receiver-general, but the Committee of Safety referred the letter to Congress and suggested that Dunmore suspend his hostilities until Congress learned the king's "ultimate intentions."

The arrival of British Captain Andrew Snape Hammond and the forty-four-gun *Roebuck* on February 9 gave Dunmore an opportunity to relieve the congestion aboard his ships and take on fresh water and provisions. A week later, Virginians watched with alarm as General Sir Henry Clinton anchored HMS *Mercury* in Norfolk Harbor along with two transports, a supply ship, and more than 1,200 troops. Thrilled by these apparent reinforcements, Dunmore was flabbergasted when Clinton informed him that he was not rescuing the royal government of Virginia. Despite the governor's protest that his was "the first Colony on the Continent for its riches and power," Clinton's orders were to support Governor Josiah Martin and a promised Tory uprising in North Carolina and then attack

Charleston, South Carolina. Politely declining Dunmore's suggestion of an attack against the Americans, the general left a scathing private assessment of Dunmore and his situation. "I could not see the Use of his Lordship's remaining longer there," Clinton reported, "especially after the failure of his Attack on the Rebel Post at the Great Bridge." Nine days later Clinton weighed anchor and set sail for the Carolinas, where Governor Martin's loyalist uprising had already failed, and where the intended assault on Charleston foundered on Sullivan's Island, ending the first British southern campaign in confusion and retreat.

ooooo

Two days after General Clinton and HMS *Mercury* cleared the Virginia Capes on February 26, Patrick Henry informed the eleven-man Committee of Safety that "he could not accept" a new commission offered him that morning as one of six colonels in the Continental service but no longer Virginia's ranking officer. Henry's resignation made obvious sense to any eighteenth-century officer faced with the indignity of being outranked by former subordinates—and it echoed similar situations in other colonies. Facing almost identical circumstances, Connecticut generals Joseph Spencer and David Wooster resigned their commissions in protest against Congress's elevation of Israel Putnam, their former subordinate, to a higher rank in the Continental line.

Assuring his troops that it was a matter "in which his honour alone was concerned," Henry made no public comment about his decision, though he later complained in private to Samuel Meredith, his brother-in-law and comrade-in-arms, about languishing in Williamsburg while William Woodford won fame and glory at the Great Bridge. Informed of Henry's resignation on Thursday, Leap Year Day in 1776, the troops camped near the capitol "went into deep mourning" and gathered at Henry's residence. His resignation filled them with "the most poignant sorrow" and a "spirited resentment" for this "most glaring indignity." Ninety of his officers also hoped that justice would promptly bring about Henry's "happy return to the glorious employment of conducting our councils."

Henry's officers insisted upon honoring him with a farewell dinner at Raleigh Tavern but soon heard reports from the regimental camp that angry enlisted men were threatening to quit and "declaring their unwillingness to serve under any other commander." In response, Henry spent the night visiting all the barracks and exhorting the troops to continue their patriotic service. Reminding them that only requirements of personal honor had forced his resignation, Henry asked the troops to dedicate themselves, as he did, to "the real interest of the United Colonies" and "the glorious cause in which they had engaged." The next day, Alexander Purdie's *Gazette* happily reassured the public that "those brave fellows are now pretty well reconciled and will spend the last drop of their blood in the country's defense," though it took a month of letters and commentary before the controversy ran its course in the newspapers.

ooooo

Dunmore's situation after Clinton's departure was now desperate. Typhus and smallpox swept through his floating city and resulted in the abandoning of so many corpses along the west bank of the Elizabeth River that "many Waggon loads of the bones of Men women and Children" remained visible in the sand three decades later. Anticipating a patriot attack, Dunmore and Captain Hammond decided to move their base of operations forty miles due north to Gwynn's Island, near the mouth of the Rappahannock River. On May 27 the frigate *Roebuck*, the sloops *Fowey* and *Otter*, and eighty-five smaller vessels evacuated Dunmore's loyalist refugees, three hundred troops, and the surviving runaway slaves to the new island sanctuary a few hundred yards offshore from Gloucester County.

Although home to four hundred head of cattle, low-lying Gwynn's Island proved less than idyllic for human habitation. Scurvy and malaria reduced Dunmore's army to about a hundred men. Hot weather dried up the island's springs. Early in June, General Andrew Lewis approached Gwynn's Island with ten companies from the First and Second Regiments and a considerable battery of artillery. At eight o'clock on Sunday, June 9, the Virginians' eighteen-pounders put a dozen holes in the *Dunmore*, formerly the merchant ship *Eilbeck*. They injured the governor, killed his skipper, damaged the *Otter*, and destroyed a battery of cannon organized by the loyalist James Parker—all within an hour. Four small tenders ran aground in the narrow channel separating the island from the mainland. One was captured and three were burned. Two more tenders and the sloop *Logan* were torched on Monday. Only Lewis's lack of boats spared the British encampment from immediate capture, and when the Virginians finally came ashore after Dunmore's hasty evacuation they found thirty ailing black soldiers left behind to die—the wretched vestige of Dunmore's Ethiopian Regiment.

As they fled Gwynn's Island, Dunmore and Captain Hammond took their fleet north to replenish their water supply before abandoning Virginia. The state navy unleashed by Patrick Henry had "become so formidable," Dunmore reported, that "Captain Hammond does not think it safe to trust one of His Majesty's Sloops alone in the Bay." Eventually the escapees found fresh water near Dumfries, about eighty-five miles up the Potomac, where the local militia enticed them into one last raid, at William Brent's Richland plantation in Stafford County. Then, after scuttling twenty unseaworthy vessels, Dunmore and Hammond headed south toward the open ocean. The *Roebuck* had lost another thirty seamen. Dunmore had left about three hundred dead at Tucker's Point in the Elizabeth River and another 150 graves at Gwynn's Island. On August 5 the refugee fleet passed the Virginia Capes into the Atlantic. The *Otter* led about fifty vessels south to St. Augustine. A few ships headed to England with the *Fowey* and its VIP passenger, Maryland governor Robert Eden. Lord Dunmore and Captain Hammond led the remaining two dozen ships to New York, where General William Howe had established headquarters on Staten Island. Fourteen eventful months after his lordship had slipped out of the palace at Williamsburg, the Old Dominion was finally rid of John Murray, Earl of Dunmore.

CHAPTER EIGHTEEN

A Free and Independent State

ON WEDNESDAY, MAY 15, 1776, the Fifth Virginia Convention announced three momentous and unanimous decisions based on motions introduced by Patrick Henry and two other delegates. Declaring that the actions of George III and Parliament had left Virginia with "no alternative . . . but an abject submission to the will of those over-bearing tyrants, or a total separation from the crown and government of Great Britain," the convention resolved to direct the Virginia delegation in Philadelphia to propose, first, that Congress "declare the United Colonies free and independent states absolved from all obedience to or dependence upon the crown or Parliament of Great Britain." Second, the convention wanted Congress to establish "foreign alliances and a confederation of the Colonies" provided that creation of state governments and "the regulation of the internal concerns of each colony be left to the respective colonial legislatures." Third, the convention named Patrick Henry and twenty-seven other prominent members to a committee charged with preparing "a Declaration of Rights, and such a plan of government as will be most likely to maintain peace and order in this colony and secure substantial and equal liberty to the people."

The next day the new "continental union flag" or "union flag of the American states," with the crosses of St. George and St. Andrew in its upper left corner and a field of thirteen red and white stripes, fluttered above the capitol as the members of the convention and Committee of Safety joined the inhabitants of Williamsburg to celebrate. After a parade and military review at Waller's Grove, northeast of the statehouse where Henry had established the First Regiment's base camp, citizens and soldiers raised their glasses in toasts to the independent American states, to the Continental Congress, and to General Washington and victory—each toast followed by an artillery salute and the shouts of all present. That evening the town was illuminated with candles, and the next morning Virginians gathered for services of fasting and prayer called by the Congress back in March. The Reverend Thomas Price, chaplain to the convention, delivered his sermon at Bruton Parish Church on a well-chosen text from Second Chronicles: "Be not afraid nor dismayed by reason of this great multitude; for the battle is not yours, but God's."

ooooo

Soon after resigning his command, Patrick Henry had marked his return to civilian leadership with another essay signed by An American. Henry had expressed impatience with those who still wished for the "liberty that we enjoyed in 1763"—a time when British regulations prevented Americans from making nails or hats, or from trading directly with the European nations that produced wine, silk, olives, oranges, and lemons. A time when the tobacco trade was entirely controlled by British merchants. A time when the king repealed American laws at will, dissolved assemblies without reason, and kept troops in the colonies as he pleased. "This was our situation in 1763, and yet some people are weak enough to wish to be left as we were then," Henry wrote. "Good God! were we not abject slaves?"

An American's renewed call for "the independence of the colonies" had reiterated Henry's arguments about foreign assistance from the Liberty or Death speech twelve months earlier. Heaven had provided rich resources for America's "just and holy war." Virginians could rely upon foreign trade for commodities, arms, and ammunition, not to mention the income with which planters and farmers would pay their taxes, settle their debts, and maintain their families. "We should declare ourselves independent," Henry had advised, and open American trade to the world.

The problem that confronted Henry and other gentry leaders was their uncertainty about whether potential allies would risk a war with Britain if there were any chance of reconciliation. If Americans kept "dutifully *whining* after our *mother country*," Henry had warned, European powers might give up on Congress and be tempted by an offer from Britain to "share the plunder of America" by swapping some of the English colonies for other concessions—as France had abruptly given Louisiana to Spain and surrendered Canada to Britain in the 1760s. "God be praised," Henry had exclaimed, "France has waited with patience."

Covert French and Spanish support for America had already begun, along with critical financial and logistical support from the Dutch republic, although open diplomatic and military treaties were not signed until after the British surrender at Saratoga in 1778. Between 1775 and 1778 Virginia played a central role in the importation of European weapons, gunpowder, and other provisions through the French island of Martinique, the Spanish port of New Orleans, and the Dutch island of St. Eustatius—in part because America's secret allies in Europe valued tobacco, flour, and rice above the mainland colonies' other exports.

Henry's second essay as An American had taken intercolonial unity for granted while urging Virginians to link independence with foreign trade and support. He had declared this position in a letter to John Adams: good-faith affirmations of unity among the colonies were "sufficient" lest anything more ambitious "delay the French alliance, which with me is everything." Another Virginian, writing as "Phil-Americus," had offered similar reassurance in Purdie's *Gazette*. "Why should we shudder at the thoughts of a *perpetual independence?*" he had asked. "Have the *Dutch* repented, or the *Swiss*, that they *shook off the yoke of their tyrants?*" Virginians faced the stark alternatives "either to be *slaves* or to *fight for independence*," Phil-Americus had declared. "But who can hesitate in the choice?"

ooooo

Public enthusiasm for independence seems not to have extended to the details of a new government. Although gentry leaders discussed constitutional issues among themselves, in pamphlets, and in the pages of the *Virginia Gazette*, only the freeholders of Buckingham County offered much advice about the "free and happy constitution" they expected from the Fifth Convention. Citing principles that went back to John Locke and the "revolution" that had crowned "the present royal family" on the throne in place of the Stuarts, Buckingham's petitioners proudly declared their God-given right to choose whatever government they pleased for their civil and religious happiness. When existing institutions of government became defective beyond correction, "the people may form themselves into another." Buckingham's electorate wanted a new government "as soon as the general consent approves and the wisdom of our counsils will admit." But beyond three specific attributes—"full representation, free and frequent elections," and "no standing armies . . . in times of peace"—the freeholders left all the details of the new government to their elected leaders. They expected convention delegates to examine the merits and defects of other governments, consider the causes that either "raised them from slavery to liberty" or "reduced them from freedom to slavery . . . and learn by these examples." The result, they modestly hoped, would give Virginia the most free, happy, and permanent government "that human wisdom can contrive and the perfection of man maintain."

Edmund Pendleton put Archibald Cary in the chair and appointed nearly a third of the delegates as members of the committee charged with preparing a declaration of rights and new plan of government, including James Madison, a promising twenty-five-year-old admirer of Patrick Henry from Orange County. But it was Pendleton's final appointee who made the greatest contribution. Detained at Gunston Hall for several days by "a smart fit of the Gout," George Mason reached Williamsburg late on the 17th, joined the convention the next day, and promptly found himself appointed to all four major committees. Delighted by the convention's unanimous resolution for independence, Mason was initially skeptical about writing a constitution with a committee "overcharged with useless Members" from whom he anticipated only "a thousand ridiculous and impracticable proposals." Mason urged Richard Henry Lee to slip away from Congress and help him in Williamsburg, where the convention needed "a few Men of Integrity and Ability" capable of "undertaking this Business and defending it ably through every stage of opposition."

Pendleton was confident of the outcome because "Colonel Mason seems to have the Ascendancy in the great work." "The Political Cooks are busy," he informed Jefferson. Of the things that contributed to Pendleton's confidence and Mason's achievement, perhaps the most significant was a general consensus shared by almost all politically active Virginians about the desired nature of the new government. At one extreme, most Virginians were horrified by Thomas Paine's radical suggestion in *Common Sense* for imposing annually elected unicameral legislatures on all the colonies, subservient to Congress but unrestrained by governors or upper houses. At the other extreme, Patrick Henry spoke for many when he dismissed as "a silly thing" the plan advanced in Carter Braxton's *Address to the Con-*

vention of the Colony and Ancient Dominion of Virginia . . . by a Native of that Colony. Braxton proposed a government with a lower house elected every three years, an upper house whose members served for life, and a governor whose term would be limited only by good behavior. Henry regarded Braxton's ideas as "shallow and evasive," his pamphlet as "an affront and disgrace to this country," and the author himself as "suspect [in] his whiggism"—all of which he also saw as good reasons for engineering Braxton's removal from Congress.

Between the extremes of Paine and Braxton, gentry leaders generally agreed that the lineaments of Virginia's existing government—which they had been vigorously defending against British authorities since the Parsons' Cause—could be adapted for an independent commonwealth and committed to parchment as a written framework for government. But that was only half the challenge. Americans generally accepted the logic of prefacing their written charters of government with explicit statements of liberties, but apparently Henry's friend Meriwether Smith of Essex County was the first American to translate that logic into an explicit call for a written "Declaration of Rights" prefixed to "a Plan of Government." Arriving three or four days after Smith had introduced his resolution, George Mason quickly embraced the idea in his drafts for both documents. Virginia's plan of government should begin, Mason wrote, with "A Declaration of Rights, made by the Representatives of the good People of Virginia, assembled in full Convention; and recommended to Posterity as the Basis and Foundation of Government."

ooooo

From a twenty-first-century perspective, it may seem strange that Patrick Henry and his contemporaries were not quite sure what to call their plan for a new republican government, but the word *constitution* had overtones in 1776 that Americans altered after 1787. The much admired English Constitution, after all, was not (and has never been) one written document. It was rather, as Montesquieu described it, a "noble system" of institutions, a configuration that preserved English liberty through its intricate balance of functional authorities.

In his early drafts for the Virginia convention, George Mason entitled his handiwork "A Plan of Government" or just "A Plan." Thomas Jefferson gave no title to his first draft, called his second draft "A Bill for new modelling the form of government and establishing the Fundamental principles of our future Constitution," and then deleted the term *constitution* in his third and final draft of "A Bill for new modelling the form of government and for establishing the Fundamental principles thereof in our future."

When the Virginia convention adopted the term in June 1776 for its final published version of "A Constitution, or Form of Government," the usage seemed sufficiently novel to require a grammatical appositive (*form of government*) clarifying its meaning. Even after the states' widespread adoption of written constitutions during the American Revolution, the word itself still retained aspects of its original English meaning. The preamble to the Pennsylvania Constitution of 1776, for example, declared that "the following *Declaration of Rights* and *Frame of Government*" comprised "the CONSTITUTION of this commonwealth." Echoing the original English meaning, Patrick Henry spoke of the *constitution* in this inclusive sense during the 1787–1788 debates over whether to ratify the document thereafter known as the U.S. Constitution. Distinctions drawn between written and unwritten constitutions remained points of contention in antebellum disputes about states' rights and the federal judiciary, just as English legal authorities long had debated the nature of their "ancient constitution."

ooooo

George Mason drafted most of the Virginia Declaration of Rights during the week of Monday, May 20, and then discussed his draft with the committee on Saturday, May 25. Two days later the committee presented its list of eighteen rights for discussion and had Alexander Purdie print copies for the delegate's convenience during the deliberation that began on Wednesday. Copies of Purdie's handbill reached Philadelphia within the week, and Mason's draft appeared in the *Pennsylvania Evening Post* on June 6. Four other papers printed it the following week, and by the end of the year Mason's draft Declaration of Rights had been published in virtually every American newspaper and several British periodicals as well.

Although the convention refined the Virginia Declaration of Rights before its final adoption on June 12, the committee draft had a much greater influence in history. Jefferson, Franklin, and Adams borrowed its phrases for the Declaration of Independence. It shaped the declarations of rights adopted by Pennsylvania, Maryland, Delaware, and North Carolina in 1776, and by Vermont in 1777, Massachusetts in 1780, and New Hampshire in 1781—as well Madison's Bill of Rights for the United States Constitution, the French Declaration of the Rights of Man and Citizen in 1789, Olympe de Gouges's Declaration of the Rights of Woman and the Female Citizen in 1791—and the nineteenth-century bills of rights adopted by Maine, Montana, New Mexico, South Dakota, Vermont, and Wisconsin.

Three elements of Mason's Declaration of Rights excited debate when Archibald Cary presented the committee draft on Wednesday, May 29. Robert Carter Nicholas led a conservative slaveholder's attack on Mason's statement "that all men are by nature free and independent." Did gentlemen really believe that their slaves were their political and social equals? Nicholas saw the first article of the declaration as a dangerous prelude to "civil confusion." Other delegates countered that since slaves were never regarded as "constituent members" of Virginia society they could never benefit from the statement, but two days into the debate Thomas Ludwell Lee complained that the convention was still "stumbling at the threshold." Nicholas and other "Aristocrates," Lee explained to his brother Richard in Congress, "have to this time kept us at bay on the first line which declares all men to be born equally free and independent." Lee felt that "a very great majority" favored Mason's statement but that Nicholas and his aristocratic "monsters" were dragging their feet with procedural "strategems" and "maneuver." With his characteristic attention to detail, Edmund Pendleton eventually defused the conflict by inserting the phrase "when they enter into a state of Society"—which was taken to exclude slaves, Indians, and women from the Lockean social contract.

If race was one lightning rod for controversy, religion offered another. Mason's draft projected "the fullest *toleration* in the exercise of religion according to the dictates of conscience." Dodging a visible role in the debate owing to his youth and inexperience, Madison got Patrick Henry to propose an amendment that would replace *toleration* with "the full and free exercise" of religion. More ominously for supporters of the established church, the Madison-Henry proposal also aimed at preventing the new government from imposing "penalties or disabilities" or granting "emoluments or priveleges" for any person or "class of men" on account of religion.

Patrick Henry's known sympathy for religious dissenters prompted an immediate challenge. Was the proposed amendment "designed as a prelude to an attack on the Established Church," critics demanded. Henry said no. Madison said nothing, and the amendment died for lack of a second. Then, abandoning the provisions seen as threatening to the Anglican establishment, Madison promptly reworked Mason's original language into a more direct endorsement of religious liberty. Introduced by an unknown third party (probably the conservative churchman Edmund Pendleton, eager to bury the abandoned provisions) Madison's second attempt was successful. As adopted by the convention, the historic sixteenth article of the Virginia Declaration of Rights read:

> That Religion or the Duty which we owe to our Creator and the manner of discharging it can be directed only by reason and Conviction not by force or Violence and therefore all Men are equally intitled to the free exercise of Religion according to the Dictates of Conscience. And that it is the mutual Duty of all to practice Christian Forbearance Love and Charity towards each other.

Although George Wythe later tried to assert that this article itself undermined Virginia's established church, that would not happen until the passage of Jefferson's Statute for Religious Freedom in 1786.

Patrick Henry was solely responsible for the third major change to the Declaration of Rights. The committee had augmented Mason's draft with bans on ex post facto legislation (laws that retrospectively punished acts that were legal at the time they were committed) and acts of attainder (criminal convictions enacted by a legislature without any trial). Henry disagreed with the prohibition of acts of attainder, arguing that such a ban might hamstring the legislature in a dire emergency. As Edmund Randolph described the debate, Henry won his point by painting "a terrifying picture of some towering public offender against whom ordinary laws would be impotent." The vision proved slightly prophetic—two years later Governor Henry would enlist Thomas Jefferson to draw up a controversial act of attainder against Josiah Philips, a persistent loyalist, for treason, murder, and arson in Princess Anne and Norfolk counties.

ooooo

The convention's progress with the Declaration of Rights gave many delegates reason for optimism about a new plan of government. George Washington's brother John Augustine was confident. He saw "no great difference of opinion among our best speakers, Henry, Mason, Mercer, Dandridge, Smith," and expected Pendleton to "concur with them in sentiment." Thomas Ludwell Lee agreed, although he worried that keeping a "just and equal" constitution from being cluttered with "discordant, unintelligible parts will demand the protecting hand of a master." As early as November 1775, Richard Henry Lee and John Adams had devoted several evenings of conversation in Philadelphia to the features they hoped to see when the colonies began to create new governments. Spurred by their mutual disdain for Paine's suggestions in *Common Sense*, Lee and Adams pushed each other to commit their ideas to paper. Lee issued his *Proposals for a Form of Government* about April 10 as an anonymous broadside in Philadelphia that Alexander Purdie reprinted a month later in Williamsburg. John Adams's pamphlet, which Henry, Lee, Jefferson, and Wythe admired in manuscript, appeared a week later as *Thoughts on Government: Applicable to the Present State of the American Colonies. In a Letter from a Gentleman to His Friend.*

George Mason's draft promptly "swallowed up all the rest by fixing the grounds and plan" for the new government. Mason's draft borrowed nothing from Paine or Braxton but relied heavily on Lee, Adams, and the powerful example of Virginia's colonial institutions. "Printed for the perusal of the members" about June 8, Mason's plan provided for a bicameral legislature, a separate executive branch composed of a governor and advisory council, and an independent judiciary. Political power was concentrated in the lower house, which had sole authority for initiating legislation and amending "money bills." The legislative chambers would jointly elect the governor (who had no power of veto) as well as members of an advisory council, the judiciary, delegates to Congress, and the secretary, treasurer, and attorney general. Under Mason's guidance, work on the constitution went smoothly and a new printing of the revised "Plan" was distributed on Saturday, June 22.

That Sunday, however, George Wythe suddenly arrived from Congress bearing an entirely new proposal drafted by Thomas Jefferson. Without consulting anyone in Williamsburg, Jefferson had worked his plan for a constitution through three successive drafts and then sent two copies of his final proposal to Williamsburg (as he had done with the text later published as *A Summary View*). Wythe kept one copy and gave the other to the convention's presiding officer, Edmund Pendleton.

Despite the urgency felt by most Virginians and by Congress, Jefferson also urged postponement of the convention's adoption of a permanent government based on his scruples over the abstract principle that "the people should elect deputies for the special purpose" of writing a constitution—an argument that Patrick Henry, Edmund Pendleton, George Mason, and other Virginians rejected because (as Jefferson admitted in private correspondence) they believed the electorate had clearly expected the convention to declare independence and create a new government. Busy as he was composing the Declaration of Independence for Congress, Jefferson would much rather have been in Williamsburg working on Virginia's new government. His plan arrived, however, just as the delegates were eager to wrap things up and go home after seven weeks of hard work in Williamsburg's summer heat and humidity. Ultimately the convention adopted only Jefferson's vigorous preamble listing two dozen "Acts of Misrule" by George III, a few provisions about landholding, some refinements to the judiciary, and an important statement about western lands and boundaries so carefully crafted that it was adopted entirely without comment or debate. Weeks later, Pendleton teased Jefferson that his preamble had so "exhausted the Subject of complaint" against the king that he doubted whether Congress could address his failures in the Declaration of Independence "without copying."

Jefferson later suggested that his plan was more democratic than Mason's, but on the crucial matter of representation the convention's endorsement of direct popular elections for the upper house went far beyond either man's plan. Jefferson would also complain after his own experience as governor that the legislature overshadowed the executive and judicial branches, but in 1776 his proposed executive "administrator" was far weaker than the office of governor created by the convention. Based on their recent experience with Lord Dunmore and George III, Edmund Randolph reported that the delegates yielded to "their horror of a *powerful* chief magistrate" without anticipating that occasions might arise when only a strong governor, properly restrained by "a republican bridle," could act decisively for the good of the commonwealth.

Only Patrick Henry, Randolph continued, was willing to risk his popularity by advocating "as strenuously as he did for an executive veto on the acts of the two houses of legislation." Arguing from Montesquieu and other political theorists, Henry warned that a governor without the power of veto would become "a mere phantom, unable to defend his office from the usurpation of the legislature." Such a weak executive, Henry argued, would ultimately threaten public order and liberty by degenerating into "a dependent instead of a coordinate branch of power." The revolutionary generation's contempt for executive authority proved impervious to Henry's eloquence on the subject, but many of his fellow delegates "were astonished" by the political courage and intellectual depth of his futile effort to strengthen the executive office in Virginia's new constitution. Although often overshadowed by other aspects of his reputation, Henry consistently argued that weak and ineffective governments often led to tyranny and despotism.

The convention's final adjustments to the new constitution on Friday, June 28, included the introduction of the names *Senate* and *House of Delegates* for the upper and lower houses of the General Assembly. The next day the delegates formally confirmed Virginia's independence by adopting the new Plan of Government for the Commonwealth of Virginia, directing Richard Henry Lee to prepare an ordinance establishing senatorial districts, and setting the annual salaries of the governor at £1,000 and of the advisory council at £1,600 divided proportionally among its members. As a transitional step, all the current members of the convention, unless they were elected to other offices, would continue in October 1776 as members of the new House of Delegates.

ooooo

Turning immediately to the choice of a governor and council, the convention elected Patrick Henry, probably nominated by George Mason, over President Thomas Nelson by a margin of 60 to 45. An uncle of Henry's ally Thomas Nelson, Jr., and a member of the royal Governor's Council since 1749, President Nelson appealed to Pendleton and his circle simply because he was not Patrick Henry—but the sixty-year-old former secretary of the colony and president of the Council also won votes from some delegates who thought he would bring experience and social luster to the new office. Someone, perhaps Henry himself, also cast a single vote for John Page of Rosewell, who was soon thereafter elected to the advisory council and designated as lieutenant governor. Nelson declined a seat on the advisory council "on Account of his age and infirmities," but he later accepted the office of secretary of the commonwealth as a virtual continuation of his old colonial post.

The vast majority of Virginians probably expected Patrick Henry's election as governor in 1776 just as the delegates at the Constitutional Convention of 1787 silently anticipated George Washington's election as president. Pendleton, Landon Carter, and a few gentry leaders may have grumbled in private, but the unspoken logic of Henry's many admirers was simple. Who better to direct their new government than the person "who opened the breath of liberty to America"? as John Adams wrote when he sent Henry a copy of his pamphlet, *Thoughts on Government.* "The author of the first Virginia Resolutions against the Stamp Act . . . will have the Glory with Posterity of beginning and concluding this great Revolution. Happy Virginia, whose Constitution is to be framed by so masterly a Builder."

Closer to home, the officers and men of the First and Second Regiments saluted Henry's election on behalf of "a grateful people" and promised to sustain his "authority as chief magistrate." Citing the new governor's proven record of advocacy for the rights of mankind, his private and public virtue, and his fair-minded commitment to the general good of his country, the men of both regiments proclaimed their delight at having "lived to see the day when freedom and equal right, established by the voice of the people, shall prevail through the land." In his replies to the convention and to his regimental comrades, Governor Henry accepted his "high and unmerited honor" with calls for unity, cooperation, and order that reflected a civic victory more than a dozen years in the making. Acknowledging his leadership in Virginia's earliest protests against king and Parliament, Henry proclaimed that America's war against British tyranny would determine "the lasting Happiness or Misery of a great proportion of the human Species."

Patrick Henry's vision extended well beyond the boundaries of the Old Dominion, whose continued efforts were essential "throughout the extended continent." Protecting the commonwealth "from Anarchy and its attendant Ruin" meant giving "Vigour to our Councils" and energy to the "infantine State." Toward that goal, Governor Henry promised his "unwearied Endeavours to secure the Freedom and Happiness of our common

Country." He closed by asking his civilian colleagues for their "Wisdom and Virtue" and commending Virginia's men-in-arms to "the glorious task of saving by your valour all that is dear to mankind."

Finally, at the culmination of the long struggle for outright independence, Henry's health collapsed, probably from complications of malaria. The new governor was "very ill" when John Page administered the oath of office on Saturday, July 6, 1776—indeed Page worried that if Henry died before the councilors could muster a quorum and choose a president "the Country will be without any head" and "every Thing must be in Confusion." By Tuesday a rumor of Henry's death had spread from the town of Hampton into the Northern Neck, although the governor had actually retired to Scotchtown to regain his health, leaving John Page in charge of the advisory council.

Early in August Alexander Purdie happily reported that Governor Henry was sufficiently recovered from "his late severe indisposition that he walks out daily" at his plantation—and that Lord Dunmore and "his motley band of pirates and renegadoes" at last were fleeing Chesapeake Bay. Although Patrick Henry did not return to Williamsburg until September, during his convalescence at Scotchtown the ailing governor set the commonwealth of Virginia on a new course, especially in regard to religion and the west.

CHAPTER NINETEEN

Visitors at Scotchtown

THE THREE YOUNG MEN who visited Scotchtown in mid-August of 1776 could scarcely have been more different. The Baptist preachers Jeremiah Walker and John Williams, thirty and twenty-nine respectively, arrived about Monday, August 12, bearing "cordial congratulations" to Patrick Henry from the ministers and lay leaders of seventy-four Baptist churches gathering at Thompson's meetinghouse in nearby Louisa County. The next week's arrival was a twenty-three-year-old frontier warrior, George Rogers Clark. Widely respected as a militia captain in Dunmore's War and for his prowess as a frontier warrior, Clark came seeking Governor Henry's support for the defense of Kentucky—and twenty-five barrels of gunpowder. Now that the united colonies had declared independence, Virginia's long debate about how best to fend off British tyranny was over. The pilgrims visiting Scotchtown in August of 1776 reflected a significant shift in the political issues facing the Old Dominion. The new commonwealth and its citizenry were engaged in a war for independence, but Patrick Henry's visitors signaled that religious freedom and the destiny of the west were now issues second in importance only to the military confrontation with Great Britain.

Jeremiah Walker had come a long way from the persecution he had faced exactly three years earlier when Archibald Cary had jailed him in Chesterfield County for preaching without a license. Despite complaints from some congregations that he and Williams expressed "too much concern in political matters," Walker had won the grudging respect both of his gentry inquisitors at the Third Virginia Convention and many Baptist leaders when the convention had adopted Henry's resolution permitting Baptist chaplains to minister to Virginia troops.

The believers who gathered in Louisa were fragmented by a host of theological wrangles and personal rivalries and the often corrosive effects of their commitment to absolute congregational autonomy, but despite their contentious internal disputes most Virginia Baptists *did* agree about the Revolution and the war against Britain—and their admiration of Patrick Henry. Unlike the Old Dominion's small communities of pacifist Moravians, Quakers, and Mennonites, the Baptists readily acknowledged, as Walker and Williams had explained to the convention, "that in some Cases it was [religiously] Lawful to go to War." Virginia Baptists embraced the war for independence as an opportunity to supplant their reputations as religious fanatics and social radicals with new identities as patriotic citizens. Although religious principles set them apart "in respect to Matters of a civil Nature," Walker and Williams reminded the convention that they considered themselves "as Members of the same Community" and were determined to support the "military Resistance against Great Britain." Virginia Baptists used the American Revolution to demonstrate their commitment to the Old Dominion and its secular leadership, according to historian Jewel L. Spangler's perceptive observation, "in much the same way that Presbyterian preacher Samuel Davies had employed the Seven Years' War a generation earlier."

Since about 1774 Regular Baptists throughout Virginia had petitioned for religious liberty and expanded civil rights in exchange for their support for the common cause—calling attention to the Baptists who had already signed up for military service and the "many more [who] were ready to do so." A typical petition from Occoquan Baptist Church of Prince William County, for example, affirmed their standing offer of support for secular authorities "in this most critical conjuncture of public affairs" in exchange for three basic privileges. First was the freedom "to worship God in our own way without interruption." Second was permission to support their own ministers "and no other"—in effect, exemption from the parish duties collected for the Anglican Church. Third, they wanted to "be married, buried, and the like without paying the Parsons of any other denomination." Quid pro quo—"These things granted," declared the Occoquan Baptists, "we will gladly unite with our Brethren of other denominations and to the utmost of our ability promote the common cause of Freedom."

This was the Baptist agenda that Walker and Williams carried to Governor Henry at Scotchtown. On the one hand, their message expressed the Baptists' "unspeakable pleasure" for the election of a governor known for his "constant attachment to the glorious cause of liberty and the rights of conscience." On the other, their message carefully honored the Baptists' traditional detachment from secular institutions by assuring Henry that "*as a religious community*, they had nothing to request from [him]." In sum, while gesturing to the evangelical rank and file about the sanctity of their religious autonomy, Walker and Williams also signaled the Baptists' promise of support *as citizens* in exchange for religious freedom and reform.

Patrick Henry's reply—his first public message as governor—pounced on this opportunity to endorse religious toleration, boost both his own popularity among dissenters, and encourage their support for the war and the new government. Henry promised "to guard the rights of all my fellow citizens from every encroachment." After years of sectarian persecution, he was "happy to find a catholick spirit prevailing in our country." Borrowing a few significant phrases from the Virginia Declaration of Rights, Henry expressed his earnest wish "that Christian charity, forbearance, and love may unite all our different persuasions as brethren who must perish or triumph together." Finally, Henry invited the Baptists to embrace the "just and equal system of liberty adopted by the last Convention" and join in his prayer for the commonwealth of Virginia—"may GOD crown our arms with success."

ooooo

Although the redheaded frontiersman who visited Scotchtown about August 20, 1776, was eager to help Providence answer Henry's prayer for victory, when George Rogers Clark thought about heaven it looked a lot like Kentucky. "A richer and more Beautiful Cuntry has never been seen in America," Clark told a younger brother. "One would think it was a new found Paradise," a Presbyterian minister from Staunton agreed.

Kentucky may have seemed like Eden, even compared to Albemarle and Caroline counties, where Clark was born and reared, but he and his neighbors felt passionately that their corner of paradise belonged to the Old Dominion. Clark and his Virginia compatriots had most recently "fought and bled for it" in Dunmore's War. Without their victory at Point Pleasant "the interior parts of Virginia" would have remained "inaccessible" to settlement. But now the frontier settlers faced a new threat. Usurpers from North Carolina led by Richard Henderson were scheming to steal their territory and create an independent province called Transylvania. To counter that threat, the settlers on the Kentucky River had gathered at Harrodsburg in June, declared themselves "Subjects" of Virginia's revolutionary convention, and sent Clark and John Gabriel Jones to seek admission "as our delegates from this western part of Fincastle County."

Clark's arrival at Scotchtown seemed almost miraculous. After their election in Harrodsburg, he and Jones had raced in nearly constant rain toward Williamsburg—a distance of 540 miles—taking turns riding and walking after Jones's horse gave out. Unwilling to build fires to dry their moccasins lest they expose themselves to Indian attack, Clark and Jones had been immobilized by "Scald Foot" and forced to hide in an abandoned cabin until they healed enough to reach Botetourt County. Learning there that the convention had ended and that Henry was convalescing in Hanover County, Jones headed south to join another battle against the Cherokee while Clark continued north toward Scotchtown.

Virginia's defense of the west during the American Revolution demanded a veil of secrecy that to this day cloaks these initial discussions between Patrick Henry and George Rogers Clark. At the very minimum, Henry wrote the newly created Council of State, which shared his executive authority, urging its members to give Clark the gunpowder he needed—and Clark left Scotchtown with Henry's assurance that the autumn session of the legislature would, as it did, formally welcome his neighbors into the commonwealth as citizens of a new county named Kentucky.

Uncertain of their authority under the new constitution, Lieutenant Governor John Page and the Council of State initially hesitated to comply with Henry's request. When Clark observed "that if a Countrey was not worth protecting it was not worth Claiming," however, Page and his colleagues suddenly discovered their authority and made good on Henry's promise of supplies. That investment brought a significant return over the course of the next five years, as George Rogers Clark devoted his remarkable talents to the enforcement of Virginia's claim to Kentucky and the Old Northwest—the modern states of Ohio, Indiana, Illinois, Michigan, and Wisconsin.

When Clark began to explain Richard Henderson's threats to the Kentucky settlements, he may not have known that Patrick Henry was well aware of the Transylvania Company and its aspirations. Henderson's company was only the most recent of many speculative schemes since 1768, when the Treaty of Fort Stanwix altered British Indian policy by allowing groups of private investors to purchase western land directly from any Native American tribe willing to claim ownership and sell the title—as distinct from earlier speculative ventures (such as Virginia's Ohio Company and Loyal Company) that had aimed at securing large grants of western land from the crown. As recently as 1774 Henry had himself conferred with William Byrd III, John Page, and William Christian about a private purchase from the Cherokee of land on the Clinch, Holston, and Powell Rivers near the Virginia-Tennessee line west of modern Bristol. "Some of the Indian chiefs" were willing to negotiate a deal, their on-site agent reported, but with the collapse of royal government the prospective investors abandoned the project. Aside from that inquiry in 1774, as Henry later declared in a sworn deposition, he had no other involvement with any purchases of Indian lands.

Later in 1774, however, Patrick Henry not only met Richard Henderson at the First Continental Congress in Philadelphia but declined his repeated invitations to invest in the Transylvania Company. Henry cited several reasons for his change of heart about "Indian purchases," but the main one was the prospect of independence. Like George Mason, George Washington, and other speculators who long had jockeyed for advantage with imperial officials, Henry was appalled when rival entrepreneurs from other colonies began lobbying American congressmen about backcountry territory claimed by Virginia. Washington expressed grave suspicions about Henderson, and in the face of his activities Mason worried about Virginia's "inexcusable" neglect of its western land claims. Henry decided that it was "improper" for a member of Congress to hold any interest in companies whose fates "he might decide as a Judge."

Despite Mason's worries, Virginia leaders promptly closed ranks behind their belief that independence entirely undermined the legitimacy of private treaties aimed at the purchase of land from Native tribes. When Henderson repeatedly pressed Henry to join his company, Henry finally declared that Kentucky belonged to "the People of Virginia" by virtue of "their Charter and the Blood and Treasure they expended on that account." The commonwealth of Virginia, Henry contended, was the proper claimant for "the Sovereignty and Right of . . . the soil of America." Virginians preferred not to mention the possibility that independence might transfer ownership of the west from Great Britain directly to Congress.

ooooo

With Governor Henry's encouragement, George Rogers Clark became
an able and enthusiastic champion of Virginia's territorial interests in
the west. Equally important, however, were the political leaders who supported the commonwealth's territorial claims with legal expertise, legislative experience, and tactical savvy. The achievements of Clark and his
frontier warriors during the Revolution might easily have suffered the fate
of other soldiers whose gains in the field were lost by inept diplomats or
vacillating politicians. Despite their divergent opinions on many other issues, Virginians agreed upon the interrelated issues of state sovereignty,
boundaries, and western lands. With regard to land companies, rival colonies or states, and the crown or the Congress, Virginia policy was as solid
as the bedrock at the falls of the Ohio: others had no authority in the
west. Western settlers were subject to Virginia's sovereignty and protection. Only Virginia could authorize partitions of its territory.

Virginians had voiced their first opposition to private land companies in October 1770, days after the death of Governor Botetourt, when
the acting governor and Council defended the colony's control of western land against the Walpole Company of Philadelphia and London,
whose projected Vandalia colony would have supplanted Virginia's control
over nearly all the territory of modern West Virginia and most of eastern Kentucky. Prominent among the Walpole partners were Benjamin
Franklin and the former colonial administrator John Pownall, whose exaggerated allegations of misconduct triggered Virginia's defense. Although
the Vandalia project failed, the dispute gave birth to a comprehensive
report—"A Vindication of Virginia's Claim Against the Proposed Colony
of Vandalia"—documenting the colony's western claims with a solid chain
of title that extended back to the 1609 charter of the Virginia Company—
the same "Charter" that Patrick Henry had cited against the Stamp Act
and thrown in the face of Richard Henderson.

Just four days after Henry's Liberty or Death speech, a second frontier
development had occurred in the heated debate over military preparedness at the Second Virginia Convention. Responding to a proclamation
by Lord Dunmore and intimations of Richard Henderson's negotiations
with the Cherokee, Peyton Randolph had appointed a seemingly innocuous five-man committee to examine "the established usage of granting

lands within this colony" and report back to the next convention or Assembly. The five men chosen to safeguard Virginia's land claims and sovereignty could scarcely have been more powerful. Patrick Henry, Richard
Bland, Thomas Jefferson, Robert Carter Nicholas, and Edmund Pendleton may have disagreed about tactics of resistance, but when they looked
to the west, Virginia leaders sang the praises of their historic charters and
eventually imposed their vision for the west upon the new republic.

If George Rogers Clark had any lingering doubt about Virginia's commitment to Kentucky, Governor Henry had only to show him the penul-
timate paragraph of the new constitution—added just weeks earlier while
Clark and Jones were scrambling through the rainy wilderness toward the
Cumberland Gap. Prompted in part by a lobbyist who came to Congress
advocating statehood for the Transylvania project, Thomas Jefferson had
so perfectly summarized Virginia's western policy in the draft constitution
he proposed to the convention that it had adopted his suggestions without
changes, comment, or debate.

Starting with the boundaries set forth in 1609, Virginia rather imperi-
ously confirmed the legitimate existence of Pennsylvania, Maryland, and
the Carolinas as usurpations of Virginia territory that nevertheless had
been "ceded, released, and forever confirmed to the People of those Colonies." It acknowledged the Mississippi River as Virginia's western boundary according to the treaty of 1763 at the end of the French and Indian
War. Third, the constitution stipulated that only the legislature of Virginia
could create territories and establish state governments westward of the
Allegheny Mountains. Finally, in a direct repudiation of the private companies, the new constitution prohibited the purchase of land from "the *Indian* Natives" except "on behalf of the Publick, by authority of the General
Assembly." So popular was this final declaration against the likes of Richard Henderson that the convention adopted it both as a freestanding resolution on June 24 and as a clause in the constitution five days later. If an
independent republic was unable to maintain the integrity of its boundaries and territory, how could it possibly protect the liberty and property of
its citizens?

During Henry's first year as governor, the General Assembly made extensive provisions for "the Infancy of the Government" in the west. In October 1776 it divided the district of West Augusta, north of the Ohio River,
into three counties. Then it complied with local petitions to split Pittsyl-

vania and Cumberland counties by creating Henry and Powhatan counties in the usual fashion—one named for the governor and the other for
the seventeenth-century Indian chieftain. Finally, despite pressures from
Richard Henderson, the Assembly made good on Henry's assurances to
Clark by carving Fincastle County into Montgomery and Washington
counties in southwestern Virginia and creating Kentucky County beyond
the mountains and south of the Ohio River.

oooooo

Patrick Henry and his colleagues recognized that Virginia's vast western
territories would eventually need to be divided into smaller states. Conventional wisdom held that republican governments were not well suited
for large territories—an outlook bolstered both by the widespread influence of Montesquieu's political theories and their direct experience dividing parishes and counties in response to population growth. Eventually, as
Edmund Pendleton reminded Virginia's congressional delegation in July
1776, any sustained effort to govern the Ohio Valley from Williamsburg
would prove "exceedingly inconvenient."

Nevertheless, the one point upon which all politically active Virginians
agreed was that they alone—without meddling from the other states or
from Congress—should determine the future of their commonwealth and
its western lands. On this point, outspoken men like Henry and Jefferson stood in agreement with moderate souls like Edmund Pendleton and
deeply conservative planters such as Carter Braxton. The constitutional
suggestions in Braxton's *Address to the Convention* had prompted Henry
and his friends to doubt his loyalty to Whig principles—but most everyone concurred with his suggestion that Virginia sell its western lands "and
apply the monies to the payment of the vast burden of taxes we shall incur
by this war." And they were alarmed by his report from Philadelphia of
talk in Congress about "seizing all unappropriated lands for the use of the
Continent."

The target of Braxton's wrath was the suggestion in John Adams's
Thoughts on Government that the authority of Congress should extend to
"the unappropriated lands of the Crown, as they used to be called." More
ominous, however, were Benjamin Franklin's and John Dickinson's drafts
for a confederation of the thirteen colonies. Virginians were already wary
of Franklin's involvement with the Walpole Company and its Vandalia

project. Dickinson's draft posed the greater threat. Born in Maryland and politically active in Pennsylvania until he returned to Delaware, the celebrated author of the Federal Farmer essays was associated with two of the five so-called landless states (whose boundaries denied them any claims to western territory).

Dickinson's plan would have given Congress authority to abridge the boundaries of the landed states (whose colonial charters extended to the Pacific or the Mississippi), redraw any boundaries that seemed vague, and create new states. Virginians objected vehemently, while Maryland became the champion of the landless states and refused to ratify the Articles of Confederation until the matter was resolved. Henry and his Virginia colleagues recognized that the dispute also invoked larger constitutional issues. If Congress could deny Virginia "the disposition of our Lands," Edmund Pendleton wrote, the stipulation that each state retained "the Sole Power of regulating their internal concerns will have no force."

The dispute between the states over western lands that began in 1776 raised constitutional debates over provincial and central authority that shaped American politics for the rest of the century. A denunciation of the Vandalia Company adopted by the General Assembly in 1779 warned against "a most dangerous precedent" if Congress were allowed to meddle in "the internal policy, civil regulations, and municipal laws of this or any other state." Such a violation of public faith would subvert the sovereignty of the states and "establish in congress a power which in process of time must degenerate into intolerable despotism." When an agent for the new Indiana Company (corporate successor to the Walpole Company) suggested that Congress might adjudicate his investors' dispute with Virginia, James Madison and William Grayson replied that Virginia would never countenance "an appeal from its own decisions to a *foreign tribunal*"!

Their long confrontation with Great Britain had taught Henry and his colleagues to equate their interests with the greater good of all the colonies. Again and again in 1774 and 1775 the people of Virginia, through their county committees, had acknowledged the Congress as an embodiment of American sovereignty. Virginia, a Maryland congressman observed, was "ever desirous of taking the lead in this great Contest" and "enjoyed a secret pride in having laid the corner stone of a confederated world." Although the Old Dominion's "fixt determination against British Tyranny" held firm until the war was won, however, Henry and other Virginia leaders were beginning to see that independence exposed old rivalries and created new tensions between the states. "One thing is certain" in Congress, Richard Henry Lee advised Governor Henry early in 1777, that "Virginia has many enemies arising from Jealousy and envy of her wisdom, vigor, and extent of Territory."

When Congress sent the "Articles of Confederation and Perpetual Union" to the states for ratification in November 1777, Virginia was ready to adopt the plan immediately. The so-called landed states (those with claims to western territory) had successfully replaced Dickinson's clauses with a guarantee that no state could be deprived of territory for the benefit of the United States. In Annapolis, however, the Articles were virtually dead on arrival. The Maryland legislature's immediate reaction was that the Confederation must have authority to "fix the western limits of those states that claim to the Mississippi or South Sea" and to treat western lands as "a common estate . . . on terms beneficial to all the United States."

"The bare mentioning of the Subject rouses Virginia," a Maryland congressman observed. "Conscious of her own importance, she views her vast Dominion with the surest expectations of holding it unimpaired." Congress rejected Maryland's demand on June 23, 1778, by a vote of seven states to five (with North Carolina absent). Not until February 1781, threatened by a British invasion in the Chesapeake and prodded by a suggestion from the Chevalier de La Luzerne that ratification would strengthen America's military alliance with France, did the Maryland legislature break its deadlock with Virginia. Even so Maryland's ratification of the Articles of Confederation came with the stipulation that "this state doth not relinquish . . . any right or interest she hath with the other United or Confederated States to the back country."

Maryland's willingness to register its objections with Congress and rely "on the justice of the several states" implicitly recognized Virginia's declared intention of ceding its claims north of the Ohio River while retaining control and possession of Kentucky to the south. Virginia had announced that possibility in its constitution of 1776. Two years later Governor Henry and Congressman Richard Henry Lee suggested that Virginia make the Ohio River its northwestern boundary and cede "the Country beyond," thereby avoiding the difficulty and expense of sustaining "republican laws and government . . . so far from the seat of Government"—and the Assembly endorsed the idea in its denunciation of the Indiana Company in 1779.

With Patrick Henry, Richard Henry Lee, Thomas Jefferson, and George Mason all in agreement, it came as no surprise that on January 2, 1781, the General Assembly of Virginia formally offered Congress all the territory north of the Ohio River, which came to be known as the Old Northwest. Only one of the conditions that Virginia placed on its cession was controversial—a stipulation that Congress deny recognition of private purchases of Indian lands. A last-ditch effort by the land companies—including generous offers of Indiana Company stock to sitting congressmen and a pamphlet with the audacious title *Public Good* for which Thomas Paine accepted three hundred shares—delayed congressional acceptance of Virginia's donation for nearly three years. The best safeguard for the virtue of Congress, James Madison wrote from Philadelphia, was to deny his colleagues the power to "gratify the avidity of the land mongers."

Congress finally accepted the Virginia cession on September 13, 1783—ten days after British and American diplomats in Paris signed the treaty that ended the war for independence. Both houses of the General Assembly confirmed the terms of the gift in December. The Old Dominion's congressional delegation—Samuel Hardy, Thomas Jefferson, Arthur Lee, and James Monroe—signed the deed conveying the Old Northwest to the nation on March 1, 1784. That same day, Congressman Thomas Jefferson introduced a committee proposal that became the famous Ordinance of 1784, establishing the principle that new states would enter the Confederation as independent entities equal to the original thirteen—though Congress rejected the committee's provision for barring slavery north of the Ohio River after 1800. In retrospect, Virginia's cession of the Old Northwest proved to be the high-water mark for the Old Dominion's unanimous and enthusiastic commitment to Congress and the new nation—a commitment rooted in the colony's long-standing strategy of courting intercolonial unity in the struggle against George III and Parliament.

ooooo

While Virginians wrestled with Congress and the other states over legal claims to the Old Northwest, Patrick Henry and George Rogers Clark were deeply engaged in protecting the west from British conquest. Beginning in January 1778, Henry supported Clark and his frontiersmen as the American Revolution's equivalent of modern special forces—small groups of experienced hunters capable of moving rapidly over impossibly long and often flooded expanses of the Illinois Country from camps near modern-day Paducah, Kentucky, to defeat British troops and their Native American allies along the Wabash, Illinois, and Ohio Rivers. Area inhabitants generally welcomed Clark and his men once they learned that France had joined the war against Great Britain in 1778. Although Clark's forces were few and stretched too thin for a successful attack against Detroit, their presence intimidated dozens of Native tribes into neutrality, prevented the British from capturing the Old Northwest, and reinforced Virginia's claims against those of rival states.

Important as the western lands were themselves, Patrick Henry's strategic vision subordinated Clark's mission to the safety of Virginia's eastern settlements. The "one great Good expected from holding Illinois," Governor Henry and his Council had reminded Clark and his compatriots, was "to overawe the Indians from warring on our settlements on this side of the Ohio." Announcing to Congress and the public the success of Clark's previously secret mission, Henry pointed to promises of peaceable conduct from the Delaware, Fox, Mascouten, Miami, Ottawa, Peoria, Piankashaw, Potowatami, Sauk, Wabash, Winnebago, and "some of the Shawanese Chiefs." George Rogers Clark and his frontiersmen had given Virginia command of its newly created county of Illinois—extending from the Ohio River to the Mississippi and the Great Lakes—for the remainder of the war.

By January 1781, when George Rogers Clark's intended second expedition against Detroit departed from Richmond, few Virginians still shared his or Jefferson's enthusiasm for the mission. With Cornwallis's army moving through the Carolinas toward the Old Dominion, Virginians east of the mountains were skeptical about diverting forces toward the Great Lakes. Governor Jefferson had given Clark the rank of brigadier general for his Virginia regiment and secured nominal cooperation from George Washington, who encouraged the Continental commander at Pittsburgh to assist the expedition. But the prospect of the Continental Army's participation in Clark's military adventure did not sit well with influential Virginia leaders, Patrick Henry prominently among them, who worried that it could undermine Virginia's territorial claims against Congress, land companies, and the landless states. Clark's potential recruits in Virginia's frontier counties also felt less urgency about fighting for territory claimed by Pennsylvania and likely to be given up by Virginia. The necessity of secrecy in Clark's earlier recruitment efforts had also eroded his credibility. Prospective recruits had grown wary of Clark's bait-and-switch recruiting tactic of signing up men for an ostensibly local campaign that turned out to have secret objectives hundreds of miles away (and for which no one until 1791 actually saw the delivery of promised grants of land).

With British troops repeatedly invading Virginia in 1781, Henry pushed a resolution through the Assembly in June recommending that Governor Jefferson "put a stop to the Expedition lately ordered against Detroit" and apply its men and matériel to coastal needs. Jefferson ignored the advice and let Clark continue westward, but as his expedition rambled from Wheeling to Louisville, Clark was ultimately forced to abandon his plans to attack Detroit. "My chain appears to have run out," Clark confessed early in October to Jefferson's successor, Governor Thomas Nelson, Jr., a few days before Cornwallis surrendered at Yorktown.

ooooo

The Virginia statute creating the county of Illinois stipulated that its inhabitants, many of whom were French- or Spanish-speaking Roman Catholics, would enjoy "their own religion . . . together with all their civil rights and property" upon taking an oath of allegiance to the commonwealth. Virginia's commitment to religious toleration had come a long way since Jeremiah Walker and John Williams called upon Patrick Henry at Scotchtown in August 1776. Early that autumn, the Baptists had led a petition campaign in which thousands of Virginians agitated for religious reform. Nearly 10 percent of the electorate signed the famous tenthousand-name petition, presented to the House of Delegates in October 1776, calling for "Equal Liberty!" and an end to tax support for the established church.

Faced with the formidable task of recruiting men and supplies for Washington's army, Governor Henry and the commonwealth struck a deal with the Baptists. In exchange for religious toleration—including freedom of worship, exemption from parish duties supporting the Anglican

Church, and permission for Baptist clergy to conduct marriages and serve as military chaplains—Virginia Baptists volunteered in great numbers to fight for "the common cause of Freedom."

In December the Virginia legislature declared "all dissenters, of whatever denomination . . . totally free and exempt from all levies, taxes, and impositions" for the support of the Anglican Church and its ministers. Citing the great variety of opinions about how Virginians should support their churches, however, legislators deferred the question of public support for religion to some "future assembly." The choice between "a general assessment" for religion or "voluntary contributions . . . of different persuasions and denominations" would have to wait until "the opinions of the country in general may be better known."

Three years later—as the Anglican Church continued to suffer from attrition among its clergy and the wartime impediments to their replacement—Virginians pushed further. In October 1779 the legislature cut all tax support "heretofore given to the clergy of the church of England" while carefully upholding the parish vestries' governmental responsibilities for the care of orphans and the poor. A year later, with Patrick Henry out of the governorship and back in the House of Delegates representing the newly formed county that bore his surname, the legislature ended the Anglican marriage monopoly by making all clergy eligible for licenses to "celebrate the rites of matrimony" for a maximum fee of twenty-five pounds of tobacco. Under pressure from religious dissenters whose support was critical for the war effort, Virginians replaced the Anglican system of 1748–1749 that had stabilized gentry control of the established church after the death of Commissary James Blair with a policy of virtually complete religious toleration.

CHAPTER TWENTY

A War to Win

IMPORTANT AS RELIGION and the west may have been, Patrick Henry's first priority as governor was to win the war for independence—for which his contributions included money, men, matériel—and political support for Congress and General Washington. Colleagues in politics since the 1760s, Patrick Henry and George Washington had risked their lives and fortunes in opposition to king and Parliament. Now, working together in the recruitment of troops and raising of provisions for the common cause, the governor and the general built a solid relationship that lasted for the rest of their lives. But it was Henry's loyal support in the so-called Conway Cabal of 1777–1778, an alleged plot to dismiss Washington as commander in chief, that cemented a mutual trust between the two patriots that endured their profound disagreement when Washington favored and Henry opposed ratification of the Constitution ten years later.

The winter of 1777–1778 found both General Washington and Governor Henry deeply engaged in the war for independence. In Williamsburg, Henry was spearheading Virginia's response to the "alarming accounts" of the plight of Washington's army, which they feared must either "Starve, Dissolve or Disperse." On January 14 the Council of State endorsed Henry's plan to dispatch an agent "to buy up all the Pork Beef and Bacon that can be procured, and . . . Waggons for conveying such Salt and other Necessaries as his Excellency may think can best be supplied from hence." That same day Henry also dispatched a messenger to New Orleans to carry money and supplies back upriver from the Spanish port in support of George Rogers Clark's defense of the Ohio Country. Six days later he was writing Virginia's congressional delegation both to summarize the commonwealth's recent "Large Loans of Flour, Meat, and Salt" and urge a thorough reform of the "mismanagement" of the commissary department. While Virginia "abounds with the provisions for which the Army is said to be almost starving," Henry wrote, drastic improvements were necessary in "the Conduct of those whose business it was to forward [supplies] to the Army."

While Henry and his colleagues were engaged in mitigating the shortages of food, shoes, blankets, and clothing that plagued Washington's troops during their winter encampment at Valley Forge, the Virginians were unaware of a tempest festering among a few of America's top generals. Throughout the previous summer, a British expedition led by John Burgoyne had begun moving south from Canada aiming to sever the American states along the Lake Champlain–Hudson River axis, while William Howe and the main British army prepared to attack Philadelphia. Washington had been forced to surrender the City of Brotherly Love in late September and then retreat into winter quarters, while late in October his subordinate, General Horatio Gates, had accepted the surrender of Burgoyne's entire army at Saratoga, New York—a victory that helped bring France into open support of the American cause and thereby change the course of the war.

Inevitably the contrast between Washington's apparent failures and Gates's evident success aroused comment among politicians that shocked the Marquis de Lafayette. "Stupid men who without knowing a single word about war," he informed Washington, "make ridiculous comparisons ... without thinking of the different circumstances." More immediately dangerous than the intemperate comments of a few congressmen, however, was the prospect of serious conflict within the officer corps of the Continental Army—where jealousies were already rife after Congress promoted a few men (notably the vain and ambitious Irish-born Frenchman Thomas Conway) over other generals with equal or better records and more seniority.

Most careful scholars agree that amid all the rumors, letters, and misunderstandings associated with the alleged plot to replace Washington with Gates, the so-called cabal consisted principally of several genuinely incendiary letters written by General Conway, a flurry of secondhand accounts of defamatory remarks about Washington being "out-generaled" by William Howe in the Philadelphia campaign, and one bogus quotation attributed to Conway by Colonel James Wilkinson in the infancy of the latter's long career as a conspirator: "Heaven has determined to save your

Country," Conway reportedly told Gates, "or a weak General [i.e., Washington] and bad Councellors would have ruined it."

By mid-January 1778 rumors of these disputes were dissipating in the echo chambers of Congress, where president of the Congress Henry Laurens assured Lafayette that "our brave and virtuous General may rest assured that he is out of the reach of his enemies, if he has an enemy . . . nor do I ever hear his military abilities questioned but comparatively." Aside from the obvious contrast between Washington's disappointments in Pennsylvania and Gates's good fortune at Saratoga, Laurens believed that everyone in Congress retained confidence in Washington's virtue, bravery, and leadership. On the very day that President Laurens offered Lafayette these assurances about Washington, however, the Philadelphia physician Benjamin Rush posted a letter from York, Pennsylvania, where Congress was meeting, that breathed new life into the alleged conspiracy by blaming Washington for the deplorable condition of American military hospitals.

Henry had won Rush's admiration in Philadelphia in 1774. Although Rush never heard him speak in public, he remembered Henry as "a zealous advocate of the claims of his country" whose "private opinions upon men and things shewed a deep and correct knowledge of human nature." Two years later, Rush had closed a letter congratulating Henry upon his election as governor with his hope that when Henry had "an idle minute it will give me pleasure to hear that you still remember your Old friend and humble Servant, B. Rush." While Henry probably remembered meeting Rush, who had inoculated him against smallpox during the First Continental Congress and conversed with him on several occasions, Henry's recollection of the outspoken doctor did not include any familiarity with Rush's handwriting.

Early in February an unsigned letter dated January 12 addressed to "His Excellency Patrick Henry Esqr: Governor of Virginia" arrived from York, Pennsylvania, where Congress had convened after the British took Philadelphia. Governor Henry may have been puzzled when he opened the letter, but its mysterious author was not trying to cloak his identity. Benjamin Rush expected Henry to remember him and recognize his handwriting. The risk of wartime correspondence being intercepted by the British had prompted many American patriots to withhold their signatures on the assumption that recipients would recognize their identities from their handwriting and from references to shared experiences.

Rush's unsigned letter to Henry opened with clues about his identity: "The common danger of our country first brought you and me together. I recollect with pleasure the influence of your conversation and eloquence upon the opinions of this country in the beginning of the present controversy. You first taught us to shake off our idolatrous attachment to royalty, and to oppose its incroachments upon our liberties with our very lives. By these means you saved us from ruin. . . ."

Then Rush lamented the nation's plight and focused his attack on Washington: "Is our case desperate?" he asked. "By no means. . . . The northern army [under Gates] has shown us what Americans are capable of doing with a GENERAL at their head. . . . A Gates, a Lee, or a Conway would in a few weeks render them an irresistable body of men." Rush then called for Washington's dismissal by quoting Conway's remark that "A great and good God hath desired America to be free, or the G[eneral] and weak counselors would have ruined her long ago."

"You may rest assured of *each* of the facts related in this letter," Rush concluded. "The author of it is one of your Philadelphia friends. A hint of his name if found out by the hand writing, must not be mentioned. . . . Even the letter *must* be thrown in the fire. But some of its contents ought to be made public in order to awaken, enlighten, and alarm our country. I rely upon your prudence . . . with my usual attachment to *you* and to our beloved independence."

Rush had written Henry under the impression, which proved erroneous, that "there is a rupture between General Gates and General Washington" and that Congress was "determined to support the authority and influence of Gates and Conway." Once they had taken over, Rush informed his wife, he expected they would implement his remedies for the hospitals through "a reformation of every department of the army."

Why Rush chose to lobby Henry about these matters remains a puzzle. He seems to have entirely forgotten about the "deep and correct knowledge of human nature" he had discerned in Henry when they first met. Henry detested conspiratorial subterfuge. Without hesitation, Henry forwarded Rush's unsigned letter directly to Washington on February 20, 1778, along with a summary of everything he knew about it. "Dear Sir," Henry wrote, "you will no doubt be surprised at seeing the inclosed letter, in which the encomiums bestowed on me are as undeserved as the censures aimed at you are unjust. I am sorry there should be one man who counts himself my friend who is not yours.

"The writer of it may be too insignificant to deserve any notice," Henry continued. "But there may possibly be some scheme or party forming to your prejudice," Henry concluded, and "I really think your personal welfare and the happiness of America are intimately connected." Although Henry may not have recognized Rush's handwriting, it was immediately obvious to Washington, who had recently read the doctor's scathing report on the state of the American hospital corps.

A few weeks later Henry wrote Washington again, to make sure that the earlier letter had not gone astray and to report that the Virginia Assembly had finally authorized providing "Clothes etc." for Washington's Virginia troops. "Your friendship, Sir, in transmitting me the anonymous letter," Washington replied, "lays me under the more grateful obligations . . . for the very polite and delicate terms in which you have been pleased to communicate the matter. I have ever been happy in supposing that I had a place in your esteem, and the proof you have afforded upon this occasion makes me peculiarly so." The next day Washington wrote again to thank Henry for his friendship. "The anonymous letter with which you were pleased to favor me was written by Dr. Rush" and it reflected "the intrigues of a faction" whose machinations Washington had been wary of bringing to public attention, lest it expose "our internal dissentions," but now had "recoiled most sensibly upon themselves."

As events played out, Washington not only survived his critics but saw his command of the army strengthened by the episode. Benjamin Rush had hitched his wagon to a falling star. Conway resigned and returned to France. Rush resigned from the hospital corps three weeks after posting his letter to Henry and later referred to his conduct as "indiscreet zeal." Gates joined with Henry Laurens in denouncing Conway as "guilty of the blackest hypocricy" and rebuilding their working relationships with Washington. And from this time forward Patrick Henry enjoyed the hearty gratitude and enduring trust of George Washington.

Sixteen years after Thomas Conway had returned to France, President George Washington testified to his lifelong regard for Patrick Henry in a letter to his former comrade in arms Light-Horse Harry Lee. "On the question of the Constitution Mr. Henry and myself, it is well known, have been of different opinions," the president observed in 1794, "but personally I have always respected and esteemed him; nay more, I have conceived myself under obligations to him for the friendly manner in which he transmitted to me some insidious anonymous writings that were sent to him in the close of the year 1777 with a view to embark him in the opposition that was forming against me at that time." Five years later, a few weeks after Henry's death, Washington pointed back to these events as "the most unequivocal proof" of the fact that despite the efforts of scoundrels who poisoned the private fountains of friendship and sowed seeds of distrust among honorable men, he knew that his old friend Patrick Henry "was not to be worked upon by Intriguers."

ooooo

Patrick Henry had favored ending the importation of slaves since the 1760s, but he was serving as governor in 1777 and cannot claim the honor of being the "*Mr. Henry* [who] presented to the House [of Delegates] . . . a bill *To prohibit the importation of slaves*" on Saturday, November 22. The credit for introducing Virginia's first successful ban on slave importation, which took effect in 1778, belonged to one James Henry, a delegate from Accomack County on the Eastern Shore, speaking for a committee that represented all corners of the commonwealth—Philip Alexander, George Mason's colleague from Fairfax County on the Potomac River; Bolling Starke, of Dinwiddie County near Petersburg; and the former Quaker Isaac Zane, of Frederick County, on the frontier near Winchester. Despite its limitations (and a cluster of adjustments during the following decade) scholars agree that Virginia's 1778 anti-importation law, which imposed a stiff penalty of £1,000 for each violation, did effectively end the slave trade into the commonwealth.

Governor Henry was not personally responsible for the 1778 anti-importation law (or a simultaneous but unsuccessful attempt to make it easier for slaveholders to manumit individual slaves), but he was deeply engaged with the Virginia Quakers, led by his old friend Robert Pleasants, who were lobbying hard for these antislavery measures. Only five official manumissions—sanctioned by the legislature in accord with a fifty-year-old colonial law—occurred between 1776 and 1782, when Henry came back into the legislature and helped adopt the less restrictive provisions for Virginia's landmark manumission statute. During those six years, however, Pleasants and other Quakers freed several hundred slaves in wills and private deeds of manumission that some of their neighbors regarded as illegal.

In addition to his religious and humanitarian motives, Pleasants sought to demonstrate that manumissions could be structured to preserve community safety and even contribute to economic growth. With legal advice and support from Governor Henry, Pleasants in 1777 freed dozens of his own slaves and set them up with land and farming equipment adjacent to his plantation at Curles, in the fertile tidal flats of the James River just downstream from Richmond. To encourage industrious habits and "remove every inducement to theft and dishonesty," Pleasants supplemented the fruits of their labor by extending his material support for his former slaves through their first year of freedom. Despite his good intentions, Pleasants soon discovered that some of his neighbors ("busie medling people," he called them) aimed to revive an "unjust and unreasonable" colonial law empowering church wardens to take possession of informally manumitted slaves and sell them back into slavery—a threat that apparently dissipated in light of concurring legal support from Governor Henry and the local commonwealth's attorney.

During Henry's first term as governor, Pleasants and his Quaker colleague Edward Stabler lobbied him both to acknowledge that the state's existing restrictions upon manumission contradicted the Virginia Declaration of Rights and to contemplate plans for gradual emancipation. The Quakers felt the time for change was overdue, as Virginians grew increasingly aware "of the injustice of holding our fellow men in Bondage." They felt it was impossible to justify slavery without denying the principles of the Revolution, for if acts of political tyranny by "the mother Country can justify the expense of so much Blood and Treasure," Pleasants and Stabler asked Governor Henry, who owned more than seventy slaves himself, "how can we impose . . . absolute slavery on others?"

As Pleasants recounted a visit with Governor Henry in 1777 to an abolitionist uncle in Philadelphia, the governor welcomed them "very kindly" and expressed optimism about the prospects of liberalizing the manumission law in the next Assembly session. In the meantime, "as a bar against any unjust attempts" by meddlesome neighbors, Henry advised Pleasants to keep those he had freed on his own land. He also assured his Quaker visitors that George Wythe, Thomas Jefferson, and a select legislative committee engaged in a wholesale revision of the state's legal code were drafting legislation for the manumission of slaves (as well as the disestablishment of the Episcopal clergy) that Henry expected to be "passed into a law." It took longer than he anticipated, but Henry did support the easing of restrictions on private manumissions adopted by the legislature in 1782.

Henry and his colleagues were less receptive to the Quakers' suggestions for the gradual abolition of slavery. When they met with him in the spring of 1777, Pleasants and Stabler urged Henry to embrace their plan for "a general freedom without the dangers and inconveniences which some apprehend from a present [i.e., immediate] total abolition of slavery." They proposed setting a date after which "all children of slaves to be born in future" would become "absolutely free at the usual ages of 18 and 21"—an approach that several northern states successfully adopted. A policy of gradual emancipation, Pleasants and Stabler assured Henry, would make freedmen "better fitted for the enjoyment of [freedom] than many now are," protect the commonwealth from "intestine Enemies and convulsions" (which detractors linked to the idea of immediate abolition), and increase the proportion of residents "interested in [the community's] peace and prosperity"—all simply by extending to Virginia slaves "that justice . . . which we contend for and claim as the unalterable birthright of every man."

Henry responded that he was "clearly convinced of the justice of such an Act" and that he even thought some delegates "who had great influence in the Assembly were for abolishing Slavery altogether." Nevertheless, Henry also "intimated" that so long as the nation was engaged in its desperate war against Great Britain any attempt to introduce a plan for gradual emancipation was premature—or, as Pleasants summarized Henry's opinion, "not . . . at this time consistent with common prudence or the real advantage of that people." Evasive as it may seem, Henry's reluctance to push faster and further against slavery still reflected the tension between action and acquiescence that he had expressed in 1773. Slavery remained evil and abhorrent. Now that Virginia prohibited further importation of slaves and authorized private manumissions, however, Henry's views no longer seemed as progressive as they had in 1773. His bromide about treating slavery's "unhappy victims" with benevolence (regardless of its apparent sincerity) sounded increasingly like an excuse for doing nothing.

ooooo

The war for independence took a drastic turn toward the south on Saturday, May 8, 1779, just three weeks before the end of Patrick Henry's third one-year term as governor, when twenty-eight British warships entered the Virginia Capes and anchored near Norfolk. Just a few weeks earlier their energetic and capable commander, Commodore Sir George Collier, had taken charge of the naval forces assigned to North America and persuaded his commander in chief, General Sir Henry Clinton, to approve a surprise raid on Virginia. Collier regarded Virginia as "the province which of all others gives sinews to the rebellion," and his immediate objectives were precise—a "desultory expedition" aimed principally at disrupting the dispatch of two thousand troops that Virginia was sending to reinforce Washington's army in New York. His secondary objective was to raid Virginia's garrison, shipyards, and warehouses at Portsmouth, a major entrepôt for American trade with France and the West Indies.

From the capitol in Williamsburg, Governor Henry dispatched an express rider to Philadelphia to apprise Congress of Virginia's situation, knowing full well that "Success . . . will be precarious in the present Situation of Things." Henry's tiny shallow-draft navy, despite its respectable record of operations in the Old Dominion's extensive coastal waters, was no match for a fleet that comprised the sixty-four-gun HMS *Raisonable*, the forty-four-gun *Rainbow*, the sloops *Otter, Diligent,* and *Haerlem*, the galley *Cornwallis*, twenty-two transports carrying two thousand marines, and several private ships-of-war. Fort Nelson, which guarded Portsmouth, was well built, with fourteen-foot parapets and forty-eight cannon, but its garrison, depleted by smallpox, numbered fewer than a hundred troops. Forced to abandon the fort on May 11, Major Thomas Mathews ordered his patriot troops to destroy a nearly finished twenty-eight-gun warship and two French merchantmen loaded with more than a thousand hogsheads of tobacco. The invaders then captured six partially completed vessels, including two frigates commissioned by Congress, and burned all the seasoned timber, buildings, and storehouses they found at what Collier described as "the finest [navy] yard on this continent." Advancing inland to the town of Suffolk, the British burned the village and its warehouses full of tobacco, salt, and naval stores, and three thousand barrels of pork.

"Last Night brought me the fatal account of Portsmouth being in possession of the enemy," Henry informed Congress on May 12. "Their force was too great to be resisted, and therefore the Fort was evacuated— Goods and Merchandize however of very great value fell into the Enemy's Hands." With Collier's warships controlling the waterways between Williamsburg and Portsmouth, the governor found it difficult to get timely and reliable intelligence about the enemy's forces and movements. Fully two weeks after the invasion, Henry was still only "*pretty certain* that the Land Forces are commanded by General Matthews [*sic*] and the Fleet by Sir George Collier."

Despite these uncertainties, Henry reacted to news of the invasion by alerting Congress on May 11 and the governor of Maryland on the 12th. He also began calling out the militia in central Virginia. Although he and his Council did not announce a full statewide mobilization until May 14, Henry's May 12 order to the county lieutenant of Charlotte County, Thomas Read, was typical of his immediate response to the invasion. "No time is to be lost!" Henry insisted as he directed Read to rush one third of the country's militia to Petersburg and to expect further instructions from General Charles Scott. Even so, as Henry explained to Richard Henry Lee a week later, when he had some three thousand troops on alert, "our militia could not be embodied in time to attack the ravagers on their march." Deciding where to deploy those troops remained a challenge, for as the governor reminded the congressman, "the extent of our shores hinders the possibility of defending all places."

The mobilization did some good, however, for intelligence about advancing Virginia militiamen sent the British raiders back to their beachhead at Portsmouth before they could attack Smithfield. A few days later the British loaded their ships with captured goods, ninety Tory refugees, and 518 slaves, "without being incommoded in the least by the Enemy," and sailed for New York on the morning of May 24—leaving optimistic Virginians with the mistaken impression that their patriot militia had repulsed the invaders. Predictably, a few armchair critics of the commonwealth's lack of military preparation may have focused their ire on the chief executive, but most Virginians recognized that the "melancholy fact that there were not arms enough to put in the hands of the few militia who were called down" owed more to legislative frugality than executive leadership.

In his private correspondence with Henry's old rival William Woodford, even Edmund Pendleton, no friend of the governor, initially attributed Virginia's inadequate response to Collier's raid as the kind of "inconvenience we must ever be subject to unless we keep a body of men below"—that is, stationed in the Tidewater area—"ready to repel those pirates or to stop their progress 'til the Militia can be collected." Pendleton said more about Henry later in the summer, however. Despite the reservations he had expressed about Henry's military acumen three years earlier (or the civic republican scruples many felt about the dangers of demagoguery or the mingling of civilian and military authority), Pendleton groused that Henry, "whose term was near expiration and his thoughts turned the contrary way," had not personally led the militia against the invaders (as New York governor George Clinton had done on two recent occasions).

ooooo

Virginians drew three lessons from the Collier invasion. One was the solid wisdom of moving the capital to Richmond, "which is more safe and central than any other town situated on navigable water." The other two lessons—confidence in the responsive capacity of the militia and anticipation that Portsmouth would remain the principal target of British attack—would prove disastrous for Henry's successor as governor. And that disaster, in turn, would forever poison the once friendly relationship between Thomas Jefferson and Patrick Henry.

Relieved by the departure of Collier's expedition and overconfident about the efficacy of the state militia, Governor Henry and the General Assembly, which had convened a week before the invasion, carried on with business as usual (except for the decision to move the seat of government). Four days before Collier's force had even departed for New York, the House of Delegates boldly affirmed Virginia's steadfast commitment to the national cause, ordering its newly recruited troops to march away into Continental service without further delay. Emboldened by their perception of recent events, the delegates reaffirmed their confidence that "the immediate defense of [the commonwealth] shall be rested on its militia and regular troops." Governor Henry also notified the House of Delegates that he had ordered the jailing of two disaffected residents who were assisting the invaders—thereby exercising "a power not expressly given [him] by law" made necessary by his "apprehension for the public safety."

With Collier's expeditionary force safely on its way back to New York and only a few days left before his term of office ended, Henry could finally attend to the commonwealth's first transfer of executive authority from one governor to a successor—a precedent-setting step complicated only by the fact that the Assembly had not yet chosen his successor! On Friday, May 28, Governor Henry politely informed Speaker Benjamin Harrison that since the constitution limited him to three successive terms as governor, he intended "to retire in four or five days." Seemingly prodded by Henry's reminder, on the following Tuesday, June 1, the Assembly got around to choosing Thomas Jefferson as Virginia's new governor on the second ballot by a margin of 67 to 61 over John Page. As soon as the new chief magistrate had been decided, both houses then sent Patrick Henry unanimous expressions of public gratitude "for his faithful discharge of that important trust and his uniform endeavours to promote the true interests of this state and of all America." Then, as if to emphasize their approval of his three-year tenure as governor, the legislators elected Henry to Congress, an honor he declined in favor of a brief return to private life and his law practice. Finally, before vacating the Governor's Palace, the "late Governour of this commonwealth" sent gracious notes of acknowledgment to both houses of the Assembly. Their publication in the Saturday gazettes signaled that the peaceful transfer of executive authority Henry had initiated a week earlier was complete.

Early in June 1779 Patrick Henry and his family made a long trek to their newly acquired home on Leatherwood Creek, a tributary of the Dan River, a few miles east of modern Martinsville. Shortly after he had sold Scotchtown and a tract of land in Kentucky, Henry had bought the ten-thousand-acre plantation in Henry County, which had been carved from Pittsylvania in 1776 and named in his honor. Dolly was approaching her first birthday. Her full name, Dorothea Spotswood Henry, honored her mother and her great-grandfather Alexander Spotswood, the first royal governor who lived in the palace, where she was born. At Leatherwood, according to the property tax records, Henry and his immediate family held seventy-five slaves as well as thirty-three horses and seventy-nine head of cattle. John Fontaine and his wife, Martha, Henry's eldest daughter, lived nearby on two thousand acres with eighteen slaves, nine horses, and twenty-six cattle.

Among other attractions, the high rolling plateau near the North Carolina line offered a respite from the swamps around Williamsburg and the mosquitoes that had infected Governor Henry and his son-in-law Fontaine with debilitating malaria. As though emphasizing both his infirmities and the geographical elevation of his namesake county, Henry worried aloud about whether his health would permit him to "remain *below* long enough to serve in the [next] assembly." Leatherwood also offered a stark contrast to the luxurious Governor's Palace in Williamsburg: a two-room brick structure built over a sturdy ground-level basement and outfitted with "portholes" through which muskets and rifles could be fired in the event of attack. The residence was suitably designed for the rugged and thinly populated frontier situation of Henry County, where the earlier danger of Indian raiders was supplanted by roving bands of Tories, emboldened by the British advance, whose violence blurred the line between guerrilla warfare and frontier criminality. "The Tories have been plotting hereabouts as well as over the Mountains," Henry reported in August 1780, "but I hope they are pretty well suppressed. We have partys out in pursuit of them, and several have been detected."

Henry's health concerns were not the only thing weighing on his spirits. Replying in February 1780 to a hand-delivered letter from Governor Jefferson, Henry expressed "many anxieties for our commonwealth, principally occasioned by the depreciation of our money ... fostered by a mistaken avarice." He also shared Jefferson's dismay about "our disguised Tories," whose dishonesty he had witnessed "when I lived below." Patriotic Virginians needed to speak out against the disaffected "miscreants [and] wretches ... laboring for our destruction," he thought—enemies of the people who deserved to be "shunned and execrated" in lieu of "legal conviction and punishment." Witnessing the "impunity and even respect which some wicked individuals have met with while their guilt was clear as the sun," Henry confided, "has sickened me and made me sometimes wish to be in retirement for the rest of my life." Was there ever in history, he wondered, an occasion when "tyranny was destroyed and freedom established on its ruins, among a people possessing so small a share of virtue and public spirit?" If Jefferson found time to answer Henry's observations, his response does not survive.

Henry did far more than brood about the character of his countrymen, however. His new neighbors placed him first on their list of "proper persons" to serve as justices of the county court, and he channeled his anxieties about patriotism (and his animosity toward the disaffected) into strategically active roles in the southern campaign against the British and local operations against roving Tories. The local records reveal many occasions when Henry supplied provisions for the war effort. He provided his neighbor Captain Eliphaz Shelton with 960 pounds of beef, a hog, and a bushel of cornmeal. Later he supplied General Nathanael Greene's southern army with thirty bales of fodder, 164 bushels of corn, and forage for twenty-eight horses. But the logistical support documented in the county records only begins to suggest the full range (or strategic significance) of Henry's wartime activities at Leatherwood. Until very recently, the evidence for Henry's efforts to ensure that Tories along the Virginia-Carolina frontier were "pretty well suppressed" has been buried along with eighty thousand Revolutionary War pension applications in the National Archives.

Henry and other leaders recognized that popular support for the Revolution depended upon their neighbors' self-confidence in their own strength and security. Early in the summer of 1780 Henry took the lead in rallying the population and "getting up" about three hundred volunteers for expeditions against bands of Tories lurking in the rugged terrain that extended on both sides of the state line from Leatherwood west into the Smoky Mountains, according to war veteran George Turnley. These borderlands "were very mountainous and in many places almost inaccessible by any human beings," a county militia officer explained, "excepting Tories who always fled to these places for security when pursued by the liberty men." Honoring the authority of the county lieutenant, Colonel Abraham Penn, Henry gave "counsel and advice in regard to our movements and [rode] with the expedition," Turnley recalled, "but he did not [take] command."

It was Patrick Henry's son-in-law Captain John Fontaine who led Turnley and his compatriots into the Smoky Mountains about two hundred miles to the west. Although many Tory bands scattered before Fontaine's company reached their hideout at "the Rich-Hollow in North Carolina" (near modern Erwin, Tennessee), the volunteers "compelled" area inhabitants to swear "the oath promising obedience to the State and Congress." Fontaine's company then "scoured the Country on the waters of the Yadkin River." After they "put down and quelled the Tories who had been about to rise in that quarter," Turnley recalled, they marched back to Henry County and were discharged in September 1780.

That same summer, John Redd responded to Henry's call to arms by signing up as an ensign to suppress another band of Tories lurking "at a place called the Hollow near the head of Dan and Arrarat Rivers," in the county's rugged terrain sixty miles west of Leatherwood (now in Patrick County). Unlike the people of Henry County, who overwhelmingly supported the Revolution, "nearly half the population in what was called the Hollow ... were disaffected," another volunteer recalled, "and the whigs were kept constantly on the alert." An experienced frontier warrior, Redd had fought the Cherokee under Henry's brother-in-law William Christian. A year later, when Redd served as a wagon master for General Greene's army, Henry supplied him with 228 sheaves of oats and nineteen pounds of fresh pork. Redd subsequently ended his service in the Revolution as one of Henry County's participants in the siege of Yorktown.

Twenty-seven-year-old James Tarrant led a third company of volunteers carrying out Henry's campaign against area Tories in 1780. Commissioned as a captain under Colonel Penn, Tarrant led his company on a six-week pursuit of "a Gang of Tories" who had murdered William Letcher, a patriot justice of the county court, at Flower Gap, near the Wilderness Road about forty miles east of the Cumberland Gap. "When the Tories heard of our approach they fled into the hills and mountains," Tarrant recalled, but "we pursued them and scoured that region for a long time ... [until] we had cleared this part of the settlements from danger."

ooooo

By the time Henry's neighbors had carried out their expeditions against the frontier Tories, the war for independence had taken several turns against the patriots. On May 12, 1780, General Charles Cornwallis captured Charleston, South Carolina, along with 3,400 American soldiers, including hundreds of Virginians in two brigades commanded by William Woodford. Then, in mid-August, the southern army lost another six hundred Americans, killed, wounded, or captured at Camden, South Carolina, where Cornwallis routed General Horatio Gates, the hero of Saratoga. The southern theater quickly became a vicious civil war, exacerbated by the British policy of enforcing oaths of allegiance among the populace and

Cornwallis's tolerance of brutality by loyalists and British officers eager to teach the Americans a lesson. "Whigs and Tories pursue one another with the most relentless fury," wrote General Nathanael Greene after he took command of the southern army in December. "Rapes, murders, and the whole catalogue of individual cruelties," wrote James Madison, "are the acts which characterize the sphere of their usurped Jurisdiction."

Rather than intimidating the general population, however, this ferocious violence had the counterintuitive effect of arousing American resistance, especially in the frontier backcountry. In October 1780 a combined force of Virginia and Carolina patriot militia routed a thousand loyalist militia led by British Colonel Patrick Ferguson at King's Mountain, South Carolina, thirty miles southwest of Charlotte, North Carolina. The lopsided patriot victory engineered largely by Henry's brother-in-law William Campbell proved to be one turning point in the southern campaign. King's Mountain interrupted Cornwallis's progress, shattered his hope of creating an effective Tory militia, reinvigorated patriot resistance—and bought time for General Greene's move from West Point, New York, to his new southern command.

Patrick Henry's entire career as a revolutionary leader—in the gunpowder expedition of 1775, throughout his tenure as governor, and most recently in his local campaigns against frontier Tories—demonstrated his profound sympathy with Nathanael Greene's keen appreciation of the political dimension of the war for independence. "Every Thing here depends upon Opinion," Greene recognized upon his arrival in the South. "If you lose the Confidence of the People you lose all support." In order to win this war, American civilian and military leaders had to convince the populace that they could rely upon the patriot regime to protect its citizens and their liberties and property better than the British could. If the enemy ever convinced the American people that they were conquered and powerless, that would be their fate. "It was [as] necessary to convince the Carolinians that they were not conquered," Greene explained to Governor Jefferson, as it was for his army to avoid anything like his predecessors' defeats at Charleston and Camden.

During the early months of 1781, Greene played cat-and-mouse with Cornwallis in a brilliantly orchestrated retreat toward Virginia—known later as the race to the Dan River—all the while looking for opportunities to strike back without incurring disaster. The Henrys may well have joined in the celebration of Greene's tactics in verses sung to the tune of "Yankee Doodle":

> Cornwallis led a country dance
> The like was never seen, sir.
> Much retrograde and much advance
> And all with General Greene, sir.

Then at last, early in February, Greene sensed that he might be able to inflict serious damage on Cornwallis and his eight thousand redcoats—if only he could augment his forces with an influx of volunteers.

On February 10, Greene informed Governor Jefferson that he had written directly to Henry and asked him "to collect 14 or 1500 Volunteers to aid us." It turns out that Henry had been following Greene's fateful dance with Cornwallis. Not content with initiating militia excursions against local Tories, Henry had been alert for opportunities to help Greene's army. With that in mind Henry had sent a courier (probably one of his slaves) who had intercepted Greene near Guilford Courthouse (modern Greensboro, North Carolina) about thirty-five miles due south of Leatherwood. The two men had probably met briefly in November when Greene addressed the General Assembly in Richmond en route to his new command, but having worked closely with George Washington for several years the former Rhode Island Quaker already knew that he could trust Henry's character. From Greene's experience as quartermaster general for Washington's army, he had surely witnessed Governor Henry's assistance with recruitment and provisions. As one of Washington's most trusted lieutenants Greene may well have known about Henry's role in exposing the Conway Cabal. The one certain truth is that Henry's courier could not have arrived at a more opportune moment.

As Greene led the remnants of the southern army toward the Dan River, he informed Henry that his forces were "too inconsiderable . . . to check the rapidity of [the enemy's] march through this unhappy country"—but that he anticipated that Cornwallis was about to move the British army into a vulnerable position, if only he could muster enough men to take advantage of the enemy's expected blunder. Two days before his forces commandeered all the available boats on the Dan River and found a brief sanctuary on the north bank Greene explained to Henry that his "influence in Virginia may terminate the war greatly to the honor and advantage of the southern states."

"If it is possible for you to call forth fifteen hundred volunteers and march them immediately to my assistance, the British army will be exposed to a very critical and dangerous situation," Greene advised Henry. Using a colloquial synonym for *pregnant*, Greene told Henry that "the present moment is *big* with the most important consequences, and requires the greatest and most spirited exertions. You, I know, are equal to them, and I trust no step will be omitted that may be necessary to call forth the power of your part to the country." Two days later Greene told a fellow officer that he had "confidence in a reinforcement from Virginia." Greene's confidence was promptly confirmed. Early in March, two thousand volunteers from the Old Dominion headed south, including 281 volunteers from Henry County—12 percent more than the county quota, a rough measure of Henry's effectiveness as a recruiter.

With four thousand men now under his command, Nathanael Greene could prepare to confront Cornwallis at Guilford Courthouse on March 15, 1781. If they prevailed "it would prove ruinous to the Enemy," he explained to the president of Congress, but if not "it would prove only a partial evil to us." After a long day of fierce combat in which the Virginia militia "did themselves great honor," the outcome presented another pivotal moment in the southern campaign. Cornwallis claimed the honor of wresting the battlefield from Greene's troops, but that honor cost him almost a third of his army. "I wish it had produced one substantial benefit to Great Britain," General Charles O'Hara concluded after the battle, in which he, too, was wounded. Instead, the loss of "nearly one half of our best Officers and Soldiers . . . has totally distroy'd this Army."

ooooo

Unlike Washington, who carefully coordinated the actions of his subordinates with regular correspondence, Sir Henry Clinton, the British commander in chief, and Lord Cornwallis acted virtually independently of one another and sometimes went for months without any communication whatsoever. The distances separating these two generals, both geographically and in temperament, soon meant that the British were fighting two distinct wars in the southern theater, according to a perceptive historian, "one in the Carolinas and one in Virginia." From Clinton's perspective in

New York, occasional forays into the Chesapeake were ancillary tactics meant to make things more difficult for Greene's and Washington's armies by interrupting Virginia's contributions of troops and supplies.

In October 1780, for example, Clinton had dispatched Major General Alexander Leslie and two thousand troops to the Chesapeake as "a diversion in favor of Lieutenant General Earl Cornwallis." Portsmouth was Leslie's principal target, but after entering the bay he moved slowly because he was uncertain about what Cornwallis wanted him to accomplish, or, for that matter, where Cornwallis and his army were at that moment. Aided by timely warnings from Washington's headquarters and the experienced leadership of three officers recently retired from Continental service, Virginians were able to stymie Leslie's forces for more than a month. Then, during the night of November 15–16, General Leslie suddenly herded his force aboard ship and abandoned Portsmouth, stranding several hundred slaves who had fled to his lines. Virginians once again attributed the British withdrawal to the effectiveness of their militia defenses. In fact, however, General Leslie had simply responded to new orders from Clinton sending him to bolster the British garrison at Charleston after news reached New York of the American victory at King's Mountain.

Although Governor Jefferson led Virginia's response to Leslie's invasion in 1780 as capably as Henry had led the response to Collier's raid in 1779, few of his contemporaries knew how intensely he reacted to his experience during the crisis. Soon after Leslie left Virginia, Jefferson implored his friend John Page, the former lieutenant governor and the man he had defeated for the governorship by a margin of six votes, to help him resign his office. Jefferson felt himself "unprepared by his line of life and education for the command of armies," and in the face of invasion increasingly unwilling, as he later wrote, "to stand in the way of talents better fitted than his own."

ooooo

Six weeks after Leslie's forces left Virginia, Clinton sent another expedition, led by the turncoat General Benedict Arnold, that caught Virginians completely by surprise on Saturday, December 30, 1780. With no advance warning from New York (where Washington did not learn that Arnold had sailed until January 2), 1,600 British troops set sail aboard twenty-seven small warships capable of navigating the Chesapeake's tributaries. Blessed with favorable winds they bypassed Portsmouth and sailed directly up the James River. By the time Jefferson summoned the militia on Tuesday it was already too late. Arnold landed his forces at Westover on Thursday, January 4. By one o'clock on Friday, eight or nine hundred troops reached Richmond, about twenty-five miles to the west. Overawed by the invaders, two hundred raw militiamen assigned to defend the capital scattered without firing a shot.

After dispatching Colonel John Simcoe's cavalry upstream to destroy the state foundry and arsenal at Westham (near the modern campus of the University of Richmond), Arnold sent Jefferson an offer to spare Richmond if he were permitted to bring in ships, claim all the tobacco in the city's warehouses as "prize goods," and pay the owners half its value. When Jefferson rejected the ransom offer, Arnold's troops set fire to several buildings and then retired downstream, first to Westover and ultimately to Portsmouth, plundering tobacco and other commodities on their way.

According to the official British tallies, during their twenty-four hours in Richmond, Arnold's troops destroyed two warehouses, 503 hogsheads of rum, countless barrels of grain and flour, twenty-one carriages, 2,200 small arms, and fifty bolts of canvas. A Hessian officer was more candid. "Terrible things happened on this excursion," Johann von Ewald confided to his diary. "Churches and holy places were plundered," and with "half the place in flames" more than forty ships "were loaded with all kinds of merchandise for the corps' booty." Once Arnold had established his base at Portsmouth, however, his troops continued their intermittent raids up and down the river from Jamestown to Petersburg for several months.

Virginians were far more critical of Jefferson's leadership during Arnold's invasion than they had been during earlier raids. Edmund Pendleton complained privately to George Washington that Jefferson had delayed "calling the Neighbouring Militia 'til it was too late." He was confident that the governor's "intentions [were] the very best, but he was Incredulous and not sufficiently attentive on this Occasion." John Page was livid. "Arnold the traitor," he wrote a friend, "has disgraced our country . . . so much that I am ashamed and shall ever be so to call myself a Virginian!" From Congress in Philadelphia, even Jefferson's bosom friend James Madison jeered that he was "glad to hear that Arnold has been at last fired at." There is no evidence of any criticism from Patrick Henry, who had firsthand experience with both the Assembly's parsimony in defense expenditures and the impossibility of securing timely and reliable information about an invader's movements and objectives. Not to mention the geographical fact that, as Henry had confided to Richard Henry Lee after the Collier raid, "the extent of our shores hinders the possibility of defending all places."

ooooo

After his expensive victory at Guilford Courthouse, prudence might have sent Cornwallis back toward Charleston, at the far end of his supply train, to bolster his garrisons, secure his control of South Carolina and Georgia, and thereby honor the policy set by the British government and his New York–based superior, Henry Clinton, of protecting Charleston at all costs. Instead, Cornwallis headed toward the coast at Wilmington, North Carolina. Greene promptly took advantage of the opportunity to move south and, by September, except for the port towns of Wilmington, Charleston, and Savannah, he reclaimed the Carolinas and Georgia without ever winning a major battle.

From Wilmington, still without consulting Clinton in New York, Cornwallis marched "into Virginia in search of Adventures," as one experienced observer sneered in a top-secret memorandum later published as *The Folly of Invading Virginia.* By May 20 Cornwallis and his army, now down to fewer than 1,500 troops, reached Petersburg, Virginia, at the confluence of the Appomattox and James Rivers thirty miles south of the newly designated capital at Richmond—where the only improvement in the state's meager defenses had been the arrival of a small French army belatedly dispatched by Washington in response to Arnold's invasion and skillfully led by the Marquis de Lafayette.

Things only got worse for Governor Jefferson after Arnold's forces and additional reinforcements from New York joined Cornwallis at Petersburg. With about seven thousand men now under his command, on June 3 Cornwallis sent two raiding parties up the James River. One led by Colonel John Simcoe captured the Continental depot at Point of Fork, where the Rivanna flows into the James River just south of Charlottesville, and destroyed badly needed supplies intended for Nathanael Greene's army. The other squadron, led by the dashing and ruthless twenty-six-year-old Colonel Banastre Tarleton, aimed at capturing Governor Jefferson and the

General Assembly at Charlottesville, where the legislature had reconvened on May 24 after fleeing Richmond.

Riding hard through Hanover and Louisa counties, Tarleton's cavalry stopped to eat and spell their horses at Cuckoo Tavern, forty miles east of Charlottesville. While they rested, twenty-six-year-old John Jouett, Jr., a local militia captain, guessed the nature of Tarleton's mission. Mounting his horse and taking shortcuts along back roads and mountain trails, Jouett reached Monticello well ahead of the British, who paused again east of Charlottesville at Castle Hill to capture Henry's half-brother, John Syme, Jr., and several other legislators at Dr. Thomas Walker's house near Keswick.

Just before daybreak on Monday, June 4, Jack Jouett alerted Jefferson to Tarleton's advance and then rode down the hillside to warn the legislators who had gathered in town. After sending his wife, Martha Wayles, and their children south toward Poplar Forest, his plantation near Lynchburg, Jefferson scrambled to gather up his official papers until the sight of redcoats ascending toward his hilltop sanctuary forced him to mount his own horse and follow his family through the woods. Technically his second one-year term of office had ended on Sunday, but amid all the confusion nothing had been done to choose his successor. At the foot of his mountain, meanwhile, the Assembly met briefly in Charlottesville and promptly adjourned to reconvene in Staunton, across the Blue Ridge in the Valley of Virginia some forty miles to the west. As a temporary precaution, the House of Delegates also reduced its required quorum to forty, a procedural expedient that would enable the House to resume its work in Staunton several days before the Senate achieved a quorum.

That evening, as Patrick Henry, John Tyler (who told the story), and several other legislators crossed Afton Mountain toward Staunton, they stopped their horses at a small cabin. When they asked its sole occupant for refreshments, the country woman demanded to know who they were. "We are members of the Legislature," Patrick Henry replied, "and have just been compelled to leave Charlottesville on account of the approach of the enemy."

"Ride on then, ye cowardly knaves," the woman replied. "Here have my husband and sons just gone to Charlottesville to fight . . . and you running away with all your might. Clear out—ye shall have nothing here."

"But," said Henry, "we were obliged to fly. It would not do for the Legislature to be broken up by the enemy. Here is Speaker [Benjamin] Harrison; you don't think he would have fled had it not been necessary?"

"I have always thought a great deal of Mr. Harrison till now," said the cabin dweller as she moved to shut the door, "but he had no business to run from the enemy."

"Wait a moment, my good woman," Henry said. "You would hardly believe that Mr. [John] Tyler or Colonel [William] Christian would take to flight if there were not good cause for so doing?"

"No indeed," she replied, "that I wouldn't."

"But Mr. Tyler and Colonel Christian are here," Henry said.

"Well, I never would have thought it," the woman responded. "I didn't suppose they would ever run away from the British, but since they have, they shall have nothing to eat in my house."

Finally, as a last resort, John Tyler (for whom this became a favorite story) stepped forward and asked, "What would you say, my good woman, if I were to tell you that Patrick Henry fled with the rest of us?"

"Patrick Henry!" she exclaimed, "I would tell you there wasn't a word of truth in it. Patrick Henry would never do such a cowardly thing."

"But," said Tyler, pointing out his companion to the astonished woman, "this *is* Mr. Henry."

"Well . . . if that's Patrick Henry it must be all right," the woman ventured after a long pause. "Come in, and ye shall have the best I have in the house."

ooooo

"We have now no Executive in the State," Speaker of the House Benjamin Harrison wrote from Staunton to a member of Congress on June 8, before the state Senate gathered a quorum and while only one member of the Governor's Council was in the area. Four days later, after a ten-day constitutional hiatus, the legislature finally elected General Thomas Nelson, Jr., of Yorktown, as the commonwealth's third governor on Tuesday, June 12. In the aftermath of Tarleton's raid, the delegates also contemplated drastic emergency measures to adapt Virginia's republican constitution to the grim realities of war—including a controversial proposal to create a temporary dictator on the classical Roman model and provisions for imposing martial law when necessary.

On June 7 delegate George Nicholas, a political novice who represented Hanover County, announced his intention of moving "to have a Dictator appointed" and named Generals Washington and Greene as possible candidates. Nicholas "referred to the practice of the Romans on similar occasions." Some delegates felt "that neither of them will or ought to [ac]cept of such an appointment"—and at least one agrarian republican believed that the appropriate legislative response to the military emergency was not to appoint a temporary dictator but to call another convention! When Nicholas sat down, according to one of Staunton's leading jurists, Patrick Henry seconded his motion. "It was immaterial to him whether the Officer proposed was called a Dictator or a Governor with enlarged powers or by any other name," Henry was reported to have said, for "surely an Officer armed with such powers was necessary to restrain the unbridled fury of a licentious enemy." The idea also had substantial public support. "At present we are without a Governor," a Hanover County physician noted on June 11, but "it is expected that our Assembly will appoint a Dictator at this dangerous crisis, and that General Washington will be Dictator."

Although the proposed dictatorship was defeated in committee (and therefore never mentioned in the official legislative journal), Nicholas and Henry were not the only Virginians contemplating such a drastic emergency measure. On several previous occasions the legislature had acknowledged that public safety in wartime sometimes required executive actions unforeseen by formal legislation (as when Governor Henry and his Council had ordered the restraint of disaffected residents early in the war or when Henry had two persons jailed for aiding the British during the Collier invasion). Time and again the General Assembly routinely endorsed (and officially excused) responsible emergency measures with formal acts of indemnity. Richard Henry Lee also advised Virginia's congressional delegation to send Washington "immediately to Virginia . . . with Dictatorial power" (as Congress had contemplated in a similar emergency a year earlier). Writing independently from his home in distant Westmoreland County on the same day the legislature finally elected General Nelson as Virginia's new governor, Lee suggested that both ancient and modern history offered Congress "precedents to justify this procedure" and that "the present necessity not only justifies but absolutely demands the measure."

Immediately after the announcement of Governor Nelson's election, the House of Delegates adopted a resolution that "at the next session of

Assembly an enquiry be made into the conduct of the Executive of this State for the last twelve months"—two dozen words that triggered a controversy that echoed through Virginia history for decades to come. The journal does not tell us, but it is generally accepted that the same George Nicholas who had suggested a dictatorship introduced the resolution for a legislative inquiry into the executive. Accounts vary as to who seconded Nicholas's motion. Archibald Cary told Jefferson that his friends seconded the motion, "confident that an Inquir[y] would do you Honor." The controversial question, however, was not just who? but why?

No responsible government could evade the necessity of comprehending its recent failures and taking steps to avoid them in future. Back in 1776 Henry had warned about the constitutional restrictions on gubernatorial authority with which only he and Jefferson yet had contended. Clearly, in the months after Leslie's and Arnold's invasions, Jefferson had not enjoyed adequate support from the members of his Council of State, who left a dismal record of abrupt resignations and casual absences. Not to mention the ten-day hiatus when Virginia had no governor, or the loss of property worth as much as £3 million, or the fact that after six months enemy forces were still prowling the countryside. In light of all these problems, how could responsible legislators look the other way?

As George Nicholas explained when Jefferson accused him of seeking to "stab a reputation," he considered it both his right and duty as a legislator "to call upon the executive to account for our numberless miscarriages and losses"—starting with "the total want of opposition to Arnold on his first expedition to Richmond." What Nicholas may not have told Jefferson was how directly his family and neighbors had suffered during the British raids. Cornwallis had set up temporary headquarters in his widowed mother's house. The general and his lieutenants discovered and confiscated jewels and silver that Ann Cary Nicholas had hidden in the chimney, pulled down fences, and feasted on her cattle, hogs, sheep, and chickens—while two soldiers from the Queen's Rangers who robbed a house in the neighborhood and raped nine-year-old Jane Dickinson were summarily hanged for their offense.

Although Jefferson felt that he was being personally attacked, Nicholas had aimed the inquiry not at the chief magistrate alone (as legislative references to the governor were usually phrased) but at the "Executive of this State." His target was not any single officeholder but the entire branch of government comprised of members of the Council of State and scores of lesser appointed officials as well the governor. Pointedly, the House of Delegates directed copies of its resolution not just to Jefferson but also to the five men who had served on his executive council—and they felt its sting. Invoking "the rectitude of their intentions" at their meeting on July 16, the targeted councilors protested that "however unsuccessful their honest endeavors may have been" they now felt "most sensibly this implied censure on them." Only the state's dire situation prevented them from stepping down while the legislators examined their conduct, because if they resigned it "would leave the State without a legal Executive" and "be productive of the most fatal consequences."

In light of Patrick Henry's own direct experience with the challenges of responding to an invasion, he surely recognized that Nicholas's inquiry could lay the groundwork for needed enhancements and clarifications of emergency governmental authority. Henry, after all, had vigorously advocated a stronger governorship during the drafting of the state constitution. And from years of experience, he was inured both to the rough-and-tumble of legislative debate and the jostling that accompanied practice in the county court, where attorneys regularly faced off against each other at one courthouse and then amicably shared meals and often beds as they traveled to face one another again in the next county.

None of these considerations comforted Jefferson. Archibald Cary, speaker of the Senate, could not have been more wrong when he assured the former governor that "if I know you" Nicholas's call for an inquiry "will Give you no pain." When it came to criticism and conflict, Jefferson did not have Henry's easygoing temperament. Cary and Henry could easily have anticipated that an inquiry would lay to rest all doubts about Jefferson's leadership (as a similar inquiry would have done for Henry's handling of the Collier invasion). Neither man anticipated the intensity of Jefferson's reaction or the anxieties he was feeling about his wife's health. Nor could Henry anticipate that when Jefferson learned of Nicholas's resolution he would lay the blame entirely at Henry's feet and construe the call for an inquiry as a personal attack.

Jefferson said that nothing in his public life wounded his feelings more deeply than George Nicholas's resolution for an inquiry into the conduct of the executive. Its implicit accusation, Jefferson told James Monroe after his wife died from complications of childbirth the following spring, "inflicted a wound on my spirit that nothing in this world could ever heal." Jefferson characterized Nicholas as "trifling," "below contempt," and "an object of pity." Brooding through the summer in the solitude of his Poplar Forest retreat, Jefferson convinced himself that the young man's "natural ill temper" was a tool worked "by another hand." He deployed a vividly scatological metaphor to describe his alleged tormentors. Nicholas, Jefferson wrote, "was like the minn[ow]s which go in and out of the fundament of a whale." Patrick Henry "was the whale himself . . . discoverable enough by the turbulence of the water under which he moved."

Just how clearly Jefferson could see below the surface remains an open question. During the writing of the state constitution, he and Henry had implicitly disagreed about the requisite authority of the executive branch. Jefferson, then serving in Congress, had submitted a draft plan of government with such a weak executive officer that he had opted for the title "administrator" rather than governor. Henry had strenuously urged the Virginia convention to create "a powerful chief magistrate" capable of "defend[ing] his office from the usurpation of the legislature." In light of the state's ineffective responses to British invasions during both his and Jefferson's administrations, Henry may well have advocated the necessity of a forceful executive as eloquently in Staunton in 1781 as he had in Williamsburg in 1776—quite possibly with rhetoric that led Jefferson to distrust Henry's motives.

After hearing about the legislative discussion of a dictatorship from young Archibald Stuart, an aspiring attorney from Staunton, Jefferson heaped additional blame on Henry for allegedly seeking to subvert the constitution. Without addressing the legislature's actual deliberations about enhancing the powers of the governor (for which he had only brief secondhand reports), Jefferson channeled his rage into the text of the new project that eventually became his famous *Notes on the State of Virginia.* Jefferson denounced the delegates for having reduced their required quorum to forty before adjourning to Staunton and for considering the creation of a Roman-style dictator. In a curious way, Jefferson conjured the delegates' precautionary decision to reduce the quorum "during the present dangerous invasion" into a subversive first step down a dangerous slope aimed at diminishing the quorum from forty to four and then to "a despotic one"—a monstrous scheme in which Jefferson thought he saw the movements of the nefarious whale plotting "treason against the people" and "treason against mankind in general" in order to create "a dictator invested with every power legislative, executive, and judiciary, civil, and military, of life and death over our persons and properties."

As Henry had probably expected, in October 1781 when John Banister of Dinwiddie County reported from the committee charged with investigating "the administration of the late Executive," he announced that the rumors that had prompted the inquiry "were groundless." Expressing regret that "popular rumors" had rendered the inquiry necessary, the Assembly proclaimed Virginia's belated gratitude to Thomas Jefferson "for his impartial, upright, and attentive administration of the powers of the Executive." Patrick Henry was prominent among the delegates who voted unanimously to affirm "Mr. Jefferson's ability, rectitude, and integrity"— and Henry was surely in agreement with the Assembly's observation that their endorsement should have "tenfold value" because it was "founded on a cool and deliberate discussion." Nevertheless, the result of George Nicholas's call for an investigation was the permanent end of any friendship between Jefferson and Henry. And despite the Assembly's effort "to obviate all future, and to remove all former, unmerited censure," the circumstances of Jefferson's escape from Monticello in 1781 fueled unfair accusations by his political adversaries from the presidential election of 1796 through his death in 1826.

ooooo

Henry spent the summer and autumn at Leatherwood, where Dorothea had borne her second child and his eighth child, Sarah Butler Henry, a few months after their arrival and her third child, Martha Catherine, in November. Thomas Jefferson and his family spent the summer at Poplar Forest, where he prepared a defense of his reputation for the next session of the General Assembly and poured his resentment toward Henry into angry diatribes about conventions and dictators for the pages of *Notes on the State of Virginia*. Meanwhile, British and American units, as well as French troops led by the Marquis de Lafayette, rambled up and down the James River Valley.

Although Cornwallis had abandoned his supply link to Charleston immediately after the battle of Guilford Courthouse, he did not establish a new base for naval operations in Virginia until early August. While the fleets commanded by Admiral Thomas Graves and the Comte de Grasse jockeyed for strategic advantage on a transatlantic chessboard that extended from Canada to the Caribbean, Cornwallis finally resolved to entrench his army at Yorktown. Quickly hemmed in by Lafayette's army and Virginia militia units, Cornwallis's fate ultimately would be decided by the contest at sea. In mid-August, when Washington received word from the West Indies that de Grasse and his fleet had sailed for the Chesapeake, he and the Comte de Rochambeau began moving their armies south. While the French and American armies marched toward Virginia, de Grasse outmaneuvered Graves and inflicted enough damage to send the British fleet back to New York. Laying siege to Yorktown on September 30, the combined American and French forces—including dozens of Patrick Henry's neighbors—forced Cornwallis and his seven thousand troops to surrender on October 19, 1781.

CHAPTER TWENTY-ONE

Making Peace

"*O GOD!* It is all over!" exclaimed Lord North, the British prime minister, when word of Cornwallis's surrender reached 10 Downing Street between one and two o'clock on Sunday, November 25, 1781. But two days later, George III barely mentioned the "very unfortunate" fate of Cornwallis when he informed Parliament of his intention to continue the fight against his rebellious American subjects and "his perfect conviction of the justice of his cause."

Until Virginians could be certain that Lord North's position would prevail, they endured anxious months of tenuous peace before the formal treaty ending the war and acknowledging American independence was signed in Paris in September 1783. From the Northern Neck, where the notorious loyalist Goodrich family was exploiting the ambiguous situation with privateering raids along both shores of the Potomac River, George Mason informed Henry in May that news of parliamentary antagonism to the treaty negotiations made "People in this Part of the Country . . . very uneasy," fearing that perceived infringements of the preliminary articles of peace might bring military "Reprisals" along Virginia's exposed and vulnerable coastline.

The months between the surrender at Yorktown in the autumn of 1781 and the ratification of preliminary articles of peace by Congress in the spring of 1783 were a period of anxiety and confusion for Patrick Henry and his contemporaries—and a period that sometimes perplexes historians because many newspapers, government records, and personal letters have been lost. Inevitably, after nearly a decade of war, it was a period of transition in which Americans who had focused on winning their independence now confronted both new uncertainties arising from their altered situation and old problems now carried over into altered and complicated new circumstances. Two clusters of issues were prominent: complex financial and constitutional wrangling over government debts, taxation, and paper money; and equally complicated debates about trade policies, treaty deliberations, and the return of exiled loyalists, many of whom were merchants.

ooooo

Patrick Henry's lifelong skepticism about paper money had begun with his earliest experiences in the House of Burgesses, when he had challenged a Loan Office scheme designed to protect the beneficiaries of John Robinson's illicit generosity as "calculated to feed extravagance and revive expiring luxury." Paper money had been an essential wartime measure, however, though its loss of value was a constant problem. Virginia's determined efforts to repay its wartime debts were reasonably well managed and, by 1786, largely successful. Heavy taxes payable in military certificates, which could also be exchanged for western land, reaped £625,000 and substantially reduced the state debt. The Confederation Congress, however, was hamstrung by the states' noncompliance with its requisitions and powerless to prevent the depreciation of the national currency—a grim reality reflected in the proverbial phrase "not worth a continental."

By May 1, 1780, when the General Assembly convened in Richmond, Congress had stopped making interest payments on its acquired debt and asked the states for $195 million in support of a new issuance of Continental paper money. Parting company with his longtime associates Richard Henry Lee and George Mason, who supported this congressional plan, "Patrick Henry poured forth all his eloquence in opposition," according to Edmund Randolph. By a 2-to-1 majority, the House of Delegates endorsed Henry's alternative to the congressional proposal. Henry's three-part plan would have paid the state's quota "for the support of the war for the current year," created a special state fund to repay Virginia's share of the continental debt in fifteen years, and imposed a state tax dedicated "for the use of the continent."

What Henry's approach avoided—by insisting that Virginia and the other states accept proportionate responsibility for the expenses of national defense—was any surrender of the national debt to the exclusive authority of Congress. In short, Henry wanted to pay Virginia's rightful share of national expenses without playing into the hands of the Pennsylvania financier Robert Morris and other nationalists, whose not-so-hidden agenda was a virtual forerunner of Alexander Hamilton's program a decade later: expand the national debt as the rationale for increasing the powers and revenues of the central government and thereby, as Morris would inform Congress, "give stability to Government by combining together the interests of moneyed men for its support."

The day after the adoption of his resolutions about the war debt, Henry's lingering health concerns prompted him to request a leave of absence from the legislature. Later in the session, after biding their time, Lee and Mason reintroduced the congressional plan as part of an ambitious program of new state taxes (which Henry would likely have endorsed) and won its approval. A year later Henry introduced legislation that redeemed (and terminated) Virginia's wartime paper currency along with a comprehensive tax program to create "a permanent revenue" and pay down Virginia's war debt.

Other states were not as forthcoming. By May of 1783, Congress was again forced to abandon all its paper money, as Morris and a wide range of statesmen turned their energies toward a plan to give Congress a modest permanent revenue through a 5 percent tax, or impost, on imports. When the legislature convened in Richmond that spring, Jefferson believed that Henry's opinions were "as usual involved in mystery," but by the end of the session he reported that Henry's support had clinched Virginia's approval of the impost. Describing Henry as "its strenuous supporter," Edmund Randolph quipped that with Henry "fixed in his opinion" the delegates heard no opposition "from the *Lee*ward quarter," a reference to Richard Henry Lee. Ultimately, however, despite the endorsement of twelve states, the impost fell victim to the Articles of Confederation's requirement that all thirteen states agree to any proposed amendment.

During the course of Patrick Henry's long political career, Americans had frequently resorted to issuing paper money for the public good, especially in wartime. After a general discussion of the Old Dominion's scarcity of circulating currency in 1787, however, Henry joined all his colleagues in unanimous support of a resolution drafted by George Mason declaring that "an emission of paper currency would be ruinous to trade and commerce, and highly injurious to the good people of this commonwealth." A year later, Henry voiced his final considered opinion about "the distresses produced by paper money" in the debates about the merits of the proposed Constitution. "We are at peace on this subject," he assured his colleagues in the Virginia convention. "Though this is a thing which that mighty Federal Convention had no business with, yet I acknowledge that paper-money would be the bane of this country. I detest it. Nothing can justify a people in resorting to it, but extreme necessity. It is at rest however in this Commonwealth. It is no longer solicited or advocated."

ooooo

During his initial tenure as governor, the Virginia legislature had expelled loyalist merchants as a wartime security measure early in 1777. Now, with the war apparently ended, many Americans were as eager to resume the sale of American produce and replenish their stocks of imported goods as foreign merchants were to buy their commodities, especially Virginia to-bacco and South Carolina rice, and take their orders for imports—even in advance of a formally ratified peace treaty. Although Congress feared that popular pressure for the resumption of trade could undermine American diplomacy and urged the states to confiscate British manufactured goods illegally imported before March 1, 1782, the continued interruption of commerce also exacerbated the depreciation of paper currency, aggravated fluctuations in commodity prices, and tempted some who had money to indulge their pent-up demand for imported and luxury goods. Although all three were reelected to the Assembly, neither Henry, Jefferson, or Rich-ard Henry Lee attended the October 1782 session, which endorsed "a strict adherence" to the continued exclusion of British subjects and goods.

At the opening of the May 1783 Assembly session, after successfully nominating his friend John Tyler for the speaker's chair, Henry moved for the repeal of all prohibitions against the importation of British goods. Speaker Tyler, who opposed the measure, gave biographer William Wirt his recollection of Henry's remarks in support of the measure, which took effect on May 13, eight days after its passage. "After painting the distress of the people, struggling through a perilous war, cut off from commerce so long that they were naked and unclothed," Henry's voice rose to a pinnacle that Tyler said he would never forget. Beautiful as his imagery was in itself, Tyler described its effect as "heightened beyond all description" by the way Henry "acted what he spoke"—first slumping and gazing despondently at his feet and then rising to his full height in "proud defiance":

Why should we fetter commerce? If a man is in chains, he droops and bows to the earth, for his spirits are broken. . . . But let him twist the fetters from his legs and he will stand erect. . . . Fetter not commerce, sir—let her be as free as the air—she will range the whole creation, and return on the wings of the four winds of heaven, to bless the land with plenty.

Speaker Tyler, who shared with many of his constituents a passionate animus toward the Tories, also found himself at odds with Henry over legislation permitting the return of loyalists to the commonwealth. Introduced along with Henry's free trade measure, the bill to repeal the wartime expulsion of the Tories encountered fierce opposition in May—as did similar measures in other states—and was held over for further consideration at the next Assembly session. Spirited debate resumed in November, prompting the Assembly to publish the bill in the newspapers and post copies at every courthouse—a legislative tool for gauging public sentiment that Henry seems always to have favored. Two weeks later, however, the House and Senate agreed to amend the bill in unspecified ways that led to its adoption.

During the November debates, Speaker Tyler had challenged Henry to explain "how he, above all other men, could think of inviting into his family an enemy from whose insults and injuries he had suffered so severely?" Henry replied that in his opinion, "the personal feeling of a politician ought not to be permitted," for the question "was a national one, and . . . if they acted wisely nothing would be regarded but the interest of the nation." Once again, although Speaker Tyler had disagreed with his friend, he supplied Henry's biographer and posterity with a vivid record of his arguments—which echoed the support for immigration and economic growth Henry had first articulated in the 1760s.

"*People*, sir, form the strength and constitute the wealth of a nation," Henry asserted, and America was destined to become a great agricultural and commercial power. Already there were young people, he believed, who would live to see "this favoured land" take its place "amongst the most powerful on earth. . . . Great in arts and in arms—her golden harvests waving over fields of immeasurable extent, her commerce penetrating the most distant seas, and her cannon silencing the vain boasts of those who now proudly affect to rule the waves." But to achieve that destiny America needed skillful and industrious immigrants as well as "commercial men and commercial capital."

What should be done? he asked. "Open your doors, sir, and they will come in." Henry envisaged the people of the Old World "standing on tiptoe upon their native shores and looking to your coasts with a wishful and longing eye." America was "a land blessed with natural and political advantages . . . not equalled by those of any other country upon earth"—"a land over which Peace hath now stretched forth her white wings, and where Content and Plenty lie down at every door!" And America offered even greater attractions than its resources. Prospective immigrants could see "that Liberty, whom they had considered as a fabled goddess existing only in the fancies of poets," reigned in America—"her altars rising on every hand throughout these happy states—her glories chanted by three millions of tongues—and the whole region smiling under her blessed influence." Bid them welcome! Henry cried. Let the celestial goddess of Liberty "stretch forth her fair hand toward the people of the old world" and "your wildernesses will be cleared and settled—your deserts will smile—your ranks will be filled—and you will soon be in a condition to defy the powers of any adversary."

Shifting at last from his grand vision of America's future to the point of John Tyler's challenge, Henry acknowledged that many gentlemen objected "to any accession from Great Britain—and particularly to the return of the British refugees." For his part, however, Henry felt "no objection to the return of those deluded people." The loyalists had mistaken their own interests most woefully—and many had suffered for their blunders. But the situation was different. "Their king hath acknowledged our independence—the quarrel is over—peace hath returned, and found us a free people."

"Let us have the magnanimity, sir, to lay aside our antipathies and prejudices, and consider the subject in a political light," Henry urged. "Those are an enterprising moneyed people," capable of contributing to the public good by marketing American produce and "supplying us with necessaries during the infant state of our manufactures." Even if some loyalists remained "inimical" to American principles, Henry had no objection, "in a political view," to welcoming their contributions "to our advantage." Good public policy would "mak[e] this use of them," not cower in fear that they might do mischief. Finally, as Henry prepared to clinch his argument, Tyler remembered him rising to a lofty stance as though he were confronting a pitiful loyalist with utter contempt. "Afraid of *them*!" Henry thundered. "Shall *we*, who have laid the proud British *lion* at our feet, now be afraid of *his whelps*?"

ooooo

Late in the autumn of 1783 Philip Mazzei returned to Virginia to settle his accounts and seek payment for his wartime labors in Europe as an agent of the commonwealth seeking £1 million in loans for the war effort. The obstacle Mazzei now faced (as did George Rogers Clark and others) was the extensive destruction in January 1781 of records from the governor's and state auditor's offices in a raid led by the turncoat Brigadier General Benedict Arnold. Before he sailed for Virginia, Mazzei had conferred with Jefferson in Paris about documenting his claims for payment with testimonials from the wartime officials he had worked for—and had visited Monticello to retrieve some documentation for his services during Jefferson's terms as governor. Mazzei then found it necessary "to travel about quite a bit in order to secure statements" of support from Patrick Henry, who had initiated Mazzei's commission in January 1779, and former members of his Council of State, including James Madison.

The trek from Albemarle County to Leatherwood and back took Mazzei five days each way, but on the trip back the Italian adventurer carried a significant overture from Henry to Madison, both of whom were preparing for the upcoming session of the General Assembly. "Mr. Mazzei did me great pleasure in telling me you were well," Henry wrote, "and not averse to render still further Services to our Country" in the legislature. Henry was eager to confer about "several Matters of the greatest Moment" when the House of Delegates convened in Richmond on May 3. The perennial impoverishment of the national Treasury suggested that "the federal Government [was] on a bad Footing," but that was "not the only Matter that wants Correction and Improvement." Virginians needed to confront the moral and political challenges of their postwar situation if they hoped to reap the Revolution's "rich Harvest of Happiness."

During the previous Assembly session, an astute German tourist had chanced to visit Richmond as the legislature gathered in its "small frame building," a former warehouse at the corner of Fourteenth and Capitol Streets that was used between sessions "for balls and public banquets."

"It is said of the Assembly that *It sits*," the visitor observed, but in fact he seldom saw the delegates "sitting still with dignity and attention." What he did see were Virginia legislators clad in "boots, trowsers, stockings, and Indian leggings; great-coats, ordinary coats, and short jackets, according to each man's caprice or comfort," chattering about "horse-races, runaway negroes, yesterday's play, [or] politics"—until some strong leader commanded their attention for an important issue. On one occasion the German visitor witnessed General Robert Lawson of Prince Edward County gain the attention of the House and explain the necessity of payments owed to revolutionary veterans. In general, however, he learned that among the men "who lead the debate and think and speak for the rest," it was "a certain Mr. Henry who appears to have the greatest influence over the House," while "the other members, for the most part farmers . . . with little education or knowledge of the world, are merely there to give their votes."

By the following spring, however, as his affectionate letter to Madison suggests, Henry was anticipating both that the 1784 Assembly session would contend with serious postwar challenges facing the new republic *and* that the presence of James Madison, despite his youth and his limitations as public speaker, would change the dynamic in the legislature. For his part, the thirty-three-year-old genius from Montpelier was acutely aware of Henry's influence. Henry held "very friendly views toward the confederacy" and supported measures to ensure the payment of British debts in accord with the peace treaty of 1783, Madison reported to Jefferson in April. Henry's attitude toward revising the state constitution (a project that had become something of a theoretical obsession for Madison and Jefferson) was uncertain, though it was known that he was preparing a plan for public support of religion.

Henry and Madison had worked together during the Convention of 1776 that wrote the state constitution and Declaration of Rights and again during Madison's two years on Governor Henry's Council of State in 1778 and 1779. Their paths had then diverged in 1780 when Virginia sent Madison to the Confederation Congress while Henry entered the House of Delegates. Now they were coming back to the legislature to grapple with problems rooted both in postwar economic dislocation and moral failure— depreciation of the state's currency, difficulties collecting taxes, and the lingering taint of wartime profiteering both by private citizens and, worse, by state and Continental requisition agents "who have plundered and empoverished the People to enrich themselves." Madison and Henry worked together to pass several significant measures, but firmly opposed one another on several major issues. Together, for example, they passed a measure aimed at reducing smuggling and regulating international commerce by confining foreign vessels to five major ports by a close vote of 64 to 58 over strong opposition from Speaker John Tyler, Wilson Cary Nicholas, John Marshall, and John Taylor of Caroline.

Madison and Henry also disagreed with the angry delegates led by Speaker Tyler and the populist John Taylor of Caroline who sought an outright repudiation of prewar debts owed by Virginia planters to British merchants. Both men concurred with George Mason's contention that settling these debts was both a matter of honor and of good business— but they found no firm grounds for agreement on the complex issues of postwar finance raised by the provisions of the Treaty of 1783. During the war, Henry had strongly supported measures to expel loyalists unwilling to swear allegiance to the commonwealth and severe limits on their ability to collect debts incurred before 1777—the formal date of the expulsion of British merchants. Madison's camp wanted to make sure that the states honored the treaty, lest a breach lead to renewed bloodshed, while Henry advocated withholding the settlement of debts until Britain complied with the treaty's requirements about the surrender of military posts in the west and compensation for slaves taken during the war. In the end, Virginia's stalemate over the handling of British debts lingered until after the creation of the national court system under the Constitution of 1787 and litigation in which Patrick Henry would play a major role.

Many people viewed the American debates about taxation, paper money, domestic credit policies, and British debts as evidence of "the degeneracy of the times" and a decline in civic virtue resulting from "sordid and selfish love of gain." Henry shared a widespread postwar anxiety about the state of public morality with his political soul mate George Mason. "We are now to rank among the Nations of the World," Mason reminded him, "but whether our Independence shall prove a Blessing or a Curse, must depend on our own Wisdom or folly, Virtue or Wickedness." At his death, Henry made the same observation in his note to posterity—but for the moment it was Mason who echoed Henry's Liberty or Death speech: "Judging of the future from the Past, the Prospect is not promising. Justice and virtue are the vital Principles of republican Government, but among us a Depravity of Manners and Morals prevails." Despite his reservations, however, Mason exhorted his friend to champion the distinction between right and wrong and "restore that Confidence and Reverence in the People for the Legislature which has been so greatly impaired by a contrary Conduct." "It is in your Power to do more Good and prevent more Mischief than any Man in this State," Mason admonished Henry, "and I doubt not that you will exert the great Talents with which God has blessed you in promoting the public Happiness and Prosperity."

∞∞∞∞

On the question of Henry's attitude toward revising the state constitution, Madison wrote hopefully at the beginning of the spring 1784 session that "the general train of his thoughts seemed to suggest favorable expectations." In June, apparently at the behest of Philip Mazzei, both men stood among the thirty-two prominent leaders who created a short-lived Constitutional Society of Virginia as a forum devoted to keeping "a watchful eye over the great fundamental rights of the people" and a forum for discussion "on every subject which may either tend to amend our government, or to preserve it from the innovations of ambition, and the designs of faction." Structured as a private club (similar to the debating clubs of revolutionary Paris), the society aimed at encouraging forthright conversation among Virginians who favored revisions to their state government and those who "feared to run into Scylla trying to avoid Charybdis."

Patrick Henry surely favored some revisions to the state constitution. A decade earlier he had sought to strengthen the office of the governor—and recent experience suggested that enhancements he had then sought might have averted problems in the executive department during Jefferson's second term as governor. But these were not the changes sought by Madison and Jefferson. Their passion for a new convention was more theoretical than practical—rooted more in concerns about ideological purity than the actual operation of government. On this question Madison was carrying Jefferson's water, and Jefferson still contended that the adoption of Virginia's constitution should have been delayed until a new convention had been elected expressly for the purpose. Despite the attention given to

Jefferson's complaints by many historians, his objections never gained credence. "Happily," concluded Edmund Randolph, "practical utility will always exterminate questions too refined for public safety."

Fastening upon a few lines in a quirky petition from Augusta County that sought permission for paying taxes with hemp just as colonial Virginians had once paid them with tobacco, Madison used the valley freeholders' mundane request to push for consideration of his and Jefferson's theories. When he tried to convince the legislature that the "Convention of 1776 [had acted] without due power from [the] people," however, Henry and the vast majority of delegates simply would not be persuaded. Nor did they share Madison's objection to the fact that Virginia had adopted its constitution on June 29, 1776, "before independence [was] declared by Congress"—a point of provincial pride that would later become a matter of national dispute. Despite Madison's claim that Virginia's stability was at risk, Henry and other senior statesmen regarded his campaign as a pointless, expensive, and empty exercise.

Although historians treat Jefferson's and Madison's attack on the constitution of 1776 as "an intellectual critique of very great interest . . . but of little political consequence," their attempt to summon a new convention revealed a profound disagreement with Henry over the fundamental nature of the existing state constitution. Henry must have been astonished when Madison declared that the convention of 1776 had failed to acknowledge that it derived its "power from [the] people." Article 2 of Virginia's Declaration of Rights could not have been clearer: "That all power is vested in, and consequently derived from, the people; [and] that magistrates are their trustees and servants and at all times amenable to them."

From Henry's perspective, the problem was that Madison and Jefferson were misrepresenting one of Virginia's great achievements. The constitution of 1776 had two components—one was the Declaration of Rights adopted on June 12, which laid out the reasons for which governments existed, and the other was "A Plan of Government" adopted on June 29 that defined the legislative, executive, and judicial apparatus of the new commonwealth. Because Virginia's Declaration of Rights "was not the work of an Assembly but of a Convention," a self-styled "Friend to the Bill of Rights" declared in an Alexandria newspaper, "all Assemblies should consider it as a rule of conduct given them by the people."

Patrick Henry's response to Madison's proposal for a convention to re-vise the state constitution should have been no surprise. Henry was al-ways inclined to assess public policy by the light of experience rather than theory. The attempt to summon a new convention aroused "the adverse temper of the House," Madison reported to Jefferson in July. "Mr. Henry shewed a more violent opposition than we expected" (a miscalculation perhaps born of the dreamy quality of Madison's fixation on this issue). Fi-nally, in answer to Madison's allegation that their constitution was unsta-ble because it was "subject to change by subsequent legislature," the House of Delegates pointedly placed the subject off limits for the future.

Jefferson's response to all this was ferocious. "The proposition for a Convention has had the result I expected," he wrote. If a convention could have been summoned, he wasn't sure "whether it would not do more harm than good." Although none of Jefferson's informants had specified which changes, if any, they thought Henry favored, Jefferson had no need for facts to inform his opinion that "while Mr. Henry lives another bad con-stitution would be formed and saddled for ever on us." And then Jeffer-son bared his teeth. "What we have to do I think is devoutly to pray for his death," Jefferson declared, and "in the mean time to keep alive . . . [in] the minds of the young men" (who had not themselves witnessed the de-liberations of the convention of 1776) "the idea that the present [constitu-tion] is but an ordinance." In the end those young Virginians were content to outwait Jefferson. Not until 1829, three years after his death, did they summon a convention to revise the state constitution—with former pres-idents James Madison and James Monroe present as its honorary chair-men. Many years later an acquaintance recalled that Patrick Henry once told him "that he could forgive everything else in Mr. Jefferson, but his corrupting Mr. Madison."

ooooo

Like its sister states and Congress, Virginia had struggled throughout the war to collect revenues equal to its wartime expenses. Despite the accusa-tions of a few wealthy detractors who regarded him only as a spokesman for ne'er-do-well debtors, however, Henry's approach to taxation and pub-lic finance was complex. He knew from personal experience the adversities faced by struggling planters. As an attorney he represented debtors and creditors alike in suits over debts. As a creditor himself, he witnessed all too vividly the financial woes of his aging father and, increasingly, his half-brother, John Syme, Jr. As a legislator he sought to balance the needs of his constituents and the requirements of government.

Two years earlier Henry had sought to align the collection of taxes with the seasonal patterns of harvests and markets by pushing for legislation that extended the tax deadline and allowed payments in two installments. Henry's legislation also added marketable deer hides to the list of commodities acceptable for tax payments, guaranteed the acceptance at face value of notes issued by Congress, and prohibited the acceptance of discounted military certificates. Historians have long recognized that these extended deadlines were "particularly welcome to the residents of Henry's region of the state, where specie was exceptionally scarce," but not that his plan also bolstered the value of Continental currency and discouraged speculation in military certificates. Moreover, as at least one of his contemporaries noticed, Henry's tax measure outmaneuvered the advocates of paper money whose political pressure might otherwise have "sullied" the legislature "by the revival of paper credit"—or worse.

Archibald Stuart, who represented Botetourt County in the Assembly in 1784, wrote a vivid account of "the extraordinary effects of Mr. Henry's eloquence" when a group led by Speaker John Tyler, Henry Tazewell, Mann Page, and Richard Henry Lee introduced a bill to raise taxes. "Mr. Henry, on the other hand, was of the opinion that . . . the people should have some repose after the fatigues and privations to which they had been subjected during a long and arduous struggle for independence." The advocates of a tax increase were delighted when their bill passed its first reading by a majority of about thirty votes. Confident that their measure would sail through its second reading, they displayed more disdain than anxiety when Patrick Henry stepped forward "in all the majesty of his power." Speaker Tyler scowled from the chair and Tazewell diverted himself by reading a pamphlet as Henry opened his remarks. Within a few minutes, however, the effect of Henry's words became increasingly "legible" on Tyler's face as his demeanor began to change. At first he glanced at Henry occasionally, Stuart recalled, then he began to smile. Soon Tyler was leaning forward to catch every word, "charmed and delighted, and finally lost in wonder and amazement."

Henry painted a vivid picture of the hardships that Virginians in the western counties still suffered from the war—"delineations of their wants

and wretchedness . . . so full of feeling" that they engaged "every sympathetic mind." He contrasted the frontier families' backbreaking toil with
the abundance enjoyed by the Virginians in the Tidewater who drew their
provisions with ease "from the waters that flowed by their doors." Henry
then "filled the house with a roar of merriment" as he imagined the advocates of higher taxes "peeping and peering along the shores of the creeks
to pick up their mess of crabs or paddling off to the oyster rocks to rake
for their daily bread." Now even Henry Tazewell "laid down his pamphlet
and shook his sides with laughter" as a shift of opinion "prevailed through
the ranks of the advocates of the bill." From a thirty-vote majority upon its
first reading, the increase was now rejected by a similar margin. Reflecting
upon Henry's effective use of both humor and pathos, Tyler recalled the
tax debate of 1784: "I have seen him reply to Page, H. Tazewell, R. H. Lee,
and others with such a volume of wit and humour that the house would
be in an uproar of laughter," Tyler wrote, "but this talent he not often in-
dulged, deeming it beneath a statesman."

The postwar tax measures advocated by Patrick Henry helped Virginia escape the kind of violent insurgence that afflicted Massachusetts in
Shays' Rebellion. Contrary to myths spun by partisan observers then and
since, the overwhelming majority of leaders and participants in that revolt
were not debtors but property-owning farmers incensed by a rapacious
scheme of taxation foisted upon the Bay State's rural population. Unlike
Henry's tax legislation, Massachusetts policies under its new constitution
of 1780 required the immediate payment of taxes in hard currency (always
a challenge for American farmers) as well as the redemption of discounted
military certificates at full value (a boon to speculators who bought them
from veterans for pennies on the dollar). After years of complaint from
constituents, things exploded in 1785 after the legislature once again refused to mitigate its draconian scheme for paying off the Bay State's entire
war debt in just two years—a program pushed through the legislature by
a clique of influential speculators. Facing a threefold increase in their tax
burden—two thirds of which went straight into the pockets of the speculators who had engineered the scheme—citizens throughout Massachusetts reacted by shutting down their local courts, intimidating judges and
magistrates, refusing to answer summons when the governor called on the
militia to stifle their revolt, and generally scaring the hell out of gentlemen
of property from Beacon Hill to Mount Vernon. "There are combustibles

in every State which a spark may set fire to," George Washington grumbled in 1786, without realizing how much Virginia's "perfect calm" owed to the mediating tax policies advanced by Patrick Henry—policies that also yielded respectable income for the commonwealth. Virginia's tax revenues for 1784 exceeded expenditures by £22,542.

ooooo

As Patrick Henry contemplated Virginia's need for virtuous citizens and the place of the church in a republic, his own outlook was shaped by three rival perspectives. On the conservative side were the traditionalist churchmen (who were now calling themselves Episcopalians) such as House of Delegates Speaker John Tyler, Senate Speaker Archibald Cary, the rising jurist John Marshall, and former governor Benjamin Harrison. Devoted to the religious heritage in which they had been raised, they shared an authentic devotion to the established church and its liturgical traditions. They represented an older generation committed both to political independence and to the established church as an essential component of society. Religion was the "duty we owe to our Creator," not just personal opinion. Their responsibility as magistrates was to see that duty carried out by the state. The prospect of disestablishment was abhorrent, and they regarded the promise of the "free exercise of religion" in the Declaration of Rights as a grant of toleration for the people whom they still viewed as dissenters. As a wartime expedient, the traditionalists had reluctantly agreed to end religious taxation for dissenters (and suspend it for Episcopalians) but had been careful to stipulate that the glebes (farms and parsonages provided by the vestries for their ministers' support) and all other church property was "reserved to the use of the church by law established." The traditionalist churchmen diverged from the established clergy only to the extent that they favored the existing system of lay dominance within the church, enshrined in laws that kept the clergy under the thumb of the Assembly and the vestries. During the Assembly sessions of 1784 and 1785 they voted to incorporate the Episcopal Church and pass Henry's bill for a general assessment in support of religion and against Jefferson's statute for religious freedom.

Independence from Great Britain had drastically altered the situation of Virginia's established clergy. Some ministers who felt that their oaths of ordination required sustained allegiance to the monarch returned to

England. Others resigned from the ministry, and many older men simply died—all without any prospect of replacements. And clergymen who clung to their pulpits saw their income cut and their social status eroded. The Revolution had proved "fatal to the Clergy of Virginia," one survivor complained to his brother, "the Establishment abolished, every sect upon the same level, and every man at liberty to contribute or not to the support of the Minister of his own persuasion as he judges best."

Directly opposed to the traditionalists were the younger and strongly rationalist legislators led by Madison and Jefferson who generally supported immediate disestablishment and complete religious equality. They regarded the church as an institution of minimal value whose clergy made only minor contributions to society. Religion was a matter of private opinion. Churches deserved only voluntary support of their adherents. "The legitimate powers of government extend to such acts only as are injurious to others," Jefferson believed, but "for my neighbor to say there are twenty gods or no god . . . neither picks my pocket nor breaks my leg."

Evangelical dissenters, especially Presbyterians and Baptists in their petitions to the General Assembly, voiced a third church-state outlook. While they echoed Madison and Jefferson in their concern for equal liberty, their outlook was rooted less in Enlightenment rationalism than in scriptural truth and religious history. When Jesus declared that his kingdom was not of this world, the Hanover Presbytery informed the legislature in 1776, he renounced "all dependence upon State Power." They saw proof for the benefits of disestablishment in the rapid growth of Christianity in the centuries before Constantine corrupted the church by linking it with his empire.

Patrick Henry's views about church and state comprised a fourth position—favoring religious freedom and the equality of all religious groups, willing to consider disestablishment, but also convinced that republican virtue needed religious support and therefore government backing for Protestant churches and clergy. For two decades Henry had characterized the established clergy's social functions as promoting civic responsibility and censuring vice—and he recognized that many Episcopal and Presbyterian clergy ran schools on weekdays. Henry also sympathized with the traditionalists who regarded religion as a duty that individuals and society owed to their creator rather than a matter of private opinion. While Jefferson agreed with Henry about the importance of virtue in a republic, he stressed the necessity of education rather than religion. For that reason, in addition to proposing secular reforms for the College of William and Mary along with his Statute for Religious Freedom, Jefferson had outlined a comprehensive public system of primary and secondary education for Virginia. The only element of his "Bill for the More General Diffusion of Knowledge" that ever became law—three decades later—was the founding of the University of Virginia.

Despite their differences about the best methods for encouraging civic virtue, many Virginians shared Henry's concerns. Outside the ranks of the evangelicals, a German visitor noticed in 1784, Virginians "freely and openly admit that zeal for religion and religion generally is now very faint among them." The government no longer collected tithes for the Protestant Episcopal Church (as it was now called). Nearly half its clergy had died, resigned, or retired. Many of its buildings were in disrepair. Yet state laws tied the church to the government and prevented its leaders from managing its own affairs. "The Episcopal Church in Virginia is so fettered by Laws," one of the activist clergy complained in July 1784, "that the Clergy could do no more than petition for . . . liberty to introduce Ordination and Government and to revise and alter the Liturgy."

Prompted by a petition from a gathering of Episcopal clergy and freeholders from Warwick and Powhatan counties, Patrick Henry and his friends began work on a bill to give the Protestant Episcopal Church the legal status of a corporation. The clergy sought permission to create rules and bylaws for public worship, with the vestries taking responsibility for managing church property, but transferring caring for the poor and infirm from the vestries to the county courts. Madison's friend Joseph Jones, a staunch churchman who sided with Henry on these religious issues, brought the bill to the floor of the House of Delegates on June 16—but after two weeks of debate it was postponed until the Assembly reconvened that autumn. "Extraordinary as such a project was," Madison reported to Jefferson, "it was preserved from a dishonorable death by the talents of Mr. Henry." In these debates, according to Spencer Roane, a young delegate who voted with Madison on the religious issues but was courting and would soon marry Henry's daughter Anne, "Mr. Henry demolished Madison with as much ease as Sampson did the cords that bound him before he was shorn." By December, when the Assembly passed an extensively revised incorporation act that carefully enshrined lay control of the Prot-

estant Episcopal Church, traditionalist clergy and churchmen were laud-
ing Henry as "the great Pillar of our Cause." Even Madison voted *for* the
incorporation law, but only as a tactic in his effort to postpone a vote on
Henry's bill for support of teachers of the Christian religion, which he regarded as "a much greater evil."

ooooo

Henry had come to Richmond in May of 1784 hoping to enact a general assessment for the support of religion, but as usual he sought to
gauge public opinion before he acted. "A general assessment...has
H[enr]y for its patron in private," Edmund Randolph observed at the
beginning of the session, "but whether he will hazard himself in public cannot yet be ascertained." Encouraged by petitions of support from
several counties for "a general assessment upon all Tythables of this
Commonwealth...countenancing the Propagation of the Holy Christian Religion," the House of Delegates endorsed the idea late in May, but
then turned its attention to the legislation for incorporating the Episcopal
Church. In October, citing religion's "happy influence upon the morality
of the citizens," the Hanover Presbytery endorsed an "alliance" between
church and state as "wise policy." So long as the legislature refrained from
meddling in "spiritual" affairs and distributed the money raised by a general assessment on "the most liberal basis," the Presbytery welcomed the
"Smiles and Support of Government."

   In November the delegates resolved by a vote of 47 to 32 "that the people of this Commonwealth...ought to pay a moderate tax or contribution annually for the support of the Christian religion, or some Christian
church, denomination, or communion of Christians, or of some form of
Christian worship"—and named Patrick Henry as chairman of a ten-
man committee charged with drafting the bill. In its final form Henry's
bill for "Establishing a Provision for Teachers of the Christian Religion"
would let every taxpayer designate the religious group that would receive
his money, which could be used both for the support of clergy and the
maintenance of church buildings. Henry's plan treated the clergy in general as educators responsible for teaching religiously based moral values
and civic virtues, but it implicitly recognized that well-educated Episcopal and Presbyterian clergymen often operated local schools in which
they taught reading, writing, mathematics, and languages during the week.

With scrupulous care for the equality of all the Christian churches and religious groups in Virginia, including the Quakers and Mennonites, Henry's bill encouraged "a general diffusion of Christian knowledge . . . to correct the morals of men, restrain their vices, and preserve the peace of society"—but it explicitly recognized the need "for learned teachers who may be thereby enabled to devote their time and attention to the duty of instructing" Virginians whose "circumstances and want of education" held them back. In addition to payments earmarked for specific denominations, Henry's bill allotted all undesignated payments toward "the encouragement of seminaries of learning within the Counties whence such sums shall arise and to no other use or purpose whatsoever." Although the principle of state support for religion excited controversy and aroused opposition, in the context of Virginia's eighteenth-century practice Patrick Henry's bill looked backward toward the limited educational system in which he had studied with his father, Thomas Jefferson had studied for college in a school operated by the Reverend James Maury, and James Madison had studied with a resident tutor, the Reverend Thomas Martin.

Virginia's legislature might well have adopted Patrick Henry's provision for teachers of the Christian religion by the close of 1784 had not its most influential supporters abandoned the measure and given Madison time to rally public opposition. Late in November the Assembly reelected Henry as governor. "The father of the Scheme," Madison reported to James Monroe with great relief, had gone home to Leatherwood to retrieve his family soon after the election "and will no more sit in the House of Delegates, a circumstance very inauspicious to his offspring." Richard Henry Lee, who strongly endorsed the assessment and could have replaced Henry as its chief advocate in the Assembly, had been reelected to the Confederation Congress. In addition, sentiment among Presbyterians, especially in the Valley of Virginia, was shifting toward opposition. On Christmas Eve 1784, after acquiescing to the passage of the Incorporation Act for the Episcopal Church, James Madison persuaded the delegates to publish Henry's assessment bill for discussion and postpone their decision until the sentiments of the people could be taken into account.

That spring and well into the summer of 1785, Henry's assessment bill inspired a vigorous public debate. On Sundays at churches and meetinghouses and at Court Days in virtually every county, thousands of Virginians signed petitions to the legislature. Advocates for the assessment circulated more than a dozen distinct memorials expressing the social importance of religion and its need for government support. For every freeholder who signed his name or placed his mark on the petition in favor of the assessment, however, ten more subscribed their opposition. Printed copies of a Memorial and Remonstrance composed by James Madison, with fifteen arguments against the proposed assessment and its dangers, circulated for signatures in about a dozen Piedmont and Northern Neck counties. But the explicitly religious petitions drawn up by church groups proved much more popular, according to the definitive scholarship of historian Thomas E. Buckley. When the Presbyterians and Baptist laymen joined the fray, "they viewed the Incorporation Act and the assessment proposal as a combined effort to restore the Episcopal Church." Responding to the anger of its congregations, the Hanover Presbytery reversed itself and attacked both the Incorporation Act and the assessment. Virginia Baptists were even more strident.

Responding to these concerns in a volatile political climate, the Separate Baptists saw an obvious need for concerted action against their political grievances. Despite their belief in the autonomy of local churches and their distrust of any centralized church government, they organized a General Committee that represented their four district associations. Functioning until the end of the century as the political action wing of the Baptist churches, the committee organized a massive petition campaign that galvanized resistance to the assessment and support for the passage of Jefferson's statute for religious freedom. Their petitions argued that the assessment was "contrary to the Spirit of the Gospel and the Bill of Rights," and that Christianity had flourished before Constantine and would prosper again if the clergy proved themselves called to the ministry by the Holy Spirit through scriptural preaching and blameless lives.

When the legislature met again in the autumn of 1785, Henry's assessment bill never came to a vote. Instead, Madison brought forward the bill for religious freedom that Jefferson had drafted years earlier as part of a package of legislative reform proposals. Adopted by a wide margin in January 1786, the Virginia statute and its unprecedented commitment to absolute religious liberty became a defining moment in world history— and one of the three accomplishments Jefferson had inscribed on his tombstone.

Forty years later one of the young delegates who had supported the Incorporation Act and opposed Madison's effort to defer consideration of Henry's bill recalled that "previous to the revolution we had an established church and all were taxed for its support," but "from one extreme we passed to the other and individual contributions became purely voluntary." As to the proposal for a general assessment for religion, future Chief Justice John Marshall observed that "its supporters incurred so much popular odium that no person has since been found hardy enough to renew the proposition." Despite his authorship of the bill, however, Governor Henry lost no sleep over its rejection by the public. Indeed, as might be expected from his long-standing commitment to the concept of religious toleration enshrined in the Virginia Declaration of Rights, within two years Henry found occasion (in the debates over the ratification of the Constitution) to celebrate Jefferson's statute as the highest and best expression of Virginia's commitment to religious freedom.

ooooo

The final major issue that Patrick Henry and his colleagues in the General Assembly tackled in 1784 and 1785, was one of the "Matters of the greatest Moment" for which Henry had sought James Madison's counsel in the letter Philip Mazzei had carried from Leatherwood to Montpelier prior to the legislative session. The perennial difficulty of getting the states to supply "the federal Government" with sufficient revenue, Henry had written, "wants Correction and Improvement."

On Friday, May 14, nine days into the spring Assembly session of 1784, Henry dismounted from his own long ride from Henry County to Richmond and immediately went looking for refreshments and a conversation with James Madison. He found both at a Richmond coffeehouse, where Madison was sitting at a table with Jefferson's friend William Short, then serving as a member of the Council of State, and Joseph Jones, an influential delegate from King George County, on the Potomac River. Henry "arrived yesterday," Madison wrote to Jefferson on Saturday, "and from a short conversation I find him strenuous for invigorating the federal Gov[ernmen]t though without any precise plan." The description of this meeting that William Short sent to Jefferson was more detailed. Henry approached them and suggested that "Mr. Jones and Mr. Madison should sketch out

some Plan for giving greater Powers to the fœderal Government," Short
reported, "and that Mr. Henry should support it on the Floor":

> A bold Example set by Virginia would have Influence on the other
> States. Mr. Henry declared that was the only Inducement he had
> for coming into the present Assembly. He saw Ruin inevitable un-
> less something was done to give Congress a compulsory Process [to
> collect revenues from] delinquent States &c.

The Confederation Congress resembled the General Assembly of the
United Nations more than its modern congressional namesake—indeed
Henry's old friend John Adams had described his delegation to Abigail
as "our Embassy" when he hoped that its conduct would "merit the Approbation of our Country"—by which he (like many Americans) meant
his state. Each state legislature chose its delegates to Congress and reined
them in with detailed instructions to ensure that political power stayed at
home. Chronic poverty, constitutional restrictions, and congressional ab-
senteeism also kept the national government in a tight harness. Amendments to the Articles of Confederation required the full agreement of all
thirteen states—a practical impossibility when states such as Rhode Island
failed to send delegates at all.

   Once the war had been won, many states also kept their ablest men at
home. "The members of Congress are no longer, generally speaking, men
of worth or of distinction," Jefferson told a Dutch visitor, "for Congress
is not, as formerly, held in respect . . . [because] the government[s] of the
States and the foreign missions absorb the men of first rank in the Union."
As the largest and most populous state in the union, the Old Dominion
perhaps enjoyed a greater pool of talent—for the Virginia legislature generally populated its congressional delegations (as it did for the executive
council) with one or two seasoned leaders and some promising youngsters
eager to test their wings. The fact that Virginia paid its congressmen a
per diem helped, too. Delegates from many states had fewer incentives for
diligence and often had difficulty getting paid at all. By sending talented
delegates and paying them adequately, of course, Virginia leaders were also
upholding the commitment to national unity that had characterized their
relations with their sister colonies since the 1760s.

Although, like other states, Virginia owed money to the Confederation, the Old Dominion had reasons for optimism. There was a small surplus in its Treasury, and with market prices for corn and tobacco on the rise, farmers were increasingly able to pay all or part of their taxes without anguish. Circulating forms of paper currency (such as tobacco warehouse receipts) kept the economy fluid. Nobody was starving, and the prospects for prosperity seemed good. Despite their disagreements about religious issues, Henry and Madison could join forces in the hope of bolstering the Articles of Confederation and guaranteeing a stream of national revenue. The operating expenses for Congress and its tiny bureaucracy were small, but by 1784 the nation's accumulated debt after seven years of war exceeded £27 million. Just as Virginia had already repaid $3.25 million in state debt since the victory at Yorktown, retiring the national debt was seen as a matter of financial solvency and national honor.

Five days after Henry and Madison agreed over coffee to strengthen the powers of Congress, the House of Delegates adopted half a dozen resolutions that accomplished their intentions. The house endorsed an amendment to the Articles of Confederation that would compute congressional requisitions on state populations rather than land area. The delegates also endorsed compliance with "all requisitions . . . for discharging the national debts incurred during the war." They instructed Virginia's congressional delegation to seek "a fair and final settlement of the accounts . . . between the United States and the individual states" and enforce the collection of money owed by "defaulting states." And finally, to strengthen America's bargaining position in negotiations for commercial treaties and in retaliation against British restrictions that prevented the resumption of Virginia's lucrative trade with the British West Indies, the delegates offered Congress regulatory authority over foreign trade for fifteen years. The Senate concurred with these measures on June 8. Although their "bold Example" meant less to the other states than he and Madison hoped, Patrick Henry made good on their agreement about augmenting congressional revenues.

CHAPTER TWENTY-TWO

Governor Again

SIXTY YEARS BEFORE a New Orleans journalist coined the phrase, Governor Patrick Henry conducted a *land-office business* during his fourth and fifth terms at the helm of the commonwealth of Virginia. Land-hungry Virginians were moving south and west, whether they claimed property based on their military service in the Revolution or bought "treasury certificates" at the rate of £1 per hundred acres. The population of Kentucky jumped from about eight thousand residents in 1783 to thirty thousand in 1784 as it climbed toward the 73,677 souls tallied by the first federal census of 1790. Virginia's Land Office was achieving its declared purposes of encouraging immigration, peopling the west, and raising revenue both for operating expenses and paying down the public debt. The process kept Governor Henry's pen busy. Between November 1784 and November 1786 Patrick Henry affixed his distinctive signature to nine thousand land grants—the highest number of Virginia land grants issued during any two years from independence to the present day. Henry signed an average of seventeen grants each weekday for two full years—seven times the number he signed during his earlier gubernatorial terms and eight times more than virtually all Virginia governors before and since.

In addition to the stack of oversized vellum land grants that came to Patrick Henry's desk for signature each week, frontier lands and their migrating settlers brought more complex matters to Henry's attention during his fourth and fifth terms as governor. In some ways, Virginia's vast territory—even after the commonwealth ceded to Congress its land claims north of the Ohio River—confirmed Montesquieu's ideas about the geographical limits suitable for republican government. In that regard, based on experience that paralleled the familiar growth and division of counties, the General Assembly had long since authorized the creation

of Kentucky as a separate state. During 1785 and 1786, however, Governor
Henry confronted crises of frontier separatism, Indian warfare, and a congressional conspiracy against Virginia's western interests. All three situations involved thorny issues of state and national authority. And all three
were handled out of public view without a single speech by a governor as
capable of statesmanship as oratory.

ooooo

"Hasty and excitable and disposed to be overbearing," a nephew recalled,
Arthur Campbell "was often engaged in violent personal quarrels." Born
in 1743 to Scots-Irish immigrants who had settled in Augusta County, west
of the Blue Ridge, Campbell was among frontier Virginia's most prominent political and military leaders. A tall and impressive man, well-read,
widely traveled, and articulate, Campbell had commanded a company of
volunteers in Dunmore's War and had voted for independence, the Declaration of Rights and constitution, and Virginia's first elected governor at
the convention of 1776. During the Revolutionary War he had served as
the county lieutenant and presiding justice in Washington County, adjacent to the North Carolina line, and led backcountry military operations
against hostile Indians and loyalists in the region.

By 1785, dissatisfied by the Richmond-based state government's indifference to Washington County's needs for better roads and improved defenses against Indian raids, Campbell and some of his neighbors were in
league with land speculator and war hero John Sevier and his movement
to create a separate state of Franklin in western North Carolina. Early
in the year, the Confederation Congress received two memorials from
Arthur Campbell and several dozen prominent landowners seeking affir-
mation of their claimed right to secede from Virginia and "introduce such
alteration in their present situation and government as they think will increase their happiness."

Governor Henry learned of the separatist memorial almost
immediately—both from Congressman Samuel Hardy and from a former
Indian agent who had recently moved to western North Carolina. That
spring, Henry also received several letters directly from Arthur Campbell
asserting that his government had "become so weak or corrupt as to . . .
be incompatible with the sovereignty of the People whose rights . . . they
ought to maintain."

Acting "swiftly and shrewdly" both to suppress Campbell's separatist movement and sidestep any congressional involvement, Henry invoked his authority under a year-old militia reform act that had transferred power to appoint and remove militia officers from the General Assembly to the executive. Henry issued a proclamation removing Arthur Campbell from the office of county lieutenant and replacing him with General William Russell—a man of impeccable military credentials whose loyalty to Virginia (and to Henry) was certain. Russell had served in the Continental Army, was present for the surrender at Yorktown, and had recently married Henry's sister Elizabeth, with whom he later converted to Methodism.

General Russell confronted Campbell at the courthouse in June 1785. After removing him from office, the general and the governor then displaced all of Campbell's supporters with county residents who had rejected the movement for separation. But Henry went further. With his encouragement, the General Assembly enacted legislation, soon dubbed the Treason Act, declaring that anyone who attempted to create a government "separate from or independent of the government of Virginia . . . shall be adjudged guilty of high treason." Unable to use the law retroactively (and too shrewd to make Campbell a martyr), Henry appointed a special investigative commission, composed of prominent Washington County residents, that found Campbell guilty of urging his neighbors "to separate from this commonwealth" and advising citizens not to pay their taxes or vote in Virginia elections. With their report in hand, the governor had the Council of State strip Campbell of his remaining office as a justice of the peace. Henry's suppression of the separatist movement in Washington County was prompt and thorough—and within a few years the "wild men of Franklin State" were forgotten after the ratification of the Constitution, the admission of Tennessee to statehood in 1796, and the election of John Sevier as its first governor.

ooooo

A year after Governor Henry crushed Arthur Campbell's separatist schemes, he was confronted with recurrent skirmishes between Kentucky settlers and Wabash Indians in the Ohio Valley near Vincennes (in modern Indiana). Many of these incidents were triggered by Kentuckians encroaching upon the Indian territory ceded to Congress north of the Ohio River. "You are drawing so close to us," one tribal chieftain complained,

"that we can almost hear the noise of your axes felling our trees and settling our Country." But the area's tribes were also getting ammunition,
supplies, and encouragement from British agents in Detroit. In the spring
of 1786 several hundred Shawnee warriors began raiding south of the
Ohio River near its confluence with the Miami River (just west of modern Cincinnati)—and when the Virginia militia prepared to respond, the
Shawnee enlisted several other tribes in a combative alliance.

From Governor Henry's perspective, Congress was not living up to its
responsibilities both to protect settlers from Indian attack and to push the
British to evacuate their forts on the Great Lakes in compliance with the
peace treaty of 1783. When Henry reported the attacks near Vincennes to
Congress in May, he complained of its "seeming inattention" to Indian affairs and specifically its failure either to have negotiated a treaty with the
Wabash or at least "given [him] Notice of a hostile Disposition among
them." That same day, Henry wrote the Virginia delegation and urged
Congress to send troops against the Wabash for "experience clearly proves
that attacking their towns is the only mode of effectual defence." In addition to his belief that Congress should share the expense and send a federal army to assist the Kentucky militia, Henry was carefully fulfilling the
requirement of Article VI of the Articles of Confederation, which stipulated that unless they were under imminent attack the states must petition
Congress for assistance before engaging in military action.

Congress referred Henry's letter to a committee comprised of William
Grayson, James Monroe, and Massachusetts delegate Nathan Dane, whose
sympathy for Virginia's needs arose from a shared desire for congressional
military support: Dane and the Bay State delegation wanted Congress to
send troops to assist in the suppression of Shays' Rebellion—a mission
for which Virginia was the only state that offered troops and resources.
On the recommendation of Grayson's committee, Congress agreed to raise
two companies under the command of Philadelphia-born Colonel Josiah
Harmar, who had served under Washington and Light-Horse Harry Lee
during the Revolution and was now senior officer of the U.S. Army. Congress dispatched Harmar to the Ohio River, near modern Louisville, but it
did not authorize his use of force. A skeptical Yankee congressman wrote
that the committee proposal had been "more hostile than we conceived existing Circumstances would warrant," but that "a soothing answer however
is to be given to the Governor of Virginia."

ooooo

Governor Henry was in no mood for soothing rhetoric from armchair generals in Congress. Not only his citizens and constituents but his sister Annie and many friends were caught up in the bloodshed in Kentucky. A year earlier, Annie and her husband, Colonel William Christian, had moved their family from Botetourt County, near modern Roanoke, to Jefferson County, near modern Louisville, Kentucky. The following spring, after a party of Wabash warriors raided his neighborhood, Christian and a neighbor, Captain Isaac Keller, were mortally wounded on April 9 after pursuing the Wabash warriors back across the Ohio River. Five weeks later, after news that William Christian had "fallen a sacrifice" finally reached him in Richmond, Henry expressed both his grief and his faith in a private letter to his widowed sister.

"My dear sister," Henry wrote Annie Christian, "while I am endeavoring to comfort you, I want a comforter myself." Her husband had read law with him in the 1770s and served under him in the First Virginia Regiment before their marriage, and Henry loved him like a "friend and brother." Together they could find consolation, Henry believed, only in "the many precious lessons of piety given us by our honored parents" and their shared Christian faith, which offered "a refuge that no misfortunes can take away." Separated by ranges of mountains and six hundred miles, Henry regretted that distance might have prevented Annie from knowing "how much I loved you or your husband." Knowing that his sister and her family had found temporary refuge near Danville, Kentucky, and that she had support from her daughter Priscilla and her husband, Alexander Scot Bullitt, Henry offered his assurance that although they might never see one another again "in this world," they would surely "meet in that heaven to which the merits of Jesus will carry those who love and serve him."

ooooo

Reflecting upon Colonel Christian's death in a letter to his sister's neighbor and his own long-time friend William Fleming, Governor Henry spoke of his "aching Heart" and his dutiful submission to "that gracious Providence whose Ways are unsearchable, and who sends his Summons for us from this World as in his Wisdom sees best as to Time and Manner." The remainder of Henry's letter answered Fleming's reports of the discovery of gold ore in Montgomery County in southwestern Virginia (near modern Wytheville). Although the enterprise ultimately fell short of everyone's hopes, Henry's astute reaction to the opportunity revealed his wide-ranging legal, entrepreneurial, and political savvy—and, in a curious way, his general attitude toward the constitutional issues that would soon confront Virginia and the nation.

Earlier in the month, Fleming had sent Henry a few ounces of ore and sought his advice on behalf of perhaps a dozen frontier associates. Henry, in turn, had entrusted an ore sample to a Petersburg goldsmith and jeweler, probably Noel Waddill, for "a very careful and exact Tryal." Henry had full confidence in Waddill's report that the ore might yield gold worth £600 per ton. He was more skeptical of Fleming's assurance that the area had "an inexhaustible Stock of it." The prospect, however, was "so big with consequences public and private" that Henry wanted to act promptly. He arranged to send Waddill westward "tomorrow or next Day" to test more samples of the ore and confer with Fleming and the others. As a way of securing his and Fleming's investments, Henry also forwarded a land warrant for 1,800 acres and his promise to reimburse Fleming for any other expenses.

Henry vouched for Waddill's honesty and discretion—and assured Fleming that in addition to the goldsmith's training and experience he would come armed with "the best Treatise on the Subject." It was important to obtain ore samples from many locations, search creek beds and rivers, and "Sink Shafts in many places." Meticulous testing, for which Waddill would bring equipment, was essential—as was discretion. Beyond the dozen men already involved, Henry urged Fleming and Waddill to "be very carefull in making known the Result to none but a very few . . . confidential persons."

Gold mania was as old as Virginia. Captain John Smith had sneered about "the Almighty Power of Gold" at Jamestown, where a mistaken frenzy for "gilded Dirt" had distracted early settlers from their crops, trade, and defenses. Gold fever was also as old as America. Spanish conquistadors had been dazzled by visions of El Dorado (as Henry recognized when he compared Fleming's news with the storied mines of South America). Indeed, gold madness was as old as civilization itself. History since the days of King Midas was replete with tales of crime, fraud, political machination, and personal ruin provoked by mankind's obsession with gold.

"Where Gold is in question," Henry cautioned, "Roguery in all its Shapes, Robberys, Murders, and every Enormity may be expected."

Mindful of the roving criminals who had plagued the Virginia back-country during the last years of the Revolutionary War, Henry warned that it could be dangerous to begin smelting the ore too close to the mines, where "Gangs of Robbers will certainly carry it off and take Refuge in the Wilderness." Far better to ship the ore eastward "in its crude state to some place of entire Safety." Virginia had demonstrated that lead could be processed and shipped from a backwoods site, but Henry had no illusions about gold's irresistible temptation for the frontier cousins of the Caribbean pirates who had preyed upon the Spanish treasure fleets. "If a large Quantity of Gold is lodged far back in the Woods," Henry warned, "Robbery and Murder will ensue."

As an attorney with business experience, Henry routinely valued clear and well-documented transactions. He was eager to team with Fleming's local partners provided all agreements were put "in writing so as to put it out of all Dispute." If the discovery did bring a bonanza, imperfect contractual agreements would only breed confusion and contention.

Gold fever could also breed "Envy and Hatred" in the corridors of government. "If our Riches are really great," Henry advised, "don't let too much Noise be made until next Assembly"! Henry knew that English law had reserved 20 percent of the value of precious metals for the crown. In addition, having signed hundreds of land warrants, Henry knew that the act creating the state Land Office had specifically (and retroactively) nullified "the reservation of royal mines . . . under the former government" for all property titles in the commonwealth. Nevertheless, Henry cautioned that "although the Law may as it stands give it to us, yet you know how easy a discontented party may sound the alarm of Danger to the State from private People having so much Gold."

Henry urged Fleming and his friends to "remember how the Lead Mines have been ruined for want of power in the several partners"—alluding both to the insufficient capital and leadership void that had prompted the commonwealth to take over the lead mines (also in Montgomery County) as a wartime emergency in October 1776. Government intervention in the operation of the lead mines posed an ominous precedent. Arguably, a well-run privately owned gold mine would benefit the entire economy of Virginia and the nation. But if the General Assembly could confiscate the lead mines on the grounds that lead was a commodity "necessary at this time for the continent in general as well as this country in particular," jealous legislators could easily project a similar rationale against the interests of Fleming and his neighbors "and perhaps succeed in getting the Law altered to suit some party purpose." Should any legislators attempt that, Henry believed that by taking "a resolute Stand . . . consistent with what is right" he could persuade the Assembly to agree upon measures that promoted "the public Interest along with our own"—but unless the investors organized their enterprise well "it will ruin them instead of enriching them."

Despite Henry's admonitions about discretion and secrecy, news of the gold discoveries along Reading Creek in Montgomery County made the newspapers not only in Richmond but as far away as Boston and Charleston, Massachusetts; New York; Hartford and Norwich, Connecticut; and Trenton, New Jersey. Had the ore's quality and quantity lived up to Fleming's reports, the discovery would surely have left a greater impression on the history of the Old Dominion (where commercial gold mining prospered from 1806 through 1947) just as the discovery in 1799 of gold in Cabarrus County made North Carolina the leading producer of American gold prior to the California Gold Rush of 1849.

Although the gold deposits of Montgomery County ultimately fell short of everyone's hopes, Patrick Henry's reaction to the discovery revealed more than his legal and business savvy. In sharp contrast with James Madison, whose disappointment in a contemporary business opportunity energized an intense commitment to curbing the powers of state governments, Henry's anticipation of the prospective challenges to Fleming's gold mining project revealed his own fundamentally democratic instincts and temperament in regard to constitutions and governance.

ooooo

In the spring of 1786, while Governor Henry was advising William Fleming about gold mining, James Madison was entering a speculative partnership with James Monroe to acquire nine hundred fertile acres of frontier land along the Mohawk River near modern Rome, New York, where Madison and the Marquis de Lafayette had witnessed government negotiations with the Iroquois two years earlier. The acreage they had been able to afford comprised only a few modest farmsteads, Madison lamented to

Thomas Jefferson, because "the difficulty of raising a sufficient sum" for a more ambitious investment "restrained us from making a larger one." Jefferson not only confirmed Madison's observation by declining to invest himself, he also dashed Madison's hope of borrowing European capital. French investors, Jefferson reported, were discouraged by America's reputation for "want of punctuality" in loan payments and "habitual protection of the debtor" when creditors went to court.

Madison's disappointment in this speculative venture, as historian Woody Holton has observed, gave him "a personal stake in government reform." Unmarried and still living with his parents at the age of thirty-six, Madison despaired of ever being able to borrow sufficient working capital to achieve personal independence unless American legislators and judges bolstered the nation's credit rating. Madison believed that the state governments' widespread reluctance to levy taxes and enforce the property rights of creditors fostered a "prevailing and increasing distrust of public engagements and alarm for private rights." State legislators, he contended, were guilty of subverting the public good by ignoring "the rules of justice and the rights of the minority" and yielding to "the superior force of an interested and over-bearing majority." If the states were unable to "crack down on delinquent debtors and taxpayers," Holton wrote, rewriting the Articles of Confederation "was like appealing an unfavorable jury verdict to a higher court." Madison now focused his energies on creating a national government equal to the task—a central government empowered to collect its own revenues, protect the sanctity of contracts, and even (in his unsuccessful pet scheme) veto state laws.

Patrick Henry's inclinations, as revealed in his advice for William Fleming, differed from Madison's in virtually every significant way. Rather than seeking investors, Henry preferred buying a stake in joint ventures using his own resources (money, landholdings, or land warrants) without relying on "too many people, as they will perplex us, and hinder the Work." Henry wanted sound business practices, a clear "Plan of Proceeding," and an executive "Agent" with sufficient "powers of Management." If the General Assembly of Virginia were tempted to disregard the public good, Henry's remedy was not to rewrite the Articles of Confederation or surrender provincial autonomy to any external higher authority. His inclination—confirmed by decades of his successful political experience—was to exert his "good Counsel" within Virginia's democratic institutions, insist that his fellow citizens and legislators act "consistent with what is right," and make sure that "the public Good [was] promoted along with our own."

ooooo

After privately consoling his sister with thoughts of heaven and advising his friend about gold mines, Henry poured his outrage over the plight of her husband and neighbors into a damning letter to Virginia's congressional delegation that they, in turn, read aloud in Congress. In language that came close to the war-cant rhetoric of his famous speeches, Henry declared himself "mortified" by the delegation's report "that opposition might be expected in Congress to the active measures agreed on all hands to be necessary for the preservation of our Western Settlements." Were congressmen too selfish to feel "sympathy for that part of the Union whose extermination seems to be attempted by an Enemy thirsting for blood" and numb to the "Tenderness and fellow feeling which every Social Compact avows as its best Foundation"?

Now more than ever, Henry demanded action. Virginia had ceded its claim to the northwest for the good of the nation and the Articles of Confederation specifically prevented him from waging war against the Wabash "till the united states in congress assembled can be consulted." Henry now insisted "that a decided answer be given to the Question, 'Will Congress defend and protect our Frontiers?'" With the same candor he had voiced on the eve of the Revolution, Henry wanted to know the worst and prepare for it. If Congress was not going to defend the frontier he wanted "to know it as quickly as possible. Otherwise the Lives of our Citizens will be the forfeit of their Indecision and want of Foresight, which I am sorry to say are too apparent in this Department of public Affairs." If on the other hand Congress did intend to defend the western settlers, he demanded that the Virginia delegation point out "the exceeding great Danger of procrastination." As Henry saw it, frontier defense was "a prerogative of Congress" and the fate of the nation was at stake. If Americans discovered "that no reliance can be placed in Congress for protection," he warned, "all the Western people [will be] driven into a separation from us," and the states with western territories would be forced to the dilemma either of "abandoning them or the present Confederation!"

Henry wanted Congress to invest in resident frontier agents posi-

tioned to monitor and encourage peaceful relations in the Ohio Country
(much as British frontier agents had worked to maintain frontier justice
and peace between the 1750s and independence). He readily admitted that
"it [was] urged by some, and with too much Truth, that our own people
are the Aggressors"—but that fact only made the deployment of federal
agents more critical. "At present if any Injury is received by an Indian, to
whom can he make known his Complaint?" Henry asked. "To trust his
person amongst the people who Committed the Injury would be too haz-
ardous," for the offending frontiersmen "would feel an interest in killing
[the Indian] to prevent a discovery of their Villainy."

Without federal agents present to mitigate complaints, Indians were
forced either to "take Vengeance . . . or forgive the Injury"—and Henry
had no illusions about "which of the two [was] like to happen." Anyone with even "a slight knowledge of the Indian character" or an honest impression of "the Character of such Americans as usually frequent
the Indian Borders," knew that their proximity "necessarily produces contention." Although it was "perhaps impossible" to prevent all "mischievous
Consequences" on the frontier, Henry felt it was unwise "to leave the peace
of the United States depending upon the bare possibility of a total change
of National character on both sides."

ooooo

Soon after dispatching his vehement letter to the Virginia delegation,
Governor Henry received a resolution from Congress directing him to
hold the Virginia militia "in readiness to unite with the federal troops in
such operations as the officer commanding the troops of the United States
may judge necessary." Although this response fell short of what Henry
wanted, it had useful implications. Most significantly, it implied a federal
commitment to the costs of frontier peacekeeping. Secondly, it answered
the constitutional stipulation about notifying Congress before waging war.
And third, it gave Henry an opportunity for creative initiative.

Immediately upon receipt of the resolution from Congress, Governor
Henry wrote to Colonel Josiah Harmar and informed him that two of his
nine companies of federal troops should be sent to Ohio "to cooperate
with such numbers of militia in the district as the occasion shall render
proper." Although his Council of State had endorsed the congressional
authorization verbatim, Henry omitted both the phrase "hold in readiness"

and any reference to the authority of "the officer commanding the troops of the United States" from his letter to Harmar. As a result, lacking any direct instructions from Congress, Harmar followed Henry's instructions and dispatched two companies of federal troops commanded by Captain Walter Finney to fight "under the command of the militia"—just as Governor Henry evidently intended.

Early in August, however, before Harmar's orders reached Finney, George Rogers Clark raised two thousand Kentucky militia and put Finney's troops on garrison duty at the falls of the Ohio (modern Louisville). Clark then led 1,200 men westward against the Wabash near Vincennes while Benjamin Logan led 790 troops eastward against the Shawnee near the Miami River. Logan's force destroyed several Shawnee towns and large quantities of provisions, killed ten chiefs, and took thirty-two prisoners. Clark's expedition ran low on supplies, however, lost half its men to desertion, and returned to Kentucky without firing shots at their enemy. After Henry's term as governor ended, Virginia continued to demand that federal troops protect its western settlers—and for this reason would offer similar support for federal troops sent to intervene in Shays' Rebellion. Nevertheless, owing in large part to slow communications between Philadelphia and the Ohio frontier, the only actual support that Clark's and Logan's expeditions got from Congress was the garrison at the falls of the Ohio.

That autumn, faced with requests for military intervention against the insurrection in western Massachusetts, an impoverished Congress imposed a special requisition on the states to back an emergency $500,000 loan to the Bay State. Mindful of Virginia's western military needs and eager to keep Harmar's troops in Ohio, the General Assembly responded to the congressional request for troops and money by raising the state's quota of sixty cavalry and adding 6 shillings per hogshead to the export tax on tobacco. Within a year the strategy that Patrick Henry had initiated— seeking national support for Virginia's western security interests by supporting congressional assistance for Massachusetts—paid off. After Shays' Rebellion had been put down, six companies of federal troops were sent to the Ohio frontier and Congress gave Virginia full credit for the expenses of the Clark and Logan expeditions.

This effort to engage federal troops in the defense of frontier settlers reflected Henry's lifelong devotion to the idea that the protection of American liberty demanded unanimity between the people of Virginia and their compatriots in the other states. But to Henry's great dismay, some of the same Massachusetts congressmen who welcomed Virginia's support for Congress in the autumn of 1786 had spent the summer intriguing to stab the Old Dominion in the back over the navigation of the Mississippi River.

ooooo

Virginia's delegation to the Confederation Congress had a cipher on hand to encode sensitive communications with the governor, but James Monroe (who seems never to have grown comfortable using codes) could not find the key to their cipher when he wrote home to Virginia about an apparent conspiracy to surrender America's claim to the use of the Mississippi in exchange for a commercial treaty with Spain. Monroe spent Saturday, August 12, composing a detailed summary of the crisis and its origins in a long letter to Governor Henry. Monroe sent his letter unencoded because he felt the crisis was "of such high importance" that it warranted the "risque [of] communication without that cover."

"This is one of the most extraordinary transactions I have ever known," Monroe warned Governor Henry,

> a minister negotiating expressly for the purpose of defeating the object of his instructions, and by a long train of intrigue and management seducing the representatives of the States to concur in it. . . . Certain it is that Committees are held in this town of Eastern men . . . upon the subject of a dismemberment of the States East of the Hudson from the Union and the erection of them into a seperate government.

Monroe's third year in Congress was nearly over. He urged Governor Henry to convene the legislature "sufficiently early" so that Virginia had its new congressmen ready to take their seats "precisely on the day that those of the present delegation expire. Affairs are in too critical a situation for the State to be unrepresented a day—eminent disadvantage may result from it."

For more than a year, John Jay, secretary for foreign affairs, and the savvy Spanish diplomat Diego de Gardoqui had been negotiating toward a treaty of amity and commerce. Their situation was deceptively simple. Spain had not been party to the Anglo-American treaty that ended the Revolution in 1783, no boundary line had been drawn between Spanish West Florida and the Tennessee country; and in 1784 Spain's King Carlos III had closed the port of New Orleans and the lower Mississippi to American trade. As their talks continued, neither man could yield on the critical point of disagreement. Gardoqui was bound by instructions to deny the Americans use of the river, while Congress held Jay to the policy advocated by Virginia and the southern states seeking open navigation down the Ohio from Pittsburgh to the Gulf of Mexico and full use of the essential docks and warehouses at New Orleans, where cargo was transferred from riverboats to oceangoing vessels.

The more time Gardoqui spent in America the more people he met who did not care about exporting bulky agricultural products downstream from the fields and forests of Kentucky. He discovered that congressmen representing desperate New England fishermen, ship owners, and merchants were as keen to learn about the ports of the Spanish empire and the Lenten market for cod among the subjects of His Most Catholic Majesty Carlos III as they were to smoke his "Havanna Segars." Although the peace treaty of 1783 had guaranteed American fishermen access to the waters off Newfoundland, the British Navigation Acts were hammering American merchants by restricting their former access to English ports. New England's maritime economy was a live coal that a shrewd negotiator like Gardoqui could easily fan into flame. In short, America's diplomatic situation in 1785–1786 was anything but simple—and it was rife with deception.

ooooo

Gardoqui exploited an intrigue begun by Bay State congressman Rufus King when his quest for trade regulations to protect American merchants against British competition carried him from thoughts of a subconfederation to ideas of regional secession. "The Confederation admits of Alliances between two or more States, provided the purpose and duration thereof are previously communicated to and approved by Congress," King wrote. "The seven Eastern states have common commercial interests ... and are competent to give the Approbation of Congress to such sub-confederations, as they might agree upon." In short, the northern states had the votes necessary to authorize a sub-confederation of, voilà, the northern states.

King had complained that even "if Congress had the power to regulate Trade, they would be without the Disposition to do it," because "the Southern States will [never] relinquish their partial, and unfederal, policy concerning commerce, until they find a decided disposition in the Eastern States to combine for their own security." Only if the northern states joined together as a commercial sub-confederation or a separate confederation would "the southern states ... sensibly feel their weakness, and accede to such measures as may be adopted by the majority of the Confederacy." "The Southern States have much to fear from a dissolution of the present Confederacy," the Harvard-trained attorney Nathan Dane wrote in January 1786 to his fellow Essex attorney Edward Pulling. "They surely must be alarmed even at the suggestion of a confederacy of the States north of the Potomac or even the Delaware."

Men who saw each other every day in Congress and every evening at their boardinghouses had little need to write to one another, except when somebody left town. When Nathan Dane went home that summer he wrote guardedly to assure Rufus King that "all the men I have conversed with appear to have adopted ideas similar to ours." King replied with equal discretion that he was "happy to lea[r]n that prudent and discreet men concur with us in Opinion concerning the Spanish negotiation," for "it would appear strange to me if a contrary Opinion was entertained by any sensible man North of the Potomack." Congressman Theodore Sedgwick was less circumspect in a letter home to a state senator in central Massachusetts. The eastern and middle states ought to reconsider their connection with the southern states, Sedgwick wrote in August 1786. "They can give us nothing" and "even the appearance of a union cannot ... long be preserved," he thought. "It becomes us seriously to contemplate a substitute; for if we do not controul events we shall be miserably controuled by them. No other substitute can be devised than that of contracting the limits of the confederacy to such as are natural and reasonable."

These New Englanders assumed that the southern states—whether out of weakness (King), fear (Dane), or incapacity (Sedgwick)—needed New England more than New England needed them. Their assumption

of superiority reflected a widespread perception that slavery made the
South vulnerable (in the felicitous language of the Declaration of Independence) to "domestic insurrection," for as Luther Martin of Maryland
reminded the Philadelphia convention of 1787, "Slaves weakened one part
of the Union which the other parts were bound to protect." In addition,
however, *these* New Englanders were closer to the congressmen that Jefferson disparaged as "obscure men who do its business badly" than to such
men as John and Samuel Adams, James Bowdoin, Elbridge Gerry, and
John Hancock, who had partnered with Patrick Henry and other Virginians since the Stamp Act Crisis. Even Rufus King's biographer ranked him
only as "foremost in the second rank of political figures in the early years
of the United States." The separatist schemers of 1785–1786 were drawn
more narrowly from a conservative eastern faction whose draconian fiscal
policies under the Massachusetts constitution of 1780 had caused Shays'
Rebellion—steadfast men whose views carried the Federalist party of the
"rich and wise and good" into regional exile and political oblivion in the
nineteenth century.

Until August 1786 Gardoqui and the New England schemers had effectively kept their conversations to themselves, but when James Monroe
began comparing their indiscreet remarks with certain actions in Congress
he knew it was time to alert the governor of Virginia. The tipoff came
when Jay reported to Congress that his negotiations with Gardoqui were
hopelessly stalled and asked that Congress relax its restrictions about the
Mississippi River. When the southern states balked, Jay suggested an alternative toward the same end by asking Congress to appoint a committee
with full authority to direct his negotiations with Gardoqui. Once again
Virginia and the southern delegations objected. In August Congress began
weeks of secret debates about the future of the Mississippi that ended in
a slightly different stalemate—one that was pregnant (as Henry's generation liked to say) with implications for the future.

Called to testify before Congress, Jay spoke in favor of relinquishing
navigation of the Mississippi for twenty-five or thirty years in exchange
for the commercial and maritime advantages with which Gardoqui had
dazzled his Yankee audience. In fairness to the urbane New Yorker, Jay
so badly underestimated the pace of western settlement and the necessity of river-borne exports that he apparently regarded a temporary surrender of the river as a harmless concession to strengthen the Union by

stealing the separatists' thunder. Although the northern states successfully rescinded the Mississippi restriction in Jay's instructions by a 7-to-5 majority (with Rhode Island absent as usual), the Virginia delegates promptly served notice that the Articles of Confederation required nine states to ratify a treaty and that the southern states would never endorse any treaty that threatened the Mississippi. In short, Rufus King's secessionist ploy had already collapsed when Congress heard the first rumblings from western Massachusetts of the agrarian rebellion triggered largely by the harsh fiscal policies of the same eastern statesmen involved in the secessionist scheme. Suddenly uncertain about their ability to control New England itself, the secret separatists abruptly scuttled the whole episode and, with few exceptions, threw their support into a patriotic movement for a stronger national government. Although Nathaniel Gorham, Rufus King, and others abandoned their scheme so quickly that they are remembered today as vigorous adherents of ratification of the Constitution, the intense feeling of betrayal and distrust they aroused among southern and western leaders was not as easily healed.

ooooo

From December 1785 until August 1786, congressional rules about the secrecy of its deliberations that were meant to protect freedom of debate created a greenhouse environment for political intrigue. Nevertheless, the dispute over the Jay-Gardoqui negotiations did not escape the notice of the French chargé d'affaires Louis-Guillaume Otto. "The negotiations relating to the treaty of commerce with Spain," he reported to his superiors, "have . . . been the constant subject of the deliberations of congress." The southern states were attempting to dissuade Pennsylvania and New Jersey from joining "the league of the North," while their northern colleagues argued that "the navigation of the Mississippi [was] . . . far from being advantageous to the confederation" because it might encourage an exodus "of the most industrious inhabitants of the northern states" to the fertile lands of the Ohio Valley, thereby crippling the fleets, decimating the market values of land, and consigning New England to a minority role in national affairs. "Who would hesitate an instant," Otto reflected, "to exchange the arid rocks of Massachusetts and of New Hampshire for the smiling plains of the Ohio and the Mississippi"?

The intensity of regional animosity did not escape Otto's notice, either.

"The secret reasons for the heat with which each side supports its opinion" was rooted in calculations of regional political and economic self-interest. Otto thought the westward movement of population was a two-fisted blow to New England, "since on the one hand it deprives her of industrious citizens, and on the other it adds to the population of the southern states. These new territories will gradually form themselves into separate [state] governments; they will have their representatives in congress, and will augment greatly the mass of the southern states." A treaty containing "only stipulations in favor of the northern fisheries," he continued, would enhance the prosperity, commerce, and "preponderance of the northern states" in national politics. Grateful that none of this was his problem, Otto closed his report by nothing that "the conduct of this thorny negotiation is in the hands of Mr. Jay."

Otto's assessment of the clash over the Jay-Gardoqui negotiations was perceptive as far as it went, but the French diplomat was not as well informed as Monroe. The Virginia congressman had been skeptical when he first overheard his New England colleagues talking about secession in their boardinghouses and New York taverns in December of 1785. Perhaps it was just the exaggerated hyperbole of weary legislators after long hours of debate and a few pints of ale, as some historians have supposed. By spring, however, after Jay approached him privately about the impasse with Gardoqui and then asked Congress for a special committee to guide his negotiations, Monroe realized that the talk about a separatist maritime confederation was becoming serious. "In conversations at which I have been present," Monroe reported to Governor Henry on August 12, 1786, they generally spoke about "a dismemberment so as to include Pen[nsylvani]a," but occasionally hoped to include Delaware and perhaps even Maryland, too. "Sometimes," Monroe said, they envisaged a northern confederation embracing "all the states south to the Potowmack."

By emphasizing that his information came from conversations he had personally witnessed, Monroe invoked a gentleman's code of honor signaling that he took personal responsibility as a gentleman for the accuracy of his report. Monroe was alerting Henry that although they were not intimate friends, the governor and his Council of State could rely on his candid belief that his warnings were well-informed, reliable, and deadly serious.

Rufus King's motion to transfer supervision of Jay's negotiation to a special advisory committee might have worked if the southerners who cared about the Mississippi had been looking the other way. Three years of careful attention to business, however, had taught Monroe some tricks, too. Nothing was easier (some tricks are timeless) than to persuade Congress to duck an issue by consigning it to further study. Instead of a committee empowered to direct Jay's negotiations and alter his instructions, Monroe wangled a committee to study Jay's request and report back later: its members were Monroe, Rufus King, and Charles Pettit of Pennsylvania, who was ostensibly neutral. The Monroe-King-Pettit committee met the next day and immediately settled into a permanent deadlock that brought the issue of Mississippi navigation to the floor and triggered the most divisive congressional debate of the revolutionary era.

Despite the constraints of house rules, honor, and prudence, there were practical political limits to the secrecy of congressional debates. It is true, as *Poor Richard's Almanack* put it, that "three may keep a secret, if two of them are dead," but congressmen of the Confederation period were accountable to the state legislators and governors who sent them to Philadelphia or New York—men who wanted to know, at least in summary, what their agents and the other states' agents were up to. Term limits enforced this primary allegiance, for a man could serve no more than three successive one-year terms in Congress. Owing their seats not to independent citizen voters but to the state legislatures, Confederation congressmen had little incentive to go public with the details of congressional deliberations, and congressmen in general did well at keeping their deliberations secret, especially in wartime.

On August 20, 1786—two weeks after his secret meeting with a group of northern congressmen and eight days after Monroe wrote Governor Henry—Diego de Gardoqui sent a report across the Atlantic to the Comte de Floridablanca and Carlos III by the French diplomatic pouch. This remarkable document confirmed Monroe's suspicions. "Not finding a better occasion," Gardoqui wrote, "I take advantage of the French mail to tell you that we are in a critical time. Never in Congress has there been a controversy more combated than that of our Mississippi." Gardoqui felt obliged "to keep secret what I have done" except "to say that it has even been [asked of] me ... whether I have come to disunite the Confederation." The prospect of a commercial treaty was now bleak—"The opposition is insurmountable, even though they flatter me that I have spoiled more of it than I believe"—but he was pleased that congressmen from all the states spoke "with the greatest respect of His Majesty and with approbation of my conduct." Gardoqui's own well-kept secret was that as long as he helped keep the Americans away from the riches of Mexico, the success or failure of his commercial negotiations had never really mattered to Carlos III—on that point the southerners were right about Spain's willingness to buy what it wanted from America, treaty or no.

Ill will engendered by the Jay-Gardoqui negotiations festered in Congress for two full years. The Spanish treaty was dead in the water by a 7-to-5 margin, but everybody had to stay on guard just in case. An air of suspicion now permeated national politics—especially in a political culture that believed in conspiracies. Distrust made routine business more difficult, aborted a promising movement for congressional reform prior to the Philadelphia convention of 1787, and inflamed regional jealousies in the debate over the new federal Constitution. The Jay-Gardoqui negotiations revealed attitudes toward the Mississippi River and the west that shaped the events of the next decade and the subsequent history of North America—hostility from New England, competitive neglect from the middle states, expansive hopes from the south, and impatient frustration in Kentucky and the Ohio Country.

ooooo

And finally, regardless of what Gardoqui, Jay, and the New Englanders may have had in mind—and regardless of the ratio of flames and smoke in their activities—Monroe's letter of August 12, 1786, to the governor of Virginia sent its own distinctive shock wave rippling through American history. Few people remember that it was Patrick Henry, in his capacity as governor, who signed Virginia's circular letter in February 1786 inviting the other twelve states to send delegates to the convention at Annapolis, Maryland, which then called for the meeting of the convention of 1787. Better known is Patrick Henry's refusal to participate in the Philadelphia convention of 1787 and his opposition to the ratification of the new government it proposed.

What changed Henry's outlook so drastically between his coffeehouse conversation in May of 1785 and both his decision not to attend the Philadelphia convention and his vigorous opposition to the Constitution in

1788? As the recipient of Monroe's letter, Henry may have been shocked by the dirty linen of the Jay-Gardoqui negotiations and the secret talk about secession among the New England congressmen. Much more profoundly, however, Henry and other prominent Virginians felt betrayed by erstwhile friends. The northern secessionist scheme of 1785–1786 utterly destroyed decades of trust between the Old Dominion and New England—the core partnership that had sustained the united colonies through their success-ful resistance to Parliament and war for independence. "Many of our most federal leading men are extremely soured," Madison lamented to Wash-ington. Virginians felt themselves treacherously *betrayed!*

Virginians had virtually always linked their future with the greater good of British North America—especially in regard to the trans- Appalachian west. Call it pride if you wish, but for thirty years—from the skirmish led by Major George Washington and his Virginia troops that triggered the French and Indian War in 1754 to the generous statemanship of Virginia's cession of the Old Northwest in 1784—most Virginia leaders equated the destiny of the Old Dominion with the future of an expansive American republic. This was the noble heritage that some New England politicians had been ready to scuttle.

Although cautionary voices had never been absent, before 1786 Vir-ginians had been remarkably united in identifying their future with the future of the nation. Many Virginians still clung to their grand conti-nental vision after the Jay-Gardoqui debacle and secessionist crisis of 1786—Washington, John Marshall, and James Madison come to mind. But for Patrick Henry and others—such as James Monroe, William Grayson, and Richard Henry Lee—the Jay-Gardoqui affair was an alarm bell in the night—a warning that a stronger national government could easily play into the hands of northern politicians hostile to Virginia's long-term interests.

The rift that opened in 1786 was by no means as deep as the chasms that would come later. Nevertheless, for Henry the long revolutionary honey-moon between Virginia and New England had eroded into a relationship haunted by the distrust that follows intense personal betrayal. Rufus King was not the only Confederation-era politician who could count noses. For Patrick Henry, the sectional distrust provoked by the Jay-Gardoqui nego-tiations surely figured in his decision to decline the honor when the General Assembly elected him as a delegate to the Philadelphia convention of 1787. The 7-to-5 alignment of states in Congress on the issue of Mississippi navigation also shaped the Virginia debates in 1787–1788 over the merits of a proposed national government in which congressional majorities would enact legislation and a two-thirds majority of the Senate could ratify treaties.

Frederick William Sievers's portrait bust of Patrick Henry.

Studley, Henry's birthplace near Totopotomoy Creek, was one of the largest houses in Hanover County when it was built about 1720.

George Cooke's 1834 portrayal of Henry's speech in the Parsons' Cause at Hanover Courthouse in 1763. Henry, center, gestures toward the justices, seated below the symbols of royal authority. His father, senior and presiding justice, dabs tears of pride.

Patrick Henry, Edmund Pendleton, and George Washington rode together to Philadelphia as three of Virginia's seven delegates to the First Continental Congress in 1774.

St. John's Church in Richmond was the site of Patrick Henry's Liberty or Death speech when the Virginia convention met there in 1775. It was built in 1741.

John Murray, Earl of Dunmore (1732–1809), Virginia's last royal governor, came to the colony in 1771 and clashed repeatedly with "Henry and his deluded followers."

Scotchtown was the earliest and largest manor house in the western part of Hanover County when it was built about 1719. Henry bought the property in 1771, but after the death of his first wife, Sarah Shelton Henry, he put the plantation up for sale in 1777.

Published in London, Thomas Kitchin's "Map of the United States in North America . . . according to the Treaty of 1783" shows the Commonwealth of Virginia administered by Governor Patrick Henry from 1776 to 1779 as a lopsided triangle, four times larger than Great Britain, with half the territory and 40 percent of the population of the new republic.

Henry and his family lived in the Governor's Palace in Williamsburg from 1776 through 1779. Destroyed by fire in December 1781, the palace was reconstructed in the early 1930s using inventories compiled by Thomas Jefferson during his residency as governor.

James Madison (1751–1836) worked with Henry on the Virginia Declaration of Rights in 1776. After they opposed one another in the ratification debates of 1788, Henry's influence denied Madison a seat in the new U.S. Senate and enforced his campaign promise to secure adoption of the Bill of Rights.

Richard Henry Lee (1732–1794) served with Henry in the House of Burgesses and the Continental Congress. Lee presented Virginia's motion for independence to Congress in 1776. He was Henry's choice as one of Virginia's first two U.S. senators in 1789.

George Washington's neighbor George Mason (1725–1792) was a principal author of the Virginia Declaration of Rights and the state's first constitution. He joined Henry in opposing ratification of the U.S. Constitution in the Virginia convention of 1788.

Edmund Pendleton (1721–1803) served with Henry in the House of Burgesses and the Continental Congress, but they frequently disagreed, especially about religious toleration. Pendleton confronted Henry in the 1788 convention debates over the ratification of the Constitution.

This portrait of Thomas Jefferson (1743–1826) was painted by Mather Brown in 1786, during Jefferson's tenure as American minister to France. Henry and Jefferson were friends and close political allies until 1781, when the General Assembly's call for an inquiry into the state government's ineffective response to the British invasions of that year permanently strained their relationship.

Edmund Randolph (1753–1813), governor of Virginia from 1786 to 1788, had followed his uncle, Peyton Randolph, president of the First Continental Congress, in support of the revolution rather than his loyalist father, John Randolph, who exiled himself to England. Randolph declined to sign the Constitution but supported its ratification in the Virginia convention of 1788.

Although John Marshall (1755–1835) and Henry disagreed about ratifying the Constitution in the Virginia convention of 1788, they began a strong friendship when they argued the British debts cases before the U.S. Supreme Court in the early 1790s after Henry's retirement from public office.

Virginia Sct:

Pursuant to an Act of the General Assembly of this Commonwealth, intituled "An Act for the appointment of Electors to choose a president, pursuant to the "Constitution of Government for the United States" We the Subscribers, being ten of the Electors appointed for this Commonwealth (our respective appointments having been duly advertised by the Governor and Council, according to the directions of the said Act,) this day assembled in the City of Richmond, and having proceeded to discharge the duty of our appointment, do hereby Certify and make known the following list of all the persons voted for, and of the number of Votes for each, agreeable to the first Section of the Second Article of the Constitution of Government for the United States, to wit;

For George Washington, Esquire, of Mount Vernon, ten votes.
For John Adams, Esquire, of Massachusetts, five Votes.
For George Clinton, Esquire, of New York, three Votes.
For John Hancock, Esquire, of Massachusetts, one Vote.
For John Jay, Esquire, of New York, one vote.

Certified and Given under our hands and Seals at the City of Richmond aforesaid, on Wednesday, this fourth day of February 1789.

P Henry

John Pride

James Wood.

As the senior statesman among the ten electors who met in Richmond on February 4, 1789, Henry was the first to sign the official certification of Virginia's electoral vote for president. All ten electors voted for George Washington.

Created about 1795, this miniature bears the initials of artist Lawrence Sully. It is one of only four portraits of Henry made during his lifetime.

CHAPTER TWENTY-THREE

The New Constitution

IMMEDIATELY UPON HIS RETURN to Mount Vernon after presiding all summer at the Philadelphia convention of 1787, George Washington sent Patrick Henry a copy of the proposed constitution. "In the first moment after my return," Washington wrote, "I take the liberty of sending to you a copy of the constitution." Confident that Henry's "judgment will at once discover the good and the exceptionable parts of it" and that Henry knew as well as he did the challenges of reconciling "such a variety of interest and local prejudices as pervade the several States," Washington offered no comments or explanations of the plan. He acknowledged that the proposal was imperfect, but he sincerely believed "it is the best that could be obtained at this time." Despite its imperfections, however, because it opened "a constitutional door ... for amendments hereafter," Washington felt that its adoption was desirable. "The political concerns of this country are in a manner suspended by a thread," he concluded, and if the convention had failed "anarchy would soon have ensued."

Washington's letter reached Henry in Richmond, where after completing his term as governor he was representing Prince Edward County in the autumn session of the General Assembly. Henry replied promptly, expressing both his thanks for the proposed constitution and his heartfelt gratitude "as a Citizen" for Washington's "great Fatigue ... attending the arduous Business of the late Convention." As to the merits of the plan, Henry was candid but not specific. "I have to lament that I cannot bring my Mind to accord with the proposed Constitution," he wrote. "The Concern I feel on this Account is really greater than I am able to express." He ventured politely, without revealing any details, that "perhaps mature Reflection may furnish me Reasons to change my present Sentiments into a conformity with the opinion of those personages for whom I have the highest Reverence." Henry closed his letter with assurances of his "unalterable Regard and Attachment."

Henry had two good reasons for not informing Washington of his specific reactions to the proposed constitution. First, he was genuinely undecided both about the details of the plan and about the political response that would best serve the common good of Virginia and the nation. Second, even after he clarified his thinking on those matters, Henry's inclination was to keep his own counsel and leave all his options as open as possible in order to accomplish his political objectives. Once again relying upon the "habit of close and attentive observation" that had impressed his friends, Henry sought to gauge both public sentiment and the opinions of his peers without divulging the details of his own mature reflections. As the thirteen states deliberated about the constitution, Henry strengthened his political bargaining position and gave himself room for tactical maneuvers in the contest by cloaking the exact nature of his objectives—even if his reticence prompted wild speculation (as it did in the months ahead) about his motives and objectives.

Henry could afford to be circumspect because others were quick to express their reservations about (or support of) the proposed constitution. Each of the three men who had refused to sign the Constitution at Philadelphia—George Mason and Edmund Randolph from Virginia, and Elbridge Gerry from Massachusetts—went public with their reservations. Mason's *Objections*, twice published as a pamphlet and widely reprinted in newspapers between October and December, opened with a thunderous complaint: "There is no Declaration of Rights, and the laws of the general government being paramount . . . the Declarations of Rights in the separate States are no security." Eight hundred words later, after listing all manner of shortcomings, Mason predicted that the proposed government, unless amended, would begin as "a moderate aristocracy," then "vibrate" for several years between a monarchy and a corrupt and tyrannical aristocracy, and finally "terminate in the one or the other." Elbridge Gerry announced his objections, which were similar to Mason's, in October and they were widely reprinted in Massachusetts and throughout the nation.

Edmund Randolph, now governor of Virginia, consigned his objections to paper in October and consulted privately with Henry, Madison, and others before he formally presented his comments to the General Assembly in December. Augustine Davis published Randolph's "Letter on the Federal Constitution" in his *Virginia Independent Chronicle* in December and as a pamphlet early in January. Randolph advocated a second constitutional convention to remedy the flaws of the plan adopted at Philadelphia and clarify "all ambiguities of expression." He wanted clearer lines "between the powers of Congress and individual states" to protect the states from being "swallowed up . . . under the cover of general words and implication," as well as some structural changes and several specific limits upon delegated powers.

Henry's and Randolph's reservations about the Constitution overlapped in significant ways. Both men were strongly committed to amendments. Both men welcomed the prospect of a second federal convention. Henry and Randolph "had several animated discourses," the governor told James Madison late in October, "but he recedes so far from me that we must diverge after a progress of half a degree further." Their initial disagreement was over political tactics—but their divergence was one of temperament as well as politics. Bold and self-confident, the experienced Henry puzzled and perhaps frightened the chronically indecisive Randolph. Henry believed that the unamended constitution posed such threats to Virginia's sovereignty and interests, and to American liberties in general, that the situation demanded political savvy. Henry, Mason, and other critics of the Constitution were appalled by Governor Randolph's naïveté when he not only disclosed his fallback position at the very outset of the public debate but openly acknowledged "the advantage which such a declaration may give to the enemies of [his] proposal." Within just three weeks of his return from the Philadelphia convention, Randolph had virtually surrendered his goal of improving the new system by declaring that "if after our best efforts for amendments they cannot be obtained" he would nevertheless "accept the constitution" as it stood. "Good God!" exclaimed Spencer Roane, echoing both his father-in-law's rhetoric and his opinions. "How can the first Magistrate . . . after a feeble parade of opposition, and before his desired plan of amendments has been determined upon, declare that he will accept a Constitution which is to beget either a monarchy or an aristocracy?" The governor, Roane sneered, "has let the cat out of the bag."

Of the former governors to whom Washington sent copies of the Constitution, only Benjamin Harrison replied with specific reservations about the document. Harrison acknowledged that he was unfamiliar with "the general situation of America" beyond the borders of Virginia. But if the situation was "not very desperate" he feared "that the seeds of civil discord are plentifully sown in very many of the power given both to the president and congress, and that if the constitution is carried into effect the States south of the Potowmac will be little more than appendages to those to the northward." Harrison also objected to "the unlimited powers of taxation and the regulations of trade." A national government armed with both "the sword and such powers," he concluded, "must sooner or later establish a tyranny."

During and even after the contest over the ratification of the Constitution, Patrick Henry's attitudes were the subject of extensive and varied speculation in Virginia and elsewhere, and the nuances of his rhetoric were always subject to the changing circumstances of the national debate. From October of 1787 until his retirement from politics early in the 1790s, however, Henry's constitutional objectives remained stable. Once he accepted the fact that the proposed constitution, rather than the old Confederation, was destined to serve as the framework for any future national government—a political reality that Henry silently recognized by the end of October—he bent all his efforts toward the single goal of changing that system to make it more compatible with his ideas of liberty and federalism. "I can never agree to the proposed plan without Amendments," Henry told his brother-in-law Thomas Madison, an attorney in Botetourt County, "tho' many are willing to Swallow it in its present Form." Of course from the nationalist perspective, James Madison (a cousin of Henry's brother-in-law), presumed that Henry's desired amendments would "strike at the essence of the System."

At first—as is evident in the arrangements he proposed for Virginia's deliberations—Henry favored either a second federal convention or cooperative efforts among the states to revise the proposed constitution—as did Edmund Randolph, George Mason, Elbridge Gerry, and a cluster of New Yorkers led by Governor George Clinton. When federalist Francis Corbin (whose father had paid for the gunpowder in 1775) moved that a convention be summoned for the first Monday in June 1788 "according to the recommendation of Congress," nobody quibbled about the date—eight months in the future—because nobody was confident of victory, nobody could foresee the immediate future, and everybody wanted time to rally the voters to their side. Although the calendar ultimately worked against them, Henry's and Mason's immediate response to Corbin's motion aimed at giving Virginia's convention "the power of proposing amendments." If Corbin's resolution were adopted, Henry argued, "the Convention would only have it in their power to say that the new plan should *be adopted or rejected*; and that however defective it might appear to them they would not be authorized to propose amendments." Corbin and George Nicholas promptly objected to Henry's alternative language lest it suggest to the public that amendments were needed. Ultimately it fell to John Marshall, "with his usual perspicuity" according to an admiring newspaper account, to sever the partisan knot by proposing simply "that a Convention should be called, and that the new Constitution should be laid before them for their free and ample discussion." Marshall's resolution passed without opposition—but Henry's assertion "that there were errors and defects" in the proposed constitution appeared in some two dozen newspapers from Georgia to New Hampshire by the end of November.

Early in December, taking advantage of the need to authorize funding for the upcoming convention and confident that the calendar was working to his advantage, Henry introduced a resolution authorizing payments not only for the expenses of the delegates meeting in Richmond but also—"in case the said Convention should judge it expedient to propose Amendments to the said Fœderal Constitution"—for "Deputys to a second fœderal Convention" or "Deputys to confer with the Convention or Conventions of any other State or States in the Union on the Subject of the proposed plan of fœderal Government."

A week later, after some jockeying between the House and Senate that toned down Henry's explicit references to a second federal convention, the Assembly authorized £8,000 for the June convention by a comfortable margin of sixteen votes. While proclaiming Virginia's "friendly sentiments" toward her sister states and hope that "the greatest unanimity should prevail ... during the deliberations concerning the great and important change in government ... proposed by the fœderal convention," the authorization also extended to any reasonable expenses for "communications with any of the sister states or the[ir] conventions" or "collecting the sentiments of the union respecting the proposed fœderal constitution."

Federalists in the Assembly regarded the outcome as a significant victory for Henry and Mason. "Since they have discovered their Strength," one gloomy federalist anticipated that Henry's majority would likely "adopt other Measures" against the Constitution—and that might have happened had Henry sought the outright rejection of the entire plan. In the three months since the end of the Philadelphia convention, however, Henry had made enormous strides toward his real goal of forcing substantive alterations in the proposed government. To promote that goal among like-minded patriots beyond the borders of the Old Dominion, Henry and his majority ordered that their final resolution and its call for amendments (now entitled "An act concerning the Convention to be held in June next") be published as a broadside and sent to all the other states.

Two days after Christmas, as directed, Governor Edmund Randolph dispatched two copies of the convention broadside to the other governors with cover letters asking them to keep one copy for their "own perusal" and have "the other . . . submitted to the Legislature of your State." In light of Randolph's well-known refusal to sign the Constitution, recipients were likely to assume that he was in complete sympathy with the Assembly's call for interstate communication about amendments. His letter and its enclosures reached most state governors by January 22—but the message for New York did not reach Governor Clinton until March 7. This fateful six-week delay prevented the legislature of the Empire State from acting on the Old Dominion's invitation before their adjournment. Governor Clinton's reply lamented the tardy receipt of Randolph's letter on a subject "of such vast Importance to the Happiness of America." Nevertheless, he assured Randolph that the people of New York were eager to embrace "the Object of the Act of your Legislature and . . . commence the Measures for holding such Communications."

At this moment the whole episode took a partisan turn. Although the exact date that Clinton's reply reached Governor Randolph is unknown, late May would be a reasonable guess. "Immediately on receiving it," Randolph said that he brought the letter to his Council of State for a judgment as to "whether it was of a public or private nature"—although the official journal of the Council does not confirm this. Based on the opinion that Clinton's letter was an official public communication, Randolph kept it secret until the legislature convened on June 23, just three days before the Virginia convention ratified the Constitution. Regardless of his earlier insistence upon amendments and a second convention, the governor's decision to withhold Clinton's letter dashed any possibility of effective cooperation between the opponents of ratification, or antifederalists, in New York and Virginia.

ooooo

By early January 1788 five state conventions had ratified the Constitution. The votes in Delaware, New Jersey, and Georgia were unanimous, and the plan was adopted by substantial majorities in Pennsylvania (46 to 23) and Connecticut (128 to 40). With these victories, as most observers agreed, the federalists had harvested all the low-hanging fruit. The Constitution would face its first serious opposition when the Massachusetts convention met on January 9. In New York, where the convention was scheduled for mid-June, the antifederalists led by Governor George Clinton outnumbered their rivals. Like Henry, Clinton had supported moderate enhancements of congressional powers for many years and was now pressing for a second convention and substantive amendments to make the Constitution safe for liberty and federalism. Had Henry and Clinton been able to join forces early in 1788, the combined efforts of Virginia and New York antifederalists would surely have bolstered the opposition in Massachusetts and forced significant changes in the Constitution prior to its ratification by the remaining states.

Mount Vernon emerged as a center for communications from proponents of the Constitution throughout the country who were worried about Henry's political influence. Writing from the legislature in Richmond, one of Washington's protégés expressed great relief about Henry's October declaration that the Constitution "must go before a Convention," as it had been "insinuated [that] he would aim at preventing this." Days before the arrival of Henry's letter acknowledging receipt of the Constitution, Washington's private secretary informed a New Hampshire federalist that they had "not yet been able to learn the sentiments of Mr. (formerly Governor) Henry," but that as "a man of great popular influence in the lower parts of Virginia much will depend upon his dictum." Writing from New York, where he was serving in Congress, Madison told Jefferson that "the part Mr. Henry will take is unknown here" but that "much will depend on it." Madison "had taken it for granted from a variety of circumstances that he would be in opposition" (and still thought that likely) but had also heard reports "which favor a contrary supposition."

"This gentleman fires his shot at the new constitution every opportunity," one Virginia legislator told a friend. "Henry digresses from every
subject to assault it," another wrote. In November, although the Assembly
had previously addressed Congress about its concerns for the navigation
of the Mississippi River, Henry introduced an "unnecessary" resolution on
the subject "to show in a forcible manner how the commercial interests of
the Southern States are sacrificed by the Northern." Many federalists were
bewildered by the circulating reports of Henry's activities. His real views
were "unaccountable," Washington's private secretary believed. He "reviles
the proposed constitution and yet points out nothing that is better." By
early December, confusion was breeding speculation. "If I may be allowed
to form an opinion from his conduct of what would be his wish," Washington's secretary guessed, "it is to divide the Southern States from the
others. Should that take place, Virginia would hold the first place among
them, and he the first place in Virginia—But this is conjecture."

Many federalists speculated about separatism as a scare tactic, but in
their private correspondence a few were more candid about Henry's real
objectives. "Mr. Henry has declared his intention," a Tidewater legislator reported to Madison, "of promoting a second Convention at Philadelphia to consider amendments" and "communicat[ing] with our sister
states on that subject." He "is determined to amend," Edward Carrington
told Madison, and was ready to let the fate of the Constitution "depend
on all the other States conforming to the Will of Virginia." Henry argued
that "the other States cannot do without us," Carrington continued, "and
therefore we can dictate to them what terms we please" for "the Value of
our Staple [i.e., tobacco] is such that any Nation will be ready to treat with
us separately."

ooooo

While Virginia federalists anxiously speculated about Henry in the early
weeks of 1788, developments in Massachusetts suddenly shifted the dynamic of the entire ratification contest drastically in their favor. A clear
majority of the Bay State delegates wanted to amend the Constitution, but
they were divided about how to accomplish that objective—and so long
as the delegates remained divided the state's savvy and ambitious governor, John Hancock, had taken refuge in a convenient illness that prevented
his attendance at the convention. Early in February the governor's health

suddenly improved, however, assisted both by a promise from the federalists of political support in the next gubernatorial election and their observation, whispered to his well-known vanity, that Hancock would be "the
only fair candidate for President" if nine states ratified before Virginia and
pushed Washington to the sidelines. Rising from his sickbed and wrapping himself in flannel, Governor Hancock had his ailing body carried
dramatically into the convention hall. There he surprised everyone by suggesting that Massachusetts adopt the Constitution *and* simultaneously insist that, after the new government was operational, their delegates to the
Congress must "exert all their influence" to make a series of specific and
substantive changes. Freed from the constraint of choosing between all
or nothing, Massachusetts adopted Hancock's compromise—ratification
with recommended amendments—by a vote of 187 to 169 on February 6,
1788.

"The decision of Massachusetts is perhaps the most important event
that ever took place in America," exulted Edward Carrington, whose
neighbors south of the James River had generally been hostile to the Constitution. "Had she rejected [it] . . . there would not have been the most remote chance for its adoption in Virginia." The news from Boston, which
reached Virginia midway through the March elections for delegates to the
state convention, forced Henry to adjust his public arguments in ways that
caused greater anxiety among his opponents. Facing the prospect that nine
states might now ratify before the Virginia convention met, Henry now
had to explain why, in order to insist upon amendments, the Old Dominion could risk a strategic delay that might temporarily keep Virginia and
like-minded states out of the new union.

Not surprisingly, federalist observers throughout the country played up
Henry's arguments as dangerous threats to the union—whether prompted
by their own fears (as happened with federalists who lived or traveled in
Virginia) or the perceived fears of undecided voters (as happened elsewhere). After traveling through Cumberland, Powhatan, and Chesterfield
counties—all south of the James River in the central Piedmont—Edward
Carrington found Henry's "politics to have been so industriously propa-
gated that the people are much disposed to be his blind followers." Henry
"does not openly declare for a dismemberment of the Union," he informed
Jefferson, "but his Arguments in support of his opposition to the constitution go directly to that issue. He says that three Confederacies would

be practicable and better suited to the good of America than one." Henry "and his Minions," a Fredericksburg merchant told a friend, "declare that they would rather see the Union dissolved than adopt the Constitution."

Further afield, Pennsylvania lawyer Cyrus Griffin informed a Philadelphia merchant that "Henry and others [were] promoting a southern Confederacy," and in New York the disconcerted author of *Letters from an American Farmer*, St. Jean de Crèvecoeur, worried that the country would "plunge into anarchy and divisions if it forms two Confederacies as P. Henry wishes." From Congress, Madison played on Edmund Randolph's fears by suggesting that, although the governor was "better acquainted with Mr. Henry's politics than I can be . . . I have for some time considered him as driving at a Southern Confederacy." In February and again in April, the allegation that Henry sought the creation of separate confederacies made it into the newspapers.

When the French ambassador wrote home about the ratification contest he singled out Henry as the antifederalist leader who was "distinguished from all the others by his talents, his ambition, and his influence on the people." Although it was not really true, as the Comte de Moustier reported, that "Mr. Patrick Henri . . . plan[ned] to detach his State from the confederation," the ambassador certainly shared the perspective of Henry and Governor Clinton when he noted that "without Virginia and New York the new Government will exist more in name than in fact." As Henry saw it, the prospect of a union without the Old Dominion and the Empire State was such an absurdity that the threat of holding out was a powerful weapon in their fight for substantive amendments.

"You may think it of Consequence that some other States have accepted of the new Constitution," Henry's ally William Grayson told his northern Virginia constituents according to a North Carolina merchant who attended his election to the June convention. "What are they?" the former congressman and future senator asked as he showed the voters a box not much larger than a coin. "When compared to Virginia they are no more than this snuff Box is to the Size of a Man." It was an argument with great appeal, the Tar Heel observed to his friend at home, "to the feelings of Virginians."

ooooo

Throughout the winter Henry had spoken about the proposed constitution when people gathered for the monthly meetings of county courts
where he practiced law, but in February 1788 he announced his candidacy
for the June convention at Prince Edward courthouse about eighty miles
southwest of Richmond. Rather than moving all the way back to Leatherwood after his fifth term as governor, Henry had bought 1,690 acres on
a hill overlooking the Appomattox River west of Farmville. Known as
Pleasant Grove, the house was a two-story frame structure, built over a
brick English basement, with a columned two-story portico at the front.
A law office stood near the road, linked to the house by a double row of
locust trees several hundred feet long. When weather permitted, Henry
"walked and meditated . . . in this shaded avenue of fine black locusts," recalled a grandson who lived nearby.

Leatherwood plantation—where he left forty slaves, three dozen
horses and mules, and more than sixty head of cattle—remained Henry's
main agricultural enterprise, but Pleasant Grove was closer to the newly
created district courts at Farmville and New London where his practice of
law could retire the debts accumulated during his last terms as governor.
Nevertheless, with twenty-five slaves, four horses, and four cattle at Pleasant Grove, Henry stood among the top one percent of county residents
in 1787—and one of only two men who owned more than one taxable vehicle. Henry and his fellow delegate to the Convention of 1788, Robert
Lawson, each owned a two-wheeled buggy, or "riding chair," as well as a
four-wheeled coach. Since both men were lawyers, the larger vehicle was
probably used for family travel and the smaller buggy devoted to his legal
practice.

Patrick Henry "had never been in easy circumstances," a friend remembered, but when he worried aloud to a Prince Edward County neighbor
about the debts he had accumulated, "the reply was to this effect: 'Go back
to the bar; your tongue will soon pay your debts. If you will promise to go,
I will give you a retaining fee on the spot.'" For the next six years Henry
practiced before the district court at Prince Edward Courthouse during its
eight-day sessions from April 1 and September 1 and then traveled to New
London (near modern Lynchburg) where a district court began its sessions on April 12 and September 12. In effect these new courts brought the
common-law jurisdiction of the old general court at the capital closer to

Virginia's sprawling population, and in criminal cases the new courts had exercised "full power to hear and determine all treasons, murders, felonies, and other crimes and misdemeanors which shall be brought before them." It was a grueling schedule, but in these courts Henry exploited his skills as a defense attorney and polished his reputation as one of America's greatest lawyers.

As always, Henry's family increased at Pleasant Grove when Dorothea gave birth to her fifth child, Alexander Spotswood (named for his great-grandfather), on the opening day of the Virginia convention of 1788, her sixth child, Nathaniel West, in 1790, and in 1792 her seventh child, Richard, who died in infancy. In addition, after the death of his son-in-law, Colonel John Fontaine, Henry's eldest daughter, Martha, brought their four children to live with their grandfather Patrick. He and Dorothea Henry also took charge of his nephew Johnny Christian after the death in 1790 of Henry's sister Annie. "John Fontaine's widow . . . has been here ever since the death of her husband" along with Mrs. Spencer Roane (Henry's daughter Anne) "and her family also," a neighboring attorney noted in his diary after he and his brother spent a day and dined at Pleasant Grove. "What a weight of worldly concerns rest upon this old man's shoulders," the neighbor continued. "He supports it with strength and fortitude, but nature must sink under the load ere long."

Pleasant Grove's proximity to Hampden-Sydney College, a few miles south, was another feature that attracted Henry—and his sons—to the county. Organized as an academy in 1775 by the Hanover Presbytery and named for two martyred heroes of the English struggles against Stuart tyranny, John Hampden and Algernon Sydney, the college was chartered in 1783 by legislation that Henry steered through the Assembly along with the charters for Liberty Hall Academy in Rockbridge County (forerunner of Washington and Lee University) and Transylvania Seminary (now Transylvania University) in Kentucky—all of which drew heavily from Princeton for their faculties. Henry served on the Hampden-Sydney board of trustees, sent seven of his sons to its classes, and along with his fellow trustee General Robert Lawson jousted politically with the college's headstrong second president, thirty-two-year-old John Blair Smith, during the ratification contest.

"You will have perceived how unfortunately this County is represented in Convention," President Smith informed James Madison, his former classmate at Princeton and now a trustee of the college, as the debates in Richmond began. "Before the Constitution appeared," Smith wrote, "the minds of the people here were artfully prejudiced against it so that all Opposition at the election for delegates ... against Mr. Henry was in vain." Vastly outnumbered by Henry's supporters in the county and on his own board of trustees, the divisive (and short-tenured) young president expressed "contempt and indignation" for Henry's "gross and scandalous misrepresentations of the New-Constitution and ... its enlightened authors." Claiming that he had felt the lash of "popular odium" for trying "to diffuse his poison," Smith informed Madison that "the idea of Virginia standing independent of the other states or forming a partial confederacy or a foreign alliance is more openly avowed by some people in this quarter than any where else." He was "certain the sentiment originated with the old Governor."

Prevented by the death of a parishioner from attending the February 1788 meeting of the Prince Edward county court, John Blair Smith sent a student to record Henry's remarks when, as anticipated, he announced his candidacy for the upcoming convention. A few days later, at an exhibition of public speaking during the college's annual celebration of Washington's birthday, the president enlisted two students to humiliate Patrick Henry in front of a large audience. The first student recited a verbatim summary of Henry's political remarks at the courthouse and the second presented a vigorous rebuttal written for him by President Smith. Henry confronted Smith about the insult, and after the president refused to apologize Henry stopped attending his worship services—a gesture that reflected more than retribution. As it happened, in addition to his unpopular political stance, Smith had been courting disaster with his trustees by preaching with an evangelical zeal that contradicted the trustees' efforts to protect Hampden-Sydney students from the sectarian "religious phrensy" associated with Methodist revivals "which their parents had no taste for." Accused of "unfair and underhanded methods to proselyte students to a particular sect," Smith resigned the presidency of Hampden-Sydney in 1789 and soon thereafter left Virginia for the pulpit of Pine Street Church in Philadelphia and later the presidency of Union College in Schenectady, New York.

Certain details in John Blair Smith's letter to James Madison tend to confirm a story about the March 1788 elections for the convention told later by Virginia historian Hugh Blair Grigsby. When the freeholders of Prince Edward County gathered to choose their delegates, the story goes, President Smith challenged Henry to explain "why he had not taken a seat in the [Philadelphia] Convention and lent his aid in making a good Constitution, instead of staying at home and abusing the work of his patriotic compeers?" Patrick Henry is said to have replied, "I smelt a rat."

Henry's suspicions about northern hostility toward Virginia's interests had blossomed two years earlier—along with his growing aversion to entrusting greater power to the national government—when James Monroe had reported the apparent betrayal in Congress of the Old Dominion's claims to the free use of the Mississippi River. In advance of the March elections, Smith and his neighbors had repeatedly heard Henry's denunciation of "the measure proposed in Congress for a perpetual relinquishment of the Navigation of the Mississippi to the Spaniards." Henry had also "written many letters to Kentucky," Smith reported, alarming his neighbors and the westerners alike "with an apprehension of their interests being about to be sacrificed by the Northern States." As Henry saw things, the new Constitution would give too much authority to a consolidated national government likely to use its power against what he regarded as Virginia's best interests.

CHAPTER TWENTY-FOUR

We the States

AFTER NEARLY TEN MONTHS of public deliberation and debate, Virginia's long anticipated convention began on Monday, June 2, 1788, "to take into consideration the proposed plan of federal government" issued by the Philadelphia convention in September of 1787. Patrick Henry was fifty-two years old and at the peak of his powers—personal, intellectual, and political. He saw Virginia's heritage of liberty and self-government as once again threatened, as it had been a quarter of a century earlier at Hanover Courthouse. This time, however, the danger arose not from the misconduct of a distant king but from the misguided decisions made in Philadelphia by the "Gentlemen who formed the Convention"—men for whom Henry still felt "the highest respect"—men in whom "America had on a former occasion put the utmost confidence"—but gentlemen whose "perilous innovation" ignored the great principles of independence and set us "wandering on the great ocean of human affairs" with "no landmark to guide us."

ooooo

With craftsmen still working to finish the new capitol before the legislature convened on June 23, Virginia's delegates met briefly in a small public building near the lower edge of Capitol Square to organize themselves for their historic assignment. The convention delegates (who would eventually number 170) chose John Beckley, clerk of the House of Delegates, as secretary of the convention and then Edmund Pendleton as president. Former chair of the revolutionary Committee of Safety, former Speaker of the House of Delegates, and now the presiding judge of the state's highest court, Pendleton arranged the appointment of the Reverend Abner Waugh as chaplain responsible for reading prayers every morning before

Secretary Beckley rang the bell calling the convention to order. The rector of Saint Mary's Parish in Pendleton's home county since 1773, Waugh had served as chaplain to William Woodford's regiment during the war and was reputed to be "the best dancer of the minuet in Virginia." Edmund Pendleton, Jr., was appointed clerk of the twenty-three-man Committee of Privileges and Elections, whose members reflected all shades of opinion about the proposed constitution as they assumed the critical task of examining the delegates' credentials and resolving any disputed elections.

The delegates ended their first day by directing Augustine Davis, whose *Virginia Independent Chronicle* had welcomed commentary both for and against ratification, to print for the delegates' use two hundred copies both of the "plan of federal government" and the General Assembly's October 1787 resolutions summoning the convention. Finally, on a motion from George Mason, who joined Henry as the convention's leading opponents of ratification, or antifederalists, the convention adjourned until the following morning at eleven o'clock, when it would reconvene in Richmond's largest available building, "the New Academy on Shockoe Hill" a few blocks north of the nearly finished capitol. After the frame structure burned in 1803, it was eventually built over by the Medical College of Virginia.

Henry's friends believed the sides "were as nearly equal as possible" when the delegates gathered at the New Academy on Tuesday morning, June 3. After the convention agreed to follow the procedural rules of the House of Delegates, George Mason urged the convention to examine the proposed constitution "freely and fully" before making any final decisions about its adoption or rejection. Both James Madison, one of the chief federalist leaders, and John Tyler, a prominent antifederalist, quickly voiced their agreement—whereupon the delegates unanimously resolved to withhold all final decisions until the proposed constitution had been debated "clause by clause, through all its parts."

Patrick Henry took no visible part in these procedural discussions, despite their tactical implications for the debates ahead. A few observers felt that Mason's insistence upon clause-by-clause deliberation worked against Henry's intention of challenging the Philadelphia convention's decision to abandon rather than revise the Articles of Confederation, but in practice the rule placed no restraints on Henry's arguments—and some of his allies thought it worked to their advantage. Henry and Mason heartily

agreed that although time was "precious" it was essential to give the delegates opportunity for careful deliberation rather than "hurrying them
precipitately" toward any decision. Their insistence upon a thorough and
careful examination of the proposed government alarmed Light-Horse
Harry Lee, an arch-federalist who wanted to push ahead lest the convention be forced to adjourn without reaching a decision when the state legislature met on June 23—but the delegates ignored his fears.

Virginia's great debate began in earnest on Wednesday, June 4, with an
exchange between Patrick Henry and his ancient rival Edmund Pendleton, who could directly participate in the debate because George Wythe
was chairing the committee of the whole. To set up his intended criticism of the Philadelphia convention Henry wanted the clerk to read aloud
Virginia's Acts of Assembly appointing deputies to the meetings at Annapolis and Philadelphia. Pendleton immediately objected. Regardless of
"whether the federal Convention exceeded their powers," Pendleton declared, "the people have sent us hither to determine whether this government be a proper one or not." Henry promptly withdrew his motion,
recognizing that it was not worth a protracted dispute.

After John Beckley read aloud the Preamble to the Constitution and
portions of Article I creating the Senate and House of Representatives—
the clauses now subject to debate—George Nicholas was the first to speak.
A lawyer from Albemarle County, future attorney general of Kentucky,
and instigator of the 1781 inquiry into the conduct of the executive, Nicholas spoke at length about the proposed legislature and expressed support
for the Constitution as a system upon which "he was willing to trust his
own happiness and that of his posterity"—sentiments with which the next
speaker vehemently disagreed.

"The public mind," Henry declared as he rose to speak for the first
time, "is extremely uneasy at the proposed change of government." Describing himself as a servant of the people and caretaker of their rights,
liberty, and happiness, Henry reminded the delegates that, contrary to the
gloomy visions of the federalists, Virginians had enjoyed "a general peace
and a universal tranquility" prior to the Philadelphia convention of 1787. "A
year ago the minds of our citizens were in perfect repose." Now the republic was in extreme danger, menaced less by the admitted shortcomings of
the Confederation than by the treacherous conduct of delegates at Philadelphia and their "fatal . . . proposal to change our government." As a re-

sult of the convention's reckless overreach, Virginia now faced a needlessly perilous situation: "A wrong step, made now, will plunge us into misery and our republic will be lost." Their decision to replace the Confederation with "a great consolidated government" was "demonstrably clear," Henry continued, "and the danger of such a government [was] to [his] mind very striking."

"What right had they to say *We the People*," Henry demanded. "Who authorized them to speak the language of *We the People* instead of *We the States*? States are the characteristics and the soul of a confederation. If the States be not the agents of this compact, it must be one great consolidated National Government. . . . The people gave them no power to use their name. That they exceeded their power is perfectly clear. . . . The Federal Convention ought to have amended the old system—for this purpose they were solely delegated: The object of their mission extended to no other consideration."

Rather than answering Henry, Governor Edmund Randolph now took the floor to explain why he had refused to sign the Constitution at Philadelphia but now favored its ratification. Then and now, Randolph sought significant amendments and for many months had lobbied for a second convention to refine the proposed government. "Wholly to adopt or wholly to reject," he believed, was "too hard an alternative for the citizens of America." As he watched state after state ratify the Constitution, however, Randolph had shifted his tactics—especially after Massachusetts struck an appealing compromise in February by ratifying the plan *and* recommending amendments to it. "With me the only question has ever been between previous and subsequent amendments," Randolph declared. With eight states already on board, Randolph now believed it was impossible to insist upon amending the Constitution before adopting it "without inevitable ruin to the Union." The American Union was "the anchor of our political salvation." Raising his arm for dramatic effect, Randolph declared that he would consent "to the lopping of this limb . . . before [he would] assent to the dissolution of the Union."

"Whether the Constitution be good or bad," George Mason announced as he rose to answer Randolph, "it is a National Government and no longer a Confederation." Mason was especially troubled by "the power of laying direct taxes, [which] does of itself entirely change the confederation of the States into one consolidated Government." How, Mason demanded, could anyone suppose "that one National Government will suit so extensive a country, embracing so many climates, and containing inhabitants so very different in manners, habits, and customs?" History demonstrated that monarchs and despots could rule extensive countries, "but that popular governments can only exist in small territories." No man was "a greater friend to a firm Union of the American States," Mason declared, but "why should we recur to such dangerous principles?" The preferable alternative, he suggested, was to have the central government assign quotas to the individual states "with an alternative of laying direct taxes in case of non-compliance." That way, Mason concluded, "the sums necessary for the Union would be then laid by the states . . . who know how it can best be raised." If proper amendments can be introduced, Mason promised that he would "concur in any reasonable measure to obtain the desirable end of conciliation and unanimity"—but he felt that the "indispensable amendment" was to restrain "the power of raising direct taxes till the states shall have refused to comply with the requisitions of Congress."

In the closing minutes of Wednesday's debate, Madison announced his "great pleasure to concur with [his] honorable colleague [Mason] in any conciliatory plan." He promised to address the subject of taxation "when we come to that part of the Constitution." Madison briefly addressed Henry's and Mason's concerns about consolidation by suggesting that "the general watchfulness of the states," together with the limited powers delegated to the proposed government, "will be a sufficient guard" against consolidation—and then the convention adjourned for the day.

ooooo

"Two unlucky circumstances happened today," William Grayson informed a friend in Boston at the end of the first full day of debate: "Governor Randolph declared in favor of adopting the Constitution and news has come to town that South Carolina has ratified." That same evening, Madison informed a friend in New York that the governor had "thrown himself fully into our scale" after declaring that the time for previous amendments had passed.

For the next three weeks, convention leaders and observers constantly gauged the sentiments of delegates, tallied prospective votes, monitored developments in other states, and reported their impressions to friends—some of whom shared their letters with newspaper editors and the American public. Scholars have identified more than thirty extracts from private letters about the Virginia convention published in out-of-state newspapers. Many were reprinted several times in Boston, New York, and Philadelphia.

Portions of a letter from Henry to the New York antifederalist John Lamb, who as chair of the Federal Republican Committee of New York was working to coordinate an interstate coalition to force amendments to the proposed constitution, appeared in the *New York Journal* (under a typical eighteenth-century headline, "*Extract of a letter from a gentleman in Richmond to his friend in this city*") on June 19, ten days after Henry wrote them: "It is a Matter of Great Consolation to find that the Sentiments of a vast Majority of Virginians are in Unison with those of our northern Friends," Henry had written. "I am satisfyd that 4/5 of our Inhabitants are opposed to the new Scheme of Government. In the part of the Country lying south of James River I am confident 9/10 are opposed to it. The Friends and Seekers of Power have with their usual Subtlety wriggled themselves into the Choice of the People by assuming Shapes as various as the Faces of the Men they address on such Occasions." Within a month the gentleman from Richmond's remarks were reprinted in three more New York newspapers, three in Pennsylvania, one in Maryland, and in Winchester's *Virginia Gazette*—but Colonel Lamb only shared the rest of Henry's letter with the governor of New York, George Clinton, and a few other prominent antifederalists.

ooooo

First to speak on Thursday, June 5, was Edmund Pendleton, who responded to Henry's objections about the Philadelphia convention's overreach and use of the phrase *We the People.* The expression was "a common one and a favorite one," Pendleton said, and as to the convention's authority, "suppose the paper on your table dropped from one of the planets, the people found it, and sent us here to consider whether it was proper for their adoption—must we not obey them?" On the question "between this government and the Confederation" he favored the new plan. Light-Horse Harry Lee agreed—and then challenged Henry directly. Declaring his respect for "the honors with which he has been dignified and the brilliant talents which he has so often displayed," Lee asked why Henry was devoting "his powers of oratory . . . to the fears of this house" rather than "proceeding to investigate the merits of the new plan of government"?

Henry's response was immediate, for the fate of the Constitution and America depended "on that poor little thing—the expression, *We, the people*, instead of the States of America." Had the convention said "We the states," it would have signaled the objective of improving the Confederation rather than creating what he saw as "most clearly a consolidated government." Instead, the convention had taken a step "as radical as that which separated us from Great Britain" because "our rights and privileges are endangered and the sovereignty of the states will be relinquished." The new plan threatened freedom of conscience, trial by jury, liberty of the press, and all other protections for "human rights and privileges."

Henry also saw the necessity of commenting on yesterday's news of South Carolina's ratification. "Eight states have adopted this plan," Henry acknowledged, but then declared "that if twelve states and a half had adopted it, I would, with manly firmness, and in spite of an erring world reject it." The chief aim of government, he insisted, was neither the promotion of trade nor imperial visions of becoming "a great and powerful people" but the protection of personal liberties. "Liberty ought to be the direct end of your government." Was it necessary to abandon trial by jury and liberty of the press? "Liberty, the greatest of all earthly blessings—give us that precious jewel, and you may take every thing else!"

Henry admitted that he had "lived long enough to become an old-fashioned fellow" if "an invincible attachment to the dearest rights of man may, in these refined, enlightened days, be deemed old-fashioned." Twenty-three years earlier, he reminded the delegates, he had been called a traitor and "said to be the bane of sedition, because I supported the rights of my country." His friend Light-Horse Harry Lee might think that his fears were groundless, Henry said, but there were many others who shared his fears for the public good. "We are come hither to preserve the poor commonwealth of Virginia." History was replete with "instances of the people losing their liberty by their own carelessness and the ambition of a few." The proposed constitution posed exactly that threat. "When power is given to this government to suppress sedition and licentiousness or for any other purpose, the language it assumes is clear, express, and unequivocal," Henry observed, "but when this Constitution speaks of privileges, there is an ambiguity, sir, a fatal ambiguity." The great rights of a free people were endangered.

"What, sir, is the genius of democracy?" Henry demanded. "Let me read that clause of the bill of rights of Virginia which relates to this:

> That government is, or ought to be, instituted for the common benefit, protection, and security of the people, nation, or community. . . . And *that whenever any Government shall be found inadequate . . . a majority of the community hath an indubitable, unalienable, and indefeasible right to reform, alter, or abolish it in such manner as shall be judged most conducive to the public weal.*

"This, sir, is the language of democracy," he proclaimed, "that a majority of the community have a right to alter government when found to be oppressive. But how different is the genius of your new Constitution."

Henry was convinced that the Constitution would result in a consolidated government that, when it proved oppressive to Virginians, could not be altered. A hostile minority could easily defeat its cumbersome mechanisms for amendment—a danger exacerbated by the clause that gave Congress control of "organizing, arming, and disciplining the militia"— unlimited control over "our last and best defense." Despite the nasty accusations of detractors who called him "a designing man," a prospective autocrat, "a demagogue," and other "illiberal insinuations," Henry felt a "conscious rectitude" when he spoke out as "an advocate of the liberty of the people." Virginia's Declaration of Rights ensured that a majority of the community retained an absolute right to re-form its government. Under the new plan "a despicable minority at the extremity of the United States" could prevent needed changes, exercise "an unlimited and unbounded power of taxation," and enforce it with their control of the militia. Suppose that Virginia's ten congressmen unanimously opposed the imposition of a tax, Henry asked, "What will it avail?" Congress could easily overrule them and, "in direct opposition to the spirit and express language of [Virginia's] Declaration of Rights," impose oppressive taxes "not by your own consent but by people who have no connection with you."

Henry was only willing to give Congress "the power of direct taxation . . . *conditionally*; that is, after non-compliance with requisitions." To convince even the most skeptical listeners that he was "a lover of the

American Union," he was even willing to stipulate that "in case Virginia shall not make punctual payment, the control of our custom-houses, and the whole regulation of trade, shall be given to Congress, and that Virginia shall depend on Congress even for passports, till Virginia shall have paid the last farthing, and furnished the last soldier"—"but let it depend upon our own pleasure to pay our money in the most easy manner for our people." Despite his insistence upon restricting the power of taxation, however, Henry also insisted that "the dissolution of the Union is most abhorrent to my mind. The first thing I have at heart is American liberty: the second thing is American union."

Although Henry had now spoken for several hours, there were two more subjects on his mind before the convention closed its debate for the evening—the presidency and the dynamics of the ratification process. The Constitution "squints toward monarchy," he believed. "Your President may easily become king," he declared, in league with a Senate that was "so imperfectly constructed that your dearest rights may be sacrificed by . . . a small minority" (a margin of seven states to five in the recent clash over navigation of the Mississippi) capable of dominating the national government "forever."

Madison and his colleagues regarded Henry's portrayal of an imperial presidency as such an apocalyptic fantasy that they did not bother to refute it, but in the decades after these debates were published, Henry's grim vision has resonated with many readers. "If your American chief be a man of ambition and abilities," Henry warned, "how easy is it for him to render himself absolute! The army is in his hands, and if he be a man of address, it will be attached to him. . . . At the head of his army [the President] can prescribe the terms on which he shall reign master. . . . If ever he violates the laws . . . his crimes [will] teach him to make one bold push for the American throne. . . . Where is the existing force to punish him? Can he not, at the head of his army, beat down every opposition? Away with your President! we shall have a King: the army will salute him Monarch. Your militia will [be forced to] . . . assist in making him King and fight against you—and what have you to oppose this force? What will then become of you and your rights? Will not absolute despotism ensue?" At this point in the torrent of Henry's oratory, David Robertson, who was taking notes so he could print the convention speeches, was unable to keep up, stopped taking shorthand, and later placed this note in his published debates: "Here Mr. Henry strongly and pathetically [i.e., passionately] expatiated on the probability of the President's enslaving America and the horrid consequences that must result." Regardless of whether these sinister speculations were outrageous or prophetic, as a matter of debate strategy Henry's opponents chose to ignore rather than answer them.

Closing out Thursday's debate, Henry addressed the national context of Virginia's deliberations. Imagine that nine other states have agreed to the Constitution but that Virginia held to her scruples and refused to join them. Will they not "continue in friendship and union with them? If she sends her annual requisitions in dollars, do you think their stomachs will be so squeamish as to refuse her dollars? Will they not accept her regiments?" The federalists, he warned, aimed at intimidating Virginia into "an inconsiderate adoption" with forecasts of imaginary evils and the dissolution of the union. "'Tis a bugbear," Henry sneered. "The fact is, sir, that the eight adopting states can hardly stand on their own legs."

Even if Virginia delayed its ratification until the necessary amendments were adopted, Henry was confident that "those States will be fond to be in confederacy with us"—just as Maryland had participated in the Revolution and voted in Congress without ratifying the Articles of Confederation until 1781. "If we pay our quota of money annually, and furnish our ratable number of men, when necessary," Henry concluded. "We have a right to have time to consider; we shall therefore insist upon it. Unless the government be amended, we can never accept it." Based on decades of commitment to intercolonial and interstate cooperation, the other states had no cause to suppose that Virginia "has any intention of seceding from the Union. . . . Would they not, therefore, acquiesce in our taking time to deliberate? Deliberate whether the measure be not perilous, not only for us, but the adopting states?" Henry did not intend "to breathe the spirit nor utter the language of secession"—but he did believe that Pennsylvania and other states had been rushed, misled, and "perhaps tricked . . . into its adoption." And he hoped that before the Old Dominion chose to "abandon the present system," Virginians would insist upon remedying the Constitution's defects rather than discovering them later "by fatal experience."

ooooo

"Mr. H made a great effort yesterday," Madison wrote on Friday, June 6, "and having spun his harangue until a late hour . . . his party were much revived." Now Henry and his allies yielded the floor to Edmund Randolph, James Madison, and George Nicholas. "I think they are less [happy] this morning," Madison crowed, because "the Governour is become *active* in favor of the adoption." *Active* was an understatement: Governor Randolph had declared his support of the Constitution two days earlier, on the first day of debate, but on Friday morning the governor launched a somewhat puzzling personal attack upon Henry over a ten-year-old capital case that neither Randolph nor his listeners remembered accurately.

More than a decade earlier, with initial encouragement from Governor Dunmore, Josiah Philips of Princess Anne County, near Norfolk, had led a band of "insurgents" and "evil-disposed persons" in a series of thefts, murders, and "atrocious actions" that terrorized the southeastern corner of Virginia during the early years of the Revolutionary War. Governor Henry and his Council of State offered a $250 reward in 1777 for the capture of Philips and two lieutenants and later doubled the reward. Early in 1778 the Assembly targeted Philips with a bill of attainder—a legislative act inflicting punishment upon a person without a judicial trial. Prepared by Thomas Jefferson, the bill of attainder declared Josiah Philips guilty of "high treason," sentenced him to "suffer the pains of death," and declared him an outlaw subject to being lawfully captured or killed by any person. Once Philips was taken into custody, however, Henry, Jefferson, and Attorney General Edmund Randolph consigned the prisoner to the General Court, where Philips was convicted in a jury trial and then executed at the gallows near Williamsburg on November 23, 1778. In short, Josiah Philips was hanged in accord with a judicial verdict not a legislative act of attainder—a fact that Edmund Randolph either forgot or chose to ignore when he ambushed Patrick Henry on Friday morning, June 6.

Intending to prove that Virginia had not enjoyed the tranquility that Henry had described on Thursday, Randolph opened Friday's debate with a puzzling barrage of accusations about "violations of the state constitution"—puzzling because Randolph got all the major facts wrong. "There is one example of this violation in Virginia of a most striking and shocking nature," Randolph declared. "An example so horrid" that he would rather flee the commonwealth than see it repeated. "A citizen was deprived of his life," Randolph declared, "from a mere reliance on general reports."

Randolph's narrative of the perilous "legislative vortex" put Patrick

Henry in the role of villain although in fact the things he recounted had
been done by Thomas Jefferson, then a member of the House of Delegates, not Henry, who was then governor. "A gentleman in the House of
Delegates," Randolph's story began, with a clear inference that he meant
Henry, "informed the house that a certain man (Josiah Philips) had committed several crimes, and was running at large, perpetrating other crimes."
That same legislator "therefore moved for leave to attaint him," was immediately granted permission to introduce a bill, and "no sooner did he
obtain it than he drew from his pocket a bill ready written for that effect."
The bill of attainder "was read three times in one day and carried to the
Senate" (by Jefferson, according to the official journal). "I will not say that
it passed the same day through the Senate" (although it did) "but [Philips]
was attainted very speedily and precipitately without any proof better than
vague reports."

Governor Randolph's narrative then took flight, soaring into the realms
of fiction and moral outrage and conveniently omitting any mention of
Philips's trial before the General Court: "Without being confronted with
his accusers and witnesses, without the privilege of calling for evidence in
his behalf," Josiah Philips "was sentenced to death and was afterwards actually executed," Randolph contended. "Was this arbitrary deprivation of
life, the dearest gift of God to man, consistent with the genius of a republican government? Is this compatible with the spirit of freedom? This, sir,
has made the deepest impression on my heart," Randolph declared, "and I
cannot contemplate it without horror."

At first glance it seems puzzling that Henry offered no objection to
Randolph's accusations, for the convention debates are replete with other
moments when one delegate or another (including Henry) objected to remarks that could be perceived as personal affronts. The explanation for
Henry's apparent silence seems to be that Henry was so familiar with the
actual passage of Jefferson's bill of attainder that he failed to perceive (at
least at that moment) that in Randolph's mind he rather than Jefferson
was the villain.

After Governor Randolph finished with an assertion that Virginians
were "unsafe without the Union," James Madison countered Henry's portrayal of tyrants as the history's prevailing cause for the failure of republics with his own belief that despotism came more frequently as the result

of "turbulence, violence, and abuse of power by the majority trampling on the rights of the minority. According to the note-taker, David Robertson, however, Madison "spoke so low that his exordium could not be heard distinctly." George Nicholas closed Friday's debate by characterizing Henry's general arguments "that the powers given to any government ought to be small" as "a new idea in politics." Powers granted for any purpose, Nicholas countered, "ought to be proportionate to that purpose, or else the end for which they are delegated will not be answered."

ooooo

Saturday's debate began with a speech by twenty-nine-year-old Francis Corbin, whose loyalist father had paid Henry for the gunpowder Dunmore removed from the magazine. Adorning his remarks with learned references to Holland, England, and the ever popular Amphictonic League of ancient Greece—the proud fruits of his years of study at Cambridge University and the Middle Temple during the Revolutionary War— Corbin offered the standard federalist response to reservations drawn from Montesquieu about whether republics were suited to the governance of large territories. "The powers of the general government are only ... to protect, defend, and strengthen the United States," Corbin explained, "but the internal administration of government is left to the state legislatures," which "retain such powers as will give the states the advantages of small republics." For clarity, therefore, Corbin urged that the proposed government be described as "a Representative Federal Republic, as contradistinguished from a Confederacy."

Taking little notice of Corbin's arguments, Henry rose to express his hope that Governor Randolph would "continue his observations on the subject he had left unfinished the day before ... as he wished to be informed of every thing that gentlemen could urge in defence of that system which appeared to him so defective." Given enough rope and sufficient opportunity, Henry could reasonably expect that Randolph, who surely was the most vulnerable of his major federalist opponents, might entangle himself in his ongoing effort to explain why he now supported the document he had refused to sign. In addition, while Henry had listened calmly to Randolph's tales from the legislative vortex on Friday and was now willing to give his extended remarks "a patient hearing," Saturday also brought a visitor to Richmond from Philadelphia bearing damning revelations about the governor's handling of the overtures from George Clinton inviting cooperation with the antifederalists of New York.

In response to Henry's invitation, Governor Randolph reiterated his belief in the necessity of union under "a national rather than a federal government" and his opposition to Mason's and Henry's proposal for permitting direct taxation only after requisitions had been refused. "Requisitions," Randolph declared, "however modified . . . strike me with horror and disgust." Madison, speaking next, agreed that the clauses that gave "the general government the power of laying and collecting taxes [were] indispensable and essential to the existence of any efficient or well-organized system of government." Madison then set out to prove the point with lessons about the Amphictonic League, the Achaean League, Philip of Macedon, the feudal Germanic League, and the Swiss cantons that he and Alexander Hamilton had used in three essays of *The Federalist*.

Henry had hoped that Randolph might entangle himself in contradictions. Instead it was Madison's decision to clinch his arguments by reading from John de Witt's *Political Maxims of the State of Holland* (London, 1743)—a book found in few American libraries but familiar to at least a few Virginia delegates—that set up Henry's response. Indeed this may well have been one of the moments that Madison described to a historian many years later—a moment when Madison felt that "he had made a most conclusive argument in favor of the Constitution" only to watch Patrick Henry "rise to reply to him and by some significant action, such as a pause, a shake of the head, or a striking gesture, before he uttered a word . . . undo all that Madison had been trying to do for an hour before."

"There are certain maxims," Henry began—picking up on the title from which Madison had just read "sundry passages"—"which no free people ought ever to abandon—maxims of which the observance is essential to the security of happiness. . . . Poor little humble republican maxims [that] have attracted the admiration and engaged the attention of the virtuous and wise in all nations and have stood the shock of ages." But now, he continued, perhaps with some gesture in Madison's direction, some men seemed enthralled by "maxims of a different but more refined nature—new maxims, which tend to the prostration of republicanism."

One of Virginia's familiar and trusted maxims, Henry reminded the delegates, was "that all men are by nature free and independent, and have certain inherent rights, of which, when they enter into society, they cannot by any compact deprive or divest their posterity"—a direct quotation from the first article of the Virginia Declaration of Rights. In addition, Virginians claimed a whole "set of maxims" admired by all friends of liberty, virtue, and mankind: "Our bill of rights contains those admirable maxims."

Henry then turned his attention to Governor Randolph—whose remarks (as anticipated) supplied the experienced orator with several easy targets. "The Honorable member has said that it is too late in the day for us to reject this new plan," Henry observed. The Constitution "once execrated by the Honorable member, must now be adopted" despite its glaring defects. "*Too late in the day?*" Henry sneered. "I never can believe, sir, that it is too late to save all that is precious." Was it not "very strange and unaccountable" that the same plan that had previously been "the object of his execration, should now receive his encomiums?

"The Honorable member has given you an elaborate account of what he judges tyrannical legislation and an ex post facto law in the case of Josiah Philips," Henry remarked—but "he has misrepresented the facts. That man was not executed by a tyrannical stroke of power. Nor was he a Socrates. He was a fugitive murderer and an outlaw—a man who commanded an infamous banditti . . . [and] committed the most cruel and shocking barbarities. He was an enemy to the human name." Philips "was not executed according to those beautiful legal ceremonies which are pointed out by the laws in criminal cases," Henry continued (forgetting that Philips *had* received a regular trial before the General Court), but given "the enormity of his crimes . . . the occasion warranted the measure."

Pressing Randolph even harder, Henry called attention to the governor's recent statement (which either eluded David Robertson's note taking or was amended before publication) referring "to the people at large" as "a *herd*"—reducing "respectable independent citizens" into "abject dependent subjects . . . by degradingly assimilating our citizens to a herd." Randolph leapt to his feet, declaring that he had "not use[d] that word to excite any odium, but merely to convey an idea of a multitude." Nevertheless, Henry replied, the condescending remark "made a deep impression on his mind." Then, having made his point, Henry playfully offered to swap Randolph's "*abominable*" word *herd* for his own "*darling* word requisitions"—a reference to Thursday's debate over powers of taxation.

ooooo

While Patrick Henry and Edmund Randolph were sparring at the New Academy on Shockoe Hill on Saturday, June 7, the arrival of Eleazer Oswald, publisher of Philadelphia's *Independent Gazetteer*, sharply intensified the Virginia antifederalists' exasperation with the governor. Oswald bore letters to Henry, George Mason, William Grayson, and Richard Henry Lee from General John Lamb, chair of the Federal Republican Committee of New York, calling for cooperation in obtaining amendments to the Constitution before it was ratified. Inevitably, however, this second attempt at a collaboration between like-minded statesmen in Virginia and New York brought the earlier effort to mind—and with it questions about the fate of Governor Clinton's response, dispatched to Governor Randolph in May, welcoming the General Assembly's call for interstate cooperation in pursuit of amendments. Or, more accurately, Oswald's visit alerted Henry and his colleagues to the fact that Governor Clinton *had* responded—in a letter they had not yet seen because Governor Randolph intended to put it before the General Assembly in two weeks.

Oswald met with Virginia's "Committee of Opposition," the name given by William Grayson to a group that George Mason characterized as the "Members of the Convention who meet to prepare such Amendments as they deem necessary" and that Henry described as "our Republican Society," chaired by George Mason. As the Virginians conferred with Oswald, two things became evident. First, although the Virginia convention was barely a week old, the antifederalist committee had already agreed upon two slates of thirty-three amendments—a "Bill of Rights" based on the Virginia Declaration of Rights and thirteen structural amendments. Prominent among the latter was the provision to prohibit direct federal taxation in the states unless funds raised through import duties were insufficient for public needs *and* "Congress shall have first made a Requisition upon the States." On Monday, June 9, Eleazer Oswald hurried northward bearing letters for the New York antifederalists from Grayson, Henry, and Mason, as well as their current draft of thirty-three amendments, and their hopes for cooperation in the campaign to amend the Constitution before it went into effect.

The second insight raised by Oswald's visit was more troubling. Although Henry and his compatriots remained fully committed to their fight for amendments, both the calendar and the Massachusetts example were now working against them. The interruption of the earlier communication with the New Yorkers had done serious, perhaps irreparable, damage to their cause. Mason did not equivocate when he fumed about the governor's apparent treachery—Randolph was nothing less than a "young [Benedict] Arnold." Nor was it surprising, with the conversations between Eleazer Oswald and the antifederalist leaders fresh in mind, that the delegates who gathered again at the New Academy on Monday morning witnessed an angry confrontation between Henry and Randolph that some onlookers feared could result in a duel.

ooooo

When Henry renewed his campaign on Monday morning, he announced that he would put off an inquiry into the dispute with Spain over navigation of the Mississippi River to focus instead upon Governor Randolph's exaggerations about the danger of disunion. Henry believed that four fifths of the people of Virginia wanted amendments—and that there was still merit in Jefferson's suggestion, offered months earlier, that nine states should ratify and the remaining four hold out for amendments. "His sentiments coincide entirely with ours," Henry declared: Jefferson "thinks yet of bills of rights—thinks of those little, despised things called maxims."

Governor Randolph had said a great deal about disunion and its dangers, Henry observed, but "how will his present doctrine hold with . . . that noble and disinterested conduct which he displayed on a former occasion? Did he not tell us that he withheld his signature? Where, *then*, were the dangers which *now* appear to him so formidable?" Henry was relentless, cloaking his sarcasm in seemingly innocent praise. "Knowing that system to be defective, [Randolph] magnanimously and nobly refused its approbation. . . . I considered his opinion as a great authority. He taught me, sir, in despite of the approbation of that great federal Convention, to doubt of the propriety of that system. When I found my Honorable friend in the number of those who doubted, I began to doubt also. I coincided with him in opinion. I shall be a staunch and faithful disciple of his. I applaud that magnanimity which led him to withhold his signature."

When Henry sat down, Randolph was eager to "prove the consistency of his present opinion with his former conduct," but Light-Horse Harry Lee had taken the floor in defense of the Constitution. Henry's accusations had hit their target. "I find myself attacked in the most illiberal manner by the Honorable gentleman," Randolph began at last. "He has accused me of inconsistency in this very respectable assembly," with aspersions and insinuations incompatible with parliamentary decency or friendship. "*And if our friendship must fall—let it fall like Lucifer, never to rise again.*"

And once again—as the celebrated trial lawyer had done after denouncing the Stamp Act in the House of Burgesses in 1765—Henry had made his point and stood ready to apologize. While Randolph began to read aloud from his published letter about the Constitution, "Mr. Henry arose, and declared that he had no personal intention of offending any one." He had only done his duty and "was sorry if he offended the Honorable gentleman without intending it."

Randolph was not immediately appeased. But after a cryptic personal exchange (with Randolph threatening to disclose something that "would have made some men's hair stand on end" and Henry replying that "if he had any thing to say against him he [sh]ould disclose it") the governor summarized his current reasons for supporting the Constitution. These now included his fear that if nine states ratified without them, Virginia would "lose our influence and weight in the Government." Without the Old Dominion (and therefore without George Washington) "will not the Senators be chosen and the electors of the President be appointed, and the Government brought instantly into action after the ratification of nine States?"

By the close of debate on Monday, June 9, there was one thing upon which everyone at the Virginia convention now agreed. Henry and his Committee of Opposition had already concurred on thirty-three of the forty amendments that the convention would eventually adopt. "The only question was," as Edmund Randolph put it the following morning, "with respect to previous and subsequent amendments." The convention debates so far "have been elaborate, elegant, eloquent, and consequently entertaining and instructive," a well-informed visitor told his brother. For the remaining two weeks of debate, "the only and grand point on which the parties split appears to be whether the amendments which are necessary should be prior or subsequent to adoption."

ooooo

Patrick Henry made enormous contributions to the elegance, eloquence, and entertainment that attracted scores of visitors to the convention debates. William Nelson, Jr., brother of the former governor of Virginia, reported to an American diplomat that Henry "was indefatigable, and more and more able day by day." He spoke at length on at least fourteen of the nineteen days that the convention met for debate—sometimes repeatedly and once for as long as seven hours. He was present for all its meetings (every day except Sundays from Monday, June 2 through Friday, June 27) and he spent the off hours in consultation with other delegates of the Committee of Opposition plotting their strategies and hammering out the wording of their desired amendments.

A genuine feeling of civic emergency fueled Henry's fervent efforts to amend the Constitution before it saddled the nation with institutions that he felt were hostile to liberty and to Virginia's interests and heritage. Midway through the convention he apologized to his daughter Anne Henry Roane for being unable to visit her. "I left my ever dear Wife very unwell" at Pleasant Grove in the care of Anne's sister Martha, widow of John Fontaine, he explained. Dorothea, now in her early thirties, had been "not so well as usual" during the last months of her pregnancy, but two days after he left for Richmond "she was delivered of a Son," Alexander Spotswood Henry, and she had recently written that she was feeling better. "Nothing but a sense of the Duty I owe my country at this important Crisis could have dragged me from her in such a Situation," Henry wrote. "You will therefore see the Necessity of my going [home] instantly at the rising of the Convention."

Henry had no political "News" for his daughter, however, "as nothing is yet decided by the Convention" and the delegates' sentiments for and against the Constitution remained too close to call. Neither side was confident enough to press for any kind of test vote, and the procedural agreement about clause-by-clause debate ensured that their meeting would continue for another week or two. As late as June 21 (just six days before the convention's final decision) the margin remained so narrow that the committee responsible for resolving contested elections was still grappling with the eligibility of ten residents whose disputed votes could overturn the election of a single delegate from Louisa County. In many respects, aside from bringing their principles to bear on specific aspects of the Constitution (the presidency, judiciary, etc.), both sides had rather thoroughly presented their main arguments during the first week of debate. Because the margin was so narrow (and because the question had evolved from acceptance or rejection to ratification conditioned on prior or subsequent amendments) Henry and his allies spent the second and third weeks of the convention exploiting every possible appeal that might win the vote of any wavering delegate.

The district of Kentucky's fourteen delegates comprised a significant target for the rival speakers. "It is said that we are scuffling for Kentucky votes," Henry observed at the beginning of a three-day debate about the Mississippi, but as Henry saw it the right of navigation was essential "to preserve the balance of American power" between the commercial states east of the Hudson River and the agricultural states south of the Potomac River. "Unless you keep open the Mississippi," Henry argued, the movement of settlers into the Ohio Country would cease, and Virginia would soon become "a contemptible minority" in Congress and put all of Virginia's interests at risk. Only the fact that nine states were necessary to adopt any treaty under the Articles of Confederation had prevented the betrayal of Virginia's interests by John Jay. The proposed constitution only required a majority of each house as "a Quorum to do Business" and "two thirds of the Senators *present*" to ratify a treaty. With just fourteen senators present, as Henry's ally William Grayson explained in detail, ten senators from the five "Northern States may then easily make a treaty relinquishing this river." In the end, Henry and Grayson prevailed with the Kentucky delegates, who (with one man absent) voted against the constitution by a margin of ten to three.

Although Henry was too busy with the convention to visit his daughter in Essex County, several of his friends (perhaps led by John Tyler) imposed upon his schedule in Richmond to commission a portrait bust by an itinerant Italian sculptor. One of only four known life portraits of Patrick Henry, the terra-cotta bust "was considered a perfect likeness." With its furrowed brow, prominent nose, and thinning hair, the portrait captured by the anonymous sculptor in 1788 displays many similarities to the portrait sketches drawn by Benjamin Henry Latrobe nine years later.

ooooo

At long last, exactly three weeks after its initial meeting, the Virginia convention of 1788 completed its clause-by-clause examination of the Constitution on Monday, June 23. The next morning, citing the "critical situation of America [and] the extreme danger of dissolving the Union," George Wythe spoke for the first time to present a resolution proposing that Virginia ratify the Constitution and then recommend "whatsoever amendments might be deemed necessary" for adoption according to Article V. Henry objected immediately and presented an alternative resolution—the product of the Committee of Opposition's efforts—proposing that Virginia refer "to the other States" a declaration of rights and twenty desired amendments to the Constitution "for their consideration *prior* to its ratification." With both options clearly in mind (each resolution having been read aloud by the clerk) the delegates made ready for one final day of intense, candid, and dramatic debate—a debate in which Henry forced his colleagues to face the "fatal effects" of slavery.

Weeks earlier, Henry and others had discussed the "striking differences and great contrariety of interests between the States" and the impossibility of fairly imposing national taxes on the "carrying and productive states" (as contemporaries often distinguished the commercial north from the agricultural south). None of the speakers in the Virginia convention said much about the protection given to slavery by the Three-fifths Compromise, which augmented the power of southern states by including 60 percent of their slaves in all computations for seats in Congress (and therefore ballots in the electoral college) and led nineteenth-century abolitionists to denounce the Constitution as a "wicked pact with the devil." Instead, Henry had warned that giving authority for taxation to Congress and its presumed "Northern majority" would "put unbounded power over *our property* in hands not having a common interest with us." How, he asked, could the ten congressmen allotted to Virginia in the proposed House of Representatives "prevent the adoption of the *most oppressive mode of taxation* in the Southern States" by "a majority in favor of the Northern States?" What Henry was saying, in the coded language of his day, was that a national government dominated by northern interests would inevitably seek to shift the burden of taxation from their lands, commodities, and commerce to the distinctive form of property held predominantly in the South—slaves. The result, he had said, would be "a picture so horrid, so wretched, so dreadful, that I need no longer dwell upon it."

Now that the convention was facing its final decision, however, Henry was prepared to draw that horrid picture in order to make absolutely certain that every delegate understood the dire implications he saw looming in northern control over the power of taxation. Even if Randolph urged him to retreat into euphemism and the "calm light of philosophy" rather than speaking honestly in language that Randolph feared might seem "dishonorable to Virginia," Henry felt (for reasons that are more complex than Randolph could imagine) that the subject was too important to ignore. Based on Virginia's experience with Congress since 1774, Henry recognized that the Constitution would create a government with jurisdiction both "over states where slavery was deeply entrenched *and* states where it was a marginal institution"—and that everyday political decisions, especially about levying taxes, would give northerners (regardless of their attitudes toward race or abolition) irresistible incentives to meddle with slavery and southern society.

Ironically, Henry's perception of the political problem was rooted in his conviction that slavery itself was repulsive, morally indefensible, and evil. "Slavery is detested," Henry reminded the convention, "we feel its fatal effects [and] we deplore it with all the pity of humanity"—and yet this disgust was a critical element of Henry's perspective. Henry saw the moral dynamic of the emerging nation more clearly than his opponents: The evil of slavery was so obvious that anyone not already invested in slavery and forced to think about it would favor abolition—and the creation of a national government would invite policy debates (especially over taxation) that would force northern congressmen to confront slavery. "They'll free your niggers!" Henry was said to have told the convention.

"As much as I deplore slavery," Henry claimed, acknowledging the recurrent moral dilemma that afflicted his generation, he had come to believe "that prudence forbids its abolition." Few Americans of Henry's generation could imagine that emancipation would result in a peaceful multiracial society—but they could readily imagine the bloody horrors of interracial civil war (even if the cautionary nightmare of the Haitian revolution lay a few years in the future). Henry lamented and deplored what he called "the necessity of holding our fellow-men in bondage," but thought it impossible "by any human means to liberate them without producing the most dreadful and ruinous consequences." In order to maintain sovereign control over slavery, Henry believed, Virginia had to reject the Constitution unless its provisions for direct taxation were deleted. Under the Constitution, he foresaw "a great deal of the property of the people of Virginia in jeopardy, and their peace and tranquility gone away." Decisions that affected slavery simply could not be trusted "in the hands of those who have no similarity of situation with us. This is a local matter, and I can see no propriety of subjecting it to Congress."

Madison tried to explain that several features of the Constitution protected slavery and in more general terms Madison famously argued that minority rights were actually safer in an extended republic than in smaller ones because the size of the electorate encouraged "a greater variety of parties and interests" and made it "less probable that a majority of the whole will have a common motive to invade the rights of other citizens." Borrowing heavily from the philosophical writing of David Hume, Madison contended that the expanded republic "will be broken into so many parts, interests, and classes of citizens that the rights of individuals or of the minority will be in little danger from interested combinations of the majority." Henry's perspective, on the other hand, derived from direct political experience, including Virginia's use of high import duties to restrain the importation of slaves in the 1770s and his participation in congressional debates about taxation and representation in 1774 and 1775. Although modern scholars revere Madison's abstract theories about "a Republican remedy for the diseases most incident to Republican Government," the nasty truth may well be that after two and a quarter centuries Henry's worries about hostile majorities have proven more accurate than Madison's attempt to overturn eighteenth-century dictums about small republics. For better or worse, America's subsequent history, not only with slavery but with countless other issues about which national majorities maintain strong opinions (such as prohibition, labor unions, communism, abortion, drugs, education, or religion) may suggest that Henry rather than Madison more clearly anticipated how the political process of levying national taxes could eventually result in federal intervention on a wide array of subjects and overpower the protections for minorities that Madison attributed to an expanded republic.

While Henry thundered against the catastrophic dangers facing America, a violent summer storm swept into Richmond. Wind and rain pummeled the New Academy as the heavens seemed to confirm the orator's evocation of "*beings* of a higher order" anxiously watching their deliberations. As Henry invited the delegates to peer "beyond the horizon that bounds human eyes . . . and see those intelligent beings which inhabit the ethereal mansions reviewing [America's] political decisions and . . . the consequent happiness or misery of mankind," a loud clap of thunder exploded overhead. Henry's rhetoric had aroused "the feelings of the audience to the highest pitch," his son-in-law Spencer Roane recalled, "When lo! A storm at that moment arose, which shook the building in which the convention were sitting . . . and it seemed as if he had indeed the faculty of calling up spirits from the vasty deep."

According to the published record, when the thunderstorm interrupted him, Henry had just reminded the delegates that their decision would be an example to other nations. By insisting upon amendments "we have it in our power to secure the happiness of one half of the human race," he declared, while ratification without amendments "may involve the misery of other hemispheres."

∞∞∞

The next morning, Wednesday, June 25, George Nicholas moved that George Wythe's resolution for ratifying the Constitution be read aloud and voted on. Then John Tyler moved that Patrick Henry's structural amendments and declaration of rights be read aloud "for the same purpose." Of the nine delegates who spoke, it seems fitting that the last two speakers were Patrick Henry and Edmund Randolph. Fearful that "some future annalist" might misconstrue his actions, Governor Randolph wanted history to remember that although he still had objections to the Constitution, "the accession of eight States reduced our deliberations to the single question of Union or no Union." Whether history looked kindly on Randolph's shifting opinions was a petty detail, however, compared to the worrisome question that Patrick Henry addressed in his final remarks. Everyone knew that the final vote was going to be close. If the convention adopted Wythe's resolution rather than Henry's—and if the consequences were as serious as had been portrayed during three weeks of intense debate—would the defeated antifederalists peacefully accept the verdict of the convention?

After appealing one last time for votes in support of his position, Henry closed by thanking the delegates for their patience and attention. "If I shall be in the minority," he said, "I shall have those painful sensations which arise from a conviction of being overpowered in a good cause. Yet I will be a peaceable citizen." He would not "go to violence," but would dedicate his head, hand, and heart "to retrieve the loss of liberty and remove the defects of that system in a constitutional way." Hoping that the public spirit that had prevailed during the Revolution was not yet gone, "nor the cause of those who are attached to the revolution yet lost," he promised to work patiently "in expectation of seeing that government changed so as to be compatible with the safety, liberty, and happiness of the people."

Once the speeches had ended, the convention took its first official vote at midday on Wednesday. Eighty-eight delegates chose George Wythe's resolution for ratification. Eighty delegates favored Henry's alternative. Soon thereafter, with two delegates absent and one apparently changing his mind, the convention ratified the Constitution by a vote of 89 to 79. Randolph, chair of a five-man committee dominated by federalists, then presented a "Form of Ratification" by which Pendleton would report the convention's decision to Congress. Adopted without dispute, the resolution spoke for the people of Virginia and stipulated that powers being granted under the Constitution "may be resumed by them whenever the same shall be perverted," that "every power not granted thereby remains with them," and that "among other essential rights the liberty of Conscience and of the Press cannot be cancelled abridged restrained or modified by any authority of the United States." Finally, the resolution urged that "imperfections . . . in the Constitution" be amended according to Article V rather than "bring the Union into danger by a delay with a hope of obtaining Amendments previous to the Ratification."

Washington was delighted when news of the ratification reached Mount Vernon—and happy to reassure his excitable new private secretary, Tobias Lear, "that the Minority will acquiese with a good grace." Patrick Henry will not be "*reconciled* to the Government in its *present* form," the general acknowledged, "and will give it every *constitutional* opposition in his power." Yet "he will submit to it peaceably," Washington wrote approvingly, "and by precept and example will endeavour, within the sphere of his action, to inculcate the like principles into others." Despite their conflicting assessments of the Constitution, George Washington knew that he could trust both Patrick Henry's patriotism and his tenacity.

ooooo

Although the federalists had won the first vote, everyone knew that a majority of the delegates wanted substantial amendments. If Virginians hoped to remedy the defects of the new government "in a constitutional way," as Henry had promised the convention, they needed to adopt the Committee of Opposition's declaration of rights and substantive amendments as their platform for change. The victors could scarcely object after pushing so hard for subsequent rather than previous amendments—but of course the more ardent federalists did not want to recommend alterations that would, as Madison put it, "strike at the essence of the System and . . . [adhere] to the principle of the existing Confederation."

On Friday, June 27, two days after the vote to ratify the Constitution, the committee charged with drafting a slate of recommended amendments brought forward twenty "essential and inalienable rights of the people" (based on the Virginia Declaration of Rights) and twenty substantive "Amendments to the Constitution" based in large part on the earlier work of the antifederalist Committee of Opposition. Of these forty proposed changes, the federalist delegates objected only to one item, the proposed Amendment Three, which outlined the requisition system for national revenue that Henry and his friends had advocated throughout the debates. Congress would be required to apportion quotas among the states according to population and give state authorities an opportunity to raise the money, but only if a state failed to comply could Congress resort to direct federal taxation. States could avoid federal collectors and—most significantly—choose the kinds of taxes that suited them, while Congress held the power of internal taxation as a last resort.

Amendment Three distinguished sovereignty from solvency. If adopted it paired revenues sufficient for national purposes with local control of taxation and administration. In many respects, the delegates' votes on this recommended amendment revealed their attitudes toward government more accurately than Wednesday's vote on ratification itself. Nationalists eager to grant substantial powers to a central government could not cloak their objectives with memories of an impoverished Congress and freezing soldiers at Valley Forge. On the other hand, the Virginians who wanted to keep Amendment Three saw it as a way to sustain local control of taxation without emasculating the nation and threatening the Union, to empower the central government for its necessary functions without undermining virtue and threatening the republic, and to keep Congress from meddling with slavery.

By a vote of 65 to 85, Madison and his friends failed in their attempt to delete Amendment Three. Thirteen delegates who had voted for the Constitution two days earlier now joined Henry and his allies by voting to retain it. This pivotal group of moderate federalists, including Edmund Pendleton, sought "some middle course," as Monroe put it, because they recognized that, more than any other aspect of governance, the powers of taxation and tariffs raised the prospect of conflict between state and national government. Henry may have lost his fight for a conditional ratification based on previous amendments, but Friday's vote on Amendment Three demonstrated that a substantial majority of the delegates stood firmly behind his continued insistence upon significant alterations in the newly ratified Constitution.

ooooo

The convention's decision to ratify the Constitution "has been distressing and awful to great Numbers of very respectable Members," Henry's son-in-law Spencer Roane informed another son-in-law, Philip Aylett, husband of Elizabeth. "There is no rejoicing on Account of the Vote of ratification," Roane reported from Richmond. "It would not be prudent to do so; and the federalists behave with moderation and do not exult in their Success." In contrast to several other states, where public celebrations had been held after their conventions voted, a gentleman from Richmond informed Eleazer Oswald's Philadelphia newspaper that the citizens of Richmond seemed "either wise enough, or polite enough, to make no procession or other parade." A gentleman from Alexandria offered a similar assessment to the *Connecticut Gazette*: "Both parties have conducted themselves with great moderation and candour," he wrote, "and no rejoicings were permitted to aggravate the feelings of so respectable a minority."

George Mason, however, took their defeat less gracefully. Never as genial a man as Henry, Mason had run out of patience after defending his principles through two successive conventions. Mason was furious about the treachery of Randolph's interruption of communication between the Virginia antifederalists and their New York compatriots—furious to the point that he prepared a formal resolution reprimanding Randolph for his failure to present Governor Clinton's letter to "the late Convention" and for "delaying to lay the [letter] before the General Assembly until the Day after the Ratification." In addition (like the disgruntled antifederalist minority after the Pennsylvania convention), Mason drafted a minority report and called a meeting of his disappointed allies on Friday evening.

Henry was not present when the group gathered in the Senate chamber of the new capitol building, nor had he conferred with Mason, whose draft statement, ostensibly intended "to reconcile the minds of their constituents to the new plan of government," turned out to be "a fiery, irritating manifesto." Benjamin Harrison and John Tyler apparently objected with the observation that because the Constitution had been adopted "by a majority of their countrymen it became their duty to submit as good citizens." As the delegates pondered their options, "a deputation was sent to Patrick Henry inviting him to take the chair," and "the venerated patriot accepted." When Henry realized that Mason was offering "a plan of resistance to the operations of the Federal Government, he addressed the meeting with his accustomed animation upon important occasions." He "had done his duty strenuously in opposing the Constitution in the *proper place*—and with all the powers he possessed," Henry reminded the assembled former delegates. "The question had been fully discussed and settled," he declared, and now, "as true and faithful republicans, they had all better go home!"

CHAPTER TWENTY-FIVE

Amendments and Abolition

EAGER, AS USUAL, to get home after the convention and the short leg-islative session that ended on Monday, June 30, Patrick Henry collected his mileage and per diem expenses, a total of £16 5s 3d, and rode south toward Pleasant Grove as quickly as possible. James Madison, after col-lecting £14 for his convention expenses, headed north to Congress, where news of the ratifications by New Hampshire and Virginia triggered the cluster of decisions necessary to put the new government into operation. By the end of July, Congress had decided upon Wednesday, January 7, 1789, as the deadline for the selection of presidential electors; Wednesday, February 4, as the date for their meetings in every state; and Wednesday, March 4 as the day for "commencing proceedings" of the new govern-ment. Congress then descended into a protracted squabble over where the new government should meet. After playing down interstate rival-ries during the Virginia convention, Madison now complained vigorously to George Washington and Governor Randolph that the decision about where to convene the new government had "become a question now be-tween North and South," with New York City the likely choice despite the location's implicit "injustice and oppression to the Southwestern and Western parts of the Union."

By October, when the General Assembly met again in Richmond's newly finished capitol, Governor Randolph had renewed his enthusi-asm for amendments. As soon as the legislators met, Randolph presented without delay a fresh circular letter from New York urging all the states to push Congress for a second constitutional convention. On the 29th Henry introduced a resolution calling for another convention and declared that until Virginia acted to secure "the most precious rights of the people," he would block every measure introduced to set the new federal government into motion. Henry's legislative influence had always been notable, but at the head of a majority with a fifteen-vote margin in the autumn 1788 session his political clout now was extraordinary. "The Edicts of Mr. Henry" are enacted by this Assembly "with less opposition . . . than those of the Grand Monarch are in the Parliaments of France," Washington remarked. "He has only to say let this be Law—and it is Law."

Bolstered not only by his majority and his experience "in parliamentary science," Henry was rendered all the more powerful because the federalists were weak. None of the prominent federalists who had sustained the convention debate—Madison, Marshall, Nicholas, or Pendleton—were members of the Assembly. "Mr. Henry is the only orator we have amongst us," one of his adversaries grumbled, "and the friends to the new government, being all young and inexperienced, form but a feeble band against him." When Francis Corbin offered an alternative resolution aimed at watering down Henry's call for a second convention, it was crushed by a vote of 85 to 39. "The triumph of Antifœderalism is compleat," one of Corbin's allies lamented. Watching these developments from his seat in the lame-duck Confederation Congress, Madison worried that his handiwork was being "successfully undermined by its enemies"—especially when he learned that Edmund Pendleton had expressed support for a second convention.

Speaking against a second convention in this debate, Francis Corbin, whose loyalist father had sent him to study in England during the war, made the rookie mistake of attacking Henry directly. Challenging Henry's contention that Virginians overwhelmingly demanded amendments, Corbin focused on a statement Henry made about his readiness, on all occasions, "to bow, with the utmost deference, to the majesty of the people."

Corbin asserted that Henry's opposition to the Constitution contradicted his claim to honor the sentiments of the people, "and yet the gentleman tells us that 'he bows to the majesty of the people'"—whereupon Corbin bowed gracefully to his listeners. "The gentleman had set himself in opposition to the people throughout the whole course of this transaction," Corbin insisted, "and yet the gentleman is ever ready and willing, at all times and on all occasions, to bow to the majesty of the people"—and again Corbin bowed gracefully to his audience. It made little difference whether a country was tyrannized "by a despot with a tiara on his head or by a demagogue in a red cloak [and] a caul-bare wig" who professed "on all occasions to bow to the majesty of the people," Corbin declared—yet again bowing gracefully to his increasingly apprehensive listeners. While his sarcastic onslaught continued—accompanied by a total of "thirteen of the most graceful bows" one observer had ever seen—Henry's friends seethed, Corbin's friends stifled nervous giggles, and the target of Corbin's attack listened "without any apparent mark of attention" until the young federalist took his seat with a look of triumph on his face. Recounting this episode in 1817, Henry's first biographer interjected a quotation from Virgil's *Aeneid* as his comment on Corbin's impending fate: *Nescia mens hominum fati sortisque futurœ*—Not knowing doom, nor of events to be!

Rising slowly as though reluctant to respond, Patrick Henry observed that he was "a plain man," and "educated altogether in Virginia." His whole life had been "spent among Planters . . . who have never had the advantage of that polish which a court alone can give and which the gentleman over the way has so happily acquired." For two decades he had only been "engaged in the arduous toils of the revolution," Henry reminded his listeners, "while that gentleman was . . . acquiring a foreign education, mixing among the great, attending levees and courts, basking in the beams of royal favor at St. James's, and exchanging courtesies with crown heads." And now—with an apology for his inability to compete with Corbin "in those courtly accomplishments of which he has just given the house so agreeable a specimen"—it was Henry's turn to emulate Corbin's gestures at court.

Henry had to admit that his own experiences during the war had been as far from Corbin's "polite accomplishments" as Corbin "was from sharing in the toils and dangers in which his unpolished countrymen were engaged." Nevertheless, Henry assured his audience, "such a bow as I can make shall ever be at the service of the people"—and with that Henry performed a bow "so ludicrously awkward and clownish as took the house by surprise and put them in a roar of laughter." Apologizing profusely for the inadequacies of his own education and social skills, Henry observed that he had "never been a favorite with that monarch whose gracious smile [Mr. Corbin] has had the happiness to enjoy." Finally, in a devastatingly calm voice and "without the smallest token of resentment," Henry scrutinized the contrasts between his and Corbin's experiences for fifteen or twenty excruciating minutes while the younger man hung his head and "sank at least a foot in his seat."

ooooo

In addition to his efforts toward a second convention, Patrick Henry exploited the electoral provisions of the new Constitution for his announced goal of retrieving American liberty and correcting the defects of the new government in a constitutional way. Article I of the Constitution gave the state legislatures authority over the management of congressional elections—including the initial creation of election districts—and the selection of United States senators (until 1913 when the Seventeenth Amendment introduced the direct popular election of senators). Henry had no interest in holding a federal office himself, but he and his allies were not shy about using these opportunities to elect senators and encourage the election of congressmen "wedded to freedom and the rights of men, and . . . steadily opposed to whatever shall tend to trample on those rights."

Throughout the ratification contest, Henry had grown increasingly suspicious about the zealous advocates of a stronger national government. They might not be guilty of "manifest Enmity to public Liberty," he commented to Richard Henry Lee, but they "show too little Sollicitude or Zeal for its preservation." Henry's nominees for the U.S. Senate, the antifederalists William Grayson and Richard Henry Lee, easily defeated the sole federalist candidate, James Madison—whose friends felt that Madison was somehow entitled to a seat in Congress "as a sort of Right." Henry disagreed. "The universal Cry is for Amendments, and the federals are obliged to join in it." His belief that "the American Union depends on the Success of Amendments" reflected the serious implications of his insight about the inexorably divisive consequences of legislative deliberations about taxation and slavery. Nevertheless, he told Lee, "the old Charges of Turbulence and Ambition have been plentifully bestowed on . . . us."

The creation of new electoral districts—twelve for presidential electors and ten for Congress—gave the legislators an opportunity to configure the latter to their liking, but the charge that Henry gerrymandered the congressional districts to keep Madison out of the new House of Representatives is exaggerated, though both Madison's and Henry's supporters did seek to align the new districts to their advantage. The boundaries drawn for the new Fifth Congressional District, which included Orange

County (Madison's home) and seven other counties, substantially coincided with three existing state senatorial districts. Unlike the contorted Massachusetts district that unleashed America's original "Gerry-mander" in 1812, or the outrageous computer-generated precincts of today's partisan redistricting schemes, all ten of Virginia's original congressional districts were responsibly contiguous adaptations of the state's senatorial districts.

With bipartisan support, the Assembly also implemented a residency requirement for congressional candidates that prevented the voters of any other district from offering a safe seat to Madison (who was then in New York serving in the Confederation Congress) or anyone else. Madison did not like campaigning, claimed to have ethical scruples about electioneering, and was suffering from hemorrhoids. Because he had hoped to win a seat in the new Congress without the agonies of traveling all the way back home to conduct a campaign, a few of Madison's friends regarded the residency requirement as evidence of Henry's partisanship. Which is not to say that Henry was indifferent about Madison's electoral ambitions. Before the vote for senators, he told the legislature that Madison was "not to be trusted with amendments since [he] had declared [in convention] that not a letter of the Constitution could be spared." As the legislature contemplated formal instructions requiring its congressional delegation "to vote against direct taxation," Henry pounced when a federalist expressed doubt as to whether Madison would comply. "There gentlemen," Henry swooped, "the secret is out: it is doubted whether Mr. Madison will obey instructions." In the public debate Henry assessed Madison's "political character [as] . . . unworthy of the confidence of the people," Light-Horse Harry Lee reported, and suggested that his election would bring "rivulets of blood throughout the land"—while in private (until a mistaken rumor was scotched) "it was whispered among the members that [Madison] was an advocate for the surrender of the navigation of the Mississippi."

Amendments to the Constitution became the overriding issue in the Fifth District when Madison ran for Congress against James Monroe, who lived in adjacent Spotsylvania County and had voted against ratification. Madison's great fear was that a second convention would scuttle the Constitution. Faced with a popular insistence upon amendments, however, Madison determined that the safest course was to formulate a bill of rights in Congress (evading the substantive alterations sought by Henry, Mason, and the rest) and send it to the states for endorsement. Accordingly, Madison's friends spread the word, in what amounted to a solemn campaign promise, that he would push for amendments during the first session of Congress. In addition, Madison traveled back to Virginia and won the support of the district's two prominent Baptist ministers—George Eve and John Leland—with convincing assurances of his dedication to religious liberty. In the end, despite ten inches of snow and subzero temperatures, Madison bested Monroe by 336 votes, a margin of 14 percent. Overall, on February 2, 1789, Virginia freeholders elected seven federalists, two antifederalists, and one candidate who seemed unaffiliated with either faction to the first session of the new Congress.

ooooo

Two days prior to the congressional elections, Virginia's twelve presidential electors gathered in Richmond to cast their ballots for president and vice president. Beyond the occasional local rivalry, the Old Dominion saw little controversy in the January voting for presidential electors because Virginians were unshakably committed to the candidacy of George Washington. Voting had occurred at county courthouses throughout the state on January 7, and by the end of the month the sheriffs from all but one district had reported their results. Henry apparently had no opposition when he was chosen as the presidential elector from the district bounded to the west by the Blue Ridge Mountains, to the south by the Carolina line, and to the northeast by the James and Appomattox Rivers.

As the senior statesman among the ten electors who met at the capitol on February 4, 1789 to cast their ballots for president and vice president, Henry served as informal chairman of the group. The Constitution was written before the advent of political parties, so although voting procedures in the electoral college would be altered by the Twelfth Amendment, between 1789 and 1800 every presidential elector voted simultaneously for two candidates. The presidency went to the one who got the most votes, the vice presidency to the candidate in second place. Henry's signature appears first on the official certification of Virginia's electoral vote, which listed ten votes "for George Washington, Esquire, of Mount Vernon," everyone's favorite; five for John Adams, the federalists' favorite; three (including Patrick Henry's) for George Clinton of New York, the antifederalists' favorite; and one each for John Hancock and John Jay. The fact that two districts went unrepresented in Virginia's first electoral balloting without much comment (one because the January voting was hopelessly confused and the other because Warner Lewis failed to attend) suggests the degree to which Washington's candidacy eclipsed all others. When the final result was tallied on February 4, 1789, Washington had 69 electoral votes, John Adams took the vice presidency with 34, and 9 other candidates garnered a total of 35 votes.

∞∞∞∞∞

Despite Patrick Henry's doubts, after his election to the House of Representatives James Madison *did* follow through on his campaign pledge by pushing our modern Bill of Rights through Congress. By channeling these amendments through Congress rather than another convention, however, Madison also fulfilled Henry's predictions by stifling the movement for a second convention and sidelining the antifederalists' substantive amendments. Reporting to Henry in June, Senator William Grayson wrote that "from motives of *policy*"—a word that implied sinister images of Machiavellian cunning—Madison was advancing a program of "amendments which shall affect personal liberty alone, leaving the great points of the judiciary, direct taxation, etc., to stand as they are." His objective, Grayson warned, was to "break the spirit" of the movement for substantive change and "go on coolly in sapping the independence of the State legislatures."

Henry, who was in constant communication with both senators, was disappointed but not surprised by these developments in Congress. Madison's feeble amendments, he advised Richard Henry Lee, "will tend to injure rather than serve the cause of liberty," as they were clearly intended "to lull suspicion . . . on the subject." Henry remained steadfast in his opinion that "the single amendment proposed in our Convention respecting direct taxes [was] worth all the rest."

Mason heartily agreed, describing Madison's "Milk and Water Propositions" as a "Farce . . . by way of throwing out a Tub to the Whale"—a popular reference to a trick employed on whaling vessels of tossing an empty barrel overboard as a diversion to discourage an angry whale from bashing the ship. When the House of Representatives sent Madison's amendments to the Senate, Virginia's senatorial delegation made a futile attempt to add the substantive changes recommended by the Richmond convention. As William Grayson informed Henry, however, they might as well have tried "to carry Mount Atlas on their shoulders."

In September Congress was able to send twelve amendments to the states for ratification. The first two (aimed at limiting the size of the House of Representatives and discouraging increases in congressional salaries) were not approved by enough states to become part of the Constitution. Over the next two years, ten states ratified the ten articles now revered as the federal Bill of Rights. By November 1791 only one more endorsement was required.

Despite Virginia's vigorous clamor for amendments, Madison's proposed amendments encountered furious opposition in the commonwealth. Senators Grayson and Lee issued a public letter to the General Assembly condemning them as inadequate and urging Virginia to hold out for more severe restrictions on the federal government. Although the House of Delegates voted to ratify the proposals, Henry's friends in the state Senate said No. Announcing that the proposals were "far short of what the people of Virginia wish" and "by no means sufficient to secure the rights of the people or to render the government safe and desirable," the state Senate warned its constituents "not to be put off with amendments so inadequate."

Restrained by Patrick Henry, the General Assembly dragged its feet for two years. When the Assembly met in October 1791, however, a refined and graceful young federalist took advantage of Henry's retirement from the House of Delegates. Francis Corbin engineered the passage, first, of the amendment to curtail the size of Congress. Then, early in December, he got the lower house to approve the remaining eleven amendments almost unanimously. The state Senate concurred on December 15, 1791. Fifteen years after Virginia had adopted its original Declaration of Rights, Francis Corbin's achievement brought the convoluted story of Patrick Henry's and James Madison's roles in the legislative history of America's Bill of Rights to a fitting conclusion. Virginia's ratification clinched its adoption. The remaining three states, Connecticut, Georgia, and Massachusetts, did not formally ratify the Bill of Rights until its 150th anniversary in 1941.

ooooo

As Americans embraced the new government, Patrick Henry's promi-nence in the ratification contest and especially his strenuous exertions on behalf of subsequent amendments made him a lightning rod for politi-cal animosity. During the next two decades the new republic experienced some of the most viciously partisan journalism in American political history—and just as Henry had been in the forefront of the Revolution, now he found himself targeted as an early victim of a malicious character assassination that astonished even his political adversaries. "Decius," as the perpetrator signed himself, began his attack with an essay in the *Virginia Independent Chronicle* on December 1, 1788, announcing his aim to expose "the treachery, hypocrisy, and deceit of some men's political lives."

In his second essay Decius focused his malice more narrowly on the object of his hatred, abandoning the polite conventions of eighteenth-century newspaper discourse to assail the man he regarded as a tyrant whose despotism "lurks under the disguise of republican zeal"—a man "whose plainness of manners and meanness of address first should move our compassion, steal upon our hearts, betray our judgments, and finally run away with the whole." Within a few weeks, however, readers disgusted by the severity and prejudice of Decius's accusations were submitting angry rejoinders defending Patrick Henry in print and by name. "A Fed-eralist" chastised Augustine Davis, the paper's editor, for publishing "false-hoods" directed against "that amiable character." Henry may have stood in "opposition to me in the convention last June," A Federalist wrote, but he "did credit to his cause and thereby added to his political fame." Another citizen challenged the patent falsehood of Decius's allegation that Henry had distorted Madison's electoral district (the boundaries of which fol-lowed county lines) "into a thousand excentric angles."

The "miserable scribbler" hiding behind the pen name Decius turned out to be a deputy clerk in Albemarle County, John Nicholas, Jr., whose "passion was to get into the newspapers and correspond with eminent men." The Decius campaign against Patrick Henry proved to be only the earliest of several intrigues that marred Nicholas's career, including elabo-rate schemes directed against Presidents Washington and Jefferson and a fraudulent effort to collect on a deceased cousin's military pension. Jeffer-son, who was returning from France when the Decius letters were initially published, later met with Nicholas and in 1790 accepted a copy of *Decius's Letters on the Opposition to the New Constitution in Virginia*. (The book, which bears Jefferson's marginal notations identifying many of Nicholas's prey, is now in the collections of the Library of Congress.) After Nicholas turned on Washington and Jefferson in intricate plots known as the Langhorn affair and the Geoffrey episode (named for the false identities Nicholas adopted in each incident), Jefferson characterized the man who had been Decius as "a malignant neighbor."

In addition to the published denunciation of Decius by A Federalist, Henry heard directly from one federalist who had spoken several times in the recent convention. James Innes wanted Henry to know that a rumor identifying him as the author of the Decius letters was false. "I neither am the author nor do I know who he is," Innes wrote. "I am not directly or indirectly concerned in the publication, nor have I ever approved of it." Innes closed his letter "with sentiments of very high respect and esteem." Equally revealing was the opinion that Edmund Randolph expressed in private to Madison. Virginia was enjoying "a general calm of politicks," and Randolph wanted to prolong it. He worried that the "very injudicious and ill-written publication . . . under the signature of Decius" might revive animosities from the ratification contest among those who were "the object of his bitterness." His assertions were "not always correct," his "facts [were] of a trivial cast," and his conclusions were "vulnerable." And although Decius might claim protection from the liberty of the press, Randolph had felt the lash of hostile pseudonymous authors and believed that men in public life deserved better than to be "assailed by an enemy in disguise and have their characters deeply wounded before they can prepare for defence."

By inclination and counsel, Henry agreed with the advice proffered by his friend Senator Grayson. "With respect to the unmerited attacks on your character," Grayson wrote from New York, "I think they deserve nothing but contempt. . . . Nothing would please the author so well as to enter into a literary altercation with you." It had become a regrettable fact, Grayson concluded, that "attacks on characters that are high in the public estimation have been so frequent . . . as not to deserve a moment's attention. Envy and detraction, says Mr. Addison, is a tax which every man of merit pays for being eminent and conspicuous"—a literary allusion that emphatically contradicted Decius's contention that Grayson was poorly educated.

Henry shared Randolph's assessment of the general calm in state politics. "Federal and anti seem now scarcely to exist," he told Grayson, "for our highest toned Feds say we must have amendments." As to the Decius letters, Henry lightheartedly claimed to have only seen about five of them—and "in these [the author] was not lucky enough to hit up on one charge that is warranted by Truth." Then, in an introspective mood that transcended politics, Henry suggested that he was also "lucky" that Decius did not know better, for as a man of faith he acknowledged "many Deficiencies in [his] own conduct" and could easily conceive of himself as "an *unprofitable Servant*"—a direct reference to parable of the talents in Matthew's Gospel—"but alas! how difficult is it for human pride to submit to that appellation from others!" Decius, Henry believed, was merely one of those "political understrappers who ever follow the footsteps of power and whine and fawn or snarl or bark as they are bid." Such petty men, "who ape their Betters and are content with their Leavings as the wages of the dirty Work assigned them," were found in all governments "and no doubt in the American," too. Whether their superiors would exhibit "a more tolerant spirit," Henry concluded, was yet to be seen.

ooooo

For better or worse, Patrick Henry's core outlook toward slavery had not shifted at all during the decade after independence—a fact that has eluded all his previous biographers because they were unaware that the dialogue he began with the Quaker Robert Pleasants in 1773 continued into the 1790s. What had happened around him in the mid-1780s, however, was a growing divergence in attitudes toward slavery as many Virginians reacted against both the growing number of private manumissions and new appeals for emancipation and abolition.

Robert Pleasants continued to emphasize religious arguments against slavery in his dialogue with Henry—"While ye have the light, walk in the light," said our blessed Lord, "lest darkness come upon You"—in contrast to the appeals to revolutionary ideals that he emphasized when urging George Washington and Thomas Jefferson to support his cause. Pleasants was confident that he knew Henry's "sentiments on this important Subject," he wrote in 1790, for his "Judgment [had been] clear more than seventeen years ago, that freedom is the Natural and inalienable right of all descriptions of mankind." The Quaker activist addressed Henry as a fellow Christian less in need of "arguments to convince [him] of the injustice

and bad policy of Slavery" than of prodding "to forgo the honors and profits of a delusive World" and embrace "humility, self denial, and a faithful
reliance on the divine promise."

November 1785 may have been the high-water mark of post-
revolutionary Virginia's short-lived willingness to consider the abolition
of slavery. Throughout that year, Methodist circuit riders carried antislavery petitions in their saddlebags and solicited signatures from citizens in
all corners of the commonwealth. Presented to the House of Delegates on
Tuesday, November 8, these petitions declared that slavery was "contrary
to the fundamental principles of the Christian religion" and an "express violation of the principles upon which our government is founded." Accordingly, these petitioners sought nothing short of "a general emancipation"
of slaves in Virginia—which the Assembly unanimously rejected.

As Virginians discussed slavery, manumission, and emancipation,
however, concerns for the rights of property began to modify and supplant more noble arguments. In the debates that had shaped Virginia's
new manumission law, Quakers had found that pragmatic Virginia legislators who seemed indifferent to the sway of religion or natural law were
often receptive to the idea that the property rights of slave owners should
permit them to dispose of their property as they saw fit. The relaxation of
restrictions upon private manumission would simply allow slaveholders to
honor their personal beliefs about slavery (whatever they were) by exercising their legal rights either to hold or dispose of their human property.

On the other hand, when Quakers, Methodists, or civic republican
reformers sought to undermine the institution of slavery with talk of a
general emancipation, the same rights of property posed a virtually insurmountable obstacle. Indeed, in 1785 many of Patrick Henry's neighbors
sent counterpetitions to the legislature justifying the institution of slavery
according to biblical injunction, property rights, and even the Revolution
itself. None of these Virginians argued that slavery was a positive good (as
antebellum southern apologists eventually would) but they did assert that
if slavery was evil it was a regrettably necessary evil. "The property is here
on our hands, and what shall we do with it?" the Reverend William Graham asked every senior class at Liberty Hall Academy (now Washington
and Lee University) in the annual lectures on Human Nature that he delivered from the 1780s to 1796. "It is a fact that none are imported now,"
Graham continued, "but thousands have been imported and are here in

our country, and the question is, would it be right and safe to emancipate them?"

Fear defined Graham's answer, as it did for many Virginians. Fear rooted in an honest perception of the degrading and violent evil of slavery, for how could any person be expected to survive enslavement without feeling a deep urge for revenge? Fear—as it was expressed in petitions from three hundred freeholders of Amelia, Mecklenberg, and Pittsylvania counties in November 1785—of free blacks committing "Outrages, Insolences, and Violences destructive to the Peace, Safety, and Happiness of Society." Fearful Virginians, as the rector of Liberty Hall put it, saw their only options as either "freeing the negroes and thereby putting it in their power of uniting in one body against us" or continuing "their present situation" as slaves in an increasingly desperate hope of making "such a combination . . . wholly impracticable."

Fearful Virginians also perceived Virginia's antislavery advocates as new threats to the liberty and property they had fought for in the Revolution. Their language may shock today's sensitivities, but petitions protesting the new manumission laws and any talk of emancipation expressed prevalent values and ideology of the post-revolutionary culture in which Patrick Henry and his colleagues now lived. These petitions from Henry's neighborhood merged religious and secular arguments against manumission and emancipation with Lockean ideas about property rights and civic republican concerns about virtue and independence—all to insist that the American Revolution itself supported the continuation of slavery.

"When the British Parliament usurped a Right to dispose of our Property without our Consent," 1,200 citizens from eight Piedmont counties explained, "we dissolved the Union with our Parent Country" and established a republican government "grounded on a full and clear Declaration of such rights as naturally pertain to Men born free"—as distinct from those *not* born to freedom. In order to place their "property on a Basis of Security not to be shaken in future" they had "risked [their] Lives and Fortunes, and waded through Seas of Blood." With victory came the promise of full "Possession of our Rights of Liberty and Property"—including "the most valuable and indispensable Article of our Property, our Slaves." Seen in this way, talk of emancipation displayed "a flagrant Contempt of the constituent Powers of the Commonwealth" and comprised "a daring attack on that sacred Constitution." It also threatened "ruin to the free Citizen [and] the Horrors of all the rapes, Robberies, Murders, and Outrages which an innumerable Host of unprincipled, unpropertied, vindictive, and remorseless Banditti are capable of perpetrating."

Only by recognizing the polar opposition of these extremes of opinion in post-revolutionary Virginia can we comprehend the middle ground that Patrick Henry attempted to maintain. He would speak honestly in the Virginia convention of 1788 when he admitted both that "as much as I deplore slavery, I see that prudence forbids its abolition" and that "a great deal of the property of the people of Virginia [is] in jeopardy." The obstacles to emancipation seemed insurmountable. On the one hand, as a prominent Baptist critic of slavery complained, it was "unconstitutional for government to take away the property of individuals." On the other hand, the cost of their "ransom"—£8,307,690 computed at an average value of £30 per slave—seemed "infinitely beyond what the commonwealth could pay to the holders of slaves" as well as "an intolerable burden upon" taxpayers who did not own slaves, whether from "conscience or poverty." Seven decades later, the estimated cost of the American Civil War would be $9.23 billion.

In the early weeks of 1790, Robert Pleasants also recognized the obstacle posed by property law when he called an organizational meeting for April 5 to establish a Virginia abolition society, "similar to those in other parts of the world," and solicited Henry's endorsement for the fledgling organization. Expressly hoping that Henry would "sacrifice ... what an unrighteous law of men calls thy property," Pleasants couched his appeal entirely in religious terms—but Henry declined either to join his association or advance its cause when the Assembly met the following October. The best that Henry and other moderate delegates would accomplish was to fend off efforts to rescind the manumission law, but he and the House of Delegates remained steadfast in their refusal to consider emancipation.

When Henry and Pleasants met again during the Assembly session in the autumn of 1790, their conversation turned to developments in Congress that Henry had expressly anticipated during the ratification debates. Driven by an abhorrence of slavery, Henry had predicted in 1788, Congress would inevitably "search that paper [i.e., the Constitution] and see if they have power of manumission." And they would discover that authority in "the power to provide for the general defence and welfare,"

Henry had warned. "May they not think that these call for the abolition of slavery."

Nineteen months later, after carefully avoiding any discussion of slavery during its initial session in 1789, the First Congress had confirmed Henry's forecast and sent shock waves into Virginia when northern congressmen brought three antislavery petitions to the floor of the House of Representatives in February 1790. Two came from Quaker groups associated with Pleasants's friend Anthony Benezet. The third was signed by Benjamin Franklin, president of the Pennsylvania Society for Promoting the Abolition of Slavery. Although they were short on specifics, the petitions urged Congress to assert its authority over the future of slavery and "step to the very verge of the power vested in you for discouraging every species of traffic in the persons of our fellow men." The Senate summarily dismissed all three petitions, but the angry debate that immediately engulfed the House of Representatives quickly spread to Richmond and points south.

Virginians were alarmed by "the very circumstances of such a subject being taken up in Congress," Edward Carrington wrote. "It has disturbed the Minds of our People, and lessened their Confidence in Congress," Adam Stephen reported from the Potomac Valley near Winchester. A friend from Raleigh, North Carolina, told James Madison that congressional discussion of "the subject of Slavery hath excited great uneasiness here and will probably Cause still greater [disquiet] to the southward"— and that the furor had given rise to "a prevailing Wish that Mr. Henry was in Congress"!

Nor were southerners the only people troubled by the controversy. Vice President John Adams, presiding officer of the Senate, condemned "the silly petition of Franklin and his Quakers" for distracting the lower house from more important issues, including Alexander Hamilton's financial measures. Massachusetts congressman Nathaniel Gorham spoke for many when he complained that the Quakers were pushing their petitions "so zealously . . . in the infancy of the government" when responsible statesmen were trying to avoid "everything that would tend to irritate."

By autumn, when Robert Pleasants and Patrick Henry met and discussed the Quaker petitions during Henry's last term in the Virginia legislature, the House of Representatives had squelched the antislavery

petitions with a clear declaration that Congress had "no authority to inter-
fere in the emancipation of slaves or in the treatment of them within any
of the States." Henry nevertheless dreaded the fact that Congress was deliberating about slavery at all, and once again advised the Virginia Quakers that it was "an improper time" to push for antislavery measures in the
Virginia legislature. Pleasants, by contrast, could not see why Henry found
the congressional resolution "exceptionable" when, from his perspective,
Congress had "been decisive in *not* passing Laws" about slavery.

ooooo

One reason that the congressional discussion of slavery was more troubling for Patrick Henry than for Robert Pleasants was its immediate constitutional context. When the antislavery petitions came to the floor of
the House of Representatives, they quite literally interrupted the heated
congressional debates about Alexander Hamilton's controversial financial program that were being reported in the Richmond newspapers. Especially controversial among Virginians was the treasury secretary's plan
for paying off the states' wartime debts with federal funds. "The people
of Virginia are, I believe, almost unanimous against the assumption," Edmund Randolph advised James Madison, not only because they felt they
had already struggled to pay down the commonwealth's debts, but because
this aspect of Hamilton's program lacked any specific authorization in the
Constitution and thus posed "the real danger of consolidation" by expanding the federal government under what came to be called the elastic clause
of Article I, which granted Congress authority "to make all Laws which
shall be necessary and proper."

Defeated in its initial formulation by a narrow vote of 29 to 31 in June
1790, Hamilton won the necessary votes in one of the most famous compromises in American history. The political bargain, struck between Hamilton and Madison at a dinner hosted by Jefferson, fixed the future site
of the nation's capital on the Potomac River in exchange for congressional passage of Hamilton's assumption plan in July. The bargain delighted
President Washington but was not well received back in Richmond. "The
mad policy which seems to direct the doings of Congress" appalled Light-
Horse Harry Lee, who had vigorously supported the ratification of the
Constitution. "Every day adds new testimony of the growing ill will of the
people here to the [federal] government," Lee told Madison. "Henry al-

ready is considered a prophet," Lee reported, for "his predictions are daily verifying." Even worse, according to Lee and other disillusioned Virginia federalists, Patrick Henry's anticipation of the sectional divisions that would "exist under the constitution and predominate in all the doings of the government already has been undeniably proved." Just twenty months after he had voted to ratify the Constitution, Lee was now entertaining serious thoughts of "disunion" rather than living "under the rule of a fixed insolent northern majority."

President Washington's confidant David Stuart confirmed Lee's observations. "The late transactions of Congress have soured the Public mind," Stuart reported, "which was just recovering from the fever which the Slave business had occasioned when the late much agitated question of the State debts came on. Both the antislavery petitions and assumption of state debts were "subversive of the true principles of the Constitution," Stuart declared, especially since congressional adoption of Hamilton's plan "rests solely on a construction of their powers." Stuart also informed Washington that a story was circulating in Richmond to the effect that when a member of the Governor's Council of State asked Patrick Henry whether he would accept an appointment to the U.S. Senate as successor to the recently deceased William Grayson, Henry had declined because "he was too old to fall into those awkward imitations which were now become fashionable." Stuart believed the comment meant that "the old Patriot has heard some extraordinary representations of the Etiquette established at [the president's] levees," which many republican critics felt were more pompous than the royal levees at the Court of St. James's—though if the rumor were true Henry could as easily have been referring to Vice President John Adams's preoccupation with exalted titles in the Senate.

Regardless of what Patrick Henry may have thought about the president's weekly levees or the vice president's penchant for honorific titles, he clearly did see Hamilton's assumption plan as a dangerous and unauthorized extension of federal power. Early in the next session of the General Assembly, on Wednesday, November 3, Henry presented, and the House of Delegates adopted, a succinct and forceful declaration that the Senate endorsed soon thereafter:

Resolved, That so much of the act intitled "An act making provision for the debt of the United States," as assumes the payment

of the state debts is repugnant to the constitution of the United
States, as it goes to the exercise of a power not granted to the general government.

Two weeks later, by another overwhelming majority vote, the Assembly endorsed Henry's resolution with a formal statement, directed at Congress,
passing judgment on the constitutionality of Hamilton's assumption plan.

On Thursday, December 16, the General Assembly asserted that neither policy, justice, nor the Constitution warranted the assumption of
state debts by the general government of the United States. Well aware of
Hamilton's admiration for British institutions, the Virginians noted the
"striking resemblance" between his program and the system that created
England's "enormous debt" after the Glorious Revolution and enabled Sir
Robert Walpole and the king to exert "unbounded influence [in] . . . every
branch of the government" and thereby threaten "the destruction of every
thing that appertains to English liberty." In an agricultural country, the
Assembly asserted, pandering to "a large monied interest" would inevitably
crush agriculture beneath "the feet of commerce" and render "the present
form of fœderal government fatal to the existence of American liberty."
Hamilton's program seemed "calculated to extort from the General Assembly the power of taxing their own constituents . . . in such a manner
as would be best suited to their own ease and convenience"—a familiar
theme from the antifederalist critique of the Constitution.

Just as Lee and David Stuart found themselves echoing Henry's arguments from the ratification debates, now the entire legislature of the commonwealth demanded that Congress live up to the constitutional promises
made by the federalists. "During the whole discussion of the fœderal constitution by the convention of Virginia," the Assembly reminded Congress, "your memorialists were taught to believe 'That every power not
granted [to the central government] was retained [by the states].'" Men
who in 1788 had disagreed mainly about whether to seek previous or subsequent amendments now remembered with perfect clarity that they had
adopted the Constitution "under this impression and upon this positive condition," which they had expressly "declared in the instrument of
ratification." However, the Assembly declared, "your memorialists can find
no clause in the constitution authorizing Congress to assume the debts of
the states!"

With the new federal government entering its third year of existence, Hamilton's assumption plan was confirming Henry's forecasts even as it contradicted the contractual agreement that Virginia made when it rat-ified the Constitution. Describing themselves as guardians of the rights of their constituents and sentinels "over the ministers of the federal gov-ernment," Henry and his colleagues asserted their constitutional authority to protect the commonwealth from congressional "encroachments." Ham-ilton's assumption plan deserved "the censure of the General Assembly" not only "because it is not warranted by the constitution of the United States, but [also] because it is repugnant to an express provision of that constitution . . . 'That all debts contracted and engagements entered into before the adoption of this constitution shall be as valid against the United States under this constitution as under the confederation.'" In light of these considerations—the explicit promises made when Virginia rati-fied and the language quoted from Article VI—the General Assembly of Virginia asserted that "the rights of states as contracting parties with the United States must be considered as sacred." Serving notice that Virginia would seek to enforce a strict adherence to the letter of the Constitution, Henry and his colleagues called upon Congress—as they had repeatedly called upon Parliament in the imperial crises of the 1760s—to revise and amend Hamilton's financial plan and, specifically, repeal everything that "relates to the assumption of the state debts."

Both Henry's succinct resolution declaring Hamilton's assumption "re-pugnant to the constitution" and the Assembly's more lengthy address to Congress were picked up by newspapers throughout the country. Although at odds with the emerging doctrine of divided political sovereignty that Hamilton, Jay, and Madison espoused in their *Federalist* essays, these res-olutions were, as historian Richard Beeman recognized, "in complete har-mony with the principles upon which Virginia had fought the Revolution and with the spirit with which it had agreed to ratify the Constitution." It was significant that while Henry and his colleagues asserted Virginia's right to enforce the limits of congressional power, they did *not* pronounce the assumption law null and void.

Although at least one gloomy federalist worried that Virginia's reac-tion to Hamilton's programs put Henry in an ideal position "to aim a blow at [the] existence" of the new government, the dissolution of the Union was not then and never had been Henry's objective. In precise legal terms,

Henry and the Assembly were advocating *interposition* not *nullification*—concepts that remained distinguishable in 1790. Long before the Supreme Court asserted its role as arbiter of the Constitution, and long before the sectional crises of the 1830s rendered the terms virtually interchangeable, the word carried the connotations of its eighteenth-century scientific and astronomical origins, as something that came between two other things in a relationship. In the American political context of the 1790s, a successful interposition began with a public challenge to a government for failing to honor its constitutional mandate and ended either in a reversal of policy or an amendment or clarification of the Constitution. Unlike nullification, interposition was not an act of sovereignty—it did not hazard the ties between a people and their government or threaten anarchy or rebellion by declaring a law null and void.

By declaring that the assumption of state debts was repugnant to the Constitution, Patrick Henry and the General Assembly asked Congress to repeal those parts of Hamilton's plan that exceeded the powers delegated to the federal government—just as Virginia had asked Parliament to repeal the Stamp Act, the Townshend Duties, and the Intolerable Acts. Before resorting to the dangers of nullification and its explicit threat of resistance, Henry sought to exhaust every opportunity of reversing unsound congressional policies "in a constitutional way"—as he had promised the convention of 1788 and counseled the disgruntled antifederalists who were contemplating resistance after their loss.

Nevertheless, as the first of antebellum Virginia's many affirmations of state rights and strict constitutional interpretation, the General Assembly's 1790 address to Congress looked back to principles forged in the conflict with Parliament and George III and squinted forward toward the Virginia and Kentucky Resolutions of 1798 and antebellum theories of nullification. By articulating the interests of an agrarian slaveholding society and linking Alexander Hamilton's financial policy with northern interests and English tyranny, Henry and the Virginia legislature set forth a vision of constitutionalism that comprised, as Richard Beeman put it, "a practical guidebook for anyone wishing to attack the federal government in the future."

CHAPTER TWENTY-SIX

For the Defense

PATRICK HENRY REACHED the pinnacle of his postwar legal career with the British-debt cases, argued before Richmond's newly formed U.S. Circuit Court in 1791 and again in 1793. Throughout these hearings, Henry and John Marshall worked together, with Marshall writing the briefs and both men presenting oral arguments. The defense of Virginia planters against British creditors suing to recover debts incurred before the Revolutionary War comprised a substantial part of Marshall's legal practice, and the creation of the federal court system now exposed his clients to collection efforts that Virginia's state courts long had discouraged.

The British debt case subject to the first hearing in November 1791 was *Jones v. Walker*, pitting the surviving partner of the Bristol firm of Farell & Jones against Albemarle County's elderly frontiersman, Dr. Thomas Walker. The three judges hearing the case were the Old Dominion's U.S. District judge Cyrus Griffin and U.S. Supreme Court justices Thomas Johnson of Maryland and John Blair, Jr., of Virginia. Each side was represented by four of Virginia's leading attorneys: Jerman Baker, Andrew Ronald, Burwell Starke, and John Wickham for Jones; Marshall, Henry, Alexander Campbell, and James Innes for Walker. One clear sign of the importance that Virginians attached to the case was the presence of the stenographic reporter David Robertson, who had recorded and published the debates of the Virginia convention of 1788. Robertson's record of the arguments in *Jones v. Walker* was lost sometime after 1817, but Henry's first biographer, William Wirt, had access to Robertson's manuscript and published Henry's speeches in the case.

Although the Peace Treaty of 1783 specified that creditors should be permitted to recover legitimate prewar debts, many Virginians remained furious about the wartime destruction and theft of property by British invaders. Pointing to the British refusal to return (or pay for) slaves and property carried off during the war as a violation of the peace treaty, Virginians rationalized their refusal to open the state courts to their former enemies as a way of pressuring the British government into compliance with the treaty. When the U.S. Circuit Court for Virginia opened in May 1790, British merchants filed more than a hundred suits for the collection of debts. Despite their formal and legalistic language, the British debt cases raised difficult questions of law and policy. Under the new Constitution, must the laws of Virginia yield to the peace treaty as the "supreme law of the land"? Could the judiciary declare that a treaty had been violated? If so, did British actions render it void? Not surprisingly, these were vexing questions (and hot political potatoes) that few American judges were eager to decide. It took eighteen months for *Jones v. Walker* to reach the courtroom, and years passed before it was finally decided.

Patrick Henry did not disappoint the large audience that gathered to hear him in the courtroom upstairs in the capitol—an audience that included so many members of the legislature that the House of Delegates was unable to convene a quorum until Henry finished his arguments three days later. After two of Jones's lawyers opened the case, Henry answered for the defense on November 25, delivering what many regard as his career masterpiece of legal argument. He demonstrated that he was both a surpassingly eloquent speaker and an accomplished lawyer at the height of his powers—a lawyer who had clearly done his homework in international law.

Preparing himself for the case in his law office at Pleasant Grove, Henry could turn to his own library for the copy of Pufendorf's *Law of Nature and Nations* he had purchased in Williamsburg in 1764. He also owned and consulted Hugo Grotius's *Of the Rights of War and Peace*, but for this case he also needed to consult Emmerich de Vattel's *Law of Nations*, which he did not own. Remembering that a friend had a copy, however, Henry dispatched his namesake grandson, Patrick Henry Fontaine, who was studying law with his grandfather, on a sixty-mile errand to borrow Vattel's treatise. "From this and other works," the young man recalled, Henry filled a small leather-bound commonplace book ("convenient for carrying in his pocket") with a closely written "syllabus of notes and heads of arguments."

As the court date drew near, Fontaine occasionally glanced up from his own studies to watch his grandfather walking "with his notebook in his hand" along a path shaded with black locust trees between his house and the law office at Pleasant Grove. "From his gestures while promenading alone in the shade of the locusts" and his occasional stops to read something from the notebook, Fontaine realized that he was watching his grandfather formulate and commit to memory "much of that celebrated speech . . . which occupied three days of the attention of the United States Court."

The case presented intricate questions arising from the law of nations, but Henry was in full command of the subject. In addition, with an apparent ease that cloaked his weeks of careful study, Henry exploited his knack for translating dry questions of law into compelling personal terms. He began with a bold condemnation of British conduct during and after the war to assert that the king's hostile actions toward Virginia had terminated Jones's right of recovery. Expressing regret at the necessity of revisiting the "animosities which the injustice of the British nation hath produced," Henry prefaced his remarks with a religious and philosophical insight about the consequences of George III's war against his former subjects that Henry had first learned from Samuel Davies in 1756. Individual Christians were duty bound "to forgive injuries done us as individuals," Henry acknowledged, "but when to the character of Christian you add the character of patriot, you are in a different situation." Christ's admonition to turn the other cheek "cannot apply . . . to your country," Henry explained, for "when you consider injuries done to your country, your political duty tells you of vengeance." God rewarded and punished sinners as individuals in the world to come, Davies had taught him, but He held nations accountable in this world for it was "only in this World that they subsist in a national Capacity."

The two objectives of Henry's three-day speech were to drive home the points raised in Marshall's written pleas and to deflect the arguments advanced by Jones's lawyers. Tailoring his presentation to the panel of senior judges (rather than a jury of country farmers), Henry quoted passages and even cited page numbers from the classic treatises on international law. He read a passage from Grotius, for example, "to prove that property of an enemy is liable for forfeiture" as an exigency of war "and that debts are as much the subject of hostile contest as tangible property." Then he followed up by observing that "Vattel, p. 484 . . . enumerates *rights* and *debts* among such property of the enemy as is liable to confiscation."

From the authority of these respectable authors "and the clearest principles of the laws of nature and nations," Henry concluded that "these debts became subject to forfeiture or remission." But then he clinched this portion of his argument with humor—one of the courtroom techniques that were his stock-in-trade as a trial lawyer. Jones's counsel had tried to assert that Virginia had not attained the status of a nation (and was therefore incapable of exercising the power of confiscation) until George III formally acknowledged American independence by the treaty of 1783. Henry retorted that America became a completely sovereign nation "when her sons stepped forth to resist the unjust hand of oppression and declared themselves independent" in 1776. "Yes, sir," Henry reminded the court, "we were a nation long before the monarch of that little island in the Atlantic Ocean gave his puny assent to it"—accompanying his words by "rising on tiptoe, pointing as to a vast distance, and half-closing his eyelids as if endeavoring with extreme difficulty to [see an] . . . object almost too small for vision—and blowing out the words *puny assent* with lips curled with unutterable contempt."

Thomas Jefferson reluctantly expressed admiration for Henry's efforts: "He never distinguished himself so much as on the . . . question of British debts in the case of Jones and Walker," Jefferson advised Henry's first biographer. "He had exerted a degree of industry in that case totally foreign to his character, and not only seemed, but had made himself really learned on the subject." In another respect, however, Jefferson's grudging compliment demonstrates once again how thoroughly he misunderstood the nature of Henry's genius. Naturally Jefferson admired an oration bejeweled with citations and quotations from the world's great legal authorities. What he failed to recognize, however, was that Henry knew his audience, and for the first time in many years he was pitching his arguments not to a jury of country farmers but to a well-educated panel of senior justices. John Marshall's judgment was more perceptive: Henry was "a great orator . . . and much more, a learned lawyer, a most accurate thinker, and a profound reasoner."

The first round of courtroom drama in *Jones v. Walker* extended into December 1791, but when one of the justices withdrew after a death in his family, the remaining two judges declined to make a ruling in the case. Seventeen months later, on May 27, 1793, Henry, Marshall, and their associates joined forces in Richmond to argue another British debts case before another three-judge panel. District Judge Cyrus Griffin, back from the earlier hearing, now was joined by John Jay of New York, chief justice of the United States, and Associate Justice James Iredell of North Carolina. The new case, *Ware v. Hylton*, involved exactly the same issues as *Jones v. Walker* and the same cast of lawyers revisited the same fundamental arguments. The only real change was in the identity of the defendant, Richmond merchant Daniel L. Hylton. The new plaintiff, John Tyndale Ware, was the estate administrator for the late William Jones, who had died before his case against Dr. Walker was decided.

John Randolph of Roanoke, who had followed Henry to Richmond, recalled hearing the chief justice tell James Iredell, who had never heard Henry speak, that he was the greatest of orators. Iredell was doubtful, especially as Henry approached the bar looking like a decrepit old man, wrapped up for warmth and protesting that his client had unwisely consigned his case to a man with trembling hands, "one foot in the grave, weak in his best days, and far inferior to his able associates." Although Randolph knew Henry's protests were exaggerated for effect, "such was the power of his manner and voice," he recalled, that for a moment he would "forget and find himself enraged with the Court for their 'cruelty.'"

Ever the horseman, Randolph compared Henry's arguments to a four-mile practice run by a thoroughbred alternately "displaying his whole power and speed for a few leaps" and then slowing to a trot until at last he got up to full speed. When Henry reviewed British depredations when they had been successful in battle and sketched the dire fate that awaited America had they been victorious, "the color began to come and go in the face of the Chief Justice, while Iredell sat with his mouth and eyes stretched open in perfect wonder." At last Henry "arrived at his utmost height and grandeur. He raised his hands in one of his grand and solemn pauses.... There was a tumultuous burst of applause, and Judge Iredell exclaimed: "Gracious God! He is an orator indeed!"

Two weeks later the court ruled against three of the four arguments advanced by Marshall and Henry, but Judges Iredell and Griffin outvoted Jay to uphold their fourth argument, in support of Virginia's wartime commission established in 1777 to manage the properties of exiled British subjects and accept payments for debts owed to British creditors. Three years passed before Ware's appeal came back to the Supreme Court, with Marshall once again representing the Virginia debtors. This time, however, Justice Iredell was overruled by his colleagues and Marshall lost the only case he ever argued at the bar of the Supreme Court.

Despite their ultimate defeats, Henry's and Marshall's brilliant efforts on behalf of the Virginia debtors did not go for naught. As legal historian Charles Hobson explains, "they had served their clients well by postponing the debtors' inevitable day of reckoning for at least six years, giving them time to recover from the war's devastating effects." Although British creditors now began winning judgments in state courts, too, juries routinely deducted eight years' interest for the war in defiance of instructions from the courts—a vindication of the continuing power of local Virginia juries to decide both law and fact. A payment of $9,574.29 from the estate of the late Dr. Walker was finally settled in May of 1799. Judgments totaling $6,014 wiped out Daniel Hylton and sent the former merchant briefly to debtor's prison and then to a ten-year stint as clerk of the Council of State prior to his death in 1811.

Throughout the 1790s Patrick Henry consistently declined several offers of federal office, including a prospective appointment to the Supreme Court for which his exemplary work in the British debt cases was an obvious commendation. For Marshall, these cases started him on the path that eventually led to his appointment in 1801 as chief justice. While in Philadelphia to argue the appeal of *Ware v. Hylton* in 1796, Marshall impressed several leading Federalists, including John Adams. A year later President Adams sent Marshall on a diplomatic mission to France, and then, after serving one term in Congress, he joined Adams's cabinet as secretary of state—the office he held when Adams nominated him to be chief justice. Henry's and Marshall's partnership in the British debt cases also laid the basis for a decade of personal and political friendship.

ooooo

By the summer of 1792 Virginia's leading advocate for emancipation knew his cause was losing ground. Over the previous two decades, Robert Pleasants and Patrick Henry had worked together to end the importation of slaves and make it easier for slave owners to ease their consciences by private acts of manumission. Now that those two goals had been accomplished, however, Pleasants perceived "that men of the first abilities" were increasingly "backward in promoting some General plan for a gradual Abolition of Slavery." Pleasants wanted to push forward with a program of gradual emancipation—"a law declaring the Children of Slaves born after a certain time to be Free etc."—for which he sought not only Henry's approval but his public endorsement: "I hope thou wilt so far at least countenance the design as to give it the Sanction of thy Name." But the intrepid Quaker was finding that men "blest not only with abilities but influence" who had been sympathetic to manumission "from some Cause or other, seem to hold back as yet from engaging in so righteous and noble a Cause."

As Patrick Henry prepared to retire from political office, events were forcing him to acknowledge that he and his Quaker friend were reaching the limits of their two decades of cooperation. Pleasants wanted to abolish the evil of slavery. Henry increasingly sought only to mitigate the horrors of what he had come to accept as a *necessary* evil and keep it from tearing the nation apart. Henry may still have believed, as he had told Pleasants in 1773, that "a time will come when an opportunity will be offered to abolish this lamentable evil"—but whenever Pleasants sought his help that wondrous moment seemed to recede even further into a distant future.

Although Pleasants feigned ignorance about reasons that able men were backing away from his righteous cause, the pamphlet he sent Henry in July of 1792 shows that the Quaker was monitoring world events. Pleasants hoped that Jean-Philippe Garran de Coulon's forty-page *Inquiry into the Causes of the Insurrection of the Negroes on the Island of St. Domingo* would persuade Henry that only "the woeful effects of Pride and prejudice" were responsible for horrors afflicting on the Caribbean island of Hispaniola. The author, a liberal member of France's revolutionary National Assembly, took pains to show that the slave revolt that erupted in 1791 was the result not of ideas about *liberté, egalité,* and *fraternité* emanating from Paris but of vicious hatreds that were as endemic to the sugar islands of the Caribbean as yellow fever and torrential rains.

Regardless of how the island rebellion began, however, the pamphlet that Pleasants sent to Henry was more likely to alarm than soothe its recipient—for the bloody spectacle of the racial warfare that eventually led to Haitian independence played a major role in the decline of America's post-revolutionary antislavery movement. Americans were horrified by the brutal stories coming out of Haiti—tales of men and women hacked to death with cane knives and of severed heads mounted on pikes along the roadways and at the gates of burned plantations—that seemed to confirm the nightmare of "rapes, Robberies, Murders, and Outrages" that many Virginians feared as the fruits of manumission and emancipation. Indeed, in May of 1792 Henry's friend Light-Horse Harry Lee investigated reports of conspiratorial conversations citing "the example of the West Indies" for an intended uprising, followed the next summer by the "Secret Keeper" conspiracy, which implicated slaves in Richmond, Norfolk, and Charleston, South Carolina.

In the end, Henry declined to join Pleasants's antislavery society or endorse his petition for gradual emancipation. Over the course of nearly two decades, the patriot and the Quaker had accomplished everything they could agree on. Henry remained convinced that slavery was evil and repugnant. He remained uneasy about its inevitably divisive effect in national politics—a prospect he had anticipated in 1788 and seen confirmed in 1790. As he retired from public life, Henry had come to believe that after ending slave importations and relaxing the rules for manumission, the best he now could do was to treat his own slaves decently, teach them to read the Bible, and encourage his descendants to do the same. In a wider perspective, as historian David Brion Davis observed, this attenuation of grand principles into a mundane program of better care for slavery's unfortunate victims marked the general collapse of the post-revolutionary antislavery movement in the southern states. For Patrick Henry, as for many other eighteenth-century Virginians, the ongoing compromise between noble political and religious ideals and the acceptance of slavery as a necessary evil continued, as it had in 1773, to lend "a gloomy perspective to future times."

ooooo

Midway between the British debt cases, a sensational scandal brought Henry and Marshall together again at the courthouse of Cumberland County—a salacious story of unwed pregnancy, possible infanticide, and alleged incest within the elite Randolph family of Virginia. No one knows exactly what had happened at Glenlyvar plantation, on the James River in Cumberland County on Monday, October 1, 1792, but the aftermath of whatever had happened demanded the skills of Virginia's most famous defense attorney.

The soap opera that had played out among the overnight guests at Glenlyvar had begun about nine months earlier and thirty miles to the southeast at Bizarre plantation, on the Appomattox River (near modern Farmville) a few miles north of Patrick Henry's home in Prince Edward County. Bizarre was home to twenty-two-year-old Richard Randolph and his twenty-year-old wife, Judith, as well as her eighteen-year-old sister, Anne Cary, known as Nancy, who had been engaged to (and probably impregnated by) Richard's brother Theodorick prior to his death at twenty-one (probably from tuberculosis) on February 14, 1792. As well-informed gossips knew at the time, Richard and Theodorick (as well as their younger brother John Randolph of Roanoke) were all descendants of the Curles branch of the family, named for their grandfather's plantation east of Richmond. Judith and Nancy (as well as Nancy's friend and sister-in-law Martha Jefferson Randolph, daughter of Secretary of State Thomas Jefferson) were their cousins from the Tuckahoe branch of the family, named for their great-grandfather's plantation west of Richmond.

According to the rumors, which spread rapidly through the Randolphs' extensive kinship network, after traveling that Monday from Bizarre, Nancy was said to have given birth that evening and Richard was said to have killed the baby and disposed of the body. The likely truth was more benign—a late-term miscarriage or stillbirth. Nevertheless, several relatives who felt that "Mr. Randolph and Miss Nancy were too fond of each other" now insinuated that Richard had also fathered the dead infant—compounding the imputation of infanticide with a suspicion of incest.

Early in the new year, forced to confront the rumors that he had seduced his sister-in-law and murdered their child, Richard Randolph engaged Patrick Henry as his attorney. Then he boldly announced in the newspapers that he would attend the April meeting of Cumberland Court and "answer in the due course of law, any charge or crime which any person or persons whatsoever shall then and there think proper to allege against me." By Virginia law, the Cumberland Court's role in a capital crime was similar to that of a grand jury—to determine whether a crime had been committed and whether the alleged perpetrator should be held for trial at the next session of the district court of Prince Edward.

As promised, Richard and his attorney reported on the first day of court, April 22, and he was arrested and committed to jail on the charge of "feloniously murdering a child said to be born of Nancy Randolph." Witnesses and the full county court then were summoned for the hearing a week later. As Richard's defense attorney, it was Henry who led the examination of thirteen witnesses, although Marshall was also present and made detailed summaries of their testimony. A distant cousin of the Randolphs through his mother, the future chief justice had an extensive clientele among the family and was probably looking after Nancy Randolph's interests in case the hearing led to criminal charges.

According to family tradition, Henry was reluctant to subject himself to a seventy-five-mile journey to Cumberland County and declined Richard Randolph's initial offer of 250 guineas (£262 10s) to defend him. A few days later, however, when Randolph sent a higher offer of 500 guineas Henry is said to have consulted his wife. "Dolly," the story goes, "Mr. Randolph seems very anxious that I should appear for him, and 500 guineas is a large sum. Don't you think I could make the trip in the carriage?" Court records indicate that Randolph actually paid Henry £140 with a promissory note—still a remarkably high legal fee for the time.

Another family story (generally corroborated by Marshall's notes) recounted Henry's adroit examination of a hostile witness, Nancy Randolph's inquisitive aunt Mary Cary Page. Mrs. Page admitted that after overhearing a conversation between Nancy and a maid she had approached her niece's room, "being then suspicious of her situation." Finding the door locked, Mrs. Page looked "through a crack" and saw that Nancy was undressed and appeared to be pregnant. At this point, according to the family account, Henry "resorted to his inimitable power of exciting ridicule by the tones of his voice and in a manner which convulsed the audience asked her, 'Which eye did you peep with?'" Flushed with anger and humiliation, her credibility impugned, Mrs. Page could say nothing as Henry turned to the justices and exclaimed, "Great God, deliver us from eavesdroppers!" Although the salacious rumors never quite disappeared, the hearing ended with the justices of Cumberland County (with all sixteen in attendance for such a high-profile inquiry) ruling that Richard Randolph was "not guilty of the felony wherewith he stands charged" and ordered him immediately "discharged out of custody."

CHAPTER TWENTY-SEVEN

Last Call

IN THE INTERIM between the first and second court sessions in the British debt cases, Patrick Henry and his family moved southwest from Pleasant Grove to Long Island on the Staunton River in Campbell County and from there to his final home at Red Hill, a dozen miles downstream in Charlotte County. The residence at Long Island—a one-and-a-half-story frame house with two large rooms on the first floor and one room with large dormer windows above stairs—overlooked the river and the six-hundred-acre, mile-long island for which the plantation was named. It was here that Dorothea buried her eighth child, seventeen-month-old Richard, in August 1793, and gave birth to her ninth child, Edmund Winston Henry, the following January.

It was also at Long Island—which the former governor bought from then governor Light-Horse Harry Lee in an unrecorded gentleman's agreement between friends—that Patrick Henry finally cleared himself from debt and retired (almost permanently) from politics. Boasting some of the most fertile soil in the southern Piedmont, the 2,506-acre farm (to which Henry added another thousand acres prior to his death) produced tobacco worth more than £200 a year as well as vegetables, sheep, cattle, and hogs for the family and about seventy slaves. Tobacco and other marketable produce—corn, wheat, oats, and rye—could be transported downstream for sale at Petersburg or carried overland to market at Lynchburg or the county seat at Rustburg. In addition to its agricultural advantages, Long Island and its ferry across the Staunton River were conveniently situated midway between the district courts at New London (near modern Lynchburg) and Prince Edward Courthouse, where Henry practiced most frequently.

Matters of health—his own and his family's—often weighed on

Henry's mind. In October 1793 he advised his daughter Elizabeth Aylett that "the flux"—a term usually associated with diarrhea or dysentery—was ravaging the neighborhood. "Many died of it and the whole country here abouts has been sickly," he wrote, "but it has pleased God we escaped it." Young Johnny Christian and Elizabeth's brother Patrick had been ill and were "recovering fast," but "Neddy has been at the point of death at Colonel Meredith's"—the home in Amherst County of Henry's sister Jane and her husband, Henry's boyhood friend Samuel Meredith. Henry regretted that he had been unable visit Neddy: "I should have gone to him, but had a pain in my hip." Nevertheless the family was going "to Red Hill, eighteen miles below this, in a few days, to spend eight months," intending to return and "spend the sickly season here."

A year later, back at Long Island, Henry told Elizabeth that he felt "great cause of Thankfulness for the health I enjoy . . . for not one of us have been sick for a long time." High above the river, Henry and his family had "providentially escaped the flux as yet, whilst many around us have died of it," though his "working Negroes on the River [were] indeed very sickly" with some kind of "Ague," or fever, though "not of an inveterate kind" (that is, probably not malaria). Henry worried about Elizabeth's health "at so sickly a place," along the tidal streams and wetlands of King William County east of Richmond. Expressing his wish that Elizabeth might "enjoy the agreeable society of your sisters at this place," Henry also acknowledged that Long Island was somewhat isolated, or as he put it, "very retired, indeed so much so as to disgust Dolly and Sally," Elizabeth's younger sisters Dorothea, now sixteen, and Sarah, now fourteen. "But as we go to Red Hill in August for five weeks they will be relieved from this Solitude," Henry concluded, "as that is a more public place"—a statement that astonishes modern visitors who find their way along winding country roads to the pristine rural landscape of Henry's last home and his final resting place outside the town of Brookneal.

oooooo

Patrick Henry purchased Red Hill in January 1794 for £1,700 from Richard Booker, who had operated the ferry there and farmed the seven-hundred-acre plantation since 1772. Booker had built the modest house, a simple story-and-a-half frame structure, twenty by thirty feet, with a large single room off the entrance hall and two rooms above. Family tradition suggests that Henry added a twelve-foot master bedroom in a "lean-to" at the east end of the house so he "could hear the patter of the rain on the roof" (though documents at the Library of Congress suggest that the addition was probably made when Patrick and Dorothea Henry's youngest son, John, born in February 1796, expanded the house about 1832). Other buildings made Red Hill, which Henry expanded within a few years to 2,965 acres, into a small village—an overseer's cottage that Henry transformed into a law office, a separate kitchen east of the house, a laundry and tannery in the ravine further east, slave quarters to the northwest of the main house, a blacksmith shop somewhere in walking distance from the house, the usual array of sheds and barns, a plantation store, and as many as three licensed distilleries.

In the autumn of 1794, Patrick Henry decided to give up the practice of law "and plague myself no more with business." "Sitting down with what I have will be sufficient employment," the fifty-eight-year-old patriot told his daughter Elizabeth, "to see after my little Flock and the management of my plantation." Henry regarded his place of retirement as "one of the garden spots of the world," especially the four acres fenced off as an enclosed orchard planted with apples, figs, olives, pears, and pomegranates, according to a poem written in 1798 by Henry's sixteen-year-old daughter Martha Catharine. Red Hill was also the most productive of Henry's plantations, with an annual yield of as many as 20,011 pounds of tobacco. Estate inventories taken in July 1799, and September 1802 listed—along with Henry's books, furniture, and household goods—128 head of cattle, 186 hogs, 38 sheep, 13 horses, 7 colts, and 5 yoke of oxen. Also listed, by name and with some indications of family connections, were the sixty-nine slaves (fourteen men, seven teenage boys, fifteen women, two teenage girls, and thirty-one children under twelve years old) whose presence made Red Hill a multifamily village and whose labor made everything work.

ooooo

Henry's retirement from political office did not mean he stopped caring about America and its destiny. Distance might cushion him from the day-to-day commotion of state and national politics, as when he claimed to have seen only five of the nasty Decius letters, but Henry monitored both domestic and world events from his rustic retreat. Like many American statesmen, he watched the events of the French Revolution with initial sympathy.

The storming of the Bastille in 1789 and the abolition of the monarchy in 1792 seemed like Gallic echoes of the American Revolution. The subsequent condemnation of Lafayette as a traitor, beheading of Louis XVI, and movement to supplant Christian worship with the Cult of Reason planted seeds of doubt about French policies. Nevertheless, when France declared war against England in 1793 many Americans embraced the young republic with gratitude for French support during the American Revolution and lingering resentment over British conduct during and after the Revolutionary War. Determined to protect the nation from entanglement in European conflicts, however, President Washington responded with a proclamation of American neutrality in April 1793.

Washington's attempt to maintain official American neutrality was never popular, especially after Jefferson left his cabinet and joined Madison as de facto leaders of the emerging Democratic-Republican party. Openly espousing the French and excusing the widespread use of the guillotine in the name of necessity, the Jeffersonians charged Washington's administration with favoring England. On the other hand, Federalist friends of the administration, many of them equally open in their admiration of Britain and its parliamentary tradition, saw the events in France as infectious harbingers of anarchy and bloodshed.

Like a reflection in a fun-house mirror, the French Revolution distorted the beauties and blemishes that Americans saw in one another, polarizing Federalists and Republicans alike: "Behold France," one Federalist warned, "an open hell, still ringing with agonies and blasphemies . . . in which we see their state of torment and perhaps our future state." Look at England, came the Jeffersonian reply, a corrupt tyrant of the seas, driven into perpetual debt by its war machine, threatening "the liberty of the whole earth." Against this backdrop, Edmund Randolph cheerfully reported to President Washington that while Henry was in Richmond arguing the British debt cases, he was "loud in reprobating the decapitation of the French king, and is a friend to peace and the steps pursued for its security" by the Washington administration.

About the same time, Henry attended a dinner at Rocky Mills, the home of his half-brother, John Syme, Jr., an enthusiastic Jeffersonian and

Francophile, where "the company was composed of very respectable characters of both parties." When Syme offered "The People" as the first toast,
Henry reacted by "pushing his old black wig aside, as was his custom when
much excited, and with his elbows akimbo, exclaimed, 'What, brother, not
drink to General Washington as we used to do? For shame, brother! for
shame!' and filling up his glass with a bumper of Thomson's Madeira, announced the name of WASHINGTON."

ooooo

As America's emerging political parties clashed over foreign policy, Alexander Hamilton's fiscal policies, and the especially divisive nature of
John Jay's treaty negotiations with Great Britain, Jefferson and Madison
and their political allies increasingly perceived Henry's instinctive support
for President Washington, as well his growing personal friendships with
John Marshall and Light-Horse Harry Lee, as evidence that Henry was
abandoning his revolutionary principles and turning Federalist. Henry answered the charge in a letter to his daughter Elizabeth Aylett, whose husband had heard the accusations in Richmond.

"As to the reports you have heard of my changing sides in politics,"
Henry wrote, "I can only say they are not true. I am too old to exchange
my former opinions, which have grown up into fixed habits of thinking."
It was true that he had "condemned the conduct of [Virginia's] members
in congress" for trying to obstruct the Jay Treaty in ways that would have
had the unintended "effect of surrender[ing] our country bound, hand and
foot, to the power of the British nation." The Jay Treaty itself was "a very
bad one indeed," Henry readily admitted, but the nature of Madison's and
Jefferson's opposition was dangerous, too. "What must I think of those
men whom I myself warned of the danger of giving the power of making
laws by means of treaty to the president and senate"—referring to Madison's defense in the convention of 1788 of the Senate's role in approving
treaties—"when I [now] see these same men denying the existence of that
power which they insisted, in our convention, ought properly to be exercised by the president and senate, and by none other?" Madison's theories, "both then and now," were "void of wisdom and foresight." Such
were the sentiments that he had expressed "in conversation in Richmond,"
Henry told his daughter, "and perhaps others which I don't remember" but
his point had been to emphasize (in agreement with Virginia republicans)

that Americans "had everything to dread" from the British whenever they found "opportunities of oppressing us."

The acrimony of party politics in the last decade of his life disgusted Henry. "Every word was watched which I casually dropped," he told his daughter, and then twisted "to answer party views." He professed neither to know nor care who spread the rumor, for he no longer considered himself "an actor on the stage of public life. It is time for me to retire . . . unless some unlooked-for circumstance shall demand from me a transient effort, not inconsistent with private life." Considering the "gross abuse" that was heaped upon Washington, Henry marveled that the man whose conduct "during the whole war was above all praise" could be treated so maliciously: "what may be expected by men of the common standard of character?"

The underlying problem, however, went deeper than vicious journalism: "The rising greatness of our country," Henry believed, "is greatly tarnished by the general prevalence of deism, which with me, is but another name for vice and depravity," as was evidenced by the mayhem of the French Revolution. "Amongst other strange things said of me," Henry told his daughter, "I hear it is said by the deists that I am one of their number; and indeed, that some good people think I am no Christian. This thought gives me much more pain than the appellation of tory; because I think religion of infinitely higher importance than politics."

Henry's concerns about the growing influence of deism—a theological perspective that dismissed traditional doctrines such as divine revelation, the Trinity, and the divinity of Christ—were not exclusively the result of French Revolution. Apart from the Bible, his favorite theological works included two of the era's leading refutations of the deist position, the Anglican bishop Joseph Butler's *Analogy of Religion: Natural and Revealed* and *The Rise and Progress of Religion in the Soul* by Philip Doddridge, a prominent English dissenting clergyman. Henry also admired a succinct book by the English Baptist Soame Jenyns, a member of Parliament and certainly no friend to Henry's politics or the cause of American independence. Nevertheless Jenyn's *View of the Internal Evidence of the Christian Religion*, first published in 1776, was a vigorous defense of traditional Christianity. The proper sphere of reason was narrow, Jenyns argued. Only the doctrines and ethics of the New Testament, deriving "its origin from God," could sustain morality and promote virtuous living.

Henry was so pleased with Jenyns's book that in the 1780s he had abandoned writing a religious tract of his own and arranged instead for a new printing of Jenyns's at his expense. Now physically too frail to ride any distance on horseback, Henry traveled to court, according to his cousin Edmund Winston, "in an old-fashioned stick-gig"—probably the two-wheeled "riding chair" enrolled on the 1787 property tax list. Henry carried a stash of Jenyns's *View of the Internal Evidence of the Christian Religion* in his carriage and gave copies to people he encountered—including two circuit court judges whom he jokingly asked "not to take him for a traveling monk."

ooooo

Despite Henry's desire to retire from public life and enjoy "the fruits of his labour under his own fig-tree with his wife and children around him in peace and security"—as he had described the aspiration he shared with countless Virginiansn in the convention of 1788—Henry's name and reputation still carried weight throughout the country. President Washington formally offered Henry an appointment as ambassador to Spain and, in 1795, the cabinet post of secretary of state. Henry declined in a long and friendly letter, citing his family's needs and personal circumstances (including his fear that living in Philadelphia could expose Dorothea and his children to smallpox, "which neither herself nor any of our family ever had") but also assuring the president of his support for Washington and his administration.

President Washington considered Henry for the Supreme Court on two occasions. In 1794, after the Maryland justice Thomas Johnson resigned, Henry's masterful performance in the British debts cases made him an attractive candidate. Since Virginia already had one justice on the court, however, Washington felt that he could not appoint Henry without exciting "unpleasant sensations in other States." The second instance came after the resignations of the aging Virginia justice John Blair and of Chief Justice John Jay and the Senate's rejection in December 1795 of John Rutledge of South Carolina, whose fierce criticisms of the Jay Treaty raised hackles among senators who had supported the controversial pact. Once again Washington approached Henry about accepting the post of chief justice through their mutual friend Light-Horse Harry Lee. "Surely no situation better suits an individual," Lee advised Henry. "The salary [was] excellent and the honor very great," and since his presence would be essential only when the court was in session, he could "continue at home except when on duty" and the "change of air and exercise will add to your days." With the next session of the court only weeks away and the president impatient for an answer, Henry met with Lee in Richmond and declined the honor in a private conversation.

President Washington also considered Henry as a potential successor to James Monroe as ambassador to France in 1796, but by then he knew that Henry was in no position to accept. In general, however, as Washington explained to Lee, the president felt a "strong inducement on public and private grounds"—the latter a reference to Henry's steadfast support during the Conway Cabal—"to invite Mr. Henry into any employment under the General Government to which his inclination might lead."

ooooo

In September 1796, when Washington announced that two terms were enough, Vice President John Adams and former secretary of state Thomas Jefferson promptly emerged as the leading contenders for the presidency. In several states, however, prominent politicians such as Alexander Hamilton, Rufus King, John Marshall, and Timothy Pickering (all of them affiliated with the emerging Federalist party) wondered whether Patrick Henry might be willing either to accept the presidency or give geographic balance to Adams's candidacy by, in effect, standing for election as vice president. Initially, Henry was unaware that anyone thought of him as a prospective candidate. Nevertheless, since he was "one of the few figures with the potential to win something close to a Washington-like national consensus victory," according to the recent definitive history of the 1796 election, Henry eventually felt compelled "publicly to declare his fixed intention to decline that office."

Because Washington had twice swept the electoral balloting virtually without opposition, 1796 witnessed the first contested presidential election in the history of the republic. It differed profoundly not only from the quadrennial spectacles of our century but also from all other presidential elections. As in previous presidential elections, voting in 1796 followed the original provisions of the Constitution. The founders had frowned upon the divisive "spirit of party" and created the electoral college to ensure that the president and vice president were the "men best qualified for the purpose"—the candidates who got the most and second-most votes. Now, however, partisanship was rampant, especially after the bitter conflict over the Jay Treaty in 1795. Although as yet America had no well-organized national parties, as the election of 1796 approached voters and candidates were beginning to identify themselves as Federalists and Democratic-Republicans. Although leaders and voters had been thinking about slates of candidates, the existing procedure would inevitably award the offices to the leading rival candidates, as it did in 1796 with Adams and Jefferson as president and vice president. And things got messier four years later, when the electoral balloting for Jefferson and Aaron Burr, his ostensible running mate, resulted in a tie that threw the election of 1800 into the House of Representatives—and then prompted the adoption of the Twelfth Amendment in 1804 to accommodate the existence of political parties.

Even more peculiarly, by modern expectations, the state legislatures of Connecticut, Delaware, and South Carolina opted to choose members of the electoral college themselves without any general election. And even in states where ordinary voters did directly participate in the presidential election, their votes could be cast only for aspiring local electors, not for the major national candidates associated with the still-emerging party system.

Sometimes, but not always, these aspiring electors announced who they favored and why. Two electoral candidates in northern Virginia, Leven Powell and Charles Simms, announced their intentions of voting for Patrick Henry as their preferred candidate and John Adams as their second choice. Initially, Jefferson and his supporters feared that a Henry candidacy would work against them by splitting the vote in Virginia and other southern states. Powell believed that Henry "could unite all parties and do away with that spirit of contention which at present rages with so much violence amongst us and threatens the destruction of the Union." His friend Charles Simms, however, contrasted Jefferson's character as governor in 1781 with Henry's "diligence and wisdom while at the head of the government of this state." In a lengthy and widely reprinted statement that exacerbated the Jeffersonians' animus toward Henry, Simms proclaimed that "a man who shall once have abandoned the helm in the hour of danger . . . seems not fit to be trusted in better times, for no one can know how soon or from whence a storm may come."

As partisans jockeyed for political advantage in an election that was without precedent, even John Adams grew impatient for the final electoral vote, venting to Abigail that he "wish[ed] Patrick Henry had 138 votes and would Accept them." Henry himself did nothing to promote or disparage any presidential candidate. Indeed, early in November he issued a public letter "To the People of the United States" declining the prospect of election to the presidency. Published first in Richmond, Henry's letter was reprinted in dozens of newspapers throughout the country.

One curious aspect of Henry's letter—the date of its composition and publication—demonstrates how starkly the 1796 election differed from its twenty-first-century counterparts. In states where ordinary citizens participated in the election, most had already voted by the time Henry's letter of withdrawal appeared in their newspapers. In our century the formal actions of the electoral college barely make the news, but in 1796 Henry implicitly recognized that the selection of electors (whether by legislators or the voters at large) was only a preliminary step. The final decision would come in December when the electors gathered at their state capitols to cast their ballots for a new president. Patrick Henry, after all, had played that role himself when he cast his electoral vote for George Washington in the capitol at Richmond on February 4, 1789.

Henry's graceful letter specifically addressed both ordinary "citizens" and the newly designated "electors." Having been informed that some people wished to vote for him, Henry expressed gratitude for their "good will and favorable opinion." Although "not so vain as to suppose that a majority of *electors* would call [him] to that high appointment," Henry sought to prevent his name from being used by political schemers. He hoped that "wisdom and virtue," rather than partisan maneuvering, would "mark the choice about to be made of a President." In short, by withdrawing his name from consideration, Henry was voicing his independence from (and disdain for) the partisan spirit that had flared in the 1795 debates over Jay's treaty, that embittered the 1796 presidential contest, and ultimately led to the emergence of the republic's first political parties. In the end, when all 276 electoral votes were tallied on February 8, 1797, Patrick Henry's name did not appear among the thirteen men for whom ballots were cast. John Adams had 71 votes, Thomas Jefferson had 68, and Thomas Pinckney of South Carolina had 59—an election close enough to have been affected had Patrick Henry not spoken out "to prevent embarrassment in the suffrage."

ooooo

Patrick Henry, like George Washington and many other civic republicans, was apprehensive about the development of organized political parties in America. Drawing upon the political perspective of Henry St. John, Viscount Bolingbroke (whose influential essays were in Henry's library), American revolutionaries of their generation still equated political parties with the evils of faction, those inherently dangerous combinations of men pursuing their self-interest rather than the public good. For Henry and Washington, true patriots were men of virtue and independence whose disinterested commitment to the welfare of the community kept them aloof from factions but ready to join like-minded patriots when necessary to challenge the arbitrary exercise of power or the dreadful threat of anarchy—men, in short, who aspired to political conduct that rose above partisanship. Regardless of Jefferson's accusations of political "apostacy," however, Patrick Henry had not (and probably never did) become a Federalist.

To be sure, in the political context of the presidential election of 1796, Henry's Virginia admirers included future Federalists such as Light-Horse Harry Lee, Leven Powell, and Charles Simms (as well as national figures such as Hamilton, King, and Pickering) who disapproved of Jefferson's candidacy. But Henry's letter of withdrawal was clearly a nonpartisan gesture in keeping with his old-fashioned opinion about the divisive menace of political parties. If anything, Henry's retirement worked to Jefferson's benefit in the south by preventing either side from exploiting him as a spoiler in the electoral balloting. Moreover, outside the halls of Monticello and Montpelier, Henry's popularity among Virginia politicians of all stripes remained solid—as became evident on Friday, November 25, 1796, when the General Assembly transcended its deep political divisions to offer Patrick Henry an unprecedented sixth term as governor.

Four days later, after an express rider carried news of his election to Red Hill (a two-hour drive today), Henry offered the Assembly his gratitude "for this great Honor." It pained him to admit "that advanced age and decaying Faculties" imposed upon him "the necessity of declining this high Honor," but he was confident that others were equal to the task. That same day Henry explained his decision in greater detail to Colonel Samuel Hopkins, Jr., who had served with Washington at Valley Forge, worked

closely with Henry against the Constitution in 1787–1788, and was now
politically aligned with Jefferson and Madison as he prepared to move
west from Mecklenberg County to Henderson, Kentucky. "Could I see
any important political good in reach of the office of Governor," Henry
assured his longtime friend, "I should be strongly tempted to give up my
retirement." Instead, he wanted to express his gratitude to Virginia "for the
sweet sound of her approving voice. 'Tis all I can or want to receive. 'Tis
all a Republic ought to give."

As his letter to Hopkins demonstrates, during the final years of the
eighteenth century Henry grew increasingly vocal about the moral and
religious values that had always informed his perspective of society
and politics—whether prompted by age and infirmity or his belief that
the deism he associated with the excesses of the French Revolution was
threatening America, too. Insofar as America's "external relations" were
being shaped by hostilities between Britain and France, Henry was convinced that healing America's internal divisions stood beyond the reach of
a state governor—indeed beyond the "reach of our executives" in general.

"The Union will dissolve if parties continue," Henry told Hopkins.
"One side or other must yield." More urgently, however, Henry believed in
the necessity of "reformations" that echoed the adherence to fundamental
civic republican principles he had advocated in the Virginia Declaration
of Rights—justice, moderation, temperance, frugality, and virtue. "Vice
and depravity must be suppressed and become unfashionable or they will
undo us," Henry advised. "Let us ally ourselves to virtue," he contended,
for "without that auxiliary our appearance on the theatre of nations will
be fleeting." On the other hand, if all of America's "republican characters" stood united as virtuous citizens, their destiny could be "fixed as the
firmament."

ooooo

Patrick Henry cited his "advanced age and decaying Faculties" when he
declined a sixth term as governor and his "inability" when he declined the
presidency—but an astute statesman never says never. Henry did acknowledge two exceptional situations that might interrupt his retirement from
public life. One, as he told his daughter Elizabeth, was "some unlooked-for
circumstance" that might demand from him "a transient effort not inconsistent with private life." The other was some national emergency, as

Henry indicated to Washington in 1795, that might compel him to "obey the call of my country into service when her venerable chief makes the demand." Thus it happened early in 1799 that, from his own retirement at Mount Vernon, Patrick Henry's revered commander in chief issued the unlooked-for call to service.

American politics had only grown more bitter in the closing years of the eighteenth century. In 1798 the Federalists who controlled Congress and the presidency targeted their Democratic-Republican opponents with a cluster of repressive laws known as the Alien and Sedition Acts, authorizing the imprisonment of newspaper editors or politicians who criticized federal officials. In response, the legislatures of Kentucky and Virginia adopted fiery resolutions written by Thomas Jefferson and James Madison that declared the Alien and Sedition Acts unconstitutional and (in language that anticipated the state rights views expressed by South Carolina in the Nullification Crisis of the 1830s) threatened state-level resistance.

"At such a crisis as this," Washington wrote in an urgent confidential letter to Henry, "measures are systematically . . . pursued which must eventually dissolve the union or produce coercion." He expressed his "earnest wish that you will come forward for the ensuing elections for Congress or the state legislature. "Your weight of character and influence," Washington told Henry, "would be a bulwark against . . . dangerous sentiments" and "a rallying point for the timid."

George Washington was the one person whose call to public service Henry could not refuse. "My Children," Henry told his venerable chief early in February, "would blush to know that you and their Father were Contemporaries," if "when you asked him to throw in his Mite for the public happiness, he refused to do it." Accordingly, he reported that he had declared himself "a Candidate for this County at the next Election." His "indifferent Health" prevented him from "leav[ing] my Home" to announce his candidacy in person and "make the Declaration [as] efficacious as I could wish," when the justices of Charlotte County gathered for their monthly court days at Marysville, a mere twenty miles east of Red Hill.

Aside from a broken collarbone when he was twelve, Henry apparently had enjoyed robust health until 1776, when he had succumbed to the "notorious" disease environment of Williamsburg and spent his first months as governor convalescing at Scotchtown. And after finishing his

third gubernatorial term and moving to Leatherwood in 1779, he had declined election to Congress owing to "a tedious illness" that prevented him
from attending to business for several months. Since his final term in the
Assembly, however, Henry's health had become a recurrent problem—to
the point that in 1794 "many cases were continued" (that is, delayed) by the
district court at New London, near modern Lynchburg, because he was
sick. And finally, soon after Henry announced his candidacy for the autumn elections, he declined a presidential appointment, already endorsed
by the Senate, as a special envoy to the French Republic. "My advanced
age and increasing debility compel me to abandon every idea of serving
my country," Henry informed President John Adams, "where the scene of
operation is so far distant." Only George Washington could persuade his
ailing compatriot to contemplate the eighty-mile journey to Richmond
and the House of Delegates in December—a trek that was contingent
upon a successful eight-hour, twenty-mile trip to Marysville (now known
as Charlotte Courthouse) for the election on Monday, March 4, 1799.

After prayers on Sunday, Henry left Red Hill by carriage to have dinner and spend the night at Woodfork, the home of Joel Watkins, a fellow trustee of Hampden-Sydney College and former colleague in the
Assembly who had led the county militia during the battle of Guilford
Courthouse. Arriving at the courthouse on Monday, Henry was greeted by
several hundred people, including all the faculty and perhaps half the students from Hampden-Sydney. "He was very infirm," one of those students
recalled. "He arose with difficulty, and stood somewhat bowed with age
and weakness." Henry's face seemed "careworn," and when he began speaking "his voice was slightly cracked and tremulous." But soon this final audience witnessed "a wonderful transformation" as Henry's "features glowed
with the hue and fire of youth, and his voice rang clear and melodious."

Henry appealed for unity and moderation: "Let us not split into factions which must destroy that union upon which our existence hangs," he
said. If the members of Congress passed bad laws, they should be voted
out of office. "The people," he reminded his neighbors, "held the reins over
the head of Congress."

> If I am asked what is to be done when a people feel themselves in-
> tolerably oppressed, my answer is ready—*overturn the government*.
> But . . . wait at least until some infringement is made upon your

rights that cannot otherwise be redressed; for . . . you may bid adieu forever to representative government. You can never exchange the present government but for a monarchy."

Patrick Henry won the election and returned to Red Hill—never again to leave.

"Dear Patsy," Henry wrote his eldest daughter on June 1, "I am very unwell, and Dr. Cabell is with me." He died five days later, on June 6, 1799, "speaking words of love and peace to his family, who were weeping around his chair" as the desperate measure of last resort, a dose of liquid mercury, failed. A week later one of the *Virginia Gazette*s announced his death. The editor put heavy black border around the death notice, which was probably written by Light-Horse Harry Lee. "As long as our rivers flow, or mountains stand," said the *Gazette*, "Virginia . . . will say to rising generations, imitate my H E N R Y."

Acknowledging the partisan context of Henry's final election, the Richmond *Examiner* described him as an able statesman devoted to the rights of man, as zealous in his promotion of the American Revolution, and always committed to republican principles—and a man who, regardless of "his late political transition," had foreseen and warned of the constitutional evils "attached to the Executive branch" under President Adams. The *Petersburg Intelligencer* regretted the untimely death of a man whose proven patriotism and illustrious talents might have been able "to conciliate all parties and produce that harmony and concord" in a time of crisis, "when the national safety is endangered and the public mind so much agitated." While acknowledging a eulogist's temptation to exaggerate the qualities of the deceased in order to inspire the living, the Petersburg editor declared it "very difficult, if not impossible, to do complete justice to the character of this truly great man!" Echoing the chord sounded by Harry Lee, the *Intelligencer* called upon all Americans to "remember and imitate your HENRY!"—for "unless his virtues be imitated, his eulogy will be in vain."

ooooo

Of all the major leaders of the American Revolution, Patrick Henry was the one person who, aside from two years in the Continental Congress, never held national office—and yet he was a founder of the republic.

Henry explained the Revolution to ordinary men and women throughout America in words they understood—and inspired them to fight for liberty and justice. In the halls of the legislature, in the governor's office, and in state and local courthouses throughout the Old Dominion, he also protected and advanced both the liberties and the interests of his neighbors and constituents. Patrick Henry "was our leader in the measures of the Revolution in Virginia," said Thomas Jefferson in an honest and generous moment. "In that respect more is due to H I M than to any other person. . . . He left us all far behind."

A Note About Sources

Patrick Henry's life presents many challenges for historical research. Virtually all the local records of Hanover County, where Henry lived his first twenty-eight years, were destroyed on April 2–3, 1865, after being moved for safekeeping to the General Court building in Richmond during the Civil War. Most of Patrick Henry's personal and family papers were destroyed when the mansion at Red Hill, enlarged in 1912 by his great-great-granddaughter Lucy Grey Henry Harrison, burned in 1919. Of some 998 weekly issues of the original *Virginia Gazette* published from 1747 through 1765 only 142 issues are extant. No issues of the original *Virginia Gazette* are extant for 1747–1750, 1758, and 1764; no more than two issues survive for any year from 1753 through 1765.

Notes

Abbreviations and Short Titles

Adams Papers • Robert J. Taylor et al., eds., *Papers of John Adams* (17 vols. to date, Cambridge: Harvard University Press, 1977–).

Adams Works • Charles Francis Adams, ed., *Works of John Adams* (10 vols., Boston, 1856).

AHR • *American Historical Review.*

ANB • John A. Garraty and Mark C. Carnes, eds., *American National Biography* (24 vols., New York: Oxford University Press, 1999).

Brock Collection • Robert Alonzo Brock Collection, Henry E. Huntington Library; microfilm at Library of Virginia, miscellaneous reels 1217–18.

Burgesses Journals • John Pendleton Kennedy and Henry Reade McIlwaine, eds., *Journals of the House of Burgesses of Virginia* (13 vols., Richmond: Library of Virginia, 1905–1915). Kennedy began publishing these journals in reverse chronological order and without numbers; volumes are identified by dates.

Carter Diary • Jack P. Greene, ed., *Diary of Colonel Landon Carter of Sabine Hall, 1752–1778* (Richmond: Virginia Historical Society, 1965).

C.O. • Colonial Office, Public Record Office of Great Britain. See also VCRP.

Couvillon, *Patrick Henry's Virginia* • Mark Couvillon, *Patrick Henry's Virginia: A Guide to the Homes and Sites in the Life of an American Patriot* (Brookneal, Va.: Patrick Henry Memorial Foundation, 2001).

Davies, *Documents of the American Revolution* • K. G. Davies, ed., *Documents of the American Revolution, 1770–1783* (31 vols., Dublin: Irish University Press, 1972–1981).

DNB • H. C. G. Matthew and Brian Harrison, eds., *Oxford Dictionary of National Biography* (60 vols., New York: Oxford University Press, 2004).

DVB • John T. Kneebone, Brent Tarter, Sandra Gioia Treadway, et al., eds., *Dictionary of Virginia Biography* (3 vols. to date, Richmond: Library of Virginia, 1998–).

Evans, *Bibliography* • Charles Evans, *American Bibliography: A Chronological Dictionary of all Books, Pamphlets, and Periodical Publications Printed in the United States of America from the Genesis of Printing in 1639 down to and including the year 1820* (14 vols., Chicago: privately printed, 1903–1959).

Executive Journals Va. Council • Henry Reade McIlwaine, Wilmer L. Hall, and Benjamin J. Hillman, eds., *Executive Journals of the Council of Colonial Virginia* (6 vols., Richmond: Library of Virginia, 1925–1966).

Fauquier Papers • George Henkel Reese, ed., *Official Papers of Francis Fauquier, Lieutenant Governor of Virginia, 1758–1768* (Charlottesville: University Press of Virginia, 1980–1983).

General Assembly Register • *The General Assembly of Virginia, July 30, 1619–January 11, 1978: A Bicentennial Register of Members*, comp. Cynthia Miller Leonard (Richmond: Library of Virginia, 1978).

Governor's Letters • H. R. McIlwaine, ed., *Official Letters of the Governors of the State of Virginia*, vol. 1, *The Letters of Patrick Henry* (Richmond: Library of Virginia, 1926).

Hening, *Statutes* • William Waller Hening, ed., *The Statutes at Large: Being a Collection of All the Laws of Virginia* (13 vols., Richmond, 1809–1823).

Henry Correspondence • William Wirt Henry, ed., *Patrick Henry: Life, Correspondence and Speeches* (3 vols., New York, 1891).

House of Commons • Sir Lewis Namier and John Brooke, eds., *The House of Commons, 1754–1790* (3 vols., New York: Oxford University Press, 1964).

JAH • *Journal of American History*.

Jefferson Autobiography • Autobiography, in Merrill D. Peterson, ed., *Thomas Jefferson: Writings* (New York: Library of America, 1984).

Jefferson Papers • Julian P. Boyd et al., eds., *The Papers of Thomas Jefferson* (42 vols. to date, Princeton: Princeton University Press, 1950–).

Jefferson Retirement Papers • J. Jefferson Looney et al., eds., *The Papers of Thomas Jefferson: Retirement Series* (11 vols. to date, Charlottesville: University Press of Virginia, 2007–).

Jefferson Works • Paul Leicester Ford, ed., *The Works of Thomas Jefferson. Federal Edition* (12 vols., Washington, D.C., 1905).

Journals Va. Council of State • Henry Reade McIlwaine, Wilmer L. Hall, George Henkel Reese, and Sandra Gioia Treadway, eds., *Journals of the Council of State of Virginia* (5 vols., Richmond: Library of Virginia, 1931–1982).

JSH • *Journal of Southern History*.

Kukla, *Speakers and Clerks* • Jon Kukla, *Speakers and Clerks of the Virginia House of Burgesses, 1643–1776* (Richmond: Library of Virginia, 1981).

LC • Library of Congress, Washington, D.C.

Letters of Delegates • Paul H. Smith, Ronald M. Gephart, et al., eds., *Letters of the Delegates to Congress, 1774–1789* (26 vols., Washington, D.C.: Library of Congress, 1976–2000).

LVA • Library of Virginia, Richmond (formerly the Virginia State Library).

Madison Papers • William Hutchinson, William M. E. Rachal, et al., eds., *Papers of James Madison* (16 vols., Chicago: University of Chicago Press, 1962–1977; subsequent vols., Charlottesville: University of Virginia Press, 1977–).

Maier, *Ratification* • Pauline Maier, *Ratification: The People Debate the Constitution, 1787–1788* (New York: Simon & Schuster, 2010).

Marshall Papers • Herbert A. Johnson, Charles T. Cullen, Charles S. Hobson, et al., eds., *Papers of John Marshall* (12 vols., Chapel Hill: University of North Carolina Press, 1974–2006).

Mason Papers • Robert A. Rutland, ed., *Papers of George Mason* (3 vols., Chapel Hill: University of North Carolina Press, 1970).

Mays, *Pendleton* • David John Mays, *Edmund Pendleton, 1734–1803: A Biography* (Cambridge: Harvard University Press, 1952; Richmond: Library of Virginia, 1984).

Meade, *Patriot in the Making* • Robert Douthat Meade, *Patrick Henry: Patriot in the Making* (Philadelphia: J. B. Lippincott, 1957).

Meade, *Practical Revolutionary* • Robert Douthat Meade, *Patrick Henry: Practical Revolutionary* (Philadelphia: J. B. Lippincott, 1969).

NEQ • *New England Quarterly.*

OED • *Oxford English Dictionary.*

Pamphlets of the Revolution • Bernard Bailyn and Jane N. Garrett, eds., *Pamphlets of the American Revolution, 1750–1776* (Cambridge: Harvard University Press, 1965).

Parliamentary History • *Parliamentary History of England from the Earliest Period to the Year 1803*, ed. William Cobbett, T. C. Hansard, et al. (20 vols., London, 1806–1820).

Pendleton Letters • David John Mays, ed., *Letters and Papers of Edmund Pendleton, 1734–1803* (Charlottesville: University Press of Virginia, 1967).

Perry, *Historical Collections* • William Stevens Perry, ed., *Historical Collections Relating to the American Colonial Church: Virginia* (Hartford, Conn., 1870).

Proceedings and Debates of Parliament • R. C. Simmons and P. D. G. Thomas, eds., *Proceedings and Debates of the British Parliaments Respecting North America, 1754–1783* (6 vols., Millwood, N.Y.: Kraus International, 1982–1987).

Randolph, *History* • Edmund Randolph, *History of Virginia*, ed. Arthur H. Shaffer (Charlottesville: University Press of Virginia, 1970).

Ratification Documents • John P. Kaminski et al., eds., *Documentary History of the Ratification of the Constitution* (25 vols. to date. Madison: State Historical Society of Wisconsin, 1976–). See also *Virginia Ratification.*

Revolutionary Virginia • William J. Van Schreeven, Robert L. Scribner, and Brent Tarter, eds., *Revolutionary Virginia: The Road to Independence* (7 vols., Charlottesville: University Press of Virginia, 1973–1983).

Selby, *Revolution in Virginia* • John E. Selby, *The Revolution in Virginia, 1775–1783* (Williamsburg: Colonial Williamsburg Foundation, 1988).

VCRP • Virginia Colonial Records Project microfilm at LVA, VHS, University of Virginia Library, and Rockefeller Library of the Colonial Williamsburg Foundation. (See Jon Kukla, John T. Kneebone, et al., eds., *A Key to Survey Reports and Microfilm of the Virginia Colonial Records Project* [Richmond: Library of Virginia, 1990].)

VG • *Virginia Gazette*, Williamsburg. Newspapers are identified by editors' surnames. William Parks founded the paper in 1736. His successors (sometimes in partnership with one another) were William Hunter, Joseph Royle, Alexander Purdie, John Dixon, and Thomas Nicolson. William Rind started a rival *Virginia Gazette* in 1766 and was succeeded by his widow, Clementina Rind, and then John Pinkney. Alexander Purdie started a third *Virginia Gazette* in 1775 and was succeeded by John Clarkson and Augustine Davis. Digital images of virtually all extant issues of these *Virginia Gazette*s from 1736 to 1780 are accessible at the Rockefeller Library website of the Colonial Williamsburg Foundation.

VHS • Virginia Historical Society, Richmond.

Virginia Ratification • John P. Kaminski et al., eds. *Documentary History of the Ratification of the Constitution, Ratification of the Constitution by the States*, vols. 8–10, *Virginia* (Madison: State Historical Society of Wisconsin, 1988–1993).

VMHB • *Virginia Magazine of History and Biography.*

Washington Diaries • Donald Jackson and Dorothy Twohig, eds., *Diaries of George Washington* (6 vols., Charlottesville: University Press of Virginia, 1976–1979).

Washington Papers, Colonial • W. W. Abbot et al., eds., *Papers of George Washington, Colonial Series* (10 vols., Charlottesville: University Press of Virginia, 1983–1995).

Washington Papers, Confederation • W. W. Abbot, Dorothy Twohig, et al., eds., *Papers of George Washington, Confederation Series* (6 vols., Charlottesville: University Press of Virginia, 1992–1997).

Washington Papers, Presidential • W. W. Abbot, Dorothy Twohig, et al., eds., *Papers of George Washington, Presidential Series* (19 vols. to date, Charlottesville: University Press of Virginia, 1987–).

Washington Papers, Retirement • Dorothy Twohig, Philander D. Chase, et al., eds., *Papers of George Washington, Retirement Series* (4 vols., Charlottesville: University Press of Virginia, 1998–1999).

Washington Papers, Revolutionary War • W. W. Abbot, Dorothy Twohig, et al., eds., *Papers of George Washington, Revolutionary War Series* (24 vols. to date, Charlottesville: University Press of Virginia, 1985–).

Wirt, *Henry* • William Wirt, *Sketches of the Life of Patrick Henry* (3d ed. ["corrected by the author"], Philadelphia, 1818).

WMQ • *William and Mary Quarterly.*

Preface

xiii *twenty-third edition:* My tally of Wirt editions (twenty-five between 1817 and 1911) is based on the collections of the Library of Congress, the Library of Virginia, the Virginia Historical Society, and the libraries at the University of Virginia.

xiii *"Henry's life":* Henry Adams to John T. Morse, Jr., Nov. 19, 1882, *The Letters of Henry Adams*, J. C. Levenson et al., eds. (6 vols., Boston: Massachusetts Historical Society, 1982–1989), 1:479.

xiii *biography that he had just published:* Adams, *John Randolph*, American Statesmen, vol. 16 (Boston: Houghton, Mifflin and Co., 1882).

xiii *neither man:* Morse believed "he had made a failure in selecting Henry Adams
for *John Randolph*"; Alexander W. Williams, "The Letters and Friends of
John T. Morse, Jr.," *Proceedings of the Massachusetts Historical Society*, 3d ser., 79
(1967): 97.

xiii *"acidity":* Adams to Moses, Nov. 19, 1882: "The rule of a writer should be that
of a salad-maker; let the vinegar be put in by a miser; the oil by a spendthrift."

Chapter 1: A Serious Loss

1 *"like the Gravel":* Patrick Henry to Robert Campbell, April 1, 1799, Robert
Douthat Meade Files at Red Hill, quoted in Patrick Daily, *Patrick Henry: The
Last Years, 1789–1799* (2d ed., Brookneal, Va.: Patrick Henry Memorial Foun-
dation, 2013), 231. The sword-chair, or corner chair, in which Henry is believed
to have died is now preserved at the DeWitt Wallace Museum of Decorative
Arts of the Colonial Williamsburg Foundation.

1 *Pharmacy ads: Henry Correspondence*, 2: 625–27. *VG* (Purdie & Dixon), June 18,
1767; *VG* (Rind), November 3, 1768; *VG* (Purdie & Dixon), Jan. 24, 1771; William Buchan, "Of the Gravel and Stone," *Domestic Medicine: Or, A Treatise
on the Prevention and Cure of Diseases* . . . (11th ed., Edinburgh and London,
1790), 324–28; "An Inquiry into the Remote Cause of Urinary Gravel," *European Magazine and London Review* 23 (February 1793): 106–8.

1 *intussusception:* G. Gayer, R. Zissin, S. Apter, M. Papa, and M. Hertz, "Adult
Intussusception: A CT Diagnosis," *British Journal of Radiology*, 75 (2002), 185–
90. Accepted practice in 1799 is reflected in many sources, including J. Cheyne,
"Observations in the Effects of Purgative Medicines," *Edinburgh Medical
and Surgical Journal* 4 (1808): 317–18; and John Hull, "On Intus-susceptio,"
in T. Bradley et al., eds., *Medical and Physical Journal Containing the Earliest
Information on Subjects of Medicine, Pharmacy, Surgery, Chemistry, and Natural History* 7 (London, 1802), 32–38. Patrick Daily's assertion (*The Last Years*,
232) that Dr. Cabell administered calomel, or mercurous chloride, is incorrect.
Calomel *was* used as a purgative, but elemental or liquid mercury was used for
intussusception because it was heavy and, if successfully passed through the
bowels, relatively harmless.

1 *final conversation:* First quoted in Moses Coit Tyler's *Patrick Henry* (rev. ed.,
Boston: Houghton, Mifflin & Co., 1898, 421–23). Edward Fontaine's account
of Henry's death has been widely quoted: *Henry Correspondence*, 2: 625–26.
Mark Couvillon edited a full transcription of the 1872 Fontaine manuscript
at Cornell University Library as *Patrick Henry: Corrections of biographical mistakes, and popular errors in regard to his character* . . . *by Patrick Henry's
great-grandson Edward Fontaine* (Brookneal, Va.: Patrick Henry Memorial
Foundation, 1996), from which James M. Elson also printed the account in

his *Patrick Henry Speeches and Writings* (Lynchburg, Va.: Warwick House, 2007), 188–89.

2 *law office:* At the time of Henry's death, the law office stood about thirty yards north of its present site.

2 *Henry's will:* Patrick Henry's will is filed in the county clerk's office at Charlotte Courthouse. Biographer George Morgan published a reliable transcription in *The True Patrick Henry* (Boston: J. B. Lippincott, 1907), 455–59 (quoted at p. 457).

3 *On the desk:* The manuscript of the 1765 resolutions and Henry's message to posterity is preserved by the Colonial Williamsburg Foundation. The resolutions have been widely reprinted. Reliable transcriptions of both texts were published in William H. Gaines, Jr., *Virginia History in Documents, 1621–1788* (Richmond: Virginia State Library, 1974), 59–61, to accompany a facsimile of the manuscript.

4 *"the war":* William Wirt published St. George Tucker's reconstruction of Henry's Liberty or Death speech in his *Sketches of the Life and Character of Patrick Henry* (3d. ed. with corrections, Philadelphia, 1818), 119–23 (quotations at p. 123).

4 *great debates:* Pauline Maier, *Ratification: The People Debate the Constitution, 1787–1788* (New York: Simon & Schuster, 2010), 126, 455, and passim.

5 *"The first proposal":* Jeremy Belknap, *History of New Hampshire*, Vol. 2, *Comprehending the Events of Seventy Five Years, from MDCCXV to MDCCXC* (Boston, 1791), 78. Belknap also believed that "the name of James Madison will be equally distinguished for proposing the Convention of 1787"; ibid.

6 *"very serious loss":* Marshall to Washington, June 12, 1799, *Marshall Papers*, 4: 118.

6 *"Not only Virginia":* Washington to Marshall, June 16, 1799, *Washington Papers, Retirement*, 4: 123.

6 *obituary: Virginia Gazette* (Richmond), June 14, 1799.

6 *"surprisingly":* Richard R. Beeman, *Patrick Henry: A Biography* (New York: McGraw-Hill, 1974), 216.

6 *popular myths:* Jon Kukla, "Orator of Nature: William Wirt's *Sketches of the Life and Character of Patrick Henry*," *Reviews in American History* 44 (2016): 517–23.

7 *"Mr. Henry":* Thomas Jefferson, Notes on William Wirt's Biography of Patrick Henry, ca. Sept. 29, 1816; *Jefferson Retirement Papers*, 10: 422.

Chapter 2: Totopotomoy Creek

8 *"forest-born Demosthenes":* Byron, "The Age of Bronze" (London, 1823), in Ernest Hartley Coleridge, ed., *Works of Lord Byron: Poetry*, vol. 5 (New York: Charles Scribner's Sons, 1901), 560.

9 *Newcastle:* Alonzo Thomas Dill and Brent Tarter, "The 'Hellish Scheme' to Move the Capital," *Virginia Cavalcade* 30 (1980): 4–11.

9 *John Syme:* V. Cabell Flanagan, *John Syme's Rocky Mills Mansion in Hanover County, Virginia* (Brookneal, Va.: Patrick Henry National Memorial, 2004), 4; *General Assembly Register,* 70, 74; Martha W. McCartney, *Nature's Bounty, Nation's Glory: The Heritage and History of Hanover County, Virginia* (Hanover, Va.: Heritage and History of Hanover County, 2009), 71, 73.

9 *seven times larger:* McCartney, *Nature's Bounty, Nation's Glory,* 79.

10 *"portly, handsome dame":* "A Progress to the Mines in the Year 1732," in Louis B. Wright, ed., *Prose Works of William Byrd of Westover: Narratives of a Colonial Virginian* (Cambridge: Belknap Press of Harvard University Press, 1966), 375–76.

10 *"agreeable":* Spencer Roane, "Memoir of Patrick Henry, 1805," Manuscripts Department, LC, printed in Elson, *Patrick Henry Speeches and Writings,* 16–18, 38–39; Virginius Cornick Hall, Jr., "Notes on Patrick Henry Portraiture," *VMHB* 71 (1965): 168–84.

10 *"clean linen":* Samuel Meredith memorandum, 1805, Manuscripts Department, LC, printed in Elson, *Patrick Henry Speeches and Writings,* 210; St. George Tucker to William Wirt, 1805, in *Henry Correspondence* 1: 125–27; Archibald Alexander, "Reminiscences of Patrick Henry," *Southern Literary Messenger* 16 (1850): 366–68; Meade, *Patriot in the Making,* 255–56, 288–89.

10 *English ancestors:* Meade, *Patriot in the Making,* 24–35; Alfred Sumner Winston, *Winstons of Hanover County, Virginia, and Related Families, 1666–1992* (Baltimore: Gateway Press, 1992). Many details of Patrick Henry's maternal ancestry are uncertain, and most of the colonial records of Hanover County were destroyed in the Civil War. His grandfather Isaac Winston married twice. The identity of his first wife (who bore all his children including Henry's mother, Sarah Winston) is unknown. "His second wife, Mary, although probably a Dabney, was not the mother of his children"; A. Denny Ellerman, "A Note on Patrick Henry's Ancestry," *Magazine of Virginia Genealogy* 28 (1990): 3; Charles William Dabney, "Origin of the Dabney Family in Virginia," *VMHB* 45 (1937): 132–43; Ethan A. Schmidt, "Cockacoeske, Weroansqua of the Pamunkeys, and Indian Resistance in Seventeenth-Century Virginia," *American Indian Quarterly* 36 (2012): 304–17; Martha W. McCartney, "Cockacoeske, Queen of the Pamunkey: Diplomat and Suzeraine," in Peter H. Wood, Gregory A. Waselkov, and Thomas Hartley, eds., *Powhatan's Mantle: Indians in the Colonial Southeast* (Lincoln: University of Nebraska Press, 1989), 173–95. The spelling *Cockacoeroe* appears only in the transcription of her June 29, 1678, letter to Francis Moryson printed in *VMHB* 23 (1915): 402 and in Dabney family genealogies.

11 *Sarah Winston Syme Henry:* Winston, *Winstons of Hanover County,* 43–49, 114–20, 293–95, 305, 451, 506, 517–20; Syme's first wife was the widow of John

Geddes. V. Cabell Flanagan, *John Syme's Rocky Mills Mansion in Hanover County, Virginia*, 4, 21n9; R. T. Barton, ed., *Virginia Colonial Decisions: The Reports by Sir John Randolph and by Edward Barradall of Decisions of the General Court of Virginia, 1728–1741* (Boston: Boston Book Company, 1909), 214.

11 *Sarah's second husband:* Alexander Smith, ed., *A New History of Aberdeenshire* (Aberdeen: Lewis Smith, 1875), 572–83. Recent research by Karen Lucas Lawless indicates that John Henry's father was named Patrick Alexander Henry and that he was likely the namesake for both his eldest son, the Reverend Patrick Henry, and his grandson, the subject of this book. After the Henrys left for Virginia, agriculture in Aberdeenshire was transformed by draining bogs and moors, removing tons of stones, and other improvements; William Watt, *A History of Aberdeen and Banff* (Edinburgh: William Blackwood and Sons, 1900), 280–308; E. Patricia Dennison, David Ditchburn, and Michael Lynch, eds., *Aberdeen Before 1800* (East Linton, Scotland: Tuckwell Press, 2002), 129–58.

12 *years of instruction:* Meade, *Patriot in the Making*, 15–17. For the critical role of parish schools in the Scottish Enlightenment, see Vern L. Bullough, "Intellectual Achievement in Eighteenth Century Scotland: A Computer Study of the Importance of Education," *Comparative Education Review* 14 (1970): 98–102.

12 *acquiring land: Executive Journals Va. Council*, 4: 178, 4: 295, 339, 353, 364, 380, 387, 391, 401; 5: 11, 56, 80, 106, 150, 152, 156; 245, 391, 422, 463, 523; Land Office Patents (LVA) No. 16, 1735, p. 5; No. 17, 1735–1738, p. 213; No. 18, 1738–1739, p. 238; No. 25, 1745–1747, p. 30; No. 22, 1743–1745, p. 99; No. 25, 1745–1747, p. 30; No. 28, 1746–1749, 730; LVA microfilm reels 14, 15, 16, 20, 23, 26.

12 *Newcastle:* McCartney, *Nature's Bounty, Nation's Glory*, 88, 97–98; Dill and Tarter, "The 'Hellish Scheme' to Move the Capital": 4–11.

12 *Gooch named John Henry: Executive Journals Va. Council*, 4: 391; 5: 56, 150; C. G. Chamberlayne, ed., *Vestry Book of St. Paul's Parish, Hanover County, Virginia, 1706–1786* (Richmond: Library of Virginia, 1940), 147–577. Pastor Henry's wife, Mary, was the widow of Arthur Clayton, first clerk of Hanover County; they had one daughter, Jane, who married John Gilliam; Leon M. Bazile, ed., "Wills of the Reverend Patrick Henry and Walter Coles of Hanover County, Virginia," *VMHB* 58 (1950): 122–25. Many Virginians used *Jr.* to distinguish themselves from relatives who were not their fathers; e.g., Secretary Thomas Nelson and his nephew Thomas Nelson, Jr.

13 *"blind stupid fortune":* Hunter Dickinson Farish, ed., *Journal and Letters of Philip Vickers Fithian: A Plantation Tutor of the Old Dominion, 1773–1774* (Williamsburg: Colonial Williamsburg Foundation, 1957), 161. At horse races or cockfights, however, Fithian warned "that £10,000 in Reputation and learning does not amount to a handful of Shillings in ready Cash!"; ibid., 162.

13 *"more intimately conversant":* Hugh Blair Grigsby, *The Virginia Convention of 1776* (Richmond: J. W. Randolph, 1855), 145.

13 *philosophical debate:* John Henry to Patrick Henry, Sr., n.d., in "Sketch of Past and Present Times," [*Virginia*] *Evangelical and Literary Magazine* 5, no. 4 (April 1822): 173.

13 *private circulation of letters:* J. W. Saunders, "The Stigma of Print: A Note on the Social Bases of Tudor Poetry," *Essays in Criticism* 1 (1951): 139–64; Jon Kukla, "The Tuesday Club," *Southern Literary Journal* 24 (1991): 115–18; Earl Greg Swem, ed., "Brothers of the Spade: Correspondence of Peter Collinson, of London, and of John Custis, of Williamsburg, Virginia, 1734–1746," *Proceedings of the American Antiquarian Society* 58 (1948).

13 *transatlantic dispute:* Paul C. Davies, "The Debate on Eternal Punishment in Late Seventeenth- and Eighteenth-Century English Literature," *Eighteenth-Century Studies* 4 (1971): 257–76; D. P. Walker, *The Decline of Hell: Seventeenth-Century Discussions of Eternal Torment* (Chicago: University of Chicago Press, 1964). Philip C. Almond explores the link between theology and secular law in *Heaven and Hell in Enlightenment England* (New York: Cambridge University Press, 1994), 144–61; Kevin J. Hayes, *The Mind of a Patriot: Patrick Henry and the World of Ideas* (Charlottesville: University of Virginia Press, 2008), 19–20, 104, 142; Edward L. Bond, *Damned Souls in a Tobacco Colony: Religion in Seventeenth-Century Virginia* (Macon, Ga.: Mercer University Press, 2000), 247. Hayes (*Mind of a Patriot,* 19) confused John Blair, Jr., with his uncle, Commissary James Blair; John C. Van Horne, "Blair, John," in *DAB* 1: 543–44.

14 *"raised among men":* Hayes, *Mind of a Patriot,* 20.

14 *"a common English school":* Meredith memorandum, 1805, Elson, *Patrick Henry Speeches and Writings,* 210. In a memoir written about 1872, Edward Fontaine (1815–1884) revived the tradition attributing his great-grandfather's education to his uncle; Mark Couvillon, ed., *Patrick Henry: Corrections of biographical mistakes, and popular errors in regard to his character . . . by Patrick Henry's great-grandson Edward Fontaine* (Brookneal, Va.: Patrick Henry Memorial Foundation, 1996; 2d ed., 2011), 4. Catechetical instruction is described in Lauren F. Winner, *A Cheerful and Comfortable Faith: Anglican Religious Practice in the Elite Households of Eighteenth-Century Virginia* (New Haven: Yale University Press, 2010), 60–62.

14 *"a man of liberal education":* George Dabney, memorandum, May 14, 1805, Manuscripts Department, LC, printed in Elson, *Patrick Henry Speeches and Writings,* 222.

14 *"literature and the sciences":* Luigi Castiglione, 1787, Kaminski, *The Founders on the Founders,* 250.

14 *"not looked into":* John Adams, Oct. 11, 1774, L. H. Butterfield et al., eds., *Diary and Autobiography of John Adams* (4 vols., Cambridge: Harvard University Press, 1961), 2: 151.

14 *Virgil:* Hayes, *Mind of a Patriot,* 13–14.

15 *"learn the language":* Biographer George Morgan heard this story told at

Red Hill; George Morgan, *The True Patrick Henry* (Boston: J. B. Lippincott, 1907), 31.

15 *"the least spice"*: Henry Correspondence, 1: 10.

15 *"under some pretext"*: Nathaniel Pope to William Wirt, June 23, 1806, Patrick Henry Papers, LC; also quoted in Morgan, *The True Patrick Henry*, 30.

15 *"the gloomy retreat"*: Henry Correspondence, 1: 116. Henry's fragmentary essay about slavery is discussed more fully below.

15 *"his invariable habit"*: Meredith memorandum, 1805, Manuscripts Department, LC, printed in Elson, *Patrick Henry Speeches and Writings*, 210.

15 *tenth birthday:* Allan Kulikoff, *Tobacco and Slaves: The Development of Southern Cultures in the Chesapeake, 1680–1800* (Chapel Hill: University of North Carolina Press, 1986), 372–74; Philip D. Morgan, *Slave Counterpoint: Black Culture in the Eighteenth-Century Chesapeake and Lowcountry* (Chapel Hill: University of North Carolina Press, 1998), 134–45.

15 *unisex smocks:* Philippe Ariès, *Centuries of Childhood: A Social History of Family Life* (New York: Alfred A. Knopf, 1962), 50–61.

15 *parsimony or a deliberate strategy:* Morgan, *Slave Counterpoint*, 126–33; Anthony S. Parent, Jr., and Susan Brown Wallace, "Childhood and Sexual Identity Under Slavery," *Journal of the History of Sexuality* 3 (1993): 384.

16 *docks at Newcastle:* Margaret Arbuthnott's appeal for the return of two runaway slaves described them as "imported from Gambia, in the Brig. Ranger, and sold at Newcastle"; *VG* (Parks), Oct. 3, 1745. For newspaper notices about runaway slaves see Tom Costa's invaluable online resource, *The Geography of Slavery in Virginia*, http://www2.vcdh.virginia.edu/gos/index.html.

16 *"very artful and cunning"*: Runaway notice, *VG* (Parks), May 8, 1746.

16 *Angolan named Roger:* Runaway notice, *VG* (Parks), Oct. 26, 1739.

16 *young slave named Will:* Runaway notice, *VG* (Parks), Sept. 19, 1745; runaway notice, *VG* (Parks), Oct. 3, 1745.

16 *"ignorant Heathens"*: The Reverend Samuel Davies used this language in a January 1757 sermon entitled *The Duty of Christians to propagate Their Religion Among Heathens, Earnestly Recommended to the Masters of Negroe Slaves in Virginia* (London: J. Oliver, 1758), 22, 27.

16 *"Europeans, instead of Africans"*: Henry Correspondence, 1: 114.

16 *"vanity and sloth"*: Travels in North America . . . by the Marquis de Chastellux, trans. Howard C. Rice, Jr. (Chapel Hill: University of North Carolina Press, 1963), 435.

16 *"to tyrranize"*: Duke de La Rouchefoucauld Liancourt, *Travels through the United States of North America* (2 vols., London, 1799), 1: 557, quoted in Morgan, *Slave Counterpoint*, 380.

16 *"most pernicious effect"*: George Mason, remarks in the Philadelphia convention of 1787; *Mason Papers*, 965–66. Compare Thomas Jefferson's famous remark that the relationship "between master and slave is a perpetual exercise of the most boisterous passions" with Maria Taylor Byrd's concern for a grand-

child "whose chief time is spent with servants & Negro children"; Jefferson, *Notes on the State of Virginia*, 162–63; Byrd to William Byrd II, Feb. 1760; Marion Tinling, ed., *Correspondence of the Three William Byrds of Westover, Virginia, 1684–1776* (Charlottesville: University of Virginia Press, 1977), 682.

17 *bequests to his daughter:* Leon M. Bazile, ed., "The Wills of the Reverend Patrick Henry and Walter Coles of Hanover County, Virginia," *VMHB* 58 (1950): 121.

17 *S-O-C-I-E-T-Y:* Rena Vassar, "William Knox's Defense of Slavery (1768)," *Proceedings of the American Philosophical Society* 114 (1970): 12–13. For the Anglican ministry to Virginia slaves, see John C. Van Horne, *Religious Philanthropy and Colonial Slavery: The American Correspondence of the Associates of Dr. Bray, 1717–1777* (Urbana: University of Illinois Press, 1985); and Jon Butler, "Enlarging the Bonds of Christ: Slavery, Evangelism, and the Christianization of the White South, 1690–1790," in Leonard I. Sweet, ed., *The Evangelical Tradition in America* (Macon, Ga.: Mercer University Press, 1984), 97–111.

17 *"no fear of losing":* William Fleetwood, bishop of St. Asaph, annual sermon to the Society for the Propagation of the Gospel in Foreign Parts, 1711, quoted in Vassar, "Knox's Defense of Slavery," 311.

17 *"The better Christian a Negro became":* Philip Bearcroft, *A Sermon Preached Before the Trustees for Establishing the Colony of Georgia* (London, 1738), quoted in James R. Hertzler, "Slavery in the Yearly Sermons Before the Georgia Trustees," *Georgia Historical Quarterly* 59 (1975): 122–23.

17 *duty of a Christian:* Thomas Secker, annual sermon, 1740–41, quoted in Vassar, "Knox's Defense of Slavery," 313.

17 *"for poor Slaves":* Davies, *Duty of Christians*, 17–18; George William Pilcher, *Samuel Davies: Apostle of Dissent in Colonial Virginia* (Knoxville: University of Tennessee Press, 1971), 107–15, 197. *Duty of Christians* was reprinted as *The Duty of Masters to Their Servants: In a Sermon by the Late Reverend, Pious, and Learned Samuel Davies* (Lynchburg, Va.: William W. Gray, 1809) nearly half a century after the author's death.

17 *"civil Distinctions":* Davies, *Duty of Christians*, 23.

17 *"Christianity made no Alterations":* Ibid., 20.

17 *"Liberty, the sweetest":* Ibid.

17 *"ask my own negroes":* Davies, "On the Defeat of General Braddock, Going to Forte-De-Quesne," Hanover, July 20, 1755, in Davies, *Sermons on Important Subjects* (Boston: Lincoln and Edmands, 1810), 126.

17 *"will make them better Servants":* Davies, *Duty of Christians*, 28, 29, 34.

18 *"remarkably fond of hunting":* George Dabney, 1805, *Henry Correspondence*, I: 10; Jane Carson, *Colonial Virginians at Play* (Williamsburg: Colonial Williamsburg Foundation, 1965), 139–49.

18 *"never hunt with hounds":* Edmund Berkeley and Dorothy Smith Berkeley, eds., *The Reverend John Clayton: A Parson with a Scientific Mind: His Scientific Writings and Other Related Papers* (Charlottesville: University of Virginia Press, 1965), 110.

18 *"as you do in England"*: John Clayton to Samuel Durrent, March 21, 1739, *VMHB* 7 (1899): 174; Anne H. Hastings, "Fox Hunting: History and Change in a Mountain Sport," *Appalachian Journal* 25 (1997): 32; William H. Gaines, Jr., "John Peel in Virginia: Fox Hunting in the Old Dominion," *Virginia Cavalcade* 3, no. 2 (Autumn 1953): 22–27.

18 *"All Virginians"*: Jacob Rubsamen to Thomas Jefferson, Dec. 1, 1780, *Jefferson Papers* 4: 174.

18 *"excellent performer"*: Meredith memorandum, 1805, Elson, *Patrick Henry Speeches and Writings*, 210–11.

19 *"not an ill Dancer"*: William Gooch to Thomas Gooch, Dec. 28, 1727, quoted in Carson, *Colonial Virginians at Play*, 22.

19 *"far soaring above"*: Meredith memorandum, 1805, Elson, *Patrick Henry Speeches and Writings*, 210–11.

19 *"fond of society"*: Nathaniel Pope quoting George Dabney to William Wirt, September 27, 1805, Patrick Henry Papers, LC; *Henry Correspondence*, 1: 9–10; Andrew Burstein, *The Inner Jefferson: Portrait of a Grieving Optimist* (Charlottesville: University of Virginia Press, 1995), 42–56; Hayes, *Mind of a Patriot*, 90–91, 102, 115–16, 119. Sterne published *Tristram Shandy* in nine installments from 1759 through 1767; Tim Parnell, ed., *The Life and Opinions of Tristram Shandy, Gentleman* (London: J. M. Dent, 2000), x.

19 *"read good books"*: Roane, "Memoir," Elson, *Patrick Henry Speeches and Writings*, 30.

20 *commonplace books: The Commonplace Book of William Byrd II of Westover*, ed. Kevin Berland, Jan Kirsten Gilliam, and Kenneth A. Lockridge (Chapel Hill: University of North Carolina Press, 2001), 33–35; *Jefferson's Literary Commonplace Book*, ed. Douglas L Wilson (Princeton: Princeton University Press, 1989).

20 *"There was nothing"*: Meredith memorandum, 1805, Elson, *Patrick Henry Speeches and Writings*, 210.

20 *"for want of bookes"*: Edmund Berkeley and Dorothy Smith Berkeley, eds., *The Reverend John Clayton: A Parson with a Scientific Mind: His Scientific Writings and Other Related Papers*, 4. The Anglican clergyman Hugh Jones wrote in 1724 that Virginians "are more inclinable to read men by business and conversation, than to dive into books, and are for the most part only desirous of learning what is absolutely necessary, in the shortest and best method"; Hugh Jones, *The Present State of Virginia*, ed. Richard L. Morton (Chapel Hill: University of North Carolina Press, 1956), 81, 118. In a dubious anecdote contradicted by other evidence, William Wirt portrayed Henry telling Ralph Wormley that *"we are too old to read books: read men—they are the only volume that we can peruse to advantage."* If true (rather than another example of Henry's habitual self-deprecation), why was the encounter reported to have taken place "in a bookstore"? Wirt, *Sketches*, 406–7.

20 *"often appeared to be irrelevant":* Meredith memorandum, 1805, Elson, *Patrick Henry Speeches and Writings,* 210.

20 *In court:* F. Thornton Miller, *Juries and Judges Versus the Law: Virginia's Provincial Legal Perspective, 1783–1828* (Charlottesville: University of Virginia Press, 1994), 4.

20 *"bold, grand and overwhelming eloquence":* Thomas Jefferson's Notes on Patrick Henry, before April 12, 1812, *Jefferson Retirement Papers* 4: 599

20 *"consummate knoledge":* Thomas Jefferson to William Wirt, Aug. 4, 1805, Thomas Jefferson Correspondence with William Wirt, acc. no 5622, University of Virginia Library, Charlottesville, Va.

21 *Pole Green meetinghouse:* Confusion abounds about the times and places that Henry heard Davies's sermons (and the timing of his family's relocation to Mount Brilliant). For instance, Henry Howe got either the age or the church wrong when he wrote in his *Historical Collections of Virginia* (Charleston, S.C., 1852, p. 221) that "when fourteen years of age, Mr. Henry went with his mother in a carriage to the Fork Church," and William Wirt Henry (*Henry Correspondence,* 1: 15) changed the age to twelve. In fact Henry's family lived at Studley near Pole Green meetinghouse until 1751, then moved to Mount Brilliant in the western part of the county near both Davies's Ground Squirrel Meetinghouse and the Anglican Fork Church; V. Cabell Flanagan, *John Syme's Rocky Mills Mansion in Hanover County, Virginia,* 2004, 4–5; George H. Bost, "Samuel Davies: Colonial Revivalist and Champion of Religious Toleration" (PhD diss., University of Chicago, 1942), 109–10; Couvillon, *Patrick Henry's Virginia,* 16.

21 *George Whitefield: VG* (Parks), Dec. 14, 1739; Alan Heimert, *Religion and the American Mind from the Great Awakening to the Revolution* (Cambridge: Harvard University Press, 1966), 160.

21 What Think ye of Christ?: *The Works of the Reverend George Whitefield* (8 vols., London and Edinburgh, 1771–1772), 5: 364; Parke Rouse, Jr., *James Blair of Virginia* (Chapel Hill: University of North Carolina Press, 1971), 228–30.

21 *"His extraordinary": VG* (Parks), Dec. 21, 1739, emphasis added.

21 *"New Light":* Heimert, *Religion and the American Mind,* 159–71.

21 *"the New Preachers":* Patrick Henry, Sr., to William Dawson, Feb. 13, 1745, Dawson Manuscripts, Library of Congress. Flawed transcriptions of Henry's letter are printed in "Letters of Patrick Henry, Sr., Samuel Davies, James Maury, Edwin Conway, and George Trask," *WMQ,* 2d ser., 1 (1921): 261–66.

21 *uncle let George Whitefield preach:* Henry to Dawson, Oct. 14, 1745, ibid., 266–67; Meade, *Patriot in the Making,* 70–71.

21 *"Enthuasiastick Preachers":* Henry to Dawson, Feb. 13, 1745, *WMQ,* 2d ser., 1 (1921): 261–66.

22 *"hirelings":* Whitefield, *Works,* 5: 354, 364.

22 *"more out of necessity":* Jewel L. Spangler, *Virginians Reborn: Anglican Monopoly,*

Evangelical Dissent, and the Rise of the Baptists in the Late Eighteenth Century (Charlottesville: University of Virginia Press, 2008), 25–26; William Dawson to the Bishop of London, July 11, 1749; Bishop of London to Dr. Philip Doddridge, May 11, 1751, William Stevens Perry, ed., *Historical Collections Relating to the American Colonial Church*, vol. 1., *Virginia* (Hartford: The Church Press, 1870), 365, 373.

22 *"the terrors":* Henry to Dawson, Feb. 13, 1745, *WMQ*, 2d ser., 1 (1921): 265.

22 *"religious Phrenzy":* Henry to Dawson, June 8, 1747, ibid., 272.

22 *predestination:* Samuel Davies to John Holt, Aug. 7, 1752, Samuel Davies Papers (LVA acc. no. 43169).

23 *Watts:* William B. Bynum, "'The Genuine Presbyterian Whine': Presbyterian Worship in the Eighteenth Century," *American Presbyterians* 74 (1996): 163.

23 *"There is not so much Need":* Samuel Davies, *Virginia's Danger and Remedy* (Williamsburg, 1756), 16.

23 *"The secret of this singular power":* Daniel Pierce Thompson, "A Talk with Jefferson, [1822]," *Harper's New Monthly Magazine* (May 1863): 833–35, reprinted in Mark Couvillon, *The Demosthenes of His Age: Accounts of Patrick Henry's Oratory by His Contemporaries* (Brookneal, Va.: Patrick Henry Memorial Foundation, 2013), 55.

23 *"He will execute Justice":* Davies, *Virginia's Danger and Remedy*, 23, 29. Henry would echo this recurrent theme from Davies's sermons in his arguments over the ratification of the Constitution and in the British debts cases.

Chapter 3: Decade of Misfortunes

25 *"an English style":* Couvillon, *Patrick Henry's Virginia*, 15–19.

25 *"who hath left":* Colonel Henry's last recorded presence at a vestry meeting was Nov. 18, 1748; Chamberlayne, ed., *Vestry Book of St. Paul's Parish*, 205, 329. Officials of Hanover and other central Virginia counties moved their archives to the General Court Building in Capital Square for safekeeping during the Civil War, where they were destroyed with the court building in the Richmond evacuation fire of April 2–3, 1865.

25 *"a forest of full-grown trees":* Evelyn M. Acomb, ed., "The Journal of Baron Von Closen," *WMQ*, 3d ser., 10 (1953): 216.

25 *"large commodious dwelling":* William Byrd, "A Journey to the Land of Eden, Anno 1733," in Louis B. Wright, ed., *Prose Works of William Byrd of Westover: Narratives of a Colonial Virginian* (Cambridge: Belknap Press of Harvard University Press, 1966), 346–55; Couvillon, *Patrick Henry's Virginia*, 47–53.

26 *Thomas Nelson:* John Henry, *Map of Virginia* (London, 1770); McCartney, *Nature's Bounty, Nation's Glory*, 109.

26 *twentieth-century inventions:* Barbara A. Yocum, *The Shelton House at Rural Plains: Historic Structure Report* (Lowell, Mass.: National Park Service, 2012), 20–24.

26 *Nathaniel West Dandridge:* Eugenia G. Glazebrook and Preston G. Glazebrook, comps., *Virginia Migrations: Hanover County* (Baltimore: Genealogical
Publishing Co., 2000), viii; John Hastings Gwathmey, *Twelve Virginia Counties: Where the Western Migration Begins* (Richmond: The Dietz Press, 1937),
114–15.

26 *"On my way to the college":* Jefferson's Notes on Patrick Henry, 1812, *Jefferson
Retirement Papers* 4: 598. Although Jefferson (who first came to William and
Mary in March 1760) assigned their first meeting to "the winter of 1759–1760,"
the evidence suggests that Jefferson first met Henry a year later at Christmas
1760 (when he was seventeen and after Henry had closed his store that autumn) when Jefferson traveled through Hanover County on his way *back* to
college; Jon Kukla, *Mr. Jefferson's Women* (New York: Alfred A. Knopf, 2007),
220n8.

26 *"conversations on scientific subjects":* Thomas Jefferson to William Wirt, August 5, 1815; *Jefferson Retirement Papers,* 8: 645.

27 *The 1750s:* Fred Anderson, *Crucible of War: The Seven Years' War and the Fate
of Empire in British North America, 1754–1766* (New York: Alfred A. Knopf,
2000).

27 *"About the age of fifteen":* Meredith memorandum, 1805, Elson, *Patrick Henry
Speeches and Writings,* 213.

27 *young Scotsmen:* T. M. Devine, ed., *A Scottish Firm in Virginia, 1767–1777:
W. Cuninghame and Co.* (Edinburgh: Scottish Historical Society, 1984), xvii;
Charles J. Farmer, *In the Absence of Towns: Settlement and Country Trade in
Southside Virginia, 1730–1800* (Lanham, Md.: Rowman & Littlefield, 1993),
114–23.

27 *"continued in that employment":* Meredith memorandum, 1805, Elson, *Patrick
Henry Speeches and Writings,* 213; Meade, *Patriot in the Making,* 76.

28 *long-term credit:* J. H. Soltow, "Scottish Traders in Virginia, 1750–1775," *Economic History Review* 12 (1959): 86–95.

28 *"a woman of some fortune":* Meredith memorandum, 1805, Elson, *Patrick Henry
Speeches and Writings,* 212–13.

28 *Henry labored:* Edmund Winston's statement that Henry "was obliged to la-
bour *with his own Hands* to obtain a scanty Support for his Family" (Robert
Douthat Meade, ed., "Judge Edmund Winston's Memoir of Patrick Henry,"
VMHB 69 [1961]: 36, emphasis added) reflected the common practice of small
slaveholders working side by side with their field hands; Philip D. Morgan,
*Slave Counterpoint: Black Culture in the Eighteenth-Century Chesapeake and
Low Country* (Chapel Hill: University of North Carolina Press, 1998), 164–70.

28 *"variety of bad seasons":* Jack P. Greene, ed., *Diary of Colonel Landon Carter of
Sabine Hall, 1752–1778* (Richmond: Virginia Historical Society, 1987), 224.

28 *"parched and fading":* Samuel Davies, *Virginia's Danger and Remedy: Two Discourses Occasioned by the fever Drought in sundry Parts of the Country; and the
Defeat of General Braddock* (Williamsburg, 1756), 6.

28 *"great Scarcity": Executive Journals Va. Council*, 590–91. Exports of corn, flour, beans, salted meat, and other supplies for the Caribbean had steadily increased until they accounted for a third of the Old Dominion's export trade in the 1760s; Jacob M. Price, "Trade and Commerce: The British Colonies," in Jacob Ernest Cooke, ed., *Encyclopedia of the North American Colonies* (3 vols., New York: Charles Scribner's Sons, 1993), 1: 519; Peter V. Bergstrom, "Markets and Merchants: Economic Diversification in Colonial Virginia, 1700–1775" (PhD diss., University of New Hampshire, 1980), 136, 151; Warren M. Billings, John E. Selby, and Thad W. Tate, *Colonial Virginia: A History* (White Plains, N.Y.: KTO Press, 1986), 201–2.

29 *"Alas!": Davies, Virginia's Danger and Remedy*, 6.

29 *"in the very Jaws":* Ibid., 6–7.

29 *"Languishing with Drought":* Ibid., 45.

29 *"almost double":* Dinwiddie quoted in Richard L. Morton, *Colonial Virginia* (Chapel Hill: University of North Carolina Press, 1960), 677. After Braddock's defeat "redcoats never return[ed] to Old Dominion during the war"; Anderson, *Crucible of War*, 109.

29 *"against Ignorance":* Davies, *Religion and Patriotism the Constituents of a Good Soldier: A Sermon Preached to Captain Overton's Independent Company of Volunteers, raised in Hanover County, Virginia, August 17, 1755* (Philadelphia: James Chattin, 1755), 13. The printed sermon also disseminated Davies's prescient commendation of "that heroic Youth Col. Washington, whom I cannot but hope Providence has hitherto preserved in so signal a Manner, for some important Service to his Country"; ibid., 9.

29 *recruiting their neighbors:* Samuel Davies, *The Curse of Cowardice: A Sermon Preached to the Militia of Hanover County in Virginia at a General Muster, May 8, 1758, With a View to raise a Company for Captain Samuel Meredith* (London: Buckland, Ward, and Field, 1758; reprinted in Boston, Portsmouth, Mass., and London, 1759), 8, 16.

30 *"Flyes":* Jack P. Greene, ed., *Diary of Colonel Landon Carter of Sabine Hall, 1752–1778*, 224–36; Rhys Isaac, *Landon Carter's Uneasy Kingdom: Revolution and Rebellion on a Virginia Plantation* (New York: Oxford University Press, 2004), 60–64.

30 *"gust":* "Continuation of the Letter from a Gentleman of Virginia, begun in our last," *New-York Journal or, The General Advertiser* (John Holt), no. 1495, August 29, 1771.

30 *Wheat and oats:* Greene, ed., *Diary of Colonel Landon Carter*, 224.

30 *"hot and very drye":* Ibid., 234, 236.

30 *single hogshead:* Charles Smith Ledger, 1757–1762, Southern Historical Collection, University of North Carolina, Chapel Hill, cited in Couvillon, *Patrick Henry's Virginia*, 25.

30 *fire consumed the dwelling:* Couvillon, *Patrick Henry's Virginia*, 24–26.

30 *Shelton's ordinary: Henry Correspondence*, 1: 17; Meade, *Patriot in the Making*, 81–92.

30 *Henry's second store:* Meade, *Patriot in the Making*, 87–89, 92. Patrick Henry's three extant ledger books are readily accessible at the Library of Virginia. Bound photocopies of two manuscript volumes preserved by the Valentine History Center cover the years 1758–1763 (LVA acc. no. 20472) and 1762–1770 (acc. no. 20473) and Henry's manuscript ledger for 1764–1798 (acc. no. 20408b); Conley L. Edwards III, Gwendolyn D. Clark, Jennifer D. McDaid, comps., *A Guide to Business Records in the Virginia State Library and Archives* (Richmond: Library of Virginia, 1994), 55–56.

31 *"good, wholesome, and clean":* "An Act for regulating Ordinaries," 1705; Hening, *Statutes* 3: 395–401; *OED* s.v. ordinary. "The inns which in the other provinces of America are known by the name of taverns, or public houses, are in Virginia called 'ordinaries'": Marquis de Chastellux, *Travels in North America in the Years 1780, 1781 and 1782*, ed. Howard C. Rice, Jr. (Chapel Hill: University of North Carolina Press, 1963), 386.

31 *"indispensable":* Chastellux, *Travels in North America*, 380. An NGram analysis of the Google Books database from 1700 to 2000 dates the earliest use of the name *Hanover Tavern* to 1850 (as an index entry in B. J. Lossing's *Pictorial Field Book of the Revolution* [New York: Harper Brothers, 1850]) followed by a period of desuetude from 1870 to 1930.

31 *"wooden tavern":* Mutual Assurance Society policy 461, misc. reel 4121, LVA; Couvillon, *Patrick Henry's Virginia*, 33–34. My estimate of the capacity of Shelton's 50-by-26-foot stable is based on the 5-by-9-foot-3-inch stalls of a stable at King William Courthouse; S. P. Moorehead, "Governor's Palace Stable Report" (Williamsburg: Colonial Williamsburg Foundation, 1950, reissued 1990).

31 *"bar-keeper":* Jefferson, 1824, Kaminski, *The Founders on the Founders*, 264. Two decades earlier Jefferson had told William Wirt that Henry "acted, as I have understood, as a bar keeper in the tavern at Hanover Court House for some time"; Jefferson to Wirt, Aug. 4, 1805, Elson, *Patrick Henry Speeches and Writings*, 46.

31 *"clad in a coarse shirt":* Nathaniel Pope, "Anecdotes Relative [to] Patrick Henry for Wm Wirt, Esqr., No. 1," Sept. 27, 1805, Patrick Henry Papers, LC.

31 *"was very active":* Nathaniel Pope to William Wirt (quoting Winston), Sept. 26, 1805, Elson, *Patrick Henry Speeches and Writings*, 252n4.

31 *three reliable observers:* Meade, "Judge Winston's Memoir," 36–41; George Dabney's Memorandum, May 14, 1805, in Elson, *Patrick Henry Speeches and Writings*, 221–24; Charles Dabney, "Account of the Gun-Powder Expedition," Dec. 21, 1805, Patrick Henry Papers, LC.

32 *"the whole story":* Meredith memorandum, 1805, Elson, *Patrick Henry Speeches and Writings*, 211.

32 *"never heard"*: Roane, "Memoir," Elson, *Patrick Henry Speeches and Writings*, 17–18.

32 *"a bar-keeper by profession"*: Wirt, *Sketches*, 19.

32 *"Necessity compelled him"*: Pope, "Anecdotes Relative [to] Patrick Henry, Sept. 27, 1805," Patrick Henry Papers, LC.

32 *"When a young gentleman"*: "A Country Justice," *VG* (Rind), Dec. 30, 1773.

32 *"did not read law"*: Meredith memorandum, 1805, Elson, *Patrick Henry Speeches and Writings*, 213. Jefferson believed legal apprenticeships encroached upon a student's time for study and "recommended strongly" (despite his remarks about Henry) that an aspiring attorney "put himself into apprenticeship with no one, but . . . employ his time for himself alone"; Jefferson to Thomas Turpin, Feb. 5, 1769, *Jefferson Papers*, 1: 24.

33 *"reading such books"*: Meade, "Judge Winston's Memoir," 37.

33 *"during which time"*: Meredith memorandum, 1805; George Dabney memorandum, Elson, *Patrick Henry Speeches and Writings*, 213, 222.

33 *nine months:* Pope's opinion in Wirt, *Sketches*, 17n.

33 *a month:* Tyler quoted in Wirt, *Sketches*, 17n. Jefferson's claim to have first met Henry in Hanover County at Christmas 1760 (not 1759, see p. 411 above) undermines his recollection that Henry "called upon me at college" in *"the spring following* [the Dandridge parties when] he came to Williamsburg to obtain a license as a lawyer" and "told me he had been reading law only six weeks." *Henry Correspondence*, 1: 22, emphasis added.

33 *"if he got"*: Roane, "Memoir," Elson, *Patrick Henry Speeches and Writings*, 19.

33 *John Lewis:* Meredith memorandum, 1805, Elson, *Patrick Henry Speeches and Writings*, 213.

33 *the "Honest Attorney"*: Sarah Travers Lewis Anderson, *Lewises, Meriwethers, and Their Kin* (Richmond: The Dietz Press, 1938), 358.

33 *"learned in the law"*: "Act for regulating the practice of Attornies," 1748, Hening, *Statutes*, 6: 140–43.

34 *Henry's first interview:* Jon Kukla, *Speakers and Clerks of the Virginia House of Burgesses, 1643–1776* (Richmond: Library of Virginia, 1981), 129–33, 152–54. Three of the houses mentioned here (Randolph, Carter, and Wythe) are maintained by the Colonial Williamsburg Foundation.

34 *The second examiner:* William Edwin Hemphill, "George Wythe the Colonial Briton: A Biographical Study of the Pre-Revolutionary Era in Virginia" (PhD diss., University of Virginia, 1937), 41–52; Robert Bevier Kirtland, "George Wythe: Lawyer, Revolutionary, Judge" (PhD diss., University of Michigan, 1983), 41–44, 105–6.

34 *Henry's third examiner: Revolutionary Virginia*, 2: 11–12; Helen Bullock, *Robert Carter House Historical Report* (Williamsburg: Colonial Williamsburg Foundation, 1931, reissued 1990), 2–3; *VG* (Rind and Purdie and Dixon), Jan. 7, 1773; *VG* (Purdie), Aug. 21, 1778.

35 *candidates' fees:* Frank L. Dewey, *Thomas Jefferson, Lawyer* (Charlottesville: University of Virginia Press, 1986), 117–21.

35 *Henry's fourth interview:* Jon Kukla, *Speakers and Clerks,* 129–33, 152–54; Patricia M. Samford, Gregory J. Brown, Ann Smart Martin, et al., *Archaeological Excavations on the Tazewell Hall Property* (Williamsburg: Colonial Williamsburg Foundation, 1986, reissued 2001), 1–7. Tazewell Hall stood on South England Street between the Williamsburg Lodge and the Spa of Colonial Williamsburg. Altered and moved about 1908, Tazewell Hall was sold and dismantled in 1954 and rebuilt in Newport News by the late Lewis A. McMurran, Jr.

35 *"after much entreaty":* "Notes on a Conversation with Thomas Jefferson," in Charles M. Wiltse and Harold D. Moser, eds., *Papers of Daniel Webster: Correspondence* (Hanover, N.H.: University Press of New England, 1974), 1: 370–78.

35 *"signed his license":* Jefferson to William Wirt, August 14, 1814; *Jefferson Retirement Papers,* 7: 545.

35 *"absolutely refused":* Ibid. The license Henry presented to the Goochland county court in April 1760 was signed by George Wythe and John Randolph; Goochland County Order Book 8, p. 284, LVA microfilm reel 23. Jefferson was also wrong about Edmund Pendleton being one of the examiners.

35 *"one of the Gentlemen":* George Dabney memorandum, 1805, Elson, *Patrick Henry Speeches and Writings,* 222.

35 *Henry himself recounted the story: Henry Correspondence,* 1: 21–22. This and the next two paragraphs draw upon Patrick Henry's account of his examination by John Randolph as John Tyler told it to William Wirt; Wirt, *Sketches,* 22.

36 *"uninterrupted tranquility":* Henry to unknown recipient, June 2, 1793, *Southern Literary Messenger* 19 (1843): 316. The editor printed this text *"verbatim"* from Henry's original letter but withheld the recipient's name: Henry had written "in the confidence of private friendship to a gentleman in misfortune, and the intention of the illustrious writer is sacredly observed even to the present day."

36 *newly licensed attorney:* Goochland County Order Book 8, p. 284, LVA microfilm reel 23; Meade, *Patriot in the Making,* 96.

36 *Hanover county court: Virginia Almanac for the Year of our Lord God 1759* (Williamsburg: William Hunter, 1759); Patrick Henry ledger, 1758–1763 (LVA acc. no. 20472). The relevant Hanover and Louisa county records were destroyed during the Civil War.

37 *"Patrick Henry's Book":* Hayes, *Mind of a Patriot,* 42–43, 114. Peter Fontaine's sister had married Henry's uncle Isaac Winston.

37 *"P. Henry Jr.":* Ibid., 43–47, 122–28, 131–32, and passim.

37 *stiff competition:* "His competitors at the bar of any celebrity were Lewis, Lyons, and Semple"; George Dabney memorandum, 1805, Elson, *Patrick Henry Speeches and Writings,* 222. Born in Ayrshire, Scotland, in 1727, John Semple had immigrated to King and Queen County in 1752 and lived at

Rosemount near Walkerton, overlooking the Mattaponi River; *Genealogies of Virginia Families from Tyler's Quarterly Historical and Genealogical Magazine* (Baltimore: Genealogical Publishing Co., 1981), 99; Harris, *Old New Kent*, 491. "The Library of John Semple, deceased, attorney at law, 'consisting of history, law, novels, etc.'" was advertised for sale in 1780; "Libraries in Colonial Virginia," *WMQ*, 1st ser., 4 (1896): 269.

37 *traveling to engage clients:* Henry was admitted to practice in Augusta County on Aug. 19, 1766; Augusta County Order Book 10, 1765–1767, LVA microfilm reel 65. I am indebted to Turk McCleskey for this citation.

37 *"barren cow":* Meade, *Patriot in the Making*, 112; Clement Eaton, "A Mirror of the Southern Colonial Lawyer: The Fee Books of Patrick Henry, Thomas Jefferson, and Waightstill Avery," *WMQ*, 3d ser., 8 (1951): 531. By comparison, during his first year of practice Thomas Jefferson "collected only about one-sixth of his earnings in legal fees"; ibid., 533. Jefferson practiced from 1767 to 1774 exclusively before the General Court, and (despite many biographers' statements to the contrary) never practiced in the county courts. Frank L. Dewey, "Thomas Jefferson's Law Practice," *VMHB* 85 (1977): 289–301; Dewey, "The Myth of Jefferson's County Court Practice," in *Thomas Jefferson, Lawyer*, 122–26.

Chapter 4: The Parsons' Cause

39 *Hanover Tavern:* The road ran to the west of the tavern in the eighteenth century and did not separate it from the courthouse; Carl L. Lounsbury, *The Courthouses of Early Virginia: An Architectural History* (Charlottesville: University of Virginia Press, 2005), 279–80.

39 *chilly morning:* During the previous three years, the temperatures on Dec. 1 recorded by Governor Fauquier in Williamsburg averaged 34° at 8 a.m. and 46° at 2 p.m. Fauquier's complete weather tabulation for 1760–1763 was printed as an appendix to Andrew Burnaby, *Travels through the Middle Settlements in North-America in the Years 1759 and 1760* (2d. ed., London: T. Payne, 1775), 163–98. Only the temperatures for 1760 appeared in the 1st ed. that same year, pp. 95–106. I am grateful to Linda Rowe and Harold Gill, of the Colonial Williamsburg Foundation, for directing me to these appendixes.

40 *"Why?":* Meredith memorandum, 1805, Elson, *Patrick Henry Speeches and Writings*, 50.

40 *"disagreeable things":* John Burk, *History of Virginia from its First Settlement to the Present Day* (4 vols., Petersburg: Dickson & Pescud, 1804–1816), 3: 303.

40 *heart of the Parsons' Cause:* Scholarship on the Parsons' Cause is extensive but not definitive, and the published accounts are replete with errors and omissions. The most reliable summary is Richard L. Morton, *Colonial Virginia* (Chapel Hill: University of North Carolina Press, 1960), 751–819, who identified five clergy lawsuits (ibid., 808). Rhys Isaac listed only three lawsuits in his influential "Religion and Authority: Problems of the Anglican Establish-

ment in Virginia in the Era of the Great Awakening and the Parsons' Cause,"
WMQ, 3rd ser., 30 (1973): 19. The most recent narrative is A. Shrady Hill,
"The Parson's Cause," *Historical Magazine of the Protestant Episcopal Church*
46 (1977), 5–35. Older discussions include Arthur P. Scott, "Constitutional
Aspects of the 'Parson's Cause,'" *Political Science Quarterly* 31 (1916), 558–77;
Glenn Curtis Smith, "The Parsons' Cause: Virginia 1755–65," *Tyler's Quarterly
Historical and Genealogical Magazine* 31 (1939), 140–71, 191–206; and Joseph
Henry Smith, *Appeals to the Privy Council from the American Plantations* (New
York: Columbia University Press, 1950), 597–626.

40 *Two-Penny Acts:* Hening, *Statutes*, 6: 568–69; 7: 243–44.

40 *Thomas Sherlock:* Bishop Sherlock's June 14, 1759, letter to the Privy Council
was exposed to public view in the opening pages of Richard Bland's *Letter to
the Clergy of Virginia, in which the Conduct of the General Assembly of Virginia is
vindicated, against the Reflexions contained in a Letter to the Lords of Trade and
Plantations, from the Bishop of London* (Williamsburg: William Hunter, 1760),
iii–vi (quotation at p iii).

41 *finally ruled against him:* An unknown church official noted that "it was hoped
by the Agents for the Clergy that the Lords of Trade would have reported
their opinion that the Acts were *null and void ab initio*. But no Precedent
could be found"; Notes on Virginia Tobacco Act, n.d., Correspondence of the
Bishop of London, doc. 132, Fulham Palace Papers 15, London; VCRP microfilm reel 591.

42 *tobacco merchants:* Samuel Gist figures prominently in Charles Royster, *The
Fabulous History of the Dismal Swamp Company: A Story of George Washington's Times* (New York: Alfred A. Knopf, 1999). James McDowall was a Richmond-based merchant; *VG* (Purdie and Dixon), Sept. 16, 1766, Feb. 27, 1772,
April 15, 1773.

42 *"to advance his fortune":* Morton, *Colonial Virginia*, 575–76.

42 *Jefferson remembered James Maury:* Dumas Malone, *Jefferson the Virginian*
(Boston: Little, Brown, 1948), 40–45.

43 *"almost equal to Patrick":* Nathaniel Pope, "Anecdotes Relative [to] Patrick
Henry for Wm Wirt, Esqr., No. 1," Patrick Henry Papers, LC.

43 *gist of Henry's arguments:* The essential source for Henry's Dec. 1, 1763, speech
at Hanover Court House is a report written by James Maury in two substantially identical documents: Maury to John Camm, Dec. 12, 1763 (James
Maury Letterbook, Sol Feinstone Collection of the American Revolution, on
deposit at the American Philosophical Society, Philadelphia [microfilm edition, 1969, reel 2]) and the "Narrative of the Determination of a Suit . . . in
Hanover Court, Nov. and Dec. 1763," that Maury sent to Jonathan Boucher
(now in the Jonathan Boucher Papers, 1759–1803; Special Collections, Earl
Gregg Swem Library, College of William and Mary, Williamsburg, Virginia;
formerly in the Jonathan Boucher Papers, East Sussex Record Office, VCRP
microfilm reel 871). Another succinct report appears in the Lords of Trade's

Report on the Virginia Clergy's Petition against An Act of Assembly, July 4, 1759; Correspondence of the Bishop of London, doc. 134, Fulham Palace Papers 15, London; VCRP microfilm reel 591. William Stevens Perry printed a widely used but misdated and inaccurate transcription of this report in *Historical Collections Relating to the American Colonial Church: Virginia* (Hartford, Conn., 1870), 458–60. As noted below, Nathaniel Pope also reported Thomas Trevillians's recollection of Henry's denunciation of the established clergy. Unless otherwise designated, all quotations in the remainder of this chapter are from Maury's report to Camm.

43 *"becomes no King":* John Locke, *Two Treatises of Government,* ed. Peter Laslett (rev. ed., Cambridge, 1963), Second Treatise, §239–43 (pp. 473–77).

44 *"dependence on the Crown":* Jack N. Rakove, "The Decision for American Independence: A Reconstruction," *Perspectives in American History* 10 (1976): 237.

44 *pastors not priests:* For the context of Camm's affinity to High Church sacerdotalism in his dispute with Landon Carter and Richard Bland, see Brent S. Sirota, *The Christian Monitors: The Church of England and the Age of Benevolence, 1680–1730* (New Haven: Yale University Press, 2014), 149–86.

44 *"The only Use":* Maury to Camm, Dec. 12, 1763. Maury also reported the phrase "Duties of imperfect Obligation" in his "Narrative of the Determination of a Suit" sent to Boucher, but the phrase was omitted from a widely used bowdlerized version of Maury's letter to Camm in Ann Maury, comp., *Memoirs of a Huguenot Family* (New York: George P. Putnam & Co., 1853), 418–24.

44 *"the Rewarder of good Men":* William Warburton, *The Alliance between Church and State, or, the Necessity and Equity of an Established Religion* (London: Fletcher Gyles, 1736), 13, 59, emphasis in original; David Sorkin, "William Warburton: The Middle Way of 'Heroic Moderation,'" *Dutch Review of Church History* 82 (2002), 262–300.

45 *"left to a man's sense":* Samuel Pufendorf, *The Law of Nature and Nations: or, A General System of the most Important Principles of Morality, Jurisprudence, and Politics* (London: J. and J. Bonwicke, 1749), 77–78. See also my forthcoming article, "Patrick Henry, the Scottish Enlightenment, and Virginia's Early Resistance to Royal Authority and Parliamentary Supremacy."

45 *"Instead of useful members":* Maury to Camm, Dec. 12, 1763.

45 *"We have heard":* Nathaniel Pope, Report "No. 2" for William Wirt, n.d., Patrick Henry Papers, LC.

46 *"among the vulgar herd":* James Maury to John Camm, Dec. 12, 1763.

46 *courtroom procedures:* Maureen K. Conklin, "Power in the Piedmont: Litigation and Political Culture in Eighteenth-Century Central Virginia" (PhD diss., University of Wisconsin-Madison, 1998), 230n69. Based on a source he described as "the record of the case," William Wirt Henry identified the members of the jury as Benjamin Anderson, John Blackwell, William Claybrook, George Dabney (Patrick Henry's boyhood friend), Jacob Hundly, Samuel

Morris, Benjamin Oliver, Roger Shackelford, Brewster Sims, John Thornton, Stephen Willis, and John Wingfield. He identified three of these jurymen as dissenters—Dabney, Morris, and Shackelford—and noted that Blackwell and Oliver had been prosecuted in 1745 for allowing the New Light itinerant John Roan to preach at their houses; *Henry Correspondence*, 1: 37. Since Hanover County's colonial records were destroyed in the Civil War, "the record of the case" must have been among the family papers at Red Hill that were accessible to W. W. Henry but subsequently destroyed when the mansion there burned in 1919.

Chapter 5: Visit to Williamsburg

47 *provincial and imperial affairs:* Although only one issue of the *Virginia Gazette* (dated Oct. 25, 1765) survives for the period from Nov. 1763 through Feb. 1766, we know that Joseph Royle published John Mercer of Marlborough's alphabetical table of stamp duties in his *Virginia Gazette* on April 26, 1765 (no copies of which are extant); J. A. Leo Lemay, "John Mercer and the Stamp Act in Virginia, 1764–1765," *VMHB* 91 (1983): 24–35. Despite some evidence that Royle yielded to pressure toward censorship from Governor Fauquier, other information and comment about the Stamp Act presumably appeared in some missing issues of the *Gazette*. John Mercer sent a copy of his entire work to the New York printer John Holt, formerly of Williamsburg, who printed the alphabetical table in *Poor Roger, 1766. The American Country Almanack* (New York, 1765), 21–29, and Mercer's prefatory comments in his *New-York Gazette* (July 4, 1765) along with a letter describing the censorship in Virginia. Both were signed Anglo-Americanus. Josiah Green reprinted these letters from Holt's paper in his *Maryland Gazette* (July 18, 1765). The Huntington Library has the only known copy of Holt's *Poor Roger, 1766* (a ghost imprint in Evans, *Bibliography* #10078); I am grateful to Mary L. Robertson and Stephen Tabor, of the Huntington Library, for providing photocopies.

47 *contentious:* Violations of campaign rules in the county elections of 1752 had been so egregious that the Assembly threw out the entire election and issued writs for a new one; *Burgesses Journals, 1752–1758*, 61–62.

47 *February 1764:* The exact date of the election is not known. I concur with John Gilman Kolp that it occurred in "early February," three or four weeks after the writ issued on January 13. Kolp, *Gentlemen and Freeholders: Electoral Politics in Colonial Virginia* (Baltimore: Johns Hopkins University Press, 1998), 23.

47 *"the damned Inspecting Law": Burgesses Journals, 1761–1765*, 270.

48 *"money, meat, drink":* Hening, *Statutes*, 7: 526. The penalty for a candidate guilty of these forms of bribery was expulsion from the House of Burgesses "as if he had never been elected"; ibid.

48 *"an ill-dressed Young Man":* Meade, "Judge Winston's Memoir," 37–38. Dandridge's protest came before the House on November 1, the committee met

on November 23, and its chair reported to the House on November 26; *Burgesses Journals, 1761–1765*, 232, 235, 269.

48 *"very coarse apparel"*: Tyler quoted in Wirt, *Sketches*, 40, and *Henry Correspondence*, 1: 47. Tyler had started at the grammar school at seven, progressed to the college, and then read law with Robert Carter Nicholas until 1765; Lyon G. Tyler, *Judge John Tyler, Sr., and His Times* (Richmond: Richmond Press, 1927), 4–5.

48 *Committee of Privileges and Elections: Burgesses Journals, 1761–1765*, 230. The remaining ten members of the twenty-man committee were mostly from the Tidewater as well: John Baylor, Lewis Burwell, Dudley Digges, William Digges, Benjamin Harrison, Bernard Moore, Mann Page, Lemuel Riddick, Thomas Whiting, and John Woodbridge.

49 *Richard Bland's month-old pamphlet:* Hayes, *Mind of a Patriot*, 18, 45, 49–50, 113.

49 *"purely for amusement"*: [Richard Bland], *The Colonel Dismounted: or The Rector Vindicated, in a Letter addressed to His Reverence: Containing a Dissertation upon the Constitution of the Colony* (Williamsburg, 1764), 2. Joseph Royle sold the first copy of *The Colonel Dismounted* on Oct. 24; Paul P. Hoffman, ed., *Virginia Gazette Daybooks, 1750–1752 & 1764–1766* (Charlottesville: University of Virginia Microfilm Publications, 1967). The essay is no. 4 in Bernard Bailyn and Jane Nuckols Garrett, eds., *Pamphlets of the Revolution, 1750–1776* (Cambridge: Harvard University Press, 1965), 292–354.

For the circulation of manuscripts in the colonial Chesapeake, see Richard Beale Davis, "The Colonial Virginia Satirist: Mid-Eighteenth-Century Commentaries on Politics, Religion, and Society," *Transactions of the American Philosophical Society*, n.s., 57, no. 1 (1967): 1–74; and Kukla, "The Tuesday Club," *Southern Literary Journal* 24 (1991): 115–18.

50 *"lay at the heart"*: Bailyn, *Pamphlets of the Revolution*, 299, 707–11.

50 *"into THE POWER"*: Bland, *The Colonel Dismounted* in *Pamphlets of the Revolution*, 319, emphasis added.

50 *denial of government by conquest:* Quentin Skinner, "History and Ideology in the English Revolution," *Historical Journal* 8 (1965): 151–78; M. P. Thompson, "The Idea of Conquest in Controversies over the 1688 Revolution," *Journal of the History of Ideas* 38 (1977): 33–46; Jon Kukla, "Recipes and Rights— Cookbooks and Charters: A Study in the Development, Transmission, and Circumstances of Anglo-American Culture as Represented in Manuscript Commonplace Books from Seventeenth- and Eighteenth-Century Virginia," unpublished paper presented at the Fourth Citadel Conference on the South, Charleston, S.C., April 11, 1985.

50 *"Under an English government"*: Bland, *The Colonel Dismounted*, in *Pamphlets of the Revolution*, 320–21.

50 *"EXTERNAL Government"*: Ibid., 320.

51 *entire file of correspondence: Burgesses Journals, 1761–1765*, 254–309.

51 *St. Stephen's Chapel:* P. D. G. Thomas, *The House of Commons in the Eighteenth Century* (Oxford, 1971), 1–5.

52 *"gave birth":* Edward Montague to the Virginia Committee of Correspondence, April 11, 1764; *VG* (Purdie and Dixon), Oct. 3, 1766.

52 *revenue by consent:* Sir William Holdsworth, *History of English Law,* ed. A. L. Goodhart and H. G. Hanbury (7th ed., 12 vols., London: Methuen, 1956–72), 11: 49–50, 248–51.

52 *deliberating in private:* George III to the Earl of Bute, mid-March 1763, Romney Sedgwick, ed., *Letters from George III to Lord Bute, 1756–1766* (London, 1939), 201–2; Harvey Wheeler, "Calvin's Case (1608) and the McIlwain-Schuyler Debate," *AHR* 61 (1956): 587–97.

52 *"the least exceptionable":* *Proceedings and Debates of Parliament,* 1: 489.

52 *"towards defraying":* Ibid., 1: 494.

52 *parliamentary debates and proceedings:* The *London Evening Post* began publishing some debates in 1768, followed by a dozen papers in 1771; Graham C. Gibbs, "Press and Public Opinion: Prospective," in J. R. Jones, ed., *Liberty Secured? Britain Before and After 1688* (Stanford: Stanford University Press, 1992), 253. Some monthly periodicals in the 1760s, such as *The London Magazine, or, Gentleman's Monthly Intelligencer,* printed reports of the previous year's proceedings.

53 *"the several provinces":* Montague to the Virginia Committee, April 11, 1764. Six days after this letter, Grenville met on April 17 with Montague, Israel Mauduit (brother of the Massachusetts agent), Charles Garth, and other agents; "An Account of the Conference and the late Mr. Grenville and the several Colony Agents," *Collections of the Massachusetts Historical Society* 9 (1804): 270–71; Lewis B. Namier, "Charles Garth, Agent for South Carolina, Part II," *English Historical Review* 54 (1939): 646–48; William Knox. For the historiography about this meeting, see Michael Kammen, *A Rope of Sand: The Colonial Agents, British Politics, and the American Revolution* (Ithaca, N.Y.: Cornell University Press, 1968), 109–11.

53 *"wish to follow":* "Parliamentary Diaries of Nathaniel Ryder, 1764–67," ed. P. D. G. Thomas, *Camden Miscellany,* 4th ser., 23 (1969): 235.

53 *"might have the whole":* Namier, "Charles Garth," 646–47; Charles R. Ritcheson, "The Preparation of the Stamp Act," *WMQ,* 3d ser. 10 (1953): 556.

53 *"the power and sovereignty":* Montague to the Virginia Committee, April 11, 1764; Thomas, *British Politics,* 74–75. Bullion disagrees with Thomas, Ritcheson, and Jack M. Sosin about the role played in these debates by John Huske, the only native-born American in the House of Commons; Bullion, *Great and Necessary Measure,* 261–62; Ritcheson, "Preparation of the Stamp Act," 553–54; Sosin, *Agents and Merchants: British Colonial Policy and the Origins of the American Revolution, 1763–1775* (Lincoln, Nebr.: University of Nebraska Press, 1965), 50–54. These scholars and parliamentary sources contradict the asser-

tions of Lawrence Henry Gipson (citing the *Pennsylvania Gazette*, May 10, 1764) and Fred J. Ericson (citing other colonial newspapers as well) that "many Members warmly oppos[ed]" Grenville's stamp duty resolution; Gipson, *The Triumphant Empire: Thunder-Clouds Gather in the West, 1763–1766* (New York: Alfred A. Knopf, 1961), 258; Ericson, "Contemporary British Opposition to the Stamp Act, 1764–65," *Papers of the Michigan Academy of Science, Arts, and Letters* 29 (1943): 490. Several American newspapers credited Richard Jackson and William Allen with delaying Grenville's introduction of stamp duties; *New-York Gazette*, May 7, 1764; *Boston News-Letter and New-England Chronicle*, May 10, 1775; *Pennsylvania Gazette*, May 10, 1765; *Providence Gazette*, May 12, 1775.

53 *"The House appeared":* Montague to the Virginia Committee, April 11, 1764; Montague's letter of March 10 does not survive, nor do agent Richard Jackson's March 10 letters to his Massachusetts and Connecticut clients; Morgan, "Postponement of the Stamp Act," 359n18.

53 *"a great measure":* Whately to John Temple, Feb. 9, 1765; Thomas, *British Politics*, 86; "Bowdoin and Temple Papers," *Collections of the Massachusetts Historical Society*, 6th ser., 9 (1897): 49.

54 *hired Montague:* The records of Virginia's Committee of Correspondence from its creation in 1759 to 1767 were published in successive issues of the *VMHB*, vols. 9–11 (1901–1904) from the manuscripts in the vaults of the Library of Virginia, Committee of Correspondence, 1759–1767, Box 124, LVA. The committee's records for 1773–1775 are printed in *Burgesses Journals, 1773–1776*, 41–288, passim. Although Virginia created its Committee of Correspondence slightly earlier than Massachusetts established committees of correspondence between its legislature and towns, South Carolina's appointment in 1712 of a Committee of Correspondence to communicate with its agents in London rendered moot the regional jealousies reflected in James Miller Leake, *The Virginia Committee System and the American Revolution* (Baltimore: Johns Hopkins University Press, 1917).

54 *its own agent:* The burgesses felt that James Abercromby, who represented Virginia's governor and Council from 1751 to 1773, was too sympathetic to Parliament; John C. Van Horne and George Reese, eds., *The Letter Book of James Abercromby, Colonial Agent, 1751–1773* (Richmond: Library of Virginia, 1991).

54 *"Much alarmed":* VMHB 12 (1904–1905): 5–6.

54 *"truly alarming":* Ibid., 9–10.

54 *Wythe and Nicholas:* Speaker John Robinson was absent in July; James City county burgess Lewis Burwell, of Kingsmill, was present after missing the June meeting; and York county burgess Dudley Digges was absent in June but present in July; ibid., 5, 7.

55 *"whole weight":* Ibid., 10, emphasis added; Committee of Correspondence, 1759–1767, Box 124, LVA. For the General Assembly's emulation of Parlia-

ment, see Kukla, *Speakers and Clerks*; Kukla, *Political Institutions in Virginia, 1619–1660* (New York: Garland Publishing Co., 1989); Warren M. Billings, *A Little Parliament: The Virginia General Assembly in the Seventeenth Century* (Richmond: Library of Virginia, 2004); and Jack P. Greene, *The Quest for Power: The Lower Houses of Assembly in the Southern Royal Colonies, 1689–1776* (Chapel Hill: University of North Carolina Press, 1963).

55 *"useful to us"*: *VMHB* 12 (1904–1905): 13.

55 *"not only we"*: Ibid., 9, emphasis added.

55 *"taxing the Colonies"*: Ibid., 7.

55 *"the first ground"*: Sir William Blackstone, *Commentaries upon the Laws of England* (4 vols., London, 1765–69), 1: 69–73, quoted at 73; Neil Duxbury, *The Nature and Authority of Precedent* (Cambridge: Cambridge University Press, 2008).

55 *"What makes the approaching Storm"*: *VMHB* 12 (1904–1905): 9–10.

56 *"would rather agree"*: Ibid., 8.

56 *"a great measure"*: Whately to John Temple, Feb. 9, 1765; Thomas, *British Politics*, 86; "Bowdoin and Temple Papers," *Collections of the Massachusetts Historical Society*, 6th ser., 9 (1897): 49.

56 *slippery-slope reasoning*: Désirée Park, "The Myth of the Slippery Slope," in Niels Henrik Gregerson, ed., *Yearbook of the European Society for the Study of Science and Theology* (Geneva, 1999), 3–10.

57 *"Every mention"*: *VMHB* 12 (1904–1905): 13, emphasis added.

57 *powerful enough to extort money*: Richard Bland, *An Inquiry into the Rights of the British Colonies* (1766), ed. Earl Gregg Swem (Richmond: Appeals Press, 1922), 26–27. For evidence that Bland's essays circulated in manuscript and were read "to the Mob" at public gatherings before being "offered to the Press," see John Camm, *Critical Remarks on a Letter Ascribed to Common Sense* (Williamsburg: Joseph Royle, 1764), vii.

57 *"These things"*: *VMHB* 12 (1904–05): 13.

57 *"criminal"*: William James Smith, ed., *The Grenville Papers* (4 vols., London, 1852–1853), 3: 215–6. "Criminal" and "betrayer of his country" were recorded in Grenville's diary, not his wife's diary as stated in Thomas, *British Politics*, 130. The constitutional divergence is succinctly summarized in Greene, *Quest for Power*, 360–64.

58 *Richard Henry Lee*: Lemay, "John Mercer and the Stamp Act," 6–11; Alexander B. Haskell, "Defining the Right Side of Virtue: Crowd Narratives, the Newspaper, and the Lee-Mercer Dispute in Rhetorical Perspective," *Early American Studies* 8 (2010): 122–25.

58 *"ancient and inestimable Right"*: *Burgesses Journals, 1761–1765*, 302.

58 *"in a respectful Manner"*: Ibid., 302–4.

58 *"a matter of favour"*: "Boston Town Records, 1758 to 1769," *Report of the Record Commissioners of the City of Boston* (Boston, 1886), 121; Edmund S. Morgan, "Thomas Hutchinson and the Stamp Act," *New England Quarterly* 21

(1948): 459–92; Bernard Bailyn, *The Ordeal of Thomas Hutchinson* (Cambridge: Harvard University Press, 1974), 65; Thomas Cushing to Jasper Mauduit, Nov. 17, 1764; *Jasper Mauduit: Agent in London for the Province of Massachusetts-Bay* (Boston: Massachusetts Historical Society, 1918), 170.

58 *"their just and undoubted rights": Burgesses Journal, 1761–65,* 302–4. Morgan curiously relegates these Virginia protests to his section on the Sugar Act not the Stamp Act; Edmund S. Morgan, ed., *Prologue to Revolution: Sources and Documents on the Stamp Act Crisis, 1764–1766* (Chapel Hill: University of North Carolina Press, 1959), 14–17.

59 *"their being respectively presented": Burgesses Journals, 1761–65,* 302.

59 *"not yet seen them":* Fauquier to the Board of Trade, Dec. 24, 1764, *Fauquier Papers,* 1201.

59 *Henry visited: Virginia Gazette Daybooks,* Nov. 24, Nov. 30, 1764. Hayes, *Mind of a Patriot,* 44–47, 138. Henry bought the Pufendorf volume through Dr. George Pitt, who operated his apothecary shop "at the Sign of the Rhinoceros next door to the Printing-Office," perhaps because Joseph Royle was busy with the production of that week's *Gazette;* Harold B. Gill, *The Apothecary in Colonial Virginia* (Williamsburg: Colonial Williamsburg Foundation, 1972), 55–56.

59 *most popular continental author:* William Hamilton Bryson, *Census of Law Books in Colonial Virginia* (Charlottesville: University of Virginia Press, 1978), xiii, 29.

59 *nature created all men equal:* Samuel Pufendorf, *The Law of Nature and Nations: or, A General System of the most Important Principles of Morality, Jurisprudence, and Politics,* trans. Basil Kennet (5th ed., London: J. and J. Bonwicke and others, 1749), 224–32; Kari Saastamoinen, "Pufendorf on Natural Equality, Human Dignity, and Self-Esteem," *Journal of the History of Ideas* 71 (2010): 47.

59 *social contract:* Pufendorf, *Law of Nature and Nations,* 625–32; Jack P. Greene, *The Intellectual Heritage of the Constitutional Era: The Delegates Library* (Philadelphia: Library Company of Philadelphia, 1986), 15.

59 *"illustrious writers":* Wirt, *Sketches,* 328; David C. Henrickson, "International Law and Universal Empire: A View from the Eighteenth Century," *Proceedings of the American Society of International Law* 99 (2005): 308.

59 *"Speech and the Obligations":* Pufendorf, *Law of Nature and Nations,* 332–36.

60 *"the injured party":* Ibid., 333.

60 "Dereliction": Ibid., 707–8.

60 *James Otis:* Bailyn, *Pamphlets of the Revolution,* 437; Thomas R. Adams, *American Independence: The Growth of an Idea* (Providence: Brown University Press, 1965), 2–3.

60 *"a Part of the* Commonwealth": Pufendorf, *Law of Nature and Nations,* 877.

60 *"to submit":* "Forceably resisting the Parliament and the King's laws is high treason," Otis wrote. "Therefore let the Parliament lay what burdens they please on us, we must, it is our duty to submit and patiently bear them till they will be pleased to relieve us." Bailyn, *Pamphlets of the Revolution,* 409, 448.

60 *struck fear:* "In some respects, the recent insistence of historians upon the reluctance of the Americans to consider independence, coupled with the reaction against so-called 'whig' history that viewed everything in the colonial
period as prologue to revolution, has obscured the obvious"; J. M. Bumstead,
"'Things in the Womb of Time': Ideas of American Independence, 1633 to
1763," *WMQ* 3d ser., 31 (1974): 533–64.

60 *"laid it out":* Jack P. Greene, Charles F. Mullett, and Edward C. Papenfuse, Jr.,
eds., *Magna Charta for America: James Abercromby's "An Examination of the Acts
of Parliament Relative to the Trade and the Government of our American Colonies" (1752) and "De Jure et Guvernatione Coloniarum, or An Inquiry into the
Nature and the Rights of Colonies, Ancient, and Modern" (1774)* (Philadelphia:
American Philosophical Society, 1986), 161–62.

61 *"in the space of thirty or fifty years":* Peter Kalm, who toured America in the
1740s, quoted in Bumstead, "'Things in the Womb of Time,'" 553.

61 *"at too great a distance":* John Rutherfurd, *The Importance of the Colonies to Great
Britain* (London: J. Millar, 1761), 10; William K. Boyd, ed., "Some North Carolina Tracts of the 18th Century," *North Carolina Historical Review* 2 (1925):
360.

61 *"can never reasonably be supposed":* State of the British and French Colonies in
North America . . . In Two Letters to a Friend (London: A. Millar, 1755), 58. Anthony Pagden identifies the author of these *Letters* as John Campbell in *Lords
of All the World: Ideologies of Empire in Spain, Britain, and France, c. 1500–c. 1800*
(New Haven: Yale University Press, 1995), 135.

61 *"dutiful and obedient":* [Benjamin Franklin], *The Interest of Great Britain Considered with regard to her Colonies and the Acquisition of Canada and Guadaloupe*
(Philadelphia: William Bradford, 1760), 31–32.

Chapter 6: Scandal and Protest

62 *a new residence:* Patrick Henry ledger, 1762–1770 (LVA acc. no. 20473); Meade,
Patriot in the Making, 155; Couvillon, *Patrick Henry's Virginia,* 39–42.

62 *Thomas Johnson:* "Johnson Family," *WMQ,* 1st ser., 21 (1912): 47; "Johnson of
King and Queen County, *VMHB* 26 (1918): 103–5; Malcolm H. Harris, *History
of Louisa County, Virginia* (Richmond: The Dietz Press, 1936), 28–30, 381–85.

63 *"false, scandalous, and malicious":* Burgesses Journals, 1758–1761, 114.

63 *convenient resignation:* Johnson's resignation was announced on May 1 and the
House immediately requested writs for a new election; ibid., 315.

64 *Henry took no chances:* Meade, *Patriot in the Making;* Sydnor, *Gentlemen Freeholders,* 103–6.

64 *Henry took the oaths:* Burgesses Journals, 1761–1765, 345.

64 *the powerful Speaker:* Kukla, *Speakers and Clerks,* 126.

65 *"When People":* Richard Corbin to Capel and Osgood Hanbury, May 31, 1765,
Richard Corbin Letter Book, 1758–1768, p. 58, VHS.

65 *"caused a great deal of noise":* William Allason Letter Book, May 21, 1765, quoted in David J. Mays, *Edmund Pendleton, 1721–1803: A Biography* (Cambridge: Harvard University Press, 1952), 331n4.

65 *quarter-of-a-million-pound scheme:* The May 17, 1765, issue of Royle's *Gazette* is no longer extant, but Thomas Jefferson had a copy at hand when he described the Loan Office debate to William Wirt; Jefferson to Wirt, Aug. 14, 1814, Paul Leicester Ford, ed., *The Writings of Thomas Jefferson* (10 vols., New York: G. P. Putnam's Sons, 1892–1899), 9: 466.

65 *borrow £240,000:* The Loan Office proposal is published in *Burgesses Journals, 1761–1765,* 350.

65 *illicit personal loans:* Appendix 2, Mays, *Pendleton,* 358–69. Many owed Robinson small debts of the sort that were incidental to Virginia's business practices, e.g. £11 6s 8d for Patrick Henry, £12 for Richard Henry Lee, and £10 11s 8d for Peyton Randolph. Henry's half-brother, John Syme, Jr., owed £522 15s 1d, and Robinson's personal attorney, executor, and political protégé Edmund Pendleton owed £1,020 12s 7d.

65 *"the debts due":* Thomas Jefferson's Notes on Patrick Henry, before April 12, 1812, *Jefferson Retirement Papers* 4: 599. Three years later Jefferson wrote "that the secret object of this scheme was to transfer those debtors to the public, and thus clear his accounts." Jefferson to William Wirt, August 14, 1814, *Jefferson Retirement Papers,* 7: 545.

65 *"in that style":* Jefferson's Notes on Patrick Henry, 1812, *Jefferson Retirement Papers* 4: 599.

65 *rejected by the Governor's Council:* *Burgesses Journals 1761–1765,* 349–63; *Legislative Journals of the Council of Colonial Virginia,* ed. H. R. McIlwaine (Richmond: Colonial Press, 1918–1919; 2d. ed., Richmond: Library of Virginia, 1979), 1344–46.

65 *"members of the upper counties":* Jefferson's Notes on Patrick Henry, 1812, *Jefferson Retirement Papers* 4: 599.

66 *"indelibly impressed":* Jefferson to Wirt, August 14, 1814, *Jefferson Retirement Papers,* 7: 545.

66 *"as a Tax":* Richard Corbin to Philip Ludwell, Aug. 2, 1765, Richard Corbin Letter Book, 1758–1768, pp. 64–65, VHS.

66 *"only to help":* Richard Corbin to Capel and Osgood Hanbury, May 31, 1765, Richard Corbin Letter Book, 1758–1768, p. 58, VHS.

66 *"Industry and frugality":* Richard Corbin to Robert Cary, Aug. 1, 1765, Richard Corbin Letter Book, 1758–1768, p. 64, VHS.

66 *"many of the Members retired":* Edmund S. Morgan, ed., "Edmund Pendleton on the Virginia Resolves," *Maryland Historical Magazine* 46 (1951): 74–75; Fauquier to the Board of Trade, June 5, 1765, *Fauquier Papers,* 1250. The Virginia agent, according to Edmund Pendleton, sent the first copy of the Stamp Act to Virginia immediately after its approval by the Lords on March 8, 1765, when Montague, "as a Master in Chancery, [had been] ordered to carry [the

act back] to the Commons, [at which time] he had taken [i.e., made] a Copy and immediately transmitted it." Pendleton to James Madison, [Jr.], April 21, 1790, *Pendleton Letters*, 565.

66 *"manly but decent":* Pendleton to James Madison, April 21, 1790, *Pendleton Letters*, 565.

67 *"the cyphers":* Thomas Jefferson to William Wirt, August 5, 1815, *Jefferson Retirement Papers*, 8: 642.

67 *the king steadfastly refused:* Andrew Jackson O'Shaughnessy, *The Men Who Lost America: British Leadership, the American Revolution, and the Fate of Empire* (New Haven: Yale University Press, 2013), 21–28.

67 *December address:* The May 1765 session met after the burgesses had adjourned on December 21, so Joseph Royle printed the autumn 1764 and spring 1765 *Journals* together. No issues of the *Virginia Gazette* survive for 1764 and only one issue (Oct. 25) is extant for 1765. The Dec. 1764 protests were reprinted in Boston in March 1765. Governor Fauquier was able to keep Henry's resolutions out of the *Gazette*, but both sets of documents appear in Royle's edition of the *Journal* (Williamsburg, 1765), 90–93, 150—from which they were reprinted in *Burgesses Journals, 1761–65*, 302–4, 360.

67 *"in Consequence": Burgesses Journals, 1761–65*, 358.

67 *committee of the whole:* Henry Scobell, *Memorials of the Method and Manner of Proceedings in Parliament* (London: Hills and Field, 1656), 35–38; Stanley M. Pargellis, "Procedure of the Virginia House of Burgesses," *WMQ*, 2d ser., 7 (1927): 148–51.

68 *"solid reasoning":* Jefferson's Notes on Patrick Henry, 1812, *Jefferson Retirement Papers*, 4: 599.

68 *"old members":* Ibid.

68 *"in a more conciliatory form":* Ibid.

68 *the "young, hot and Giddy members":* Fauquier to the Board of Trade, June 5, 1765, *Fauquier Papers*, 1250–51.

68 *legal protest:* J. A. Leo Lemay, "John Mercer and the Stamp Act in Virginia, 1764–1765," *VMHB* 91 (1983): 21–22; Alexander B. Haskell, "Defining the Right Side of Virtue: Crowd Narratives, the Newspaper, and the Lee-Mercer Dispute in Rhetorical Perspective," *Early American Studies* 8 (2010): 122–25. To the extent that the British thought about how Americans might have suitably protested the Stamp Act, they projected an unrealistic vision of Parliament's generosity in making adjustments after the passage of a law or tax.

68 *"brought with them": Burgesses Journals, 1761–65*, 360, provides accurate texts of Henry's first four resolutions as introduced on the 29th and adopted on the 30th. Variant texts of the remaining resolutions appeared in several newspapers.

69 *fifth resolution: Newport Mercury*, June 24, 1765; *Boston Gazette*, July 1, 1765.

69 *"The Gentlemen had":* Fauquier to the Board of Trade, June 5, 1765; *Fauquier Papers*, 1250.

69　*sixth resolution: Newport Mercury*, June 24, 1765; *Boston Gazette*, July 1, 1765; *Maryland Gazette*, July 4, 1765.

69　*final resolution: Newport Mercury*, June 24, 1765; *Boston Gazette*, July 1, 1765; *Maryland Gazette*, July 4, 1765.

70　*Two thirds of the elected members:* The burgesses reduced the required quorum to twenty-five during the French and Indian War and raised it back to fifty in 1766; Pargellis, "Procedure of the Virginia House of Burgesses," 83.

70　*One new face:* Murray wrote about the debate in a diary that eventually ended up in a French archive, separated from anything that identified its author. It was published in two parts as "Journal of a French Traveller in the Colonies, 1765," AHR 26 (1921): 726–47; 27 (1921): 70–89. Ninety years later, the detective work of Joshua Beatty, a graduate student at the College of William and Mary just a mile west of the spot where Charles Murray heard Patrick Henry, identified the author; Beatty, "The 'French Traveller,' Patrick Henry, and the Contagion of Liberty," paper presented to the Virginia Forum, Lexington, Va., March 26, 2011. I am indebted to our mutual friend, the late Rhys Isaac, for introducing me to Mr. Beatty via email. I found additional information about Murray in *Scots Magazine and Edinburg Literary Miscellany* 70 (1808): 398, and Desmond Gregory, *The Beneficent Usurpers: A History of the British in Madeira* (Rutherford, N.J.: Fairleigh Dickinson University Press, 1988), 35, 46. For the predominance of Scots merchants in the Atlantic wine trade, see David Hancock, "The Trouble with Networks: Managing the Scots' Early-Modern Madeira Trade," *Business History Review* 79 (2005): 467–91. Both Samuel Eliot Morison in 1923 and Edmund S. Morgan in 1959 reprinted the diarist's excerpts about the debate in Williamsburg but nothing further as the traveler witnessed Henry's influence spreading to other colonies. Many subsequent writers, following their example, have largely ignored the rest of Murray's diary. Morison, *Sources and Documents illustrating the American Revolution, 1764–1788* (Oxford: Clarendon Press, 1923), 14–15; Edmund S. Morgan, ed., *Prologue to Revolution: Sources and Documents on the Stamp Act Crisis, 1764–1766* (Chapel Hill: University of North Carolina Press, 1959), 46–47.

70　*"went immediately":* "Journal of a French Traveller," 745.

70　*"entertained":* Ibid.

70　*"torrents":* Jefferson's Notes on Patrick Henry, 1812, *Jefferson Retirement Papers*, 4: 598–604.

70　*22 to 17:* Fauquier to the Board of Trade, June 5, 1765; *Fauquier Papers*, 1250.

70　*"was most bloody":* Jefferson's Notes on Patrick Henry, 1812, *Jefferson Retirement Papers* 4: 599. Jefferson wrote "500 guineas" in his 1812 letter (ibid.) and "100 guineas" in 1814, but otherwise his recollections of Randolph's comment were identical; Jefferson to Wirt, August 14, 1814, *Jefferson Retirement Papers*, 7: 547.

71　*opposition strategy:* Archibald S. Foord, *His Majesty's Opposition, 1714–1830* (Oxford: Oxford University Press, 1964).

71　*"Tarquin and Caesar": Henry Correspondence*, 1: 86. William Wirt based his reconstruction of the Caesar-Brutus speech on firsthand accounts from Paul Carrington, John Tyler, and Thomas Jefferson; Wirt, *Henry*, 64–65. Carrington's recollection that Henry mentioned Tarquin is confirmed by Murray's diary and the *London Gazetteer*, Aug. 13, 1765.

71 *"one of those trying moments":* Tyler quoted in Wirt, *Henry*, 65.

72 *"splendid display":* Jefferson Autobiography, 6.

72 *"heard a Gentleman":* Pendleton to James Madison, April 21, 1790, *Pendleton Letters*, 565.

72 *"the cry of treason":* Wirt, *Henry*, 65.

72 *"Shortly after I came in":* "Journal of a French Traveller," 745.

72 *"Upon which":* Ibid., emphasis added. For ease of reading, I also corrected Murray's spellings of *beged, afaire,* and *droped.*

72 *Historians writing in 1953:* Morgan and Morgan, *Stamp Act Crisis*, 122–23.

73 "was ready": "Journal of a French Traveller," 745, emphasis added.

73 *"with a grace":* St. George Tucker quoted in Jane Carson, *Patrick Henry: Prophet of the Revolution* (Williamsburg: Virginia Independence Bicentennial Commission, 1979), 24.

73 *"A tactical retreat":* Isaac, *Landon Carter's Uneasy Kingdom*, 172.

73 *"who has ever watched":* George Morrow, *The Greatest Lawyer That Ever Lived: Patrick Henry at the Bar of History* (Williamsburg: Telford Publications, 2011), 26. In his meditation on Landon Carter's diary, Rhys Isaac commented that Morgan and Morgan's *Stamp Act Crisis* "is still the 'standard' history, but it is out-of-date and is written with a New England bias that tends to show Patrick Henry's debut—Williamsburg's immortal May 1765 moment—as a humiliation rather than the triumph it really was"; *Landon Carter's Uneasy Kingdom: Revolution and Rebellion on a Virginia Plantation* (New York: Oxford University Press, 2004), 369. For the dispute about the end of Henry's speech, see Elson, *Patrick Henry Speeches and Writings*, 54–57, and Morrow, *The Greatest Lawyer*, 25–26.

73 *intrigued by events:* Jefferson bought vol. 1 of Temple Henry Croker et al., *Complete Dictionary of Arts and Sciences* (4 vols., London: Croker, Clark and Williams, 1764–1766) for £5 and William Cheselden's *Anatomy of the Human Body* (5th ed., London: Knapton et al., 1763) for 13 shillings on April 20, 1765; *Virginia Gazette Daybooks*.

73 *Jefferson watched his distant cousin:* Jefferson's Notes on Patrick Henry, 1812, *Jefferson Retirement Papers*, 4: 600; Jefferson to Wirt, August 14, 1814; *Jefferson Retirement Papers*, 7: 547.

73 *"Some of the timid members":* Jefferson to Wirt, August 14, 1814; *Jefferson Retirement Papers*, 7: 547.

73 *"entering resolves":* "Journal of a French Traveller," 745–46.

74 *"in Expectation":* Ibid., 746.

74 *"Very indecent Language":* Fauquier was particularly concerned to excuse Speaker Robinson, "who has always assisted me in carrying on the Kings

Service"; in his report to the Board of Trade, June 5, 1765, *Fauquier Papers*, 1250–51.

75 *Royle's deference:* John Holt, who had learned the printing trade at the *Virginia Gazette* and whose father has been mayor of Williamsburg, published a report dated "Virginia, October 25," explaining that because Royle "was the Government's Printer," Governor Fauquier "did actually prevent the publication of any Reflections upon the unconstitutional Nature of the Stamp-Act, or that might imply a Censure upon the ministerial Conduct, or tend to rouse the People to a Sense of their just Rights; and threatened the Printer with the Loss of his Salary if he should presume to print any such Pieces." *New York Journal*, November 27, 1766.

75 *Henry's resolutions reached London: London Magazine, or Gentleman's Monthly Intelligencer*, Aug. 1765, 435; *London Gazetteer*, Aug. 13, 1765; Bullion, *Great and Necessary Measure*, 191–95; Thomas, *British Politics*, 115–19.

75 *"dangerous and desperate doctrines":* Grenville to Whately, Aug. 13; George Grenville Letter Books, George Grenville Papers, Stowe Collection, Henry E. Huntington Library, San Marino, Calif. I am grateful to Mary Robertson, chief curator of manuscripts, for photocopies of these letters and permission to quote from them.

75 *Thrown out of office:* "Something disagreeable in [Grenville's] manner and behaviour to His Majesty had so alienated him" that George III dismissed him, Lord Lyttelton wrote his brother in July; Robert Phillimore, ed., *Memoirs and Correspondence of George, Lord Lyttelton* (2 vols., London: J. Ridgway, 1845), 2: 677.

75 *"Have you seen the Resolutions":* Grenville to Robert Nugent, Aug. 13, 1765, Grenville Papers, Huntington Library.

75 *"what answer":* Grenville to Lord Lyttelton, Aug. 20, 1765, ibid.

76 *bitter opposition:* Warren M. Billings, John E. Selby, and Thad W. Tate et al., *Colonial Virginia: A History* (White Plains, N.Y.: KTO Press, 1986), 300–308. Tate's observations about the limits of seniority reflect Charles Sydnor's explication of the screening and training of talented young men in *Gentleman Freeholders*, 103–19.

76 *"While one would pay":* Edmund Randolph, *History of Virginia*, ed. Arthur H. Shaffer (Charlottesville: University of Virginia Press, 1970), 167.

76 *differing styles:* Tate et al., *Colonial Virginia*, 300–303. Tate's distinction between responsible and representative political styles has parallels in Bernard Bailyn's distinction between deliberative and locally accountable representation (*Ideological Origins of the American Revolution*, 161–75) and contrasting styles explored in Gordon S. Wood's "Interests and Disinterestedness in the Making of the Constitution," in Richard Beeman, Stephen Botein, and Edward C. Carter II, eds., *Beyond Confederation: Origins of the Constitution and American National Identity* (Chapel Hill: University of North Carolina Press, 1987), 69–109.

76 *knighthood:* Kukla, *Speakers and Clerks,* 121.

77 *"at this critical moment":* Randolph, *History of Virginia,* 187.

77 *"as a Species":* Clifford K. Shipton, "James Otis, Jr.," in *Sibley's Harvard Graduates* (14 vols., Cambridge: Harvard University Press, 1933–1975), 11: 264; Paul H. Giddens, "Maryland and the Stamp Act Controversy," *Maryland Historical Magazine* 100 (2005): 253.

77 *"was realy surprised":* "Journal of a French Traveller," 726–47. His diary ends in September but the editors' statement that Murray sailed from Philadelphia late in October (p. 86n74) is confirmed by a letter written on October 24 quoted in Arthur H. Cole, "The Tempo of Mercantile Life in Colonial America," *Business History Review* 33 (1959): 286.

78 *"Call the french":* If the French were still "in Canada," one Hanoverian told Murray, "the British parlem[en]t would as soon be D[amne]d as to offer [i.e., attempt] to do what they do now"; "Journal of a French Traveller," 747.

78 *"the King's health":* Ibid., 72, 75.

78 *"They are men!":* John Adams to Hezekiah Niles, Feb. 13, 1818, *Adams Works,* 10: 287.

78 *"the eminent patriot":* John Adams, Novanglus IV, 1774, *Adams Works,* 4: 50.

78 *"that all who maintained":* Thomas Hutchinson, *History of the Province of Massachusetts Bay from 1749 to 1774,* ed. John Hutchinson (London: John Murray, 1828), 119.

79 *"We were happy":* Massachusettensis [Daniel Leonard], "To the Inhabitants of the Province of Massachusetts-Bay," *Massachusetts Gazette and Boston Post-Boy and Advertiser,* Dec. 12–19, 1774; Joseph A. Dowling, "John Adams vs. Daniel Leonard: 'Novanglus' Opposes 'Massachusettensis,'" Lawrence H. Leder, *The Colonial Legacy: Some Eighteenth-Century Commentators* (New York: Harper & Row, 1971), 181–202.

79 *"We read them":* Massachusettensis, Dec. 12–19, 1774; Carol Berkin, "Daniel Leonard," *ANB* 13: 489–90.

79 *"I thought":* Gov. Bernard to the Earl of Halifax, Aug. 15, 1765, Morgan, *Prologue to Revolution,* 106.

79 *"Murmurs on account":* "London, August 19," reprinted in *New-York Mercury,* Oct. 28, 1765. The word *murmur* then had connotations, now obsolete, of discontent and rumor.

79 *"the Resolves of the Assembly":* Gen. Thomas Gage to Henry Seymour Conway, Sept. 23, 1765; Clarence Edwin Carter, ed., *Correspondence of General Thomas Gage* (2 vols., New Haven: Yale University Press, 1931–1933), 1: 67. Merrill Jensen emphasized Virginia's resolves as a catalyst for revolution in a "Commentary" in Randolph G. Adams, *Political Ideas of the American Revolution* (3d ed., New York: Barnes & Noble, 1958), 12.

Chapter 7: The Stamp Act

80 *Clad in leather:* Grigsby, *Virginia Convention of 1776*, 150.

80 *"the more enlightened and sensible Men":* March 12, 1766, *Fauquier Papers*.

80 *more than one third:* New men comprised 34.5 percent of the burgesses elected in July 1765; *General Assembly of Virginia*, 91–96. Legislative turnover generally declined in eighteenth-century Virginia; Jack P. Greene, "Legislative Turnover in British America, 1696 to 1775: A Quantitative Analysis," *WMQ* 3d ser., 38 (1981): 447; Kukla, "Order and Chaos in Early America: Political and Social Stability in Pre-Restoration Virginia," *AHR* 90 (1985): 296–97.

80 *"the Madness of the people":* Fauquier to Henry Seymour Conway, Nov. 8, 1765, *Fauquier Papers*, 1301.

81 *Grenville's successor:* Thomas, *British Politics*, 124–25.

81 *"to guide me":* Fauquier to the Board of Trade, Nov. 3, 1765; *Fauquier Papers*, 1295–96. "The usual practice was to send to the colonial governors printed copies of acts relating to America passed in a session of Parliament. However, the board's journal does not record the transmittal of acts passed during the session, ended on 25 May 1765, in which the Stamp Act was passed." Ibid., 1296n8.

82 *"Mr. Henry . . . took the lead":* Jefferson to William Wirt, Aug. 4, 1805, in Stan V. Henkel, ed., "Jefferson's Recollections of Patrick Henry," 400.

82 *"in a great degree executes itself":* Grenville's speech introducing the Stamp Act, Feb. 6, 1765, *Proceedings and Debates of Parliament*, 11. See also Charles Jenkinson's notes for the speech in Bullion, *Great and Necessary Measure*, 224–29. Bullion plausibly suggests that because everybody groused about stamp duties, Grenville and his associates were inclined to regard American protests as evidence of "the colonists' realization that they could not evade paying stamp duties"; ibid., 146.

82 *"It was fortunate":* David Ramsay, *History of the American Revolution*, ed. Lester H. Cohen (Indianapolis: Liberty Fund, 1990), 58–59; Arthur M. Schlesinger, "Colonial Newspapers and the Stamp Act," *New England Quarterly* 8 (1935): 65; Michael D'Innocenzo and John J. Turner, Jr., "The Role of New York Newspapers in the Stamp Act Crisis, 1764–88," *New-York Historical Society Quarterly* 51 (1967): 345.

83 *fifty-five specific taxes:* A convenient source for the full text of the Stamp Act is Edmund S. Morgan, ed., *Prologue to Revolution: Sources and Documents on the Stamp Act Crisis, 1764–1766* (Chapel Hill: University of North Carolina Press, 1959), 35–43.

83 *"Poor America!":* Edmund Pendleton to James Madison, Sr., April 17, 1765. At first glance the date of this letter (the manuscript of which is not extant) seems problematic, but a close reading of Pendleton's characteristic precise language suggests that his reaction was to news of the first reading on Feb. 13, 1765, when "the House of Commons resolved and ordered in a Bill to estab-

lish a stamp duty" and not necessarily to a draft of the Stamp Act itself; *Pendleton Letters*, 20.

83 *"every advertisement":* Morgan, *Prologue to Revolution*, 41.

84 *"the most respectable":* Thomas Whately to John Temple, May 10, 1765, "Bowdoin and Temple Papers," 52; Thomas, *British Politics*, 100, 132, 135.

84 *convenient roll call:* Lists of stamp masters were published in London in June and reprinted in the *Boston Post-Boy* on Aug. 5, the *Boston News-Letter and New England Chronicle* on Aug. 8, the *Connecticut Gazette* on Aug. 9, and the *Newport Mercury* on Aug. 12, 1765, and reprinted in other colonial papers as well.

84 *"The People of Virginia":* Boston Gazette and Country Journal, July 8, 1765; Schlesinger, "Colonial Newspapers and the Stamp Act," 73; Edmund S. Morgan, "Thomas Hutchinson and the Stamp Act," *New England Quarterly* 21 (1948): 469. Morgan attributed the July 8 essay to Oxenbridge Thacher, who drafted the resolutions Hutchinson gutted; *Stamp Act Crisis*, 135. Edes and the Loyal Nine, the secret inner circle of the embryonic Sons of Liberty, directed the activities of those Bostonians who "sometimes seemed to love violence for its own sake"; Morgan and Morgan, *Stamp Act Crisis*, 159–61. Richard Maxwell Brown suggests that Massachusetts launched "a new level of violence and intimidation during the anti–Stamp Act riots of 1765, the *Liberty* anti-customs riot in 1768, and the threat of mob violence that caused the evacuation of the two British regiments in the aftermath of the Boston Massacre"; *Strain of Violence: Historical Studies of American Violence and Vigilantism* (New York: Oxford University Press, 1975), 56.

84 *"Green-ville sole":* Morgan and Morgan, *Stamp Act Crisis*, 160–65; Pauline Maier, *From Resistance to Revolution: Colonial Radicals and the Development of American Opposition to Britain, 1765–1776* (New York: Alfred A. Knopf, 1972), 51–112; Robert Blair St. George, *Conversing by Signs: Poetics of Implication in Colonial New England Culture* (Chapel Hill: University of North Carolina Press, 1998), 206–95.

84 *the next morning:* Maier, *From Resistance to Revolution*, 51–60; Gov. Bernard to the Earl of Halifax, Aug. 15, 1765; Morgan, *Prologue to Revolution*, 106–8.

84 *"surrounded Mr. Oliver's House":* William Tudor, ed., *Deacon Tudor's Diary . . . from 1732 to 1793* (Boston, 1896), 17–18.

84 *evening of August 26–27:* Robert Middlekauf, *The Glorious Cause: The American Revolution, 1763–1789* (rev. ed., New York: Oxford University Press, 2005), 87–97; Hutchinson to Richard Jackson, Aug. 30, 1765, Morgan, *Prologue to Revolution*, 108–9.

84 *"the encouragers of the* first mob*":* Hutchinson to Jackson, Aug. 30, 1765, Morgan, *Prologue to Revolution*, 108–9, emphasis added; Bailyn, *The Ordeal of Thomas Hutchinson* (Cambridge: Howard University Press, 1974), 35; Brown, *Strain of Violence*, 41–46. The events of August 14–15 showed more evidence of the "moral economy of the English crowd" described in the seminal works of

George Rudé and E. P Thompson that began with Rudé, "The London 'Mob' of the Eighteenth Century," *Historical Journal* 2 (1959): 1–18, and *The Crowd in History: A Study of Popular Disturbances in France and England, 1730–1848* (New York: J. Wiley, 1964), and Thompson, "The Moral Economy of the English Crowd in the Eighteenth Century," *Past and Present* 50 (1971): 76–136. Dirk Hoerder found more "rudimentary class feeling" in the events of August 26–27; Hoerder, "Boston Leaders and Boston Crowds, 1765–1776," in Alfred F. Young, ed., *The American Revolution: Explorations in the History of American Radicalism* (DeKalb, Ill.: Northern Illinois University Press, 1976), 231–71. See also Gary B. Nash, *The Unknown American Revolution: The Unruly Birth of Democracy and the Struggle to Create America* (New York: Viking, 2005), 46–59, and Paul A. Gilje, *Rioting in America* (Bloomington: Indiana University Press, 1999), 40.

85 *"Enemies to the liberties":* Thomas Moffat to Joseph Harrison, Oct. 16, 1765; Morgan, *Prologue to Revolution*, 109–13; David S. Lovejoy, *Rhode Island Politics and the American Revolution, 1760–1776* (Providence: Brown University Press, 1958), 100–112; Sheila Skemp, "Newport's Stamp Act Rioters: Another Look," *Rhode Island History* 47 (1989): 41–49; Elaine Forman Crane, *A Dependent People: Newport, Rhode Island in the Revolutionary Era* (New York: Fordham University Press, 1985), 112–15; Allen Mansfield Thomas, "'Circumstances Not Principles': Elite Control of the Newport Stamp Act Riots," *Newport History* 67 (1995): 128–43.

85 *"a miserable shell":* Moffat to Harrison, Oct. 16, 1765, Morgan, *Prologue to Revolution*, 112–13; Lovejoy, *Rhode Island Politics*, 105–8; Skemp, "Newport's Rioters," 44–47.

85 *"Damnation":* "Journal of a French Traveller," 72; *Maryland Gazette*, April 18, 1765.

85 *"are most violent":* Sharpe to Lord Baltimore, July 11, 1765, "Correspondence of Governor Horatio Sharpe, 1761–1771," ed. William Hande Browne, *Archives of Maryland* 14 (1895): 210; Giddens, "Maryland and the Stamp Act," 246–47. Several of Giddens's citations are misdated 1785 rather than 1765.

85 *"will probably be worth":* Sharpe to Cecelius Calvert, Aug. 16, 1765, "Correspondence of Governor Sharpe," 220.

85 *Sons of Liberty:* Benjamin L. Carp, "Terms of Estrangement: Who Were the Sons of Liberty?," *Colonial Williamsburg* 34, no. 1 (Winter 2012): 40–45.

86 *"without a considerable Military Force":* Sharpe to Calvert, Sept. 10, 1765, "Correspondence of Governor Sharpe," 227; Carroll to Christopher Bird, Sept. 28, 1765, *Unpublished Letters of Charles Carroll of Carrollton*, ed. Thomas Meagher Field (New York: United States Catholic Historical Society, 1902), 94.

86 *"A perfect Frenzy":* Civis (Aug. 30, 1765) quoted in Schlesinger, "Colonial Newspapers and the Stamp Act," 72; Sharpe to Calvert, Sept. 10, 1765, "Correspondence of Governor Sharpe," 227; Gilje, *Rioting in America*, 38–39; Giddens, "Maryland and the Stamp Act," 246–47. My dear friend the late Bill

Abbot wrote the best account of the Stamp Act in Georgia: W. W. Abbot, *Royal Governors of Georgia, 1754–1775* (Chapel Hill: North Carolina University Press, 1959), 103–25.

86 *enthusiastic references: Fauquier Papers*, 1277. These pages rely heavily upon Alfred Procter James, *George Mercer of the Ohio Company: A Study in Frustration* (Pittsburgh: University of Pittsburgh Press, 1963) for biographical details.

86 *several tons of stamps:* C. A. Weslager described the sheer bulk of stamps and stamped paper and logistics of their manufacture and shipping in *The Stamp Act Congress, With an Exact Copy of the Complete Journal* (Newark, Del.: University of Delaware Press, 1976), 43–46. The first shipment for Massachusetts, New Hampshire, and Rhode Island weighed twelve tons.

87 *"Accompanied by hundreds": Maryland Gazette*, Sept. 12, 1765, reprinted in *Pennsylvania Gazette*, Sept. 12, and *Newport Mercury* and *Boston Post-Boy*, Sept. 30, 1765. Only one *Virginia Gazette* is extant for 1765. In this context, "Mosaic Law" generally meant thirty-nine lashes; Brendon McConville, "Rough Music: Reflections on an Ancient New Custom in Eighteenth-Century New Jersey," in Matthew Dennis, Simon P. Newman, and William Pencak, eds., *Riot and Revelry in Early America* (University Park: Pennsylvania State University Press, 2002), 96.

87 *"the infamous Projector": Maryland Gazette*, Supplement, Oct. 17, 1765; John C. Matthews, "Two Men on a Tax: Richard Henry Lee, Archibald Ritchie, and the Stamp Act," in Darrett B. Rutman, ed., *The Old Dominion: Essays for Thomas Perkins Abernethy* (Charlottesville: University of Virginia Press, 1964), 100–101; Alexander B. Haskell, "Defining the Right Side of Virtue: Crowd Narratives, the Newspaper, and the Lee-Mercer Dispute in Rhetorical Perspective," *Early American Studies* 8 (2010): 120–45.

87 *"Audience of all Ranks": Maryland Gazette*, Supplement, Oct. 17, 1765; Matthews, "Two Men on a Tax," 100–101.

88 *Born at Stratford Hall:* Richard Henry Lee is the subject of several monographs, but the best summary remains Pauline Maier's chapter in *The Old Revolutionaries: Political Lives in the Age of Samuel Adams* (New York: Alfred A. Knopf, 1980), 164–200—now supplemented by Albert H. Tillson, Jr., *Accommodating Revolutions: Virginia's Northern Neck in an Era of Transformations, 1760–1810* (Charlottesville: University of Virginia Press, 2010), 27–32, and Haskell, "Defining the Right Side of Virtue." See also James Curtis Ballagh, ed., *Letters of Richard Henry Lee* (2 vols., New York: Macmillan, 1911–1914); J. Kent McGaughy, *Richard Henry Lee of Virginia: A Portrait of an American Revolutionary* (Lanham, Md.: Rowman & Littlefield, 2004); Oliver Perry Chitwood, *Richard Henry Lee, Statesman of the Revolution* (Morgantown: West Virginia University Library, 1967; Mary Elizabeth Virginia, "Richard Henry Lee of Virginia: A Biography" (PhD diss., State University of New York at Buffalo, 1992); Paul Chadwick Bowers, Jr., "Richard Henry Lee and the Continental Congress, 1774–1779" (PhD diss., Duke Univer-

sity, 1964); Richard H. Lee, *Memoir of the Life of Richard Henry Lee . . . by his Grandson* (Philadelphia, 1825).

88 *self-serving dimension:* Tillson, *Accommodating Revolutions*, 27–32; Silas Deane to Elizabeth Deane, Sept. 10, 1774, *Letters of Delegates*, 1: 62.

88 *"Having a large family":* Virginia Congressional Delegates to George Pyncheon and John Bradford, Oct. 16, 1777, *Letters of Richard Henry Lee*, 1: 332.

88 *"wise, attentive, sober":* Richard Henry Lee to Arthur Lee, Feb. 11, 1799, ibid., 2: 33.

88 *"the eastern part of this Union":* Richard Henry Lee to James Lovell, June 12, 1781, ibid., 2: 236.

88 *"favored New England":* Richard Henry Lee to Patrick Henry, May 26, 1777, ibid., 1:300. Arthur Lee worked closely with Samuel Adams when he served as colonial agent for Massachusetts; Louis W. Potts, *Arthur Lee: A Virtuous Revolutionary* (Baton Rouge: Louisiana State University Press, 1981), 106–28; Fauquier to the Board of Trade, May 11, 1766, *Fauquier Papers*, 1359.

89 *"impose on us":* Justices of Westmoreland Co. to the Governor and Council, Sept. 24, 1765, *Fauquier Papers*, 1278; *Revolutionary Virginia*, 1: 19.

89 *"utterly inconsistent":* Justices of Stafford Co. to Fauquier, Oct. 5, Justices of Culpeper Co. to Fauquier, Oct. 21, 1765, *Fauquier Papers*, 1281–86.

89 *"properly educated":* Fauquier to the Board of Trade, Nov. 3, 1765, *Fauquier Papers*, 1291.

89 *"none that are fit":* Pendleton to James Madison, Sr., Feb. 15, 1766, *Pendleton Letters*, 23.

90 *"the inhabitants of this Colony":* *Newport Mercury*, June 24, 1765; *Boston Gazette*, July 1, 1765; *Maryland Gazette*, July 4, 1765.

90 *"whether they . . . should":* *Revolutionary Virginia*, 1: 20–21, quoting Northampton County Minute Book, 1765–1771, pp. 31–32 (LVA), and *VG* (Purdie), March 11, 1766.

90 *"Colonel Mercer is not yet arrived":* Fauquier to the Board of Trade, Oct. 2, 1765, *Fauquier Papers*, 1280.

90 *"Whether the Stamp Act":* *Executive Journals of the Council*, 6: 278. The manuscript, docketed "Obr. 1765," probably records a meeting in the second or third week of October.

91 *Fauquier had received no information:* "I found the Governour was so far from having any Order to support me," Mercer explained in April 1766, "that he assured me, he never had any Account, but from the News Papers, of the Existence of the Act, and the first authentic Assurance he had of it, was from my Commission." J. E. Tyler, ed., "Colonel George Mercer's Papers," *VMHB* 60 (1952): 412.

91 *"Absurdity":* "Colonel George Mercer's Papers," 412. A brief circular letter from the Treasury dated Sept. 14, 1765—rather late in the game!—directed American governors to aid and assist the stamp distributors. There is no indication that Fauquier ever received the letter; *Fauquier Papers*, 1277. Compare Maurice

A. Crouse, "Cautious Rebellion: South Carolina's Opposition to the Stamp Act," *South Carolina Historical Review* 73 (1972): 61–63; Abbot, *Royal Governors of Georgia*, 112.

91 *"This Concourse of people":* Fauquier to the Board of Trade, Nov. 3, 1765; *Fauquier Papers*, 1292–94; "Colonel George Mercer's Papers," 412–13; Michael Olmert, *Official Guide to Colonial Williamsburg* (Williamsburg: Colonial Williamsburg Foundation, 1985), 44–47. Reconstructed after careful archaeological research, Charlton's Coffeehouse opened in 2010.

91 *"One and all":* This and all quotations in the next five paragraphs are from Fauquier to the Board of Trade, Nov. 3, 1765, *Fauquier Papers*, 1292–94. When the crowd pushed forward during the incident, Fauquier reported that he "heard a Cry see the Governor take care [i.e., be careful] of him," which he attributed partly "to the Respect they bore to my Character, and partly to the Love they bore to my person"; ibid., 1292.

93 *"Oyes, Oyes, Oyes!":* The proclamation for opening the General Court dated to 1662; Philip Alexander Bruce, *Institutional History of Virginia in the Seventeenth Century* (2 vols., New York: G. P. Putnam, 1910), 1: 663.

94 *"as there was no Business":* This and all quotations in the next two paragraphs are from Fauquier to the Board of Trade, Nov. 3, 1765; *Fauquier Papers*, 1293–94.

95 *"by Menace or Force":* Gen. Thomas Gage to Henry Seymour Conway, Sept. 23, 1765; Clarence Edwin Carter, ed., *Correspondence of General Thomas Gage* (2 vols., New Haven: Yale University Press, 1931–1933), 1: 67; John L. Bullion, "British Ministers and American Resistance to the Stamp Act, October–December 1765," *WMQ*, 3d ser., 49 (1992): 97.

95 *cleaning up Grenville's mess:* Thomas, *British Politics*, 124–25; G. H. Guttridge, *The Early Career of Lord Rockingham, 1730–1765* (Berkeley: University of California Press, 1952), 1–49; Bullion, "British Ministers and American Resistance to the Stamp Act, October–December 1765," 99; Paul Langford, *The First Rockingham Administration, 1765–1766* (London: Oxford University Press, 1973), 98–108.

96 *"a declaratory act":* Rockingham quoted in Morgan and Morgan, *Stamp Act Crisis*, 336.

96 *"the celebrated electric philosopher":* Proceedings and Debates of Parliament, 2: 185–251.

96 *"on the throne":* VG (Purdie and Dixon), June 6, 1766.

96 *"And be it further declared":* Morgan and Morgan, *Prologue to Revolution*, 155–56.

96 *"The principal people":* [Edmund Burke], *Annual Register . . . for the Year 1765* (London, 1766), 49.

97 *"to bow":* Henry Correspondence, 2: 419.

Chapter 8: Europeans or Africans?

98 *"degeneracy in morals":* James Reid, "The Religion of the Bible and the Religion of King William County Compared," in Richard Beale Davis, ed., *Colonial Virginia Satirist, Mid-Eighteenth-Century Commentaries on Politics, Religion, and Society, Transactions of the American Philosophical Society*, new ser., 57 (1967), 56.

98 *"outward grandeur":* "To the Printer," *VG* (Purdie and Dixon), Sept. 19, 1766.

99 *"broke the influence":* Randolph, *History of Virginia*, 178. Reading the *Virginia Gazettes* and other sources from midcentury to independence, one is struck by the increased reliance upon civic republican rhetoric in Virginia after 1766.

99 *fond of imagining:* Jack P. Greene, "The Happy Retreat of True Britons: Virginia 1720–1775," *Douglas Southall Freeman Historical Review* (Spring 1996): 94–99. I am grateful to John W. Gordon for supplying a copy of this short-lived journal and Jack Greene for permission to cite his Freeman Lectures.

99 *"in a kind of independence":* William Byrd to Charles Boyle, Earl of Orrey, July 5, 1726; and Byrd to John Boyle, Baron Boyle of Broghill, June 15, 1731, Marion Tinling, ed., *Correspondence of the Three William Byrds of Westover, Virginia, 1684–1776* (Charlottesville: University Press of Virginia, 1977), 355, 443. Oddly, Daniel L. Dreisbach, "The 'Vine and Fig Tree' in George Washington's Letters: Reflections on a Biblical Motif in the Literature of the American Founding Era," *Anglican and Episcopal History* 76 (2007): 299–326, showed no awareness of Byrd's imagery.

99 *"Wherefore is it":* This and all quotations in the next three paragraphs are from the essay printed in *Henry Correspondence*, 1: 112–16. In his discussion of American manufacturing Henry expressed no concern about British mercantilist restrictions, which were easily evaded if an enterprise was viable. Generous policy incentives for military commodities (e.g., reserving tall trees for ship's masts) had some success in the colonies.

100 *"vast shoals":* Hugh Jones, *Present State of Virginia* (London, 1724), ed. Richard L. Morton (Chapel Hill: University of North Carolina Press, 1956), 130.

100 *"chief Instruments":* William Yates and Robert Carter Nicholas to John Waring, Sept. 30, 1762, in John C. Van Horne, ed., *Religious Philanthropy and Colonial Slavery: The American Correspondence of the Associates of Dr. Bray, 1717–1777* (Urbana: University of Illinois Press, 1985), 185.

101 *"To live in Virginia":* Peter Fontaine to Moses Fontaine, March 30, 1757, in Ann Maury, ed., *Memoirs of a Huguenot Family* (New York: Putnam, 1907), 352. For the general pattern of social development, see Lorena S. Walsh, *Motives of Honor, Pleasure, and Profit: Plantation Management in the Colonial Chesapeake, 1607–1763* (Chapel Hill: University of North Carolina Press, 2010); and John C. Coombs, *The Rise of Virginia Slavery* (Charlottesville: University of Virginia Press, forthcoming).

101 *"many bad consequences":* Byrd to John Perceval, Earl of Egmont, July 12, 1736, *Correspondence of the Three William Byrds*, 487–89.

101 *"the gloomy retreat": Henry Correspondence*, 1: 116.

102 *advocating intermarriage:* Meade, *Patriot in the Making*, 156–58, 264–65. Compare Jefferson's complex attitudes toward "merciless savages"; Annette Gordon-Reed and Peter S. Onuf, *"Most Blessed of the Patriarchs": Thomas Jefferson and the Empire of the Imagination* (New York: Liveright, 2016), 85–87, 138–40.

102 *"Virginia":* Thomas Lee to the Board of Trade, Sept. 29, 1750, quoted in Lawrence Henry Gipson, *British Empire Before the American Revolution*, vol. 2, *The British Isles and the American Colonies: The Southern Plantations, 1748–1754* (New York: Alfred A. Knopf, 1960), 3.

103 *£5,300 in legal fees:* Meade, *Patriot in the Making*, 259.

103 *Shelton engaged Henry:* Ibid., 229–31.

103 *first expedition:* "William Fleming," *Dictionary of American Biography* (New York: Charles Scribner's Sons, 1930), 3: 461. Daniel Boone began marking the trail between the Holston and Kentucky Rivers in March 1775.

104 *"to reconnoitre":* Patrick Henry to William Fleming, June 10, 1767; typescript supplied by Ruben Thwaites to William Wirt Henry based on a manuscript in Henry's hand with notations by Lyman Draper, William Wirt papers, VHS.

104 *"an act for the encouragement": Journal of the House of Burgesses, 1766–1769*, 122. The bill was rejected by the Council on April 10, 1767; *Legislative Journals of the Council*, 1373–74.

104 *His favorite sister:* Gail S. Terry, "Anne Henry Christian: Reluctant Revolutionary to Woman of Business," in Cynthia A. Kierner and Sandra Gioia Treadway, eds., *Virginia Women: Their Lives and Times* (2 vols., Athens: University of Georgia Press, 2015–2016), 1: 116–37.

104 *Another sister, Elizabeth:* Jon Kukla, "Elizabeth Henry Campbell Russell: Champion of Faith in the Early Republic," in Kierner and Treadway, eds., *Virginia Women*, 1: 160–79.

104 *Samuel Meredith: Henry Correspondence*, 3: 639–43.

104 *Thomas Madison: VHMB* 7 (1900): 253; Thomas Marshall Green, *Historic Families of Kentucky* (Cincinnati: Robert Clarke & Co., 1889), 68–69.

104 *Luke Bowyer:* Joseph A. Waddell, *Annals of Augusta County, Virginia, From 1726 to 1871* (Staunton, Va.: C. Russell Caldwell, 1902), 215–16.

105 *Valentine Wood: VMHB* 5 (1898): 78–79.

105 *Except for Sarah: Henry Correspondence*, 3: 639–43; *VG* (Purdie and Dixon), June 20, Oct. 17, 1766, Feb. 22, 1770; *VG* (Rind), Feb. 22, 1770.

105 *"sour":* Fauquier to the Board of Trade, Sept. 4, 1766, *Fauquier Papers*, 1382–83.

105 *"The Blood of the People":* Fauquier to the Board of Trade, Oct. 8, 1766, *Fauquier Papers*, 1388. New men comprised 35.2 percent of the burgesses elected in Feb. 1766; *General Assembly of Virginia*, 91–96. Turnover rates for 1768 and 1769

echoed the intense competition of earlier decades, while the composite turn-over rate of 22 percent in the 1770s reflected the increasingly united resistance to British policies.

105 *"In a warm debate":* George Dabney memorandum, 1805, Elson, *Patrick Henry Speeches and Writings,* 223.

105 *investigation of the Robinson scandal: Burgesses Journals, 1766–1769,* 11–24; Mays, *Pendleton,* 360. Merrill Jensen wrongly asserted that Cary owed £7,500, and his otherwise helpful summary of events in Virginia misdated the assembly of 1766 and thereby confused its actions with 1767 reactions to the Townshend Duties; Jensen, *Founding of a Nation: A History of the American Revolution, 1763–1776* (New York: Oxford University Press, 1968), 203–9.

106 *prestigious committee assignments: Burgesses Journals, 1766–1769,* ix, 11–16.

106 *"to perpetuate the Glorious Repeal":* Ibid., 33, 48, 53, 59.

106 *become "the gloomy retreat": Henry Correspondence,* I: 116.

106 *By the 1760s:* The percentage of African-born slaves in Virginia dropped from 52 percent in 1710 to 14 percent in 1760 and 9 percent in 1770. During the same period in South Carolina the percentage of African-born slaves de-clined from 67 percent in 1710 to 39 and 35 percent in 1760 and 1770; Philip D. Morgan, *Slave Counterpoint: Black Culture in the Eighteenth-Century Chesa-peake and Lowcountry* (Chapel Hill: University of North Carolina Press, 1998), 61. Drawing upon extensive scholarship, David Brion Davis concluded that "in contrast to slave societies farther south and to most examples of slavery in human history," Virginia's "slave population began by the 1720s to increase rapidly by natural means"; Davis, *Inhuman Bondage: The Rise and Fall of Slav-ery in the New World* (New York: Oxford University Press, 2006), 134. See also Walsh, *Motives of Honor, Pleasure, and Profit,* 398–401.

106 *An essay about slavery:* Richard K. MacMaster, ed., "Arthur Lee's 'Address on Slavery': An Aspect of Virginia's Struggle to End the Slave Trade, 1765–1774," *VMHB,* 80 (1972): 149. In 1772 the duty on slaves imported from mainland colonies or the West Indies was set at £5 "in lieu of the twenty per cent ad va-lorem"; Hening, *Statutes,* 8: 532. MacMaster's discussion of these duties (ibid., 143–44) is incomplete; see instead Darold D. Wax, "Negro Import Duties in Colonial Virginia: A Study in British Commercial Policy and Local Public Policy," *VMHB* 79 (1971): 29–44, and the duties themselves in Hening, *Stat-utes,* 6: 218, 353–54, 466; 7: 81, 363, 383; 8: 237, 337–38, 532.

106 *wharf-side scenes:* Joshua Fry and Peter Jefferson, *A Map of the Inhabited part of Virginia* (London, [1751]); John Henry, *New and Accurate Map of Virginia* (London, 1770).

106 *"more strenuous in our Opposition":* Associator Humanus, *VG* (Purdie and Dixon), July 11, 1771; Winthrop Jordan, *White over Black: American Attitudes Toward the Negro, 1550–1812* (Chapel Hill: University of North Carolina Press, 1968), 294–311.

107 *"slavery was a little less brutal":* Morgan, *Slave Counterpoint,* 663.

107 *"treated by too many":* Yates and Nicholas to Waring, Sept. 30, 1762, in Van Horne, ed., *Religious Philanthropy and Colonial Slavery*, 185.

107 *"Infatuated and Abandoned":* John Mercer, "Dinwiddianae," 1757, in Davis, ed., *Colonial Virginia Satirist*, 30.

107 *"dangerous to the safety":* "Arthur Lee's 'Address on Slavery,'" 153–57.

107 *"the Policy of encouraging":* George Mason to George Washington and George William Fairfax, Dec. 23, 1765, *Mason Papers*, 61–62.

107 *"to see one of the Assemblymen":* Henry Correspondence, 117. The Assembly actually met in May that year.

Chapter 9: Organizing Resistance

108 *"some Bungler":* George Mason to the Committee of Merchants in London, June 6, 1766, *Mason Papers*, 70–71.

108 *"must soon come to an issue":* Robert J. Chaffin, "The Townshend Acts of 1767," *WMQ* 3d ser., 27 (1970): 115.

108 *"the most futile":* Jensen, *Founding of a Nation*, 224–27.

108 *cluster of miscellaneous taxes:* P. D. G. Thomas, *The Townshend Duties Crisis: The Second Phase of the American Revolution, 1767–1773* (New York: Oxford University Press, 1987), 7–35; Sir Lewis Namier described Townshend's fateful peculiarities in *Charles Townshend: His Character and Career* (Cambridge: Cambridge University Press, 1959) and Namier and John Brooke, eds., *The House of Commons, 1754–1790* (New York: Oxford University Press, 1964), 3: 539–48.

109 *"a putrid fever":* Chaffin, "Townshend Acts," 115; Thomas, *Townshend Duties Crisis*, 37.

109 *Americans reacted:* Riggs, *Nine Lives of Arthur Lee*, 19–21; Riggs, "Arthur Lee, Radical Virginian," 271–72. The most accessible modern edition of Dickinson's pamphlet is Forrest McDonald, ed., *Empire and Nation: "Letters from a Farmer in Pennsylvania," John Dickinson, "Letters from the Federal Farmer," Richard Henry Lee* (Englewood Cliffs, N.J.: Prentice Hall, 1962) despite its outdated attribution of authorship of the Federal Farmer to Lee rather than Melanchthon Smith or another New Yorker; *Ratification Documents*, 14: 14–18; 15: 80; 18: 220; Gordon S. Wood, "The Authorship of the *Letters from the Federal Farmer*," *WMQ*, 3d ser. (1974): 299–308.

109 *"will have the same success":* McDonald, ed., *Empire and Nation*, 85.

109 *"their own interests":* The Farmer's and Monitor's Letters to the Inhabitants of the British Colonies (1st ed., Williamsburg: William Rind, 1769; reprinted, Williamsburg: Virginia Independence Bicentennial Commission, 1969), 62–63, 68, 95.

109 *John Locke:* McDonald, ed., *Empire and Nation*, 45n; *Farmer's and Monitor's Letters*, 33, 68, 84, 93.

110 *"subversion of our constitutional freedom":* Farmer's and Monitor's Letters, 62, 97.

110 *"the capacity of becoming Pitt"*: Randolph, *History of Virginia*, 181.

110 *"implore his Majesty"*: *Revolutionary Virginia*, 1: 64–67. "If they petition Parliament," wrote Thomson Mason, George Mason's younger brother, "it will be acknowledging their [i.e., Parliament's] right." A British American, *VG* (Rind), May 4, 1769.

110 *"so destructive"*: *Burgesses Journals, 1766–1769*, 145.

110 *"the only true"*: Ibid., 146.

111 *"the people of every county"*: *Farmer's and Monitor's Letters*, 63.

111 *sparsely attended:* Of 108 elected burgesses, the journal names only thirty-seven as having been present. Although this tally could reflect changes in record keeping by the new clerk, George Wythe, it seems more likely that Acting Governor John Blair's proclamation of March 7 (four days after Fauquier's death) calling the assembly to meet on March 31 got to outlying counties too late for many burgesses (Patrick Henry apparently among them) to reach the capital before the session adjourned on April 16; *Burgesses Journals, 1766–1769*, 135–40. Henry may also have been on his expedition to the Holston River Valley.

111 *"Don't you think"*: Letter from a Gentleman in Edenton, May 26, 1769, *Essex Gazette* (Salem, Mass.), June 20; subsequently printed in *VG* (Rind), July 13, and other newspapers.

111 *"The brave VIRGINIANS"*: *Essex Gazette*, Jan. 30, 1770.

111 *"the best heads"*: Horace Walpole to Horace Mann, Aug. 13, 1768, in W. S. Lewis et al, eds., *Horace Walpole's Correspondence* (48 vols., New Haven: Yale University Press, 1937–1983), 23: 401.

112 *"The Council"*: Hillsborough's views quoted in Thomas, *Townshend Duties Crisis*, 87.

112 *"The conduct of the Virginians"*: Measures proposed by Lord Hillsborough to the Cabinet, Sir John Fortescue, ed., *Correspondence of King George the Third* (6 vols., London: Macmillan and Co., 1927–28), 2: 83–84.

112 *"four or five ships of war"*: Hillsborough quoted in Thomas, *Townshend Duties Crisis*, 87.

112 *"a great force"*: Hillsborough quoted in ibid.

112 *abrupt removal:* Memorandum by the King, Feb. 1769, Fortescue, *Correspondence of George the Third*, 2: 85; Thomas, *Townshend Duties Crisis*, 87–91. The flap over Amherst "made a noise for a while," Ben Franklin wrote, but quieted down after promises of a lucrative pension and possible peerage soothed the general's wounded pride; Thomas, *Townshend Duties Crisis*, 91. For a contemporary American report, see "Late Transactions respecting Sir Jeffrey Amherst," *Boston Gazette*, Nov. 28, 1768.

113 *"gilded in every part"*: Timothy Pickering described the carriage and its motto when he visited Williamsburg before the siege of Yorktown; Octavius Pickering, *Life of Timothy Pickering* (4 vols., Boston, 1867), 1: 297–98. George T. Morrow II vividly portrays Botetourt's personal charms but inflates his political

effectiveness in *The Day They Buried Great Britain: Francis Fauquier, Lord Botetourt and the Fate of Nations* (Williamsburg: Telford Publications, 2011), 51–86.

113 *"to enact Laws":* George III, Additional Instructions to Lord Botetourt, Aug. 21, 1768, C.O. 5/1346, fol. 77–80, VCRP reel 1.

113 *"separately and personally":* Ibid; *General Assembly Register,* 94–98; *Burgesses Journals, 1766–1769,* 188–89.

114 *"without Passion": Burgesses Journals, 1766–1769,* 189.

114 *"is now, and ever hath been": Revolutionary Virginia,* 1: 65–67, 70–71, 6: 357; *Burgesses Journals, 1766–1769,* 214–16. While the burgesses were in debate, Mason supported petitioning the king but warned that petitioning Parliament could be seen as acknowledging its claims authority. He recommended that "without naming the act of the British Parliament" the burgesses "enter upon the journals a resolve . . . that the people of this colony cannot be taxed in any manner but by the Assembly"; "A British American," *VG* (Rind), May 4, 1769.

114 *"Royal Interposition": Revolutionary Virginia,* 1: 70–71, 6: 357; *Burgesses Journals, 1766–1769,* 214–16.

114 *"Secret and Confidential":* Botetourt to Hillsborough, May 23, 1769, C. O. 5/1347, fol. 81, VCRP reel 1.

115 *"Moderator": Revolutionary Virginia,* 1: 72–77.

115 *"a Committee":* Washington to Mason, April 5, 1769, *Washington Papers, Colonial,* 8: 177; *Mason Papers,* 96.

115 *gossipy merchant:* James Parker to Charles Steuart, June 22, 1769, Charles Steuart Papers, National Library of Scotland, LVA microfilm, misc. reel 3702.

115 *"reducing us": Revolutionary Virginia,* 1: 74–77.

116 *taking precautions:* Ibid., 1: 69–70; *Burgesses Journals, 1766–1769,* 214.

116 *"the point of no return":* Thomas, *Townshend Duties Crisis,* 137–41, 264.

117 *"soothing":* Ibid., 139.

117 *"no man should scruple":* Washington to Mason, April 5, 1769, Washington Papers, LC; *Washington Papers, Colonial,* 8: 177; *Mason Papers,* 96.

117 *Although Halifax:* Ian R. Christie and Benjamin W. Labaree, *Empire or Independence, 1760–1776: A British-American Dialogue on the Coming of the American Revolution* (New York: W. W. Norton, 1976), 26, 144–46.

117 *Of only seventeen:* The word *independence* and its variants appeared 154 times between 1769 and 1771 in colonial newspapers held by the American Antiquarian Society, but only 10 percent referred to political separation from Great Britain. These tabulations are based on key-word searches in the Newsbank American Historical Newspapers database available at many research libraries. Virginia and Maryland newspapers are not well represented in this database. *Independence* appeared frequently in reports about the controversial London politician John Wilkes, legal or legislative proceedings, accounts of European history or current events, and in praise of someone's independent character.

117 *"an absolute Independence":* Extract from a letter, *Boston Chronicle,* Apr. 27, 1769.

117 *"in effect maintain":* Letters of John Morin Scott and Isaac Low, *New-York Journal,* May 14, 24, 31, 1770. Dorothy Rita Dillon, *The New York Triumvirate: A Study of the Legal and Political Careers of William Livingston, John Morin Scott, William Smith, Jr.* (New York: Columbia University Press, 1949); "Isaac Low," John N. Ingham, *Biographical Dictionary of American Business Leaders,* vol. 2 (Westport, Conn.: Greenwood Press, 1983), 826.

118 *Virginia's organization differed:* Rhys Isaac, "Dramatizing the Ideology of Revolution: Popular Mobilization in Virginia, 1774 to 1776," *WMQ,* 3d ser., 33 (1976): 368; Isaac, *The Transformation of Virginia, 1740–1790* (Chapel Hill: University of North Carolina Press, 1982), 244; Woody Holton, *Forced Founders: Indians, Debtors, Slaves, and the Making of the American Revolution in Virginia* (Chapel Hill: University of North Carolina Press, 1999), 91; Charles McLean Andrews, "Boston Merchants and the Non-Importation Movement," *Transactions of the Colonial Society of Massachusetts* 19 (1918): 256–57; Glenn Curtis Smith, "An Era of Non-Importation Associations, 1768–73," *WMQ,* 2d ser. 20 (1940): 94.

118 *"Virginia cloth":* Revolutionary Virginia, 1: 74–77; Mrs. Martha Jacquelin to John Norton, Aug. 14, 1769, *John Norton and Sons,* 103.

118 *Association document: Revolutionary Virginia,* 1: 76. Of the burgesses present at the end of the session, eighty-eight signed the Association on May 18 and ten more sent their names to Peyton Randolph by July. Seven of thirteen burgesses who *apparently* did not sign the association were never reelected to the assembly. These computations are based on *Revolutionary Virginia,* 1: 76–77; *General Assembly Register; Burgesses Journals, 1766–1769*; and *VG* (Rind), July 27, 1769. It is possible that a few more burgesses endorsed the Association without being named in extant newspapers. Only 60 percent of the *Virginia Gazette*s survive from 1770 and 85 percent from 1771; seventy-seven weekly papers and an unknown number of supplements are lost.

119 *"The Association is Sent":* James Parker to Charles Steuart, June 22, 1769, Charles Steuart Papers, National Library of Scotland; LVA microfilm, misc. reel 3702.

119 *"upon his Word": Revolutionary Virginia,* 1: 76.

119 *Political deference:* Debates about deference began with J. R. Pole's "Historians and the Problem of Early American Democracy," *AHR* 67 (1962): 626–46, and generated an immense literature. John M. Murrin's "In the Land of the Free and the Home of the Slave, Maybe There Was Room Even for Deference," *JAH* 85 (1998): 89–91, and Michael Zuckerman, "Authority in Early America: The Decay of Deference on the Provincial Periphery," *Early American Studies* 1 (2003): 1–29, are good introductions. See also Pole, "Representation and Authority in Virginia from the Revolution to Reform," *JSH* (1958): 16–50; Pole, *Political Representation in England and the Origins of the American Republic* (New York: St. Martin's Press, 1966); Charles S. Sydnor's classic, *Gentlemen Freeholders: Political Practices in Washington's Virginia* (Chapel Hill: University

of North Carolina Press, 1952); and John Gilman Kolp, *Gentlemen and Free-holders: Electoral Politics in Colonial Virginia* (Baltimore: Johns Hopkins University Press, 1998).

119 *two rare copies:* The LVA copy was published in *Revolutionary Virginia*, 1: 76–77; the LC copy is Evans, *Bibliography* no. 11513.

119 *"principal inhabitants":* VG (Purdie and Dixon), July 14, 1769; *VG* (Rind), July 14, 1769.

119 *"widow Ladies":* VG (Rind), July 27, 1769. Lucy Bolling Randolph's late husband, Peter, had served on the Governor's Council; Anne Harrison Randolph of Wilton was the Speaker's sister-in-law; Christian Blair Burwell's father had been president of the Council; Mary Bolling Starke was the daughter of Colonel Robert Bolling; and Rebecca Acrill Watson's husband, Phillip, had been a prominent merchant at Richmond and her brother represented Charles City County in the legislatures from 1766 to 1778; "Ladies of the Association," *WMQ*, 1st ser., 8 (1899): 36; John Frederick Dorman, ed., *Adventurers of Purse and Person, Virginia, 1607–1624/5* (4th ed., 3 vols., Baltimore: Genealogical Publishing Co., 2004), 1: 134–35, 176–77, 444, 451; 2: 310; David Meschutt, "John Wollaston's Portraits of the Randolph Family," *VMHB* 92 (1984): 457–66; "The Starke Family," *WMQ*, 1st ser., 4 (1896): 270–72.

120 *"I expect to be dressed":* Mrs. Martha Jacquelin to John Norton, Aug. 14, 1769, *John Norton and Sons*, 103.

120 *"made a genteel appearance":* VG (Purdie and Dixon), Dec. 14, 1769, April 19, 1770; *VG* (Rind), Dec. 14, 1769. Weaving, generally the work of male artisans in the seventeenth century, become a female domestic chore in New England and the Chesapeake in the eighteenth century but remained the work of immigrant male artisans in the middle colonies; Laurel Thatcher Ulrich, *The Age of Homespun: Objects and Stories in the Creation of an American Myth* (New York: Alfred A. Knopf, 2001), 102–5; Patricia Ann Gibbs, *Cloth Production in Virginia to 1800* (Williamsburg: Research Department, Colonial Williamsburg Foundation, 1978), 108–11, 127–28.

120 *flax sickle:* Meade, *Patriot in the Making*, 273; Henry's accounts with George and Sampson Mathews, 1768–1770, Mercer Family Papers, VHS. The estimate of Henry's flax production from half a bushel of seed is based on information from the websites of the agricultural extension services of North Dakota State University and the University of Missouri.

120 *"apparelled in Virginia growth":* Letter of C.R. in *VG* (Purdie and Dixon), March 22, 1770. Bruce Ragsdale identified C.R. as Landon Carter; *Planters' Republic*, 82, 88. Cynthia A. Kierner has argued that wearing homespun at "genteel civic balls" gave elite southern women "a unique stage on which to display the distinctive ways in which members of their sex could express their patriotism and public spirit"; Kierner, "Genteel Balls and Republican Parades: Gender and Early Southern Civic Rituals, 1677–1826," *VMHB* 104 (1996): 192–93.

120 *"deer skins":* Buckskin in *VG* (Rind), June 1, 1769.

120 *"warmly clad":* C.R. in *VG* (Purdie and Dixon), March 22, 1770.

121 *"both Houses of Parliament":* Senex, *VG* (Rind), Nov. 23, 1770.

121 *incipient revolutionaries:* Thad W. Tate, "Point of No Return: The American Revolution and the Crisis of the 1760s," Society of Cincinnati Lecture, University of Richmond, March 24, 1976; typescript at VHS.

Chapter 10: Good and Evil

122 *"meritorious services":* Hening, *Statutes*, 4: 132.

122 *"with great civility":* Diary of Rachel Wilson, quoted in *Henry Correspondence*, 1: 117.

122 *"Noble sentiments of liberty":* Anthony Iaccarino, "Virginia and the National Contest over Slavery in the Early Republic, 1780–1833" (PhD diss., University of California, Los Angeles, 1999), 7–9. The pamphlet was likely either Woolman's *Some Considerations on the Keeping of Negroes: Recommended to the Professors of Christianity of Every Denomination* (Philadelphia, 1754) or his *Considerations on Keeping Negroes: Recommended to the Professors of Christianity, of Every Denomination. Part the Second* (Philadelphia, 1762)—both of which were frequently reprinted into the 1860s; Thomas E. Drake, *Quakers and Slavery in America* (New Haven: Yale University Press, 1950), 59–67, 83–84, 221–22.

123 *"with the grossest indecorum":* Jefferson to Edward Coles, Aug. 25, 1814, *Jefferson Retirement Papers*, 7: 603; Eva Sheppard Wolf, *Race and Liberty in the New Nation: Emancipation in Virginia from the Revolution to Nat Turner's Rebellion* (Baton Rouge: Louisiana State University Press, 2006), 12–16; Paul Finkelman, "Jefferson and Slavery: 'Treason Against the Hopes of the World,'" in Peter S. Onuf, ed., *Jeffersonian Legacies* (Charlottesville: University Press of Virginia, 1993), 188–89.

123 *enforced by violence:* Recent scholarship about Virginia's antebellum slave trade emphasizes the sustained violence inherent to America's slave economy; e.g., Maurie Dee McInnis, *Slaves Waiting for Sale: Abolitionist Art and the American Slave Trade* (Chicago: University of Chicago Press, 2011); Edward E. Baptist, *The Half Has Never Been Told: Slavery and the Making of American Capitalism* (New York: Basic Books, 2014); and Ashraf H. A. Rushdy, *American Lynching* (New Haven: Yale University Press, 2012), 146–53.

123 *"a remarkable shift":* David Brion Davis, *The Problem of Slavery in the Age of Revolution, 1770–1823* (Ithaca: Cornell University Press, 1975), 196–97.

123 *"Anthony Benezet's book":* Henry to Pleasants, Jan. 18, 1773, is printed in *Henry Correspondence*, 1: 152–53. My transcription is from a photocopy of the original manuscript at Friends House, London.

124 *"Is it not amazing":* Ibid. I have substituted *slavery* for the pronoun *it.*

124 *"Would anyone believe"*: Ibid. For ease of comprehension, I have substituted *duty* for the archaic term *devoir* and *virtue's* for the pronoun *her*.

124 *"a time will come"*: Ibid. I have substituted *Christian morality* for the pronoun *it* referring to the antecedent *religion*.

125 *"vast shoals of Negroes"*: Hugh Jones, *Present State of Virginia* (London, 1724), ed. Richard L. Morton (Chapel Hill: University of North Carolina Press, 1956), 130.

125 *"radically different"*: Richard S. Dunn, *A Tale of Two Plantations: Slave Life and Labor in Jamaica and Virginia* (Cambridge: Harvard University Press, 2014), 61–73, quotation at p. 73. In stark demographic terms, "the 2.3 million Africans imported to the British sugar islands [since the 1640s] generated a slave population of about 775,000 in 1807, while the 388,000 Africans imported to North America during the slave trade generated a population . . . [of] 1.4 million U.S. slaves in 1807"; ibid., 3.

125 *"increasingly dysfunctional"*: Ibid., 68. Virginia slaves may have "escaped the grueling and debilitating gang labor" of the sugar islands and benefited from "a much ampler and more nutritious diet," Dunn notes, but what antebellum Virginia slaves "*did* experience was continuous family breakup" as nineteenth-century planters sold their "surplus slaves to new owners or moved them to new jobs in distant places"; ibid., 183.

125 internal *slave trade*: Ibid., 70; Baptist, *The Half Has Never Been Told: Slavery and the Making of American Capitalism*; Maurie D. McInnis, *Slaves Waiting for Sale: Abolitionist Art and the American Slave Trade*.

126 *"the interest of the Country"*: "Address of the House of Burgesses to the King in Opposition to the Slave Trade," *Revolutionary Virginia*, 1: 87.

126 *"in point of law"*: Richard Jackson to the Board of Trade, July 18, 1770, Donnan, *Documents of the Slave Trade*, 4: 152. British merchants began protesting Virginia's slave importation duties in 1723; editorial note, *VMHB* 16 (1903): 85–87.

126 *From 1769 to independence*: Pauline Maier, *American Scripture: Making the Declaration of Independence* (New York: Alfred A. Knopf, 1997), 120–22, 146–47, 239. Compare Jefferson's comments in *A Summary View of the Rights of British North America* (Williamsburg, 1774): "The abolition of domestic slavery is the great object of desire in those colonies, where it was unhappily introduced in their infant state. But previous to the enfranchisement of the slaves we have, it is necessary to exclude all further importations from Africa; yet our repeated attempts to effect this by prohibitions, and by imposing duties which might amount to a prohibition, have been hitherto defeated by his majesty's negative: Thus preferring the immediate advantages of a few African corsairs to the lasting interests of the American states, and to the rights of human nature, deeply wounded by this infamous practice." Merrill D. Peterson, ed., *Thomas Jefferson: Writings* (New York: Library of America, 1984), 115–16.

126 *"by sea or land":* Hening, *Statutes,* 9: 471–72; Wolf, *Race and Liberty,* 24–25. Wolf misidentified Patrick Henry (who was then governor) as a delegate involved in drafting the anti-importation legislation of 1778. The committee comprised Isaac Zane, Philip Alexander, and James Henry of Accomack County (who was not kin to the governor).

126 *"prisoners for Christ":* James Ireland, *The Life of the Rev. James Ireland* (Winchester, Va., 1819), 156.

126 *Separate Baptists:* Robert B. Semple, *History of the Rise and Progress of the Baptists in Virginia* (Richmond, 1810), 15. Semple's work remains an essential primary source, but the best summary of modern scholarship is Jewel L. Spangler, *Virginians Reborn: Anglican Monopoly, Evangelical Dissent, and the Rise of the Baptists in the Late Eighteenth Century* (Charlottesville: University of Virginia Press, 2008).

126 *"are great disturbers":* Semple, *Rise and Progress of the Baptists,* 30.

127 *"the gnats that buzz":* Jonathan Boucher, "On the American Episcopate: A Sermon Preached at St. Mary's Church in Caroline County, Virginia, in the year 1771," *A View of the Causes and Consequences of the American Revolution* (London, 1797), 100. These remarks are probably authentic, but Anne Young Zimmer and Alfred H. Kelly warn that the 1797 volume "cannot be accepted as a literal reproduction . . . in all respects of Boucher's earlier political thought"; "Jonathan Boucher: Constitutional Conservative," *JAH* 58 (1972): 902.

127 *levying fines:* John A. Ragosta, *Wellspring of Liberty: How Virginia's Dissenters Helped Win the American Revolution and Secured Religious Liberty* (New York: Oxford University Press, 2010), 180–83. Dissenters accounted for nineteen indictments for unauthorized worship, but the eighteen accusations of nonattendance may have involved delinquent Anglicans as well as dissenters; personal communication from John A. Ragosta, March 10, 2012.

127 *Pendleton imprisoned:* Mays, *Pendleton,* 262–65.

127 *"for preaching the laws":* Mays, *Pendleton,* 264; Timothy Alden, *A Collection of American Epitaphs and Inscriptions with Occasional Notes* (5 vols., New York, 1812–1814), 5: 23; Ragosta, *Wellspring of Liberty,* 171–83.

128 *"whipped him":* Lewis Peyton Little, *Imprisoned Preachers and Religious Liberty in Virginia* (Lynchburg, Va.: J. P. Bell Co., 1938), 229–31. Three years later Pendleton and vestrymen of Drysdale Parish asked the governor and council to dismiss Moreton for unstated "Immoralities"; *Executive Journals Va. Council,* 6: 556.

128 *Cary signed:* Brent Tarter, "Archibald Cary," *DVB,* 3: 101–3; "Prosecution of Baptist Ministers, Chesterfield County, Va., 1771–73," *VMHB* 11 (1904): 415–17.

128 *More than thirty Baptist preachers:* Garnett Ryland, ed., "Baptists in Middlesex, 1771," *WMQ,* 2d ser., 5 (1925), 208–13; Spangler, *Virginians Reborn,* 119.

128 *"pulled down":* Semple, *Rise and Progress of the Baptists,* 17–23; Little, *Imprisoned Preachers,* 32–47, 58, 180–83, 269, 311–13; Ragosta, *Wellspring of Liberty,* 28–36.

128 *"The more ye mow us down"*: The quotation attributed to Tertullian is in *The Oxford Dictionary of Quotations* (2d ed., New York: Oxford University Press, 1953), 452.

128 *fifty-four congregations*: Spangler, *Virginians Reborn*, 77–118; Sandra Rennie, "The Role of the Preacher: Index to the Consolidation of the Baptist Movement in Virginia from 1760 to 1790," *VMHB* 88 (1980): 430; Ragosta, *Wellspring of Liberty*, 50–52.

129 *"May it please the court"*: Ragosta, *Wellspring of Liberty*, 50–52; Gary B. Nash, *The Unknown American Revolution: The Unruly Birth of Democracy and the Struggle to Create America* (New York: Viking, 2002), 148–49. The core of Henry's remarks (as quoted) accurately reflect an oral tradition derived from two men who claimed to have been present. Variants of the phrase "Teaching and Preaching the Gospel" that appear in writs for similar prosecutions (Ryland, ed., "Baptists in Middlesex, 1771," 209, 211) contradict Lewis Peyton Little's challenge to the veracity of "Henry's Supposed Speech" (*Imprisoned Preachers*, 107–26).

129 *"until the day"*: Semple, *Rise and Progress of the Baptists*, 24.

129 *"men of all religious persuasions"*: A Citizen of the World, *VG* (Purdie and Dixon), June 14, 1770. A subsequent essay over the same pseudonym contested the "antipathy to the Scotch which appears to be so general amongst us"; A Citizen of the World, *VG* (Pinkney), Jan. 26, 1775. I am grateful to Henry Morse, of the Virginia Newspaper Project at LVA, for confirming the text of the 1770 essay.

129 *"one among the few Lawyers"*: "Address to the Anabaptists," Aug. 8, 1771, *VG* (Purdie and Dixon), Feb. 20, 1772. Many scholars have followed Lewis Peyton Little's attribution of the address, "based solely upon the internal evidence," to Attorney General John Randolph; *Imprisoned Preachers*, 255. Jewel Spangler's suggestion of Edmund Pendleton as another "likely" author (*Virginians Reborn*, 149) seems more plausible. In addition to the obvious fact that its date was the day before Pendleton sent Lewis Craig to jail, the "Address to the Anabaptists" opens with a Lockean account of the formation of civil societies by compact that more likely reflected Pendleton's political philosophy than, for example, Randolph's view of the British constitution in the pamphlet *Considerations on the Present State of Virginia* published by Purdie and Dixon in July 1774; *Revolutionary Virginia*, 1: 206–18.

130 *"a Sameness of Religion"*: Timoleon, *VG* (Purdie and Dixon), Aug. 22, 1771.

130 *"the State of the established Religion"*: *Burgesses Journals, 1770–1772*, 157, 160–61, 182–83, 185–86, 188–89; *VG* (Rind), March 26, 1772.

130 *"laid on the table"*: *Burgesses Journals, 1770–1772*, 188–89, 194, 197, 245, 249; *VG* (Rind), March 26, 1772; Ragosta, *Wellspring of Liberty*, 47–48. Robert Carter Nicholas described the legislative deliberations on the bill in *VG* (Rind), June 10, 1773. Several errors flaw the discussion of this legislation in Rhys Isaac, *The Transformation of Virginia, 1740–1790* (Chapel Hill: University of

North Carolina Press, 1982), 201. This episode is also an early instance of an emerging and implicitly democratic legislative tactic of deferring action on divisive or controversial issues until public sentiment could be clarified.

Chapter 11: Hurrying Toward a Crisis

132 *The ambitious Scot:* James Corbett David, *Dunmore's New World: The Extraordinary Life of a Royal Governor in Revolutionary America—with Jacobites, Counterfeiters, Land Schemes, Shipwrecks, Scalping, Indian Politics, Runaway Slaves, and Two Illegal Royal Weddings* (Charlottesville: University of Virginia Press, 2013), 25–130.

132 *"Damn Virginia":* William H. Sabine, ed., *Historical Memoirs from 16 March 1763 to 9 July 1776 of William Smith* . . . (New York: Privately published, 1956), 107.

132 *"a gamester, a whoremaster":* William Aitchison to Charles Steuart, Oct 17, 1770; James Parker to Charles Steuart, April 19, 1771, quoted in David, *Dunmore's New World*, 43; *Revolutionary Virginia*, 2: 86; Hillsborough to Dunmore, Feb. 11, 1771. George Morrow details the governor's affairs with Kitty Blair and Susannah Randolph in *A Cock and Bull for Kitty: Lord Dunmore and the Affairs that Ruined the British Cause in Virginia* (Williamsburg: Telford Publications, 2011), drawing heavily upon Frank L. Dewey, "Thomas Jefferson and a Williamsburg Scandal: The Case of Blair v. Blair," *VHMB* 89 (1981): 44–63.

133 *"a very unfavorable opinion":* Richard Bland to Thomas Adams, Aug. 1, 1771, VHS.

133 *"searched through the world":* Lee to Macaulay, Nov. 29, 1775, James Curtis Ballagh, ed., *The Letters of Richard Henry Lee* (2 vols., New York: The Macmillan Company, 1911–1914), 1: 162. The best overall assessment of Dunmore's character is John E. Selby, *Dunmore* (Williamsburg: Virginia Independence Bicentennial Commission, 1977).

133 *"strong guard":* Dunmore to the Earl of Dartmouth, March 31, 1773, *Burgesses Journals, 1773–1776*, ix–xi. Dartmouth had succeeded Hillsborough as secretary of state for North America. The most detailed treatment of the Pittsylvania forgeries remains Douglas Southall Freeman, *George Washington: A Biography*, vol. 3, *Planter and Patriot* (New York: Charles Scribner's Sons, 1951), 309–15.

133 *"knowing how ineffectual":* Dunmore to Dartmouth, March 31, 1773, *Burgesses Journals, 1773–1776*, ix–xi, emphasis added.

133 *"usual mode":* Ibid.

133 *unusually powerful committee: Burgesses Journals, 1773–1776*, 19–20, 22.

134 *"the safety of the innocent":* Ibid., 22, emphasis added.

134 *news from Rhode Island:* Steven Harley Park, "The Burning of the H.M.S. *Gaspee* and the Limits of Eighteenth-Century British Imperial Power" (PhD diss., University of Connecticut, 2005), 15–27; William R. Leslie, "The *Gaspee* Affair: A Study of Its Constitutional Significance," *Mississippi Valley Historical Review* 39 (1952): 233–56; William R. Staples, *Documentary History of*

the Destruction of the Gaspee (Providence, R.I., 1845), 3–7. Often described as a single-masted sloop, the *Gaspee* had been refitted as a two-masted schooner in 1767 or 1768.

134 *"five times the magnitude":* Attorney General Edward Thurlow quoted in Thomas, *Townshend Duties Crisis,* 229, and Lawrence Henry Gipson, *The Triumphant Empire: Britain Sails into the Storm, 1770–1776,* vol. 12 of *The British Empire Before the American Revolution* (New York: Alfred A. Knopf, 1965), 30.

134 *"the inestimable priviledge":* Burgesses Journals, *1766–1769,* 214.

135 *"beyond the Sea":* "Providentia," *Providence Gazette,* Jan. 9, 1773; Lynne Withey, *Urban Growth in Colonial Rhode Island: Newport and Providence in the Eighteenth Century* (Albany: State University of New York, 1984), 15; Edward M. Cook, Jr., "Enjoying and Defending Charter Privileges: Corporate Status and Political Culture in Eighteenth-Century Rhode Island," in Robert Olwell and Alan Tully, eds., *Cultures and Identities in Colonial British America* (Baltimore: Johns Hopkins University Press, 2006), 244–68.

135 *"old and leading members":* Jefferson Autobiography, 6–7.

135 *"usual mode":* Revolutionary Virginia, 2: 6.

136 *"an understanding":* Jefferson Autobiography, 6.

136 *"contrived":* Lee to Dickinson, April 4, 1773, *Letters of Richard Henry Lee,* 1: 84; compare Lee to Samuel Adams, Feb. 4, 1773, ibid., 1: 82–83.

136 *"his great worth":* Jefferson Autobiography, 6–7.

136 *"correspondence and communication":* Burgesses Journal, *1773–1776,* 28; *Revolutionary Virginia,* 1: 91–92.

136 *"too much unanimity":* Wirt, *Henry,* 109–10. The student, then about twenty, was the future jurist St. George Tucker.

137 *"bilious fever":* Revolutionary Virginia, 2: 11–16. Carr's body was the first burial in the graveyard at Monticello; Malone, *Jefferson the Virginian,* 160–61.

137 *"If the other colonies":* Burgesses Journal, *1773–1776,* 28; *Revolutionary Virginia,* 2: 11–21; Jacob M. Price, "Who Was John Norton? A Note on the Historical Character of Some Eighteenth-Century London Virginia Firms," *WMQ* 3d ser., 19 (1962): 400–407.

137 *"a Congress will grow":* Thomas Cushing to Arthur Lee, April 22, 1773, in Bancroft, *History of the United States,* 4: 456.

137 *"Measures proposed":* Ezra Stiles to Mr. Spencer, ca. May 1773, in Abiel Holmes, *Life of Ezra Stiles* (Boston, 1798), 167–68; Ammerman, *In the Common Cause,* 22–23.

137 *"The Americans would soon":* Dunmore quoted in William Strahan to David Hall, Jan. 11, 1770, "Correspondence Between William Strahan and David Hall, 1763–1777," *Pennsylvania Magazine of History and Biography* 11 (1887): 224–25; Selby, *Dunmore,* 3–4, 9, 14.

137 *Henry closeted himself:* Acting essentially as an oral historian, Nathaniel Pope supplied William Wirt with two versions of John Overton's account of Henry's confidential remarks at his uncle's house: "Anecdotes Relative [to]

Patrick Henry for Wm Wirt, Esqr., No. 1" and Report "No. 2" for William Wirt, both in Patrick Henry Papers, LC. Robert Meade misread the location and altered the probable date of this conversation; *Patriot in the Making*, 334–35.

138 *"whether he supposed"*: Pope, Report "No. 2."

138 *"But do you think"*: "Anecdotes Relative [to] Patrick Henry, No. 1."

138 *"I will be candid"*: Ibid.

139 *"rummaged"*: Jefferson Autobiography, 7–8.

139 *"cooked up a resolution"*: Ibid.

139 *"engrossed"*: Mason to Martin Cockburn, May 26, 1774, *Mason Papers*, 1: 190–91.

139 *"opportunity of conversing"*: Ibid.

140 *"whose grave and religious character"*: Jefferson Autobiography, 7–8; *Revolutionary Virginia*, 1: 94–95.

140 *"Day of Fasting"*: *Revolutionary Virginia*, 1: 93–95.

140 *"the College Member"*: Carter Diary, 818.

140 *"It certainly deserves notice"*: Burgesses Journals, *1773–1776*, 132; Carter Diary, 818. I substituted *prayers* for Carter's liturgical term "Collects."

140 *"an attack made"*: *Revolutionary Virginia*, 1: 97–98.

141 *"We were divided"*: Ibid., 1: 101–02.

141 *"Parliament's war"*: Carter Diary, 817.

141 *more complicated in Virginia*: Ammerman, *In the Common Cause*, 30–39, explains the subtle nuances of these debates.

142 *Sunday afternoon, December 4*: VG (Pinkney), Dec. 9, 1774.

142 *"piteous and melancholy"*: *Revolutionary Virginia*, 1: 101. Deference remains a complex dynamic, but the gentry's careful attention to their constituents' opinions laid the foundation for Virginia's remarkable unanimity throughout the Revolution. The summer 1774 petitions fill sixty pages, 108–68, but students consulting vols. 1 and 2 of *Revolutionary Virginia* should be alert to their chronological overlap for the seventeen months from March 12, 1773, through Aug. 25, 1774.

142 *"Plan of Conduct"*: *Revolutionary Virginia* 1: 139.

142 *"of the future Policy"*: Ibid., 1: 139–40.

143 *"any measures"*: Ibid., 1: 112, 132, 149. Three days into the August convention, Clementina Rind announced that she did not have space to publish the "spirited and determined" statements from Amelia, King George, King William, Lancaster, Lunenburg, Mecklenburg, Northumberland, Orange, and Warwick counties and "a few other resolves." *VG* (Rind), Aug. 4, 1774.

143 *"political Orthodoxy"*: Madison to William Bradford, Jr., July 1, 1774, *Madison Papers*, 115, 117n7. The father of Madison's friend was publisher of the *Pennsylvania Journal*.

143 *"Let it suffice"*: *Revolutionary Virginia*, 1: 139.

143 *"Parliaments of their own"*: Ibid., 1: 158.

143 *"his American Assemblies"*: Ibid., 1: 167.

143 *only four:* The Culpeper resolution was reprinted in *Dunlap's Pennsylvania Packet*, July 25; Spotsylvania's in the *New-York Journal*, July 29; Fairfax's in the *Boston Gazette*, Aug. 8; and Richmond County's in the *Newport Mercury*, Aug. 15, 1774.

143 *"should preside":* **Revolutionary Virginia**, 1: 227–29; Randolph, *History of Virginia*, 206.

144 *"All America look up":* **Revolutionary Virginia**, 2: 122.

144 *"went to the Coffee House":* John Adams, *Diary and Autobiography*, ed. L. H. Butterfield et al. (4 vols., Cambridge: Harvard University Press, 1961), 2: 109.

Chapter 12: Congress in Philadelphia

145 *"very sociable":* John Adams diary entry, Sept. 2, 1774, *Letters of Delegates*, 1: 7; Robert Earle Graham, "The Taverns of Colonial Philadelphia," *Transactions of the American Philosophical Society*, n.s. 43 (1953): 323.

146 *"the Sam. Adams of Phyladelphia":* John Adams diary entry, Aug. 30, 1774, *Letters of Delegates*, 1: 4; Merrill Jensen, *The Founding of a Nation: A History of the American Revolution, 1763–1776* (New York: Oxford University Press, 1968), 490–97. Carpenter's Hall was the meeting place of the radical-leaning Committee of Forty-three, of which Thomson was secretary; Richard Alan Ryerson, *The Revolution Is Now Begun: The Radical Committees of Philadelphia, 1765–1776* (Philadelphia: University of Pennsylvania Press, 1978), 90–91.

146 *"highly agreeable":* Silas Deane to Elizabeth Deane, Aug. 31–Sept 5, 1774; *Letters of Delegates*, 1: 20.

146 *"They are sociable":* Silas Deane to Elizabeth Deane, Sept. 3 and Sept. 10, 1774, *Letters of Delegates*, 17, 61–62.

147 *"the use of such Books":* Hayes, *Mind of a Patriot*, 68; Jack P. Greene, *The Intellectual Heritage of the Constitutional Era: The Delegates' Library* (Philadelphia: Library Company of Philadelphia, 1986), 5.

147 *Henry's printed bookplate:* Hayes, *Mind of a Patriot*, 119. Henry's great-granddaughter Elizabeth Henry Lyons presented the volume to the Library of Congress on Jan. 19, 1914, thereby saving it from destruction when her home at Red Hill burned in 1919.

147 *"When we take up arms":* The quoted and earmarked passage is in the Library of Congress's copy of Leland's translation of *Orations of Demosthenes* at pp. 33–34. For John Adams's marginalia, see Zoltan Haraszti, *John Adams and the Prophets of Progress* (Cambridge: Harvard University Press, 1952).

147 *"minister's gray":* John Fanning Watson, *Annals of Philadelphia and Pennsylvania in the Olden Time . . .* (Philadelphia, 1850), 422.

147 *"But as he proceeded":* Thomson's recollection passed from William White, a chaplain to Congress and later bishop of Philadelphia, to Dr. Thomas C. James and then to John Fanning Watson, who recorded the anecdote in his *Annals of Philadelphia and Pennsylvania in the Olden Time . . .* (1st ed., Phila-

delphia, 1830) quoted from 1850 ed., 421–22. Benjamin L. Lossing cited Watson but inexplicably reworded the anecdote for his *Pictorial Field Book of the Revolution* (New York, 1850), 61.

148 *"Fleets and Armies":* John Adams's Notes on Debates, Sept. 6, 1774; James Duane's Notes on Debates, Sept. 6, 1774, *Letters of Delegates,* 1: 28, 30.

148 *"We are in a State of Nature":* Adams's Notes and Duane's Notes, Sept. 6, 1774; Samuel Ward Diary, Sept. 9, 1774, *Letters of Delegates,* 1: 28, 30, 59.

148 *"the laws":* Worthington Chauncey Ford et al., eds., *Journals of the Continental Congress, 1774–1789* (34 vols., Washington, D.C.: Government Printing Office, 1904–1937), 1: 28.

149 *"amiable in his manners":* George W. Corner, ed., *The Autobiography of Benjamin Rush: His "Travels Through Life" together with his Commonplace Book for 1789–1813* (Princeton: Princeton University Press for the American Philosophical Society, 1948), 110–11.

149 *"Broken Hints":* Adams, *Diary and Autobiography,* Butterfield et al., eds. 2: 135–38.

149 *"with great attention":* Ibid.

149 *"By God":* Ibid.

150 *"In the Congress of 1774":* John Adams to Thomas Jefferson, July 18, 1818, Lester J. Cappon, ed., *The Adams-Jefferson Letters: The Complete Correspondence Between Thomas Jefferson and Abigail and John Adams* (Chapel Hill: University of North Carolina Press, 1959), 392.

150 *Burlington meetinghouse:* Now a Society of Friends conference center, the Burlington meetinghouse had played host to the Philadelphia Yearly Meeting in alternate years from 1685 to 1750; Donald Janson, "Burlington Awaits Quakers," *New York Times,* Sept. 6, 1981.

150 *"Although a stranger":* Allinson to Henry, Oct. 17, 1774, Allinson Family Papers, 1710–1939; Quaker and Special Collections, Haverford College, Philadelphia. I am grateful to Amanda Robiolio for tracking down and photocopying this letter.

150 *"to give a Vital blow":* Allinson's letter was characteristic of the American Quakers' early antislavery lobbying in other letters to Henry. Beyond the series of rhetorical questions raising religious and philosophical arguments against slavery, Allinson outlined no concrete legislative proposal and declared that "I shall not suggest in what manner" Congress might accede to his request.

151 *"a Declaration of Warr":* Silas Deane's Diary, Oct. 1, 1774; Richard Henry Lee's Proposed Resolution, Oct. 3, 1774, *Letters of Delegates,* 1: 113, 138–39, 140; Rakove, *Beginnings of National Politics,* 56.

151 *"Preparation for Warr":* Silas Deane's Diary, Oct. 3, 1774, *Letters of Delegates,* 1: 139, 140; Washington to Mason, April 5, 1769, *Washington Papers, Colonial,* 8: 177; *Mason Papers,* 96.

151 *Cicero and Demosthenes had their way:* Rakove, *Beginnings of National Politics,* 56–58.

152 *"a horrid opinion":* John Adams diary entry, Oct., 11, 1774, *Letters of Delegates,* 1: 173.

152 *"To the KING":* Editor William Bradford acknowledged receipt of Scipio's essay on Sept. 21 (*Pennsylvania Journal,* Sept. 21, 1774) and published it on his front page Oct. 6.

152 *proprietor of the London Coffeehouse:* Graham, "Taverns of Colonial Philadelphia," 320–24; Mark Evans Bryan, "'Sliding into Monarchical Extravagance': Cato at Valley Forge and the Testimony of William Bradford Jr.," *WMQ,* 3d ser., 67 (2010): 131.

152 *chosen pen name:* Gary Remer, "The Classical Orator as Political Representative: Cicero and the Modern Concept of Representation," *Journal of Politics* 72 (2010): 1067–69; J. Jackson Barlow, "The Education of Statesmen in Cicero's 'De Republica,'" *Polity* 19 (1987): 372–74.

152 *"willful mal-administration":* Scipio, "To the KING," *Pennsylvania Journal,* Oct. 6, 1774.

153 *"the Guardian":* Ibid.

154 *"the breath of a tyrant":* John Trenchard and Thomas Gordon, *Cato's Letters,* no. 73, April 21, 1722, Ronald Hamowy, ed., *Cato's Letters: or, Essays on Liberty, Civil and Religious* (Indianapolis: Liberty Fund, 1995), 541–42.

154 *"Your sun of glory":* Scipio, "To the KING," *Pennsylvania Journal,* Oct. 6, 1774.

155 *yet another petition:* Edwin Wolf II, "The Authorship of the 1774 Address to the King Restudied," *WMQ,* 3d ser., 22 (1965): 190–224. The first page of Henry's manuscript is reproduced on p. 203.

156 *effort to foster unanimity:* David Ammerman's "A Note on Consensus" (which reflects the similar perspective in Marston, *King and Congress,* and Rakove, *Beginnings of National Politics*) demonstrated that the First Continental Congress was more radical than depicted by historians who relied too heavily on Joseph Galloway's reminiscences; Ammerman, *In the Common Cause,* 89–101.

156 *"One general Congress":* Deane to Henry, Jan. 2, 1775, *Letters of Delegates,* 1: 291.

157 *locus of American sovereignty:* On this theme, see especially Marston, *King and Congress.*

157 *continental boycott:* Jacob M. Price, *Capital and Credit in British Overseas Trade: The View from the Chesapeake, 1700–1776* (Cambridge: Harvard University Press, 1980), 162; Woody Holton, *Forced Founders: Indians, Debtors, Slaves, and the Making of the American Revolution in Virginia* (Chapel Hill: University of North Carolina Press, 1999), 102. Specific procedures for auctioning contraband according to the Continental Association are explained in *Revolutionary Virginia,* 2: 191–92.

157 *"War is unavoidable":* John Dickinson to Josiah Quincy, Jr., October 28, 1774, *Letters of Delegates,* 1: 251.

157 *"in a State of Rebellion":* Marston, *King and Congress,* 45.

Chapter 13: Blows Must Decide

158 *"bought the Scotchtown"*: Sarah Henry to Anne Henry Christian, Sept. 13, 1771, VHS.

158 *"large commodious dwelling-house"*: *VG* (Rind), Dec. 28, 1769.

158 *"eight rooms upon the first floor"*: *VG* (Richmond: James Hayes), April 22, 1782.

158 *bargain price:* Couvillon, *Patrick Henry's Virginia*, 47–53.

158 *"His children"*: Meredith memorandum, 1805, Elson, *Patrick Henry Speeches and Writings*, 220; Lorri Glover treats the family lives of Henry and his peers in *Founders as Fathers: The Private Lives and Politics of the American Revolutionaries* (New Haven: Yale University Press, 2014).

159 *"My brother Pat"*: Annie Henry Christian to Anne Christian Fleming, Oct. 15, 1774, William Fleming Papers, Cyrus Hall McCormick Library, Washington and Lee University, Lexington, VA (LVA misc. reel 432).

159 *puerperal psychosis:* Margaret G. Spinelli, "Postpartum Psychosis: Detection of Risk and Management," *American Journal of Psychiatry* 166 (2009): 405–8; *Postpartum Psychosis: Severe Mental Illness After Childbirth* (London: Royal College of Psychiatrists, 2014); Christine Hallett, "The Attempt to Understand Puerperal Fever in the Eighteenth and Early Nineteenth Centuries: The Influence of Inflammation Theory," *Medical History* 49 (2005): 1–28.

159 *"beloved companion"*: Meade wrote that Dr. Hinde's account was "written and published by his son [the Reverend Thomas S. Hinde] in 1843" (*Patriot in the Making*, 281) but like too many other careless citations in Meade's volumes, his annotation (ibid., 414n77) supplies no information about that publication. I have not yet located this passage about Sarah's illness among the recollections that the younger Hinde published (sometimes over the pseudonym Theophilus Arminius) in periodicals such as *The Methodist Magazine* 10 (1827): 260–63; *The Methodist Magazine and Quarterly Review*, n.s., 1 (1830): 121–28; and *The American Pioneer* 2 (1843): 363–68—nor has it been found in the Hinde Papers (Section Y) of the Draper Collection; Reuben Gold Thwaites, ed., *Descriptive List of the Manuscript Collections of the State Historical Society of Wisconsin* (Madison: State Historical Society of Wisconsin, 1906), 31–33.

159 *"for the support and maintenance of ideots"*: Hening, *Statutes*, 8: 378; Edward A. Chappell and Travis C. McDonald, "Containing Madness," *Colonial Williamsburg Journal* 7 (1985): 26–29; *VG* (Purdie and Dixon), Feb. 3, 1774; *VG* (Rind), Feb. 10, 1774.

159 *"The loss of his first wife"*: *Philip Mazzei: My Life and Wanderings*, trans. S. Eugene Scalia, ed. Margherita Marchione (Morristown, N.J.: American Institute of Italian Studies, 1980), 278.

160 *"advanced his Fortune"*: Nathaniel Pope, Jr., "Anecdotes Relative [to] Patrick Henry for William Wirt," Sept. 27, 1805, LC; Couvillon, *Patrick Henry's Virginia*, 50.

160 *"Action"*: Plutarch quoted in Meade, *Practical Revolutionary*, 15.

160 *"Shall we call him":* Conrad Speece, *The Mountaineer* (Staunton, Va.: Isaac Collett, 1818), 13. Couvillon, *Demosthenes of His Age*, 108, cited this Staunton edition but actually quoted a variant text from *The Mountaineer* (2d ed., Harrisonburg, Va.: Ananias Davisson, 1818), 22.

160 *"AMERICANS* unite!":* A Virginian, "To the honest Inhabitants of America and true lovers of Liberty," *VG* (Rind), Sept. 1, 1774.

160 *"wished to communicate":* Charles Dabney, "Account of the Gun-Powder Expedition made by Patrick Henry in 1775," Dec. 21, 1805, Patrick Henry Papers, LC.

161 *traditional militia companies:* William L. Shea, *The Virginia Militia in the Seventeenth Century* (Baton Rouge: Louisiana State University Press, 1983).

161 *"to execute all orders":* Dunmore to Dartmouth, Dec. 24, 1774. This account contradicts Michael A. McDonnell's imposition of a class-based interpretation upon the results of his extensive research for *The Politics of War: Race, Class, and Conflict in Revolutionary Virginia* (Chapel Hill: University of North Carolina Press, 2007). In his first chapter alone, McDonnell miscounted and dismissed the county resolutions of July 1774 as elitist propaganda and evidence of social disarray rather than vitality (pp. 33–34, 36) while treating a similar run of July 1775 county resolutions as accurate reflections of popular sentiment (pp. 69–70). His chapter also misrepresented the closing of the courts (p. 35), treated the democratic features of the independent companies as evidence both for gentry exclusiveness (pp. 41–43) and a radical threat to oligarchy (p. 54), and dated the early-seventeenth-century name of the General Assembly as "the creation of a new constitution in 1776" (p. 44n40). Perceptive reviewers of *The Politics of War* include Douglas Bradburn in *Historical Journal* 52 (2009): 836–39; Robert Middlekauff in *AHR* 113 (2008): 174–75; and Steve Rosswurm in *WMQ*, 3d ser, 64 (2008): 827–29.

161 *"universally supported":* Dunmore to Dartmouth, Dec. 24, 1774.

161 *"undutiful people":* Ibid.

162 *"partisans of government":* Ibid. For the disastrous consequences of British leaders' delusive optimism about military support from American loyalists, see Andrew Jackson O'Shaughnessy, *The Men Who Lost America: British Leadership, the American Revolution, and the Fate of the Empire* (New Haven: Yale University Press, 2013), 54, 59–60, 84–86, 136, 163, 187, 189, 193, 273, 353, 359.

162 *"the old and fatal delusion":* O'Hara to the Duke of Grafton, April 20, 1781, George C. Rogers, ed., "Letters of Charles O'Hara to the Duke of Grafton," *South Carolina Historical Magazine* 65 (1964): 177.

162 *"ports should be blocked up":* Dunmore to Dartmouth, Dec. 24, 1774.

162 *"he flew into a rage":* Philip Mazzei: *My Life and Wanderings*, 406n65.

162 *"Your object":* Dartmouth to Gage, Jan. 27, 1775, quoted in Ammerman, *In the Common Cause*, 135, 137; Vice-Admiral Samuel Graves to Philip Stevens, April 22, 1775, William Bell Clark, ed., *Naval Documents of the American Revolution* (11 vols., Washington, D.C.: Naval History Division, 1964–2005),

1: 205–6; George III to Lord North, Nov. 18, 1774, quoted in John Shy, *Toward Lexington: The Role of the British Army in the Coming of the American Revolution* (Princeton: Princeton University Press, 1965), 418.

163 *Lord Dartmouth dispatched:* Ammerman, *In the Common Cause*, 137; Vice-Admiral Graves to Stevens, April 22, 1775; Shy, *Toward Lexington*, 416.

163 *British intentions: VG* (Purdie and Dixon), Supplement, Dec. 8, 1774.

164 *"a set of miscreants":* "Freeholders of Botetourt County to Col. Andrew Lewis and Mr. John Bowyer," *Revolutionary Virginia*, 2: 324–25, printed in *VG* (Dixon and Hunter), March 11, 1775.

Chapter 14: Liberty or Death

165 *119 members: Revolutionary Virginia*, 2: 334–37.

166 *"into a posture":* Ibid., 2: 366.

166 *"mediator":* Ibid., 2: 362–66.

166 *"when we lived":* Ibid.

166 *arming themselves:* Only four counties (Chesterfield, Essex, Henrico, and Louisa) had not already created independent companies when the convention met; Mays, *Pendleton*, 353n12.

166 *"that this Colony":* Revolutionary Virginia, 2: 366.

167 *Second Amendment:* David Thomas Konig, "The Second Amendment: A Missing Transatlantic Context for the Historical Meaning of 'the Right of the People to Keep and Bear Arms,'" *Law and History Review* 22 (2004): 119–59.

167 *"Pretext of taxing":* Revolutionary Virginia, 2: 366–67.

167 *"premature":* St. George Tucker quoted in Moses Coit Tyler, *Patrick Henry* (rev. ed., Boston: Houghton Mifflin, 1898), 137; Mays, *Pendleton*, 2: 4–5; *Henry Correspondence*, 1: 258–59.

167 *"calmly":* Couvillon, *Demosthenes of His Age*, 24.

168 *"very opposite":* Wirt, *Sketches*, 120. The best discussion of the veracity of William Wirt's and St. George Tucker's reconstruction of Henry's most famous speech is Stephen T. Olsen, "Patrick Henry's 'Liberty or Death' Speech: A Study in Disputed Authorship," in Thomas W. Benson, ed., *American Rhetoric: Context and Criticism* (Carbondale: Southern Illinois University Press, 1989), 19–65.

168 *"transformed resistance":* Peter S. Onuf, *Biography* 32 (2009): 854.

168 *"I have but one lamp":* Wirt, *Sketches*, 120–21.

168 *"Shall we try argument":* Ibid., 121–22.

168 *"Our petitions have been slighted":* Ibid., 122. "When he reached that point in his speech where he said, 'We must fight!' . . . his whole manner changed," St. George Tucker recalled. "Imagine that you heard a voice from heaven uttering the words, 'We must fight,' as the doom of Fate and you may have some idea of the speaker, the assembly to whom he addressed himself, and the audi[ence], of which I was one." Couvillon, *Demosthenes of His Age*, 116–17.

169 *"They tell us that we are weak"*: Wirt, *Sketches*, 122–23.

169 *"There is no retreat"*: Ibid., 123.

169 *"Peace, Peace"*: Jeremiah 6:14.

169 *"but there is no peace"*: Wirt, *Sketches*, 123.

169 *"almost visible"*: Couvillon, *Demosthenes of His Age*, 146. John Tyler and John Roane recalled Henry's use of the letter opener in imitation of Cato of Utica, who had stabbed himself rather than submit to Caesar; ibid., 121, 147.

170 *"Men looked beside themselves"*: Ibid., 24.

170 *"Let me be buried at this spot"*: Ibid., 29; Tyler, *Patrick Henry*, 140–52; *Revolutionary Virginia*, 2: 368–70.

171 *"he would wait for no orders"*: Emory G. Evans, *Thomas Nelson and the Revolution in Virginia* (Williamsburg: Virginia Independence Bicentennial Commission, 1978), 2–12; Evans, *Thomas Nelson of Yorktown: Revolutionary Virginian* (Williamsburg: Colonial Williamsburg Foundation, 1975), 41; Evans, *A "Topping People": The Rise and Decline of Virginia's Old Political Elite, 1680–1790* (Charlottesville: University of Virginia Press, 2009), 184–91.

171 *65 to 60*: *Revolutionary Virginia*, 2: 369.

171 *"What flattened their ardour"*: James Parker to Charles Steuart, April 6, 1775, Charles Steuart Papers, National Library of Scotland; LVA microfilm, misc. reel 3704; John Taylor of Caroline to Wilson Cary Nicholas, Oct. 25, 1818, Massachusetts Historical Society, Boston. Taylor attended the convention as a protégé of Edmund Pendleton. His letter to Treasurer Nicholas's son describes the alternative motion; I am grateful to J. Jefferson Looney for a transcript of this letter. David Mays and others have focused on the larger numbers of troops Nicholas proposed but overlooked his emphasis upon gentry leadership; Mays, *Pendleton*, 2: 7, 354–55nn18–19.

171 *"infamously insolent"*: Parker to Steuart, April 6, 1775.

172 *"attempt to execute"*: Pendleton to Fleming, March 30, 1775, in Mays, *Pendleton*, 2: 8.

172 *"a redress of grievances"*: Pendleton's autobiography, in Mays, *Pendleton*, 1: 357.

172 *"His doctrines"*: *Philip Mazzei: My Life and Wanderings*, 221; "Memoirs of Philip Mazzei," trans. E. C. Branchi, *WMQ*, 2d ser., 9 (1929): 249.

Chapter 15: Gunpowder

173 *Colins and his squad*: Accounts of the magazine incident include Ivor Noël Hume, *1775: Another Part of the Field* (New York: Alfred A. Knopf, 1966), 135–51; *Revolutionary Virginia*, 3: 3–24; Selby, *Revolution in Virginia*, 1–6; and *Burgesses Journals, 1773–1776*, 223–24; 231–33; as well as contemporary reports and documents in the *Virginia Gazette*s. For Burwell's Ferry, see William M. Kelso, *Kingsmill Plantations, 1619–1800: Archaeology of Country Life in Colonial Virginia* (2d ed., Jamestown, Va.: WMK Press, 2003), 47–50.

173 *"in readiness"*: Journal of the *Magdalen*, William Bell Clark et al., eds., *Naval*

Documents of the American Revolution (11 vols., Washington, D.C.: Naval History Division, 1964–2005), 1: 204; *Burgesses Journals, 1773–1776*, 231. The schooner's journal contradicts the contention that Colins brought his marines to the palace on April 15 and hid there until the raid five days later; Hume, *1775: Another Part of the Field*, 138.

174 *"at a little distance":* Dunmore to Dartmouth, May 1, 1775, C. O. 5/1375, VCRP microfilm reel 33.

174 *"to a place":* VG (Dixon and Hunter), April 22, 1775.

174 *"in the night time":* Journal of the *Magdalen, Naval Documents,* 1: 212.

174 *"the People":* Dunmore to Dartmouth, May 1, 1775.

175 *"had no reason but the Timidity of her Sex":* Burgesses Journals, *1773–1776*, 232.

175 *"entirely overturned":* Dunmore to Dartmouth, May 1, 1775.

175 *"His Lordship then swore":* Burgesses Journals, *1773–1776*, 231.

175 *"setting up the Royal Standard":* Ibid.

176 *fire upon Yorktown:* Emory G. Evans, *Thomas Nelson of Yorktown: Revolutionary Virginian* (Williamsburg: Colonial Williamsburg Foundation, 1975), 47.

176 *damaging excerpts: Revolutionary Virginia,* 3: 65–67, 90–91; *VG* (Pinkney), April 28, May 4, 1775; *VG* (Purdie), May 5, 1775.

176 *"very disagreeable intelligence": Revolutionary Virginia,* 3: 6, 71.

176 *"upwards of 2000 men":* Ibid., 3: 6.

176 *"so many brave hearty men":* Michael Wallace to Gustavus Brown Wallace, May 14, 1775, quoted in Mays, *Pendleton,* 355n43.

177 *"firmly persuaded": Revolutionary Virginia,* 3: 6–7, 64; Douglas Southall Freeman, *George Washington: A Biography,* vol. 3, *Planter and Patriot* (New York: Charles Scribner's Sons, 1951), 414–15. Freeman disputes the assertions advanced by John Daly Burk and popularized by Charles Campbell that Edmund Pendleton and George Washington also sent written advice to the Spotsylvanians; ibid., 415n88.

177 *"well armed and disciplined men": Revolutionary Virginia,* 3: 63–65, 70–71.

177 *"defend the laws":* Ibid., 3: 69–71.

177 *Peyton Randolph left Williamsburg:* Ibid., 7, 72n4; Freeman, *Washington,* 3: 410–18; Mays, *Pendleton,* 17–19.

178 *"unsatisfactory": Revolutionary Virginia,* 3: 61, 63, 85.

178 *"voted for a march":* Ibid., 3: 70, emphasis added.

179 *"As soon as these objects":* Samuel Meredith memorandum, 1805, Manuscripts Department, LC, printed in Elson, *Patrick Henry Speeches and Writings,* 210–20. Elson expressed reservations about the accuracy of Meredith's account of the gunpowder expedition because "Meredith gives himself far too important a role in the incident" (ibid., 209, 260; cf. Morgan, *The True Patrick Henry,* 204–5)—an assessment that underestimated the collegial aspect of Henry's leadership style and Henry's shrewd encouragement of Meredith's continued participation and support.

179 *"a fortunate circumstance"*: Dabney memorandum, 1805, LC, printed in Elson, *Patrick Henry Speeches and Writings*, 83.

180 *"was generally condemned"*: Dabney memorandum, 1805, LC, printed in Elson, *Patrick Henry Speeches and Writings*, 223.

180 *"every Moment"*: Dunmore to Dartmouth, May 15, 1775, C.O. 5/1375.

180 *"actively encouraging"*: Ibid.

181 *"strict orders"*: Samuel Meredith memorandum, 1805, Manuscripts Department, LC.

181 *"Our thick-headed Treasurer"*: James Parker to Charles Steuart, May 6, 1775, Charles Steuart Papers, National Library of Scotland: LVA microfilm, misc. reel 3704.

181 *"upon the strength"*: *Revolutionary Virginia*, 3: 9.

181 *"for the gunpowder"*: Henry to Corbin, May 4, 1775, *Revolutionary Virginia*, 3: 87–88.

182 *"The affair of the powder"*: Henry to Nicholas, May 4, 1775, *Revolutionary Virginia*, 3: 88.

182 *"more safe"*: Ibid., 3: 88, 111–13, 145.

182 *"returned triumphantly"*: Dunmore to Dartmouth, May 15, 1775.

182 *"restore peace and harmony"*: *Revolutionary Virginia*, 3: 80–82.

182 *"flew into an outrageous passion"*: "[Memoir of] Governor Page," *Virginia Historical Register and Literary Notebook* 3 (1850): 149. George T. Morrow II highlights this personal rivalry in *"We Must Fight!": The Private War Between Patrick Henry and Lord Dunmore* (Williamsburg: Telford Publications, 2012).

183 *"retreat to the Man of War"*: Dunmore to Dartmouth, May 15, 1775.

183 *"were so fatigued"*: *VG* (Pinkney), May 4, 1775.

183 *"The affair of the powder"*: Henry to Nicholas, May 4, 1775, *Henry Correspondence*, 1: 284–85; *Revolutionary Virginia*, 3: 88.

183 *"a certain* Patrick Henry*"*: *VG* (Dixon and Hunter), May 13, 1775; *Revolutionary Virginia*, 3: 100–101.

184 *"to fly to arms"*: Dabney memorandum, 1805, in Elson, *Patrick Henry Speeches and Writings*, 83.

184 *"who opposed the measure"*: *Henry Correspondence*, 1: 287–90.

184 *"the hostilities to the Northward"*: Ibid.

184 *Using the pen name "Brutus"*: Commentary about the Brutus essay in vol. 3 of *Revolutionary Virginia* is confused. The editorial note that mentions Brutus's defense of Henry precedes a text published by Purdie on July 14 that did not mention Henry (ibid., 3: 125–26, 126–32), while the second Brutus letter (which defended Henry and was dated May 19 when Purdie published it in a two-page Supplement on Aug. 4, 1775) is absent from *Revolutionary Virginia* but was reprinted in Peter Force, *American Archives*, ser. 4, 2: 641–44, and *Sons of the Revolution in the State of Virginia Quarterly Magazine* 3 (1924): 19–28.

184 *"hearty approbation":* The *Virginia Gazette*s published statements from Albemarle, Caroline, Culpeper, Fincastle, Frederick, Hanover, James City, Loudoun, Louisa, Orange, Prince Edward, Prince William, and Spotsylvania counties between May 8 and July 10, 1775; *Revolutionary Virginia*, 3: 104–277 passim (quoted at 277).

185 *"pusillanimous":* Nathaniel Pope, "Particulars relative [to] Patrick Henrys Expedition," June 23, 1806, LC; *Henry Correspondence*, 1: 291; Meade, *Practical Revolutionary*, 48.

185 *one last outrage:* Selby, *Revolution in Virginia*, 42–43; Hume, *1775: Another Part of the Field*, 212–19.

185 *"with the opprobrious title":* VG (Purdie) Supplement, June 9, 1775.

186 *"the Cry among the People":* Dartmouth to Dunmore, June 25, 1775, C.O. 5/1375.

186 *"Old Dick Bland":* James Parker to Charles Steuart, June 12, 1775, Charles Steuart Papers.

186 *"deserved Assassination":* Pendleton to Joseph Chew, June 15, 1775, *Letters of Delegates*, 1: 490.

186 *"I am no longer interested":* Selby, *Revolution in Virginia*, 45; John J. Reardon, *Edmund Randolph: A Biography* (New York: Macmillan, 1975), 22.

Chapter 16: Commander in Chief

187 *"a number of armed people":* Connecticut Courant, May 15, 1775; *Pennsylvania Packet*, May 18, 1775; *Story and Humphreys's Pennsylvania Mercury*, May 19 and 26, 1775; *Pennsylvania Ledger*, May 20, 1775; *New England Chronicle or Essex Gazette*, May 25, 1775; *Connecticut Gazette*, May 26, 1775.

187 *first resounding victory:* Middlekauf, *The Glorious Cause*, 281–83.

187 *"We have nothing":* Eliza Farmer to Jack Halroyd, June 28, 1775, quoted in Mays, *Pendleton*, 2: 22.

187 *Pendleton went so far:* Charles Francis Adams, ed., *Works of John Adams* (10 vols., Boston: 1856), 2: 416–18; Mays, *Pendleton*, 2: 24–25; Douglas Southall Freeman, *George Washington: A Biography*, vol. 3, *Planter and Patriot* (New York: Charles Scribner's Sons, 1951), 434.

187 *"firmly Cements":* Eliphalet Dyer to Joseph Trumbull, June 17, 1775, *Letters of Delegates*, 1: 499.

188 *"of so important a trust":* Washington to John Parke Custis (Martha's son by her first marriage), June 19, 1775; *Washington Papers, Revolutionary War* 1: 15. He expressed the same sentiments in letters to Martha Washington, June 18, Burwell Bassett, June 19, and his brother John Augustine Washington, June 20, 1775, ibid., 1: 3–4, 12, 19.

188 *"About this time":* Autobiography of Benjamin Rush, 113.

188 *the president went home:* Randolph left Philadelphia on May 24, *Pennsylvania Ledger*, May 27, 1775. Jefferson served in Congress from June 21 to July 31; Malone, *Jefferson the Virginian*, 202–8.

188 *"Our cause is just": Jefferson Papers*, 187–92, 213–19 (quoted at p. 217, emphasis added). Dickinson toned down the peculiar explanation of imperial relations that Jefferson had repeated from his *Summary View*, but Julian P. Boyd disproved the Virginian's assertion that his drafts were "too strong for Mr. Dickinson"; Boyd, "The Disputed Authorship of the Declaration on the Causes and Necessity of Taking Up Arms, 1775," *Pennsylvania Magazine of History and Biography* 74 (1950): 51–73.

188 *"We are undoing":* Robert Wormeley Carter to Landon Carter, Aug. 5, 1775, quoted in Mays, *Pendleton*, 2: 358n67.

189 *"Bablers":* Mason to Washington, Oct. 14, 1775, *Mason Papers*, 1: 255.

189 *"obligatory Force":* Ibid.; Selby, *Revolution in Virginia*, 50–51; *Revolutionary Virginia*, 3: 409, 417, and passim.

189 *"commander in chief":* "Commission for the Colonel of the First Regiment," Aug. 26, 1775, *Revolutionary Virginia*, 3: 498.

189 *"the Majority":* *Revolutionary Virginia*, 3: 400–401; Selby, *Revolution in Virginia*, 50–51.

190 *"made a Capitol mistake":* George Washington to Lt. Col. Joseph Reed, March [7], 1776, *Washington Papers, Revolutionary War*, 3: 369.

190 *"Oh that I was":* John Adams to Abigail Adams, May 29, 1775, *Letters of Delegates*, 1: 417; John E. Ferling, "'Oh that I was a Soldier': John Adams and the Anguish of War," *American Quarterly* 36 (1984): 258–75; Charles Royster, *A Revolutionary People at War: The Continental Army and American Character, 1775–1783* (Chapel Hill: University of North Carolina Press, 1979), 25–53.

190 *mixing civilian and military authority:* H. Trevor Colbourn, *The Lamp of Experience: Whig History and the Intellectual Origins of the American Revolution* (Chapel Hill: University of North Carolina Press, 1965), 21–56.

190 *"Vexation and Disgust":* Mason to Washington, Oct. 14, 1775, *Mason Papers*, 1: 255.

191 *From their common roots:* "Cato," *VG* (Dixon and Hunter), March 30, 1776. David J. Mays devoted a few unsympathetic pages to the Henry-Pendleton relationship, but Spencer Roane challenged the report of Henry borrowing law books from Pendleton; Mays, *Pendleton*, 1: 239–48; Spencer Roane memorandum, 1805, Manuscripts Department, LC, printed in Elson, *Patrick Henry Speeches and Writings*, 19–20.

191 *"absolute direction":* Joseph Jones to William Woodford, Dec. 13, 1775, *Henry Correspondence*, 1: 341; *Revolutionary Virginia*, 3: 411, 456, 460n7; Mays, *Pendleton*, 2: 35–36; "Commission for the Colonel of the First Regiment," Aug. 26, 1775, *Revolutionary Virginia*, 3: 498. One delegate later argued that the convention had *not* intended to make the colonel of the First Regiment "commander-in-chief"; "Cato," *VG* (Dixon and Hunter), March 30, 1776.

Chapter 17: Norfolk Destroyed

192 *"a stroke of the palsey"*: A Virginian, *VG* (Purdie), Nov. 10, 1775.

192 *"ministerial squadron"*: Ibid; Selby, *Revolution in Virginia*, 63–64; Eva Sheppard Wolf, *Race and Liberty in the New Nation: Emancipation in Virginia from the Revolution to Nat Turner's Rebellion* (Baton Rouge: Louisiana University Press, 2006), 15.

193 *"distance"*: Charles Lee to Benjamin Rush, Oct. 10, 1776, quoted in Jonathan Gregory Rossie, *The Politics of Command in the American Revolution* (Syracuse: Syracuse University Press, 1975), 65.

193 *"familiarity"*: George Washington to John Hancock, Sept. 21, 1776, ibid.

193 *"regarded his"*: The quoted language is Hugh Blair Grigsby's report of Paul Carrington's "testimony" to his son Clement Carrington; Grigsby, *The Virginia Convention of 1776* (Richmond: J. W. Randolph, 1855), 52–53n.

193 *"studies had been directed"*: Cato, *VG* (Dixon and Hunter), March 30, 1776.

193 *library tells us:* Hayes, *Mind of a Patriot*, 113, 137; Ira D. Gruber, *Books and the British Army in the Age of the American Revolution* (Chapel Hill: University of North Carolina Press, 2020), 32, 39, 70–71, 149, 202.

193 *Harvey's* The Manual Exercise*:* Frederick R. Goff, "Recent Acquisitions of the Rare Book Division," *Quarterly Journal of the Library of Congress* 28 (1971): 232; Sandra L. Powers, "Studying the Art of War: Military Books Known to American Officers and Their French Counterparts During the Second Half of the Eighteenth Century," *Journal of Military History* 70 (2006): 789–92, 801, 805.

193 *On the advice of George Washington:* Fairfax County Committee, Jan. 17, 1775; "Plan for embodying, arming and disciplining the Militia," March 25, 1775, *Revolutionary Virginia*, 2: 244n3, 375, 379n11.

194 *"the Usual Exercise"*: Brent Tarter, ed., "Orderly Book of the Second Virginia Regiment, September 27, 1775–April 15, 1776," *VMHB* 85 (1977): 165.

194 *Great Bridge:* Selby, *Revolution in Virginia*, 65–66.

194 *"all indented Servants"*: A Proclamation, Nov. 7, 1775, *Revolutionary Virginia*, 4: 334.

194 *Dunmore's edict:* Selby, *Revolution in Virginia*, 66–69; *Revolutionary Virginia*, 4: 340nn6 and 7. Commentary about Dunmore's proclamation is extensive. Helpful introductions include Sylvia Frey, "Between Slavery and Freedom: Virginia Blacks and the American Revolution," *JSH* 49 (1983): 375–98; Sally E. Hadden, *Slave Patrols: Law and Violence in Virginia and the Carolinas* (Cambridge: Harvard University Press, 2001), 158–62; and Francis L. Berkeley, Jr., *Dunmore's Proclamation of Emancipation* (Charlottesville: Tracy W. McGregor Library of the University of Virginia, 1941). Again this account differs from Michael A. McDonnell's *The Politics of War*, 135–74, which projects the peculiar social and political divisions of the Norfolk area, as well as the strategic vulnerability of the Eastern Shore, to the rest of Virginia. Adele Hast's de-

tailed study of these events demonstrates that "outside the Princess Anne–Norfolk area, some semblance of normalcy existed"; *Loyalism in Revolutionary Virginia: The Norfolk Area and the Eastern Shore* (Ann Arbor, Mich.; UMI Research Press, 1982), 60.

195 *a few hundred slaves:* Casandra Pybus, "Jefferson's Faulty Math: The Question of Slave Defections in the American Revolution," *WMQ,* 3d ser., 62 (2005): 243–64.

195 *Purdie printed a broadside:* Proclamation from Head Quarters, Nov. 20, 1775, *Revolutionary Virginia,* 4: 334–35.

195 *"fatal to the publick Safety":* Henry to the County Committees, Nov. 20, 1775, *Revolutionary Virginia,* 4: 435–36, 442n2. In 1766 the General Assembly required each county to appoint slave patrols of a militia officer and up to four militiamen charged with visiting "all negro quarters and other places suspected of entertaining unlawful assemblies of slaves, servants, or other disorderly persons" at least once a month and apprehending any slave found "strolling about from one plantation to another, without a pass from his or her master, mistress or overseer." Patrollers were paid twenty pounds of tobacco for every twelve hours of duty; Hening, *Statutes,* 8: 195–97; Hadden, *Slave Patrols,* 158–62.

195 *"the most extensive good consequence":* Cary to Richard Henry Lee, Dec. 24, 1775, Lee Family Papers, UVA (LVA microfilm misc. reel 3685).

195 *"a strong Breastworke":* William Woodford to Edmund Pendleton, Dec. 4, 1775, *Revolutionary Virginia,* 5: 49.

195 *"absurd, ridiculous":* Lt. Col. John Dalrymple to the Earl of Dumfries, Jan. 4, 1776, C. O. 5/40, VCRP microfilm reel 62; *Revolutionary Virginia,* 5: 8–10; Tarter, "Second Virginia Regiment," 304–5.

195 *"Bullets whistled":* *Revolutionary Virginia,* 5: 8–9; Selby, *Revolution in Virginia,* 72–74.

196 *"to risk the success":* Pendleton to Woodford, Dec. 1, 1775, *Revolutionary Virginia,* 5: 34; Dalrymple to Dumfries, Jan. 4, 1776; Selby, *Revolution in Virginia,* 72–74.

196 *"sacrificed":* *Revolutionary Virginia,* 5: 161.

196 *"like the Mad Man":* Ibid., 5: 109.

196 *"depression":* Ibid., 5: 10.

196 *"a second* Bunker's Hill*":* *VG* (Pinkney), Dec. 13, 1775; *VG* (Purdie), Dec. 15, 1776; Tarter, "Second Virginia Regiment," 305.

196 *"Some people have expressed":* *VG* (Pinkney) Dec. 13, 1775.

197 *flotilla anchored offshore:* Dunmore's fleet anchored in the harbor formed by the Elizabeth River and Hampton Roads not "back out to sea"; McDonnell, *Politics of War,* 162, 164.

197 *"Rule of Congress":* Pendleton to Woodford, Dec. 7, 1775, *Revolutionary Virginia,* 5: 76; Selby, *Revolution in Virginia,* 74; Tarter, "Second Virginia Regiment," 307; Louis VanLoan Naisawald, "Robert Howe's Operations in Virginia, 1775–1776," *VMHB* (1952): 438.

197 *"Friends of Government":* John Johnson to unidentified addressee, Nov. 16, 1775, *Revolutionary Virginia,* 4: 414; Selby, *Revolution in Virginia,* 59–61; Intercepted letters, *Revolutionary Virginia,* 4: 58, 338, 358, 424, 439, 496, and passim.

197 *"Delenda est Norfolk":* Jefferson to Page, Oct. 31, 1775, Jefferson Papers, 1: 251.

197 *"Provisions and Water": Revolutionary Virginia,* 5: 152, 160, 171–72. When Captain Squire signaled his intention of reclaiming the brig *Molly* that he had captured as a prize, Howe and Woodford replied that they would "Fire upon any Boat that attempts to take her away"; ibid., 5: 182.

198 *"Boddy of Troops":* Howe and Woodford to Pendleton, Dec. 15, 1775, *Revolutionary Virginia,* 5: 159–60.

198 *"the ships of war":* H. S. Parsons, ed., "Contemporary English Accounts of the Destruction of Norfolk in 1776," *WMQ,* 2d ser., 13 (1933): 219.

198 *A conflagration:* Tarter, " 'An Infant Borough entirely supported by Commerce': The Great Fire of 1776 and the Rebuilding of Norfolk," *Virginia Cavalcade* 28 (Fall 1978): 52–61; Selby, *Revolution in Virginia,* 81–84.

199 *"the Inhumanity":* Dalrymple to the Earl of Dumfries, Jan. 4, 1776, C. O. 5/40. Robert Howe reported that the destruction of Norfolk was "greatly beneficial to the Public. It was a place that Government could at any time possess" inhabited predominantly by merchants and their dependents who had opposed the Continental Association and lacked "any strong prepossession in favour of America or its cause, suspicious friends therefore at best"; Howe to Pendleton, Jan. 6, 1776, *Revolutionary Virginia,* 5: 355–56.

199 *"Nine-tenths of the town": VG* (Purdie), Supplement, Jan. 5, 1776; Tarter, "An Infant Borough," 52–61; Selby, *Revolutionary Virginia,* 81–84; Howe to Pendleton, Jan. 6, 1776, *Revolutionary Virginia,* 5: 355–56, 417, 420n21.

199 *filled the remaining columns: VG* (Purdie), Supplement, Jan. 5, 1776. See also Jon Kukla, " 'We Should Declare Ourselves Independent': Three Newly Discovered *Virginia Gazette* Essays by Patrick Henry," *Newsletter of the Patrick Henry Memorial Foundation* (Spring–Summer 2008).

199 *"I hope our countrymen": VG* (Purdie), Supplement, Jan. 5, 1776.

200 *"dispirited":* Ibid.

200 *"of British cruelty":* Ibid.

200 *"Dunmore's plots":* Ibid.

200 *"prevail more than":* Samuel Adams to Joseph Warren, Jan. 7, 1776, *Letters of Delegates,* 1: 53.

200 *"The destruction of Norfolk":* Washington to Lt. Col. Joseph Reed, Jan. 31, 1776, *Washington Papers: Revolutionary War,* 3: 224–29. The British navy burned Falmouth, Massachusetts (now Portland, Maine), on October 18, 1775, and threatened another dozen port towns; Kevin Phillips, *1775: A Good Year for Revolution* (New York: Viking, 2012), 343–56.

201 *Fourth Convention: Revolutionary Virginia,* 5: 25–26, 47, 434, 437; Selby, *Revolution in Virginia,* 76.

202 *Patrick Henry's navy: Revolutionary Virginia,* 5: 227–29, 234n17; Dean C. Al-

lard, "The Potomac Navy of 1776," *VMHB* 84 (1976): 411–12; E. M. Sanchez-Saavedra, comp., *A Guide to Virginia Military Organizations in the American Revolution, 1774–1787* (Richmond: Virginia State Library, 1978), 149–74; Gaius Marcus Brumbaugh, *Revolutionary War Records: Virginia Army and Navy Forces with Bounty Land Warrants for Virginia Military District of Ohio* (Washington, D.C.: By the author, 1936), 25, 44, 55–72.

202 *negotiate a peace agreement:* Dunmore to Corbin, Jan. 27, 1776; *Revolutionary Virginia*, 6: 29–30.

202 *"ultimate intentions":* Edmund Pendleton to Corbin, Feb. 19, 1776, ibid., 6: 112–13.

202 *"the first Colony":* Selby, *Revolution in Virginia*, 85–87.

203 *"I could not see":* *Revolutionary Virginia*, 6: 4, 144–45; John Richard Alden, *The South in the Revolution* (Baton Rouge: Louisiana State University Press, 1957), 202–06.

203 *"he could not accept":* Committee of Safety proceedings, Feb. 28, 1776, *Revolutionary Virginia*, 6: 149. Moses Coit Tyler's discussion of the resignation remains useful; Tyler, *Patrick Henry* (rev. ed., Boston: Houghton Mifflin Co., 1898), 177–88.

203 *Henry's resignation":* Rossie, *Politics of Command*, 15–23.

203 *"in which his honour alone was concerned":* *VG* (Purdie), March 1, 1776; *Revolutionary Virginia*, 6: 5–7, 149. All quotations are from Purdie's newspaper, which published the texts of the communications between Henry and his officers as well as Purdie's report of events. Several texts appeared in *VG* (Dixon and Hunter), March 2, 1776. Transcriptions published in *Henry Correspondence*, 1: 348–52, are not entirely reliable.

203 *"went into deep mourning":* *VG* (Purdie), March 1, 1776.

203 *"happy return":* "Address to Patrick Henry … signed by upwards of 90 officers," *VG* (Purdie), March 22, 1776.

203 *"declaring their unwillingness":* *VG* (Purdie), March 1, 1776.

204 *"many Waggon loads of the bones":* Benjamin Henry Latrobe quoted in *Revolutionary Virginia*, 6: 8. Gwynn's Island became part of Mathews County upon the creation of that jurisdiction in 1790.

204 *formerly the merchant ship* Eilbeck: Charles Thomas Long, "Green Water Revolution: The War for American Independence on the Waters of the Southern Chesapeake Theater" (PhD diss., George Washington University, 2005), 84; Selby, *Revolution in Virginia*, 104–6, 124–27.

205 *"become so formidable":* Dunmore to George Germain, July 31, 1776, quoted in Allard, "Potomac Navy of 1776," 426.

Chapter 18: A Free and Independent State

206 *based on motions: Revolutionary Virginia*, 7: 145–48.

206 *"no alternative": Revolutionary Virginia*, 7: 143.

206 *"a Declaration of Rights":* Ibid.

206 *"continental union flag":* Marc Leepson, *Flag: An American Biography* (New York: St. Martin's Press, 2005), 16–19.

207 *services of fasting and prayer:* Worthington Chauncey Ford et al., eds., *Journals of the Continental Congress, 1774–1789* (34 vols., Washington, D.C.: Government Printing Office, 1904–1937), 6: 208–9.

207 *"Be not afraid":* VG (Dixon and Hunter) May 18, 1776; 2 Chron. 20: 15.

207 *"liberty that we enjoyed":* VG (Purdie), March 29, 1776.

208 *Covert French and Spanish support:* Donald E. Reynolds, "Ammunition Supply in Revolutionary Virginia," *VMHB* 73 (1965): 56–63. Every conceivable French motive for supporting the colonies is evaluated in Alexander De Conde, "The French Alliance in Historical Speculation," in Ronald Hoffman and Peter J. Albert, eds., *Diplomacy and Revolution: The Franco-American Alliance of 1778* (Charlottesville: University of Virginia Press, 1981), 1–37.

208 *"sufficient":* Henry to Adams, May 20, 1776, *Henry Correspondence,* 1: 413. Disagreements over issues such as representation did delay the formal adoption of the Articles of Confederation until the war was over.

208 *"Why should we":* VG (Purdie), March 8, 1776.

208 *"free and happy constitution":* Revolutionary Virginia, 7: 111–12.

209 *Archibald Cary in the chair: Revolutionary Virginia,* 6: 471n4; 7: 143, 145n6, 158, 182–83.

209 *"a smart fit of the Gout":* Mason to Richard Henry Lee, May 18, 1776, *Mason Papers,* 271.

209 *"Colonel Mason seems":* Pendleton to Jefferson, May 24, 1776, *Pendleton Letters,* 180; *Jefferson Papers,* 1: 296.

209 *Paine's radical suggestion:* John P. Kaminski, ed., *Citizen Paine: Thomas Paine's Thoughts on Man, Government, Society, and Religion* (Lanham, Md.: Rowman & Littlefield, 2002), 8; Benjamin Ponder, "Independence Unfurled: Common Sense and the Constitution of the American Public" (PhD diss., Northwestern University, 2007).

209 *"a silly thing":* Henry to John Adams, May 20, 1776, *Henry Correspondence,* 1: 413; [Carter Braxton], *An Address to the Convention . . .* (Philadelphia, 1776), 22–23 (Evans, *Bibliography,* no. 14669).

210 *Meriwether Smith: Revolutionary Virginia,* 7: 143, 145n6; Gordon S. Wood, *Creation of the American Republic, 1776–1787* (Chapel Hill: University of North Carolina Press, 1969), 271–72.

210 *"Declaration of Rights":* First draft of the Virginia Declaration of Rights, May 20–24, 1776, *Mason Papers,* 276; A. E. Dick Howard, *Commentaries on the Constitution of Virginia* (Charlottesville: University of Virginia Press, 1974), 34–35. When finally adopted on June 12 the opening text read: "A Declaration of Rights made by the representatives of the good people of Virginia, assembled in full and free Convention; which rights do pertain to them, and their posterity, as the basis and foundation of government."

210 *"noble system": View of the English Constitution by the late Baron de Montesquieu* (London: B. White, 1781), 71; Wood, *Creation of the American Republic,* 10–17; Annelien de Dijn, *French Political Thought from Montesquieu to Tocqueville: Liberty in a Levelled Society* (Cambridge: Cambridge University Press, 2008), 24–25, 54–55.

210 *"A Plan": Mason Papers,* 299; *Jefferson Papers,* 1: 366, 369; *Revolutionary Virginia,* 7: 594.

210 *"A Bill for new modelling": Jefferson Papers,* 1: 337, 347, 356.

211 *"A Constitution, or Form":* Ibid., 1: 377; *VG* (Purdie), Postcript, July 5, 1776; Broadside, *In a General Convention . . ."* (Evans no. 43207; Williamsburg: Alexander Purdie, 1776); *VG* (Dixon and Hunter), July 6, 1776.

211 *"the following* Declaration*": Constitutions of the Several Independent States of America* (Philadelphia: By order of Congress, 1781), 86. Bills of Rights were variously included or omitted from the state constitutions in successive editions of this compilation printed by order of Congress in 1781, 1785, 1786, and 1791 (Evans, *Bibliography,* nos. 17390, 19306, 20064, and 23887). Although the compilers did not include the Virginia Declaration of Rights in these four English editions, it did appear in the French translation (Evans no. 18265) reprinted in Philadelphia in 1783. I am grateful to John P. Kaminski for bringing these compilations to my attention and for pointing out that in accord with congressional practice during the confederation period, these compilations presented the state constitutions in geographical sequence from New Hampshire to Georgia.

211 *Henry spoke of the* constitution*:* F. Thornton Miller, *Juries and Judges Versus the Law: Virginia's Provincial Legal Perspective, 1783–1828* (Charlottesville: University of Virginia Press, 1994), 9–10, 68–69, 109–12.

211 *"ancient constitution":* J. G. A. Pocock, *The Ancient Constitution and the Feudal Law* (Cambridge: Cambridge University Press, 1957); Quentin Skinner, *The Foundations of Modern Political Thought* (2 vols., Cambridge: Cambridge University Press, 1978), 1: 209n.

211 *Mason drafted: Mason Papers,* 279–82; *Revolutionary Virginia,* 7: 276n6.

211 *It shaped the declarations:* R. Carter Pittman commentary, *VHMB* 68 (1960): 110–11; *Revolutionary Virginia,* 7: 277n27; Robert Allen Rutland, *The Birth of the Bill of Rights, 1776–1791* (Chapel Hill: University of North Carolina Press, 1955), 41–77.

212 *Robert Carter Nicholas led:* Randolph, *History of Virginia,* 253.

212 *"stumbling at the threshold":* Thomas Ludwell Lee to Richard Henry Lee, June 1, 1776, Lee Family Papers, UVA (LVA microfilm misc. reel 3686).

212 *"when they enter": Revolutionary Virginia,* 7: 302, 449, 454n16.

212 *"the fullest* toleration*": Revolutionary Virginia,* 7: 272, 450, 456n33, emphasis added; Thomas E. Buckley, *Establishing Religious Freedom: Jefferson's Statute in Virginia* (Charlottesville: University of Virginia Press, 2013), 53; Douglass Adair, ed., "James Madison's Autobiography," *WMQ,* 3d ser., 2 (1945): 199.

213 *"designed as a prelude"*: Randolph, *History of Virginia*, 264.

213 *"historic sixteenth article"*: *Revolutionary Virginia*, 7: 450, 456n33; Buckley, *Establishing Religious Freedom*, 53–54.

213 *"a terrifying picture"*: Randolph, *History of Virginia*, 254–55; Hening, Statutes, 9: 463–64; W. P. Trent, "The Case of Josiah Philips," *AHR* (1896): 444–54.

214 *"no great difference"*: John Augustine Washington to Richard Henry Lee, May 18, 1776, Lee Family Papers, UVA (LVA microfilm misc. reel 3686).

214 *"just and equal"*: Thomas Ludwell Lee to Richard Henry Lee, May 18, 1776.

214 *Lee and Adams pushed each other*: John E. Selby, "Richard Henry Lee, John Adams, and the Virginia Constitution of 1776," *VMHB* 84 (1976): 388–94; *Revolutionary Virginia*, 6: 367–68, 373n2, 408–14, 420–21; 7: 604–5; *VG* (Purdie), May 10, 1776.

214 *"swallowed up"*: Thomas Ludwell Lee to Richard Henry Lee, May 18, 1776; Lee Family Papers, UVA (LVA microfilm misc. reel 3686).

214 *"Printed for the perusal"*: "A Plan of Government," June 8–10, 1776, *Jefferson Papers*, 1: 366–69; *Revolutionary Virginia*, 7: 11–12; 594–608 ("money bills" quoted at p. 596). This draft is Evans, *Bibliography*, no. 43209.

214 *entirely new proposal*: *Jefferson Papers*, 1: 364–65n, 372n; *Mason Papers*, 295–310.

215 *"the people should elect deputies"*: Randolph, *History of Virginia*, 251–53; *Revolutionary Virginia*, 7: 464–65, 594–95; Selby, *Revolution in Virginia*, 119–20. In *Notes on the State of Virginia* Jefferson bolstered his objections to the constitution of 1776 with the specious argument that "Independence, and the establishment of a new form of government, were not even yet the objects of the people at large" during the April 1776 elections; William Peden, ed., *Notes on the State of Virginia* (Chapel Hill: University of North Carolina Press, 1955), 122, 283n13. His assertion is contradicted both by the evidence presented in this chapter and by Jefferson's contemporary remarks to Thomas Nelson, Jr., hoping that the convention would tell Virginia's congressmen "what to say on the subject of independence," and acknowledging that before returning to Congress in May 1776 he had taken "great pains to enquire into the sentiments of the people on that head" and "in the upper counties I think I may safely say nine out of ten are for it"; Jefferson to Nelson, May 16, 1776, *Jefferson Papers*, 1: 292; Dumas Malone, *Jefferson the Virginian* (Boston, 1948), 235–36.

215 *"Acts of Misrule"*: *Jefferson Papers*, 1: 352–53, 362–63, 385n19.

215 *"exhausted the Subject"*: Pendleton to Jefferson, July 22, 1776, *Pendleton Letters*, 188.

215 *"administrator"*: *Jefferson Papers*, 1: 359–61; Howard, *Commentaries on the Constitution of Virginia*, 570–75. Jefferson's wartime experience persuaded him that "173 despots would surely be as oppressive as one"; Peden, ed., *Notes on the State of Virginia*, 118, 120.

215 *"their horror"*: Randolph, *History of Virginia*, 255, emphasis in original; *Revolutionary Virginia*, 7: 605n23.

216 *"as strenuously as he did"*: Randolph, *History of Virginia*, 255–56.

216 *final adjustments: Revolutionary Virginia*, 7: 654. In Jefferson's draft constitution the General Assembly comprised a House of Representatives and a House of Senators; *Jefferson Papers*, 1: 358.

217 *"on Account of his age"*: *Revolutionary Virginia*, 7: 667–68; 670n10; 717n10; Richard Henry Lee to Edmund Pendleton, May 12, 1776, James Curtis Ballagh, ed., *Letters of Richard Henry Lee* (2 vols., New York: The Macmillan Company, 1911), 1: 192. In a conversation with Landon Carter, John Page characterized the vote as "a great majority"; Jack P. Greene, ed., *Diary of Colonel Landon Carter of Sabine Hall, 1752–1778* (Richmond: Virginia Historical Society, 1965), 1052.

217 *grumbled in private: Carter Diary*, 1057. Edmund Pendleton, who aspired to become Speaker of the new House of Delegates in October, later claimed that he had not sought the governorship himself and had voted for Secretary Nelson because "he did not think it became those who pushed on the revolution to get into the first offices"; *Henry Correspondence*, 1: 446.

217 *"who opened the breath"*: Adams to Henry, June 3, 1776, *Letters of Delegates*, 4: 122.

217 *"a grateful people"*: Address of the First and Second Virginia Regiments, *VG* (Purdie), July 5, 1776. A month later a short notice "demanded" by William Woodford and "cheerfully granted" by his officers "let the publick know that Col. Woodford's name was not among the subscribers of the address to the Governour" only because "the officers and their men" had not "consulted" their colonel "on the occasion"; *VG* (Purdie), Aug. 9, 1776.

217 *"high and unmerited honor"*: Answer to the Convention, *Revolutionary Virginia*, 7: 666; Answer to the First and Second Virginia Regiments, *VG* (Purdie), July 5, 1776.

218 *"very ill"*: Page to Jefferson, July 6, 1776, *Jefferson Papers*, 1: 454–55; Meade, *Practical Revolutionary*, 128–37.

218 *rumor of Henry's death:* Greene, ed., *Diary of Landon Carter*, 1057.

218 *"his late severe indisposition"*: *VG* (Purdie), Aug. 2, 1776.

Chapter 19: Visitors at Scotchtown

219 *"cordial congratulations"*: "Humble Address of the Ministers and Delegates of the Baptist Churches," *VG* (Purdie), Aug. 23, 1776; *VG* (Dixon), Aug. 24, 1776; Charles F. James, *Documentary History of the Struggle for Religious Liberty in Virginia* (Lynchburg: J. P. Bell, 1900), 101; John S. Moore, "Writers of Early Virginia Baptist History: John Williams," *Virginia Baptist Register* 14 (1975): 633–47; Moore, "Jeremiah Walker in Virginia," ibid., 15 (1976): 719–30; "Persecution of Baptists Ministers, Chesterfield County, Va., 1771–73," *VMHB* 11 (1904): 416–17.

219 *The next week's arrival:* Hugh F. Rankin, *George Rogers Clark and the Winning of the West* (Richmond: Virginia Independence Bicentennial Commission, 1976), 6–8; Donald W. Gunter, "George Rogers Clark," *DVB*, 3: 266–69.

219 *"too much concern":* James, *Documentary History,* 101.

219 *Henry's resolution:* "Address from the Baptists in this Colony," Aug. 16, 1775, *Revolutionary Virginia,* 3: 450–51, 453n3; Jewel L. Spangler, *Virginians Reborn: Anglican Monopoly, Evangelical Dissent, and the Rise of the Baptists in the Late Eighteenth Century* (Charlottesville: University of Virginia Press, 2008), 92–95; John S. Moore, "A Story at a Goochland Inn in 1772," *Virginia Baptist Register* 13 (1974): 621–22.

220 *"that in some Cases":* "Address from the Baptists of this Colony," Aug. 16, 1775, *Revolutionary Virginia,* 3: 450.

220 *"in much the same way":* Spangler, *Virginians Reborn,* 218; Charles F. Irons, "The Spiritual Fruits of Revolution: Disestablishment and the Rise of the Virginia Baptists," *VMHB* 109 (2001): 161–70.

220 *"many more":* "Address from the Baptists of this Colony, August 16, 1775," *Revolutionary Virginia,* 3: 450–51.

220 *"in this most critical conjuncture":* Petition of Baptists of Prince William County, May 19, 1776, ibid., 7: 188–89.

220 *"unspeakable pleasure":* "Humble Address of the Ministers and Delegates of the Baptist Churches," emphasis added.

221 *"to guard the rights":* "[Reply] to the Ministers and Delegates of the Baptist Churches and the Members of that Communion," *VG* (Purdie), Aug. 23, 1776; *VG* (Dixon), Aug. 24, 1776; also printed in *Governors' Letters,* 30.

221 *"A richer and more Beautiful":* George Rogers Clark to Jonathan Clark, July 6, 1775, in James Alton James, ed., *George Rogers Clark Papers, 1771–1781* (Springfield: Illinois State Historical Library, 1912), 10.

221 *"One would think":* Rev. John Brown to William Preston, May 5, 1775, in Rueben Gold Thwaites and Louise Phelps Kellogg, eds., *The Revolution on the Upper Ohio, 1775–1777* (Madison: Wisconsin Historical Society, 1908), 10.

221 *"fought and bled":* Kentucky petition, June 15, 1775; *Revolutionary Virginia,* 7: 518–19.

222 *"Scald Foot":* Rankin, *Clark and the West,* 6–7.

222 *"that if a Countrey":* Selby, *Revolution in Virginia,* 141.

223 *"Some of the Indian chiefs":* Deposition of Patrick Henry, June 4, 1777, in *Jefferson Papers,* 2: 69–71; Stephen Aron, "Pioneers and Profiteers: Land Speculation and the Homestead Ethic in Frontier Kentucky," *Western Historical Quarterly* 23 (1992): 183–86. Although contradicted by a careful reading of Henry's deposition, Clarence W. Alvord's speculation that Henry maintained connections with the Transylvania and Illinois-Wabash Companies after 1774 echoes throughout subsequent scholarship; Alvord, *The Illinois-Wabash Land Company Manuscript* (Chicago: Privately published, 1915), 20–21; Thomas Perkins Abernethy, *Western Lands and the American Revolution* (New York: Appleton-Century, 1937),

227; Merrill Jensen, *The Articles of Confederation: An Interpretation of the Social-Constitutional History of the American Revolution, 1774–1781* (Madison: University of Wisconsin Press, 1940), 207; Aron, "Pioneers and Profiteers," 185.

223 *"Indian purchases":* Henry deposition, *Jefferson Papers,* 2: 70.

223 *"inexcusable":* Mason to Washington, March 9, 1775, *Mason Papers,* 225–6; Washington to William Preston, March 27, 1775, *Washington Papers: Colonial,* 10: 312.

223 *"improper":* Henry deposition, Jefferson Papers, 2: 70.

224 *Only Virginia:* Peter S. Onuf, *The Origins of the Federal Republic: Jurisdictional Controversies in the United States, 1775–1787* (Philadelphia: University of Pennsylvania Press, 1983), 85.

224 *"A Vindication":* John C. Van Horne, ed., *The Correspondence of William Nelson as Acting Governor of Virginia, 1770–1771* (Charlottesville: University of Virginia Press, 1975), 39–46; "Virginia's Claim," *Jefferson Papers,* 6: 656–63; Onuf, *Origins of the Federal Republic,* 80.

224 *"the established usage":* On a motion by Henry seconded by Bland, this exceedingly powerful committee was created on March 27, 1775, to challenge Dunmore's "innovation on the established usage of granting [western] lands in this colony"; *Revolutionary Virginia,* 2: 383–84.

225 *"ceded, released, and forever confirmed":* Revolutionary Virginia, 7: 593, 598, 654; *Jefferson Papers,* 1: 352–53, 362–63, 383. Jefferson's hand in the constitutional provisions and the June 24 resolution goes unmentioned in Peter S. Onuf's brilliant discussion of Virginia and the west in *Origins of the Federal Republic,* 81–85.

225 *"the Infancy of the Government":* Edmund Pendleton to the Virginia Delegates in Congress, July 15, 1776, *Jefferson Papers,* 2: 464; Hening, *Statutes,* 9: 241–43, 257–61, 262–66, 322–25; Selby, *Revolution in Virginia,* 143–44.

226 *"exceedingly inconvenient":* Pendleton to the Virginia Delegates, *Jefferson Papers,* 1: 464. This letter is inexplicably absent from *Pendleton Letters.* Onuf, *Origins of the Federal Republic,* 84–85.

226 *"and apply the monies":* Braxton, *Address to the Convention, Revolutionary Virginia,* 6: 526.

226 *"unappropriated lands":* Adams, *Thoughts on Government,* ibid., 413, 533n13.

226 *More ominous:* Benjamin Franklin's Proposed Articles of Confederation, July 21, 1775, Worthington Chauncey Ford et al., eds., *Journals of the Continental Congress, 1774–1789* (34 vols., Washington, D.C.: Government Printing Office, 1904–1937), 2: 198; John Dickinson's Draft Articles of Confederation, June 17, 1776, *Letters of Delegates,* 2: 250; *Ratification Documents,* 1: 54–63.

227 *"the disposition":* Pendleton to Jefferson, Aug. 3, 1776, *Pendleton Letters,* 194; *Jefferson Papers,* 1: 484.

227 *"a most dangerous precedent":* Remonstrance of the General Assembly, Dec. 10, 1779, *Mason Papers,* 595; Hening, *Statutes,* 10: 557.

227 *"an appeal":* Virginia Delegates in Congress to George Morgan, Nov. 20, 1780,

Madison Papers: Confederation Series, 2: 188, emphasis added; Onuf, *Origins of the Federal Republic*, 90.

227 *"ever desirous"*: John Henry to Nicholas Thomas, March 17, 1778, *Letters of Congress*, 9: 304–6.

227 *"fixt determination"*: Richard Henry Lee to Patrick Henry, May 26, 1777, James Curtis Ballagh, ed., *Letters of Richard Henry Lee* (2 vols., New York: The Macmillan Company, 1911), 1: 301.

228 *"fix the western limits"*: Maryland Instructions to Delegates in Congress, Dec. 22, 1777, *Ratification Documents*, 1: 97–100.

228 *"The bare mentioning"*: John Henry to Nicholas Thomas, March 17, 1778, *Letters of Congress*, 9: 304–6.

228 *"this state doth not relinquish"*: *Journals of the Continental Congress*, 9: 637; *Ratification Documents*, 1: 100, 135–36; George L. Sioussat, "The Chevalier de la Luzerne and the Ratification of the Articles of Confederation by Maryland, 1780–1781," *Pennsylvania Magazine of History and Biography* 60 (1936): 391–407.

228 *"the Country beyond"*: Richard Henry Lee to Patrick Henry, Nov. 15, 1778, *Letters of Richard Henry Lee*, 1: 451–53.

229 *last-ditch effort*: Jensen, *The Articles of Confederation*, 233; *Public Good, being an Examination into the Claim of Virginia to the Vacant Western Territory . . . by the author of Common Sense* (Philadelphia, 1780), Evans, *Bibliography* no. 16920.

229 *"gratify the avidity"*: Madison to Joseph Jones, Nov. 21, 1780, *Letters of Congress*, 16: 372.

229 *Congress finally accepted*: "Resolution for a cession of the lands on the north west side of Ohio to the United States," Jan. 2, 1781, Hening, *Statutes*, 10: 564–66; Onuf, *Origins of the Federal Republic*, 91–102; Robert F. Berkhofer, Jr., "Jefferson, the Ordinance of 1784, and the Origins of the American Territorial System," *WMQ*, 3d ser., 29 (1972): 231–62.

229 *While Virginians wrestled*: Henry to Clark [secret instructions], Jan. 2, 1778, *Official Letters of the Governors of Virginia*, 223; public instructions to Clark, Jan. 2, 1778, *George Rogers Clark Papers*, 36; George Wythe, George Mason, and Thomas Jefferson to Clark, Jan. 3, 1778, *Mason Papers*, 409–10; Rankin, *Clark and the West*, 10–14; Selby, *Revolution in Virginia*, 189–96; Gayle Thornbrough, ed., *The Secret Orders and "great things have been Done by a few Men": Letters of Patrick Henry and George Rogers Clark* (Indianapolis: Indiana Historical Society, 1974).

230 *"one great Good"*: *Journals Va. Council of State*, 2: 234.

230 *"some of the Shawanese"*: Henry to the Virginia Delegates in Congress, Nov. 14, 1778, *Official Letters of the Governors of Virginia*, 323–25; Hening, *Statutes*, 9: 552–55.

231 *Prospective recruits had grown wary*: William Goghan to William Davies, Aug. 18, 1781, *Calendar of Virginia State Papers*, 2: 345–46; Selby, *Revolution in Virginia*, 200–203; Rudolf Freund, "Military Bounty Lands and the Origins of the Public Domain," *Agricultural History* 20 (1946): 11.

231 *"put a stop": Journal of the House of Delegates, 1781* (Charlottesville: John Dunlap and James Hayes, 1781), 43.

231 *"My chain appears":* Clark to Thomas Nelson, Aug. 4, 1781, *Calendar of Virginia State Papers*, 2: 294–95; Clark to Nelson, Oct. 1, 1781, *George Rogers Clark Papers*, 608.

231 *"their own religion":* Hening, *Statutes*, 9: 553.

231 *"Equal Liberty":* Miscellaneous Petition, Oct. 16, 1776, LVA; Church, *Legislative Petitions*, 141-P. Digital images of this and other petitions are accessible online in the Early Virginia Religious Petitions collection at the LVA and LC websites.

232 *"the common cause":* Petition of Baptists of Prince William County, May 19, 1776, *Revolutionary Virginia*, 7: 189.

232 *"all dissenters":* Hening, *Statutes*, 9: 164–67.

232 *"heretofore given":* Ibid., 10: 197–98; Irons, "Spiritual Fruits of Revolution," 170–71.

Chapter 20: *A War to Win*

233 *"alarming accounts": Governor's Letters*, 226–27. The problems of the Continental quartermasters are recounted in reliable military histories of the Revolution, e.g., Willard M. Wallace, *Appeal to Arms: A Military History of the American Revolution* (New York: Harper & Brothers, 1951), 169–74.

233 *messenger to New Orleans: Governor's Letters*, 227–29.

233 *"Large Loans":* Ibid., 231–33.

234 *"Stupid men":* Lafayette to Washington, Dec. 30, 1777, quoted in Douglas Southall Freeman, *George Washington: A Biography*, vol. 4, *Leader of the Revolution* (New York: Charles Scribner's Sons, 1951), 587.

234 *jealousies were already rife:* Rossie, *Politics of Command*, 174–91.

234 *incendiary letters:* e.g., Conway to Washington, Dec. 31, 1777, Freeman, *George Washington*, 4: 590–91.

234 *"out-generaled":* Jonathan Trumbull to Gates, Sept. 29, 1777, ibid., 180.

234 *"Heaven has determined":* Ibid., 450–51. Wilkinson was later on the Spanish payroll as a spy and involved with the Burr Conspiracy; Jon Kukla, *A Wilderness So Immense: The Louisiana Purchase and the Destiny of America* (New York: Alfred A. Knopf, 2003), 121–33, 180–87.

235 *"our brave and virtuous General":* Laurens to Lafayette, Jan. 12, 1778, quoted in Freeman, *George Washington*, 4: 609.

235 *"a zealous advocate": Autobiography of Benjamin Rush*, 111.

235 *"an idle minute":* Rush to Henry, July 16, 1776, Lyman H. Butterfield, ed., "Dr. Rush to Governor Henry on the Declaration of Independence and the Virginia Constitution," *Proceedings of the American Philosophical Society* 95 (1951): 252.

235 *"His Excellency":* Rush to Henry, Jan. 12, 1778, Lyman H. Butterfield, ed., *Let-*

ters of Benjamin Rush (Princeton: Princeton University Press for the American Philosophical Society, 1951), 182–85. Butterfield explained the distinction between unsigned and anonymous letters at 184n7. Washington's notation on the letter reads, "The Superscription on the Back (from its Similarity) proves that Doctr Rush was the Author of the Letter to Govr Henry and for that purpose is filed with it." *Washington Papers, Revolutionary War* 13: 610.

236 *"The common danger":* Rush to Henry, Jan. 12, 1778, *Letters of Benjamin Rush,* 182–85.

236 *"there is a rupture":* Benjamin Rush to Julia Rush, Jan. 15, 1778, *Letters of Benjamin Rush,* 185.

236 *"Dear Sir":* Henry to Washington, Feb. 20, March 5, 1778, *Washington Papers, Revolutionary War* 13: 609, 14: 63.

237 *"Your friendship, Sir":* Washington to Henry, March 27, 1778, ibid., 14: 328.

237 *"The anonymous letter":* Washington to Henry, March 28, 1778, ibid., 14: 336.

237 *Washington not only survived:* Rossie, *Politics of Command,* 202.

237 *"indiscreet zeal":* Autobiography of Benjamin Rush, 137.

237 *"guilty of the blackest":* Henry Laurens to John Laurens, Feb. 3, 1778, *Letters of Delegates,* 9: 18; Gates to Washington, Jan. 23, 1778, *Washington Papers, Revolutionary War* 13: 319.

237 *"On the question":* Washington to Lee, Aug. 26, 1794, *Washington Papers, Presidential* 16: 603.

238 *"the most unequivocal proof":* Washington to Archibald Blair, June 24, 1799, *Washington Papers, Retirement* 4: 150.

238 "Mr. Henry": *Journal of the House of Delegates, 1777* (Williamsburg: Alexander Purdie, 1778), 38, 41; Hening, *Statutes,* 9: 471–72.

238 *James Henry:* Although Wolf (*Race and Liberty,* 24–25) misidentified Patrick Henry (then governor) as the delegate who presented the committee's bill on November 22, the rest of her legislative history is solid.

238 *scholars agree:* Wolf, *Race and Liberty,* 27; Michael L. Nicholls, "'The Squint of Freedom': African-American Freedom Suits in Post-Revolutionary Virginia," *Slavery and Abolition* 20 (1999): 51.

238 *Only five:* Wolf, *Race and Liberty,* 50.

239 *Quakers freed several hundred:* William Fernandez Hardin, "Litigating the Lash: Quaker Emancipator Robert Pleasants, the Law of Slavery, and the Meaning of Manumission in Revolutionary and Early National Virginia" (PhD diss., Vanderbilt University, 2013), 88.

239 *community safety:* Pleasants's actions were in keeping with a national effort to demonstrate black capacity for freedom; Paul J. Polgar, "'To Raise Them to an Equal Participation': Early National Abolitionism, Gradual Emancipation, and the Promise of African American Citizenship," *JER* 31 (2011): 233–35.

239 *legal advice:* Memorial of Robert Pleasants to the Governor of Virginia, [ca. 1790?], Pleasants Family Papers, Box 12, Robert Alonzo Brock Collection, Huntington Library, San Marino, Calif. (LVA misc. microfilm reel 4239, 119–

21). If he consulted the 1769 statute "for the better government of Servants and Slaves," Henry might well have advised Pleasants that the law was directed at owners who hired out their slaves for wages; Hening, *Statutes*, 8: 360.

239 *"remove every inducement":* Pleasants to Henry, March 28, 1777, *Henry Correspondence*, 3: 49. The provision of the 1748 statute authorizing intervention by church wardens (Hening, *Statutes*, 6: 112) had not been renewed in subsequent legislation; e.g., Hening, *Statutes*, 8: 360.

239 *"of the injustice":* Pleasants to Henry, March 28, 1777, *Henry Correspondence*, 3: 49.

239 *"very kindly":* Pleasants to Israel Pemberton, April 21, 1777, Robert Pleasants Letter Book, 1754–1797, 44–45 (Quaker Manuscript Collection, Haverford College Library, Haverford, Penn.) (LVA microfilm misc. reel 506).

240 *"a general freedom":* Pleasants to Pemberton, April 21, 1777.

240 *"clearly convinced":* Ibid.

241 *"the province":* Collier quoted in Gardner W. Allen, *A Naval History of the American Revolution* (Boston: Houghton Mifflin Company, 1913), 395.

241 *"desultory expedition":* Sir Henry Clinton, *The American Rebellion: Sir Henry Clinton's Narrative of His Campaigns, 1775–1782* (New Haven: Yale University Press, 1954), 122–23; Selby, *Revolution in Virginia*, 204; Elizabeth Cometti, "Depredations in Virginia During the Revolution," in Darrett B. Rutman, ed., *The Old Dominion: Essays for Thomas Perkins Abernethy* (Charlottesville: University of Virginia Press, 1964), 140–42; Robert Fallow and Marion West Stoer, "The Old Dominion Under Fire: The Chesapeake Invasions, 1779–1781," in Ernest McNeill Eller, ed., *Chesapeake Bay in the American Revolution* (Centreville, Md.: Tidewater Publishers, 1981), 443.

241 *His secondary objective:* British inventories of vessels, weapons, and commodities captured or destroyed reflect Portsmouth's importance for wartime logistics and supply; George Collier and Gen. Edward Mathew to Sir Henry Clinton, May 16, 1779, reprinted from the *London Gazette*, June 19, 1779, in *WMQ*, 2d ser., 12 (1932): 181–86. Collier and Mathew's letter circulated widely in Great Britain; e.g., *The Rembrancer* (London, 1779), 295–97; *The Scots Magazine* (Edinburgh, 1779): 371–74.

241 *"Success":* Patrick Henry to John Jay, president of Congress, May 11, 1779, *Governor's Letters*, 366–67; *Henry Correspondence*, 3: 238. Council journals from March 22, 1779, through July 8, 1780, are not extant; *Executive Journals Va. Council*, 2; 250, 254–55.

241 *HMS* Raisonable*:* Henry to Richard Henry Lee, May 19, 1779, *Governor's Letters*, 372; Allen, *Naval History*, 395.

241 *"the finest":* Collier quoted in Allen, *Naval History*, 2: 396; Selby, *Revolution in Virginia*, 205. Gen. Mathews reported that it took his engineers "many Days with near one Hundred Blacks to destroy the Fort, which was so substantially constructed as to give us a great Deal of Trouble in the Demolition"; Mathews to Clinton, May 24, 1779, *WMQ*, 185.

241 *three thousand barrels:* Mathews to Clinton, May 16, 1779, *WMQ*, 183.

242 *"Last Night":* Henry to Jay, President of Congress, May 12, 1779, *Henry Correspondence*, 3: 240.

242 "pretty certain": Henry to Jay, May 21, 1779, ibid., 374, emphasis added.

242 *Henry reacted:* Selby, *Revolution in Virginia*, 207; Henry to Jay, May 11, May 12, 1779; Henry to Thomas Johnson, May 12, 1779, *Governor's Letters*, 366–68; Edmund Pendleton to William Woodford, May 24, 1779, *Pendleton Letters*, 285–86.

242 *statewide mobilization:* Proclamation, *VG* (Dixon and Nicolson), May 15, 1779.

242 *"No time is to be lost":* Patrick Henry to Thomas Read, May 12, 1779, Special Collections, Charles Leaming Tutt Library, Colorado College, Colorado Springs, Colo.

242 *"our militia":* Henry to Lee, May 19, 1779, *Governor's Letters*, 372.

242 *Smithfield:* Selby, *Revolution in Virginia*, 207; Henry to Richard Henry Lee, May 19, 1779, *Governor's Letters*, 371–72.

242 *"without being incommoded":* Collier and Mathew to Clinton, May 16, 1779, *WMQ*, 2d ser., 12 (1932): 185.

242 *"melancholy fact":* St. George Tucker to Theodorick Bland, Jr., June 6, 1779, Campbell, ed., *Bland Papers*, 2: 11. Tucker (who then held a grudge against Henry about remarks made about his negotiations for a shipment of indigo) worried that if newly elected Governor Jefferson followed "in the steps of his predecessor, there is not much to be expected from the brightest talents"; ibid. In 1805 Tucker confessed that his earlier opinion reflected an encounter with Henry when he sought reimbursement for his expenses as Virginia's agent purchasing indigo in Charleston, South Carolina, to be shipped abroad in exchange for arms: "Governor Henry received me like a great man; I was not asked to sit down, I was not thanked for my zeal and expedition, or for advancing my money. Mr. Henry made some remarks upon the high price I had given for the Indigo—said it was more than the State had bought it for before (which was very true, for depreciation had then begun), and that I appeared to have been too much in a hurry to make the purchase. I felt indignation flash from my eyes, and I feel it at my heart at this moment. I am therefore an unfit person to draw an exact portrait of Mr. Henry, or to give a fair estimate of his character." Later in the same letter, however, Tucker described meeting Henry socially for the first time in 1792: "His manners were the perfection of urbanity; his conversation various, entertaining, instructive, and fascinating. I parted from him with infinite regret, and forgot for the whole time I was with him, that I had so many years borne in mind an expression which might not have been intended to wound me, as it did." Tucker to William Wirt, Feb. 10, 1805, *Henry Correspondence*, 2: 37–38.

243 *"inconvenience":* Pendleton to Woodford, May 24, May 31, 1779, *Pendleton Letters*, 1: 285–86, 289–90 (quoted at p. 289).

243 *"whose term":* Pendleton to Woodford, July 26, 1779, *Pendleton Letters*, 1: 293;

Kaminski, *George Clinton*, 29–37. Aside from Pendleton's and Tucker's private comments, there seems to be little evidence (at least prior to the controversy over Jefferson's response to subsequent invasions) supporting John Selby's statement that Henry "suffered severe criticism" after the Collier raid; *Revolution in Virginia*, 207.

243 *"which is more safe":* Hening, *Statutes*, 10: 86–89.

243 *"the immediate defense":* House of Delegates Resolution, May 20, 1779, *Governor's Letters*, 373.

243 *"a power":* Henry to Benjamin Harrison, Speaker of the House of Delegates, May 25, 1779, ibid., 373–74. The House apparently took no official action about this notification, but during the 1781 invasion the Assembly would specifically authorize the imprisonment of disaffected persons without bail or benefit of habeas corpus; Hening, *Statutes*, 10: 414.

244 *"to retire":* Henry to Harrison, May 28, 1779, *Governor's Letters*, 377.

244 *67 to 61:* On the first ballot, Jefferson had fifty-five votes, Page thirty-eight, and Gen. Thomas Nelson thirty-two; *Journal of the House of Delegates, 1779* (Williamsburg: Clarkson and Davis, 1779), 36.

244 *"for his faithful discharge":* The Senate's unanimous resolution was printed in the newspapers on June 5; the House sent a committee to express in person "the thanks of that House for the faithful discharge of his important trust"; ibid., 39; *Governor's Letters*, 379.

244 *property tax records:* Blunt, *Patrick Henry: Henry County Years*, 10.

245 *malaria:* Despite its reputation as a tropical disease, malaria was introduced to Jamestown from England in the earliest years of settlement. Jon Kukla, "Kentish Agues and American Distempers: The Transmission of Malaria from England to Virginia in the Seventeenth Century," *Southern Studies* 25 (Summer 1986): 135–47.

245 *"remain below":* Henry to Jefferson, Feb. 15, 1780, *Henry Correspondence*, 2: 48, emphasis added.

245 *"portholes":* Couvillon, *Patrick Henry's Virginia*, 63–66; Meade, *Practical Revolutionary*, 224.

245 *"The Tories have been plotting":* Henry to Capt. Thomas Madison, Aug. 23, 1780, in Louise Phelps Kellogg, ed., *Frontier Retreat on the Upper Ohio, 1779–1781* (Madison: State Historical Society of Wisconsin, 1917), 264. Meade cited this letter as "in the New York Public Library" (*Practical Revolutionary*, 224, 499n5), but I am grateful to Mark Couvillon for alerting me to the published transcription from the Draper Papers. Emory G. Evans, "Trouble in the Backcountry: Disaffection in Southwest Virginia During the American Revolution," in Ronald Hoffman, Thad W. Tate, and Peter J. Albert, eds., *An Uncivil War: The Southern Backcountry During the American Revolution* (Charlottesville: University Press of Virginia, 1985), 179–212.

245 *"many anxieties for our commonwealth":* Henry to Jefferson, Feb. 15, 1780, *Henry Correspondence*, 2:48–49. Jefferson's letter is not extant, *Jefferson Papers*, 3:

293–94. In 1779 Governor Henry had exercised "a power not expressly given by law" to jail two Virginians for aiding the enemy; Henry to Benjamin Harrison, Speaker of the House of Delegates, May 25, 1779, *Governor's Letters*, 373–74. In 1781 the assembly authorized the summary imprisonment of disaffected persons; Hening, *Statutes*, 10: 414.

245 *"proper persons"*: C. B. Bryant, ed., "Henry County: From its Formation in 1776 to the End of the Eighteenth Century," *VMHB* 9 (1902): 266, 417.

246 *provisions for the war effort*: Blunt, *Patrick Henry: Henry County Years*, 17–18.

246 *960 pounds of beef*: Bryant, ed., "Henry County," 417, 420

246 *"pretty well suppressed"*: Henry to Capt. Thomas Madison, Aug. 23, 1780, in *Frontier Retreat on the Upper Ohio*, 264.

246 *Revolutionary War pension applications*: An estimated eighty thousand files, arranged by names of veterans, fill 2,670 reels of microfilm (M804); Revolutionary War Pension and Bounty-Land-Warrant Applications Files, Record Group 15, Records of the Veterans Administration, National Archives, Washington, D.C. A growing collection of searchable transcriptions of these documents is accessible online at *Southern Campaigns American Revolution Pension Statements* (http://revarapps.org); I am grateful to Michael L. Nicholls for bringing this invaluable resource to my attention. Transcriptions cited below appear to have been uploaded to this website between 2012 and 2014.

246 *popular support for the Revolution*: Ronald Hoffman, "The 'Disaffected' in the Revolutionary South," in Alfred F. Young, ed., *The American Revolution: Explorations in the History of American Radicalism* (Dekalb: North Illinois University Press, 1876), 312–13.

246 *"getting up" about three hundred volunteers*: George Turnley pension application, June 11, 1834 (National Archives file no. S21545), transcribed by Will Graves for the *Southern Campaign Pension* website.

246 *"were very mountainous"*: James Tarrant pension application, Jan. 20, 1840 (National Archives file no. R10395), transcribed by C. Leon Harris for the *Southern Campaign Pension* website.

246 *"counsel and advice"*: George Turnley pension application.

246 *"the Rich-Hollow"*: Ibid. For the oath of allegiance "to the Common Wealth of Virginia, as a Free and Independent State" and "the Freedom and Independence thereof as declared by Congress," as administered in Henry Co., see C. B. Bryant, ed., "Henry County: From Its Formation in 1776 to the End of the Eighteenth Century," *VMHB* 9 (1901): 11–12.

247 *"at a place called the Hollow"*: John Redd pension application, Oct. 14, 1833 (National Archives file no. S18174), transcribed by C. Leon Harris for the *Southern Campaign Pension* website. Henry County residents swore allegiance to the commonwealth in 1777 and 1778 by a margin of 697 to 11; Bryant, ed., "Henry County," *VMHB* 9 (1901): 11–18, 138–48, 262. Michael A. McConnell contended that most of the disaffected in 1780 "simply wanted to be left alone"; *Politics of War*, 378.

247 *"nearly half the population":* William Carter pension application, March 14, 1833 (National Archives file no. S18174), transcribed by C. Leon Harris for the *Southern Campaign Pension* website.

247 *Redd had fought the Cherokee:* John Redd pension application.

247 *228 sheaves of oats:* Bryant, ed., "Henry County," *VMHB* 10 (1903): 417.

247 *"a Gang of Tories":* James Tarrant pension application, Jan. 20, 1840 (National Archives file no. R10395), transcribed by C. Leon Harris for the *Southern Campaign Pension* website. For additional information about Letcher's murder, see the pension applications (all transcribed by C. Leon Harris) of James Boyd, Oct. 11, 1832 (National Archives file no. S12269); John Hall, Sept. 5, 1832 (National Archives file no. S2589); and Nathaniel Smith, May 3, 1836 (National Archives file no. R9817).

247 *two brigades:* "Virginia Troops at Charleston, South Carolina, 1779–1780," in Sanchez-Saavedra, *Virginia Military Organizations in the American Revolution,* 177–81.

248 *"Whigs and Tories pursue one another":* Greene to Gen. Robert Howe, Dec. 29, 1780, *Papers of General Nathanael Greene,* ed. Richard K. Showman et al. (13 vols., Chapel Hill: University of North Carolina Press, 1976–2005), 7: 17. Brutality in the southern campaign began less than three weeks after the fall of Charleston; J. Tracy Power, "'The Virtue of Humanity Was Totally Forgot': Burford's Massacre, May 29, 1780," *South Carolina Historical Magazine* 93 (1992): 5–14.

248 *"Rapes, murders":* Madison to Philip Mazzei, July 7, 1781, *Madison Papers* 3: 180.

248 *King's Mountain:* The American militia lost 28 killed and 64 wounded compared to loyalist losses of 157 killed, 163 badly wounded, and 698 captured; editorial note, Greene Papers, 7: 408n2; E. T. Crowson, "Colonel William Campbell and the Battle of Kings Mountain," *Virginia Cavalcade* 30 (1980): 22–29; Paul David Nelson, "Campbell, William," *DVB,* 2: 582–84.

248 *"Every Thing here":* Nathanael Greene to Henry Knox, Dec. 7, 1780, *Greene Papers,* 6: 547; James Haw, "'Every Thing Here Depends Upon Opinion': Nathanael Greene and Public Support in the Southern Campaigns of the American Revolution," *South Carolina Historical Magazine* 109 (2008), 212–31.

248 *"It was [as] necessary":* Greene to Jefferson, March 10, 1781, *Jefferson Papers,* 5: 111.

248 *race to the Dan River:* Larry G. Aaron, *The Race to the Dan: The Retreat That Rescued the American Revolution* (South Boston, Va.: Halifax County Historical Society); Hugh F. Rankin, *Greene and Cornwallis: The Campaign in the Carolinas* (Raleigh: North Carolina Division of Archives and History, 1976).

249 *"Cornwallis led a country dance":* Contemporary doggerel quoted in Rankin, *Greene and Cornwallis,* 84.

249 *"to collect 14 or 1500 Volunteers":* Greene to Jefferson, Feb. 10, 1781, *Jefferson Papers,* 4, 576. William Wirt Henry cited only this letter for evidence of Henry's assistance to Greene's army; *Henry Correspondence,* 2: 67–68.

249 *Henry had sent a courier:* Greene to Henry, Feb. 10, 1781, William L. Clements Library, University of Michigan, Ann Arbor. I am indebted to Janet Bloom for supplying a photocopy of this letter. Henry Mayer cited a version at the Huntington Library; *Son of Thunder,* 504n. The Clements Library letter is calendared in *Greene Papers,* 7: 270. An excerpt printed in William Johnson, *Sketches of the Life and Correspondence of Nathanael Greene* (2 vols., Charleston, S.C.: A. E. Miller, 1822), 1: 447, did not include the opening sentence that indicates Henry's initiative: "A Man from your quarter arrived in my Camp this Morning, with orders as he says, from you, to enquire into our situation." Greene's reference to a man from Henry's quarter probably indicates that the messenger was a slave.

249 *en route to his new command:* Nathanael Greene to Joseph Reed, Jan. 9, 1781, *Greene Papers,* 84–85; Greene to Jefferson, Nov. 20, 1780, *Jefferson Papers,* 4: 130–34.

249 *"too inconsiderable":* Greene to Henry, Feb. 10, 1781, Clements Library, University of Michigan.

250 *"If it is possible":* Ibid., emphasis added.

250 *"confidence in a reinforcement":* Greene to Gen. John Butler, Feb. 12, 1781, *Papers of General Nathanael Greene,* 7: 282.

250 *281 volunteers:* The muster roll of 281 Henry County volunteers who joined Greene's forces in March 1781 is printed in Blunt, *Patrick Henry: Henry County Years,* 40–41, and Bryant, "Henry County," *VMHB* 17 (1909): 189–93.

250 *"it would prove ruinous":* Greene to Samuel Huntington, March 16, 1781, *Papers of General Nathanael Greene,* 7: 433.

250 *"did themselves great honor":* Greene to Jefferson; March 16, 1781, *Jefferson Papers,* 5: 157.

250 *"I wish it had produced":* O'Hara to the Duke of Grafton, April 20, 1781, George C. Rogers, ed., "Letters of Charles O'Hara to the Duke of Grafton," *South Carolina Historical Magazine* 65 (1964): 177. "Tho you will not find it in the Gazette," O'Hara reported, "every part of our Army was beat repeatedly on the 15th of March and were obliged to fall back twice"; ibid.

250 *"one in the Carolinas":* Willcox, "British Road to Yorktown," 10. Clinton and Cornwallis exchanged no communications at all between Jan. 18 and April 10, 1781.

251 *"a diversion":* Clinton to Leslie, Oct. 12, 1780, quoted in Selby, *Revolution in Virginia,* 216.

251 *Jefferson implored his friend:* Jefferson's letter to Page "is unfortunately missing" (*Jefferson Papers,* 193n) but in his reply on Dec. 9, 1780, Page urged Jefferson "not to think of resigning. Go on serve out the Time allowed by the Constitution"; ibid., 192. Long ignored by historians, Jefferson's reservations are thoroughly explicated in George T. Morrow II, *A Wound on His Spirit: Thomas Jefferson's Disastrous Two Years as Governor of Virginia* (Williamsburg: Telford Publications, 2013), 44–70.

251 *"unprepared"*: Jefferson, "Diary of Arnold's Invasion and Notes on Subsequent Events in 1781," *Jefferson Papers*, 4: 260.

251 *Clinton sent another expedition*: Selby, *Revolution in Virginia*, 221–25; Cometti, "Depredations in Virginia," 142–47; George Green Shackelford, "Benedict Arnold in Richmond, 1781," *VMHB* 60 (1952): 591–99; Michael Kranish, *Flight from Monticello: Thomas Jefferson at War* (New York: Oxford University Press, 2010), 154–231; "Notes and Documents Relating to the British Invasions in 1781," *Jefferson Papers*, 4: 256–335.

252 *"prize goods"*: Arnold's handwritten offer is reproduced in Shackelford, "Benedict Arnold in Richmond," 597–98, and discussed in Kranish, *Flight from Monticello*, 193–94.

252 *British tallies*: Kranish, *Flight from Monticello*, 194.

252 *"Terrible things"*: Johann von Ewald, *Diary of the American War: A Hessian Journal*, ed. Joseph P. Tustin (New Haven: Yale University Press, 1979), 268–69; Kranish, *Flight from Monticello*, 195; Cometti, "Depredations in Virginia," 144.

252 *"calling the Neighbouring Militia"*: Pendleton to Washington, Feb. 16, 1781, *Pendleton Letters*, 1: 340.

252 *"Arnold the traitor"*: Page to Theodorick Bland, Jan. 21, 1781, *Virginia Historical Register and Literary Note Book*, 4 (1851): 196. "However short the notice of their approach to Richmond might be," Page continued, "we certainly had time to have secured the Great Bridge and Suffolk if not Portsmouth, and to have cut them off on their march [downriver] through so many defiles"; ibid.

252 *"glad to hear"*: Madison to Edmund Pendleton, Jan. 23, 1781, *Madison Papers*, 2: 286.

253 *"the extent of our shores"*: Henry to Richard Henry Lee, May 19, 1779, *Governor's Letters*, 372.

253 *After his expensive victory*: John Richard Alden, *The South in the Revolution, 1763–1789* (Baton Rouge: Louisiana State University Press, 1957), 259; William B. Willcox, "The British Road to Yorktown: A Study in Divided Command," *AHR* 52 (1946): 10–12; O'Shaughnessy, *The Men Who Lost America*, 272–82.

253 *"into Virginia"*: Richard Oswald, *Memorandum on the Folly of Invading Virginia*, ed. W. Stitt Robinson, Jr. (Charlottesville: University of Virginia Press, 1953), 12.

253 *a small French army*: Marc Leepson, *Lafayette: Lessons in Leadership from the Idealist General* (New York: Palgrave Macmillan, 2011), 85–114.

253 *two raiding parties*: Selby, *Revolution in Virginia*, 279–85; Kranish, *Flight from Monticello*, 269–96.

254 *term of office*: Julian P. Boyd made a sound case for June 2, 1781, as the final date of Jefferson's term of office in *Jefferson Papers*, 6: 77–79—except perhaps where Boyd asserted that "TJ was barred from exercising the Executive powers" (p. 79).

254 *"We are members"*: Lyon G. Tyler, ed., *The Letters and Times of the Tylers* (2 vols.,

Richmond: Whittet and Shepperson, 1884), 82. Harrison, Henry, and Tyler were leaders in the House of Delegates; William Christian was a state senator. For clarity I altered the phrase "he'd no business" to read "he had no business."

255 *"We have now"*: Benjamin Harrison to Joseph Jones, June 8, 1781, *Letters of Joseph Jones, 1777–1787*, ed. Worthington C. Ford (Washington, D.C.: Department of State, 1889), 83.

255 *martial law: Journal of the House of Delegates, 1781* (Charlottesville: John Dunlap and James Hayes, 1781), 20 and passim. For a dispassionate summary of these legislative measures, including "Ample Powers to the Executive," see Archibald Cary to Thomas Jefferson, June 19, 1781, *Jefferson Papers*, 6: 96–97.

256 *"to have a Dictator"*: Henry Young to William Davies, June 9, 1781, *Jefferson Papers*, 6: 84–85. The fact that the official journal has no record of this proposal suggests that discussions about appointing a dictator took place in a committee of the whole, which would leave no record unless a resolution were reported from the committee to the whole house.

256 *"referred to the practice"*: Archibald Stuart to Jefferson, Sept. 8, 1718, ibid., 6: 84n.

256 *"that neither"*: Young to Davies, June 9, 1781, ibid., 6: 85.

256 *another convention*: John Taylor of Caroline's belief in the efficacy of conventions (revealed in his letter to Jefferson in Dec. 1798, *Jefferson Papers*, 30: 601) provides an important perspective on Jefferson's fervent advocacy of conventions. "As it was the custom of the Roman aristocracy, whenever it felt itself in danger, to appoint a dictator," Taylor wrote, "so the same office [i.e., function] seemed to be peculiarly proper for a convention in a popular republic."

256 *"It was immaterial"*: Stuart to Jefferson, Sept. 8, 1718, ibid., 6: 84n.

256 *"At present"*: Richard K. MacMaster, ed., "News of the Yorktown Campaign: The Journal of Dr. Robert Honyman, April 17–November 25, 1781," *VMHB* 79 (1971): 402.

256 *acts of indemnity*: E.g., Hening, *Statutes*, 8: 373–74, 377, 387, 535, 584; 9: 10: 150, 195, 478; 11: 135, 373.

256 *"immediately to Virginia"*: Lee to the Virginia Delegates in Congress, June 12, 1781, *Jefferson Papers*, 6: 91; Committee at Headquarters Memorandum, May 14, 1780, *Letters of Delegates*, 15: 123–25; John Fell's Diary, Sept. 5, 1780; ibid., 15: 709.

256 *"precedents"*: Lee to Virginia Delegates, June 12, 1781, *Jefferson Papers*, 6: 91.

256 *"at the next session": Journal of the House of Delegates, 1781*, 21. In his otherwise reliable narrative, Michael Kranish (*Flight from Monticello*, 295) reversed the sequence of Nicholas's proposals for a dictator and an inquiry.

257 *"confident than an Inquir[y]"*: Cary to Jefferson, June 19, 1781, *Jefferson Papers*, 6: 97. Edmund Randolph wrote that Nicholson and Henry "were those who charged Mr. Jefferson" but it is not entirely clear whether he was present in Staunton or relied upon Jefferson's opinion; Randolph, *History*, 296; Reardon, *Edmund Randolph*, 41–42.

257 *"stab a reputation"*: Jefferson to Nicholas, July 28, 1781, *Jefferson Papers*, 6: 104–5.

257 *"to call upon the executive"*: Nicholas to Jefferson, July 31, 1781, ibid., 105–6.

257 *What Nicholas may not have told Jefferson*: Kranish, *Flight from Monticello*, 274; John Graves Simcoe, *Simcoe's Military Journal: A History of the Operations of a Partisan Corps called the Queen's Rangers* (New York: Bartlett and Welford, 1844), 212.

258 *"the rectitude of their intentions"*: *Journals Va. Council of State*, 2: 356. The journal clearly states that the House of Delegates addressed its resolution to the five men who had comprised Jefferson's Council of State. Three of them signed this protest at the July 16 meeting, one was absent, and one had left the council. Governor Nelson and two newly elected members present at that meeting did not sign the protest.

258 *"if I know you"*: Cary to Jefferson, June 19, 1781, *Jefferson Papers*, 6: 97.

258 *wounded his feelings*: Peden, ed., *Notes on the State of Virginia*, 284n28; Malone, *Jefferson the Virginian*, 362.

259 *"inflicted a wound"*: Draft letter, Jefferson to James Monroe, May 20, 1782, *Jefferson Papers*, 6: 185 and 187n6. For the last eight words of his draft sentence, Jefferson substituted "which will only be cured by the all-healing grave." Monroe shared Jefferson's complaints with Edmund Randolph and others; Randolph to James Madison, June 1, 1782, *Madison Papers*, 4: 306.

259 *"trifling"*: Jefferson to Zane, Dec. 24, 1781; *Jefferson Papers*, 6: 143.

259 *"administrator"*: *Jefferson Papers*, 1: 359–61.

259 *"a powerful chief magistrate"*: Randolph, *History of Virginia*, 255–56. Peter S. Onuf offers important insights about their relationship in his Fleming Lecture, "Democracy: Thomas Jefferson and Patrick Henry," in *Democracy, Constitutionalism, and Empire: Jefferson, Henry, Madison, and Washington* (Baton Rouge: Louisiana State University Press, forthcoming).

259 *"during the present dangerous invasion"*: Peden, ed., *Notes on the State of Virginia*, 125–29.

260 *"the administration of the late Executive"*: This and other quotations in this paragraph are from *The Journal of the House of Delegates, 1781* (Richmond: Thomas White, 1828), 37.

260 *unfair accusations*: Kranish, *Flight from Monticello*, is the most recent of many accounts of Jefferson's actions in 1781. George T. Morrow II (*A Wound on His Spirit*, 60–72 and passim) raised reservations about Jefferson's leadership that echo concerns expressed about Jefferson's character in the election of 1796; e.g., Charles Simms, "To the Freeholders of the Counties of Prince William, Stafford, and Fairfax," *Columbian Mirror and Alexandria Gazette*, Sept. 29, 1796. However, accusations of personal cowardice advanced during that election and later by Light-Horse Harry Lee and his family strike me as unwarranted and unfair (William Loughton Smith et al., *The Pretensions of Thomas Jefferson to the Presidency Examined . . .* [Philadelphia, October 1796], 33–34; Merrill D. Peterson, *The Jefferson Image in the American Mind* [New York: Ox-

ford University Press, 1960], 115–18; Kranish, *Flight from Monticello*, 324–31).
Any wartime executive must avoid capture by the enemy.

261 *Quickly hemmed in:* Leepson, *Lafayette*, 98–103.

Chapter 21: Making Peace

262 *"O God! It is all over":* O'Shaughnessy, *The Men Who Lost America*, 3, 41.

262 *notorious loyalist Goodrich family:* George Mason to Arthur Lee, March 25, 1783, *Mason Papers*, 767; George M. Curtis III, "The Goodrich Family and the Revolution in Virginia, 1774–1776," *VMHB* 84 (1976): 73–74; Randolph, *History*, 232–33, 206; Selby, *Revolution in Virginia*, 208.

262 *"People in this Part of the Country":* Mason to Henry, May 3, 1783, *Mason Papers*, 770–71.

263 *"calculated to feed":* Henry Correspondence, 1: 116.

263 *Virginia's determined efforts:* Merrill Jensen, *The New Nation: A History of the United States During the Confederation* (New York: Alfred A. Knopf, 1950), 302–7; Randolph, *History*, 277–78.

263 *"not worth a continental":* On March 18, 1780, Congress repudiated $200 million in debt by declaring that forty Continental dollars were worth one in gold; Edmund C. Burnett, *The Continental Congress* (New York: Macmillan, 1941), 406–26; E. James Ferguson, *The Power of the Purse: A History of American Public Finance, 1776–1790* (Chapel Hill: University of North Carolina Press, 1961); Ferguson, "The Nationalists of 1781–1783 and the Economic Interpretation of the Constitution," *JAH* 56 (1969): 241–61.

263 *Henry's three-part plan: Journal of the House of Delegates, Anno Domini 1780* (Richmond: John Dixon and Thomas Nicolson, 1780), 37–38.

264 *"give stability to Government":* Morris to the President of Congress, Aug. 1782, quoted in Ferguson, "Nationalists of 1781–1783," 247. Continental Army officers were another component of this initiative; E. Wayne Carp, "The Origins of the Nationalist Movement of 1780–1783: Congressional Administration and the Continental Army," *Pennsylvania Magazine of History and Biography* 107 (1983): 363–92.

264 *leave of absence: Journal of the House of Delegates, 1780*, 39.

264 *ambitious program:* "An act for calling in and redeeming the money now in circulation, and for emitting and funding new bills of credit, according to the resolution of Congress of the eighteenth of March last," Hening, *Statutes*, 10: 241–54.

264 *Henry introduced legislation:* "An act for calling in and funding the paper money of this state," Hening, *Statutes*, 10: 456–57; "An act for ascertaining certain taxes and duties, and for establishing a permanent revenue," ibid., 10: 501–17; Jacquelin Ambler to James Madison, Dec. 22, 1781, *Madison Papers*, 3: 335–36.

264 *imports:* Jackson Turner Main, *The Antifederalists: Critics of the Constitution, 1781–1788* (Chapel Hill: University of North Carolina Press, 1961), 72–102.

264 *"as usual involved in mystery":* Jefferson to James Madison, May 7, 1783; Jefferson to Madison, June 1, 1783, *Jefferson Papers,* 6: 266, 273.

264 *"its strenuous supporter":* Randolph to Madison, May 15, 1783, *Madison Papers,* 7: 44–45.

264 *"an emission of paper currency": Journal of the House of Delegates, October 15, 1787– January 8, 1788* (Richmond: Augustine Davies and Thomas Nicolson, 1788), 23.

264 *"the distresses produced by paper money":* Convention speech, June 9, 1788, *Virginia Ratification,* 1061.

265 *"We are at peace":* Ibid., 1055.

265 *During his initial tenure: Journal of the House of Delegates, Anno Domini 1776* (Williamsburg: Alexander Purdie, 1776), 139; Selby, *Revolution in Virginia,* 149; "Patrick Henry and the Deportation of the Royalists," *Tyler's Quarterly Historical and Genealogical Magazine* 4 (1922): 128–29.

265 *Although Congress feared:* Gov. Benjamin Harrison to John Tyler, Speaker of the House of Delegates, May 6, 1782, H. R. McIlwaine, ed., *Official Letters of the Governors of the State of Virginia,* vol. 3, *The Letters of Thomas Nelson and Benjamin Harrison* (Richmond: Library of Virginia, 1929), 214; Arthur Lee to James Madison, May 16, 1782; Edmund Randolph to Madison, May 16, 1782, ibid., 244–52.

265 *"a strict adherence":* Hening, *Statutes,* 11: 136–38. For comment on the three absentees, see Edmund Randolph to James Madison, Aug. 24, Oct. 26, Nov. 8, and Nov. 16, 1782, *Madison Papers,* 5: 78, 217, 262, 282.

265 *repeal of all prohibitions:* Hening, *Statutes,* 11: 195.

265 *"After painting the distress":* Wirt, *Henry,* 237–38.

266 *"Why should we fetter commerce":* Ibid, 238.

266 *similar measures in other states:* Douglas Bradburn, *The Citizenship Revolution: Politics and the Creation of the American Union, 1774–1804* (Charlottesville: University of Virginia Press, 2009), 58–60.

266 *Spirited debate: Journal of the House of Delegates, October 20–December 20, 1783* (Williamsburg: James Hayes, 1783), 75–76, 128–29, 136, 155; Hening, *Statutes,* 11: 324–25.

266 *Speaker Tyler had challenged Henry:* Quotations in these paragraphs are from Tyler's account of the debate in Wirt, *Henry,* 233–38.

268 *"to travel about": Philip Mazzei: My Life and Wanderings,* 276–78; Jerome O. Steffen, *William Clark: Jeffersonian Man on the Frontier* (Norman: University of Oklahoma Press, 1977), 26–29; Selby, *Revolution in Virginia,* 222–24. Mazzei's lengthy narrative about his European mission is printed in the *Bulletin of the New York Public Library* 38 (1934): 541–62. Henry's letter of support to Governor Benjamin Harrison, April 16, 1784, is in *Henry Correspondence,* 3: 245–47.

268   *"Mr. Mazzei did me great pleasure":* Patrick Henry to James Madison, April 17, 1784, Lloyd W. Smith Collection, Morristown National Historical Park (LVA misc. reel 315). This and six other documents in the Smith collection are not found in *Henry Correspondence*; this letter is in *Madison Papers*, 8: 18.

268   *"small frame building":* Johann David Schoepf, *Travels in the Confederation, 1783–1784,* trans. Alfred J. Morrison (2 vols., Philadelphia: William J. Campbell, 1911), 2: 55–57. Schoepf's mention of Robert Lawson links his observations to the session of October–December 1783, *General Assembly Register,* 150.

269   *"very friendly views":* Madison to Jefferson, April 25, 1784, *Madison Papers,* 8: 20.

269   *"who have plundered and empoverished":* "Petition and Remonstrance from the Freeholders of Prince William County," Dec. 10, 1781, *Mason Papers,* 705. For confirmation of Mason's allegations see his exchange with the state auditors; ibid., 806–7.

270   *Madison and Henry worked together: Madison Papers,* 8: 64–66.

270   *George Mason's contention:* Mason to William Cabell, May 6, 1783; Mason to Henry, May 6, 1783, *Mason Papers,* 768–73; Merrill Jensen, *The New Nation: A History of the United States During the Confederation, 1781–1789* (New York: Alfred A. Knopf, 1950), 279–81.

270   *"the degeneracy of the times":* Virginia Gazette or Weekly Advertiser* (Richmond), May 23, 1782, quoted in Isaac, *Transformation of Virginia,* 277. See also Gordon S. Wood, *The Creation of the American Republic, 1776–1787* (Chapel Hill: University of North Carolina Press, 1969), 109–14.

270   *"We are now to rank":* Mason to Henry, May 6, 1783, *Mason Papers,* 770.

271   *"the general train of his thoughts":* Madison to Jefferson, May 15, 1784, *Madison Papers,* 8: 34; *Jefferson Papers,* 7: 258.

271   *"a watchful eye":* "Rules of the Constitutional Society," June 1784, *Madison Papers,* 8: 71–72.

271   *"feared to run into Scylla":* Mazzei to John Blair, May 12, 1785, Howard R. Marraro, trans., "Philip Mazzei on American Political, Social, and Economic Problems," *Journal of Southern History* 15 (1949): 376–78.

271   *Jefferson still contended:* In a diatribe against the constitution of 1776 that he was composing about this time, Jefferson drastically misrepresented public opinion and the convention's mandate at the time of its adoption; William Peden, ed., *Notes on the State of Virginia* (Chapel Hill: University of North Carolina Press, 1955), 118–29, 283n13. Jack N. Rakove situates these concerns about ratifying conventions in a larger context in *Original Meanings,* 94–130.

272   *"Happily":* Randolph, *History of Virginia,* 253. "Mr. Jefferson's observations . . . have been disarmed of the possibility of mischief by the solemn recognitions in our courts of the validity of the constitution"; ibid., 252. St. George Tucker laid Jefferson's objections to rest once and for all in his influential edition of *Blackstone's Commentaries* (5 vols., Philadelphia: William Young Birch and

Abraham Small, 1803), 1: 79–139. Spencer Roane recalled that he "voted with [Henry] in general" at these Assembly sessions "because he was, as I thought, a more practical statesman than Madison [though] time has made Madison more practical," *Henry Correspondence*, 2: 242.

272   *quirky petition:* Madison transformed this bland comment about political reformation in a petition about hemp and taxes into his attack on the legitimacy of the constitution of 1776. "There are som things in the political Sistem of our constitution which we think are grievous at present and may in time become more so," the Augusta petitioners wrote, "and could a Reformation Take place we think it might be of great utility to the people at large—but these things we leave to the Wisdom of this H[onora]ble House not doubting but they will discover and Rectify these evils and grant Such Relief that equity and Justice will dictate." (Augusta Co. Petition, May 25, 1784, Legislative Petitions of the General Assembly, 1776–1865, Box 15, Folder 42, LVA.)

272   *"before independence":* "Notes for a Speech Favoring Revision of the Virginia Constitution of 1776," June 14 or 21, 1784, *Madison Papers*, 8: 77–78. Lincoln, Message to Congress, July 4, 1861, *Congressional Globe: Containing the Debates and Proceedings of the First Session, The Thirty-Seventh Congress*, ed., John C. Rives (Washington, D.C.: Congressional Globe Office, 1861), 2–3. For the implications of the debate over when the nation began, see Roman J. Hoyos, "Peaceful Revolution and Popular Sovereignty: Reassessing the Constitutionality of Southern Secession," in Sally E. Hadden and Patricia Hagler Minter, eds., *Signposts: New Directions in Southern Legal History* (Athens: University of Georgia Press, 2013), 241–63.

272   *"an intellectual critique":* J. R. Pole, *Political Representation in England and the Origins of the American Republic* (New York: St. Martin's Press, 1966), 297.

272   *"power from [the] people":* "Notes for a Speech," *Madison Papers*, 8: 77. Madison also argued that "revision during the war [would have been] improper" but that "on peace decency requires surrender of power to the people" by a new convention; ibid., 8: 78.

272   *"That all power is vested":* *Revolutionary Virginia*, 7: 449.

272   *"was not the work of an Assembly":* A Friend to the Bill of Rights, *Virginia Journal and Alexandria Advertiser*, April 14, 1785.

273   *"the adverse temper":* Madison to Jefferson, July 3, 1784, *Madison Papers*, 93.

273   *placed the subject of limits: Journal of the House of Delegates, May–June 1784*, 74. The resolution Madison regarded as a permanent barrier to future attempts at a convention appears in the *Journal* at p. 96.

273   *"The proposition for a Convention":* Jefferson to Madison, Dec. 8, 1784, *Jefferson Papers*, 7: 558; *Madison Papers*, 8: 178.

273   *"that he could forgive":* Timothy Pickering to John Marshall, Dec. 26, 1828, *Marshall Papers*, 11: 192–93.

273   *wealthy detractors:* John Parke Custis to George Washington, March 16, 1781, Louisiana State University Library, Baton Rouge; Fielding Lewis, Sr., to

Washington, April 24, 1781; Rosenbach Museum and Library, Philadelphia, Penn.

273 *As a creditor:* Henry's ledger of accounts with John Syme, Jr., is at the Manuscripts Dept., LC.

274 *Henry's legislation:* Hening, *Statutes*, 11: 66–71. Richard R. Beeman recognized the complexity of Henry's approach to fiscal matters in *Patrick Henry: A Biography*, 117–22. Commodities and certificates rather than specie accounted for 72 percent of the $4.6 million Virginia collected in taxes between 1782 and 1785; E. James Ferguson, *The Power of the Purse: A History of American Public Finance, 1776–1790* (Chapel Hill: University of North Carolina Press, 1961), 222.

274 *"particularly welcome":* Ferguson, *The Power of the Purse*, 118.

274 *"sullied":* Edmund Randolph to Theodorick Bland, Jr., May 25, 1782, Charles Campbell, ed., *The Bland Papers: Being a Selection from the Manuscripts of Colonel Theodorick Bland, Jr.* (2 vols., Petersburg, Va.: Edmund and Julian C. Ruffin, 1840–1843), 2: 83. Henry also avoided the radical measures of debt relief adopted to avert violence in South Carolina; Robert A. Becker, "Salus Populi Suprema Lex: Public Peace and South Carolina Debtor Relief Laws, 1783–1788," *South Carolina Historical Magazine* 80 (1979): 65–75.

274 *"the extraordinary effects":* Stuart to William Wirt, Aug. 25, 1816, Henry Papers, LC; Elson, *Patrick Henry Speeches and Writings*, 109–10.

275 *"I have seen him reply":* Henry Correspondence, 2: 214.

275 *Contrary to myths:* Robert A. Gross, ed., *In Debt to Shays: The Bicentennial of an Agrarian Revolution* (Charlottesville: University of Virginia Press, 1993); Leonard L. Richards, *Shays's Rebellion: The American Revolution's Final Battle* (Philadelphia: University of Pennsylvania Press, 2002); David P. Szatmary, *Shays' Rebellion: The Making of an Agrarian Insurrection* (Amherst: University of Massachusetts Press, 1980); Richard D. Brown, "Shays's Rebellion and the Ratification of the Federal Constitution in Massachusetts," in Richard Beeman, Stephen Botein, and Edward C. Carter II, *Beyond Confederation: Origins of the Constitution and American National Identity* (Chapel Hill: University of North Carolina Press, 1987), 113–27.

275 *a boon to speculators:* Woody Holton, *Unruly Americans and the Origins of the Constitution* (New York: Hill & Wang, 2007), 100–107; Holton, review of Richards, *Shays's Rebellion*, in *WMQ*, 3d ser., 60 (2003): 692.

275 *"There are combustibles":* Washington to Henry Knox, Dec. 26, 1786, *Washington Papers, Confederation*, 4: 482.

276 *tax revenues for 1784:* Editorial note, *Madison Papers*, 8: 218n1.

276 *three rival perspectives:* Any responsible account of church-state relations in revolutionary Virginia must rely heavily (as these paragraphs do) on the scholarship of Father Thomas E. Buckley, S.J.—especially his *Establishing Religious Freedom: Jefferson's Statute in Virginia* (Charlottesville: University of Virginia Press, 2013), *Church and State in Revolutionary Virginia, 1776–1787*

(Charlottesville: University of Virginia Press, 1977), and "Patrick Henry, Religious Liberty, and the Search for Civic Virtue," in Daniel L. Dreisbach, Mark David Hall, and Jeffrey H. Morrison, eds., *The Forgotten Founders on Religion* (Notre Dame: University of Notre Dame Press, 2009), 125–44.

276   *Tyler, Cary, Marshall, Harrison:* Buckley, *Church and State*, 192–200.

276   *"duty we owe to our Creator":* Virginia Declaration of Rights, 1776, *Revolutionary Virginia*, 7: 450.

276   *"reserved to the use of the church":* Hening, *Statutes*, 9: 165.

276   *they voted to incorporate:* Buckley, *Church and State*, 192.

277   *"fatal to the Clergy":* Alexander Balmain to John Balmain, May 8, 1783, quoted in Buckley, *Establishing Religious Freedom*, 57.

277   *"The legitimate powers":* Peden, ed., *Notes on the State of Virginia*, 159.

277   *"all dependence":* Hanover Presbytery petition, Oct. 24, 1776, quoted in Buckley, *Establishing Religious Liberty*, 61.

278   *"freely and openly admit":* Schoepf, *Travels in the Confederation*, 2: 62.

278   *"The Episcopal Church":* David Griffith to William White, July 26, 1784, quoted in Buckley, *Church and State*, 86.

278   *"Extraordinary":* Madison to Jefferson, July 3, 1784, *Madison Papers*, 8: 94; *Jefferson Papers*, 7: 361.

278   *"Mr. Henry demolished":* Roane, "Memoir," Elson, *Patrick Henry Speeches and Writings*, 24.

278   *incorporation act:* Hening, *Statutes*, 11: 532–37.

279   *"the great Pillar":* Samuel Sheild to David Griffith, Dec. 20, 1784, quoted in Buckley, *Church and State*, 102.

279   *"a much greater evil":* Madison to Jefferson, Jan. 9, 1785, *Jefferson Papers*, 7: 594–95; editorial note, *Madison Papers*, 8: 228–29.

279   *a general assessment:* Randolph to Thomas Jefferson, May 15, 1784, *Jefferson Papers*, 7: 260.

279   *"a general assessment upon all Tythables":* Warwick County petition, May 15, 1785, Legislative Petitions, LVA acc. no. 3612, Box 248, Folder 1 (microfilm reel 196).

279   *"happy influence":* Minutes of the Hanover Presbytery, Oct. 28, 1784, quoted in Buckley, *Establishing Religious Freedom*, 69.

279   *"that the people of this Commonwealth": Journal of the House of Delegates, Oct. 18, 1784–Jan. 7, 1785* (Richmond: Nicolson and Prentis, 1784), 17.

279   *"Establishing a Provision":* Henry's bill was published in the *Virginia Journal and Alexandria Advertiser*, March 17, 1785, and is printed in Buckley, *Church and State*, 188–89.

280   *Henry's bill looked backward:* Jefferson Autobiography, 4. Madison had previously studied at a school run by Donald Robertson in King and Queen County; Madison to Joseph Delaplaine, Sept. 1816, Jefferson Papers, LC; Kevin R. C. Gutzman, *James Madison and the Making of America* (New York: St. Martin's Press, 2012), 1.

280　"*The father of the Scheme*": Madison to Monroe, Nov. 27, 1784, *Madison Papers*, 8: 157–58.

280　*On Christmas Eve:* Buckley, *Establishing Religious Freedom*, 69–70.

281　"*they viewed the Incorporation Act*": Buckley, *Establishing Religious Freedom*, 70–72.

281　"*contrary to the Spirit*": Nov. 1785 petitions quoted in Buckley, *Church and State*, 148.

282　"*previous to the revolution*": John Marshall to William B. Sprague, July 22, 1828, *Marshall Papers*, 11: 168.

282　"*Matters*": Henry to Madison, April 17, 1784, Smith Collection; *Madison Papers*, 8: 18.

282　"*arrived yesterday*": Madison to Jefferson, May 15, 1784, *Madison Papers*, 8: 34; *Jefferson Papers*, 7: 258.

282　"*Mr. Jones and Mr. Madison*": Short to Jefferson, May 14, 1784, *Jefferson Papers*, 7: 257.

283　"*our Embassy*": John Adams to Abigail Adams, Sept. 18, 1774, *Letters of Delegates*, 1: 79.

283　"*The members of Congress*": Count Gijsbert Karel van Hogendorp's account of a conversation with Thomas Jefferson, translated in *Jefferson Papers*, 7: 52.

284　*£27 million:* Ferguson, *Power of the Purse*, 180.

284　"*all requisitions*": *Journal of the House of Delegates, May–June 1784*, 14–15; "An act to invest the United States in congress assembled, with additional powers for a limited time," Hening, *Statutes*, 11: 388–89; "Bill Authorizing an Amendment to the Articles of Confederation," *Madison Papers*, 8: 83–85.

284　"*bold Example*": Short to Jefferson, May 14, 1784, *Jefferson Papers*, 7: 257. Madison and Henry disagreed on other issues during this session, but the editors of the *Madison Papers* (8: 37) were wrong to accuse Henry of deceit about congressional revenues.

Chapter 22: Governor Again

285　land-office business: The *OED* dates this phrase to the New Orleans *Daily Picayune*, April 2, 1839.

285　"*treasury certificates*": Hening, *Statutes*, 11: 50–65. Nearly 120,000 land grants issued between 1776 and 2000 are accessible via the Library of Virginia's online catalogue (www.lva.gov) searching on the phrase *land office*. The information presented here is based on more detailed online searches within that data and examination of digitized pages from Land Office Grant books M (1781–1784) and N (1784–1785), LVA (also available on LVA microfilm reels 53 and 54). I am grateful to Minor Weisiger for his expert advice about the Land Office and its records.

285　*population of Kentucky:* Jon Kukla, *A Wilderness So Immense: The Louisiana*

Purchase and the Destiny of America (New York: Alfred A. Knopf, 2003), 112–13.

286 *"Hasty and excitable":* David Campbell quoted in Peter J. Kastor, "Arthur Campbell," *DVB*, 2: 555.

286 *"introduce such alteration":* Washington Co. memorial to Congress, Nov. 18, 1784, quoted in Kastor, "'Equitable Rights and Privileges': The Divided Loyalties in Washington County, Virginia, during the Franklin Separatist Crisis," *VMHB* 105 (1997): 211; Kevin T. Barksdale, *The Lost State of Franklin: America's First Secession* (Lexington: University Press of Kentucky, 2008).

286 *"become so weak":* Campbell to Henry, May 21, 1785, Patrick Henry Executive Papers, LVA, quoted in Kastor, "Equitable Rights," 213.

287 *"swiftly":* Ibid., 215.

287 *Henry's sister Elizabeth:* Jon Kukla, "Elizabeth Henry Campbell Russell: Champion of Faith in the Early Republic," in Cynthia A. Kierner and Sandra Gioia Treadway, eds., *Virginia Women: Their Lives and Times* (Athens: University of Georgia Press, 2015), 160–79.

287 *Treason Act:* Hening, *Statutes*, 12: 41–42; Kastor, "Equitable Rights," 218–19.

287 *"to separate": Executive Journals Va. Council*, 3: 497.

287 *strip Campbell:* Ibid., 3: 577.

287 *"wild men":* Kastor, "Equitable Rights," 224.

287 *"You are drawing so close to us":* Record of a Council at Wakitunikee, May 18, 1785 (British Museum), quoted in Colin G. Galloway, "'We Have Always Been the Frontier': The American Revolution in Shawnee Country," *American Indian Quarterly* 16 (1992): 47.

288 *"seeming inattention":* Henry to Congress, May 16, 1786, *Henry Correspondence*, 3: 354.

288 *"experience":* Henry to Virginia Delegates, May 16, 1786, ibid., 3: 350.

288 *Article VI:* Keith L. Dougherty, *Collective Action Under the Articles of Confederation* (New York: Cambridge University Press, 2001), 109.

288 *Congress referred:* Ibid., 110.

288 *"more hostile":* Charles Pettit to James Wilson, July 2, 1786, *Letters of Delegates*, 23: 381.

289 *"fallen a sacrifice":* Samuel McDowell to Patrick Henry, April 18, 1786, Governor's Office, Patrick Henry Executive Papers, LVA.

289 *"My dear sister":* Henry to Anne Henry Christian, May 15, 1786, *Henry Correspondence*, 2: 286–87.

289 *Danville:* John May to Henry, April 19, 1786, Governor's Office, Patrick Henry Executive Papers, LVA. May's report of Christian's death was published in *The Virginia Journal and Alexandria Advertiser*, May 25, 1786.

289 *aching Heart:* Henry to Fleming, May 15, 1786, Darlington Autograph Files, Box 3, Folder 79, Special Collections Department, University of Pittsburgh. I am grateful to Mark Couvillon for bringing this letter to my attention, and to

Dr. Palmer C. Sweet, retired state geologist, for advice about its content. Unless otherwise identified, this letter is the source of all quotations in the next few paragraphs.

290 *"a very carefull and exact Tryal"*: Ibid; "Noel Waddill," in Catherine B. Hollan, *Virginia Silversmiths, Jewelers, Watch- and Clockmakers, 1607–1860: Their Lives and Marks* (McLean, Va.: Hollan Press, 2010), 766–68. Noel Waddill's relationship with William Waddill, a less prominent and slightly older jeweler, engraver, and goldsmith, is undetermined. Henry mentioned no given name and could have consulted either man.

290 *"an inexhaustible Stock"*: Henry to Fleming, May 15, 1786.

290 *"the Almighty Power of Gold"*: Robert Beverley; *The History and Present State of Virginia* (1st ed., London, 1705), ed. Susan Scott Parish et al. (Chapel Hill: University of North Carolina Press, 2013), 24.

291 *"the reservation of royal mines"*: Hening, *Statutes*, 10: 61. Interestingly, the Land Office statute of 1779 specified Sept. 29, 1775 (not June 29 or July 4, 1776), as the operative date for land titles authorized by the commonwealth; ibid., 10: 65.

291 *"although the Law"*: Henry to Fleming, May 15, 1786.

291 *take over the lead mines*: Hening, *Statutes*, 9: 287–88.

292 *"necessary at this time"*: Hening, *Statutes*, 9: 287.

292 *"and perhaps succeed"*: Henry to Fleming, May 15, 1786.

292 *news of the gold discoveries*: *Massachusetts Centinel* (Boston), May 10; *Independent Chronicle* (Boston), May 11; *American Recorder and Charlestown Advertiser*, May 5; *Independent Journal* (New York), May 6; *American Mercury* (Hartford), May 8; *Norwich Packet*, May 18; *New-Jersey Gazette* (Trenton), May 8, 1786. The Richmond paper from which these out-of-state items were reprinted (probably dated April 19, 1786) apparently is not extant. I have not been able to locate a Reading Creek in Virginia; I am indebted to Yorktown historian Edward Ayres for calling my attention to Read Creek, described in several 1780s land grants as a tributary of the Holston and New Rivers, near modern Wytheville in what was until 1789 Montgomery County.

292 *gold mining prospered*: Palmer C. Sweet, *Gold in Virginia* (Charlottesville: Department of Conservation and Economic Development, 1980), 1–5; Sweet and James A. Lovett, "Additional Gold Mines, Prospects, and Occurrences in Virginia," *Virginia Minerals* 81 (1985): 41–52.

292 *Cabarrus County*: Richard F. Knapp, "Golden Promise in the Piedmont: The Story of John Reed's Mine," *North Carolina Historical Review* 52 (1975): 1–19.

293 *"the difficulty of raising"*: Madison to Jefferson, Aug. 12, 1786, *Jefferson Papers*, 10: 235.

293 *"want of punctuality"*: Jefferson to Madison, Dec. 12, 1786, *Jefferson Papers*, 605.

293 *"a personal stake"*: Woody Holton, *Unruly Americans and the Origins of the Constitution* (New York: Hill & Wang, 2007), 25–26.

293 *"prevailing and increasing distrust":* Madison, *Federalist* No. 10, Jacob E. Cooke, ed., *The Federalist* (Middletown, Conn.: Wesleyan University Press, 1961), 57.

293 *"crack down on delinquent":* Holton, *Unruly Americans,* 9.

293 *veto state laws:* Max Farrand, ed., *Records of the Federal Convention of 1787* (rev. ed., 4 vols., New Haven: Yale University Press, 1937), 1: 21, 131, 140, 150, 164–68; 3: 3: 134, 399, 424, 494, 516, 523, 527, 549; Kevin R. C. Gutzman, *James Madison and the Making of America* (New York: St. Martin's Press, 2012), 120; Larry D. Kramer, "Madison's Audience," *Harvard Law Review* 112 (1999): 649–53; Mary Sarah Bilder, *Madison's Hand: Revising the Constitutional Convention* (Cambridge: Harvard University Press, 2015), 70–78.

293 *"too many people":* Henry to Fleming, May 15, 1786. Henry frequently acquired property by trade. See his offer to exchange land he owned near Richmond and in Henry County for land in Charlotte, Cumberland, Halifax, or Prince Edward counties; *Virginia Gazette or American Advertiser,* Feb. 15, 1786.

293 *"good Counsel":* Henry to Fleming, May 15, 1786.

294 *"mortified":* Henry to the Virginia Delegates in Congress, July 5, 1786, *Henry Correspondence,* 3: 362–68; *Letters of Delegates,* 23: 399n3.

294 *"till the united states":* Merrill Jensen, ed., *Documentary History of the Ratification of the Constitution, Ratification of the Constitution by the States,* vol. 1, *Constitutional Documents and Records, 1776–1787* (Madison: State Historical Society of Wisconsin, 1976), 88.

294 *"that a decided answer":* Henry to the Virginia Delegates, 365–68.

295 *"in readiness":* Congressional resolution quoted in Dougherty, *Collective Action,* 110.

295 *"to cooperate":* Henry to Harmar, July 12, 1786, ibid., 111 and 111n19; Alan S. Brown, "The Role of the Army in Western Settlement: Josiah Harmar's Command, 1785–1790," *Pennsylvania Magazine of History and Biography* 93 (1969): 161–78.

296 *"under the command":* Secretary at War Henry Knox to Harmar, Jan. 22, 1787, quoted in Dougherty, *Collective Action,* 111.

296 *$500,000 loan:* Dougherty, *Collective Action,* 117–19.

296 *the General Assembly responded:* Hening, *Statutes,* 12: 288–89; Dougherty, *Collective Action,* 118–19.

297 *"of such high importance":* James Monroe to Patrick Henry, Aug. 12, 1786, *Letters of Delegates,* 23: 462–66.

297 *"This is one of the most extraordinary":* Ibid.

298 *"Havanna Segars":* Richard Henry Lee to Thomas Lee Shippen, June 4, 1785, *Letters of Delegates,* 23: 22.

298 *"The Confederation admits":* King to Caleb Davis, Oct. 17 and Nov. 3, 1785, *Letters of Delegates,* 22: 691n, 718–20. The Philadelphia convention replaced Article 6, Section 2 of the Articles of Confederation (requiring permission from Congress before any "two or more states shall enter into any treaty, confeder-

ation, or alliance, whatever, between them") with Article I, Section 10 of the Constitution, which abruptly stipulated that "No State shall enter into any Treaty, Alliance, or Confederation" (Farrand, *Records of the Federal Convention*, 2: 135), though I am grateful to John Pagan for pointing out that Article I, Section 10, Paragraph 3 does permit an "agreement or compact with another State, or with a foreign power" with "consent of Congress."

299 *"if Congress had":* King to Davis, Nov. 3, 1785, *Letters of Delegates*, 22: 718–20.

299 *"The Southern States":* Nathan Dane to Edward Pulling, Jan. 9, 1786, ibid., 23: 85. Dane practiced law in Beverly, across the harbor from Salem, and later participated in the Hartford convention.

299 *"all the men":* Dane to King, Aug. 11, 1786, ibid., 23: 488.

299 *"happy to lea[r]n":* King to Dane, Aug. 17, 1786, ibid., 23: 488–89.

299 *"They can give us nothing":* Theodore Sedgwick to Caleb Strong, Aug. 6, 1786, ibid., 23: 436.

300 *"domestic insurrection":* Max Farrand, ed., *Records of the Federal Convention of 1787* (rev. ed., New Haven: Yale University Press, 1937), 2: 364. I am grateful to Alan Taylor and Woody Holton for advice on this theme. Holton quoted Martin's observation in *Unruly Americans*, 220–22. Wartime observers had frequently mentioned the strategic weakness occasioned by slavery, exemplified by Dunmore's famous proclamation of November 7, 1776, offering freedom to slaves and indentured servants who joined "His Majesty's forces"; Selby, *Revolution in Virginia*, 65–68.

300 *"obscure men":* Count Gijsbert Karel van Hogendorp's account of a conversation with Thomas Jefferson, translated in *Jefferson Papers*, 7: 52.

300 *"foremost in the second rank":* Robert Ernst, *Rufus King: American Federalist* (Chapel Hill: University of North Carolina Press, 1968), vii.

300 *"rich and wise and good":* Stephen E. Patterson, "The Roots of Massachusetts Federalism: Conservative Politics and Political Culture Before 1787," in Ronald Hoffman and Peter J. Albert, *Sovereign States in an Age of Uncertainty* (Charlottesville: University of Virginia Press, 1981), 38–39.

300 *pace of western settlement:* Andrew R. L. Cayton, *The Frontier Republic: Ideology and Politics in the Ohio Country, 1780–1825* (Kent, Ohio: Kent State University Press, 1986), 23; Gordon S. Wood, *Empire of Liberty: A History of the Early Republic, 1789–1815* (New York: Oxford University Press, 2009), 114–23. Jay believed the United States had ample land east of the Appalachian Mountains. In 1779, as president of Congress, Jay supposed that if Spain closed the Mississippi to American trade for a period of years the interruption might force backcountry settlers to establish family farms, develop "an attachment to property and industry," and stop "living in a half-savage condition." "Would it not be wiser," he mused privately to Jefferson, "gradually to extend our Settlements than to pitch our Tents through the Wilderness in a great Variety of Places, far distant from each other, and from those Advantages of Education, Civilization, Law, and Government which compact Settlements and Neigh-

bourhood afford?" John J. Meng, ed., *Despatches and Instructions of Conrad Alexandre Gérard, 1778–1780: Correspondence of the First French Minister to the United States with the Comte de Vergennes* (Baltimore: Johns Hopkins University Press, 1939); 433–34, 494, 531; Jay to Jefferson, Dec. 14, 1786, *Jefferson Papers*, 10: 599; Kukla, *A Wilderness So Immense*; and Eli Merritt, "Sectional Conflict and Secret Compromise: The Mississippi River Question and the United States Constitution," *American Journal of Legal History* 35 (1991): 117–71.

301 *rumblings from western Massachusetts:* Patterson, "The Roots of Massachusetts Federalism," 38–39; Robert A. Gross, ed., *In Debt to Shays: The Bicentennial of an Agrarian Revolution* (Charlottesville: University of Virginia Press, 1993), 1–3, 101–30; Joseph Parker Warren, ed., "Documents Relating to the Shays Rebellion," *AHR* 2 (1896–1897): 694–95.

301 *threw their support:* The desperation felt by King and Gorham is evident in their inquiries (through Baron von Steuben) about recruiting Prince Henry of Prussia to restore a monarchy in America; Richard Krauel, "Prince Henry of Prussia and the Regency of the United States, 1786," *AHR* 17 (1911): 44–51.

301 *"The negotiations":* Louis-Guillaume Otto to the Comte de Vergennes, Sept. 10, 1786, Archives du Ministère des affaires étrangères: Correspondance politique, États-Unis, 32: 65–71; translated in George Bancroft, *History of the Formation of the Constitution of the United States* (New York: D. Appleton, 1882), 2: 389–93. I amended Bancroft's translation as shown: "The secret *reasons* ~~motives~~ for the heat with which each *side* ~~state~~ supports its opinion. . . ."

302 *exaggerated hyperbole:* e.g., Middlekauf, *The Glorious Cause*, 609.

302 *"In conversations":* James Monroe to Patrick Henry, Aug. 12, 1786, *Letters of Delegates*, 23: 466.

302 *Monroe invoked:* The seemingly innocuous phrase "conversations at which I have been present" is an example of what Joanne B. Freeman described as "references to honor disputes that are invisible to modern eyes"; Freeman, *Affairs of Honor: National Politics in the New Republic* (New Haven: Yale University Press, 2001), 174, 177. The honor code guided the secret deliberations of Congress, too. At its first session in 1774, Congress had resolved that its doors "be kept shut during the debates And that every Member be obligd under the strongest obligation of Honor to keep secret the proceedings of the Congress until they shall be ordered to be publishd"—a fact that delegates quickly learned to explain to their friends. "I am obliged to be very reserved," wrote one typical congressman (none other than John Jay), "by the Injunction of Secrecy laid on all the Members of the Congress, and tho I am aware of the Confidence I might repose in your Prudence, I must nevertheless submit to the Controul of Honour." James Duane's Notes of Debates, September 6, 1774; John Jay to John Vardill, September 24, 1774, *Letters of Delegates*, 1: 31, 95. References to *secrecy* or *secrets* occur 1,305 times in Smith's twenty-five volumes of congressional correspondence.

303 *"Not finding a better occasion":* Diego de Gardoqui to the Comte de Florida-

blanca, Aug. 20, 1786, Legajo 3.893, Ap. 6 s.n., Archivo Histórico Nacional, Madrid.

304 *conspiracies:* Bailyn, *Ideological Origins,* 144–59; Wood, "Conspiracy and the Paranoid Style," 401–41.

304 *Virginia's circular letter:* One exception was Forrest McDonald, who savored the irony in *E Pluribus Unum: The Formation of the American Republic, 1776–1790* (Boston: Houghton Mifflin, 1965), 142.

305 *"Many of our most federal leading men":* James Madison to George Washington, Dec. 7, 1786, William T. Hutchinson, William M. E. Rachal, Robert A. Rutland et al., eds., *Papers of James Madison* (Chicago: University of Chicago Press; Charlottesville: University of Virginia Press, 1962–), 9: 199–200.

305 *destiny of the Old Dominion:* Drew McCoy, "James Madison and Visions of American Nationality in the Confederation Period: A Regional Perspective," in Beeman, Botein, and Carter, eds., *Beyond Confederation,* 226–58; Peter Onuf, "Liberty, Development and Union: Visions of the West in the 1780s," *WMQ,* 3d ser., 43 (1986): 179–213.

Chapter 23: The New Constitution

307 *"In the first moment":* On Sept. 24, 1787, Washington sent copies of the Constitution to Henry, Benjamin Harrison, and Thomas Nelson, Jr. His letter to Henry was first printed in Jared Sparks, ed., *Writings of George Washington,* vol. 9 (Boston: Russell, Odiorne, and Metcalf, 1825), 265–66, and reprinted in *Henry Correspondence,* 2: 319–20. Only the letter to Harrison is printed in *Washington Papers, Confederation,* 5: 339. The letter to Nelson apparently is not extant; ibid., 6: 422 (where the editors inexplicably misidentified the offices held in 1787 by all three recipients, who were former governors of Virginia then serving in the General Assembly). Before leaving Philadelphia, Washington had also dispatched copies of the Constitution to Jefferson and Lafayette on Sept. 18; ibid., 5: 333–34.

307 *"as a Citizen":* Henry to Washington, Oct. 19, 1787, *Washington Papers, Confederation,* 5: 384; and *Henry Correspondence,* 2: 320–21.

308 *"habit of close and attentive observation":* Meredith memorandum, 1805, Elson, *Patrick Henry Speeches and Writings,* 210.

308 *Mason's* Objections: "Mason's Objections Written on the Committee of Style Report," Sept. 16, 1787, *Mason Papers,* 991–94; *Virginia Ratification,* 40–46; Maier, *Ratification,* 87.

309 *"all ambiguities": A Letter of His Excellency Edmund Randolph, Esquire, on the Federal Constitution* (Richmond: Augustine Davis, 1787), 15–16; Evans, *Bibliography* no. 20669. Randolph's *Letter* is also printed in *Virginia Ratification,* 260–75.

309 *"had several animated discourses":* Randolph to Madison, Oct. 29, 1787; *Virginia Ratification,* 133; Reardon, *Edmund Randolph,* Maier, *Ratification,* 89–90; *Ratification Documents,* 15: 117–21.

309 *chronically indecisive:* Commenting on Randolph's refusal to sign the Constitution, a Philadelphia lawyer wrote that Randolph "is said to be afraid of the democracy and Patrick Henry"; Robert Milligan to William Tilghman, Sept. 20, 1787, *Virginia Ratification*, 13. As is evident from their correspondence between Oct. 1787 and June 1788, Madison stoked Randolph's anxieties by playing up the antifederalists' reputed indifference to the union. *Virginia Ratification*, passim; *Madison Papers*, 9: passim.

309 *"the advantage":* A Letter of His Excellancy Edmund Randolph, 16. The paragraph describing Randolph's willingness to accept the Constitution (*Virginia Ratification*, 274) was omitted when his letter was reprinted along with other antifederalist essays in *Observations on the Proposed Constitution . . . Clearly shewing it to a be complete System of Aristocracy and Tyranny and Destructive of the Rights and Liberties of the People* (New York: No publisher, 1788), 45. Evans, *Bibliography*, no. 21344.

309 *"Good God!":* Spencer Roane, "A Plain Dealer," *Virginia Independent Chronicle*, Feb. 13, 1788; Jon Kukla, "A Spectrum of Sentiments: Virginia's Federalists, Antifederalists, and 'Federalists Who Are For Amendments,' 1787–1788," *VMHB* 96 (1988): 294.

310 *"the general situation":* Harrison to Washington, Oct. 4, 1787, *Virginia Ratification*, 35–36; *Washington Papers: Confederation*, 5: 353.

310 *"I can never agree":* Henry to Thomas Madison, Oct. 21, 1787, *Virginia Ratification*, 31n1, 88.

310 *"strike at the essence":* Madison to Thomas Jefferson, Dec. 9, 1787, *Virginia Ratification*, 227; *Madison Papers*, 10: 312. For the context of Madison's analysis in this letter, see Kukla, "A Spectrum of Sentiments," 277–96.

310 *"according to the recommendation":* Virginia Ratification, 110–12.

311 *"the power of proposing amendments":* Petersburg Virginia Gazette, Nov. 1, 1787; ibid., 113.

311 *"with his usual perspicuity":* Ibid., 114.

311 *"that there were errors":* Virginia Ratification, 113, 119n7.

311 *"in case the said Convention":* Draft Resolution Concerning the State Convention, Dec. 4, 1787, House of Delegates Original Bills (LVA acc. no. 35162), Box 11.

311 *"friendly sentiments":* Virginia Ratification, 190–91.

311 *"Since they have discovered their Strength":* Archibald Stuart to James Madison, Dec. 2, 1787, *Virginia Ratification*, 196.

312 *"An act concerning the Convention":* Hening, *Statutes*, 12: 462–63, Evans, *Bibliography*, no. 20842.

312 *"own perusal":* Editorial note, *Virginia Ratification*, 789.

312 *six-week delay:* Governor Randolph's letter, Dec. 27, 1787, ibid., 192.

312 *"of such vast Importance":* Clinton to Randolph, May 8, 1788, ibid., 790–91.

312 *"Immediately on receiving it":* Randolph to the Speaker of the House of Delegates, June 23, 1788, ibid., 794; *Journals Va. Council of State*, 4: 221–58, 361–62.

312 *Randolph kept it secret:* Randolph to the Speaker, June 23, 1788, *Virginia Ratification*, 794.

313 *five state conventions:* Maier, *Ratification*, 97–158.

313 *Henry and Clinton:* John P. Kaminski, *George Clinton: Yeoman Politician of the New Republic* (Madison, Wis.: Madison House, 1993), 114–21, 131–39; Jon Kukla, "Patrick Henry and George Clinton: State Governors and Opponents of the Constitution," *Newsletter of the Patrick Henry Memorial Foundation* (Spring 2005), 1–6; Keith L. Dougherty, *Collective Action Under the Articles of Confederation* (New York: Cambridge University Press, 2001), 68–69.

313 *"must go":* David Stuart to Washington, Oct. 16, 1787, *Virginia Ratification*, 66–67. Dr. Stuart, who represented Fairfax County in the legislature and the convention of 1788, had married Eleanor Custis, the widow of Washington's adopted son; ibid., 529.

313 *"not yet been able":* Tobias Lear to John Langdon, Oct. 19, 1787, ibid., 80.

313 *"the part Mr. Henry will take":* Madison to Jefferson, Nov. 1, 1787, ibid., 106–7.

314 *"This gentleman fires his shot":* John Pierce to Henry Knox, Nov. 12, 1787, ibid., 155–56.

314 *"Henry digresses":* Archibald Stuart to John Breckinridge, Oct. 21, 1787, ibid., 89.

314 *"unnecessary":* John Pierce to Henry Knox, Nov. 12, 1787, ibid., 1556–56.

314 *"unaccountable":* Tobias Lear to John Langdon, Dec. 3, 1787, ibid., 197.

314 *"Mr. Henry has declared":* George Lee Turberville to Madison, Dec. 12, 1787, ibid., 234.

314 *"is determined to amend":* Carrington to Madison, Jan. 18, 1788, ibid., 309.

315 *"the only fair candidate":* Rufus King to Henry Knox, Feb. 3, 1788, quoted in Maier, *Ratification*, 195. John Trumbull later told John Adams that "the whole affair" of Hancock's "grand manoeuvre of limping forth . . . to propose nonsensical amendments . . . was planned and conducted as a political measure by men of more discernment than himself"; Trumbull to Adams, March 30, 1790, quoted in ibid., 318n33.

315 *"exert all their influence":* Maier, *Ratification*, 192–213, quotation at p. 196.

315 *"The decision of Massachusetts":* Carrington to Henry Knox, March 13, 1788, *Virginia Ratification*, 491.

315 *"politics to have been":* Carrington to Madison, Feb. 10, 1788, ibid., 359–60.

315 *"does not openly":* Carrington to Jefferson, April 24, 1788, ibid., 755.

316 *"and his Minions":* James Duncanson to James Maury, March 11, 1788, ibid., 479.

316 *"Henry and others":* Griffin to Thomas FitzSimons, Feb. 18, 1788, ibid., 382.

316 *"plunge into anarchy":* Crevecoeur to William Short, April 1, 1788, ibid., 636.

316 *"better acquainted":* Madison to Randolph, Jan. 10, 1788, ibid., 289.

316 *the allegation:* The State Soldier II, *Virginia Independent Chronicle*, Feb. 6, 1788, ibid., 349; A Freeholder, *Virginia Independent Chronicle*, April 9, 1788, ibid., 728.

316 *"distinguished from all the others":* Comte de Moustier to Comte de Montmo-

rin, June 25, 1788, ibid., 1679. Moustier's full letter, in French, was published in *AHR* 8 (1903): 730–33. Other explicit comments about Henry's alleged separatist aims include Miles King to an unknown recipient, Nov. 26, 1787, *Virginia Ratification*, 175–76; Tobias Lear to John Langdon, Dec. 3, 1787, ibid., 197; George Gilmer to Jefferson, Dec. 23, 1787, ibid., 257; George Nicholas to Madison, April 5, 1788, ibid., 703; Madison to Jefferson, April 22, 1788, ibid., 745; and Carrington to Jefferson, April 24, 1788, ibid., 755.

316 *"You may think":* Hugh Williamson to John Gray Blount, New York, June 3, 1788, *Virginia Ratification*, 609; Jon Kukla, "William Grayson's Notes on the United States Constitution," *Virginia Phoenix* 7, no. 1 (1974): 2–14; Kukla, "'Freedom and Good Government': Antifederalist William Grayson's Intended Amendments to the United States Constitution," *Virginia Cavalcade* 36 (1987): 184–91.

317 *announced his candidacy:* Henry Correspondence, 2: 332–33; John Luster Brinkley, *On This Hill: A Narrative History of Hampden-Sydney College, 1774–1994* (Hampden-Sydney: Hampden-Sydney College, 1994), 30–37.

317 *Pleasant Grove:* Couvillon, *Patrick Henry's Virginia*, 81–83.

317 *"walked and meditated":* Couvillon, *Patrick Henry: Corrections by Edward Fontaine*, 11.

317 *forty slaves:* Netti Schreiner-Yantis and Florene Speakman Love, comps., *Personal Property Tax Lists for the Year 1787 for Henry County, Virginia* (Springfield, Va., Genealogical Books in Print, 1987), 664.

317 *newly created district courts:* Hening, *Statutes*, 12: 532–59.

317 *"riding chair":* Schreiner-Yantis and Love, comps., *Personal Property Tax Lists for the Year 1787 for Prince Edward County, Virginia* (Springfield, Va., Genealogical Books in Print, 1987), 1288–1301. At the extremes of wealth among the county's 881 householders, 299 (34 percent) owned no slaves, while 49 (.06 percent) owned 1,291 slaves (39 percent of the county's enslaved population). The county's 533 middling planters owned 2,010 slaves—about 3.8 per household. Of the other taxable items subject to the March 1787 inventory, fourteen householders owned two-wheeled chairs, eight owned four-wheeled coaches, nine owned stud horses, none owned a billiard table, two were licensed physicians, and two owned licensed ordinaries.

317 *"had never been in easy circumstances":* Edmund Winston quoted in *Henry Correspondence*, 2: 330–31. William Wirt Henry identified Col. John Holcombe as the advisor and client.

318 *"full power":* Hening, *Statutes*, 12: 548.

318 *"John Fontaine's widow":* Diary of Richard N. Venable, May 10, 1792, quoted in *Henry Correspondence*, 476–77.

318 *proximity to Hampden-Sydney:* Hening, *Statutes*, 11: 272–73; Meade, *Practical Revolutionary*, 270; Brinkley, *On This Hill*, 10n1, 19n18, 28n35.

318 *seven of his sons:* Edith C. Poindexter, "Henry Sons at Hampden-Sydney," personal communication, Nov. 26, 2014.

318 *"You will have perceived"*: Smith to Madison, June 12, 1788, *Virginia Ratification*, 607. Madison graduated from the College of New Jersey ahead of Smith but stayed on for another year of study; both men were active in Princeton's American Whig Society; Charles Grier Sellers, Jr., "John Blair Smith," *Journal of the Presbyterian Historical Society* 34 (1956): 201–25.

319 *"contempt and indignation"*: Smith to Madison, June 12, 1788, *Virginia Ratification*, 607.

319 *"religious phrensy"*: Thomas Jefferson to William Short, Dec. 14, 1789, *Jefferson Papers*, 16: 26. "Brother Sam," John Blair Smith once told his elder brother Samuel Stanhope Smith, founding president of Hampden-Sydney and later president of the College of New Jersey, "you don't preach Jesus Christ and him crucified, but Sam Smith and him dignified"; A. Owen Aldridge, "An Early American Adaptation of French Pulpit Oratory," *Eighteenth Century* 28 (1967): 238.

319 *"unfair and underhanded"*: Brinkley, *On This Hill*, 36.

319 *a story*: Hugh Blair Grigsby, *History of the Virginia Convention of 1788* (2 vols., Richmond: Virginia Historical Society, 1890), 1: 32.

320 *"the measure proposed"*: Smith to Madison, June 12, 1788, *Virginia Ratification*, 607.

Chapter 24: We the States

321 *"to take into consideration"*: *Virginia Ratification*, 909–10.

321 *"Gentlemen who formed"*: Ibid., 930–31.

322 *"the best dancer"*: Arthur Pierce Middleton, "The Colonial Virginia Parson," *WMQ*, 3d ser., 26 (1969): 426; G. MacLaren Brydon, "Clergy of the Established Church in Virginia and the Revolution," *VMHB* 41 (1933): 303–4.

322 *"plan of federal government"*: *Virginia Ratification*, 910.

322 *"the New Academy"*: *Virginia Ratification*, 910; Martin Staples Shockley, "The Richmond Theatre, 1780–1790," *VMHB* 60 (1952): 421–36; John G. Roberts, "The American Career of Quesnay de Beaurepaire," *The French Review* 20 (1947): 468–70; Adele Clark, "Academy Square, Richmond, Virginia," *Medical College of Virginia Bulletin* 25, no. 9 (Nov. 1928): 9–13.

322 *"were as nearly equal"*: William Grayson to Nathan Dane, June 4, 1788, *Virginia Ratification*, 1573.

322 *"freely and fully"*: *Virginia Ratification*, 914.

322 *Mason's insistence*: Although antifederalist William Grayson believed "this is in our favor" (Grayson to Nathan Dane, June 4, 1788, *Virginia Ratification*, 1573), Madison's influential comment that Mason and Henry "appeared to take different and awkward ground found its way into many newspapers (Madison to Rufus King, June 4, 1788; Madison to George Washington, June 4, 1788; *Massachusetts Centinel*, June 18, 1788, ibid., 1574, 1648). See also Grigsby, *Virginia Federal Convention of 1788*, 287–89, and Kukla, "A Spectrum of Sen-

timents," 286. The late Pauline Maier generously acknowledged her reliance upon my "spectrum model" for her *Ratification: The People Debate the Constitution, 1787–1788* (New York: Simon & Schuster, 2010), 504n80.

323 *"precious"; Virginia Ratification*, 915.

323 *"whether the federal Convention":* Ibid., 917.

323 *"he was willing":* Ibid., 917–29.

323 *"The public mind":* Ibid., 929–30.

324 *"What right":* Ibid., 930–31.

324 *"Wholly to adopt":* Ibid., 931–36.

324 *"Whether the Constitution":* Ibid., 936–41.

325 *"great pleasure":* Ibid., 940–41.

325 *"Two unlucky circumstances":* Grayson to Nathan Dane, June 4, 1788, *Virginia Ratification*, 1573.

325 *"thrown himself fully":* Madison to Rufus King, June 4, 1788, *Virginia Ratification*, 1573.

326 *extracts from private letters: Virginia Ratification*, 1571. Five published extracts were from members of the convention.

326 *"It is a Matter of Great Consolation":* Henry to Lamb, June 9, 1788, *Virginia Ratification*, 817. For details about the reprints, see ibid., 827n13.

326 *"a common one": Virginia Ratification*, 945–46.

326 *"the honors":* Ibid., 949.

327 *"on that poor little thing":* Ibid., 951.

327 *"Eight states":* Ibid., 951–52.

327 *"lived long enough":* Ibid., 952–53.

328 *"What, sir, is the genius of democracy?":* Ibid., 956.

328 *"organizing, arming, and disciplining":* Ibid., 957, 960–61.

328 *"the power of direct taxation":* Ibid., 961–62, emphasis added.

329 *"squints toward monarchy":* Ibid., 963.

329 *"If your American chief ":* Ibid., 964.

330 *"continue in friendship":* Ibid., 966.

330 *"those States will be fond":* Ibid., 966–68.

330 *"Mr. H made a great effort":* Madison to unknown recipient (perhaps Edward Carrington), June 6, quoted in Samuel A. Otis to Theodore Sedgwick, June 15, 1788, *Virginia Ratification*, 1629, emphasis added.

331 *ten-year-old capital case:* W. P. Trent, "The Case of Josiah Philips," *American Historical Review* 1 (1896): 444–54; Selby, *Revolution in Virginia*, 206; Malone, *Jefferson the Virginian*, 292–93.

331 *"insurgents": Executive Journals Va. Council*, 1: 435–36.

331 *$250 reward: Governor's Letters*, 267, 268n297, 300; *Executive Journals Va. Council*, 1: 435–36; 2: 58, 127, 169, 210.

331 *"high treason": Jefferson Papers*, 2: 189–93; Hening, *Statutes*, 9: 468–69. Technically the act was a *conditional* attainder (without ex post facto elements) because it imposed punishment only if the attained failed to surrender for trial;

Charles H. Wilson, Jr., "The Supreme Court's Bill of Attainder Doctrine: A Need for Clarification," *California Law Review* 54 (1966): 240.

331 *Once Philips was taken: VG* (Purdie), June 19, Oct. 30, 1778; *VG* (Dixon and Hunter), Oct. 30, Dec. 4, 1778.

331 *"violations of the state constitution": Virginia Ratification*, 972. Compare the details of Randolph's version with the factual narrative in the editorial note in the *Jefferson Papers*, 2: 190–93.

331 *"legislative vortex": Virginia Ratification*, 972.

332 *"Without being confronted":* Ibid.

332 *personal affronts:* The fact that Randolph regarded Henry as the guilty legislator in his retelling of the Philips episode is clear from his transitional remark that "The Honorable Gentleman [Patrick Henry] went on further and said that the accession of eight States is not a reason for our adoption"; ibid., 973.

332 *"unsafe":* Ibid., 983.

333 *"spoke so low":* Ibid., 989.

333 *"that the powers given":* Ibid., 999; Jeffrey Allen Zemler, "'A Conciliatory Declaration': George Nicholas, the Virginia Ratification Convention, and the Misuse of History," *Register of the Kentucky Historical Society* 112 (2014): 179–97.

333 *"The powers of the general government are only": Virginia Ratification*, 1007–15, quotations at p. 1010.

333 *"continue his observations":* Ibid., 1016.

334 *"a national rather than a federal government":* Ibid., 1020.

334 *"the general government the power":* Ibid., 1028–35, 1047n, quoted at p. 1030; Jacob E. Cooke, ed., *The Federalist* (Middletown, Conn.: Wesleyan University Press, 1961), 110–29, 616–19.

334 *"he had made a most conclusive argument":* Grigsby, *Virginia Federal Convention of 1788*, 88n.

334 *"There are certain maxims": Virginia Ratification*, 1036. For the civic-educational value of maxims recognized especially by Henry and John Marshall, see Akhil Reed Amar, *The Bill of Rights: Creation and Reconstruction* (New Haven: Yale University Press, 1998), 131–32.

334 *"that all men": Virginia Ratification*, 1036.

335 *"The Honorable member has said":* Ibid.

335 *"The Honorable member has given":* Ibid., 1038.

335 *Pressing Randolph even harder:* Robertson explained in a footnote that "Governor Randolph had cursorily mentioned the word *herd* in his second [June 7] speech"; ibid., 1047.

335 "abominable": Ibid., 1044–45, emphasis in original.

336 *arrival of Eleazer Oswald:* "Second Attempt at Cooperation between Virginia and New York Antifederalists," *Virginia Ratification*, 811–13.

336 *"Committee of Opposition":* William Grayson to John Lamb, June 9, 1788; *Virginia Ratification*, 816.

336 *"Members of the Convention":* George Mason to Lamb, June 9, 1788; ibid., 818.

336 *"our Republican Society":* Henry to Lamb, June 9, 1788; ibid., 817.

336 *"a Bill of Rights":* Ibid., 819; "Amendments to the New Constitution of Government," ibid., 821–23.

336 *"Congress shall":* Ibid., 822.

337 *"young [Benedict] Arnold":* George Mason to John Mason, Dec. 18, 1788, *Mason Papers*, 1136.

337 *Jefferson's suggestion:* Ibid., 1052. Jefferson's suggestion (expressed in letters to Alexander Donald, James Madison, and William Stephens Smith in February 1788) was widely known in Virginia and North Carolina. He later embraced the Massachusetts example of recommended amendments as "far superior"; ibid., 1088n7.

337 *"His sentiments coincide":* Virginia Ratification, 1050.

337 *"how will his present doctrine":* Ibid., 1057–58, emphasis added.

337 *"Knowing that system":* Ibid., 1058.

337 *"prove the consistency":* Ibid., 1082–83, emphasis in original.

338 *"Mr. Henry arose":* Ibid., 1082.

338 *cryptic personal exchange:* Ibid., 1082. No one has ever determined what if anything Randolph had in mind.

338 *"lose our influence":* Ibid., 1084. I have corrected *loose* to *lose*.

338 *"The only question":* Ibid., 1092.

338 *"have been elaborate":* James Breckinridge to John Breckinridge, June 13, 1788, ibid., 1620–21.

339 *"was indefatigable":* William Nelson, Jr., to William Short, July 12, 1788, ibid., 1701.

339 *"I have left my ever dear":* A photograph of Henry's letter to Anne Henry Roane, June 15, 1788, is reproduced in the Maggs Brothers auction catalogue, *Rare and Interesting Autograph Letters, Signed Documents, Manuscripts, etc.* (Leamington, U.K.: Courier Press, 1921), plate 6.

339 *contested elections:* Virginia Ratification, 594–95, 1440–44.

340 *Kentucky delegates:* Charles Gano Talbert, "Kentuckians in the Virginia Convention of 1788," *Register of the Kentucky Historical Society* 58 (1960): 187–93.

340 *"It is said that we are scuffling":* Ibid., 1245.

340 *"a Quorum to do Business":* Article I, section 5, U.S. Constitution; "two thirds of the Senators *present*," Article II, section 2, emphasis added.

340 *"Northern States":* Virginia Ratification, 1192.

340 *"was considered a perfect likeness":* George Morgan, *The True Patrick Henry*, viii. Morgan quoted an account, written in 1859 by one T. W. Walter of Washington, D.C., saying that "during the session of the great Virginia Convention," Henry sat for the bust "at the request of Judge [John] Tyler . . . Mr. Madison, Judge Marshall, and other friends," ibid.; Virginius Cornick Hall, Jr., "Notes on Patrick Henry Portraiture," *VMHB* 71 (1963): 168–69.

341 *"critical situation":* Virginia Ratification, 1474.

341 *"to the other States":* Ibid., 1479, emphasis added.

341 *"fatal effects":* Ibid., 1476; Robin L. Einhorn, "Patrick Henry's Case Against the Constitution: The Structural Problem with Slavery," *Journal of the Early Republic* 22 (2002): 549–73; Einhorn, *American Taxation, American Slavery* (Chicago: University of Chicago Press, 2006), 173–83.

341 *"striking differences": Virginia Ratification,* 1221–22.

341 *"wicked pact with the devil":* Robert F. Durden, *The Self-Inflicted Wound: Southern Politics in the Nineteenth Century* (Lexington: University Press of Kentucky, 1985), 54; John P. Kaminski, ed., *A Necessary Evil? Slavery and the Debate over the Constitution* (Madison, Wis.: Madison House, 1995), 18–23, 43–58; George William Van Cleve, *A Slaveholder's Union: Slavery, Politics, and the Constitution in the Early American Republic* (Chicago: University of Chicago Press, 2010), 114–39; David Waldstreicher, *Slavery's Constitution: Revolution to Ratification* (New York: Hill & Wang, 2009); Garry Wills, *Negro President: Jefferson and the Slave Power* (New York: Houghton Mifflin, 2003).

342 *"calm light of philosophy": Virginia Ratification,* 1483; Einhorn, "Patrick Henry's Case," 569. Einhorn noted that of Henry's major biographers all but Henry Mayer, *A Son of Thunder: Patrick Henry and the American Republic* (New York: Franklin Watts, 1986), 433 (now joined by Thomas S. Kidd, *Patrick Henry: First Among Patriots* [New York: Basic Books, 2011], 285n42) ignored the existence of his arguments about slavery in the Virginia convention ("Patrick Henry's Case," 551n4); that Herbert J. Storing omitted them from his edition of *The Complete Anti-Federalist* (7 vols., Chicago: University of Chicago Press, 1981); and that many other scholars dismissed them as a desperate effort to use "any argument he could find to oppose the Constitution"; Paul Finkelman, "Slavery and the Constitutional Convention: Making a Covenant with Death," in Richard Beeman, Stephen Botein, and Edward C. Carter II, eds., *Beyond Confederation: Origins of the Constitution and American National Identity* (Chapel Hill: University of North Carolina Press, 1987), 193n13.

342 *"over states where":* Einhorn, "Patrick Henry's Case," 553–54, emphasis in original.

342 *"Slavery is detested": Virginia Ratification,* 1476; Einhorn, "Patrick Henry's Case," 552.

342 *"They'll free":* Hugh Blair Grigsby wrote in the 1850s that he "was told by a person on the floor of the Convention . . . when Henry had painted in the most vivid colors the dangers likely to result to the black population from the unlimited power of the federal government . . . and had filled his audience with fear, he suddenly broke out with the homely exclamation: '*They'll free your Niggers!'* The audience passed instantly from fear to wayward laughter; and [Grigsby's] informant said that it was most ludicrous to see men who a moment before were half frightened to death with a broad grin on their faces." Grigsby, *Virginia Federal Convention of 1788,* 157n142. Henry Mayer inexplicably changed the wording to "They'll take your niggers from you"; Mayer, *A Son of Thunder,* 433. Thomas Kidd doubted the authenticity of the quotation

"given Henry's documented sober comments about slavery at the convention, and the belated nature of the source"; Kidd, *Patrick Henry*, 285n42.

342 *"As much as I deplore": Virginia Ratification*, 1477.

342 *"the necessity":* Ibid.

343 *"a great deal": Virginia Ratification*, 1477.

343 *"a greater variety":* Madison, *Federalist* No. 10, Cooke, ed., *The Federalist*, 64. Douglass Adair, "The Tenth Federalist Revisited," and "'That Politics may be Reduced to a Science': David Hume, James Madison, and the Tenth Federalist," in Trevor Colbourn, ed., *Fame and the Founding Fathers: Essays by Douglass Adair* (New York: W. W. Norton, 1974), 75–106. These influential essays were first published, respectively, in the *WMQ*, 3d ser., 8 (1951): 48–67, and *Huntington Library Quarterly* 20 (1957): 343–60.

343 *"will be broken":* Madison, *Federalist* No. 51, Cooke, ed., *The Federalist*, 351.

343 *"a Republican remedy":* Madison, *Federalist* No. 10, Cooke, ed., *The Federalist*, 65. Recent scholarship in the wake of Douglass Adair's classic work includes Jack N. Rakove, "James Madison in Intellectual Context," *WMQ*, 3d ser., 59 (2002), 865–68; Mark G. Spencer, "Hume and Madison on Faction," ibid., 869–96; Woody Holton, "'Divide et Imperia': *Federalist 10* in a Wider Sphere," ibid., 62 (2005): 175–212; and Marc M. Arkin, "'The Intractable Principle': David Hume, James Madison, Religion, and the Tenth Federalist," *American Journal of Legal History* 39 (1995): 148–76.

343 *For better or worse:* Larry D. Kramer, "Madison's Audience," *Harvard Law Review* 112 (1999): 611–79, argues that Madison's theory about enlarging the republic in order to curb factionalism "was simply over the heads" (p. 663) of most contemporaries; rejected by the few who understood it (Jefferson, Hamilton, and Gouverneur Morris); completely without influence either at Philadelphia or in the ratifying conventions; and abandoned by its author after the ratification, who mentioned it "no more than once or twice during the entire rest of his life" (p. 670).

343 "beings *of a higher order": Virginia Ratification*, 1506, emphasis in original.

344 *"the feelings":* Roane, "Memoir," Elson, *Patrick Henry Speeches and Writings*, 137.

344 *"we have it": Virginia Ratification*, 1506.

344 *"for the same purpose":* Ibid., 1516.

344 *"some future annalist":* Ibid., 1537.

344 *"If I shall be":* Ibid.

345 *"Form of Ratification":* Ibid., 1542, 1546.

345 *"may be resumed":* Ibid., 1546. These stipulations resurface in later debates over secession; Hoyos, "Peaceful Revolution and Popular Sovereignty," 241–63; Amar, *The Bill of Rights: Creation and Reconstruction*, 119–27.

345 *"that the Minority":* Washington to Lear, June 29, 1788; *Virginia Ratification*, 1715, emphasis in original.

346 *"in a constitutional way": Virginia Ratification*, 1537.

346 *"strike at the essence":* Madison to Thomas Jefferson, Dec. 9, 1787, *Madison Papers*, 10: 312; Kukla, "A Spectrum of Sentiments," 290–95.

346 *"essential and inalienable rights": Virginia Ratification*, 1551. For a detailed comparison of the early June drafts and the final proposed amendments, see "The Ratification of the Constitution and the Recommendation of Amendments," ibid., 1512–15, and Wythe's June 27 committee report, ibid., 1551–59.

346 *Amendment Three distinguished soveriegnty:* This paragraph draws heavily upon Kukla, "A Spectrum of Sentiments," 291–92. Because the power of taxation was of such importance, and because Amendment Three addressed several of Pendleton's objections to the Constitution, I disagree with his biographer's dismissal of Pendleton's support for the amendment as merely a gesture "to mollify Henry and Mason"; Mays, *Pendleton*, 2: 270; Kukla, "A Spectrum of Sentiments," 283–85.

347 *"some middle course":* James Monroe, *Some Observations on the Constitution* (Fredericksburg, 1788), in *Writings of James Monroe*, ed. Stanislaus Murray Hamilton (7 vols., New York: G. P. Putnam's Sons, 1898–1903), 1: 320–21; *Virginia Ratification*, 844–46, 857.

347 *"has been distressing and awful":* Roane to Aylett, June 26, 1788, "Letters of Spencer Roane, 1788–1822," *Bulletin of the New York Public Library* 10 (1906): 167; *Virginia Ratification*, 1713.

347 *"either wise enough": Independent Gazetteer* (Philadelphia), July 2, 1788, *Virginia Ratification*, 1697–98. Celebrations of Virginia's ratification *were* held in Alexandria, Norfolk, and Winchester as well as some northern cities; ibid., 1709.

347 *"Both parties": Connecticut Gazette*, July 11, 1788, ibid., 1713n2.

348 *"the late Convention":* George Mason, Draft Resolutions Reprimanding Governor Edmund Randolph, ca. June 28, 1788, *Virginia Ratification*, 792.

348 *"to reconcile":* "A Spectator of the Meeting," *Virginia Independent Chronicle*, July 9, 1788, ibid., 1560.

348 *"fiery": Massachusetts Centinel*, July 26, 1788, ibid., 1561.

348 *"a deputation":* David Meade Randolph, "Anecdotes of Patrick Henry," *Southern Literary Messenger* 1 (1834–1835): 332, reprinted in *Virginia Ratification*, 1561–62. Randolph was a Federalist who was later thrown out of office by Thomas Jefferson; his wife, Mary Randolph, wrote the famous cookbook, *The Virginia Housewife* (Washington, D.C., 1824).

Chapter 25: Amendments and Abolition

349 *£16 5s 3d: Virginia Ratification*, 1566.

349 *"commencing proceedings":* Merrill Jensen, Robert A. Becker, Gordon DenBoer, et al., eds., *Documentary History of the First Federal Elections, 1788–1790* (4 vols., Madison: University of Wisconsin Press, 1976–1989), 1: 50.

349 *"become a question":* Madison to Edmund Randolph, Aug. 22, 1788, *Madison Papers*, 11: 237; see also Madison to Washington, Aug. 11, 1788, ibid, 11: 230.

349 *"the most precious rights":* Charles Lee to George Washington, Oct. 29, 1788, *Washington Papers, Confederation,* 1: 82. Henry's resolution, adopted on Oct. 30, is printed in *Virginia Ratification,* 1764.

350 *"The Edicts":* Washington to James Madison, Nov. 17, 1788, *Madison Papers* 11: 349. Washington's private secretary, Tobias Lear, shared similar observations at greater length with John Langdon of New Hampshire; Lear to Langdon, Jan. 11, 1789, *Documentary History of the First Federal Elections,* 2: 398.

350 *"in parliamentary science":* Richard Bland Lee to James Madison, Oct. 29, 1788, *Madison Papers,* 11: 322–23.

350 *"Mr. Henry is the only orator":* Ibid.

350 *"The triumph":* George Lee Turberville to Madison, Nov. 10, 1788, ibid., 11: 340.

350 *"successfully undermined":* Madison to Edmund Randolph, Aug. 22, 1788, ibid., 11: 237; Robert Allen Rutland, *The Ordeal of the Constitution: The Antifederalists and the Ratification Struggle of 1787–1788* (Norman: University of Oklahoma Press, 1966), 285.

350 *"to bow":* Henry Correspondence, 2: 420–22.

350 *"and yet the gentleman tells us":* Ibid., 2: 420.

350 *"by a despot":* Cauls were the mesh caps upon which wigs were constructed; *OED.* A caul-bare wig is shabby or threadbare.

351 *"thirteen of the most graceful bows":* William Wirt Henry attributed this detail to "the authority of William L. Tabb, of Mecklenburg, who was present"; *Henry Correspondence,* 2: 421.

351 Nescia: Wirt, *Sketches,* 306; *The AEneid of Virgil,* ed. Theodore C. Williams (Boston: Houghton Mifflin, 1908), Book 10, line 502 (p. 351).

351 *"a plain man":* Henry Correspondence, 2: 421.

351 *"sank at least a foot":* William Wirt Henry attributed this observation to Spencer Roane, ibid., 2: 422.

352 *"wedded to freedom":* Theodorick Bland to Richard Henry Lee, Oct. 28, 1788, *Documentary History of the First Federal Elections,* 2: 267.

352 *"manifest Enmity":* Henry to Lee, Nov. 15, 1788, Henry Papers, LC.

352 *"as a sort of Right":* Ibid. Some admiring biographers and historians implicitly concur.

352 gerrymandered: E.g., Editorial note, *Madison Papers,* 11: 302; Editorial note, *Jefferson Papers,* 16: 143, 145; Thomas Rogers Hunt, "The First Gerrymander? Patrick Henry, James Madison, James Monroe, and Virginia's 1788 Congressional Districting," *Early American Studies* 9 (2011): 781–820.

353 *"Gerry-mander":* "The Gerry-mander: A new species of Monster, which appeared in Essex South District in January last," *Boston Gazette,* March 26, 1812.

353 contiguous: Maps of Virginia's congressional and presidential electoral districts are reproduced in *Documentary History of the First Federal Elections,* 2: 248–49, from Lester J. Cappon et al., eds., *Atlas of Early American History* (Princeton: Princeton University Press, 1976), 72–73. Edward Carrington told Madison

about federalist efforts to add Fauquier County to the Fifth District in a letter on Nov. 14, 1788, *Madison Papers*, 11: 345.

353 *residency requirement:* Edward Carrington to James Madison, Nov. 9, Nov. 14, 1788, *Madison Papers*, 11: 337, 345.

353 *"not to be trusted":* George Lee Turberville to James Madison, Nov. 16, 1788, *Madison Papers*, 11: 346.

353 *"to vote against direct taxation":* Edmund Randolph to Madison, Nov. 10, 1788, ibid., 11: 338.

353 *"political character":* Lee to Madison, Nov. 19, 1788, ibid., 11: 356.

353 *Madison ran for Congress:* "Election of Representatives: District 5," *Documentary History of the First Federal Elections*, 2: 317–49; Editorial note, "Madison's Election to the First Federal Congress, October 1788–February 1789," *Madison Papers*, 11: 428–29.

354 *Madison bested Monroe: Fredericksburg Virginia Herald*, Feb. 12, 1789, *Documentary History of the First Federal Elections*, 2: 346; the statewide results are at ibid., 2: 254, 356.

354 *voting for presidential electors:* Ibid., 2: 298–309.

354 *"for George Washington":* Ibid, 2: 304. The official record indicated only the total votes for each presidential candidate. The French consul Martin Oster, who attended their meeting, described the votes cast by each elector; Oster to the Comte de La Luzerne, Feb. 11, 1789, ibid., 2: 401.

355 *campaign pledge:* Introducing his slate of amendments on June 8, 1789, Madison declared that he was "bound in honor and in duty . . . not to let the first session pass over without proposing to the State Legislatures some things to be incorporated into the constitution that will render it as acceptable to the whole people of the United States as it has been found acceptable to a majority of them," so that "those who have been friendly to the adoption of this constitution may have the opportunity of proving to those who were opposed to it that they were as sincerely devoted to liberty and a Republican Government as those who charged them with wishing the adoption of this constitution in order to lay the foundation of an aristocracy or despotism." *Debates and Proceedings of the Congress of the United States*, ed. Joseph Gales, vol. 1 (Washington, D.C.: Gales and Seaton, 1834): 442, 448–49. Robert Allen Rutland's classic narrative *The Birth of the Bill of Rights, 1776–1791* (Chapel Hill: University of North Carolina Press, 1955), 194–221, tells the story of Madison's "campaign pledge fulfilled." See also Helen E. Veit, Kenneth R. Bowling, and Charlene Bangs Bickford, eds., *Creating the Bill of Rights: The Documentary Record from the First Federal Congress* (Baltimore: Johns Hopkins University Press, 1991); Jon Kukla, ed., *The Bill of Rights: A Lively Heritage* (Richmond: Library of Virginia, 1987); David J. Bodenhamer and James W. Ely, Jr., eds., *The Bill of Rights in Modern America: After 200 Years* (Bloomington: Indiana University Press, 1993); and Akhil Reed Amar, *The Bill of Rights: Creation and Reconstruction*.

355 *stifling the movement:* Linda Grant De Pauw, "The Anticlimax of Antifederalism: The Abortive Second Convention Movement, 1788–89," *Prologue: The Journal of the National Archives* 2 (1970): 98–114.

355 *"from motives of* policy": Grayson to Henry, June 12, 1789; *Henry Correspondence,* 2: 443, 3: 391, emphasis added; Napoleone Orsini, "'Policy': Or the Language of Elizabethan Machiavellianism," *Journal of the Warburg and Courtauld Institutes* 9 (1946): 122–34; George L. Mosse, "Puritanism and Reason of State in Old and New England," *WMQ,* 3d ser., 9 (1952): 67–80.

355 *"will tend to injure":* Henry to Lee, Aug. 28, 1789, *Henry Correspondence,* 2: 444.

355 *"the single amendment":* David Stuart to George Washington, Sept. 12, 1789, *Washington Papers, Presidential,* 4: 28.

355 *"Milk and Water Propositions":* George Mason to John Mason, July 31, 1789, *Mason Papers,* 1164; Kenneth R. Bowling, "'A Tub to the Whale': The Founding Fathers and Adoption of the Federal Bill of Rights," *Journal of the Early Republic* 8 (1988): 223–51.

356 *"to carry Mount Atlas":* Grayson to Henry, Aug. 24, 1789; Henry Correspondence, 2: 444.

356 *"far short":* Brent Tarter, "Virginians and the Bill of Rights," in Kukla, *The Bill of Rights: A Lively Heritage,* 13–14.

356 *Francis Corbin engineered:* Ibid., 14–15.

356 *The remaining three states:* Rutland, *Birth of the Bill of Rights,* 220.

357 *"the treachery":* Decius's Letters on the Opposition to the New Constitution in Virginia (Richmond: Augustine Davis, 1789), 11; all quotations are from this 134-page booklet (Evans, Bibliography, no. 21971), which included the Decius letters and many responses. The original letters appeared in Davis's *Virginia Independent Chronicle* from Dec. 1, 1788, through July 15, 1789; Editorial note, *Jefferson Papers,* 16: 139–45.

357 *"lurks under":* Decius's Letters on the Opposition, 12.

357 *"A Federalist":* Ibid., 66.

357 *"into a thousand":* Ibid., 59.

357 *"miserable scribbler":* Thomas Jefferson to James Monroe, Jan. 8, 1811, *Jefferson Retirement Papers,* 3: 286; Manning J. Dauer, "The Two John Nicholases: Their Relationship to Washington and Jefferson," *AHR* 45 (1940): 338–53; V. Dennis Golladay, "Jefferson's 'Malignant Neighbor,' John Nicholas, Jr.," *VMHB* 86 (1978): 306–19.

357 *"passion was to get":* Henry Stevens Randall, *Life of Thomas Jefferson* (3 vols., New York: Derby and Jackson, 1858), 2: 371; Golladay, "Jefferson's 'Malignant Neighbor,'" 306–19.

358 *"a malignant neighbor":* Jefferson, "The Anas," Feb. 4, 1818, in *Jefferson Works,* 1: 183.

358 *"I neither am the author":* Innes to Henry, March 28, 1789, *Henry Correspondence,* 2: 436.

358 *"a general calm":* Randolph to Madison, March 27, 1789, *Madison Papers,* 12: 31.

358 *"With respect":* Grayson to Henry, June 12, 1789, *Henry Correspondence,* 3: 389–90.

358 *literary allusion:* Decius characterized Grayson as "in the alphabet of his English education" and prone to "unmeaning jargon" and "clumsey jokes"; *Decius's Letters on the Opposition,* 25. The comment attributed to Addison is conflated from two essays: "Censure is the tax a man pays to the public for being eminent," from *Spectator No. 101* and the phrase "envy and detraction," from *Spectator No. 253; Works of the Right Honourable Joseph Addison, Esq.* (3 vols., London: Jacob Tonson, 1721), 3: 22, 251.

359 *"Federal and anti":* Henry to Grayson, March 31, 1789, *VMBH* 14 (1906): 202–4.

359 "unprofitable Servant": Ibid., 203, emphasis added; Matthew 22:30.

359 *"political understrappers":* Henry to Grayson, March 31, 1789, 203.

359 *previous biographers:* The 1773 letter from Henry to Pleasants and 1777 letter from Pleasants to Henry are widely known (published in *Henry Correspondence,* 1: 151–53; 3: 49–51, and elsewhere), but no previous biographer consulted the subsequent correspondence in Robert Pleasants Letter Books at Haverford College or the Pleasants Family Papers in the Brock Collection at the Huntington Library (both available on microfilm at LVA, misc. reels 506, 4238–41), or grappled with the implications of Robin L. Einhorn, "Patrick Henry's Case Against the Constitution: The Structural Problem with Slavery," *JER* 22 (2002): 549–73. Thomas S. Kidd (*Patrick Henry: First Among Patriots,* 285n42) cited Einhorn's article in regard to Hugh Blair Grigsby's report of Henry's alleged comment about "niggers" in the convention of 1788.

359 *"While ye have":* Pleasants to Henry, Jan. 25, 1790, Robert Pleasants Letter Book, 100–102. Compare his letters to Washington, Dec. 11, 1785, ibid., 103–4; and Jefferson, June 1, 1796, and Feb. 8, 1797, ibid., 235; *Jefferson Papers,* 29: 120, 287. The biblical quotation is a slight adaptation of John 12:35.

359 *"sentiments":* Pleasants to Henry, Jan. 25, 1790.

360 *"contrary": Journal of the House of Delegates, 1785–1786* (Richmond: 1786), 25.

360 *counterpetitions:* Fredrika Teute Schmidt and Barbara Ripel, eds., "Early Proslavery Petitions in Virginia," *WMQ* 3d ser., 30 (1973): 133–46. The original documents are at LVA.

360 *"The property":* David W. Robson, ed., "'An Important Question Answered': William Graham's Defense of Slavery in Post-Revolutionary Virginia," *WMQ,* 3d ser., 37 (1980): 651.

361 *Fear:* Ibid., 647; Don B. Kates, Jr., "Abolition, Deportation, Integration: Attitudes Toward Slavery in the Early Republic," *Journal of Negro History* 53 (1968): 44.

361 *"Outrages":* Schmidt and Ripel, eds., "Early Proslavery Petitions," 140.

361 *"freeing":* Robson, ed., "'An Important Question Answered,'" 651.

361 *Their language may shock:* Schmidt and Ripel, eds., "Early Proslavery Petitions," 133–46. These observations first appeared in Kukla, "The Irrelevance and Relevance of Saints George and Thomas," *VMHB* 102 (1994): 261–70.

361 *"When the British Parliament":* Quotations in this summary are drawn heavily from the Amelia, Lunenburg, Mecklenburg, and Pittsylvania petitions, which also included scriptural references and arguments; Schmidt and Ripel, eds., "Early Proslavery Petitions," 138–43.

362 *"as much as": Virginia Ratification,* 1476–77.

362 *"unconstitutional":* John Leland, *The Virginia Chronicle, with Judicious and Critical Remarks* (Norfolk: Prentis and Baker, 1790), 10. "The whole scene of slavery," Leland wrote in language that echoed the observations of Thomas Jefferson and many others, "is pregnant with enormous evils. On the master's side, pride, haughtiness, domination, cruelty, deceit, and indolence; and on the side of the slave, ignorance, servility, fraud, perfidy, and despair"; ibid.

362 *$9.23 billion:* Claudia D. Goldin and Frank D. Lewis, "The Economic Cost of the American Civil War: Estimates and Implications," *Journal of Economic History* 35 (1975): 321–22.

362 *"similar to those":* "To the Friends of Liberty," *Virginia Independent Chronicle and General Advertiser,* Jan. 20, Feb. 10, 1790. These announcements were followed by the publication of a "Plan for liberating the Negroes within the United States" (ibid., March 31, 1790), that elicited replies from "A.C." and "The Moderate Slaveholders" (ibid., June 1, July 14, 1790).

362 *"sacrifice":* Pleasants to Henry, Jan. 25, 1790, Robert Pleasants Letter Book, 100–102; Davis, *Problem of Slavery in the Age of Revolution,* 197. References to Richmond editor Augustine Davis's publication of Pleasants's proposal for a Virginia abolition society appear in the *New-Hampshire Spy,* Feb. 6, 1790, and a March 29 letter from Williamsburg excerpted in the *Philadelphia Independent Gazetteer,* Nov. 6, 1790.

362 *efforts to rescind:* For the tenuous majority that upheld manumission but rejected emancipation, see *Journal of the House of Delegates, 1785–1786,* 25, 28, 91, 107, 123, 143; and *Journal of the House of Delegates, 1787–1788,* 97, 99, 100.

362 *met again:* Pleasants referred to their conversation "the fall before last in Richmond" in Pleasants to Henry, July 21, 1792, Robert Pleasants Letter Book, 110–11.

362 *"search that paper": Virginia Ratification,* 1476.

363 *avoiding any discussion: Documentary History of the First Federal Congress of the United States of America,* vol. 8, *Petition Histories and Nonlegislative Official Documents,* ed. Kenneth R. Bowling, William Charles diDiacomantonio, and Charlene Bangs Bickford (Baltimore: Johns Hopkins University Press, 1998): 314–38; Richard S. Newman, "Prelude to the Gag Rule: Southern Reaction to Antislavery Petitions in the First Federal Congress," *Journal of the Early Republic* 16 (1996): 576.

363 *three antislavery petitions:* Howard A. Ohline, "Slavery, Economics, and Congressional Politics, 1790," *JSH* 46 (1980): 341; Van Cleve, *A Slaveholder's Union,* 191–203, 289–91.

363 *"step to the very verge":* Petition of the Pennsylvania Society for Promoting the

Abolition of Slavery, Feb. 3, 1790, presented to Congress, Feb. 19, 1790, *Debates and Proceedings of the Congress of the United States*, ed. Joseph Gales, vol. 2 (Washington, D.C.: Gales and Seaton, 1834): 1239–40.

363 *"the very circumstance"*: Carrington to James Madison, April 7, 1790, *Madison Papers*, 13: 142.

363 *"It has disturbed"*: Stephen to Madison, April 25, 1790, ibid., 13: 176.

363 *"the subject of Slavery"*: Thomas Pleasants, Jr., to Madison, July 10, 1790, ibid., 13: 271. Newman, "Prelude to the Gag Rule," 592, 597, mistakenly attributed this letter to the Virginia Quaker Robert Pleasants.

363 *"the silly petition"*: Adams to Thomas Crafts, May 25, 1790, quoted in Ohline, "Slavery, Economics, and Congressional Politics," 344.

363 *"so zealously"*: Gorham to Theodore Sedgwick, April 18, 1790, quoted in ibid., 356.

364 *"no authority"*: Resolution of the Committee of the Whole, March 23, 1790, *Debates and Proceedings of the Congress*, 2: 1239.

364 *"an improper time"*: Pleasants reminded Henry that when they last spoke, he had "intimated" that in light of the controversy in Congress "it would be an improper time to move in such a business"; Pleasants to Henry, July 21, 1792; Robert Pleasants Letter Book, 110.

364 *"been decisive in not passing Laws"*: Ibid., emphasis added.

364 *Richmond newspapers*: E.g., "Proceedings of Congress," *Virginia Independent Chronicle and General Advertiser*, June 1, June 30, July 14, 1790.

364 *"The people of Virginia"*: Randolph to Madison, May 20, 1790, *Madison Papers*, 13: 224; Richard R. Beeman, *The Old Dominion and the New Nation, 1788–1801* (Lexington: University Press of Kentucky, 1972), 67–82.

364 *The political bargain*: Stanley Elkins and Eric McKitrick, *The Age of Federalism* (New York: Oxford University Press, 1993), 155–61; Norman K. Risjord, *Chesapeake Politics, 1781–1800* (New York: Columbia University Press, 1978), 363–93; 649–51; Jacob E. Cooke, "The Compromise of 1790," *WMQ*, 3d ser., 27 (1970): 523–45; Kenneth Bowling, "Dinner at Jefferson's: A Note on Jacob E. Cooke's 'The Compromise of 1790,'" ibid., 33 (1976): 629–40; Melvin Yazaw, "Republican Expectations: Revolutionary Ideology and the Compromise of 1790," in Donald R. Kennon, ed., *A Republic for the Ages: The United States Capitol and the Political Culture of the Early Republic* (Charlottesville: University of Virginia Press, 1999), 3–35.

364 *"The mad policy"*: Lee to James Madison, April 3, 1790, *Madison Papers*, 13: 136–37; "Is your love for the constitution so ardent," Lee challenged Madison, "as to induce you to adhere to it tho it should produce ruin to your native country. I hope not." Lee to Madison, ibid., Beeman *Old Dominion and New Nation*, 76–77.

365 *"The late transactions"*: Stuart to Washington, June 2, 1790, *Washington Papers, Presidential*, 5: 458, 462.

365 *"he was too old"*: Ibid., 5: 463.

365 *exalted titles:* David McCullough, *John Adams* (New York: Simon & Schuster, 2001), 404–8.

365 *"Resolved, That so much of the act":* Journal of the House of Delegates, 1790 (Richmond: John Dixon, 1790), 36; Hening, *Statutes*, 13: 234. The vote on Henry's resolution was 78 to 51, and an attempted substitute resolution was defeated by a vote of 47 to 88.

366 *"striking resemblance":* The address is printed in *Journal of the House of Delegates, 1790*, 81–82, 141–42, and Hening, *Statutes*, 13: 237–39, and discussed in detail in Beeman, *Old Dominion and New Nation*, 79–82.

367 *"repugnant to the constitution":* In Philadelphia alone the resolutions appeared in *The Federal Gazette and Philadelphia Advertiser*, Nov. 16, *Gazette of the United States*, Nov. 17, *General Advertiser and Political, Commercial, Agricultural and Literary Journal*, Nov. 18, and *Pennsylvania Mercury and Universal Advertiser*, Nov. 25, 1790.

367 *"in complete harmony":* Beeman, *Old Dominion and New Nation*, 81.

367 *"to aim a blow":* Stuart to Washington, June 2, 1790; *Washington Papers, Presidential*, 5: 462.

368 interposition *not* nullification: Christian G. Fritz, "Interposition: An Overlooked Tool of American Constitutionalism," in Neil H. Cogan, ed., *Union and States' Rights: A History and Interpretation of Interposition, Nullification, and Secession 150 Years After Sumter* (Akron, Ohio: University of Akron Press, 2014), 169.

368 *"in a constitutional way":* Virginia Ratification, 1237.

368 *"a practical guidebook":* Beeman, *Old Dominion and New Nation*, 80; R. Kent Newmyer, *John Marshall and the Heroic Age of the Supreme Court* (Baton Rouge: Louisiana State University Press, 2001), 105.

Chapter 26: For the Defense

369 *Throughout these hearings:* Charles F. Hobson, "Patrick Henry and John Marshall: The 18th-Century Legal Dream Team," *Newsletter of the Patrick Henry Memorial Foundation* (Summer 2005): 7.

369 Jones v. Walker: *Marshall Papers*, 5: 264–94. Francis Walker acted for his father (who died in November 1794) first under a power of attorney and later as his executor.

369 *Robertson's record:* Wirt, *Henry*, 312–14; *Marshall Papers*, 5: 267–68.

370 *"supreme law":* Hobson, "The Recovery of British Debts in the Federal Circuit Court of Virginia, 1790 to 1797," *VMHB* 92 (1984): 176–200.

370 *Henry did not disappoint:* Henry Correspondence, 3: 647; Wirt, *Henry*, 320.

370 *Pufendorf, Grotius, Vattel:* Hayes, *Mind of a Patriot*, 99, 128, 138.

370 *"From this":* Ibid., 99; Couvillon, *Patrick Henry: Corrections by Edward Fontaine*, 9–10.

370 *"with his notebook":* Ibid.

371 *"animosities"*: Wirt, *Henry*, 321.

371 *"to forgive injuries"*: God "will execute Justice upon Sinners as Individuals in the eternal World," Davies had preached in *Virginia's Danger and Remedy* (pp. 23, 29), "but *now* is the Time for him to deal with . . . their national Sins."

371 *"to prove"*: Wirt, *Henry*, 326.

371 *"Vattel, p. 484"*: Ibid. Soon thereafter Henry recommended pp. 6–12 of Vattel's "preliminary discourse" and then read portions of Vattel's sections 17, 18, 19, and 20.

372 *"when her sons"*: Wirt, *Henry*, 327–28, emphasis in original.

372 *"He never distinguished"*: Jefferson to William Wirt, April 12, 1812, LC.

372 *"a great orator"*: Memorandum of conversation between John Marshall and John Scott, n.d., *Henry Correspondence*, 2: 376.

373 Ware v. Hylton: *Marshall Papers*, 5: 294–329.

373 *"one foot in the grave"*: Henry Correspondence, 2: 474–75. W. W. Henry's source for Randolph's recollection of the court case was a letter from James W. Bouldin, who heard his description of the scene.

373 *"displaying his whole power"*: Ibid.

373 *wartime commission*: Hening, *Statutes*, 9: 377–80. Between 1777 and 1780 (when the law was repealed), only 307 Virginians of more than 35,000 who owed debts to British creditors made payments totaling £272,544 in paper currency worth £12,035 sterling. Patrick Henry, George Washington, Richard Henry Lee, and George Mason were among those leaders who did not utilize the program; Emory G. Evans, "Private Indebtedness and the Revolution in Virginia, 1776 to 1796," *WMQ*, 3d. ser., 28 (1971): 352–57. Despite his accusation that Henry paid for a tract of land "in depreciated paper, not worth oak leaves," Thomas Jefferson made one of the largest individual currency payments (£2,666) through this commission; Thomas Jefferson's Notes on Patrick Henry, before April 12, 1812, *Jefferson Retirement Papers* 4: 603; Evans, "Private Indebtedness," 355; Herbert E. Sloan, *Principle and Interest: Thomas Jefferson and the Problem of Debt* (Charlottesville: University of Virginia Press, 1995), 32–41.

374 *"they had served"*: Hobson, "Henry and Marshall," 8.

374 *$9,574.29*: Marshall Papers, 5: 294–2, 328–2.

374 *"that men"*: Pleasants to Henry, July 21, 1792, Robert Pleasants Letter Book, 110–11.

375 *"a time"*: Henry to Pleasants, Jan. 18, 1773, *Henry Correspondence*, 1: 152–153. When Pleasants approached James Madison in 1791 for advice about submitting a petition against the slave trade to Congress and an emancipation plan to the state legislature, Madison advised against both as "likely to do harm rather than good." Pleasants to Madison, June 6 and Aug. 8, 1791; Madison to Pleasants, Oct. 30, 1791, *Madison Papers*, 14: 30, 70, 91.

375 *"the woeful effects"*: Pleasants to Henry, July 21, 1792; Robert Pleasants Letter Book, 110–11. The American edition (Evans no. 24426) of Coulon's *Inquiry into the Causes of the Insurrection of the Negroes on the Island of St. Domingo* (Phila-

delphia: Joseph Crukshank, 1792) was reprinted from a London edition published in 1791.

376 *"rapes, Robberies":* Amelia County petition, quoted in Schmidt and Ripel, eds., "Early Proslavery Petitions," 139; Martin Ros, *Night of Fire: The Black Napoleon and the Battle of Haiti,* trans. Karin Ford-Treep (New York: Sarpedon, 1994), 14–21; "Concise and Connected Account of the Late Disturbances at St. Domingo," *Boston Independent Chronicle,* Oct. 20, 1791; "St. Domingo Disturbances," *Carlisle [Pennsylvania] Gazette,* Nov. 30, 1791.

376 *"the example of the West Indies":* Lee to Robert Goode, May 17, 1792, quoted in James Sidbury, "Saint Domingue in Virginia: Ideology, Local Meanings, and Resistance to Slavery, 1790–1800," *JSH* 63 (1997): 539–45.

376 *general collapse:* Davis, *Problem of Slavery in the Age of Revolution,* 197.

376 *"a gloomy perspective":* Henry to Pleasants, Jan. 18, 1773.

376 *a sensational scandal:* Cynthia A. Kierner, *Scandal at Bizarre: Rumor and Reputation in Jefferson's America* (New York: Palgrave Macmillan, 2004); Alan Pell Crawford, *Unwise Passions: A True Story of a Remarkable Woman—and the First Great Scandal of Eighteenth-Century America* (New York: Simon & Schuster, 2000). Jonathan Daniels, *The Randolphs of Virginia* (Garden City, NY: Doubleday, 1972), x–xxi, has convenient genealogical charts for all six branches of the family.

377 *"Mr. Randolph and Miss Nancy":* Testimony of Anne Randolph of Curles, a cousin of the accused, April 29, 1793, *Marshall Papers,* 11: 173.

377 *"answer in the due course":* Virginia Gazette and General Advertiser, May 15, 1793, quoted in *Marshall Papers,* 11: 163.

377 *By Virginia law: Marshall Papers,* 11: 164; Hobson, "Patrick Henry and John Marshall: The 18th-Century Legal Dream Team," 5.

377 *"feloniously murdering":* Cumberland County Court Order Book, 1792–1797, 88 (LVA), quoted in *Marshall Papers,* 11: 164n7.

378 *detailed summaries:* Marshall's "Notes of Evidence," ca. April 29, 1793, are published in *Marshall Papers,* 11: 168–78, from a manuscript copy in the hand of John Randolph of Roanoke at VHS. Patrick Henry was assisted by Alexander Campbell, a lawyer of great reputation who also teamed with Henry and Marshall on the British debt cases; Charles F. Hobson, *The Great Chief Justice: John Marshall and the Rule of Law* (Lawrence: University Press of Kansas, 1996), 2.

378 *"Dolly": Henry Correspondence,* 2: 491.

378 *£140:* Randolph's note left a public record because after Henry assigned it to another person, as was commonplace, that recipient eventually had to take Randolph to court for payment; Cumberland Order Book, 217, cited in *Marshall Papers,* 11: 165. The editors of the *Marshall Papers* (11: 165n2) correct Robert Douthat Meade's "confused" account of this hearing and his mistaken belief that the county records had disappeared; Meade, *Practical Revolutionary,* 518–19.

378 *"being then suspicious":* Testimony of Mary Cary Page, a daughter of Archibald Cary and aunt of Nancy and Judith Randolph, April 29, 1793, *Marshall Papers,* 11: 169–70.

378 *"through a crack":* Ibid.

378 *"resorted to his inimitable power":* Henry Correspondence, 2: 492.

378 *"not guilty":* Cumberland County Court Order Book, 1792–1797, 88 (LVA), quoted in *Marshall Papers,* 11: 164n7.

Chapter 27: Last Call

379 *Long Island:* Couvillon, *Patrick Henry's Virginia,* 85–87.

379 *Dorothea buried her eighth child:* Edith C. Poindexter, comp., "Patrick Henry's Family," unpublished paper, Oct. 2010.

380 *"the flux":* Henry to Elizabeth Aylett, Oct. 26, 1793, *Henry Correspondence,* 3: 422–23; Wyndham Bolling Blanton, *Medicine in Virginia in the Eighteenth Century* (Richmond: Garrett & Massie, 1931), 68.

380 *"Neddy":* Edward Henry (Neddy), born in 1771 at Scotchtown, died Oct. 28, 1794, at Winton, Samuel, and Jane Meredith's home in Amherst County, where he had just been admitted to the bar.

380 *"great cause":* Henry to Aylett, Sept. 8, 1794, *Henry Correspondence,* 3: 423.

380 *"Ague":* Jon Kukla, "Kentish Agues and American Distempers: The Transmission of Malaria from England to Virginia in the Seventeenth Century," *Southern Studies* 25 (Summer 1986): 135–47.

380 *Henry purchased Red Hill:* Couvillon, *Patrick Henry's Virginia,* 93–95.

381 *"lean-to":* Morgan, *The True Patrick Henry,* 399; Memorandum and Agreement between John Henry and Jesse Staples for a house at Red Hill, Feb. 1, 1832, Patrick Henry Family Papers, LC.

381 *"and plague myself":* Henry to Aylett, Sept. 8, 1794; *Henry Correspondence,* 3: 423.

381 *"one of the garden spots":* Morgan, *The True Patrick Henry,* 396.

381 *Estate inventories:* The official copy of Henry's will and estate inventory is filed at Charlotte County courthouse. A reliable transcription is published in Morgan, *The True Patrick Henry,* 461–73.

381 *Decius letters:* Henry to William Grayson, March 31, 1789, *VMBH* 14 (1906): 202–4.

382 *"Behold France":* Works of Fisher Ames, ed. W. B. Allen (Indianapolis: Liberty Fund, 1983), 190.

382 *"the liberty":* Dumas Malone, *Jefferson and the Ordeal of Liberty* (Boston: Little, Brown, 1962), 48.

382 *"loud in reprobating":* Randolph to Washington, June 24, 1793, *Henry Correspondence,* 2: 537.

383 *"the company was composed":* William Wirt Henry attributes this anecdote to a

manuscript written by David Meade Randolph published in the *Southern Literary Messenger*, ibid., 2: 537.

383 *"As to the reports":* Henry to Elizabeth Aylett, Aug. 20, 1796, *Henry Correspondence*, 2: 568–70.

384 *"Every word":* Ibid.

384 *"The rising greatness":* Ibid.

384 *Henry's concerns:* This discussion of Butler, Doddridge, and Jenyns closely follows Thomas Buckley, *Establishing Religious Freedom*, 66.

384 *"its origin from God":* Jenyns, *View*, pp. 98–99, quoted in Buckley, *Establishing Religious Freedom*, 66.

385 *a new printing:* Hayes, *Mind of a Patriot*, 104–5; 132.

385 *"in an old-fashioned stick-gig":* Meade, "Judge Winston's Memoir," 41; Schreiner-Yantis and Love, *Property Tax Lists for 1787 for Prince Edward County*, 1288–1301.

385 *"not to take him":* Meade, "Judge Winston's Memoir," 41. "One wonders if he gave a copy to Jefferson" (who Henry regarded as a deist), Buckley asks in *Establishing Religious Freedom*, 66.

385 *"the fruits of his labour":* Convention speech, June 5, 1788, *Virginia Ratification*, 960.

385 *"which neither herself":* Henry to Washington, Oct. 16, 1795, *Henry Correspondence*, 2: 558–59.

385 *"unpleasant sensations":* Washington to Henry Lee, Aug. 26, 1794, *Washington Papers, Presidential*, 16: 603.

385 *"Surely no situation":* Lee to Henry, Dec. 26, 1795, *Henry Correspondence*, 2: 563; Maeva Marcus and James R. Perry, eds., *Documentary History of the Supreme Court, 1789–1800*, vol. 6 (New York: Columbia University Press, 1998): 2.

386 *successor to James Monroe:* Timothy Pickering to Washington, July 1, July 2, 1796, Record Group 59, Miscellaneous Letters, National Archives, Washington, D.C.

386 *"strong inducement":* Washington to Lee, Aug. 26, 1794, *Washington Papers, Presidential*, 16: 603; *Henry Correspondence*, 2: 545.

386 *whether Patrick Henry might be willing:* John Marshall to Alexander Hamilton, April 25, 1796, *Marshall Papers*, 3: 23; Marshall to Rufus King, May 24, 1796, ibid., 3: 28; King to Hamilton, May 2, 1796, Harold C. Syrett et al., eds., *Papers of Alexander Hamilton* (27 vols., New York: Columbia University Press, 1961–1987): 20: 151–53; Robert G. Harper to Hamilton, Nov. 4, 1796, ibid., 20: 372.

386 *"one of the few":* Jeffrey L. Pasley, *The First Presidential Contest: 1796 and the Founding of American Democracy* (Lawrence: University of Kansas Press, 2013), 205.

386 *"publicly to declare":* "To the People of the United States, Nov. 3d, 1796," *Virginia Gazette &c., Extraordinary*, Nov. 9, 1796, was reprinted in *The Ga-*

zette of the United States and Philadelphia Daily Advertiser, Nov. 15, 1796, and
Greenleaf's New Daily Advertiser in New York, Nov. 18, 1796, and reported in
Carlisle, Penn., Charleston, S.C., and Keene, N.H.

386 "spirit of party": Cooke, ed., The Federalist, 168, 432.

387 no well-organized national parties: Ronald P. Formisano, "Deferential-
Participant Politics: The Early Republic's Political Culture, 1789–1840," American Political Science Review 68 (1974): 474–78.

387 the state legislatures: Pasley, First Presidential Contest, 312–15.

387 "could unite all parties": Powell, "To the Freeholders of the Counties of
Loudoun and Fauquier," ibid., Oct. 1, 1796. Powell's letter was reprinted in
Philadelphia.

387 "diligence and wisdom": Simms, "To the Freeholders of the Counties of Prince
William, Stafford, and Fairfax," Columbian Mirror and Alexandria Gazette,
Sept. 29, 1796. Simms's letter was reprinted in Boston and Salem, Mass.,
Charleston, S.C., and Baltimore, Md.

388 "wish[ed] Patrick Henry": John Adams to Abigail Adams, Dec. 18, 1796,
Gregg L. Lint et al., eds. Adams Family Correspondence, vol. 11 (Cambridge:
Harvard University Press, 2013), 446. Adams was referring to the 138 electors,
each of whom cast two votes for a total of 276; Pasley, First Presidential Contest, table 3, p. 406.

388 "To the People": Henry, "To the People of the United States."

389 evils of faction: Glenn A. Phelps, "George Washington and the Paradox of
Party," Presidential Studies Quarterly 19 (1989): 733–45; Bernard Bailyn, The Origins of American Politics (New York: Alfred A. Knopf, 1968), 36–40. Bolingbroke's influential statement about the evil effects of party, A Dissertation on
Parties (2d ed., London: H. Haines, 1735), was widely reprinted throughout
the century. Kevin Hayes identified Henry's copy of Bolingbroke's writings
as the Letters on the Spirit of Patriotism; on the Idea of a Patriot King; and on
the State of Parties at the Accession of King George the First, published in many
editions between 1749 and 1783; Hayes, Mind of a Patriot, 114. Robert M. Weir,
"'The Harmony We Were Famous for': An Interpretation of Prerevolutionary
South Carolina Politics," WMQ, 3d ser., 26 (1969): 473–501, summarized the
vast literature about country Whig ideals in the eighteenth-century southern
colonies.

389 "apostacy": Jefferson to Archibald Stuart, May 14, 1799; Jefferson to Tench
Coxe, May 21, 1799, Jefferson Papers, 31: 110, 112; Jefferson to William Wirt,
before April 12, 1812, Jefferson Retirement Papers, 4: 604.

389 sixth term as governor: Journal of the House of Delegates of Virginia, 1796 (Richmond: Augustine Davis, 1796), 42, 54. The rift between the emerging Jeffersonian and Federalist groups was evident in their extended dispute over a
resolution on the subject of President Washington's retirement; ibid., 22, 26,
63–66, 70–71.

389 "for this great Honor": Henry to John Preston, Nov. 29, 1796; Henry to the

Speaker of the House of Delegates, Nov. 29, 1796, *Henry Correspondence*, 2: 573–74, 3: 424. Henry also thanked Preston, a state senator for the southwestern district that included Botetourt and adjacent counties, for his "very friendly interest" in the Assembly.

390   *"Could I see":* Henry to Samuel Hopkins, Nov. 29, 1796; in Rhoda van Bibber Tanner, *Atlantic Between* (New York: House of Field, Doubleday, 1947), 621–22. Hopkins was promoted to general when called to service in the War of 1812; "Letters of General Samuel Hopkins of Henderson, Kentucky," *Register of Kentucky State Historical Society* 41 (1943): 269–303.

390   *"external relations":* Henry to Hopkins, Nov. 29, 1796; in Tanner, *Atlantic Between*, 621–22.

390   *"The Union will dissolve":* Ibid.

390   *"advanced age":* Henry to Preston, Nov. 29, 1796, *Henry Correspondence*, 3: 424.

390   *"inability":* Henry, "To the People of the United States."

390   *"some unlooked-for circumstance":* Henry to Aylett, Aug. 20, 1796, *Henry Correspondence*, 2: 568–70.

391   *"obey the call":* Henry to Washington, Oct. 16, 1795, ibid., 2: 558–59.

391   *"At such a crisis":* Washington to Henry, "Confidential," Jan. 15, 1799, *Washington Papers, Retirement*, 3: 318–19.

391   *"My Children":* Henry to Washington, Feb. 12, 1799, *Washington Papers, Retirement*, 3: 371. Marysville was named for Mary Read, whose son Thomas was clerk of the county court and owner of the hundred acres that comprised the town; Patrick Daily, *Patrick Henry: The Last Years, 1789–1799* (2d ed., Brookneal, Va.: Patrick Henry Memorial Foundation, 2013), 198–208.

391   *"notorious":* "Williamsburg, which has hitherto been proverbial for general Health, is now notorious for the Contrary"; Edmund Randolph to Washington, Oct. 11, 1776; *Washington Papers, Revolutionary War*, 6: 540.

392   *"a tedious illness":* Henry to Benjamin Harrison, Speaker of the House of Delegates, Oct. 18, 1779, *Henry Correspondence*, 2: 43.

392   *"many cases were continued":* Diary of Richard N. Venable, Sept. 7, 1792, quoted in *Henry Correspondence*, 2: 480.

392   *"My advanced age":* Henry to Adams, April 16, 1799, *Henry Correspondence*, 2: 623.

392   *"He was very infirm":* Couvillon, *Patrick Henry: Corrections by Edward Fontaine*, 22–23.

393   *"Dear Patsy":* Ibid., 27–28; *Henry Correspondence*, 2: 624.

393   *"speaking words of love":* Henry Correspondence, 2: 626.

393   *"As long as our rivers flow":* VG (Richmond), June 14, 1799, reprinted in *Virginia Gazette or Petersburg Intelligencer*, June 18, 1799 (LVA film 51) and *The Virginia Herald* (Fredericksburg), June 18, 1799 (LVA film 49a).

393   *"his late political transition":* Richmond Examiner, ca. June 14, 1799, reprinted in *Virginia Gazette or Petersburg Intelligencer*, June 18, 1799, and *Virginia Argus*, June 21, 1799.

393 *"remember and imitate"*: *Virginia Gazette or Petersburg Intelligencer,* June 18, 1799, also reprinted in *Virginia Argus* (Richmond), June 25, 1799.

394 *"was our leader"*: Thomas Jefferson, Conversation with Daniel Webster, 1824, quoted in John P. Kaminski, ed., *The Founders on the Founders: Word Portraits from the American Revolutionary Era* (Charlottesville: University of Virginia Press, 2008), 264.

Acknowledgments

Books are not solo performances. Through more years than we expected, I enjoyed the steadfast support of my literary agent Stephen Hanselman at LevelFiveMedia, LLC. At Simon & Schuster, Bob Bender persuaded me that new insights about revolutionary America warranted a fresh biography of Henry. His perceptive editorial guidance, supported by the painstaking work of his colleagues Johanna Li and Phil Metcalf, clarified and strengthened the result.

Thorough research also requires an orchestra. At the Library of Virginia, David Grabarek, J. Christian Kolbe, and Minor Weisiger are prominent among the librarians and archivists who assisted me—as did Francis Pollard and her colleagues at the Virginia Historical Society and Karen Stuart at the Manuscript Division of the Library of Congress. My annotation gratefully testifies to Mark Couvillon's lifelong interest in Henry and our joint pursuit of previously unknown Henry documents, in concert with Susan H. Perdue and William B. Kurtz as they began a projected digital edition of Henry's papers at the Virginia Foundation for the Humanities and Public Policy.

My former colleague Edith C. Poindexter was my virtuoso for Henry family history. Janet Bloom at the William L. Clements Library of the University of Michigan, Ann Arbor; Patricia Lynn Sharp at the library of the University of Pittsburgh; Susan Riggs and Amy C. Schindler at the Earl Gregg Swem Library of the College of William and Mary; and Mary L. Robertson and Stephen Tabor at the Henry E. Huntington Library and Art Gallery supplied photocopies of documents from their institutions. Amanda Robiolio located a revealing letter in the collections at Haverford College. John W. Gordon supplied a published text of Jack P. Greene's

Freeman Lectures at the University of Richmond. John P. Kaminski brought several documents to my attention. J. Jefferson Looney shared a transcription from his files at Monticello. Joseph McAlhany transliterated the Greek terms discussed by Patrick Henry's father and uncle. Turk McCleskey provided evidence of Henry's legal practice in Augusta County. Michael L. Nicholls introduced me to the online transcriptions of Revolutionary war pension files. Harold Gill and Linda Rowe, of the Colonial Williamsburg Foundation, clarified several matters. Palmer C. Sweet, retired state geologist, advised me about early gold mining in Virginia. Edward Ayres, of the Jamestown-Yorktown Foundation, helped me understand militia activity near the North Carolina border.

Woody Holton, John R. Pagan, and Alan Taylor offered advice about a partial draft of chapter 22 presented to the Fall Line Early Americanists in Richmond. I also enjoyed extended conversations with scholars who presented the annual Governor Henry Lectures cosponsored by the Library of Virginia and the Patrick Henry Memorial Foundation between 2001 and 2012: Carol Berkin; Thomas E. Buckley, S.J.; Kevin R. Hardwick; Kevin J. Hayes; Don Higginbotham; Charles F. Hobson; John P. Kaminski; Thomas S. Kidd; Cynthia A. Kierner; George Morrow II; and C. Jan Swearingen. Years of research deepened my respect for the contributions of departed friends W. W. Abbot, Sarah Bearss, Lester J. Cappon, Jane Carson, Alonzo T. Dill, John W. Dudley, Emory G. Evans, Donald Haynes, John M. Hemphill, Rhys Isaac, John Melville Jennings, William M. E. Rachal, George H. Reese, Edward M. Riley, Robert L. Scribner, John E. Selby, and Waverly K. Winfree.

A. Roger Ekirch, Kevin R. Hardwick, Peter S. Onuf, James F. Sefcik, and Brent Tarter read the manuscript and offered very helpful suggestions and encouragement. Amy, Jennifer, and Elizabeth patiently monitored the old guy's progress—and Sandra Gioia Treadway made it possible.

Jon Kukla, Richmond

Index

Page numbers beginning with 400 refer to endnotes.